THE ART OF SEEING

FOURTH EDITION

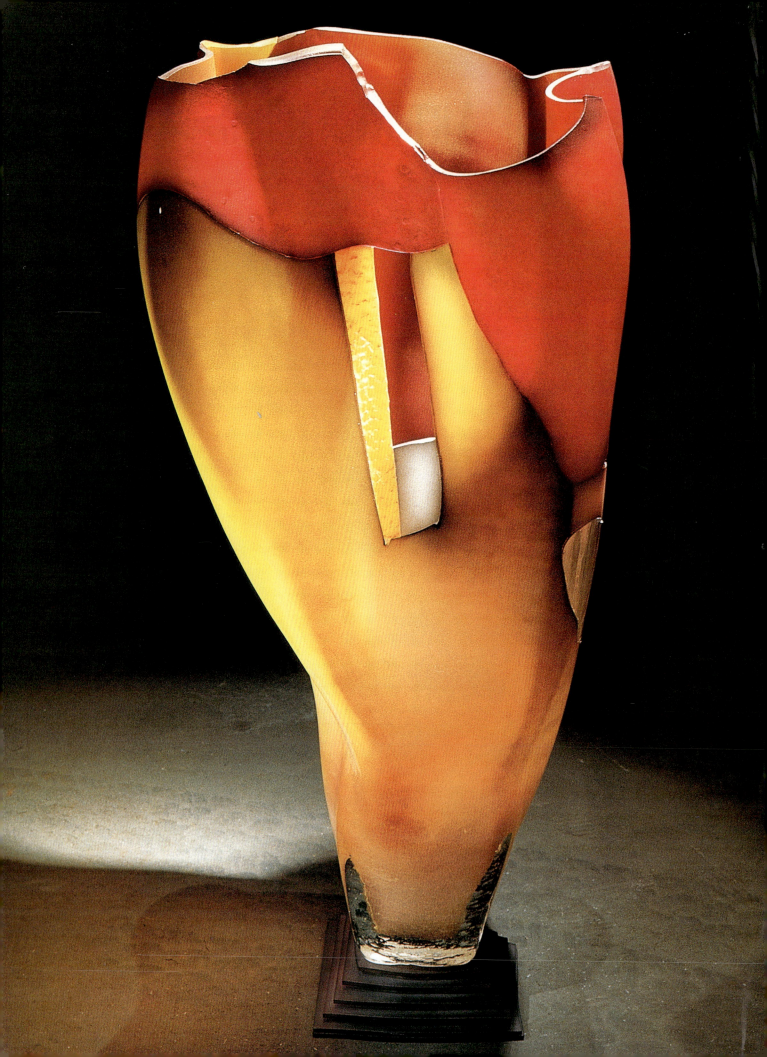

THE ART OF SEEING

FOURTH EDITION

PAUL ZELANSKI
UNIVERSITY OF CONNECTICUT

MARY PAT FISHER

PRENTICE HALL INC., UPPER SADDLE RIVER, N.J. 07458

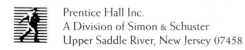

Prentice Hall Inc.
A Division of Simon & Schuster
Upper Saddle River, New Jersey 07458

10 9 8 7 6 5 4 3 2 1

ISBN 0–13–790635–8

This book was designed and produced by
CALMANN & KING LTD, LONDON

Editor: Richard Mason
Designer: Karen Osborne
Picture researcher: Callie Kendall
Maps: Eugene Fleury
Typesetter: Fakenham Phototypesetting Ltd., Norfolk
Printer: Kyodo, Singapore

Cover: (front) Giovanni Paolo Pannini, *Interior of the Pantheon* (detail), c. 1740.
Oil on canvas, 4 ft 2 ½ in (1.28 m) high; 3 ft 3 in (0.99 m) wide.
National Gallery of Art, Washington, D.C. Samuel H. Kress Collection.

Cover: (back). Vincent van Gogh, *The Starry Night* (detail), 1889.
Oil on canvas, 29 x 36 ¼ ins (73.7 x 92.1 cm).
Collection Museum of Modern Art, New York.
Acquired through the Lillie P. Bliss Bequest.

Frontispiece: Danny Perkins, White Square, 1994.
Blown glass, oil paints, 42 3 16 x 16 ins (106.6 3 40.6 x 40.6 cm).

CONTENTS

Preface 9

PART 1
LEARNING TO SEE 11

1 UNDERSTANDING ART 12

THE CREATIVE IMPULSE 12

CONTENT 14
Political Content 15
Power and Propaganda 18
Narrative 21
Inner Experiences 23
Intellectual Concepts 27
Vincent van Gogh on Emotion and Intellect 28
Ideals of Beauty 30

FORMS OF ART 30
Two- and Three-Dimensional Art 30
Degrees of Realism 32
Georgia O'Keeffe on "Saying What I Want To" 38
Fine and Applied Arts 40
Public and Private Art 42
ART ISSUES: Censorship 46

CRITICAL OPINION 48
ART ISSUES: Race and Gender Criticism 50
Greatness in Art 51

2 VISUAL ELEMENTS 55

LINE 55
Seeing Lines 55
Implied Line 59
Descriptive Line 61
Expressive Qualities of Line 63
Directional Line 65

SHAPE AND FORM 65
Degrees of Three-Dimensionality 67
Characteristics of Three-Dimensional Form 71
Henry Moore on Form and Space 74
Two-Dimensional Illusion of Form 77
Shapes 80
Arshile Gorky on The Intensity of Art 82

SPACE 88
Three-Dimensional Art in Space 88
Two-Dimensional Space 92
Scale 101
Spatial Illusion 105

TEXTURE 108
Actual Texture 110
Simulated Texture 111
Texture-Like Effects 114

VALUE AND LIGHT 114
Local and Interpretive Values 116
Lighting 118
Reflections 123
Light as a Medium 124

COLOR 127
A Vocabulary of Color 127
Natural and Applied Color 131
Local, Impressionistic, and Interpretive
    Color 134
Emotional Effects of Color 135
Warm and Cool Colors 138
Advancing and Receding Colors 142
Color Combinations 143
Interaction of Color 146
Josef Albers on The Complexity of Color 150
Limited and Open Palette 152

TIME 155
Viewing Time 155
Auguste Rodin on The Illusion of Movement 157
Actual Movement 158

Illusion of Movement   159
The Captured Moment   163
Time as the Subject   164
Ephemeral Time   168
Change Through Time   169

3 ORGANIZING PRINCIPLES OF DESIGN   170

REPETITION   171

VARIETY   175

RHYTHM   180

BALANCE   182

COMPOSITIONAL UNITY   187

EMPHASIS   190

ECONOMY   192

PROPORTION   193
Wassily Kandinsky on Underlying Harmony   196

RELATIONSHIP TO THE ENVIRONMENT   198

PART 2
TWO-DIMENSIONAL MEDIA AND METHODS   201

4 DRAWING   202

APPROACHES TO DRAWING   202

DRY MEDIA   205
Graphite Pencil   205
Silverpoint   206
Charcoal   206
Chalk   209
Pastel   211
Crayon   212

LIQUID MEDIA   213
Pen and Ink   213
Brush and Ink   215

5 PAINTING   216

APPROACHES TO PAINTING   216
Leonardo da Vinci on Chiaroscuro   220

PAINT MEDIA   222
Encaustic   222
Fresco   224
Tempera   226
Oil   228
ART ISSUES: Cleaning and Restoring
Paintings   232
Watercolor   234
Gouache   237
Synthetics   238
Collage   240
Mosaic   242

MIXED MEDIA   244

6 PRINTMAKING   245

PRINTMAKING PROCESSES   247
Relief   247
Stephen Alcorn on The Challenge of Linocuts   251
Intaglio   253
Planographic   259
Stencil   262

MIXED MEDIA   264

7 GRAPHIC DESIGN   267

THE GRAPHIC DESIGNER AND VISUAL IDEAS   267
Peter Good on The Art of Graphic Design   268

TYPOGRAPHY   270

ILLUSTRATION   272

8 PHOTOGRAPHY, PHOTOCOPY, AND FILMMAKING   276

PHOTOGRAPHY   276
Edward Weston on Photography as a Way of
Seeing   286

PHOTOCOPY AND FAX ART   291

FILM   293

TELEVISION AND VIDEO   298

9 COMPUTER GRAPHICS 301

The Computer as a Drawing Medium 301

The Computer as a Painting Medium 303

Video Graphics 305

Virtual Reality 306

The Computer as a Unique Art Medium 307

Art in Cyberspace 309

PART 3
THREE-DIMENSIONAL MEDIA AND METHODS 311

10 SCULPTURE 312

Carving 312
  Michelangelo Buonarroti on Marble-Quarrying 313
  Linda Howard on Computer-Aided Sculpture Design 316

Modeling 320

Casting 323
  Benvenuto Cellini on A Near-Disastrous Casting 326

Assembling 328

Earthworks 331

11 CRAFTS 333

Clay 333
  Paula Winokur on Working in Clay 336

Metal 338

Wood 340
  George Nakashima on A Feeling for Wood 342

Glass 344

Fibers 347
  Norma Minkowitz on The Interface Between Art and Craft 350

12 PRODUCT AND CLOTHING DESIGN 354

Industrial Design 354

Clothing Design 356

13 ARCHITECTURE 364

Function 367

Structure 374
  Hassan Fathy on Indigenous Architectural Ingenuity 380
  Alvar Aalto on Humanizing Architecture 392

14 DESIGNED SETTINGS 395

Interior Design 395

Environmental Design 401
  John Lyle on Sustainable Environmental Design 406

Visual Aspects of the Performing Arts 408

PART 4
ART IN TIME 413

15 HISTORICAL STYLES IN WESTERN ART 414

The Beginnings of Western Art 418
  Prehistoric 418
  Aegean 419
  Near Eastern 420
  Egyptian 420

Art of Ancient Cultures 422
  Greek 422
  Roman 425
  Early Christian and Byzantine 425

Medieval Art 429
  Early Medieval 429
  Romanesque 429
  Gothic 429
  Late Gothic 431

Renaissance Art 433
  Early Renaissance in Italy 433
  High Renaissance in Italy 436
    Art Issues: Protecting Famous Artworks 438
  Mannerism 442
  Northern Renaissance 442

Baroque Art 444
  Southern Baroque 444
  Northern Baroque 448
  Rococo 448

EIGHTEENTH- AND EARLY NINETEENTH-CENTURY
    ART   450
    Neoclassicism   450
    Romanticism   451

LATER NINETEENTH-CENTURY ART   453
    Realism   453
    Impressionism   453
    Post-Impressionism   455
    Paul Gauguin on Cross-Cultural Borrowings   456
    Expressionism   458

TWENTIETH-CENTURY ART   458
    Fauvism   460
    Cubism   461
    Futurism   463
    Abstract and Nonobjective Art   464
    Dada   465
    Surrealism   466
    Traditional Realism   467
    Abstract Expressionism   467
    Post-Painterly Abstraction   468
    Pop Art   470
    New Realism   471
    Technological Art   472
    Installations, Performance Art, Earthworks,
      and Conceptual Art   475
    Neoexpressionism   475
    The Craft Object   477
    Recognition of Women's Art   479
    Recognition of Multi-Cultural Art   480
    *Deborah Muirhead on Art as Ancestral
      Exploration*   482
    Recognition of Outsider Art   484
    Jon Serl Inside an Outsider's Mind   485
    ART ISSUES: Art as Investment   486

16 UNDERSTANDING ART ON ALL LEVELS 488

PICASSO'S *GUERNICA*   489

RODIN'S *GATES OF HELL*   495

MICHELANGELO'S SISTINE CHAPEL CEILING   500

MOSHE SAFDIE'S VANCOUVER LIBRARY SQUARE   507

NOTES   512

GLOSSARY/ PRONUNCIATION GUIDE   516

ARTISTS' PRONUNCIATION GUIDE   528

CREDITS   530

INDEX   532

TIMELINE

30,000 BC–2000 AD   416-17

TABLES

30,000 BC–500 AD Prehistoric to Roman   415

500–1500 AD Early Christian to Gothic   427

1425–1640 Early Renaissance to Southern
    Baroque   440

1500–1800 Northern Renaissance to Rococo   446

1750–1950 Neoclassicism to Surrealism   452

1945–2000 At the Turn of the Twenty-First
    Century   473

MAPS

The Prehistoric and Ancient World   415

Europe in the Early Twelfth Century   427

Renaissance Italy   440

Northern Europe in the mid-Seventeenth
    Century   446

Europe in the mid-Nineteenth Century   452

The World in the Late Twentieth Century   473

PREFACE

For this fourth edition of *The Art of Seeing*, we have strengthened those features that have already made the book very popular and incorporated new ways of bringing the reader closer to an informed understanding of the art, and related media, of all cultures.

In keeping with today's interests, a major new theme in this edition is the controversial aspects of arts. At relevant points in the text, we have created new art issues boxes: censorship, race and gender criticism, cleaning and restoration of paintings, protection of famous artworks, and art as investment. They are discussed not only as sources of contemporary controversy but also as problematic issues in the past. Issues such as the changing opinions of art critics, public reaction to public art, and the dubious nature of art attributions also appear throughout the text.

The final chapter of the book examines four major works of art in depth. We have enlivened and updated this chapter by adding a controversial new piece of public architecture: Moshie Safdie's Vancouver Library Square. To integrate and set the stage for that final chapter, we have now introduced four masterworks—Vancouver Library Square, Picasso's *Guernica*, Rodin's *Gates of Hell*, and Michelangelo's Sistine Chapel ceiling—in the first chapter. These threads are picked up again as the book proceeds, weaving them into discussions of particular aspects of art.

Chapter 1 has been thoroughly reworked to provide a clear and provocative introduction to the understanding of art. We have also given computer graphics a chapter of its own. It covers the historical development of the medium and current computer graphics applications, including virtual reality and art in cyberspace.

As before, we try to give insights into art from the artist's point of view. Artists' own words about their work are a treasure trove for the student of art appreciation. We have therefore added more such statements by artists. In addition, we have created twenty-three feature boxes in which artists speak at length about some facet of their work that is related to the subject under discussion. Some of these are developed from our personal interviews with these artists, some from historical documents. New artists' boxes for this edition include Stephen Alcorn speaking about printmaking and John Lyle discussing ecologically oriented landscape design. To further enhance understanding of why artists have worked as they have, we have increased discussion of the relationship between the formal means artists use and the content they wish to convey.

THE NATURE OF THIS BOOK

As before, we have taken considerable effort in *The Art of Seeing* to make art come to life. The language we use is vigorous and down-to-earth, with numerous quotations from the artists themselves to help explain, in their own words, what they were trying to do. Unfamiliar words are carefully defined when they are first used and also in an extensive illustrated glossary at the end of the book. In this edition, pronunciation aids have been added to words in the glossary which may be unfamiliar to students. There is also a new guide in the back of the book to artists' names that are difficult to pronounce.

Perhaps even more important than the writing in *The Art of Seeing* is the art. The illustrations for each concept are clearly related to the text and carefully described. There are some 607 illustrations, 275 of them in color, and many of these are reproduced at full-page size. They are taken from all the visual arts, from painting and sculpture to clothing and industrial design. Many cultures are represented, as is the work of many women artists, for their "discovery" has been a belated new area of excitement in the art world. A sampling of the new artworks introduced in this edition indicates the variety in the illustration program, which has been hailed as one of the great strengths of this book. New works include: Czech postage stamps;

a Japanese doll; Damien Hirst's animal parts in formaldehyde; stone inlay work in the Taj Mahal; a virtual reality journey; a delicate painting by Agnes Martin; Michelangelo's *Last Judgment* with and without loincloths and drapes that were added because of sixteenth-century censorship; special computer effects from the movie *Independence Day*; a contemporary kimono master at work; and Maria Martínez pinching a pot with her gnarled and ancient hands. Use of such a global variety of illustrations from both fine and applied arts, old and new, allows us to broaden tastes in art and to demonstrate the underlying principles, elements, and issues in art, no matter what form it takes. As well as being good references for the explanations in the text, the large illlustrations provide a stimulating, exciting visual gallery.

In Chapter 15, which traces the development of Western art, the discussion is enhanced by maps and timelines. The six maps show the regions where major trends in Western art developed and indicate key artistic centers, with insets of important buildings and monuments. Each map is accompanied by a timeline giving a global historical context to the evolution of Western art, up to the turn of the twenty-first century.

ITS ORGANIZATION

Part 1 of *The Art of Seeing* lays the foundation for understanding the aesthetic aspects of a work of art. In Chapter 1, we develop an initial vocabulary and an intellectual framework for considering artworks: the creative impulse, the varying forms and content of its manifestation, critical opinion of the results, and, with time, recognition of the greatness of some works. Chapter 2 is devoted to extensive analysis of the visual elements with which the artist works: line, shapes, form, space, texture, light, color, and time. Chapter 3 covers the subtle organizing principles by which these elements are used in a work of art.

The next two parts of the book approach art through the materials and techniques used by the artists. By revealing the difficulties of each method, we hope to enhance appreciation of the artists' accomplishments in the face of the intractabilities of their media. Part 2 covers two-dimensional techniques and media: drawing, painting, printmaking, graphic design, photography, photocopy, fax, film, television, video, and computer graphics. Part 3 covers three-dimensional media: sculpture, crafts, industrial design, clothing design, architecture, interior design, environmental design, and the performing arts.

Part 4 approaches art as it exists in time. We first offer a concise approach to historical styles in Western art. Some forty-five major movements, from prehistoric to contemporary, are covered, with an illustrated timeline on pages 416 and 417 as an aid to understanding how the distinctly different aesthetic movements are related in time. In addition, six maps show close-ups of particular periods so that one can see where the major artists of the time were working, in the context of major world events of the time.

The final chapter is a unique, in-depth examination of specific works of art, including their evolution in time. It approximates the actual experience of encountering a work of art, drawing on all levels of appreciation developed in the book, in order to analyze and respond to four masterworks.

ACKNOWLEDGMENTS

Many people have helped us to revise and update *The Art of Seeing*, especially Heidi N. Abbey, Heather Gross, Thomas Jacoby, and Erin Valentino. Each edition has been extensively reviewed, but our reviewers for this fourth edition have been particularly helpful with specific and general comments which guided our revisions. We would like to express our special gratitude to Eugene Hood, University of Wisconsin–Eau Clair; Dr. Susan Benforado Bakewell, Kennesaw State College; Pamela Awana Lee, Washington State University; Larry Griffin, Miami-Dade Community College, Kendall Campus; and Lily Mazurek. As always, Bud Therien of Prentice Hall has been enthusiastic and supportive, and the dedicated people at Calmann and King—Melanie White, Richard Mason, Callie Kendall, and Karen Osborne—have handled the myriad editorial and production details with intelligence and sensitivity. Annette Zelanski has again been generous with her help and her loving support.

We feel that these improvements will be very helpful to all those who seek an educated, sharpened sense of art appreciation. Our own appreciation grows each time we approach this book.

Paul Zelanski
Mary Pat Fisher

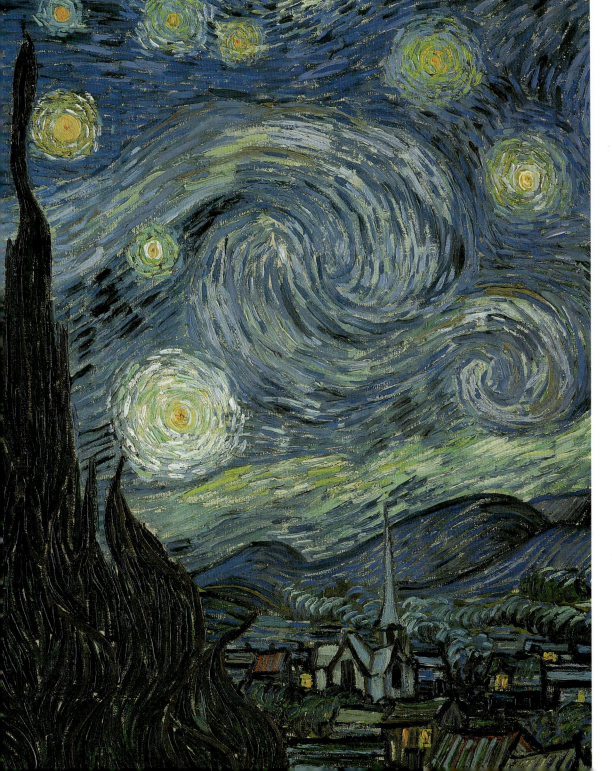

PART 1
LEARNING TO SEE

An encounter with a work of art can be deeply satisfying, provocative, or disturbing. With training, we can begin to recognize the ideas, feelings, and historical context of works of art, and the elements and principles of design that are the artist's aesthetic tools.

Vincent van Gogh,
The Starry Night
(detail of fig. 1.21)

1
UNDERSTANDING ART

In one of the world's most famous images, a grand old man on a cloud surrounded by angels reaches from heaven to earth and imparts life into the first human. The excitement of Michelangelo's *Creation of Adam* (1.1) is centered on the moment when God's finger sends the spark of life into previously inert matter. Similarly, artists of all times and places have set their hands to the raw material of the planet and produced from it new and dynamic works of art.

This chapter takes an overview of artistic creation. First we will explore the impulses and intentions from which art arises. Then we will survey the general forms of art and at the end of the chapter we will consider how the artist's creations are received by others. These topics provide an initial framework for understanding art.

1.1 Michelangelo Buonarroti, Sistine Chapel ceiling (detail, post-restoration), *Creation of Adam*, 1510. Fresco. Vatican Museums and Galleries, Rome.

THE CREATIVE IMPULSE

The impulse to create art is so strong that artworks have appeared in all cultures, from the earliest days of our species. Perhaps as early as 70,000 years ago, our Paleolithic ancestors were apparently painting with red ocher, shaping ritual objects, and fashioning simple necklaces out of animal bones and teeth. Even weapons and sewing needles had decorations scratched onto them.

A tiny bust of a woman (1.2) carved perhaps 24,000 years ago illustrates the care with which artists have worked throughout history. This piece is only 1¼ inches (3 cm) high, and yet the ivory has been carefully sculpted into a woman's likeness, including details of her hairstyle. Why did someone lavish such attention on a very small piece of bone? It was sculpted long before recorded history, so we can only speculate.

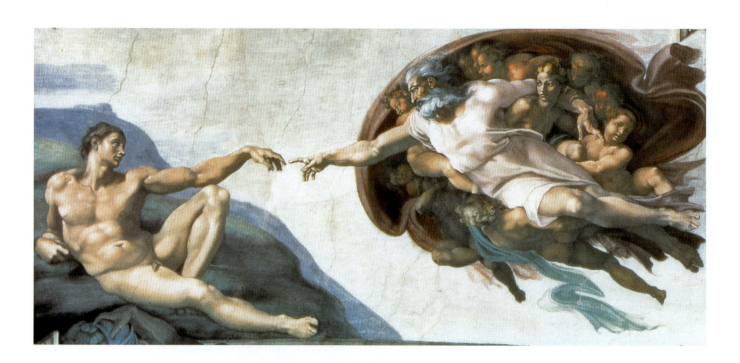

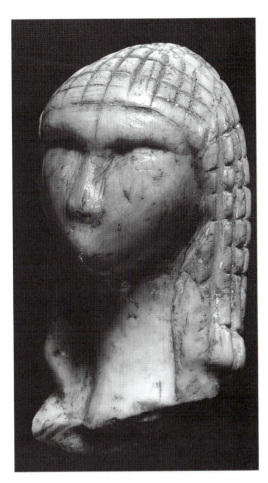

Even today, if we question artists about their feelings and ideas, we find that some cannot easily explain why they create art. For them, it is an inner calling. Whether or not the work sells, an artist is compelled to create it. Rembrandt van Rijn, the seventeenth-century Dutch painter, fell out of favor and was forced to give up his fine things, declare himself bankrupt, and live a life of poverty. Nonetheless he continued painting and at that time produced some of his very best work, such as his haunting *Self-Portrait* (1.3). Auguste Renoir, the French Impressionist painter (see pages 188-9), developed arthritis, which was so painful that he could not hold a brush. Instead he had a brush strapped to his hand, and he continued painting. What unconsciously touches us in the artist's work is perhaps in part the passionate commitment from which it is born. To be sure, there are others for whom artmaking is a profession, a craft at which they have become skillful and which provides a way of making a living.

1.2 *Woman from Brassempouy,* Grotte du Pape, Brassempouy, Landes, France, c. 22,000 BC. Ivory, height 1¼ ins (3 cm). Musée des Antiquités Nationales, St. Germain-en-Laye, France.

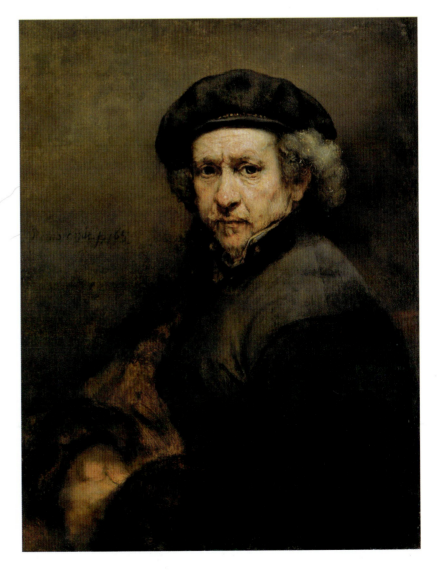

1.3 Rembrandt van Rijn, *Self-Portrait*, c. 1660. Oil on canvas, 33 × 26 ins (84 × 66 cm). National Gallery of Art, Washington, D.C. Andrew W. Mellon Collection.

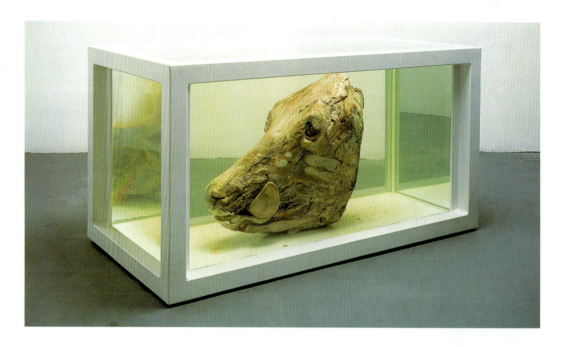

1.4 Damien Hirst, *James (The Twelve Disciples)*, 1994. Steel, glass, and bull's head in formaldehyde solution, 18 × 36 × 18 ins (45.7 × 91.4 × 45.7 cm). Courtesy Jay Jopling.

The question is not so much why people make art but why some people don't. From a very early age, we begin trying to shape materials in our environment into artistic creations. This effort usually continues unless it is stifled by those who try to teach us the "right" way to make art or those who insist that we color within the lines of somebody else's drawing. We may compare our creations unfavorably with more skillful works and give up our attempts at making art.

Training and practice are usually necessary to make the hands create what the mind can imagine. In many cases, the creation of a work of art is meticulously planned and executed. But there may also be an element of spontaneity and serendipity in some kinds of artistic expression. Creating something new requires a certain originality of thought. To create is to develop something from one's own imagination, bringing something into being which would not evolve in the natural course of things. This imagination has deep wellsprings which may lie beneath conscious thought. When some artists are working they may enter a state of intense concentration in which they may fail to notice the passage of time or the stiffness of their bodies. In this meditation-like altered state of consciousness, visual ideas may evolve without intellectual struggle, once a foundation of skills and design sensitivities has been developed. The chance to experience this direct communion with a deeper level of reality is at least part of the urge to create—and it invites others to share in the experience.

At the dawn of the twenty-first century, the creative urge persists, sometimes taking unprecedented forms, such as Damien Hirst's animal parts displayed in formaldehyde (1.4). The bull's head shown here is labeled "James." It is part of a series representing the disciples of Jesus, who faced persecution and death because they were attempting to spread their master's mission. Even given this explanation, some people are puzzled and shocked to see the disciples represented by severed bulls' heads. Hirst's use of preserved parts of dead animals as a medium for sculpture is new and unfamiliar, stretching the boundaries of what is considered art. Even Michelangelo's art was controversial in his own time, as we shall see; we are still finding new ways in which to understand it, and even new ways to criticize it.

CONTENT

One way of beginning to understand what is going on in a work of art is to try to grasp its **content**—its meaning, including the subject-matter (what it is or represents), and the emotions, ideas, symbols, stories, or spiritual connotations it suggests. As analyzed in the sections that follow, the content may be considered in terms of politics, propaganda, narrative, inner experiences, intellectual ideas, or sheer celebration of aesthetic form.

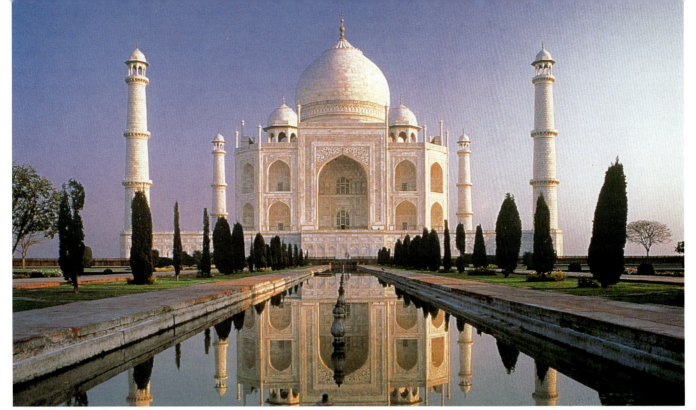

1.5 Taj Mahal, front view with pool in foreground.

The content of a work of art is not a fixed entity captured within a frame. It is shifting, evanescent, personal. It changes depending on who is looking at the artwork, and what emotions and experiences they bring to the act of viewing.

Content is also influenced by the context of the artist's life and historical setting. Visitors to the beautiful Taj Mahal (**1.5**) find it especially poignant when they learn that it was built by the emperor Shah Jahan to immortalize his beloved wife, Mumtaz Mahal, and that she had been his constant companion, even in battle, until she died while giving birth to their fourteenth child. One's appreciation of the intention behind this lovely monument to his life partner is tragically heightened when one learns that the emperor was later imprisoned by his son and could thereafter see the Taj Mahal only from his prison window, from which he gazed at it for the rest of his life.

Some works are so powerful that we can respond to them directly, without knowing anything of the artist's personal life or of the historical context. We don't think of Rembrandt as a period artist; we know him as one of the greatest artists of all time. Hundreds of years after his self-portrait was painted in 1660 (1.3), that face, executed with such compelling truth, such strength in design, and such technical skill, looks out at us from the darkness with an appeal that is timeless.

Political Content

One outlet for the creative impulse is the creation of works intended to record something in the political or social rather than the physical environment, to inform the public, or to preserve an event for history. Some art historians look at all art from a sociopolitical point of view. They see it as providing information about the cultural and social background of its time. They also attach importance to the fact that the individual viewer's response to a work of art is culturally influenced.

Some art is created as social criticism. Sometimes the message is blatant, immediately apparent; sometimes it is subtle and complex. W. Eugene Smith's photograph *Tomoko in a Bath* (**1.6**) is part of a series illustrating industrial pollution in Minamata, Japan. Tomoko is a victim of mercury poisoning; her mother is giving her a bath. The scene—dramatized by composition and lighting—is one of the most powerful photographs ever taken. It may evoke a strange mixture of feelings, from horror at the effects of pollution to compassion for the tenderness with which Tomoko's mother is holding and looking at her. The pose and expression of great love in the midst of tragedy may remind some of Michelangelo's *Pietà* (15.22).

Art may be used intentionally to provoke a reaction to political or cultural situations, not just to

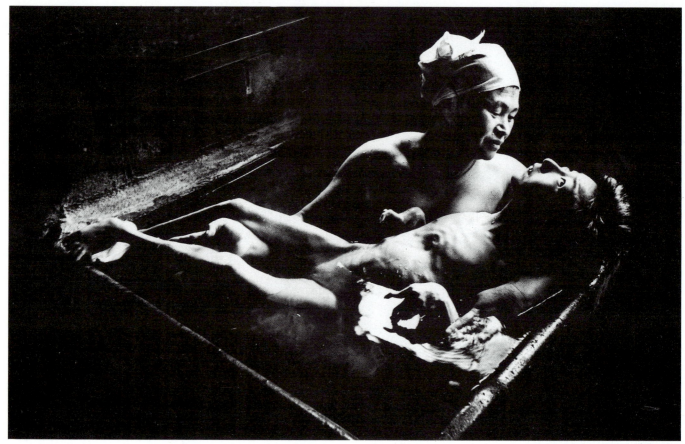

1.6 W. Eugene Smith, *Tomoko in a Bath*, 1972. Photograph. © 1972 Aileen & W. Eugene Smith.

inform the viewer or record events for posterity. One cannot be unaffected by Pat Ward Williams's *Accused/ Blowtorch/Padlock* (**1.7**). Any photograph carries a sense of immediacy and truth. Williams goes beyond that: by taking apart this photograph, presenting it in broken close-ups, she brings us face to face with its horror. She says, "Come in closer; notice this!" Hand- written text surrounding the construction adds the agony of an observer's voice to engage our emotions more fully. As the handwriting makes us notice, this man seems still to be alive. How could anyone take his picture and not do something to stop his torture? Then, by implication, how can anyone be indifferent to racial violence? Williams comments:

1.7 Pat Ward Williams, *Accused/Blowtorch/Padlock*, 1986. Mixed media and photograph, 5 ft × 8 ft 4 ins (1.52 × 2.54 m). Collection of the artist. Courtesy Williams College Museum of Art.

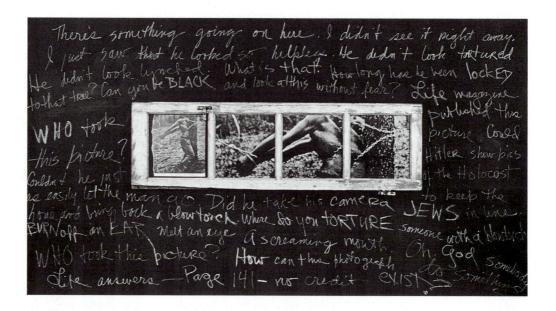

A single, documentary shot is usually too little to express a broader idea about racism. That's why I started to make photographic constructions ... My constructions promote discussion. People can talk about the provocative or controversial images. Someone's curiosity might be sparked to look further into a situation or issue.[1]

By contrast, the political intent of some art may be to soothe rather than to inflame passions. The Vietnam War deeply divided the people of the United States. There was a desire to create a memorial to those who died fighting the war, but how could this be done in a way that did not antagonize either the relatives of the deceased or the opponents of the war? In an open competition, the winning solution was created by a young architecture student, Maya Lin. Her Vietnam Veterans' Memorial in Washington, D.C. (1.8), is a very quiet but nonetheless profoundly moving statement about the deaths of Americans in the war. Elegantly and starkly simple, it consists of an angled wall

of polished black granite, incised with the names of all the Americans who died in the conflict, and then tapering down to disappear into the earth. In the face of bitter divisions that once existed between proponents and opponents of American involvement in the war, Lin intentionally avoided presenting a blatant political idea. The meaning of the wall is to be discovered individually by each viewer. Lin explains:

Many earlier war memorials were propagandized statements about the victor, the issues, the politics, and not about the people who served and died. I felt a memorial should be honest about the reality of war and be for the people who gave their lives.... I didn't want a static object that people would just look at, but something they could relate to as on a journey, or passage, that would bring each to his own conclusions.... I didn't visualize heavy physical objects implanted in the earth; instead it was as if the black-brown earth were polished and made into an interface between the sunny world and the quiet, dark world beyond, that we can't enter.[2]

1.8 Maya Ying Lin, Vietnam Veterans' Memorial, Washington, D.C., 1982-4. Black granite, length 250 ft (76.2 m).

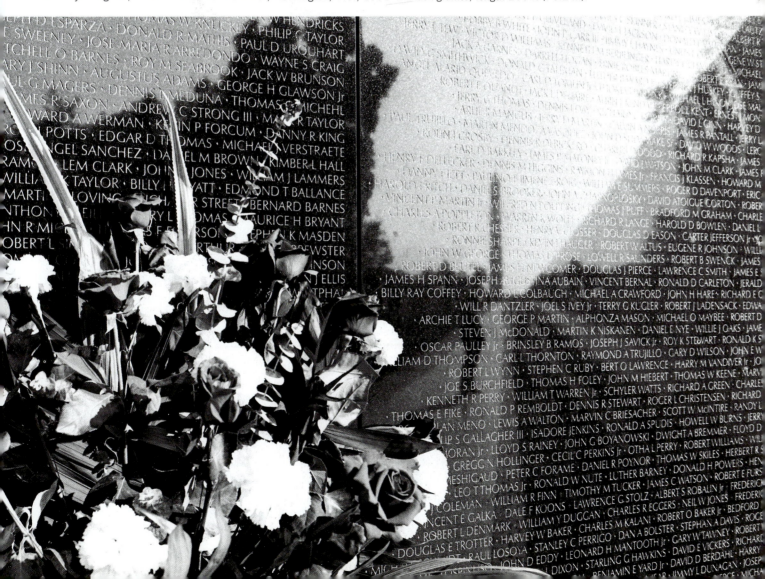

Power and Propaganda

Another way in which artists' talents and creativity have been engaged is in the creation of works that allow the person or group who paid for them to gain prestige. Certainly this was an intention behind the commissioning of many monumental pieces, such as Louis XIV's colossal palace at Versailles (1.9). A huge corps of architects, interior designers, sculptors, painters, and landscape artists worked for almost half a century to create not only the largest and grandest palace the world had ever seen, surrounded by an immense and elaborate park, but also an entire city for government officials, courtiers, servants, and the military. Their buildings radiate along avenues that intersect in the king's bedroom, symbolizing the vast wealth and power of the absolute monarch.

Mingled with a show of wealth is the desire to impress the public with one's good taste in art. Today corporations often choose for this purpose large, nonobjective paintings and sculptures. These can suggest a sophisticated, contemporary corporate image, and they have no subject matter that would offend anyone. But it takes wealth and a certain daring to commission monumental modern sculpture to occupy expensive urban real estate. The point of using valuable Manhattan ground-level space for a huge cube resting precariously on one corner (1.10) may escape the uninitiated, but this sculpture by Isamu Noguchi is a signal to those who know something about art that its owner, the Marine Midland Bank, is imaginative, forward-looking, and prestigious.

1.9 Louis le Vau and Jules Hardouin-Mansart, Palace of Versailles, France, 1669-85.

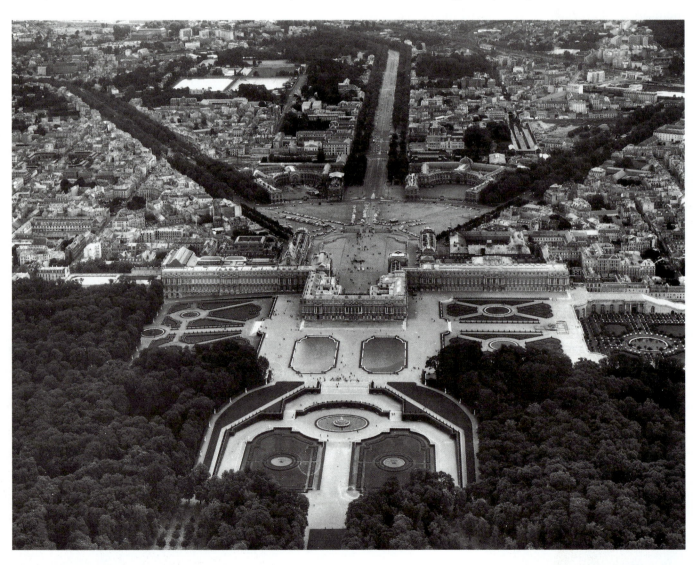

1.10 (opposite) Isamu Noguchi, *Red Cube*, 1968. Marine Midland Plaza, New York.

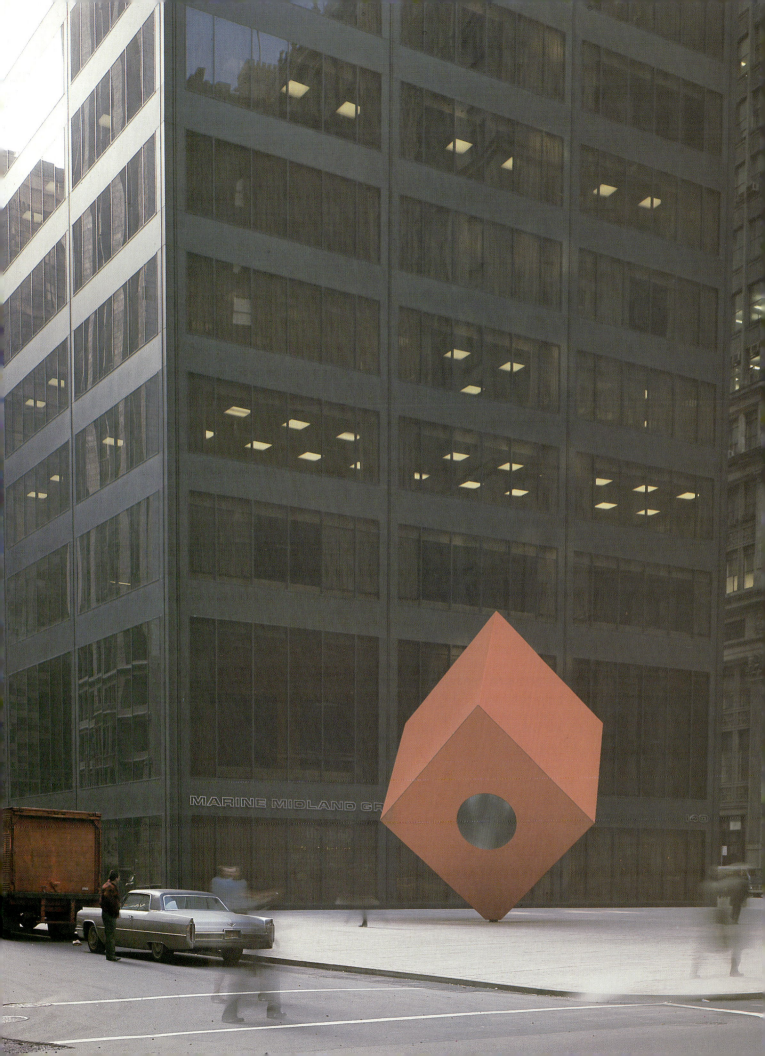

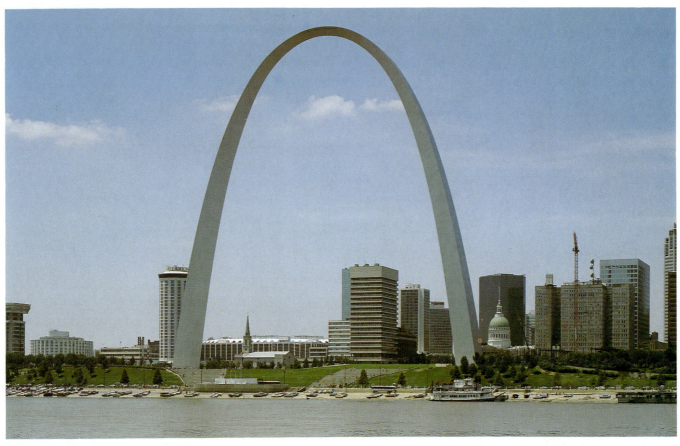

1.11 Eero Saarinen, Jefferson National Expansion Memorial (*The Gateway to the West*), St. Louis, Missouri, 1966.

Patronage plays a major part not only in financing but also in determining the content of commissioned artworks. Governments like to project positive self-concepts, presenting a proud image to both citizens and visitors. Such a monument to civic pride is the Jefferson National Expansion Memorial, magnificently engineered by architect Eero Saarinen (**1.11**). It was part of a federal project originally funded under the then president, Franklin D. Roosevelt, to glorify the territorial expansion of the United States. The great arch presents a visible symbol of St Louis as "The Gateway to the West." From a distance, it appears as a line thrown against the sky. From nearby, its girth becomes apparent: its triangular form is 54 feet (16.2 m) along each side at its bases, and carries stairways and elevators connecting with an observation room at the top. This soaring structure can be seen not only from the city but also from miles around.

The same artistic skills that can express civic pride can also be used coercively. The advertising executives who commission graphic designers are skillful at tapping into consumers' pride to convince them to buy products. Advertisements for expensive cars often speak to people's aspirations to wealth and good taste; ads for clothing often manipulate people's desire to exert sex appeal. Adolf Hitler had a clear sense of the tremendous impact of media propaganda and used it extensively and ultimately with tragic effect, to build popular support for his regime. Ludwig Hohlwein's poster commissioned for the Nazi regime (**1.12**) presents such a powerful visual image that the mere words *"Und du?"* ("And you?") convey the aggressive challenge to the civilian to become part of the war machine. We are shown only the storm-trooper's masculine features, nothing of his individuality; he becomes an abstraction for the idea of The German Soldier, a super-humanly strong man with the power of the group and the group's history behind him. The angle from which he is shown makes us look up at him, and the deliberate mingling of hero worship, intimidation, and brooding power is characteristic of the totalitarian values of the Nazi regime.

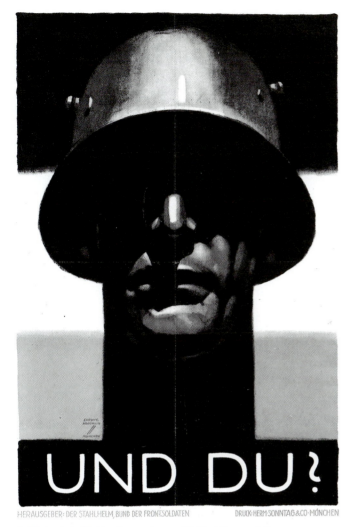

1.12 Ludwig Hohlwein, poster, c. 1943. Library of Congress, Washington, D.C. Poster Collection.

Narrative

Many artworks tell a story. Quite often the story is a spiritual one, commissioned by a religious institution, perhaps intended to give a lesson or to inspire worshippers. The Baroque sculptor and architect GianLorenzo Bernini was commissioned by the Roman Catholic Cardinal Cornaro to build an intimate and ornate chapel honoring himself and his family. As its altarpiece, Bernini created a lifesized sculpture of *The Ecstasy of St. Teresa* (**1.13**). It illustrates the story in which the saint is speared by an angel in a vision, leaving her "completely afire with love of God."

Visual stories are often told by means of symbols, such as the representation of God in Michelangelo's *Creation of Adam* (1.1) as a wise old man in the sky. Symbols are usually designed to be understood by the audience for whom they are made. People from cultures that regard the Ultimate Power as formless or as female would be puzzled by Michelangelo's depiction of God.

Sometimes, even though a story is being told in an artwork, its symbols are understood only by the artist or by an initiated few. In Australian aboriginal culture, the unseen world—the Dreaming—is understood as the ground of existence and the abode of powerful ancestral beings. Only the elders are initiated into the secrets of this world, but they are authorized to depict it symbolically. When acrylic paints were introduced to the indigenous people in the 1970s, the elders' paintings of the Dreaming took on new exuberance. On a superficial level, these paintings are aerial views of the sacred landscapes, but they are said to have many more levels of interpretation understood only by the elders.

Another kind of narrative can be perceived in some works of art, forming part of their visual content. This is the story of their artistic creation. In the aboriginal painting of *Burrowing Skink Dreaming at Parikirlangu*, supervised by Darby Jampijimpa (**1.14**),

1.13 GianLorenzo Bernini, *The Ecstasy of St. Teresa*, 1645-52. Marble, stucco, and gilt bronze, lifesize. Cornaro Chapel, Church of Santa Maria della Vittoria, Rome.

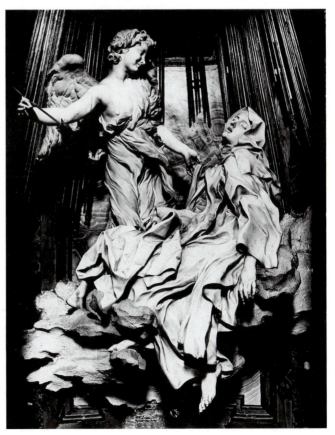

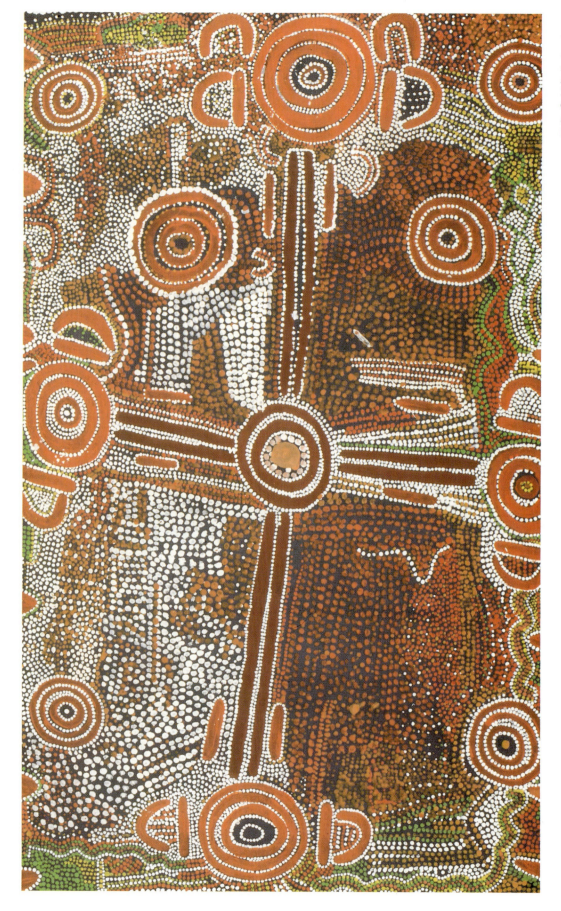

1.14 Darby Jampijimpa, *Burrowing Skink Dreaming at Parikirlangu*, 1986. Acrylic on canvas, 57¼ x 37 ins (145.3 x 94.2 cm). © Asia Society Galleries and South Australia Museum.

we can imagine the aboriginal artists at work, for the asymmetrical circles laid down are clearly the tracks of their brushstrokes. By contrast, Bernini in his *The Ecstasy of St. Teresa* (1.13), took pains to conceal traces of his own hand.

Inner Experiences

Rather than taking images or events outside themselves as their subjects, many artists have explored their own interior worlds. One aspect of this inner world is the capacity for fantasy—for imagining things that have never been seen, as in Paul Klee's *Twittering Machine* (1.16). Despite the delicate playfulness of this painting, Klee spoke about the act of artistic creation very seriously. For him, it seemed to be a way of approaching the unseen and the creator of all realms, both seen and unseen. In his *Creative Credo* he asserted that "visible reality is merely an isolated phenomenon latently outnumbered by other realities." He approached his materials with no preconceived subject matter, allowing unconscious understandings to guide his hand. "My hand is entirely the implement of a distant sphere,"[3] he explained. "What artist does not yearn to dwell near the mind, or heart, of creation itself, that prime mover of events in time and space?"[4]

Another artist who delved into the unconscious to bring forth fantastic images was Henri Rousseau. A retired Parisian customs collector, he painted exotic landscapes and creatures that he had never seen, as in *The Dream* (1.15). The narrative within the painting suggests the illogical happenings and inventive landscapes we experience in our dreams. Rousseau was a **naive artist**, one who had never been trained in the principles and techniques of art. For instance, the lighting in *The Dream* does not seem to come from the direction of the moon; Rousseau placed highlights and shadows where he wanted them, rather than

1.15 Henri Rousseau, *The Dream*, 1910. Oil on canvas, 6 ft 8½ ins × 9 ft 9½ ins (2.045 × 2.985 m). Collection Museum of Modern Art, New York. Gift of Nelson A. Rockefeller. Photograph © 1997 MOMA.

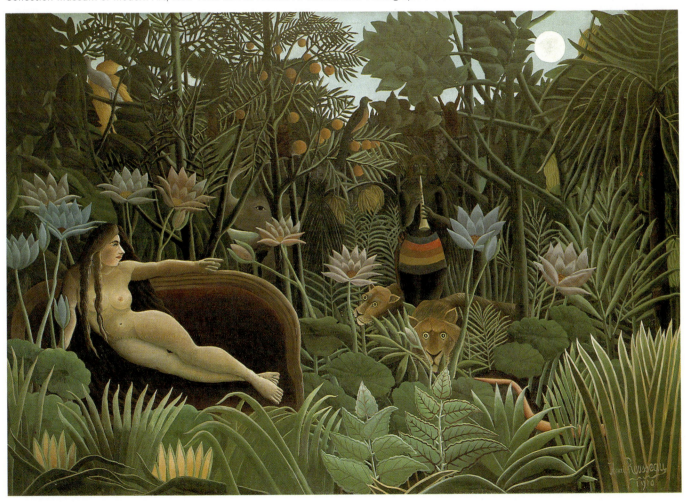

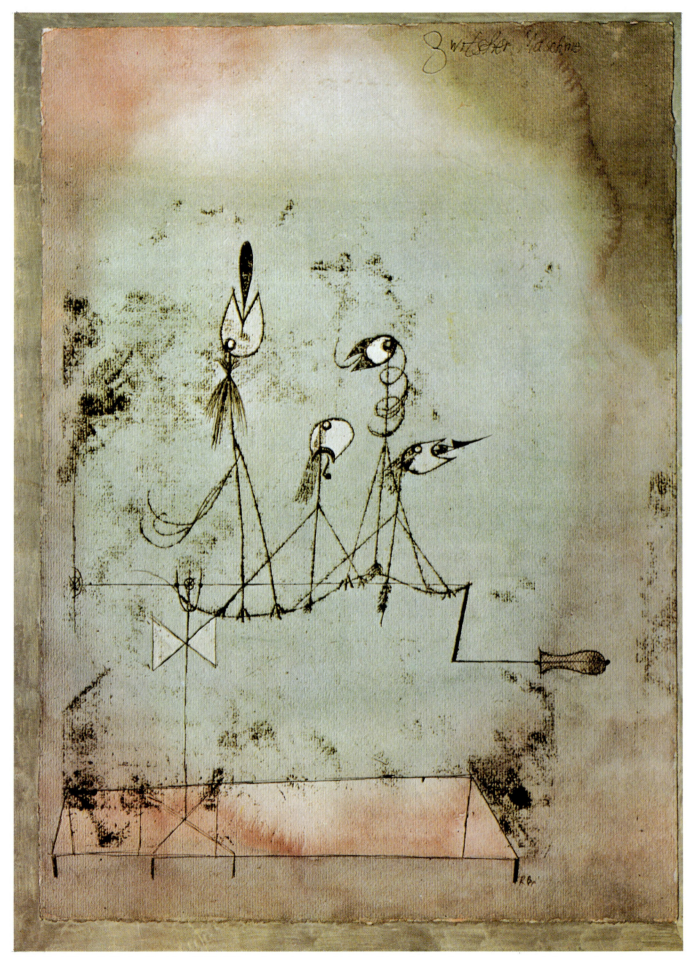

1.16 Paul Klee, *Twittering Machine*, 1922. Watercolor and pen and ink on oil transfer drawing on paper, mounted on cardboard, 25¼ × 19 ins (63.8 × 48.1 cm). Collection Museum of Modern Art, New York. Purchase. Photograph © 1997 MOMA.

where they would logically fall. Unencumbered by ideas of the way things "should" look or be represented, he was highly successful in entering the uncharted territory of the subconscious. Be that as it may, we respond to Rousseau's images on some level beneath conscious thought. Rousseau's untaught, natural sense of design and his detailed treatment of mysteriously juxtaposed figures give a haunting power to these landscapes of the soul.

Often artworks refer to cultural symbols for inner experience, which are best understood by people from that particular culture. For Korean women, "wrapping the bundle" is an expression that means packing up one's things and leaving the family, perhaps to avoid tension, perhaps to live with another person. To a Korean, the sight of a bundle of possessions evokes personal responses to change, impermanence, and uprooting of one's life, as poignantly suggested in Soo-ja Kim's installation piece *Deductive Object* (1.17). But although the symbolism here comes from a specific culture, it can have universal meanings, allowing people from other cultures to respond well to the work. Can you deduce any personal meaning from *Deductive Object?*

Inner experiences may also be depicted directly, as it were, without the use of any imagery from the outer world. Mark Rothko's subject-matter was sheer emotion, beyond form. His sublime nonobjective paintings, such as *Green on Blue* (1.18), offer large, hovering, soft-edged fields of color for quiet contemplation. People often respond to them with powerful emotion, as was Rothko's intention. He said:

> I am interested only in expressing the basic human emotions—tragedy, ecstasy, doom, and so on—and the fact that lots of people break down and cry when confronted with my pictures shows that I *communicate* with those basic human emotions. The people who weep before my pictures are having the same religious experience I had when I painted them. And if you . . . are moved only by their color relationships, then you miss the point.[5]

In some cases, artists draw their imagery from external realities but project their own state of mind

1.17 Soo-ja Kim, *Deductive Object*, Yangdong village, South Korea, 1994. Used clothes and used bedcovers.

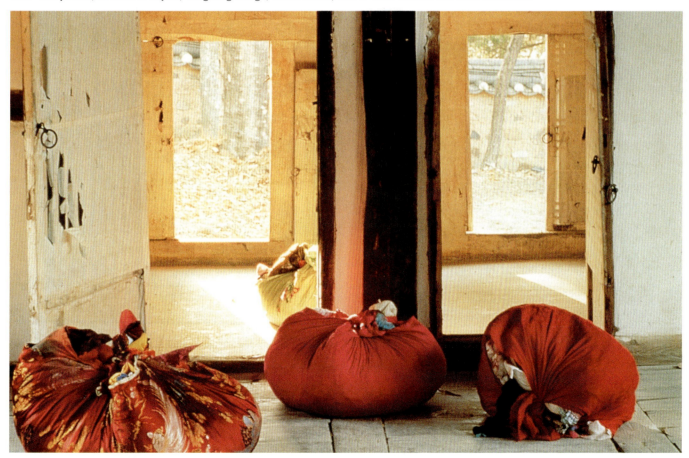

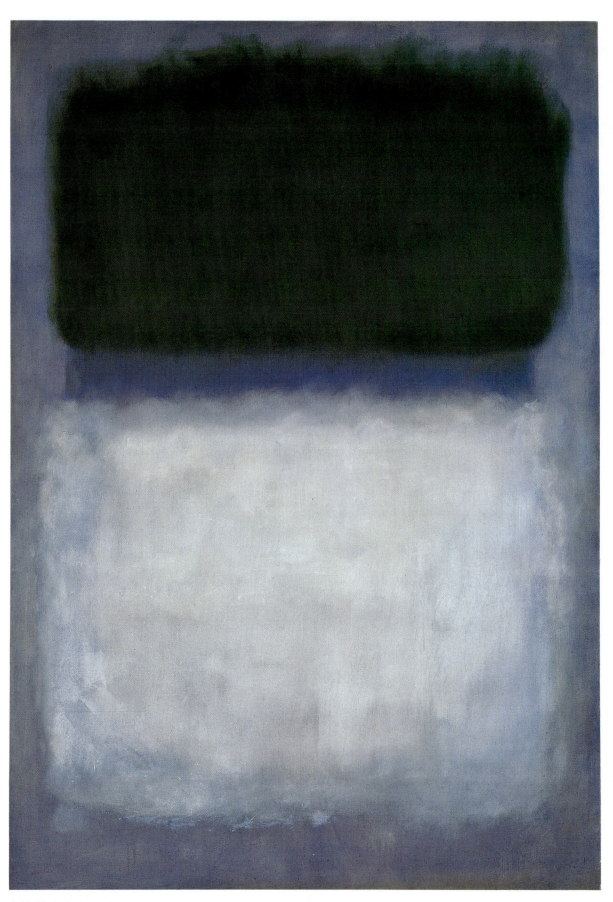

1.18 Mark Rothko, *Green on Blue*, 1956. Oil on canvas, 7 ft 5¾ ins × 5 ft 3¼ ins (2.28 × 1.61 m). University of Arizona Museum of Art, Tucson, Arizona. Gift of Edward J. Gallagher, Jr.

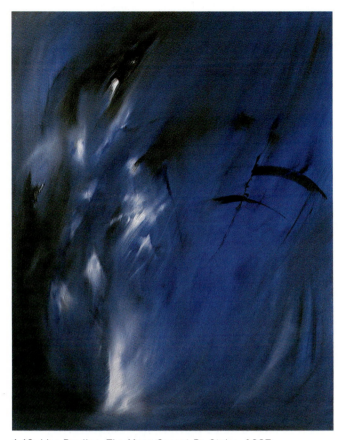

1.19 Lisa Bradley, *The Moon Cannot Be Stolen*, 1987.
Oil on canvas, 4 ft 2 ins × 3 ft 4 ins (1.27 × 1.02 m).
Courtesy of the artist.

onto them. Some quality inside the artist finds its counterpart in the outer world, revealing inner truths. One who worked in this way was Vincent van Gogh. His *The Starry Night* (1.21) reflects a dynamic vision of nature as ever-changing, in continuous motion. The sky boils with swirling energy patterns; the hills roll like waves; the trees writhe upward like flames. The houses in the village seem dwarfed by the cosmic drama, with the possible exception of the church spire. It is clear that, to see this pastoral landscape thus, van Gogh must have been highly sensitive and seething with inner energy (see Box).

Personal spirituality without reference to a particular religious tradition permeates much of artistic creation. Without theology, without historical references, such direct experiences of mystical dimensions of life are difficult to express, either in words or in images. Lisa Bradley says of her luminous paintings (1.19):

> In them you can see movement and stillness at the same time, things coming in and out of focus. The light seems to be from behind. There is a sense of something like a

permeable membrane, of things coming from one dimension to another. But even that doesn't describe it well.

How do you describe truth in words? That's what I want to reach—that nonverbal level of truth. These are things that go beyond our ability to communicate verbally, but perhaps we can suggest them visually. At a certain point in the process of the painting, every stroke is in perfect accord; there is a sense of the rightness in every stroke, a resonance with what is true.[6]

Intellectual Concepts

The impulse for some art is an intellectual idea. Vera Mukhina's huge *Machine Tractor Driver and Collective Farm Girl* (1.20) was a visual expression of the mid-twentieth-century communist theory that men and women of all classes could work side by side for the common good and so create a new egalitarian society.

These muscular figures bespeak Youth, Strength, Optimism. They appear to be moving forward so powerfully into the future that their clothing is blown back by the wind. In them is no hint of the weaknesses that caused the dream to collapse less than three-quarters of a century after the Russian Revolution of 1917.

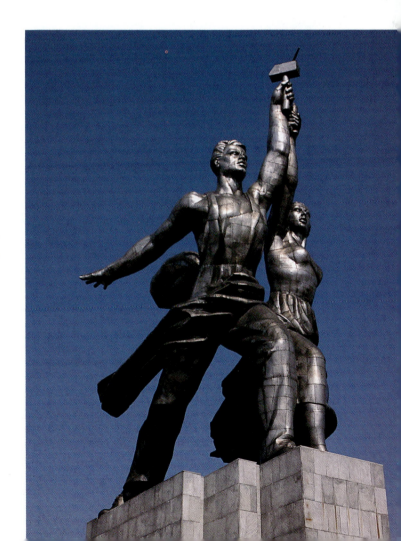

1.20 (right) Vera Mukhina, *Machine Tractor Driver and Collective Farm Girl*, undated, Moscow.

VINCENT VAN GOGH
on EMOTION AND INTELLECT

The Dutch Post-Impressionist painter Vincent van Gogh (1853–90) did not consider himself an artist at first. His father was a clergyman, and Vincent initially wanted to help people by being a missionary or lay preacher among the peasants. When that and other odd jobs did not work out, he discovered a love for painting. He spent all the money his supportive brother Theo sent him on paints and canvases, totally neglecting his physical health. But his work did not sell. He painted his famous sunflowers just to have something pretty to hang on the wall when Gauguin came to visit. At length he had to place himself in an asylum for protection during his periodic mental disorders. In July 1890 he tried to end his life, and died from the effects two days later. Although van Gogh is commonly characterized by his psychological imbalance and emotional intensity, he approached painting in a calculated, deliberate, albeit passionate, way, as he reveals in his letters to the faithful Theo:

"The cypresses are always occupying my thoughts, I should like to make something of them like the canvases of the sunflowers, because it astonishes me that they have not yet been done as I see them.

1.21 Vincent van Gogh, *The Starry Night*, 1889. Oil on canvas, 29 × 36¼ ins (73.7 x 92.1 cm). Collection Museum of Modern Art, New York. Acquired through the Lillie P. Bliss Bequest. Photograph © 1997 MOMA.

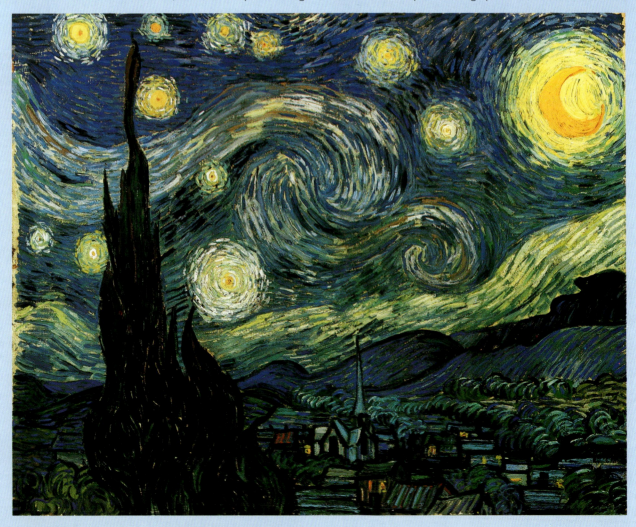

[The clump of cypresses, which rise in the left foreground of *The Starry Night* (1.21) but occurred in other van Gogh paintings as well] . . . is as beautiful of line and proportion as an Egyptian obelisk.

And the green has a quality of such distinction.

It is a splash of black in a sunny landscape, but it is one of the most interesting black notes, and the most difficult to hit off exactly that I can imagine.

But then you must see them against the blue, *in* the blue, rather. To paint nature here, as everywhere, you must be in it a long time."

Letter 596, June 25, 1889

"I am quite sure that *color*, that *chiaroscuro* [the effects of light and shadow], that *perspective* [degrees of light and dark] and that *drawing*, in short, everything has fixed laws which one must and can study, like chemistry or algebra. This is *far from being* the easiest view of things, and one who says, 'Oh, one must know it all instinctively,' takes it very easy indeed.

I do not at all intend to think and live less passionately than I do. By no means—I may meet with rebuffs, I may often be mistaken—often be wrong—but that only as far as it goes—basically I am not wrong."

Letter 381, October 1884

"I must warn you that everyone will think I work too fast.

Don't you believe a word of it.

Is it not emotion, the sincerity of one's feeling for nature, that draws us, and if the emotions are sometimes so strong that one works without knowing one works, when sometimes the strokes come with a sequence and a coherence like words in a speech or a letter, then one must remember that it has not always been so . . . So one must strike while the iron is hot, and put the forged bars on one side."

Letter 504, Summer 1888

"When I come back myself from the mental labor of balancing the six essential colors . . . sheer work and calculation, with one's mind utterly on the stretch, like an actor on the stage in a difficult part, with a hundred things at once to think of in a single half hour.

Don't think that I would artificially keep up a feverish condition, but do understand that I am in the midst of a complicated calculation which results in quick succession in canvases quickly executed, but calculated long *beforehand*. So now, when anyone says that such and such is done too quickly, you can reply that they have looked at it too quickly."

Letter 507, Summer 1888[7]

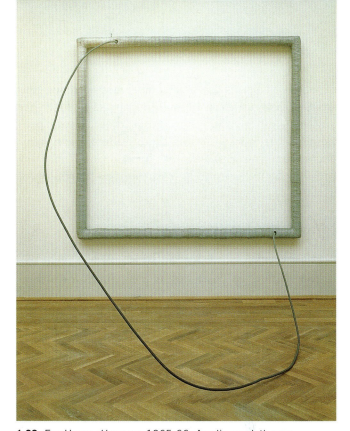

1.22 Eva Hesse, *Hang-up*, 1965-66. Acrylic on cloth over wood and steel. 5 ft 10 ins × 6 ft 9 ins × 6 ft 6 ins (1.82 × 2.13 × 1.98 m). Art Institute of Chicago, Chicago, Illinois.

To give visual expression to something so immaterial as a thought with only a bare reference to form is a challenge taken up by certain artists in the latter half of the twentieth century. Their work is known as **conceptual art**. In conceptual art, physical form is stripped away or de-emphasized, so that the emphasis falls upon the idea. Some conceptual works consist merely of a set of directions or a photograph of a temporary construction. Others are minimal in form, such as Eva Hesse's *Hang-up* (1.22). The thin, eccentric loop projecting from an empty frame seems to express the idea of not fitting in, of being isolated or breaking away like a mutation from a meaningless base, but still being attached to it, bound by it, and thus unsure of its own identity. Hesse speaks of such sculptures as embodying the "absurdity" and "contradictions" in her life. Hesse was a Jew born in Germany who, with her sister, barely escaped being sent to a concentration camp in 1939, when she was two. She was reunited with her parents, but they later divorced and her mother committed suicide. Hesse struggled as a young female artist in New York developing new directions in an art world dominated by men. How can one express something that has not been articulated before? If one is insecure, one will feel absurd judged by mainstream standards. Hesse also despaired of being able to fulfill all the roles expected of her as a woman, wife, housekeeper, and artist—"I cannot even be myself," she said. After her husband left her and her father died, Hesse proclaimed, "Art and work and art and life are very connected, and my whole life has been absurd."[8] *Hang-up* can thus be understood as a bare-bones expression of her idea of herself.

Ideals of Beauty

Far from eschewing form, many artists have had the strong impulse to create art as a celebration of form. There may be some narrative content, or expression of feelings or ideas, or some political context, but the emphasis in such cases is to create forms that are the most beautiful creations of human hands. Ideals of beauty are culturally influenced, but elegance of form often transcends culture to appeal to people everywhere.

Perhaps the world's most dramatic example of this impulse to create beauty is the Taj Mahal (1.5). The Mughal Emperor Shah Jahan's desire was to immortalize his wife's memory in a mausoleum of matchless beauty. For twenty-two years, the greatest masons and twenty thousand laborers worked under his direction to execute his ideal. Their materials were pure white marble, sandstone, and precious stones gathered from as far afield as Persia, Baghdad, Tibet, and Sri Lanka. Across the exquisite surfaces are sculpted verses from the Qur'an, and inlays of diamond, lapis lazuli, sapphire, carnelian, turquoise, agate, coral, garnet, onyx, and amethyst to create flowers of subtly varying colors, such as those on the cenotaphs overlying the graves (1.23). The regal symmetry of the great

1.23 Taj Mahal, detail of cenotaph showing inlay of flowers.

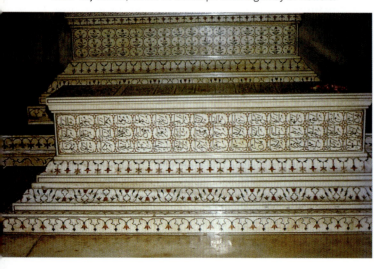

the towers that flank it, like ladies-in-[wait]ing a lovely princess, is beautifully reflecting pool. For three centuries as amazed and touched throngs of the world.

...derstanding and appreciation of such ...hs, Chapter 2 of this book will expl... f **design**, which are the visible char... line, shape and form, space, textur... color, and movement or change ...ts study these characteristics and ...sciously to achieve their ends. Ch... **principles of design**— how a wo... nified and engaging effect. The ...e will be exploring include ...trast, rhythm, balance, con... ...phasis, economy, proportion, ...p to the surrounding environment. ... arts 2 and 3 of the book will explore two- and three-dimensional media and their methods, revealing the difficulties as well as the potential of each medium.

FORMS OF ART

Just as the content of artworks differs widely, so do their forms. In general, artworks can be described in terms of their two- or three-dimensionality, their degree of realism, their usefulness or nonfunctionality, and their intended audience, be it public or private. The ever-changing evolution of formal styles in art will be examined in Chapter 15, with particular reference to historical styles in Western art.

Two- and Three-Dimensional Art

Three-dimensional works have spatial depth as well as height and width. Degrees of three-dimensionality are discussed in Chapter 2. **Two-dimensional** works, by contrast, are developed on a flat plane without depth (though the surface may be somewhat built up with paint). Both types of art are shown in Figure 1.24, a scene from an exhibit at New York's Whitney Museum of American Art. Claes Oldenburg's *Soft Saxophone* is three-dimensional. Visitors to the exhibit could walk around the soft sculpture, puzzling over its contours. (Is it like a balloon being deflated to near-nothingness? Or is it in the process of being inflated?) The museum

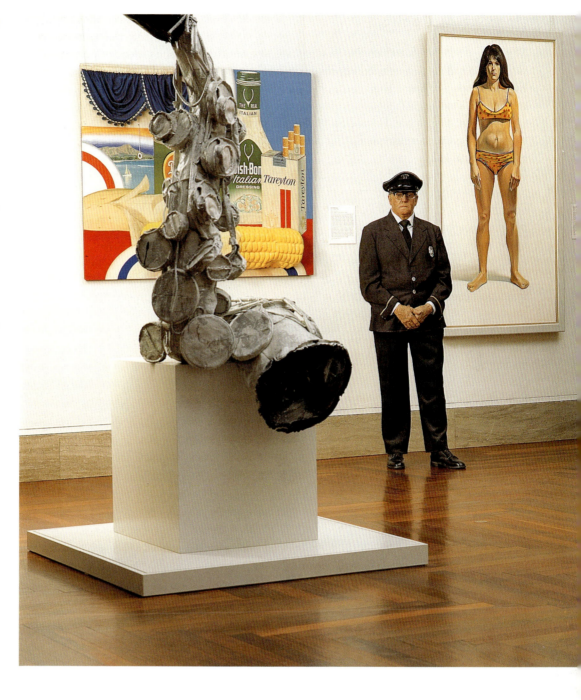

1.24 Duane Hanson, *Museum Guard,* 1975. Polyester, fiberglass, oil and vinyl, 69 x 21 x 13 ins (175.3 x 53.3 x 33 cm); Claes Oldenburg, *Soft Saxophone: Scale B*, 1992. Canvas, wood, clothes line, dacron, resin, and latex paint, 69 × 35 × 36 ins (175.3 × 89 × 91.4 cm). On long-term loan from the Hall Family Foundation; Tom Wesselmann, *Still Life no. 24,* 1962. Acrylic polymer on board, fabric curtain, 48 × 59⅞ × 7⅞ ins (122 × 152.1 × 20 cm); Wayne Thiebaud, *Bikini*, 1964. Oil on canvas, 72 × 35⅞ ins (182.9 × 91.1 cm). Parker-Grant Gallery installation, 1994. The Nelson-Atkins Museum of Art, Kansas City, Missouri. Photo by E. G. Schempf.

guard standing near by is also a three-dimensional sculpture, Duane Hanson's *Museum Guard*, a fiberglass and polyester cast of a real human being, dressed in guard's clothing. Hanson's human sculptures are so lifelike that viewers often mistake them for real people.

On the wall are hung two two-dimensional paintings. In Wayne Thiebaud's *Bikini* a woman stares straight out at us, her body language and the starkness of the painted background emphasizing the direct visual confrontation. Tom Wesselmann's *Still Life* gives presence on a grand scale to items of pop culture, almost like icons of the times: cigarettes, canned food, Midwestern corn, and the American landscape seen through the window. These pictures are painted larger than life in a way that makes them appear almost more real than a photograph. Thus, as this exhibit shows, whether art exists in rarefied two-dimensional space or in the three-dimensional world we experience, it is equally capable of engaging our attention.

Degrees of Realism

When art attempts to represent what we see in the world around us, it is called **representational** or **figurative** work. Within this category there are many degrees of realism.

William Beckman's *Power Lines* (**1.25**) illustrates the highest degree of **realism**. Rather than painting only the conventionally "pretty" aspects of this rural scene, he included what might be considered blots on the landscape—the road and power lines. Nevertheless, the slice of life is carefully chosen, just as a photographer carefully selects views that work well aesthetically. In *Power Lines*, the road and power lines curve in flowing relationship and opposition to each other, creating a harmony of movement that is balanced by the staid quietness of the rural scene.

A step removed from this realism is **idealization**—transforming the real world into one that approximates one's ideas of perfection. If you look ahead at the Classical Greek sculpture of a spear bearer in Figure 2.31, you can see that the man's head is more than humanly perfect: the eyes, nose, mouth, and hair have a smoothness and symmetry that are not seen in real human beings. Similarly, Peter Paul Rubens's *Landscape with Rainbow* (**1.26**) offers a romanticized picture of country life. Everyone seems healthy and happy, even the animals, and the sun's appearance after a shower of rain floods the scene with light, bringing out a double rainbow in the sky. The pastoral idyll expresses Rubens's own apparent pleasure with his life in the Flanders countryside.

Another kind of shift from absolute realism is **stylization**—emphasizing design rather than exact repre-

1.25 William Beckman, *Power Lines*, 1982. Pastel on paper, 24⅜ × 33 ins (61.9 × 83.8 cm). San Francisco Museum of Modern Art, San Francisco, California. The Glenn C. Janss Collection.

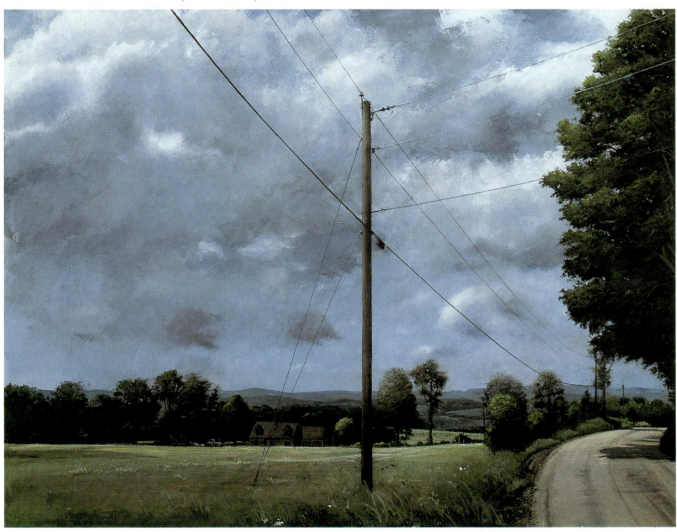

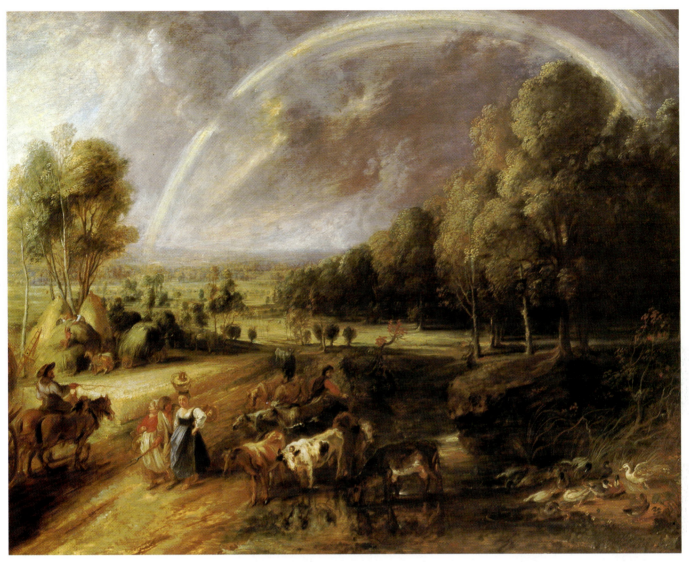

1.26 Peter Paul Rubens, *Landscape with Rainbow*, c. 1635. Panel, 37¼ × 48½ ins (94.6 × 123.2 cm). Alte Pinakothek, Munich.

sentation when working with natural forms. Diego Rivera's *Flower Day* (1.27) stylizes human figures into massive forms. The simplified outlines turn arms and garments into interlocking blocks of color, shaded at the edges for a monumental three-dimensional effect. The seated local women and the flower carrier are thus transformed into sacred statues honoring the abundance of the earth.

A somewhat different approach to figurative art is called **abstraction**—extracting the essence of real objects rather than faithfully representing their surface appearance. A series of trees by Dutch artist Piet Mondrian illustrates the process of increasing abstraction. The first one shown, *Tree II* (1.28), is a fairly representational depiction of what appears to be an old apple tree, with riotous interplay among the lines of the main branches and the secondary suckers that shoot upward from them. In the second, *The Gray Tree* (1.29), Mondrian has in effect pruned away the suckers, leaving only the branches that form a rhythmic series of arcs, echoing and counterbalancing the strong leftward arc of the main trunk. Mondrian also develops interest in the shapes of the spaces between the branches by painting them as if they had textures of their own. In the third, most abstract, tree image, *Flowering Apple Tree* (1.30), the thickness of trunk and branches is also pared away, leaving only the interaction of arcing lines and the spaces between them. Here Mondrian has reduced the visual essence of a tree as lines in space to its bare bones.

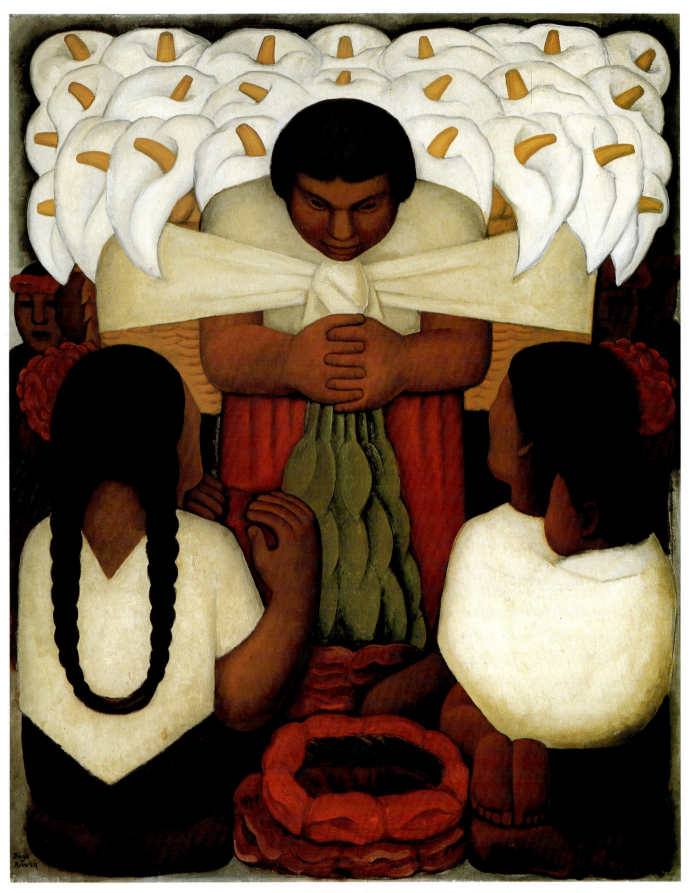

1.27 Diego Rivera, *Flower Day*, 1925. Encaustic on canvas, 4 ft 10 ins × 3 ft 11½ ins (1.47 × 1.20 m).
Los Angeles County Museum of Art, Los Angeles, California. County Funds.

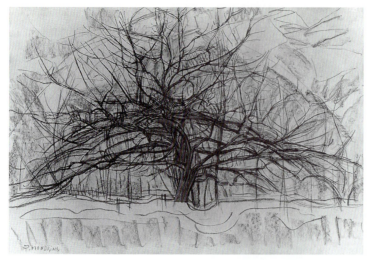

1.28 (left) Piet Mondrian, *Tree II*, 1912. Black crayon on paper, 22¼ × 33¼ ins (56.5 × 84.5 cm). Haags Gemeente Museum, The Hague, Netherlands.

1.29 (below) Piet Mondrian, *The Gray Tree*, 1912. Oil on canvas, 31 × 42 ins (78.5 × 107.5 cm). Haags Gemeente Museum, The Hague. On loan from S. B. Slijpen.

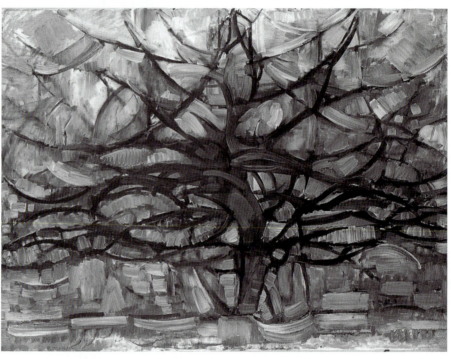

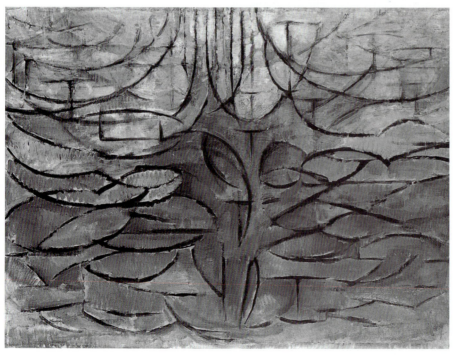

1.30 (left) Piet Mondrian, *Flowering Apple Tree*, 1912. Oil on canvas, 30¾ × 41¾ ins (78 × 106 cm). Haags Gemeente Museum, The Hague.

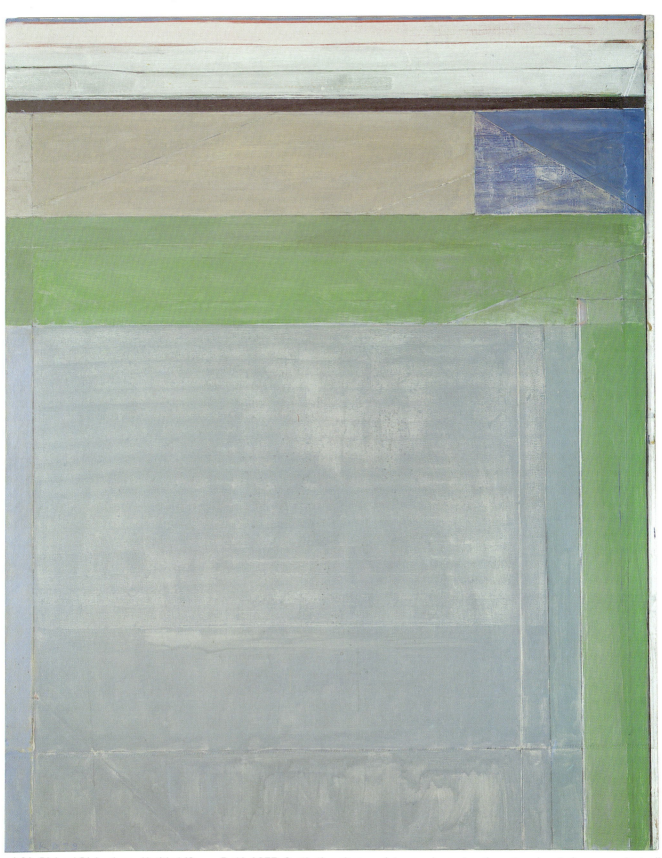

1.31 Richard Diebenkorn, *Untitled (Ocean Park)*, 1977. Synthetic polymer paint, gouache, watercolor, cut-and-pasted paper, and pencil on cut-and-pasted paper, 18⅝ x 33 ins (47.4 x 84 cm). Museum of Modern Art, New York. Purchase. Photograph © 1997 MOMA.

The opposite extreme from realism is **nonobjective** or **nonrepresentational** work, in which no reference at all is made to objects from the physical world. Here one sees only pure elements of design—lines, shapes or forms, space, textures, colors. Richard Diebenkorn's *Ocean Park* painting shown in Figure **1.31** is clearly nonobjective. The title refers to the area of Santa Monica, California, where he has his studio. He is working not with physical imagery but with the pure elements and principles of design, particularly a counterplay between rigidly geometrical lines and shapes and a more organic sense of weathered, light-and-color-filled spaciousness created by repeated **scumbling** (dry-brush applications of thin layers of paint) and scraping of paint pigments. In the end, the colors and textures may be subtly reminiscent of an oceanside park, even in the absence of any figurative imagery.

The less representational a work is, the more we must bring to it if we are to appreciate it. In Mondrian's more abstract trees, we have to use our memories of trees to interpret the images. We are also asked to become intellectually involved in discovering relationships between lines and spaces. When all figurative imagery is deleted, our response no longer has any base in our experiences of the physical world. Instead, we can explore the work as we would explore virgin territory. Indeed, nonobjective art has historically been used in many cultures to suggest spiritual realities that lie beyond form. The Yoruba divination bag shown in Figure **1.32** incorporates many common motifs for the intangible dimensions of life, including swirling circles within circles, the four directions of the universe, and intertwined lines.

1.32 Yoruba diviner's bag.

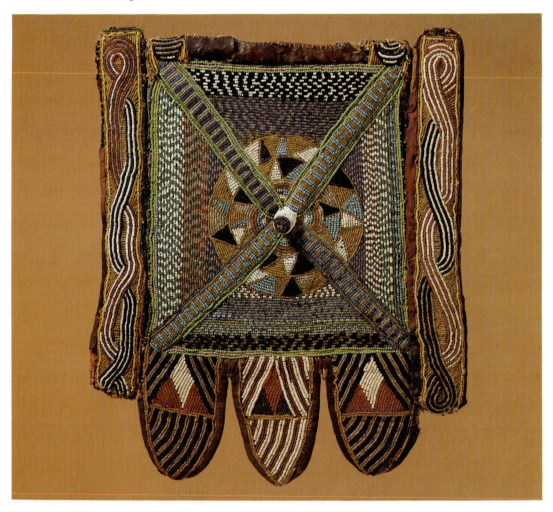

GEORGIA O'KEEFFE
on "SAYING WHAT I WANT TO"

Georgia O'Keeffe (1887–1986), an austere, strong-minded woman who painted until her death at the age of ninety-nine, is considered one of the greatest American artists of the twentieth century. She is particularly famous for her large abstractions of flowers, as shown in *Lily—White with Black* (**1.33**), animal bones, mysterious organic forms, and landscapes of the New Mexico desert, where she spent her later years as a near-recluse. For her, painting was a way of communicating about experiences and sensations that could not be expressed in any other way. And, although she had studied and practiced previous artists' methods, she was also determined to use her skills to communicate in a different way. She explains in her letters:

"It was in the fall of 1915 that I first had the idea that what I had been taught was of little value to me except for the use of my materials as a language—charcoal, pencil, pen and ink, watercolor, pastel, and oil. I had become fluent with them when I was so young that they were simply another language that I handled easily. But what to say with them? I had been taught to work like others, and after careful thinking I decided that I wasn't

going to spend my life doing what had already been done . . . I decided I was a very stupid fool not to at last paint as I wanted to and say what I wanted to when I painted . . ."[9]

Among her letters are these comments:

"The large White Flower with the golden heart is something I have to say about White—quite different from what White has been meaning to me. Whether the flower or the color is the focus I do not know. I do know that the flower is painted large to convey to you my experience of the flower—and what is my experience of the flower if it is not color.

I know I cannot paint a flower. I cannot paint the sun on the desert on a bright summer morning but maybe in terms of paint color I can convey to you my experience of the flower or the experience that makes the flower significant to me at that particular time.

Color is one of the great things in the world that makes life worth living to me and as I have come to think of painting it is my effort to create an equivalent with paint color for the world—life as I see it."

November 1, 1930

"From experiences of one kind or another shapes and colors come to me very clearly—Sometimes I start in very realistic fashion and as I go on from one painting after another of the same thing it becomes simplified till it can be nothing but abstract—but for me it is my reason for painting it I suppose.

At the moment I am very annoyed—I have the shapes—on yellow scratch paper—in my mind for over a year—and I cannot see the color for them—I've drawn them again—and again—it is from something I have heard again and again till I hear it in the wind—but I cannot get the color for it—only shapes."

April 22, 1957

"I think [walking in the desert] is almost the best thing to do that I know of out here—it is so bare—with a sort of ages old feeling of death on it—still it is warm and soft and I love it with my skin . . ."

Early 1940s

"I liked it that you liked the blue and the red of the bone series. It is a kind of thing that I do that makes me feel I am going off into space—in a way that I like—and

that frightens me a little because it is so unlike what anyone else is doing. I always feel that sometime I may fall off the edge—It is something I like so much to do that I don't care if I do fall off the edge—No sense in it but it is my way . . ."

December 24, 1945[10]

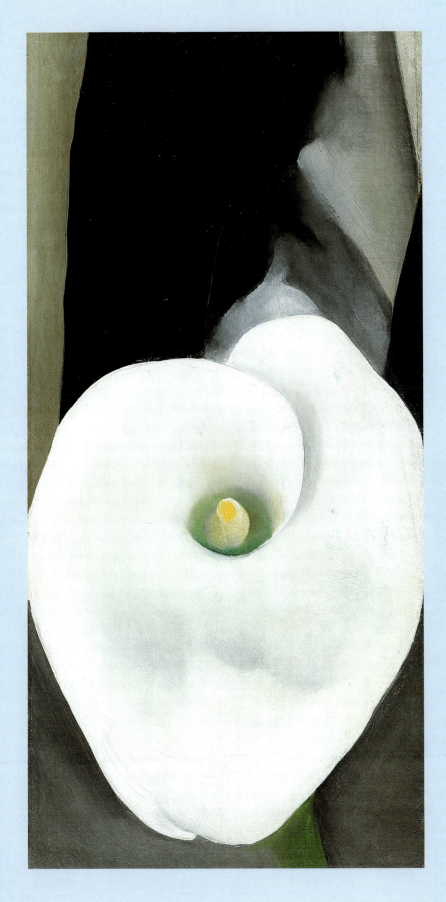

1.33 Georgia O'Keeffe, *Lily—White with Black*, 1927. Oil on board, 12 × 6 ins (30.5 × 15.2 cm). Estate of Georgia O'Keeffe.

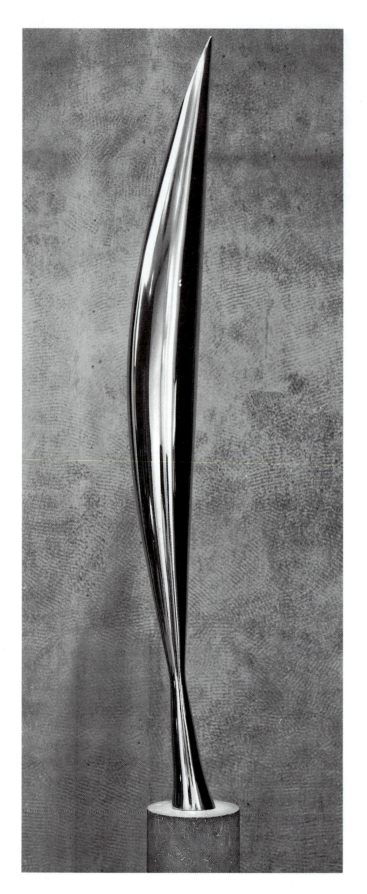

Fine and Applied Arts

In addition to dimensionality and realism, another distinction that can be made among works of art is whether they were originally intended as objects to be looked at or as objects to be used. The **fine arts**, such as drawing, painting, printmaking, and sculpture, involve the production of works to be seen and experienced primarily on an abstract rather than practical level. Pieces of fine art may evoke emotional, intellectual, sensual, political, or spiritual responses in us. Those who love the fine arts feel that these responses are very valuable, perhaps especially so in a highly materialistic world, for they expand our awareness of the great richness of life itself. Auguste Rodin, the nineteenth-century sculptor whose work *The Gates of Hell* we explore in depth in Chapter 16, offered a passionate challenge to artists—and to those who are touched by their works: "The main thing is to be moved, to love, to hope, to tremble, to live."[11]

Constantin Brancusi's elegant *Bird in Space* (**1.34**) has no utilitarian function whatsoever. It is solely "art for art's sake," a highly refined suggestion of that ephemeral moment when a bird in flight catches the light. Indeed, the effect captured Brancusi's imagination, and between 1910 and the early 1950s he created a series of twenty-eight similar birds in bronze and marble, explaining that "The Bird has fascinated me and will not release me."[12] It is based on the Rumanian legend of Maiastra, a magical golden bird whose feathers shone like the sun, illuminating the darkness. When struck by light that brings out their highly polished surface, Brancusi's bronze birds become radiant, light-giving sources, formless points of light in the immensity of space. Brancusi said:

> As a child, I used to dream that I was flying among trees and up into the sky. I have always remembered this dream and for forty-five years I have made birds. It is not the bird that I want to express but the gift, the taking off, the *élan* ... God is everywhere. One is God when one forgets oneself and if one is humble and makes the gift of oneself, there is God in your work ... One lady in New York felt that and, kneeling, wept before one of my Birds.[13]

Unlike the nonfunctional appeals of the fine arts, the first purpose of the **applied arts** is to serve some

1.34 Constantin Brancusi, *Bird in Space*, 1928. Bronze (unique cast), 54 × 8½ × 6½ ins (137.2 × 21.6 × 16.5 cm). Museum of Modern Art, New York. Anonymous donation. Photograph © 1997 MOMA.

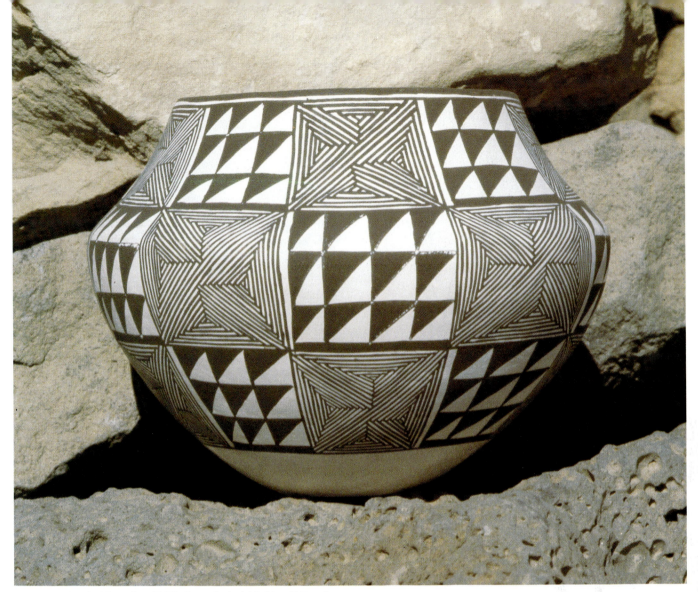

1.35 Lucy Lewis, Water jar, 1979. Ceramic, height 6 ins (15 cm).

useful function. Traditional basket-makers, furniture-makers, potters, and weavers around the world create objects to hold things, to sit upon, to cover the body. But many craftspeople have not been content solely to do the bare minimum of work to create functional objects. Everywhere, their creative urge has burst the confines of functionality, leading to infinite variations in design. Lucy Lewis, a traditional potter from Acoma Pueblo in New Mexico, used the chewed end of a yucca cactus spine to paint the fine lines of an elaborate design on the surface of her water jar (**1.35**). But the jar's main purpose is to hold water. Until recently, the people of Acoma, which may be the oldest continually inhabited city in the United States, still followed the old ways, carrying water for drinking, cooking, and washing up to their adobe homes from natural rock cisterns on the cliff walls below. The forms of their water jars were therefore designed to prevent spilling and to balance readily on the carrier's head. The pots also had to be light in weight, so Acoma ware is some of the world's thinnest-walled pottery. Interestingly, the languages of most Native American peoples do not include a word that means "fine art"; although they traditionally created pottery, basketry, and woven materials with a highly sophisticated sense of design, they used these pieces simply as part of their everyday lives.

The applied art of pottery-making is one of the **crafts**, the making of useful objects by hand. Other applied art disciplines are similarly functional. **Graphic designers** create advertisements, fabrics, layouts for books and magazines, logos for corporate identification, and so on; **industrial designers** shape the mass-produced objects used by high-tech societies, from cars, telephones, and teapots to the carefully sculptured Coca-Cola bottle (**1.36**). Other

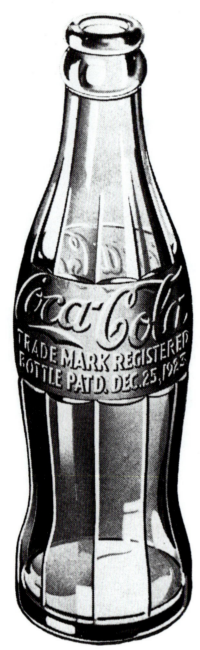

1.36 Alex Samuelson, Coca-Cola bottle, designed 1913, patented (with minor modifications) 1915, 1923, 1937.

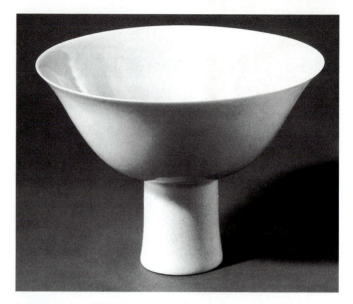

1.37 Stemcup, Ch'ing dynasty, Ch'ien Lung reign, 1736-39. Porcelain, 3⅞ ins (9.8 cm) high. Yale University Art Gallery, Connecticut. Gift of Dr. Yale Kneeland, Jr., B.A. 1922.

Many functional pieces have been made with the accent on their visual appeal rather than their functional qualities. The fine porcelain stemcup shown in Figure **1.37** is so beautifully designed that we cannot consider it simply as a functional piece. It is equally a work of fine art, created for those who could afford to surround themselves with costly beauty, even in the functional furnishings of their homes.

Another reason for the blurring of the distinction between fine and applied arts is that the artistic sophistication of many functional pieces and the time and skill involved in handmade crafts are increasingly appreciated by Western viewers. The everyday pottery of people who still follow their culture's traditional lifeways, along with many other examples of applied design, are now included in major museum collections, as objects both of cultural significance and of pure visual delight.

Public and Private Art

Some art is intended chiefly for private use or enjoyment; some for the public at large. Private works are of a scale and character that invite intimate participation, though they may secondarily be displayed in museums as well. In a traditional Japanese home, the *tokonoma* alcove, like the one shown in Figure **1.38**, is a quiet spot for private contemplation, usually decorated only by a single scroll painting and a vase with flowers, whose natural beauty is thought to humble anything created by humans. Originally set aside for the worship

applied arts include clothing design, interior design, and environmental design.

Having made this traditional distinction between the fine and applied arts, we must note that the boundary between them is blurred. For one thing, certain works had functions when they were created that are now overlooked by those who consider them solely as fine arts. The sculptures and stained-glass windows of Gothic cathedrals were functional in the sense that they were designed to teach and inspire people of the Christian faith.

1.38 (opposite) *Tokonoma* alcove in a private home, Japan.

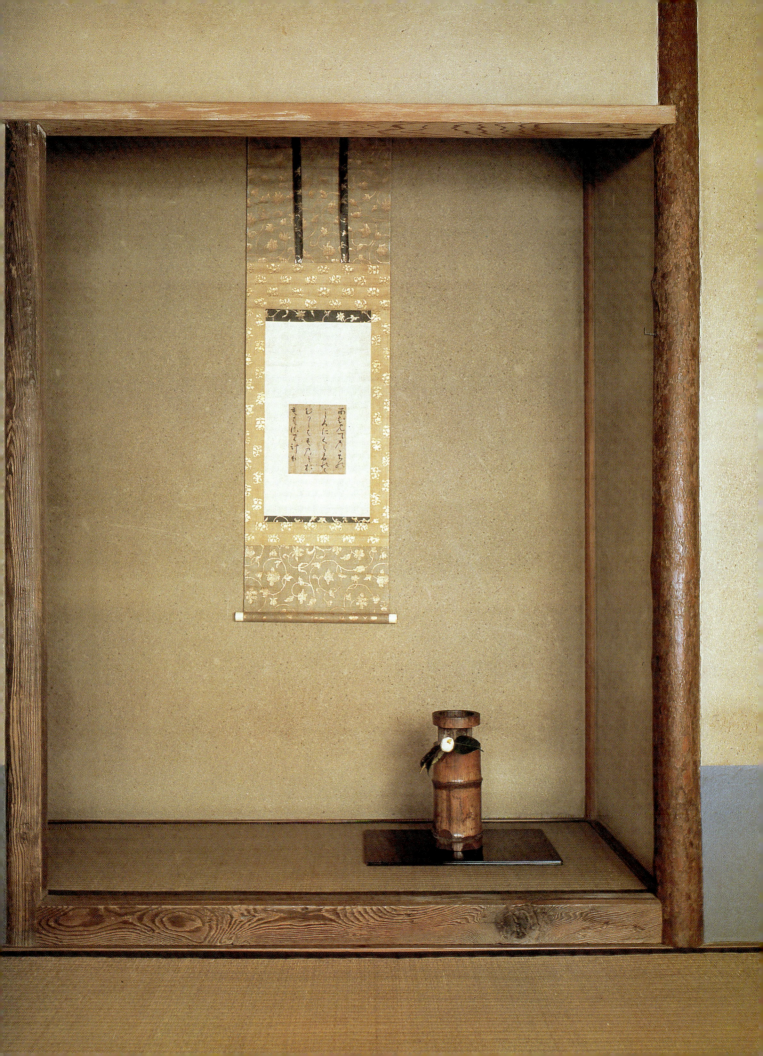

of ancestors, the alcove still invites contemplation of the sacred in the midst of ordinary life.

By contrast, governments and public institutions have long commissioned art on a grand scale as public statements. Rome's Arch of Constantine (1.39) was designed to glorify Constantine's victory over his greatest rival, a victory that made him absolute ruler of the Roman Empire. Its surface is decorated with a series of reliefs used to honor the emperor (though some were actually plundered from monuments to earlier rulers). The massiveness of the arch is a symbol of the emperor's public stature.

In all cultures, religious institutions have been major patrons of artists, commissioning paintings and sculptures to help tell the story of their tradition to the masses and inspire them with the same beliefs. Much of our greatest architecture has been created in the service of centralized governments and religious bodies, who had the power or commanded the devotion to raise the large sums of money needed for monumental projects.

Business corporations and multinational conglomerates are now also centers of wealth and power. In recent years, they have become patrons of the arts as

1.39 Arch of Constantine, Rome, 312-15 AD.

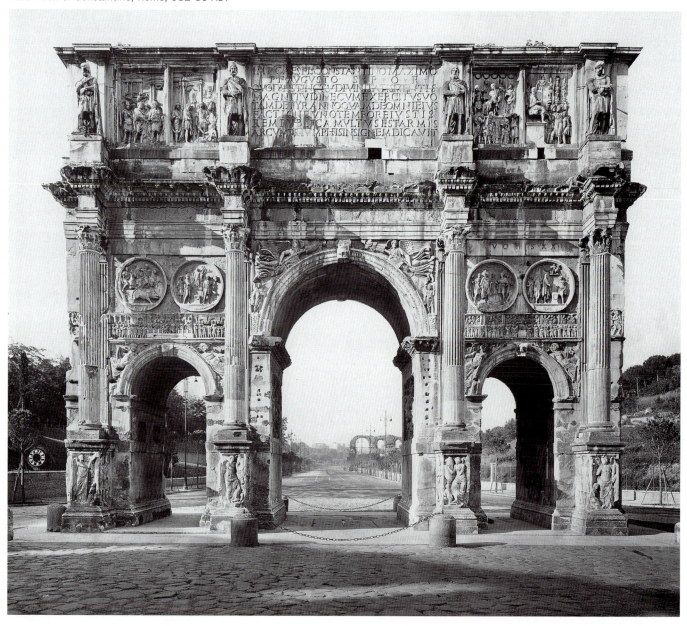

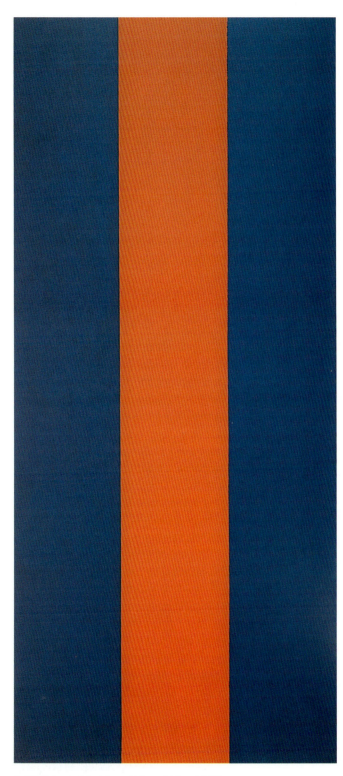

1.40 Barnett Newman, *Voice of Fire*, 1967.
Acrylic on canvas, 17 ft 10 ins × 8 ft (5.44 × 244 m).
The National Gallery of Canada, Ottawa.
Collection Annalee Newman, New York.

well. They buy and display large paintings and sculptures, partly to impress their clients and partly as good investments, for the commercial gallery and auction-house system has fostered a vigorous market in art as a financial commodity.

The increasing appreciation of art as investment has raised new issues for public consumers of art, such as museums, municipalities, and governments. One is the issue of ethical censorship (see Box). Other issues raised in this area will be examined in an Art Issues box in Chapter 15.

People feel that when public money is used for the purchase of art—as when it is used for any other purpose—they have a right to express their disapproval, whether on the grounds that they do not like the art or that they consider it simply a waste of money. The purchase of the American artist Barnett Newman's *Voice of Fire* (**1.40**) by the National Gallery of Canada for the equivalent of US$1.5 million raised a howl of protest. Some objected to spending two-thirds of the Gallery's annual acquisitions budget on a work by a non-Canadian artist. Others did not place such high value on modern, nonrepresentational paintings. A pig farmer, who was then Chairman of the Canadian House of Commons Cultural Affairs Committee, said he could have created the same 18-foot-high (5.5-m) red stripe on blue ground himself, "given two cans of paint, a roller, and about ten minutes."[14]

The Gallery director defended the decision to buy the work of a US artist, affirming that "Art is universal; it knows no boundaries, and artists know no boundaries."[15] The Head of Collections and Research at the National Gallery explained the aesthetic reasons for the purchase:

> In the spacious, sunlit gallery where the work is presently installed, *Voice of Fire*'s soaring height strengthened by the deep cadmium red center between darker blue sides is for many visitors an exhilarating affirmation of their being wholly in the world and in a special space where art and architecture compliment each other.[16]

As you study the material and examples in this book, you can begin to develop informed opinions about art that may have been unfamiliar to you. Was the pig farmer right?

ART ISSUES
CENSORSHIP

Does the pursuit of art require complete freedom of expression for all artists? Should limits be drawn as to what is acceptable in publicly displayed art or publicly funded art?

These questions came to the fore in 1990 in the United States when funding by the National Endowment for the Arts for a traveling exhibition of sexually explicit photographs by Robert Mapplethorpe became the subject of intense debate and even an obscenity court case It was filed against the director of the Contemporary Art Center in Cincinnati. Jurors were shown only the seven most controversial photographs from the exhibit. They were asked to determine whether they met all three criteria of obscenity, as defined in a landmark US Supreme Court ruling from 1973. The Supreme Court had ruled that a work is obscene if it depicts sexuality "in a patently offensive way," if "the average person, applying contemporary community standards" finds that it appeals to "prurient interest," and if it "lacks serious literary, artistic, political, or scientific value."[17]

None of the jurors had any background in art appreciation and they did not like the pictures. Nevertheless, they acquitted the director after ten days of expert testimonies designed to prove that Mapplethorpe's work did indeed have serious artistic value and therefore should not be judged legally obscene. The director of the Cleveland Museum of Art argued that the photographs are metaphoric "images of rejection, aggression, anxiety." The director of the Walker Art Center in Minneapolis told the jury:

"I recognize that they are difficult. I recognize that they are confrontational. I recognize that they tell us things maybe we would rather not hear. But they do shine lights in some rather dark corners of the human psyche. And they symbolize, in disturbing, eloquent fashion, an attitude. And they do reflect an attitude that is not necessarily limited to the artist."[18]

As one of the jurors later said, "We learned that art doesn't have to be pretty."[19] Nevertheless, the potential for funding for art on the edge to be withdrawn continues to hang over the heads of artists and museums.

Censorship of art has long been an issue. Michelangelo's monumental painting at the end wall of the Sistine Chapel, *The Last Judgment* (detail in Figure **1.41**) was violently attacked in the sixteenth century shortly after it was painted. In the Council of Trent, Roman Catholic Church officials had ruled that sacred images must adhere closely to scriptural descriptions, lest any viewer be misled. Critics felt that Michelangelo had taken too much artistic license. His angels did not have wings, for instance, and the angels blowing trumpets announcing the apocalypse were all grouped together, rather than at the four corners of the earth in accordance with scripture. The most controversial aspect of the work was the voluptuous nudity of the figures, which prompted one critic to refer to Michelangelo as "that inventor of filthiness."[20] People tried physically to attack *The Last Judgment.* So as to save the masterpiece, two succeeding popes ordered that the naked figures should be overpainted with loincloths to cover their genitals and breasts; the bits of clothing (Figure 1.41, right) did not exist in Michelangelo's original work.

More recently, in 1937 Nazi Germany confiscated over 16,000 pieces of modern German art of all sorts, burned much of it in a huge fire, and exhibited some of the rest with the label "Degenerate Art". At the opening of the exhibit, the president of the Reich Chamber of Visual Arts explained:

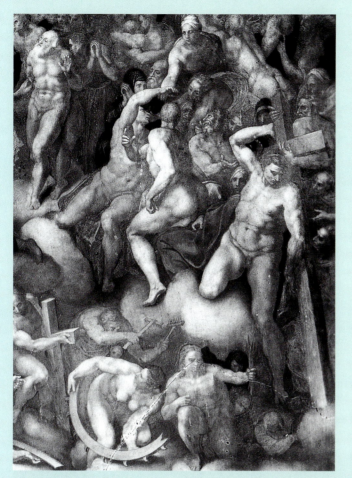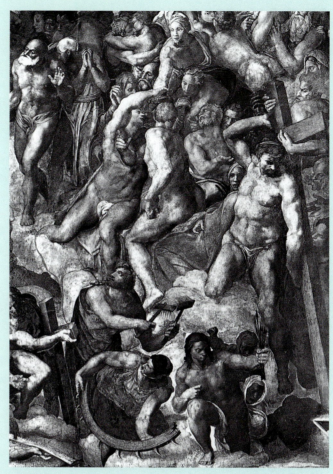

1.41 Michelangelo Buonarroti, the *Last Judgment* (detail), end wall of the Sistine Chapel: *left*: original condition; *right*: present condition.

"We now stand in an exhibition that contains only a fraction of what was bought with the hard-earned savings of the German people and exhibited as art by a large number of museums all over Germany. All around us you see the monstrous offspring of insanity, impudence, ineptitude, and sheer degeneracy. What this exhibition offers inspires horror and disgust in us all."[21]

Among the works confiscated from German museums were fifty-seven paintings by Wassily Kandinsky, whose delicate explanations of spiritual harmony in art are quoted in a special feature box on pages 196-7.

Questions arise: What are the ramifications of institutional censorship of artistic creation? Can art be dangerous for social health?

Can censorship of art be dangerous for social health? If there should be limits, who should define them? Should depiction of violence, sexism, racism, or sacrilege be censored, or only overt depictions of sexual activity?

CRITICAL OPINION

Art does not exist in a vacuum. The mood of the times and the opinion of the professionals in art appreciation, such as art critics and museum curators, have a telling effect on our response to works of art. There are no absolute guidelines for judging quality in art. People tend to respond negatively to anything unfamiliar, but what was originally shocking and unprecedented may in time become quite familiar and acceptable. In the early 1960s, the average person thought Jackson Pollock was a fraud or a trickster, because he presented his works done with flung or dripped paint as serious art (1.42). But the critics declared Pollock a serious artist, worthy of being studied and collected. Nonobjective art became highly respectable and also began to attract high prices.

Critical tastes have changed dramatically over time. Some artists who were praised to the skies in art magazines ten years ago are almost unknown today. When the French Impressionists such as Monet, Renoir, and Seurat began their experiments with depicting the play of light and how it determined what they saw, they were utterly rejected by the reigning French Academy. At one point, a bankrupt dealer tried to sell van Gogh's canvases in bundles of ten for 50 centimes to one franc per bundle. Today the works of the Impressionists and Post-Impressionists are considered so valuable that only the very wealthiest collectors can afford them. Van Gogh's *Portrait of Dr. Gachet* was sold in 1990 for US$82.5 million.

Referring to a painting by Auguste Renoir (see his work in Figure 3.28), a critic once wrote, "Evidently, the models spent several days under water."[22] A painting by Paul Cézanne (see Figure 2.40) was at first

1.42 Jackson Pollock, *Number 1, 1948*, 1948. Oil and enamel on unprimed canvas, 5 ft 8 ins × 8 ft 8 ins (1.73 × 2.64 m). Collection Museum of Modern Art, New York. Purchase. Photograph © 1997 MOMA.

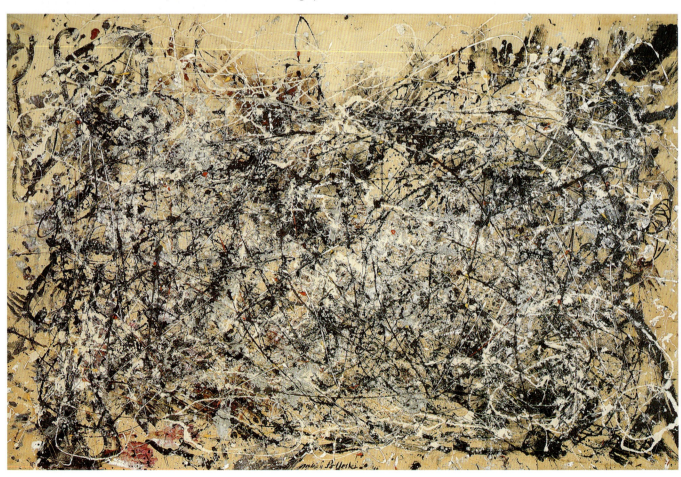

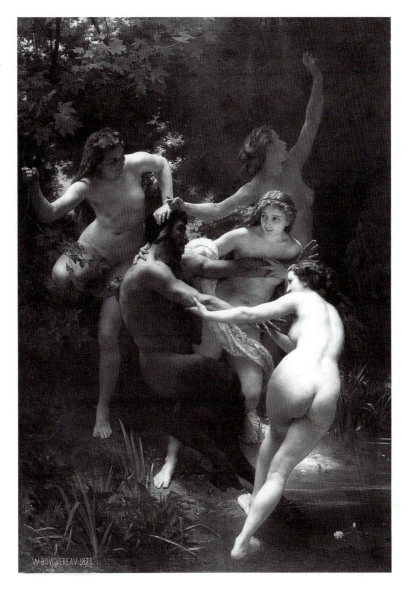

1.43 William Bouguereau, *Nymphs and Satyr*, 1873. Oil on canvas, 8 ft 6 ins × 5 ft 11 ins (2.59 × 1.8 m). Sterling and Francine Clark Art Institute, Williamstown, Massachusetts.

dismissed as "a few palette scrapings,"[23] but is now in the collection of the Philadelphia Museum of Art.

While the Impressionists were struggling to survive, a member of the French Academy named William Bouguereau was the favorite of the critics. In his romantic paintings, such as *Nymphs and Satyr* (**1.43**), he achieved flowing groupings of figures by applying traditional formulas for composition. But as Impressionism and later contemporary movements gradually took hold, accustoming viewers to more offbeat and abstract effects, Bouguereau's work lost favor. For a long time, it was considered too contrived and romanticized to be taken seriously. In recent years, however, some critics have reassessed this opinion: Bouguereau's work is being shown again at certain museums, and realistic figurative work has come back into vogue.

In recent years, handcrafts, political art without great aesthetic merit, "outsider" art by untrained individuals, and multicultural art have also earned critical appreciation. Peter Schjeldahl, art critic for *The Village Voice*, asserts that "Anyone who doesn't change his mind doesn't have one."[24] Arthur Danto, art critic for *The Nation*, concludes that it is important to work at appreciating art. He cites his own example: when he first moved to Rome, he went to see Bernini's *Ecstasy of St. Teresa* (1.13). He found it "absurd and silly." Then, as he continued living in the city, he read about Baroque art and made a point of visiting the Baroque churches in Rome. When he went back to see the St. Teresa nine months later, he was "moved to tears."[25]

ART ISSUES
RACE AND GENDER CRITICISM

At present, art is undergoing intense scrutiny on the basis of criteria that are new to art criticism. At issue is the extent to which women artists and artists of color have been marginalized by the white, male-dominated, Western art establishment and their humanity trivialized or oppressed through art.

One problem has been racial and gender stereotyping, rather than recognition of the full humanity of those without political power. Women have often been depicted as seductive sex objects rather than as complete and independent individuals. From the 1970s onward, some women artists have themselves begun creating art about the female body, not as an object but as a subject. To redefine their own sexuality, they have explored the female body in images, celebrated its links with nature and natural processes, and documented its abuses.

Another issue is the low value placed on the work of women and people of color. In the art market centered on New York, it has been difficult for many such artists to be accepted or taken seriously. Women have rarely been acknowledged as fine artists—as painters or sculptors or printmakers, for instance. And traditional crafts which they have mastered, such as quiltmaking, have not been recognized as valuable art until recent years. In 1969, a prominent show at the Whitney Museum of American Art of what were considered the major living artists included only eight women. If the work of women or people of color is shown, it may be specifically as "feminist" or "black" art, rather than simply as art, or it may be shown only in alternative spaces, such as cooperative galleries. Daryl Chin asserts:

"The art world, so tied to an ideology of a market economy, reflects the sociopolitical consciousness of that ideology. And that ideology maintains a hierarchy of stratification, with minority artists lacking a definable place within the structure . . . If the majority fails to recognize the exclusionary tactics now being practiced, then the realm of aesthetics is no longer imaginary; it is downright pathological."[26]

One could argue that the art of disempowered peoples should be judged by the same aesthetic standards as the art of the powerful. But it can also be argued that the criticism of art is based on aesthetic principles developed in the mainstream of Western culture. How then to judge quality in works that are not part of that tradition? Are there eternal, universal principles that can be applied to any work of art, from any culture? To consider this question, study the principles of design and the wide-ranging illustrations in Chapter 3.

Another aspect of marginalization in art lies in the political content of some artists' work. Some art by women calls attention to women's unique experiences, both positive and negative. Joyce Scott's bead sculpture often makes references to the ironies of race relations. Her *Evolution* (**1.44**) shows a white-skinned mother-of-the-world figure whose skin has been parted on the head, revealing an ancient African woman beneath. This piece refers to new genetic discoveries suggesting that the common ancestor of the entire human race is a 200,000-year-old black African woman. Scott says:

"If it's true that the mother of the human race is a 200,000-year-old African woman, then inside everyone, even if you're white, is your black mother. It's very difficult for people to hear that, because of the relationship of people of color with people of European stock. We've had so many horrendous problems between us. Your central self could be the same person you abuse. That makes us cousins, fiftieth or sixtieth cousins. There is absolutely no way I can't look at you and see me. If that's true, that means that we humans have to examine everything we do to each other."[27]

GREATNESS IN ART

If art critics and public opinion are culturally biased and subject to change, how then can the quality of a work of art be judged? Throughout this book, you will be gaining critical faculties that will help you to judge the form and content of artworks. By the end of the book, you should be able to analyze a work of art from many perspectives and thus come to some conclusions about its worth. In the last chapter, we will be looking in depth at three artworks that have been considered great through the centuries, and also a new work, which is loved by some and vigorously opposed by others. We will also be examining aspects of these key works at relevant points throughout the book. Here we will look briefly at the circumstances under which they were created, and how all have been enmeshed in some kind of controversy.

One of these featured works is Michelangelo Buonarroti's Sistine Chapel ceiling (**1.45**). Early in the sixteenth century, Pope Julius II commissioned him to paint the Twelve Apostles and some simple decorations on the Vatican Palace Chapel ceiling. Michelangelo later wrote that he convinced the pope that if he limited himself to this idea, the result would be "a poor thing." The pope thus gave him *carte blanche* to create whatever he thought best. The result was an extraordinarily complex project to paint in fresco the Christian story of humanity's beginnings. It is considered one of the world's greatest art treasures. Nevertheless, Michelangelo was soon under criticism from counter-reformers in the Roman Catholic Church. In a backlash against Renaissance humanism, the Counter-Reformation attempted to reestablish the Church's voice of authority, as opposed to the voice of individual reason, which was subject to potential errors. Art commissioned for Church purposes was included in restrictions outlined by the Council of Trent in 1563. As indicated in the Censorship feature box (page 46), Michelangelo's work was criticized for its inventive and metaphorical spiritual approach, for the artist had not used biblical descriptions literally. Michelangelo was a very wealthy artist, but his letters indicate that he had continually to remind his patrons, including the pope and the Church, to pay him.

In recent years, the Sistine Chapel ceiling has again been at the center of a raging controversy. This time the issue is its radical restoration, which some people feel has ruined this great work. The issues

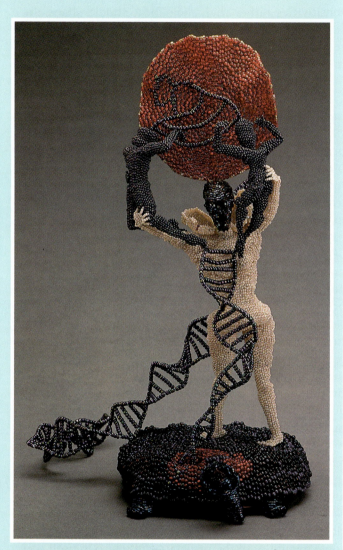

1.44 Joyce J. Scott, *Evolution*, 1992. Beads, thread, wire, approx. 20 × 10 × 11 ins (50.8 × 25.4 × 28 cm). Courtesy of the artist.

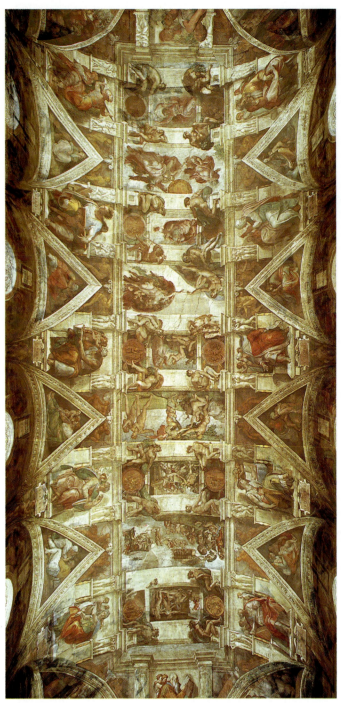

1.45 Michelangelo Buonarroti, Sistine Chapel ceiling (before restoration), Vatican Palace, Rome, 1508–12.

involved in restoration of famous artworks will be examined in an Art Issues box in Chapter 5, as well as in the last chapter.

Just as Michelangelo had trouble in collecting the money owed to him for this work, so did the nineteenth-century French sculptor Auguste Rodin, artist of the monumental *The Gates of Hell*, explored in the last chapter of the book. He also had difficulty in dictating how his work should be displayed, and it was hard for him to convince his patrons that his aesthetic sensitivities rather than their ideas should shape the sculptures they commissioned. Many of his projects remained unfinished. *The Gates of Hell* (1.46) was commissioned for a proposed museum which was never built; the plaster molds that Rodin created for the Gates (as shown here) were not cast into bronze, as he had planned, until after he had died (see Figure 2.22).

Pablo Picasso's monumental twentieth-century painting *Guernica* (1.47) was also a commissioned piece. During the Spanish Civil War, Picasso was a loyalist, an anti-fascist, living in exile in France. He was asked in January 1937 by the Spanish government in exile to paint a commemorative piece about the war for the 1937 World's Fair in Paris. He had not yet begun when, in April 1937, the ancient city of Guernica in northern Spain was destroyed by German bombers acting to support General Franco. There was no strategic reason to bomb Guernica; it was just a rehearsal to test the new military technique of saturation bombing. Most of Guernica was reduced to rubble; many civilians were killed. When Picasso heard the news, he began to work on the huge and profound painting, expressing his anguish over this atrocity. As soon as the painting was finished, it was put on display at the Spanish Pavilion in Paris. Picasso may have intended that the work would incite protest against modern warfare in general. Franco's supporters interpreted the painting in a specific political sense, and they recommended that the painting should be removed from the Pavilion as "an anti-social and ridiculous picture, wholly inadequate for the wholesome mentality of the proletariat." Picasso himself had it transferred to the Museum of Modern Art in New York to protect it.

The final key work to be examined will be Moshe Safdie's Vancouver Library Square (1.48). Completed in 1995, it was to be the central symbol of the city of Vancouver, as well as a place for learning, public gatherings, and civic office work. Safdie's solution wraps a curving, freestanding wall, reminiscent of the ruins of

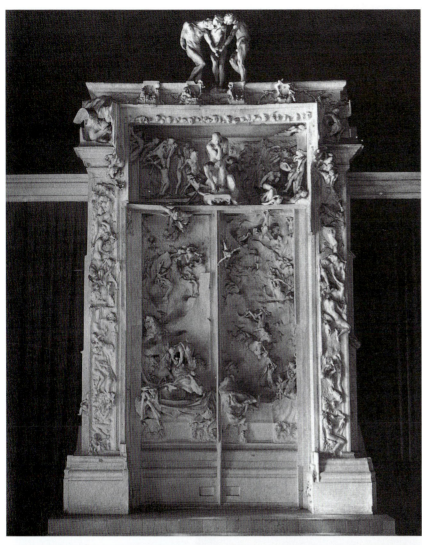

1.46 Auguste Rodin, *The Gates of Hell*. Plaster. Photographed in 1917. Musée Rodin, Paris.

1.47 Pablo Picasso, *Guernica*, 1937.
Oil on canvas, 11 ft 5 ½ ins × 25 ft 5 ¼ ins
(3.49 × 7.75 m).
Reina Sofia Museum of Modern Art, Madrid.

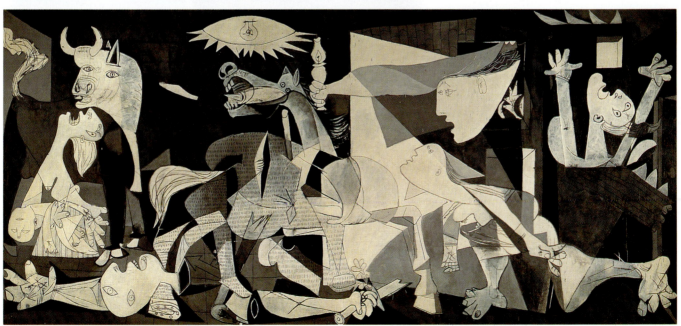

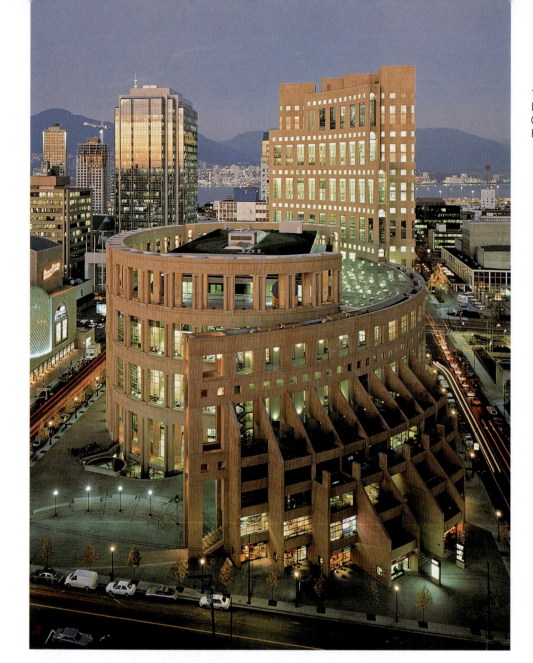

1.48 Moshe Safdie, Vancouver Library Square, Vancouver, British Columbia, opened May 1995. Photo by T. Hursley.

the Roman Colosseum, around a semicircular structure containing small reading nooks, which in turn embraces a cube containing the library stacks. The design has triggered some intense opposition. Architecture students in Vancouver protested at the library's inauguration, wearing togas to mock its apparent reference to the Colosseum. They considered it an historical anomaly, which did not fit into Vancouver's modern architectural scene. Others complained that the design was "silly," "like Disneyland." However, when Vancouver citizens were asked to choose one of three designs by competing firms, 70 per cent preferred Safdie's design, finding it "most memorable and different."[28] The jury is still out.

Great artistic creation, rooted in the immediate context, nonetheless manages to communicate something to spectators centuries later. People could compare Safdie's work with the Roman Colosseum because, after two thousand years, the Colosseum is still well known and impressive, even in ruins. Picasso's *Guernica* was provoked by, and refers to, a war about which most people now living know nothing, yet the painting still stirs us today. The cries of those opposing the radical restoration of the Sistine Chapel ceiling are anguished precisely because they recognize the work as a great and irreplaceable work of art. What is communicated by great works varies—be it anger, compassion, spiritual inspiration, or elegance of form—but what all great works have in common is their ability to fascinate us over the ages.

2

VISUAL ELEMENTS

The elements of design with which artists work are the observable properties of matter: line, shape and form, space, texture, value (lights and darks) and lighting, color, and time. Although these elements are unified in effective works of art, we will isolate and deal with one at a time to train our eye to see them and to understand how artists use them.

LINE

A mark or area that is significantly longer than it is wide may be perceived as a line. In the world around us, we can see trees and grass, legs and telephone posts as lines if we learn to apply the mental abstraction "line" to the world of real things. A tree bare of its leaves can be perceived as a medley of lines, as

Mondrian noted in his tree abstractions (1.28–1.30). The sections that follow will develop the ability to discern lines in artworks and to understand the aesthetic functions they serve.

Seeing Lines

It is easiest to see lines in works that are primarily linear and two-dimensional, such as the lovely piece of calligraphy shown in Figure 2.1. **Calligraphy** is the art of fine writing, so highly developed in Arabic cultures, Japan, and China that some pieces are meant first as art and only secondarily as figures to be read. Those who do not read Arabic will see the lines in this piece as purely abstract anyway, because they do not know how to interpret them as words. Arabic characters are usually set down in straight lines, but the master

2.1 Sami Efendi, *Levha in Celi Sülüs*, 1872. Private collection, London.

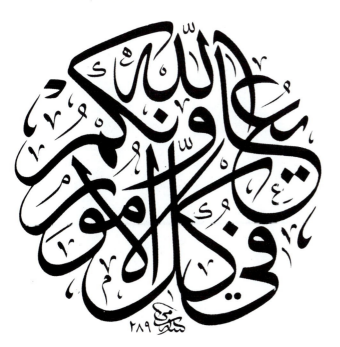

2.2 Agnes Martin, *Untitled X, 1982.* Acrylic and pencil on canvas, 72 ins sq. Courtesy Pace Gallery, New York.

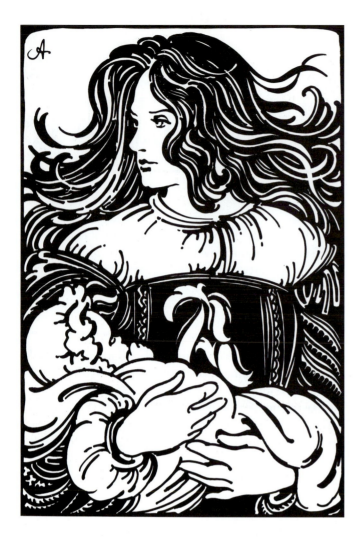

calligrapher Sami Efendi worked the strokes into a flowing circular pattern to enhance their beauty and the unity of the design. When lines are made with a flat-pointed instrument, such as the reed pen used here, their thickness grows and diminishes as the lines swing through curves.

Agnes Martin's work has for decades consisted largely of thin parallel lines, as in *Untitled X*, (2.2). She uses only this simple line, which one critic has called "a signature without an ego,"[1] laid down with an 18-inch (45-cm) ruler, and subtle washes of paint. Paradoxically, viewers respond spiritually to these linear paintings as if they were seeing fields of luminous space. Martin speculates:

> I think that our minds respond to things beyond this world. Take beauty: It's a very mysterious thing, isn't it? I think it's a response in our minds to perfection. My paintings are certainly non-objective. They're just horizontal lines. There's not any hint of nature. And still everybody responds, I think.[2]

Lines may be seen in unworked as well as worked areas of a design. In John Alcorn's drawing to represent Hawthorne's novel *The Scarlet Letter* for television audiences (2.3), we can see not only black lines on white but also white lines defined by black-inked areas. Notice how gracefully Alcorn handles the rapid transi-

2.3 (above) John Alcorn, *The Scarlet Letter*, 1980. Exxon Corporation, for Public Broadcasting Great Performances.

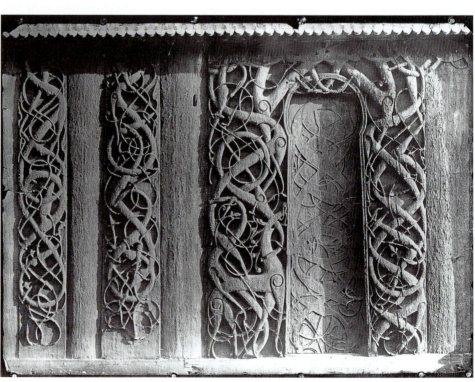

2.4 Doorway panels, parish church, Urnes, Norway, c. 1050–70. Carved wood.

tions from the white of the background to the white lines defining the hair, leading us to see the former as **negative**, or unfilled, space, and the latter as **positive**, or filled, space.

Even more subtly, we perceive lines along **edges** where two areas treated differently meet. Along the left side of Hester Prynne's face, as we see it, there is a strong white line belonging to and describing her profile; the black of her hair shadows is pushed behind it in space. On the right side of her face there is a strong edge belonging to the black of her hair, with her face appearing to be behind it in space.

In three-dimensional works, we may find lines that are incised, raised, or applied to forms. In the eleventh-century Norwegian door panels (2.4), some superb but now unknown craftsman has carved wood into complex patterns of lines. These patterns continually shift from elongated animals to serpents to plant vines. They are carved in such a linear fashion that what we perceive at first is a maze of interlacing lines rather than distant objects.

Edges may be "read," or interpreted, as lines in three-dimensional works as well as in two-dimensional works. Part of the effectiveness of Barnett Newman's *Broken Obelisk* (2.5) lies in the sharp edges where flat planes meet, creating visual lines that emphasize the form and define its three-dimensionality (2.6). If the top and bottom segments were rounded, without the lines of the edges, the effect would be quite different.

In some three-dimensional pieces, entire areas are so thin in relation to their length that they are seen as lines. The human figure is sometimes handled as abstract lines in space, a perception that is carried to an extreme in the attenuated figures of Alberto Giacometti, such as *Walking Man* (2.7). This reduction of a human to something less than a skeleton can be seen as a statement about the isolation and loneliness of the individual in modern civilization. Giacometti himself insisted that his focus lay not so much on the gaunt figure as on the vast, empty space that surrounds and presses in on it. It is hard to grasp this perspective when looking at a photograph, but in actuality, the small scale of the battered figure—only 27 inches (69 cm) high—does make the space surrounding it seem even greater.

Earthworks—large-scale environment-altering projects in which the surface of the earth becomes the artist's canvas—sometimes create immense lines that can best be seen from a distance. From near by, *Running Fence* (2.8) by Christo and Jeanne-Claude appeared as

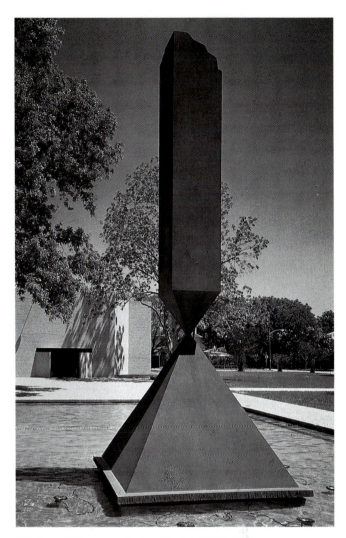

2.5 Barnett Newman, *Broken Obelisk*, 1963–67. Steel, height 25 ft 1 in (7.65 m). Institute of Religion and Human Development, Houston, Texas.

2.6 Lines formed by the edges of *Broken Obelisk*.

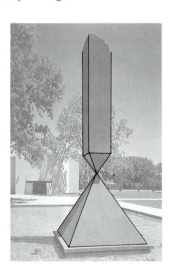

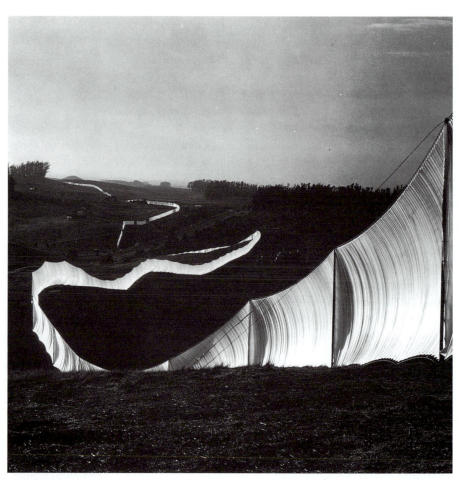

2.8 Christo and Jeanne-Claude, *Running Fence*, *Sonoma and Marin Counties*, California, 1972–76, erected 1976. Nylon fabric, steel poles, cable, 18 ft × 24½ miles (5.5 m × 40 km). © Christo and Jeanne-Claude 1976. Photograph © Jeanne-Claude 1993.

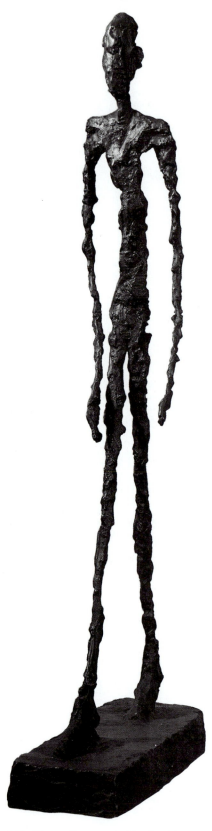

2.7 Alberto Giacometti, *Walking Man*, c. 1947–49. Bronze, height 27 ins (69 cm). Hirshhorn Museum and Sculpture Garden, Smithsonian Institution, Washington, D.C. Gift of Joseph H. Hirshhorn, 1966.

a great fabric curtain, 18 feet (5.5 m) high. Its even more memorable aspect was the beautiful line it created over 24½ miles (40 km) of northern Californian countryside, until it ultimately disappeared into the Pacific Ocean. To erect this temporary structure for only two weeks in 1976, Christo, Jeanne-Claude, and a large crew of engineers and lawyers spent three years threading their way through public hearings and legal battles; they were also required to produce a 265-page environmental impact statement. These struggles with a disbelieving society are part of Christo's art form; the temporary end-product is not the only goal. Neither was the line of the fence the only visual element in the design. Its existence also called attention to the contours and features of the land. Speaking of the ranchers who gave their support to Christo and Jeanne-Claude in obtaining the permits and who were sorry when, as intended, it was taken down and all traces of it removed, Christo and Jeanne-Claude were pleased that "they can find that a part of *Running Fence* is their cows, and the sky, and the hills and the barns and the people."[3]

Implied Line

Some lines are not physically created; they are merely suggested by the artist. Our mind, with its penchant for trying to read order into the messages from the senses, does the rest, perceiving lines where there are none. Part of the visual excitement of the ad for *Harper's Magazine* (**2.9**) by the Beggarstaffs (a far-sighted but short-lived British design studio around the turn of the twentieth century) is the filling in of lines that have been left out. Just enough information is given for us to see the famous figure of a beefeater in his distinctive uniform. The illusion works particularly well along the right side of his lower tunic, where an edge is suggested by very slight upward swings of the dark bands.

Implied lines may project beyond the work itself. In many two-dimensional works, the artist asks us to make assumptions about what "happens" beyond the edges of the picture. For this we need to be given enough information to draw inferences based on our experiences of the physical world. Geometric figures are perhaps easiest to predict. Shown part of a square or a circle, we may automatically fill in the rest with our imagination. In *Fox Trot A* (**2.10**), Piet Mondrian shows us a cropped segment of a linear image that by implication extends beyond the picture area. The challenge he sets for us is to determine how much larger the uncropped "original" would be. We automatically assume that the left vertical and the horizontal will continue as straight lines and intersect just beyond the

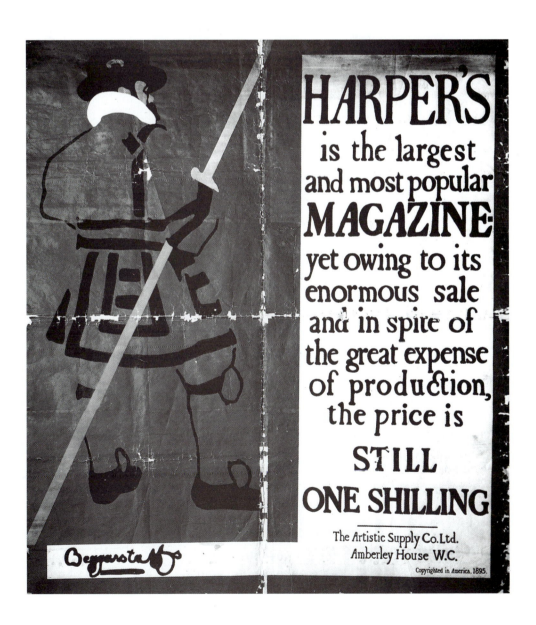

2.9 William Nicholson and James Pryde, called the Beggarstaff Brothers, poster for *Harper's Magazine*, 1895. Victoria and Albert Museum, London.

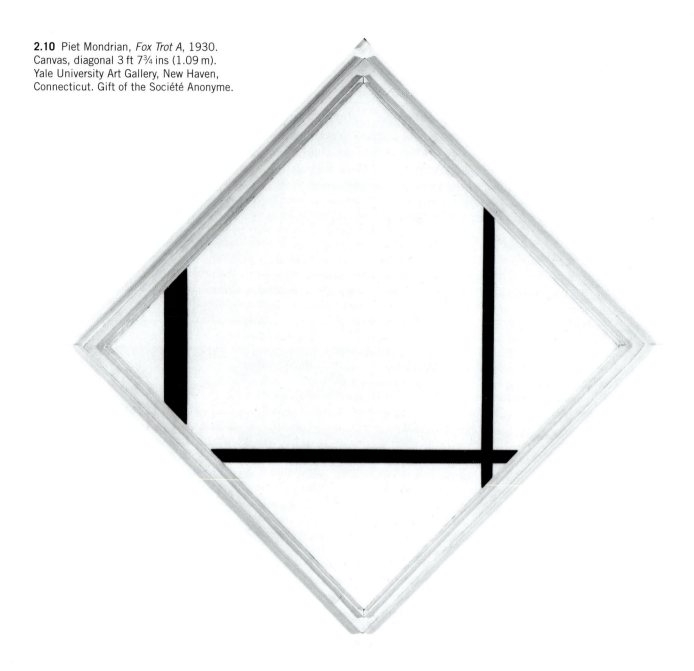

2.10 Piet Mondrian, *Fox Trot A*, 1930. Canvas, diagonal 3 ft 7¾ ins (1.09 m). Yale University Art Gallery, New Haven, Connecticut. Gift of the Société Anonyme.

picture. But what about the two verticals? Will they be joined by a crosspiece above the top? The only clue that the cropped segment shown may be part of a hypothetical series of rectangles—like a multi-paned window—is the crossing of the two lines at lower right. The suggestion that the figure doesn't end here leads the mind outward to imagine a much larger series of lines that cannot be seen at all.

In addition to drawing the viewer into participating in a work, implied lines are often used for compositional ends. **Eyelines**—the implied lines along which a subject's eyes appear to be looking—are a common device for directing the viewer's eye or pulling a composition together. Usually eyelines occur between figures, as in Bouguereau's *Nymphs and Satyr* (1.43), in which each person in the circle is looking at someone who is looking at someone else, so tying them all together. But in the Hellenistic bronze *Thorn Puller* (2.11), we follow the "line" between the youth's eyes and his own foot, for his concentration is so clearly fixed on his foot that our eyes go in the same direction. His limbs are also arranged to form lines

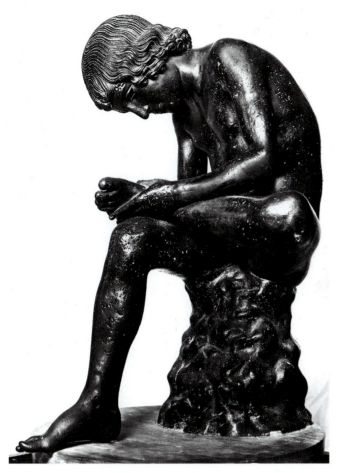

2.11 *Thorn Puller* (*Spinario*), 1st century BC. Bronze, height 28¾ ins (73 cm). Capitoline Museums, Rome.

that lead our eye toward the foot. Our attention is often drawn to points where many lines intersect. If our eye then strays to examine the figure as a whole, the lines of the body carry us around in a circle to arrive back at the same point.

Descriptive Line

Decorative line is that which provides surface embellishments, such as the A on Hester Prynne's dress (**2.3**). By contrast, line that is **descriptive** tells us the physical nature of the object we are seeing and how it exists in space.

In *Narcissus* (**2.12**), the spare inked line is purely descriptive. Although the paper has the same tone everywhere, the line tells us to read certain unfilled areas as positive leaves and flowers and the rest as negative unfilled space. Line is used here as **outline**—an

imaginary line defining the outer boundaries of an object but not its internal modeling, color, shading, or texture. Not only do the outlines allow us to "see" the narcissus plant; they also describe the space around it. The plant has been carefully placed on the page in such a way that the negative areas become satisfying in themselves as a series of shapes that alternately curve softly outward (such as the large unfilled space at lower left) and plunge in pointed tips into the heart of the stem. The lines also describe two enclosed pointed spaces below the flowers.

Whereas the narcissus drawing is quite flat in space, with only its outlines described, lines may be used in two-dimensional work to describe three-dimensional form—to create the illusion that a figure's **mass**, or solid content, occupies a certain **volume** in space and has a certain **weight**. In *Head of an Apostle* by the German artist Albrecht Dürer (**2.13**), the head appears to have continually varying contours, to be fully rounded in spatial volume, and to have convincing weightiness. Dürer achieved this extremely detailed depiction of a venerable, beetle-browed head largely by highly skillful use of line. Drawn close

2.12 After Zhu Da (1625–1705), *Narcissus*. Ink on paper, 12⅛ × 10½ ins (30.8 × 26.5 cm). British Museum, London.

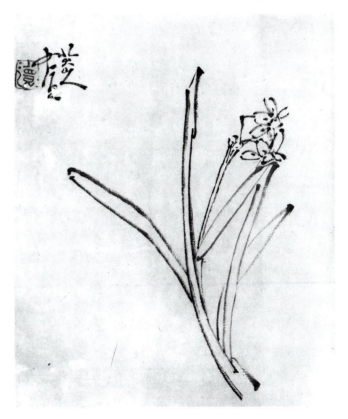

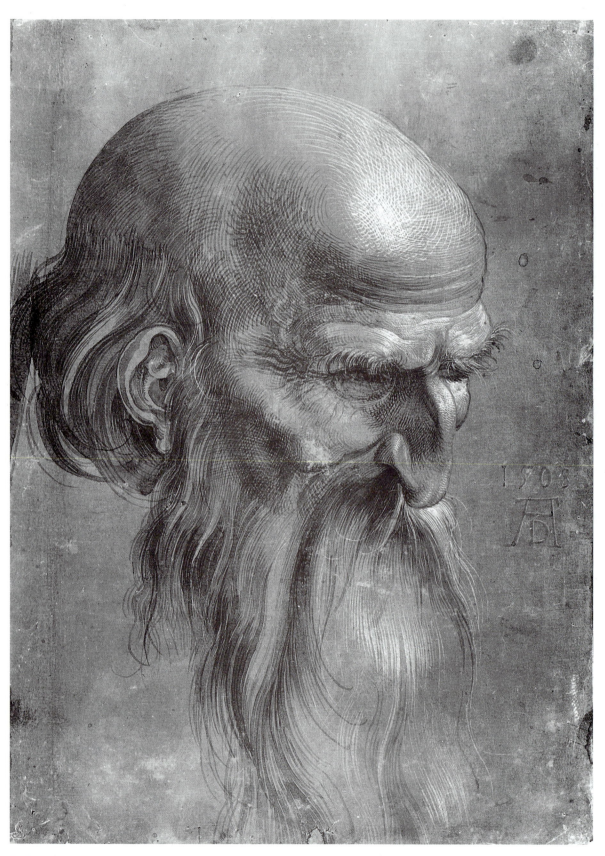

2.13 Albrecht Dürer, *Head of an Apostle*, 1508. Brush on paper, 12½ × 8⅓ ins (31.7 × 21.2 cm).
Graphische Sammlung Albertina, Vienna.

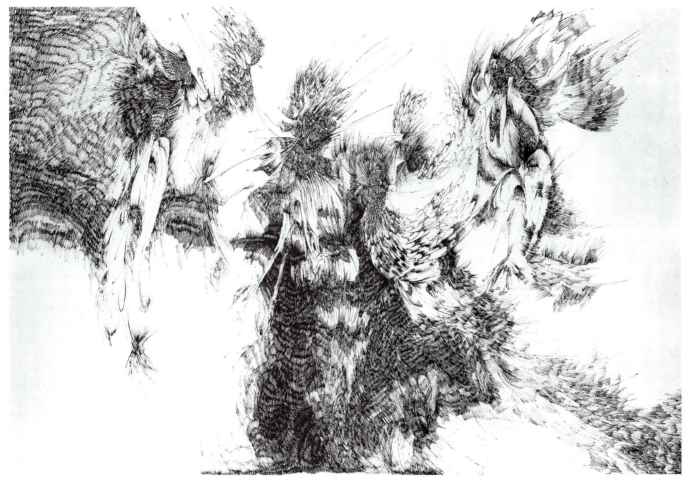

2.14 Arnold Bittleman, *Martyred Flowers*, c. 1957. Pen and ink, 26 × 38¾ ins (66 × 98 cm). Fogg Art Museum, Harvard University, Cambridge, Massachusetts.

together, dark parallel lines (**hatching**) and crossed parallel lines (**cross-hatching**) suggest shadows where contours curve away from the light. Where the lines seem to loop in visually incomplete ovals around an axis, a technique known as **bracelet modeling**, they imply the contours of the unseen back side of the form.

Many small lines placed close together may also be used to suggest texture. In Arnold Bittleman's *Martyred Flowers* (**2.14**), we readily perceive textural effects even though we cannot be sure what forms are being described. The title refers to flowers; yet in places the textures appear feathery, wing-like. These are not hastily scribbled strokes; each line has been placed with great care. Where many are juxtaposed, dark areas develop that create a mysterious undulation in space. Note that variations in thickness and spacing of lines create a range of degrees of darkness, or value, with many shades of gray.

Expressive Qualities of Line

As our eyes move along a line, "reading" it, our visual perception system seems to interpret our eye movements as characterizing the line itself. If a line creates sharp peaks (see the uppermost line in Figure **2.15**), the eye cannot scan it easily. Its progress is constantly interrupted, giving us a rather uneasy feeling. A line without sharp angles or curves can be read quickly and easily, but if there are breaks in it, as in the second line in Figure 2.15, they slow the scanning process. Such characteristics of lines tend to make us assign emotional qualities to them. Artists use this tendency to control our emotional response to a work. For example, sharply angled lines may be used to evoke feelings of excitement, anger, danger, or chaos. A relatively flat line may be used to give a sense of calmness. A wide line that can be read quickly may be used to

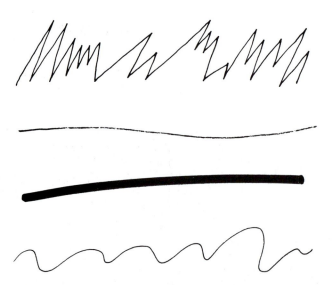

2.15 Lines with varying expressive qualities.

2.16 Gebrüder Thonet, *Reclining rocking chair with adjustable back*, c. 1880. Steam-bent beechwood and cane, 30½ × 27½ × 68½ ins (77.5 × 70 × 174 cm). Collection Museum of Modern Art, New York. Phyllis B. Lambert Fund and Gift of the Four Seasons. Photograph © 1997 MOMA.

suggest bold strength, directness. A gently curving line may be used to suggest unhurried pleasure.

The reclining rocking chair by the Austrian firm of Thonet (**2.16**) suggests visually, by its long, flowing lines, the restful feeling that one expects to experience when lying in the chair. As the lines flow through lengthened curves, it is difficult to follow a single line. Rather, we are drawn visually into the abstract expressive quality of the lines: the sense of languid movement. In the mid-nineteenth century, Michael Thonet had perfected a process of steaming and bending wood that allowed the creation of these plant-like lines and greatly reduced the need for structural joints in furniture. Many of his graceful bentwood furniture designs have continued in production to this day.

Expressive lines in two-dimensional art often have a **gestural** quality. That is, they directly reveal the artist's arm at work, transferring expressive gestures into marks on a surface. In Eliza Schulte's *Alphabet* (**2.17**), two very different kinds of calligraphic gestures are contrasted. The wide lines spelling ALPHABET convey the sense that they have been carved forever in stone; we can picture the artist with feet firmly planted, making exaggerated vertical strokes with her brush. The thin letters seem to dance lightly and gracefully around them. One imagines their being

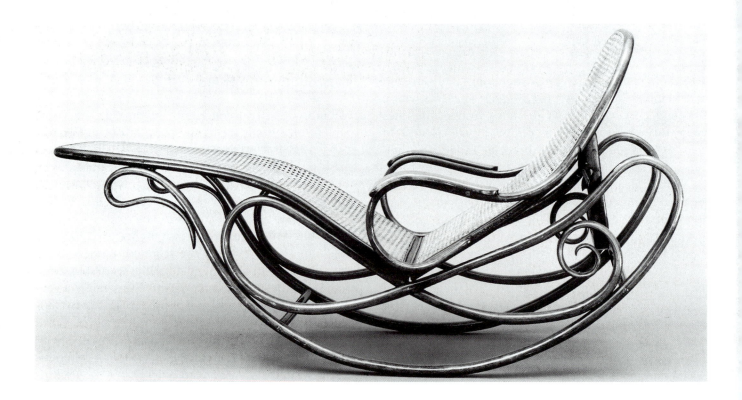

made with large, flowing gestures with no breaks in the arm movement.

For another example of the expressive possibilities of pure line, consider John Crocker's album cover for Schubert's violin music (2.18). A blank set of staves goes through a gradual, comically plausible metamorphosis into a visual equivalent of Schubert's romantic music, with flourishes and embellishments. Such lines can quite literally be called *lyrical*, a term used in describing art that is the visual equivalent of intimately emotional melodies.

2.17 Eliza Schulte, *Alphabet no. 101*, 1988. Gouache on paper, 11½ × 7½ ins (29.2 × 19 cm). Courtesy of the artist.

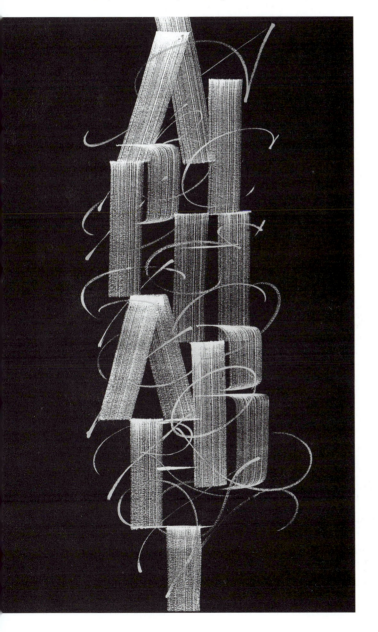

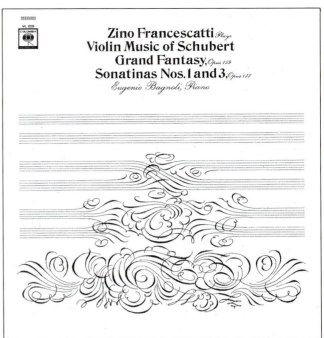

2.18 John Crocker, CBS album cover, 1968.

Directional Line

Lines may also be used by artists to steer the eye in a certain direction. In the poster for a luxury train by the French poster designer A. M. Cassandre (2.19), our eye is directed from the bottom to the top of the poster. We are placed squarely on top of the rail that is perpendicular to the bottom edge of the poster. Our eye races along the rail to the point where all the rails converge and disappear on the horizon. The immediate impression is that of speed and elegance in covering great distances. These directional lines lead us effortlessly to our destination, as the poster suggests the train will do—and even beyond, to the North Star (the name of the train).

SHAPE AND FORM

Throughout this book, we will be using the word **shape** to refer to defined two-dimensional areas. As we use the term, a shape is flat. We will reserve the word **form** for three-dimensional areas, also called "volume" or "mass." But flat shapes may appear on the surface of three-dimensional forms, and two-dimensional works may create on a flat surface the illusion of forms.

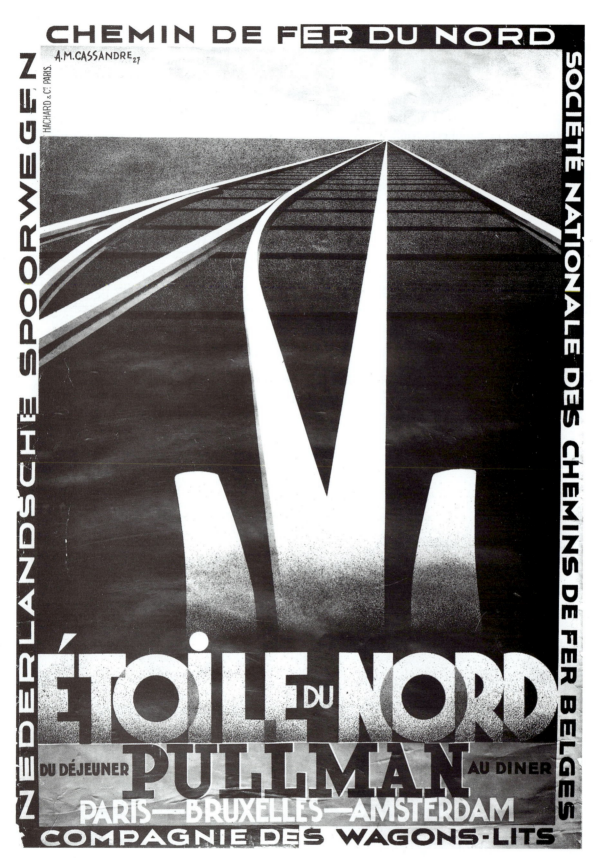

2.19 A. M. Cassandre, poster, 1927. Colored lithograph, 41½ × 29½ ins (105 × 75 cm).
Victoria and Albert Museum, London.

Degrees of Three-Dimensionality

Within the category of three-dimensional art there are various degrees of three-dimensionality. The flattest works approach two-dimensionality: in these an image is developed outward or inward from a two-dimensional ground. These are called **reliefs**. In a **low relief** (or "bas relief"), figures exist on nearly the same plane as the background, almost as in a drawing, but are carved with enough depth for shadows to appear on surfaces where the light is blocked. In the low-relief Moon House post used to support a roof beam by the Kwashkan Tlingit of the northwest coast of North America (**2.20**), the shadows enhance the drama of the piece, drawing attention to the moon and wolf symbols of the family's membership in the wolf clan. Nevertheless, no area is entirely detached from the ground.

Technically, a work is considered a **high relief** only if at least half of the figures' natural spatial depth projects forward from the background. The fact that far more of the substrate is carved away than in a low relief creates a greater range of light and dark shadows that help to define the forms.

In the sculpted exterior of this Roman sarcophagus, or coffin (**2.21**), some limbs are completely undercut, lifting them away from the background entirely, while other, more shallowly carved figures merge with the background. These variations in depth create a dynamic flow of darks and lights and of projections toward, and recesses from, the viewer.

Whether figures are carved or created by attaching materials to a closed backplane, the basic orientation of a relief is the association of three-dimensional figures with a backing. Reliefs are principally designed to be seen straight on; the farther to the side the viewer moves, the less sense the images make.

Another form of three-dimensional art that is designed principally to be seen from the front only is called **frontal** work. Although it is totally freestanding, allowing the viewer to walk all around it or turn it over if it is small, it does not invite viewing from more than one side. Necklaces are typically designed as frontal pieces; the interesting, worked side faces outward, while the back is often minimally worked since it is not designed to be seen. Auguste Rodin's *The Gates of Hell* (**2.22**) was not meant to be seen from the back. The artist's concept, never fully implemented, was that people would walk toward it up a flight of stairs, contemplate the agonies of hell as described or imagined in Christian traditions, and then open the doors and

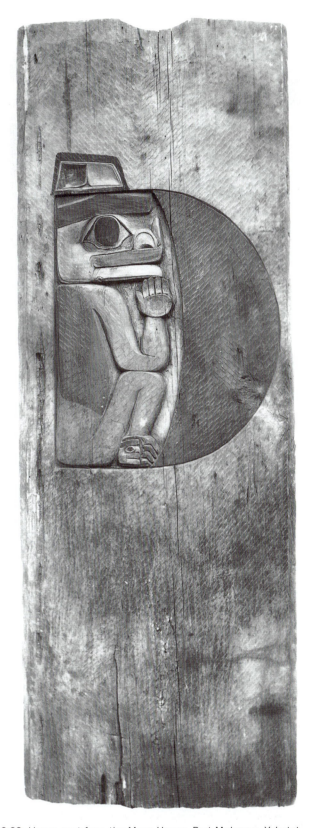

2.20 House post from the Moon House, Port Mulgrave, Yakutat, c. 1916–17. Wood with red, black, and green pigment and nails. Museum of the American Indian, Heye Foundation, New York.

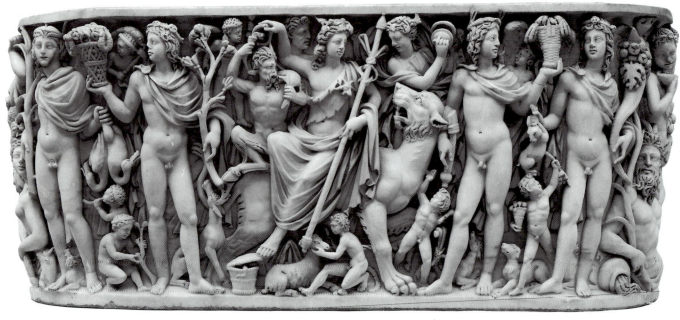

2.21 Sculpted sarcophagus representing Dionysos, the Seasons, and other figures, c. 220–30 AD. Marble, 35½ × 87¾ × 36¾ ins (90.2 × 222.9 × 93.3 cm). Metropolitan Museum of Art, New York. Purchase 1955 Joseph Pulitzer Bequest.

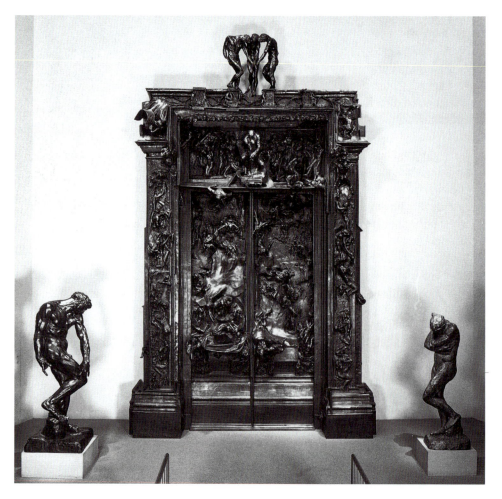

2.22 Auguste Rodin, *The Gates of Hell*, c. 1880. Bronze, 20 ft 10 ins × 13 ft 3 ins × 2 ft 9 ins (6.38 × 4.01 × .83 m). Musée Rodin, Paris.

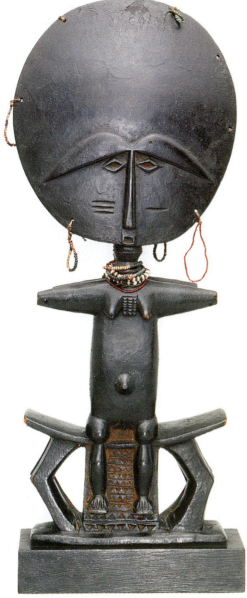

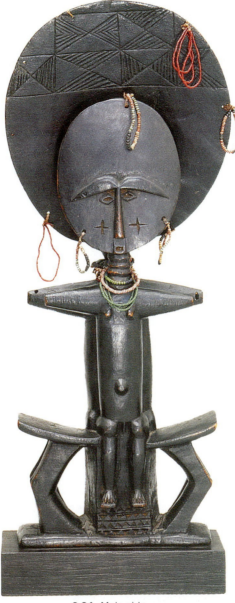

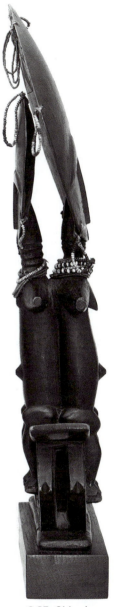

2.23 Female side **2.24** Male side **2.25** Side view

2.23–2.25 Akua'ba figure, Ghana. Wood, double figure of seated male and female. National Museum of African Art, Smithsonian Institution, Washington, D.C.

walk through, as if confronting their own destiny upon dying. They were to look at the work itself from the front only, facing the distress of its writhing figures.

Three-dimensional art in the **full round** is free-standing and designed to be seen from all sides. When a full-round piece is effective, it often makes people want to walk all the way around it or turn it around in their hands to discover how it changes. A common device artists use is to pique our curiosity to see what happens out of sight. If a leg disappears around a curve in the piece, we are likely to follow it to find the foot.

If we walk around the Akua'ba wood figure from the Akan people of Ghana, we discover that the female image on one side (**2.23**) has a smaller male image behind it (**2.24**). Even though both are conceived rather frontally, it is interesting to look at the piece from the side (**2.25**) to see how they fit together, back-to-back on a stool, and thus compare their relative sizes. Most of these pieces, used for fertility and for blessing a pregnancy, have only the female image; the addition of the male figure in this matrilineal society adds intriguing sociological as well as aesthetic puzzles.

The ever-changing quality of three-dimensional works in the full round can barely be imagined from the single, two-dimensional photographs used to represent them. To appreciate a full-round piece completely, one must explore the real thing, from as many angles as possible, for each step and each movement of the head reveals new facets and new relationships among the parts of the piece.

An even fuller degree of three-dimensionality occurs in **walk-through** works, which become part of the environment through which we move. Landscape artists throughout history have planned gardens as walk-through aesthetic experiences. A contemporary version of this experience is available to visitors to the Smithsonian Institution's central court, in Elyn Zimmerman's *Marabar* (2.26). We are invited to walk among the granite boulders, sensing and perhaps feeling their rough, organic strength and discovering the contrasting extremely smooth textures of the faces of those boulders that Zimmerman has cut and polished. These polished faces can be seen only from certain angles, so to experience the totality of the work we must walk varying paths through it, exploring what can be seen from many points.

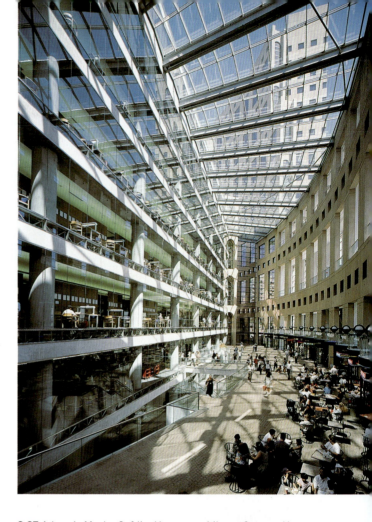

2.26 (below) Elyn Zimmerman, *Marabar*, 1984. Plaza and garden sculpture, National Geographic Society, Washington, D.C. Five natural cleft and polished carnelian granite boulders, height 36 to 120 ins (91.4 to 305 cm), surrounding a pool of polished carnelian granite.

2.27 (above) Moshe Safdie, Vancouver Library Square, Vancouver, British Columbia, completed May 1995, inner promenade. Photo by T. Hursley.

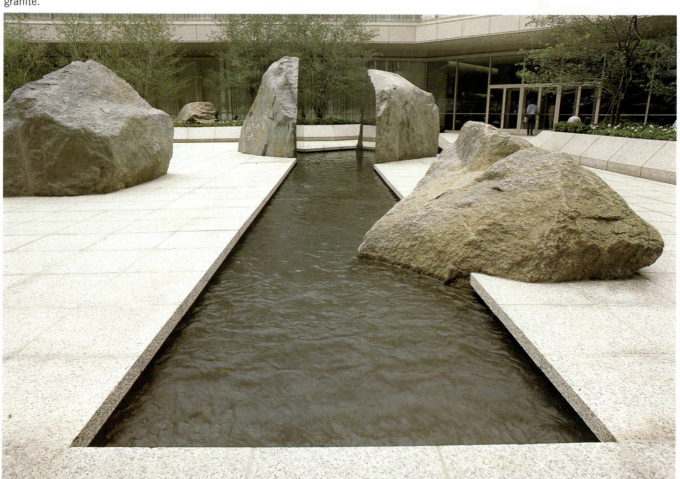

All effective three-dimensional work subtly defines a certain area as "belonging" to it and to a certain extent influences our movements within this space. Work that surrounds the viewer—such as architecture—is the final step in this control, not only becoming an encompassing structure that we enter but also perhaps surrounding us with a certain psychological atmosphere.

Moshe Safdie's controversial Vancouver Library Square (2.27) creates a rather happy mood among public users of the space. The glass-roofed, six-story "urban room" between the inner glass-walled library and the outer structure places pedestrians and library users in visual relationship to each other, as well as to the structures that surround them. People become part of the architecture, like fellow players in a three-dimensional chess game.

Characteristics of Three-Dimensional Form

Artists have approached three-dimensional form in various ways. They may create exterior or interior contours, open or closed forms, and static or dynamic forms.

The surfaces of a three-dimensional work are sometimes called its **contours**. They may project outward (convex) or inward (concave) relative to the general body of the form. Philip Grausman's monumental *Leucantha* (2.28) exaggerates the inward and outward contours of a woman's head, such as the swelling muscles in the neck and the cleft between lips and nose. Highlighting these strong contours gives the figure an impression of great strength.

Some three-dimensional works have both **exterior** and **interior contours** that can be examined. In architecture, the exterior form of a building gives quite a different impression from its interior structure. The lovely flask shown in Figure 2.29 invites us to look at

2.28 Philip Grausman, *Leucantha*, 1993.
Cast aluminum, no. 1/3, 9 ft × 9 ft 10 ins × 9 ft 10 ins.
Photo by Ricardo Barros. Courtesy of Grounds for Sculpture.

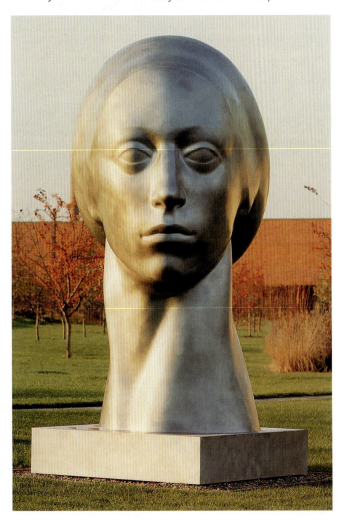

2.29 Maurice Mainot, Flask, 1931. Clear crystal glass with bubbles, height 4⅞ ins (12.4 cm). Victoria and Albert Museum, London.

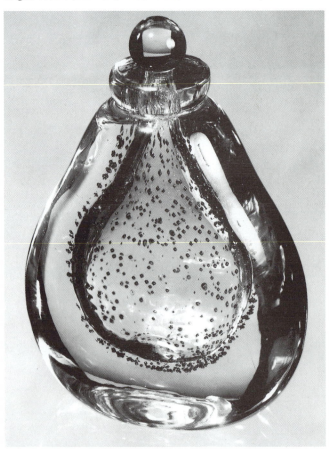

both exterior and interior contours simultaneously. It is made of clear crystal, revealing the concave, pear-shaped contour within a similar but convex exterior contour. The interior contour is emphasized and elaborated by the bubbles surrounding it.

A more subtle kind of interior form can only be sensed, rather than seen. Barbara Hepworth, whose work is shown in Figure 2.33, had a loving awareness of unseen interior forms. She wrote:

> There is an inside and an outside to every form. When they are in special accord, as for instance a nut in its shell or a child in the womb, or in the structure of shells or crystals, or when one senses the architecture of bones in the human figure, then I am most drawn to the effect of light. Every shadow cast by the sun from an ever-varying angle reveals the harmony of the inside and the outside.[4]

2.30 *Senmut with Princess Nefrua*, Thebes, Egypt, c. 1450 BC. Black stone, height 3 ft 4 ins (1.20 m). Egyptian Museum, Berlin.

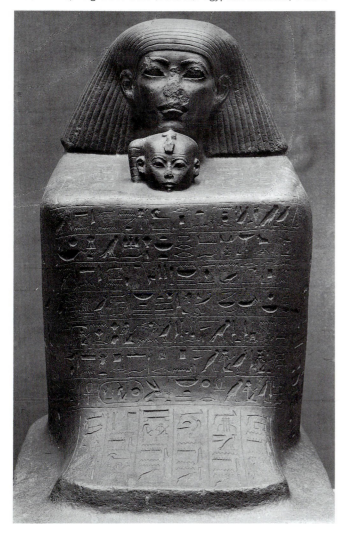

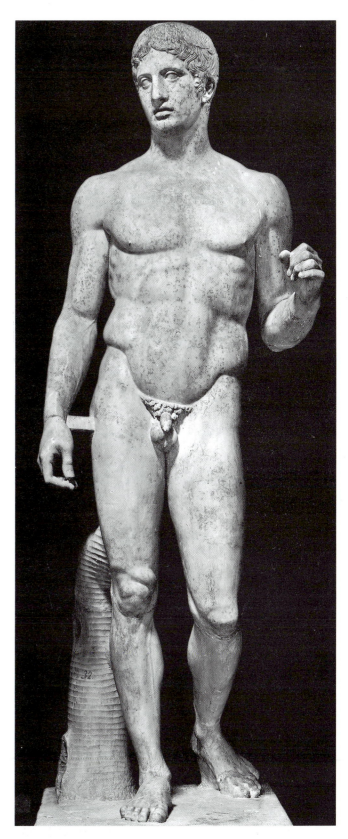

2.31 After Polyclitus, *Spear Bearer (Doryphorus)*, Roman copy after a Greek bronze original of c. 450–400 BC. Marble, height 6 ft 6 ins (1.98 m). National Museum, Naples.

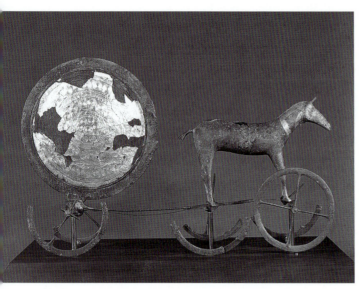

2.32 Horse and Sun Chariot, from Trundholm, Zealand, Denmark, c. 1800–1600 BC. Bronze, length 23¼ ins (59.2 cm). National Museum, Copenhagen.

Another set of distinctions may be made between closed and open forms. Many early Western sculptures were **closed forms** that reflected the raw mass from which they had been carved. The early Egyptian sculpture of *Senmut with Princess Nefrua* (**2.30**) is developed from a cut stone block which is still quite apparent. To create the heads—particularly that of the

child—much of the original block has been removed, yet the overall impression is that of a solid mass. As stone carving evolved, sculptors learned how to open the forms without losing their structural strength. In the *Spear Bearer* (**2.31**), the legs are placed apart and the arms are lifted slightly away from the body. Yet to keep the limbs from breaking off—as they often did—several props have been maintained.

The development of metal casting allowed fully **open forms**, such as the horse and chariot from ancient Denmark (**2.32**). The slender, open spokes of the wheels and long shaft of the chariot could not be executed in stone, whereas the tensile strength of bronze allows it to be cast into elongated forms without bending or breaking. Bronze casting was a major technological innovation, found from about 3500 BC. in Mesopotamia and perhaps as early as 3650 BC. in Thailand.

In the twentieth century, a number of sculptors opened voids through the center of their works. In Barbara Hepworth's *Pendour* (**2.33**), it is the holes piercing the center of the form that are the focus of attention. These ambiguous voids are accentuated by contrast with the solidity and simplicity of the outer form. Defined by wood painted white, in contrast with the darker exterior, they suggest a quality of tender, hidden purity protected from the outside world.

2.33 Barbara Hepworth, *Pendour*, 1947–48. Painted wood, 12⅛ × 29⅜ × 9⅜ ins (30.6 × 74.5 × 23.8 cm). Hirshhorn Museum and Sculpture Garden, Smithsonian Institution, Washington, D.C. Gift of Joseph H. Hirshhorn, 1966.

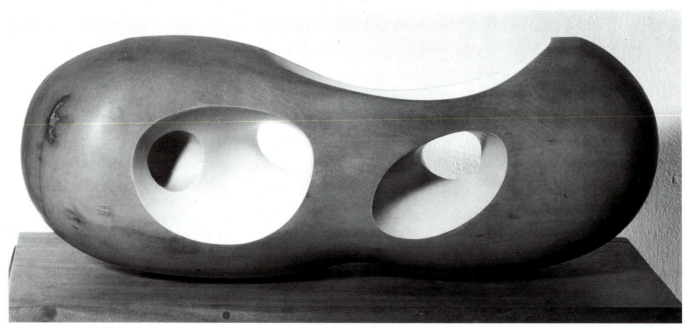

HENRY MOORE
on FORM AND SPACE

When Henry Moore (1898–1986) was a student at The Royal College of Art in London, he visited the British Museum twice a week to explore the riches of the world's sculptural traditions. The one that spoke to him the most was the sculpture of ancient Mexico, with its powerful closed forms. He also had a lifetime interest in organic forms, such as weather-worn bones and water-smoothed pebbles. From these and other elements, he evolved a distinctive personal sculptural style that was characterized by abstract, rounded contours interwoven with shapely voids, as in his *Sheep Piece* around which sheep cluster at his homestead (**2.34**). Whether he was working in stone, wood, or bronze castings, Moore was consistently interested in the interplay between positive form and negative space, and in how a piece looks from all sides:

"Appreciation of sculpture depends upon the ability to respond to form in three dimensions. That is perhaps why sculpture has been described as the most difficult of all arts . . . Many more people are 'form-blind' than colour-blind. The child learning to see first distinguishes only two-dimensional shape; it cannot judge distances, depths. Later, for its personal safety and practical needs, it has to develop (partly by means of touch) the ability to judge roughly three-dimensional distances. But having satisfied the requirements of practical necessity, most people go no farther . . . They do not make the further intellectual and emotional effort needed to comprehend form in its full spatial existence.

This is what the sculptor must do. He must strive continually to think of, and use, form in its full spatial completeness. He gets the solid shape, as it were, inside his head—he thinks of it, whatever its size, as if he were holding it completely enclosed in the hollow of his hand. He mentally visualises a complex form from all round itself; he knows while he looks at one side what the other side is like; he identifies himself with its centre of gravity, its mass, its weight."[5]

"At one time the holes in my sculpture were made for their own sakes. Because I was trying to become conscious of spaces in the sculpture—I made the hole have a shape in its own right, the solid body was encroached upon, eaten into, and sometimes the form was only the shell holding the hole. Recently I have attempted to make the forms and the spaces (not holes) inseparable, neither being more important than the other."[6]

"If you hold your hand as I am doing now, the shape that those fingers could enclose if I were holding an apple would be different from the shape if I were holding a pear. If you can tell what that is, then you know what space is. That is space and form. You can't understand space without being able to understand form and to understand form you must be able to understand space. If I can really grasp in my mind the shape of your head, I must know what distance there is from your forehead to the back of your head, and I must know what shape the air is between your eyebrows and your nostrils, or down to the cheeks. The idea that space is something new in sculpture is only spoken of by people who can't know what space and form are."[7]

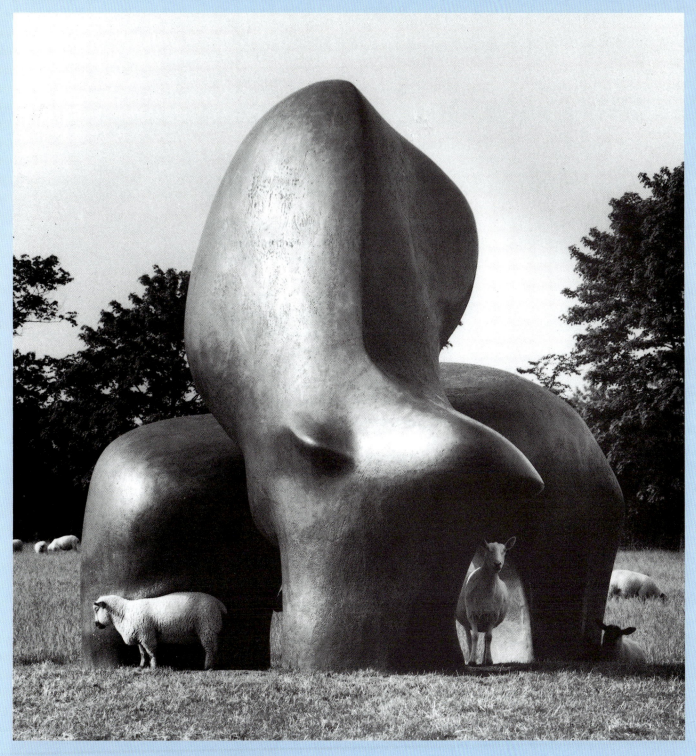

2.34 Henry Moore, *Sheep Piece*, 1971–72, Hoglands, Hertfordshire.
Bronze, length 19 ft (5.8 m).
Courtesy of the Henry Moore Foundation, Hertfordshire, England.

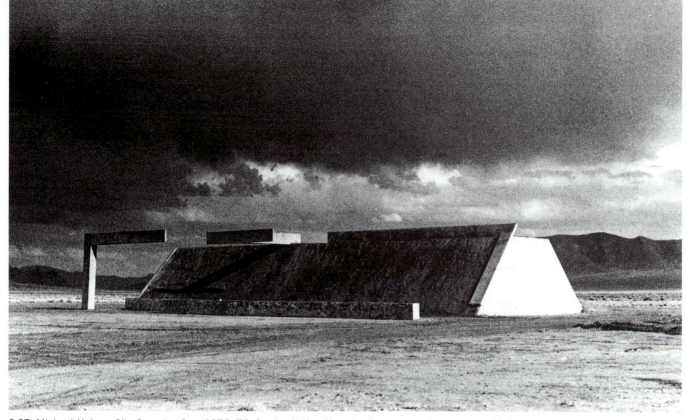

2.35 Michael Heizer, *City Complex One*, 1972–76, Garden Valley, Nevada. Cement, steel, and earth, 23 ft 6 ins × 140 ft × 110 ft (7 × 43 × 34 m). Collection of the artist and Virginia Dwan.

Finally, we can draw a distinction between static and dynamic forms. **Static** forms appear to be still, unchanging. The pyramid is a supremely static form, for its broad base seems to guarantee an immovable stability. Michael Heizer's *City Complex One* (**2.35**) has an enduring, monumental effect. Like the surrounding mountains, it looks set to remain standing a very long time. Indeed, in contrast to the more temporary nature of many earthworks, this structure was built to last, with concrete and steel reinforcing packed earth. The sense of historical permanence that Heizer's structure evokes is increased by its reference to ancient structures: the rectangular base and sloped sides derived from the mastabas (tombs) of ancient Egypt, and the framing from an ancient Maya ball court at Chichén Itzá.

Dynamic forms are those that appear lively, moving, and changing, even though they are actually stationary. The Art Nouveau movement in applied art often worked with dynamic forms, such as Louis Comfort Tiffany's exquisite *Flower-form Vase* (**2.36**). From chairs to vases to stair railings, Art Nouveau designs appear to be growing as though they are organic forms. Tiffany's vase exposes the dynamic process by which the glass was blown, pulled, and shaped when in a molten state. Although the end result is hard and fixed, it appears still to be in fluid motion, like a bud in the process of reaching upward and growing outward.

2.36 Louis Comfort Tiffany, Flower-form vase, c. 1900–05.
Height 12¾ ins (32.3 cm). Colorless, transparent green and translucent opalescent white glass; blown, trailed threading pulled into chevron patterns, iridized. Corning Museum of Glass, New York.

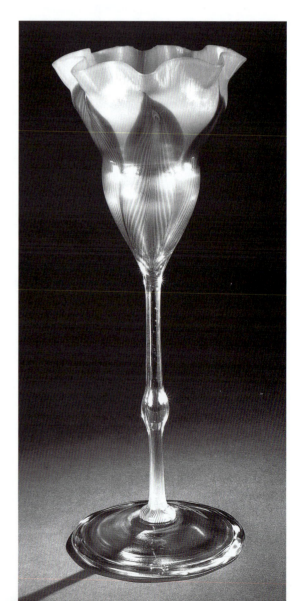

Two-Dimensional Illusion of Form

Many two-dimensional works of art are designed to represent the three-dimensional world, but they exist on a flat plane rather than the three-dimensional world of our experience. Jan Vermeer makes us very aware of this process in his *The Art of Painting* (**2.37**). We see the artist—some think it is Vermeer himself—observing a three-dimensional model and translating her form into a two-dimensional painting. The drawing aside of a curtain gives us what appears to be an intimate view into this process. The scene seems to have realistic spatial depth, with the curtain very close to us, the artist somewhat farther, and the model, seen as though over the artist's shoulder, farther away still, against the wall. The impression we have of seeing three-dimensional forms in three-dimensional space is an illusion, for the painting consists of marks on a flat surface, like the painting being started on the artist's easel. Vermeer's skill lies in convincing us that we are seeing figures with mass, volume, and weight, rather than flat figures.

2.37 Jan Vermeer, *The Art of Painting*, c. 1665–70. Oil on canvas, 3 ft 11¼ ins × 3 ft 3⅜ ins (1.2 × 1 m). Kunsthistorisches Museum, Vienna.

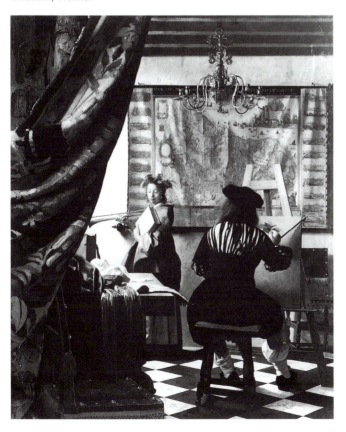

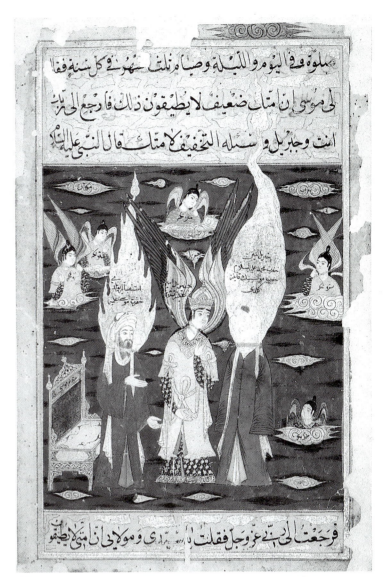

2.38 *The Prophet Mohammad with the Archangel Gabriel Meeting Moses in Heaven*. Persian miniature painting, 12¼ × 8 ins (31.1 × 20.3 cm). From Mustafa Zarir's *The Book of the Life of the Prophet*, c. 1594. Museum für Islamische Kunst, Berlin-Dahlem.

One of the earliest devices used to suggest three-dimensional form is **overlapping**. From our experience in a three-dimensional world, we know that if one thing covers another from our view, it must exist in front of it in space.

In the Persian miniature painting (**2.38**), the hands and sleeves of Moses (the figure on the left) and the archangel Gabriel obscure part of their garments, which tells us that the arms are closer to us than the rest of their bodies. Likewise, Gabriel's crown slightly overlaps his wings, placing crown spatially in front of wings. Nevertheless, the figures are painted in solid colors, and have a slightly flat appearance, like paper dolls.

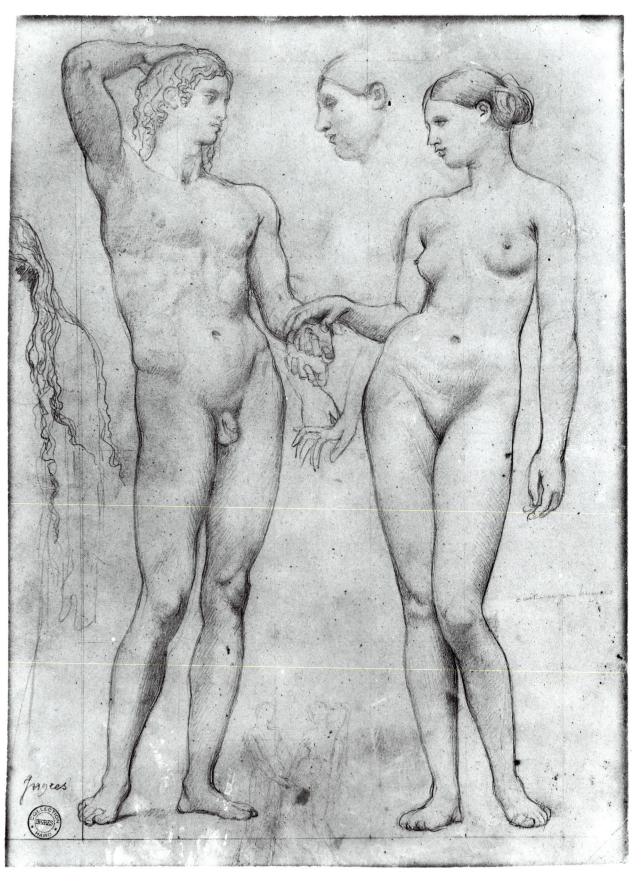

2.39 Jean Auguste Dominique Ingres, *Two Nudes*, study for *The Golden Age*, 1842.
Graphite on paper, 16⅜ × 12⅜ ins (41.6 × 31.4 cm). Fogg Art Museum, Harvard University, Cambridge, Massachusetts.

Another set of devices—**shading** and **modeling** of contours—brings out a sense of spatial depth. In the elegantly understated Ingres figure study (2.39) just the slightest indication of shading within the primary contours develops a full-bodied illusion of form, for we understand that the shaded areas exist behind contours which block the light. Curving lines of bracelet modeling, such as those on the woman's left leg, suggest that the form is also fully rounded on the side we cannot see. In areas such as the heads, where bracelet modeling is not added, the figures read more like reliefs than fully rounded forms.

Another device for giving a two-dimensional surface the appearance of three-dimensional forms is to show more than one side of a form, indicating how it recedes into the distance. If we see only the front wall of a building, we have no idea of the building's depth in space. But if an artist depicts the building from an angle that allows us to see one of the sides as well as the front, we immediately grasp the idea of its form. Paul Cézanne studied nature—and human perceptions of natural objects—with great care to determine how we see them and therefore how a painter might truthfully represent the optical sensations. In *Mont Sainte-Victoire seen from Les Lauves* (2.40), a complex array of buildings, trees, and facets of the mountain he so often painted are reduced to abstract geometric structures. Some are painted in clear linear perspective, with sides angling back toward the horizon. (The topic of linear perspective is covered in depth later in this chapter in the discussion of Space.) Others are brushstroked suggestions of geometric form. In letters to an art student, Cézanne advised:

> To achieve progress nature alone counts, and the eye is trained through contact with her. . . . In an orange, an apple, a bowl, a head, there is a culminating point; and this point is always—in spite of the tremendous effect of light and shade and colorful sensations—the closest to our eye; the edges of the objects recede to a center on our horizon. . . . Treat nature by the cylinder, the sphere, the cone, everything in proper perspective so that each side of an object or a plane is directed toward a central point.[8]

2.40 Paul Cézanne, *Mont Sainte-Victoire seen from Les Lauves*, 1902–4. Oil on canvas, 27½ × 35¼ ins (69.8 × 89.5 cm). Philadelphia Museum of Art, George W. Elkins Collection.

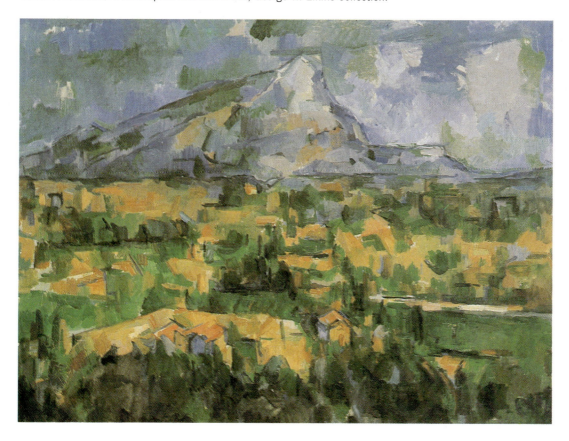

Shapes

In the terminology we are using, **shapes** are relatively flat areas. In *The Snail* (**2.41**), for instance, Henri Matisse was working primarily with large shapes that had been painted and then cut and organized into a dynamic composition in which each painted shape touches and is related to the sequence forming the whole. Shapes are particularly noticeable here because they have been physically cut out with clearly defined edges and then glued down. Note that the white shapes created between the colored shapes are active and interesting in themselves, and more varied in configuration than the colored patches.

There are a number of general kinds of shapes with which artists have worked. One is the distinctive result of tearing or cutting paper, as in the Matisse. Another is the flattening of objects from the three-dimensional world into two-dimensional shapes.

In his *Hiroshima Series: Boy with Kite* (**2.42**), Jacob Lawrence depicts the horror of the atomic bombing by reducing human figures into a series of disjointed, flattened shapes. The deformed shapes of skull-like heads and agonized hands stand out as disembodied parts of a whole that is no longer unified, that no longer works, as flat and broken as the torn shapes of the kite. We read such a composition from shape to shape across a relatively flat surface in which the only indication of depth is the continual overlapping of one shape by another. In Picasso's *Guernica* (1.47), which also depicts the horrors of war, you can see shapes used in a similar way to convey a feeling of fragmentation, dislocation,

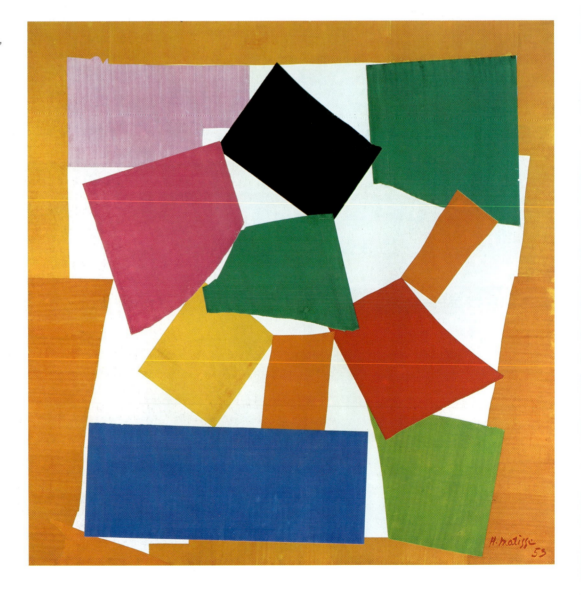

2.41 Henri Matisse, *The Snail*, 1953. Painted, cut, and pasted paper, 9 ft 4¾ ins × 9 ft 5 ins (2.86 × 2.87 m). Tate Gallery, London.

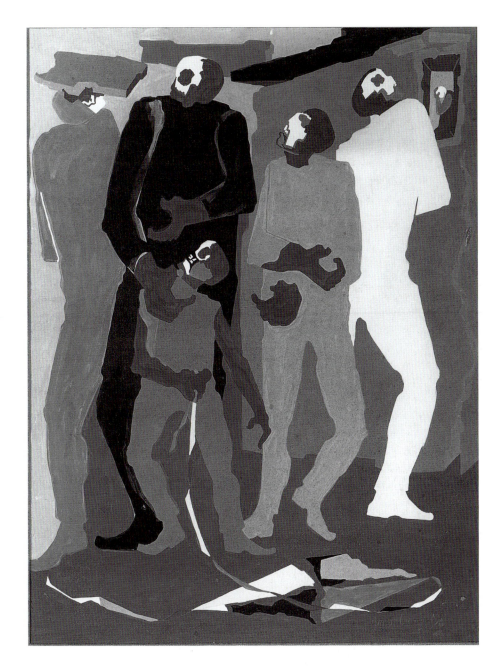

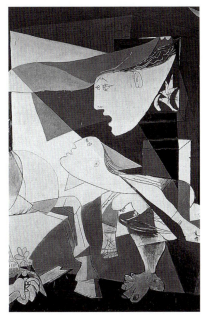

2.42 Jacob Lawrence, *Hiroshima Series*, # 7: *Boy with Kite*, 1983. Gouache on paper, 23 × 17½ ins (58.4 × 44.5 cm). Seattle Art Museum, Seattle, Washington. Collection of Gwendolyn and Jacob Lawrence.

2.43 (below) Pablo Picasso, *Guernica* (detail), 1937. Oil on canvas, 11 ft 5½ ins × 25 ft 5¼ ins (3.49 × 7.75 m). Reina Sofia Museum of Modern Art, Madrid.

and horror. The detail in Figure **2.43** focuses on two human heads which are painted without any three-dimensional modeling, like flat arrowheads directing our eye to the horror in the skies and the devastation it has wrought on the ground.

Abstracted shapes may be so extensively reworked that they begin to lose their representational identity, for everyone except the artist. Arshile Gorky's shapes in *Making the Calendar* (**2.44**) appear to be purely imaginative inventions, but they are derived from a family scene. One of his daughters sits on the left before a window view of the Connecticut countryside. In the center of the painting, there is a dog on the floor in front of a fireplace. To the right, Gorky stands reading a magazine with one hand on the shoulder of his wife, who is rocking their baby in a cradle. Gorky says of such work, "Though the various forms all had specific meaning to me, it is the spectator's privilege to find his own meaning."[9]

ARSHILE GORKY
on THE INTENSITY OF ART

Arshile Gorky's work revolves around lines, shapes, and fields of color. At first glance, they may seem fanciful, spontaneous, playful, but his own life and words correct this impression. Born in Armenia in 1904 as Vosdanik Adoian, Gorky experienced both the joys of life in a well-to-do family in the Armenian countryside and the terrible sufferings of the Armenian people. His father left for America when Gorky was four years old, to avoid being drafted by the Turks to fight other Armenians. The Turks killed all his grandparents, six uncles, and three aunts, in some cases before his eyes. His family residence was shelled, and his people were forced to undertake a 150-mile (240-km) death march. That year, 1915, two million Armenians were massacred by the Turks. Gorky and his younger sister worked to bring home what food they could in the face of a Turkish blockade, but when he was fifteen his beloved mother died of starvation in his arms while dictating a letter to his father.

In 1920 Gorky emigrated to America, where he faced hunger and poverty but gradually achieved recognition and considerable influence as an artist, only to see some of his best works destroyed in a barn fire. In 1948, his father died. The same year Gorky's neck was broken and his painting arm paralyzed in an automobile crash. His wife also left him, taking their two children with her. He ended this life of suffering that year by hanging himself. Gorky's words about art therefore ring with the intensity of his personal experience:

"My Armenian experiences have quickened my consciousness to a greater sensitivity of feeling and a higher level of discrimination. In revealing myself, it is my purpose to reveal people to themselves. An artist must see and feel and understand as opposed to those who merely glimpse but do not really see.

The camera has rendered impotent any attempt to compete with it. What reason, therefore, remains to sit in the stagnation of realism? Art is more than mere chronicle. It must mirror the intellect and the emotion, for anyone can portray realism. The mind's eye in its infinity of radiations. It is left for the artist to forge the new metal, to resurrect his ancient role as the uncoverer and interpreter, but never the recorder, of life's secrets.

When I speak of the great influence of Armenia on my art, some here mistakenly call it chauvinism. It is decidedly not chauvinism at all and they do not understand; for good or bad I believe that I have experienced more than most of my fellow artists. This does not automatically enable me to know more. But it does enable me to respond necessarily to more experiences than they have had the ability to observe directly. As Armenians of Van, we were forced to experience with greater intensity and in a shorter time what others can only read about while sitting in comfort. We lived and experienced it. The blood of our people at the hands of the Turks, the massacres and genocide. Our death march, our relatives and dearest friends dying in battle before our eyes. The loss of our homes, the destruction of our country by the Turks, Mother's starvation in my arms.

We have been made privy to mankind's evil secrets as well as its glorious achievements. And the living, sensitive, thinking man cannot help but respond with greater than normal intensity. And the remembrance of Armenia's beauty prior to the bloodshed. The art and accomplishments of our unfortunate people. Great art's problem, that is to say my goal, is to enable those who have not experienced certain elements of reality to experience them through

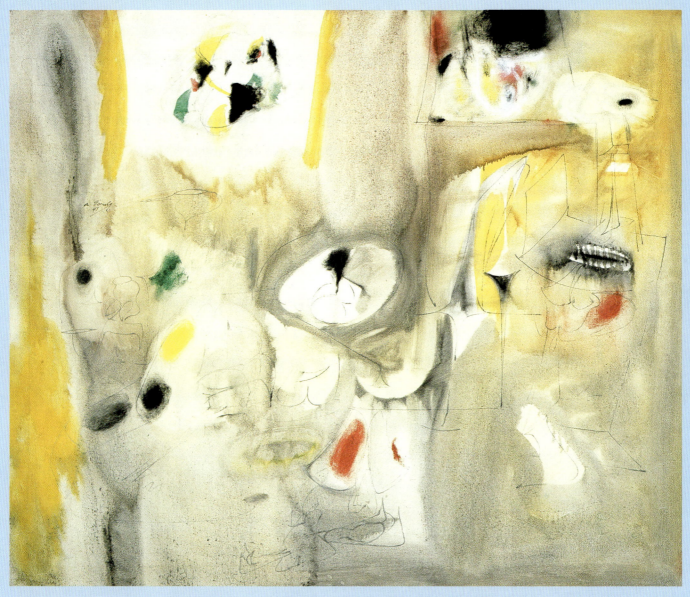

2.44 Arshile Gorky, *Making the Calendar*, 1947. Oil on canvas.
The Munson-William-Proctor Institute, Utica, New York. Edward W. Root Bequest.

the power of my work on their mind and eyes and imagination. To enable them to come as close to realization of reality as possible, simply through my work.

To be alive is to feel, to be sensitive, and above all to be aware. Art must always remain earnest. Great art contains great topics. What do I mean by great? Not kings, rich men, and clerics, not publicized political scoundrels. I mean love of man, love of nature, love of beauty, love of progress in the well-being of man. Sarcasm has no place in art because it verges on cynicism, which is weakness and the inability to face reality, to master reality.

The history of our Armenian people has shown us the secret of creativity. The secret is to throw yourself into the water of life again and again, not to hang back, no reservations, risk everything, but, above all, strike out boldly with all you have."[10]

Geometric shapes have long been used as a design element in many cultures. The water jar by the pueblo potter Lucy Lewis (1.35) is decorated with black and white triangles within squares, alternating with diamond-like shapes created by lines, woven into squares of the same size. A Liberian gown (2.45) is composed largely of geometric shapes—circles, squares, rectangles, and triangles—whose symmetry is a striking counterpoint to the asymmetrical style of the gown. Although the shapes are worked flat on the cloth, when the gown is worn they will become more three-dimensional as the cloth drapes over the contours of the body.

Shapes can be created in unfilled as well as filled areas of a design. We perceived unworked white shapes in Matisse's *The Snail* (2.41), but they were not the focus of the work. In Helen Frankenthaler's *Mauve District* (2.46), an unpainted white area appears as a

positive shape that is as important as the painted areas. We are meant to perceive the unworked space as "filled" rather than "empty." Frankenthaler explains:

That area not painted on didn't need paint because it had paint next to it. So it operated as forcefully, and the thing was to decide where to leave it and where to show it and where to say, "This doesn't need another line or another pail of color." In other words, the very ground was part of the medium. Red, blue, against the white of cotton duck or the beige of linen, has the same play in space as the duck. Every square inch of that surface is equally important in depth, shallowness, space, so that it isn't as if background meant the background is a curtain or a drape in front of which there is a table, on which there is a plate, on which there are apples. The apples are as important as the drape, and the drape is as important as the legs of the table.[11]

2.45 Gown made by the Mandingo, Liberia. Dyed and woven cotton cloth, decorated with embroidery and appliqué, height 36½ ins (93 cm). British Museum, London.

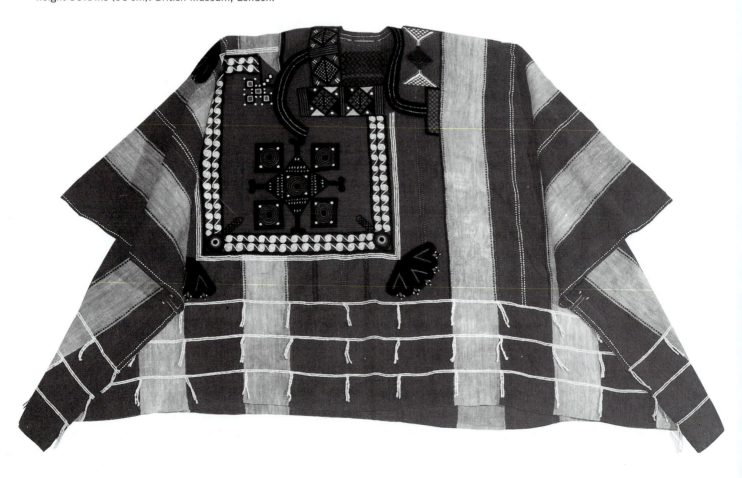

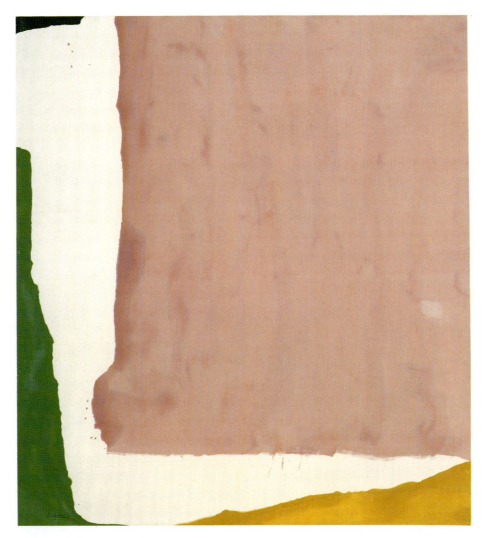

2.46 Helen Frankenthaler, *Mauve District*, 1966.
Synthetic polymer on unprimed canvas, 8 ft 7 ins × 7 ft 11 ins (2.62 × 2.41 m).
Collection Museum of Modern Art, New York. Mrs. Donald B. Strauss Fund.

The shapes in Frankenthaler's painting are **hard-edged**. That is, their boundaries are clearly distinguished from surrounding areas by contrasts in color along the edges where they meet. The fact that Jacob Lawrence turns body parts into hard-edged shapes in his Hiroshima painting (2.42) forces the eye to focus on the frighteningly erratic outlines of those shapes.

Some artists work instead with **soft-edged** shapes, in which edges are not precisely delineated. In this case, it may be hard to pinpoint where one shape stops and another begins, but we may still get a sense of the presence of shapes. Odilon Redon, one of the fore-most Symbolist painters of the late nineteenth century, created a dream-like atmosphere for *Orpheus* (2.47) by using softly diffused lights and shadows and a barely defined outline for the severed head of Orpheus. The blue cloth is an even more soft-edged shape. Redon, who sought visible expression of the products of the unconscious, saw the mythical head of the dead Orpheus, still singing, as a symbol of art's immortality.

Shapes may also be created to express a certain emotion. In the context of martial law in Poland in 1983, there was no ambiguity about the emotion being expressed by the Polish poster artist Henryk

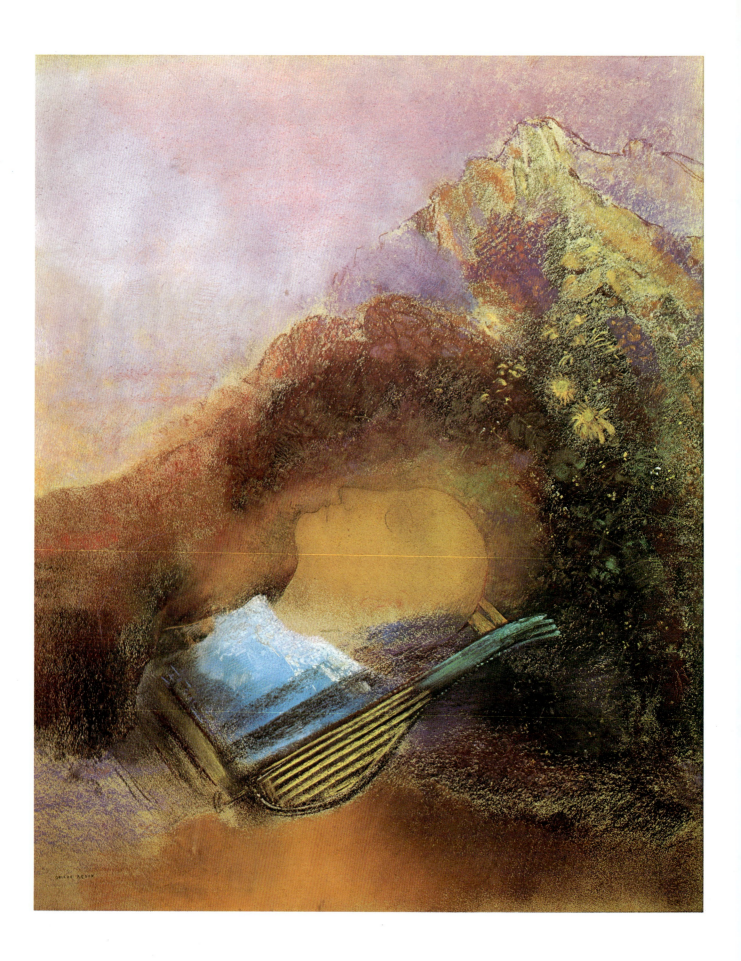

2.47 (opposite) Odilon Redon, *Orpheus*, after 1903. Pastel, 27½ × 22¼ ins (70 × 56.5 cm). Cleveland Museum of Art, Cleveland, Ohio.

2.48 (right) Henryk Tomaszewski, poster for the work of Witold Gombrowicz, 1983. Stedelijk Museum, Amsterdam.

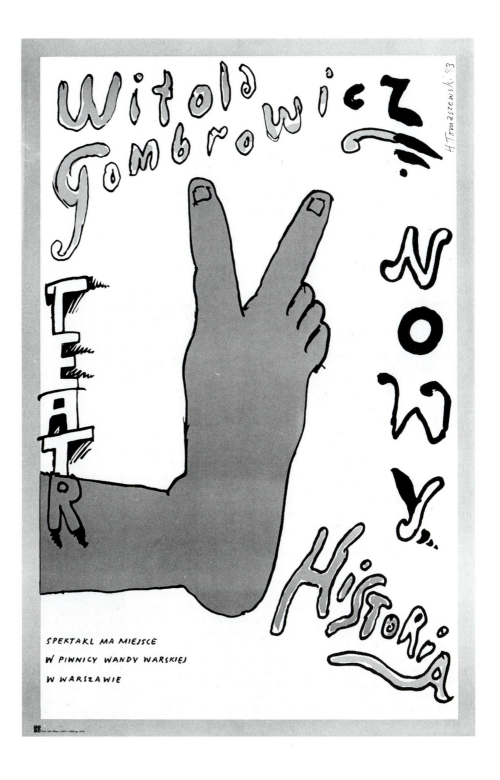

Tomaszewski in his poster advertising an art show (2.48). Prohibited by censorship from showing a "V for victory" hand signal, Tomaszewski presented a foot that clearly bespeaks a defiant, playful freedom. With its slightly bumpy, hairy edges, this shape immediately suggests a down-to-earth populace who will persist in asserting their inner freedom, no matter what restrictions may be imposed by the government.

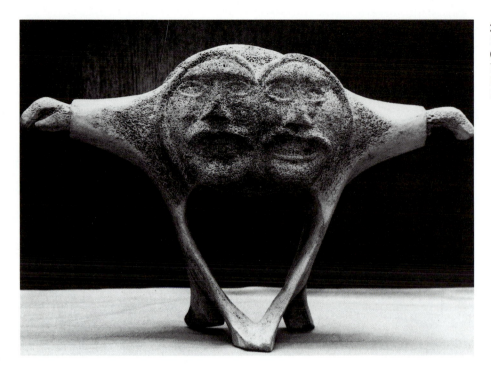

2.49 Manasie Manaipik, *Good Spirit*, 1969, Pangnirtung, Northwest Territories, Canada. Whale vertebra, 12½ × 18⅝ × 7½ ins (32 × 48 × 19 cm). Macmillan-Bloedel Ltd., Vancouver, British Columbia.

SPACE

In art, as in life, space is an intangible element. Yet artists work quite consciously with spatial aspects of our existence to achieve the effects they desire. Those we will explore here are the ways in which three-dimensional art controls space, the differing ways space is handled in two-dimensional work, the concept of scale, and the mystery of spatial illusions.

Three-Dimensional Art in Space

On the most basic level, three-dimensional art physically occupies space. It has its own very obvious spatial reality—the volume of air it displaces. Less obvious are other ways in which certain works exist in space.

Some works delineate forms in space, shaping the intangible into contoured areas. In Manasie Manaipik's *Good Spirit* sculpture (**2.49**), the open area in a whale's vertebra that once housed the spinal cord is brought to our attention as an interesting form in itself. The hard edges of the opening and its regular contours help us to "see" the form of the unfilled space. Certain architectural forms work the same way, defining a volume in space by enclosing it. In the great Byzantine church of Hagia Sophia (**2.51**), the central interior space is a vast domed square rising 183 feet (56 m) above the floor. A model of the interior (**2.50**) reveals the form of this space as though it were a solid mass. This delineated space surrounds worshippers—originally restricted to the emperor, his court, and the clergy—with an awe-inspiring microcosm of the vastness of the universe and the greatness of its Creator.

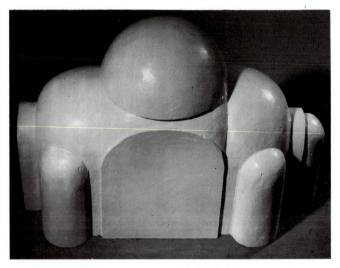

2.50 Model of the interior space of Hagia Sophia.

2.51 (opposite) Hagia Sophia, Istanbul, AD 532–37. Dome height 183 ft (56 m).

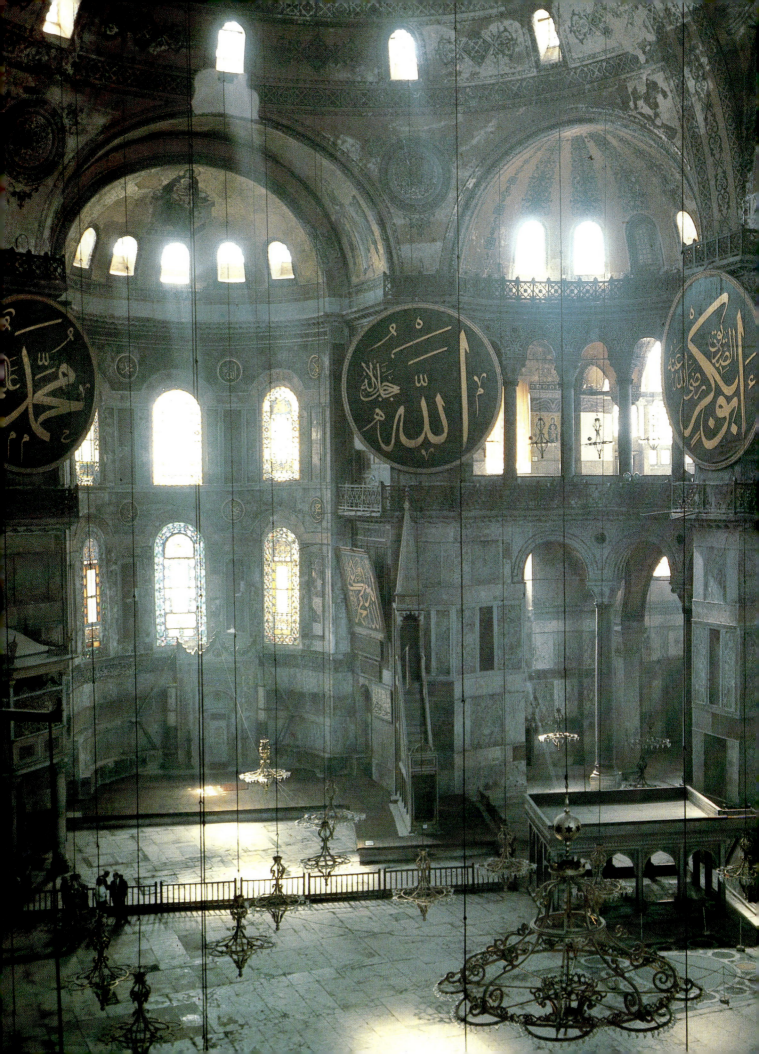

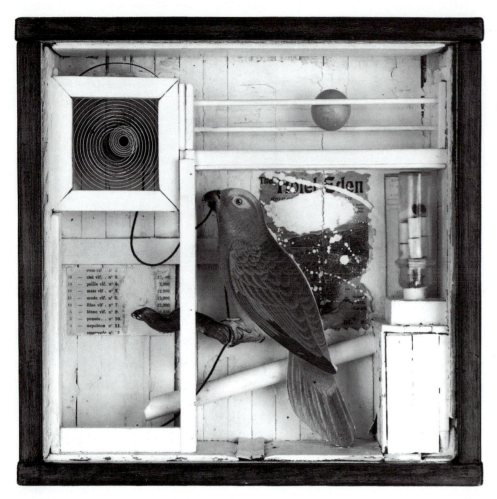

2.52 Joseph Cornell, *The Hotel Eden*, 1945. Assemblage with music box, 15⅛ × 15⅝ × 4¾ ins (38.3 × 39.7 × 12.1 cm). National Gallery of Canada, Ottawa, Ontario. Copyright © The Joseph and Robert Cassell Memorial Foundation. Photo by Bruce C. Jones, courtesy of Xavier Fourcade, Inc.

Some sculptures carve out their own small world in a confined space. Joseph Cornell has done many works of this sort, defining an area by means of a glass case and then building up enigmatic compositions within it from **found objects**. In his *The Hotel Eden* (**2.52**), there is a sense of faded Victorian romance—the exotic paper parrot, listings in French, the remains of a poster for what appears to be a large seaside hotel. Beyond these relatively identifiable clues to content, the identity, meanings, and relationships of the found objects exist in a private fantasy world of the artist. Why the ball? The concentric circles to which the parrot holds a string? The glass of white cylinders? Cornell collected all sorts of objects that delighted him, from marbles and toys to sky charts, and created small scenes with them that tempt the mind beyond its usual frame of reference. Within a space so defined and set apart, everyday objects lose their usual identities and become whatever the artist and the viewers' imaginations perceive them to be.

It is possible for a three-dimensional work to "control" an area larger than it physically occupies. Sculp-tures with pointed linear projections may seem to acti-vate the space around them, as if the lines continued for some distance into that space. The bold lines of Mark di Suvero's sculpture *She* (**2.53**) are so strong that their commanding presence is felt beyond the edges of the steel. Furthermore, when the three movable parts of this participatory sculpture are set in motion, the sculpture seems to command an even greater volume of space.

It is also possible for three-dimensional art to con-trol us in space. Architecture provides defined rooms, halls, stairways, and ramps that guide our movements. Gardens may also be planned to manipulate people's movements through space, using pathways and bar-riers. In the Japanese garden shown in Figure **2.54**, the way across the pond is defined by a path and then by stepping stones, all carefully arranged to imitate nature. The artistry of Japanese garden design leads us to step in specific places, at a specific pace, so that we are invited to enjoy artfully composed views of the landscape. When these devices work well, we are unaware of being manipulated.

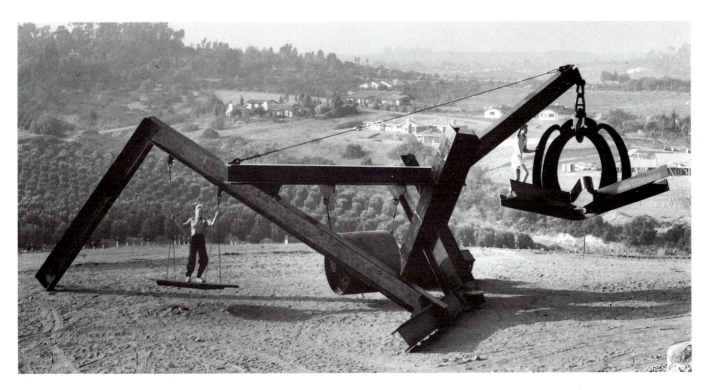

2.53 Mark di Suvero, *She*, 1976–79.
Steel, length 55 ft (16.76 m).
Collection of Eugene M. Klein.

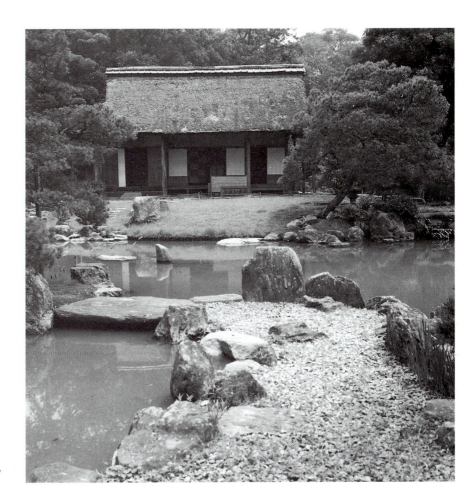

2.54 Garden of Katsura Palace, Kyoto, Japan,
Edo period, early 17th century.

Two-Dimensional Space

The two-dimensional surface is by definition a flat plane. This plane may be referred to as the **ground**; if a discrete shape is placed on it, it may be called a "figure on a ground," or a **figure-ground relationship**. In the most direct case of a figure-ground relationship, the ground is unworked and the figure can be clearly distinguished as lying on top of it. In this Australian Aboriginal bark painting (**2.55**), the painted spirit is the positive figure; the bark on which it is painted is the ground, which seems to lie behind it in space. Since there is a strong contrast in colors between figure and ground, we can discern an edge where they meet and we interpret it as belonging to the figure. However, even in this case, the spatial relationship between figure and ground is not necessarily so straightforward. As a second look at this painting will reveal, the figure is not fully demarcated from the ground by an outline; the figure is open, leaving some mystery about where the spirit stops and the surrounding environment begins. Indeed, they may not be entirely separate.

If figure and ground are approximately equal in area, artists can create a **figure-ground reversal** in which either color can be interpreted as lying on top of the other. Is a checkerboard red on black or black on red? Those of us who are accustomed to reading black type on white paper may initially assume that when we see black and white work, black is the figure and white the ground. The poster for *"Master Harold" ... and the Boys* (**2.56**) calls this assumption into question, for we can continually flip between seeing the black head of Master Harold as a positive figure and seeing it as the background for a white figure. The white itself alternately reads as the African continent and a white boy's head. In this case, the visual puzzle not only holds our attention but also draws us into the theme of the play: race relations in South Africa.

Two-dimensional picture planes are often treated to create the impression of space that recedes from the viewer—or sometimes even extends forward. A

2.55 Attributed to Dick Nangulay, *Spirit Figure*, 1972, Western Arnhem Land, Northern Territory, Australia. Ocher on bark, 14½ × 22½ ins (37 × 57 cm). Copyright by The Asia Society Galleries and the South Australian Museum.

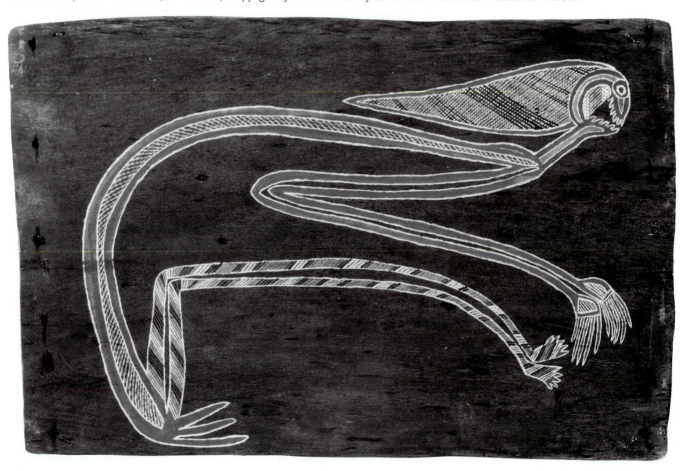

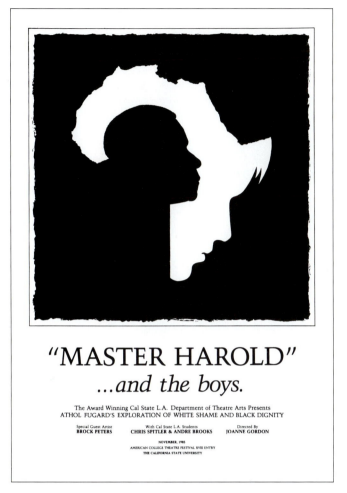

"MASTER HAROLD"
...and the boys.

The Award Winning Cal State L.A. Department of Theatre Arts Presents
ATHOL FUGARD'S EXPLORATION OF WHITE SHAME AND BLACK DIGNITY

Special Guest Artist **BROCK PETERS** With Cal State L.A. Students **CHRIS SPITLER & ANDRE BROOKS** Directed By **JOANNE GORDON**

NOVEMBER, 1985
AMERICAN COLLEGE THEATRE FESTIVAL XVIII ENTRY
THE CALIFORNIA STATE UNIVERSITY

2.56 David McNutt, designer, *"Master Harold" . . . and the boys*, 1985. Poster for the Department of Theater Arts, California State University, Los Angeles, California. Courtesy of the artist.

number of devices have been developed that fool the eye into thinking it is looking into a space that has depth. As illustrations, we will use works that primarily use only one device, though many pieces of three-dimensional art use all of them at once.

One such device is the **placement** of images on the picture plane. In general, we tend to interpret figures that are lower on the picture plane as being closer to us in space. In Muqi's *Six Persimmons* (**2.57**), we do not interpret the fruits as floating in the air. Even though there is no visible surface for them to be sitting on, we perceive them as resting on something because of their placement in relationship to each other. We see the one that is lowest as closest to us, implying a surface that extends at least as far forward as that fruit seems to come. The other persimmons line up behind it at slightly different depths in space, the highest one

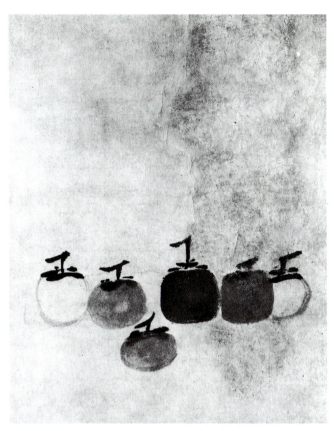

2.57 Muqi, *Six Persimmons*, Southern Song Dynasty, China, late 13th century. Ink on paper, width 14½ ins (37 cm). Daitokuji, Kyoto, Japan.

in the center seeming farther away than the ones to either side. The artist tells us to look from object to object, observing the many subtle ways they differ, including their very slightly differing placement in space.

Another device giving the illusion of spatial depth is **overlapping** space: the obscuring of images to be interpreted as farther away from us by objects designed to appear closer to us. In Romare Bearden's collage, *She-Ba* (**2.58**), even though the cut-out shapes are flat and intentionally ambiguous, the obscuring of some parts by others offers clues to their relative positions in space. Across the queen's torso, for instance, overlapping tells us that her scarf is in front of her sleeve, which is in front of her right arm, which is in front of her breasts, which are in front of the other side of her scarf, which is in front of her left arm. The staff is not floating in the air, for part of her hand is in front of it and there is a suggestion that the ends of her fingers are hidden by it in the back.

A device which adds a tremendous feeling of depth to a two-dimensional painting is **scale change**. In art, the term "scale" refers to relative size. One of the

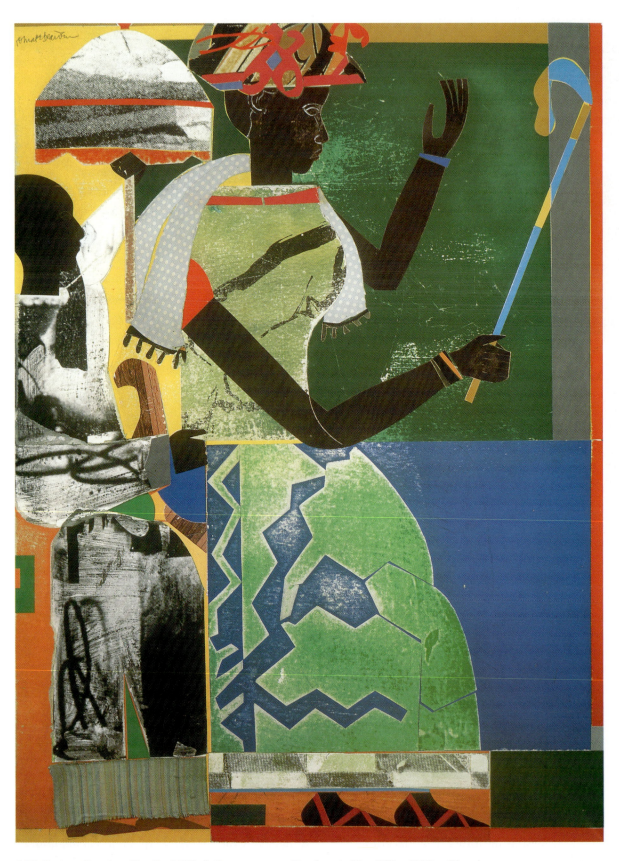

2.58 Romare Bearden, *She-Ba*, 1970. Collage on composition board, 48 × 36 ins (122 × 91 cm).
Wadsworth Atheneum, Hartford, Connecticut. The Ella Gallup Summer and Mary Catlin Summer Collection.

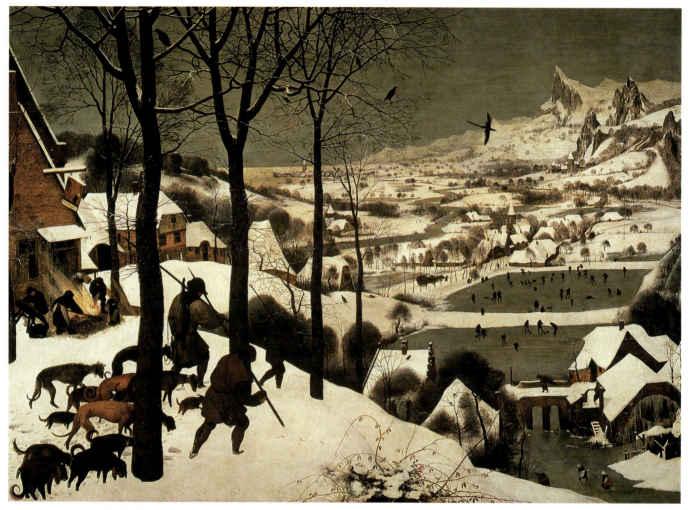

2.59 Pieter Bruegel the Elder, *Hunters in the Snow*, 1565. Oil on canvas, 3 ft 10 ins × 5 ft 4 ins (1.17 × 1.62 m). Kunsthistorisches Museum, Vienna.

most dramatic examples of the use of scale change is Bruegel's *Hunters in the Snow* (2.59). We perceive the hunters on the left as closest to us in space because they are by far the largest of the human figures. The people down on the frozen pond are pushed way back in space because they are so much smaller in comparison. The same kind of rapid scaling down can be traced in the houses and the trees from foreground to distant background. Bruegel makes us feel that we are looking across an immense distance, all the way to another village with a church spire and even beyond that.

Another device used to create the illusion of extremely deep space is **linear perspective**. This technique was refined and translated into precise mathematical terms by Renaissance artists in the fifteenth century. It portrays all parallel horizontal lines of forms that recede from the viewer's position as converging diagonally toward the same **vanishing point** in the distance (in simple **one-point perspective**), determining the changing scale of the forms. Figure **2.60** demonstrates the effect of standing on a railroad track while holding a window before one's eyes. This window represents the **picture plane**—the flat surface on which a two-dimensional work is created. The tracks, which are parallel in actuality but perpendicular to the picture plane, appear on the picture plane as lines drawn toward a single point at a great distance. The horizontal line on which they seem to converge appears as the horizon; it is at the height of the viewer's **eye-level line**.

A dramatic demonstration of this principle can be seen in Anselm Kiefer's *Athanor* (**2.61**), in which architectural lines rapidly converge toward an eye-level line somewhere beyond the doors of this war-ravaged Third Reich building. The heightened emphasis on

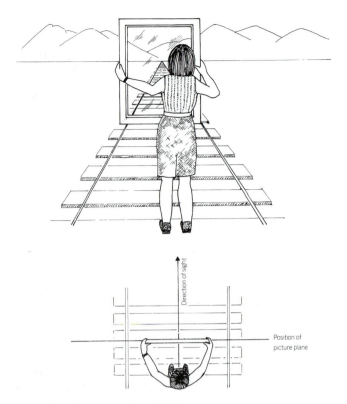

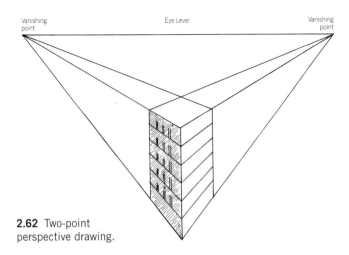

2.62 Two-point perspective drawing.

2.60 One-point perspective drawing.

the spaciousness of this building makes its emptiness all the more eerie, as if what appeared strong and invincible was actually vulnerable and empty at the core, damaged from the inside out. As is characteristic in Kiefer's work, this feeling is intensely personal, as

the artist explores dark and destructive elements in his own psyche and in twentieth-century German history.

When parallel lines appear to diverge toward two different vanishing points (as when we look at the corner of a building or the intersection of two hallways), the visual illusion is known as **two-point perspective** (**2.62**). The engraving of *The Crystal Palace* shown in Figure **2.63** is rendered in two-point perspective. The parallel lines of the hall to the right seem to converge toward one vanishing point, while those in the hall to the left apparently converge toward another, both on the same eye-level line. Note that the vertical lines of the supports remain of even width from top to bottom, for they are parallel, rather than perpendicular, to the picture plane.

2.61 Anselm Kiefer, *Athanor*, 1983–84. Oil, acrylic, emulsion, shellac, and straw on photograph mounted on canvas, 7 ft 4½ ins × 12 ft 5⅝ ins (2.25 × 3.80 m). Private collection.

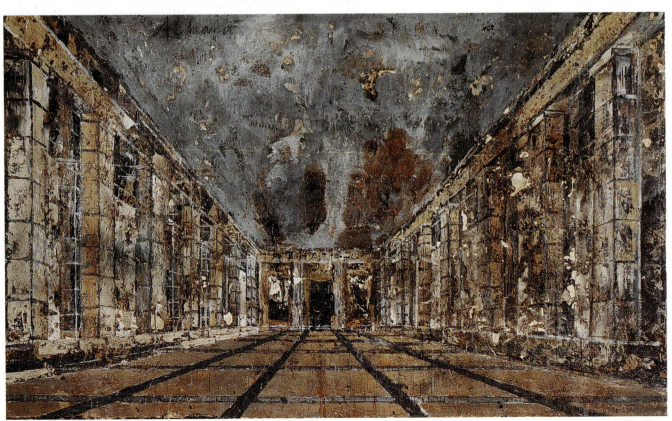

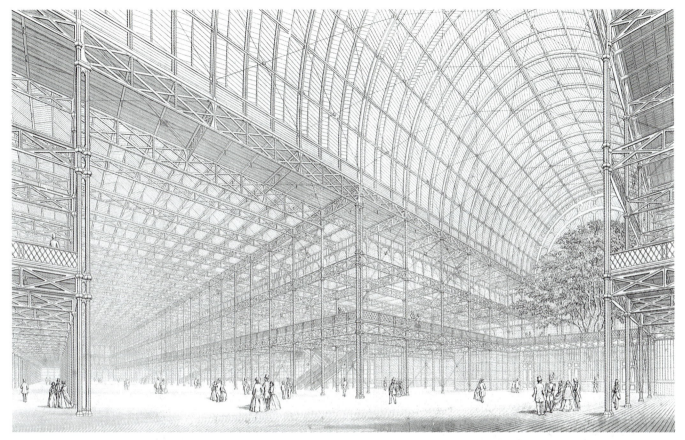

2.63 Joseph Paxton, *The Crystal Palace*, London, 1851. Engraving by R. P. Cuff after W. B. Brounger, 18¼ × 25¼ ins (46.5 × 64 cm). Drawings Collection, Royal Institute of British Architects, London.

2.64 Albert Bierstadt, *The Rocky Mountains, Lander's Peak*, 1863.
Oil on canvas, 6 ft 1½ ins × 10 ft ¾ ins (1.86 × 3.06 m). Metropolitan Museum of Art, New York. Rogers Fund 1907.

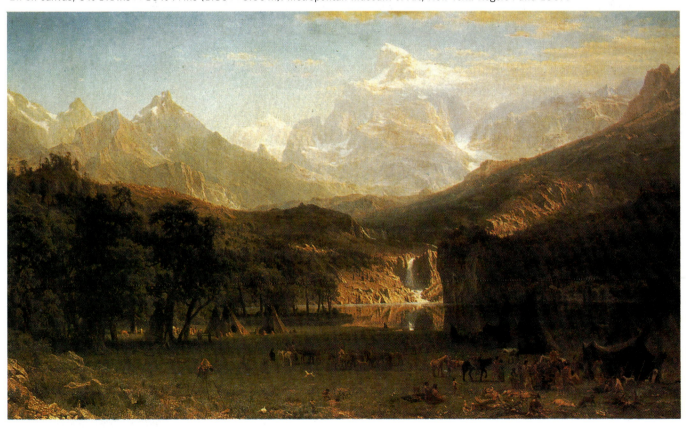

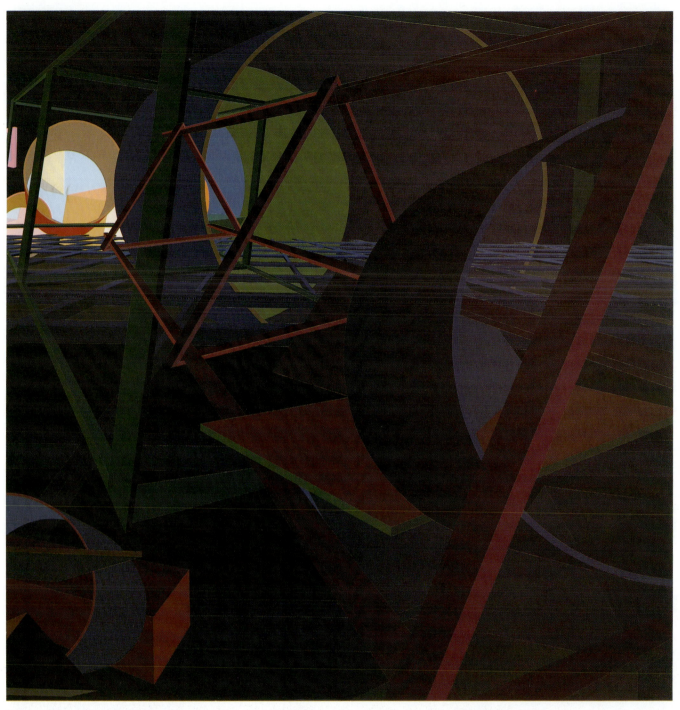

2.65 Al Held, *Vaporum VI*, 1988. Acrylic on linen, 7 × 7 ft (2.13 × 2.13 m). Andre Emmerich Gallery, New York.

Artists may also use **atmospheric perspective**, by representing the tendency of things in the distance to be less sharply defined in form, hues, and value contrast than forms that are closer to us, because of the effect of atmospheric haze. This device is used naturalistically to push areas back in space, especially when a truly vast scene is depicted, as in Albert Bierstadt's scene from the Rocky Mountains (2.64). In contrast with the details of the Shoshone Indian encampment in the foreground, the land gradually loses sharpness and value contrast to the point where the details of the mountains in the distant background are so faint as almost to blend with the sky.

Atmospheric perspective is a rather subtle spatial

clue and may sometimes be overridden by use of the stronger illusory devices: overlapping, scale change, and linear perspective. In Al Held's *Vaporum VI* (2.65), the latter three devices create a great sense of depth, despite the paradoxical placement of the brightest colors to the rear rather than in the foreground, contradicting expectations that colors will become grayer as they recede from us. Strong use of multiple-point linear perspective steers the eye through a complex maze of imagined structures. However, Held notes, the perspective lines "are not systematized—they're empirical."[12] That is, like many artists, he uses linear perspective in a way that reminds us of our experience in a three-dimensional world rather than abiding by theories about precisely where and how lines should converge.

In working two-dimensionally with illusions of three-dimensional space, artists also manipulate the **point of view**. By the angle from which they show us figures, they are telling us exactly where we are placed in spatial relationship to them. The invention of the camera encouraged artists to experiment freely with the points of view they used, rather than rely on conventional frontal views.

Edgar Degas explored unusual points of view in many of his works. In *Dancer with a Bouquet* (2.66), we can barely see the bouquet. What we see instead is the fan of the woman whom Degas has placed between us

2.66 Edgar Degas, *Dancer with a Bouquet*, c. 1878. Pastel and wash over black chalk on paper, 12½ × 19¾ ins (31.7 × 50.2 cm). Museum of Art, Rhode Island School of Design, Providence, Rhode Island. Gift of Mrs. Murray S. Danforth.

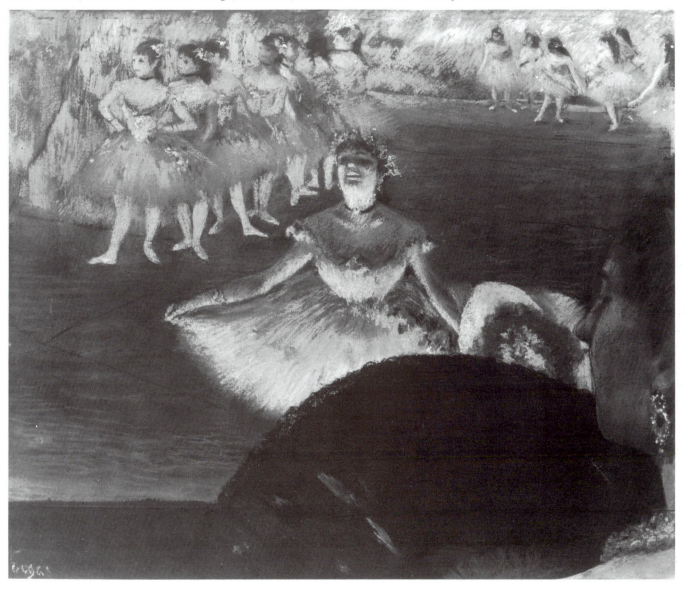

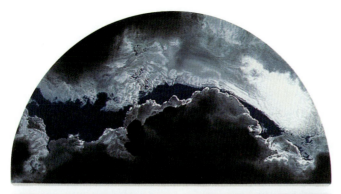

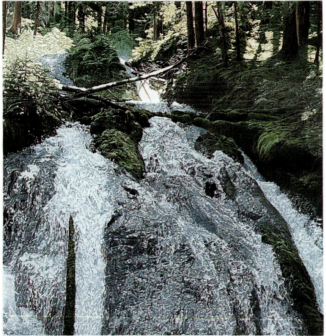

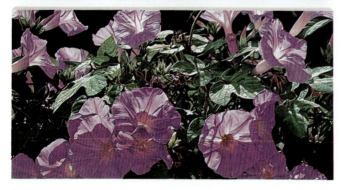

2.67 Don Eddy, *Imminent Desire/Distant Longing II*, 1993. Acrylic on canvas, 6 ft 2½ ins × 3 ft (1.89 x .91 m) Nancy Hoffman Gallery, New York.

and the ballerina, telling us exactly where we are sitting: behind and to the left of the woman with the fan, perhaps in a box slightly above the stage. Degas even makes it very clear where we are looking: down and back across the stage. This precise and unexpected point of view brings us intimately into the scene, as

though we were really sitting at the ballet rather than looking at a picture of a ballet.

Don Eddy's *Imminent Desire/Distant Longing II* (**2.67**) seems to offer three different views of a natural scene from a single vantage point: looking up, looking straight out, and looking at the plants near the ground. Eddy further controls our viewing position by exaggerating the different angles of view and scale of the images. The lowest panel gives us the impression of being very close to the flowers and grass, for their scale is much enlarged, as if one were lying among them and seeing them from very close range. The natural scene in the middle panel is painted in a smaller scale that makes it seem much farther from us. The uppermost panel is painted in such a way that we are placed lying on our back, as it were, looking up at the sky. Today it is easy for viewers to accept this manipulation of viewing angles, for it is commonly used in television and films.

Another relatively recent innovation in points of view is the **aerial view**, in which the point of view is above the scene depicted. It takes considerable visual sophistication to interpret such images as horizontal when they are hung on a vertical surface. Janet Good's *Floor Show* (**2.68**) may make sense to you if you are holding this book horizontally. But if you tip it to the vertical, as the picture would be if it were hanging on a wall, you must make a strong mental adjustment to recognize that you are looking down on cats who are lying on a wooden floor instead of across at cats splayed acrobatically against a wall. In such cases, artists require us to use our model of the world to interpret their creations. We just know from experience that cats sleep on the floor, not on the wall.

We can also examine two-dimensional use of space by considering the extent to which the artist has filled it or left it open. Hieronymus Bosch's *The Carrying of the Cross* (**2.69**) is so full of people that the canvas seems crowded with degenerate life forms. For this crowd effect, Bosch packed more heads into the picture than could in reality fit bodily into the space. Amid this leering and hateful mob, the serene, resigned face of Jesus carrying the cross (repeated in the veil carried by Saint Veronica on which his image is said to have appeared) is a striking counterpoint—the image of the divine, unrecognized in the midst of human ugliness.

By contrast, leaving large areas of the picture plane unfilled may be used to create a quiet effect or to draw attention to an image isolated within this emptiness. In traditional Japanese painting, the areas left unfilled were considered just as important as the filled

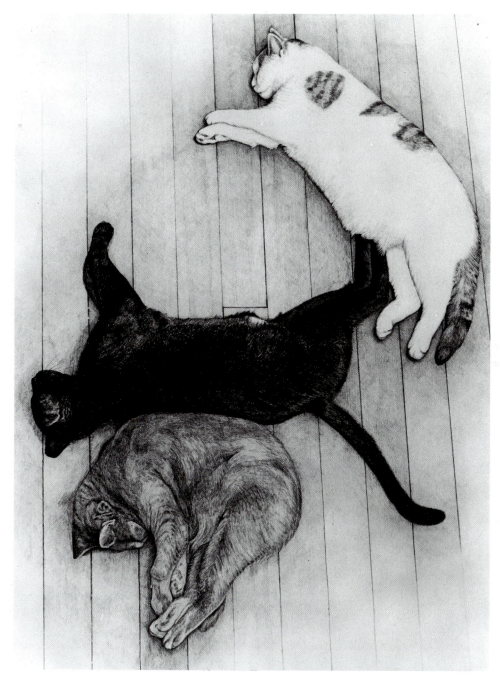

2.68 Janet Cummings Good, *Floor Show*, 1983. Ink drawing, 40 × 30 ins (101.6 × 76.2 cm). Collection of the artist.

areas. The sixteenth-century Japanese artist Hasegawa Tohaku dares to leave two of the large panels of his painted screen (2.70) almost completely unfilled and provides only suggestions of form in the others to create the effect of trees fading into the mist. By a supremely subtle use of contrast, the unfilled areas and the barely seen, washed out tree forms heighten our appreciation of the darkest strokes.

Scale

We are accustomed to objects that are "lifesized." When an artist presents a familiar form in an unfamiliar size, our interest is often heightened, for the experience is immediately something out of the ordinary.

Claes Oldenburg presents mundane objects— such as a clothespin, a lipstick, a hamburger, a baked

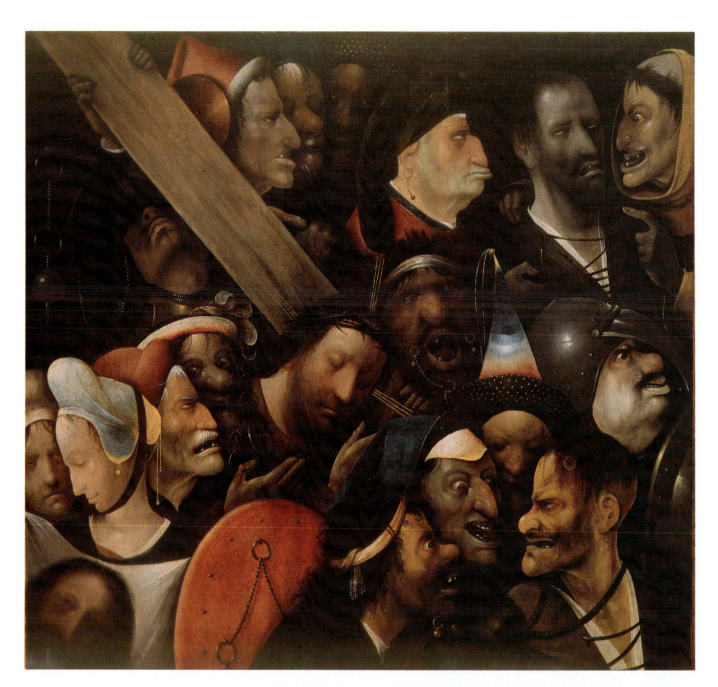

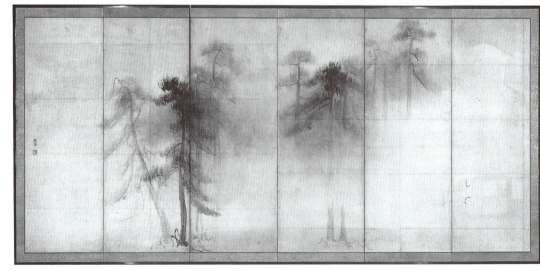

2.69 Hieronymous Bosch, *The Carrying of the Cross*, c. 1510. Oil on board, 30 × 32 ins (76.2 × 81.3 cm). Musée des Beaux-Arts, Ghent, Belgium.

2.70 Hasegawa Tohaku (1539–1610), *Pine Trees*, Momoyama period, Japan. Ink on paper, height 5 ft 1 in (1.55 m). Collection Tokyo National Museum, Tokyo.

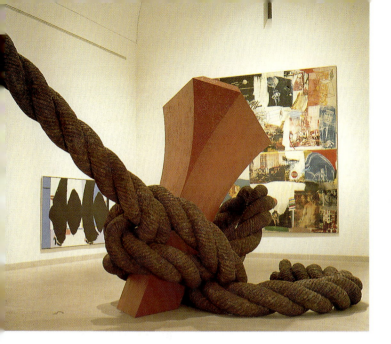

2.71 Claes Oldenburg, *Stake Hitch*, 1984. Aluminum, steel, urethane foam, 53 ft 6 ins × 15 ft 2 ins × 44 ft 6 ins (16.3 × 4.6 × 13.6 m). Dallas Museum of Art, commissioned to honor John Dabney Murchinson, Sr., for his arts and civic leadership, and presented by his family.

2.72 (below) Buddha from Gal Vihara, near Polonnaruwa, Sri Lanka, 11th to 12th centuries AD. Stone, length 46 ft (14 m).

potato—as colossal monuments to the familiar banalities of our lives, greatly exaggerated in scale. By their great size, these inflated monuments to the ordinary make viewers feel dwarfed. Visitors to the Dallas Museum of Art discover that *Stake Hitch* (**2.71**) is so huge that the 20-inch-thick (51-cm) rope runs all the way to the vaulted roof of the gallery and the point of the stake is "hammered through" the floor and can be seen in the basement. Oldenburg sketched and proposed far more monuments than municipalities have dared to build. Approaching the absurdities of modern civilization with humor as a survival tactic, Oldenburg explained his first inspiration:

> The first suggestion of a monument came some years ago as I was riding in from the airport. I thought: how nice it would be to have a large rabbit about the size of a skyscraper in midtown. It would cheer people up seeing its ears from the suburbs.[13]

By contrast, vast scale is often used to evoke awe and reverence. Such is the case with the many colossal statues of the Buddha in Asia. The great dying Buddha in Polonnaruwa, Sri Lanka (**2.72**), is 46 feet (14 m) long, dwarfing devotees and inspiring a sense of the greatness of the eternal Buddha principle.

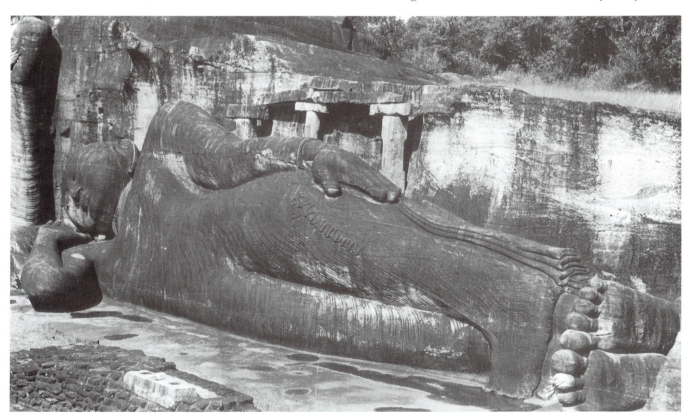

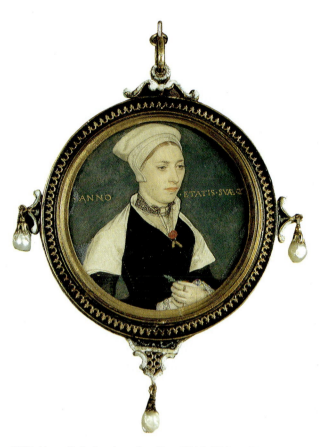

2.73 Hans Holbein, *Jane Small*, c. 1540. Watercolor on vellum, diameter 2¹⁄₁₆ ins (5.3 cm). Victoria and Albert Museum, London.

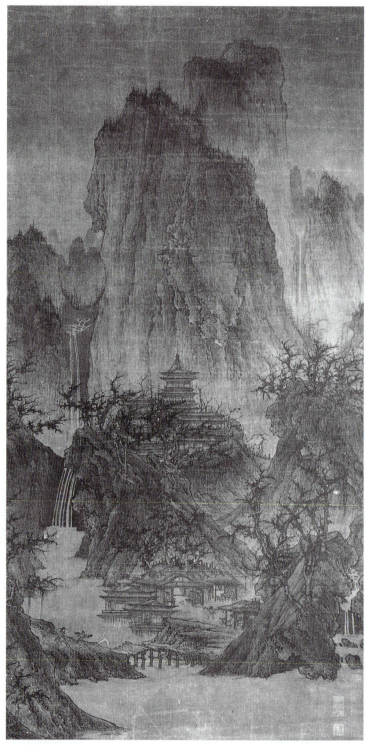

2.74 Attributed to Li Cheng, *Buddhist Temple in the Hills after Rain*, Northern Song Dynasty, China, c. 940–67 AD. Ink and slight color on silk, 44 × 22 ins (111.8 × 55.8 cm). William Rockhill Nelson Gallery of Art, Atkins Museum of Fine Arts, Kansas City, Missouri.

At the other end of the scale of exaggerations are **miniatures**, artworks that draw us in because they are so much smaller than we would expect. Hans Holbein's miniature portrait of Jane Small (**2.73**) was actually painted in the same size as it is shown here, requiring extreme delicacy and skill. Imagine how small a brush Holbein must have used to paint the details on the cuffs and neckpiece. Despite the minuscule scale of this meticulous work, it is considered one of the world's great portraits. Precise miniature paintings were very popular as illustrations for medieval European and Persian manuscripts and as jewelry pieces for sixteenth- through eighteenth-century English aristocrats.

Scale may also be used to make a statement about the relative importance of forms within a work. In *Buddhist Temple in the Hills after Rain* (**2.74**), as in many early Chinese landscape paintings, the figures of pilgrims are tiny and unobtrusive in comparison with the impressive mountains. In Taoist thought, this scale reflected the importance of humanity in the universe—a barely significant part of the totality, subordinate to nature. By contrast, religious works from the Christian tradition tend to emphasize human forms, especially those of holy figures. In the large altarpiece *Madonna Enthroned with Angels and Prophets* (**2.75**), the Madonna is larger than life and larger than the angels on either side and the prophets below, a spatial device that speaks of her importance on the throne of heaven.

Spatial Illusion

One intriguing way in which some artists work with space is to twist it into situations that seem at first glance to work but turn out on closer inspection to be quite impossible, given what we know of the three-dimensional world. William Hogarth's frontispiece for Kirby's *Perspective* (**2.76**) is a visual game with space as its subject. For instance, the fishing pole held by the man at the far right cannot possibly be long enough to reach all the way out to the pond, where it is shown neatly catching a fish. The scale of the sheep rounding the corner at the left is exactly backwards: those farthest away are the largest. To introduce the study of perspective, Hogarth has humorously created a scene full of spatial "mistakes." It may look initially plausible, but the longer you examine it, the more spatial impossibilities you will discover.

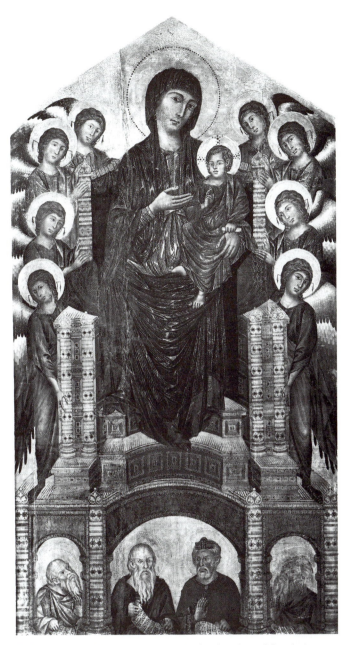

2.75 Cimabue, *Madonna Enthroned with Angels and Prophets*, c. 1280–85. Tempera on wood, 12 ft 6 ins × 7 ft 4 ins (3.85 × 2.23 m). Galleria degli Uffizi, Florence.

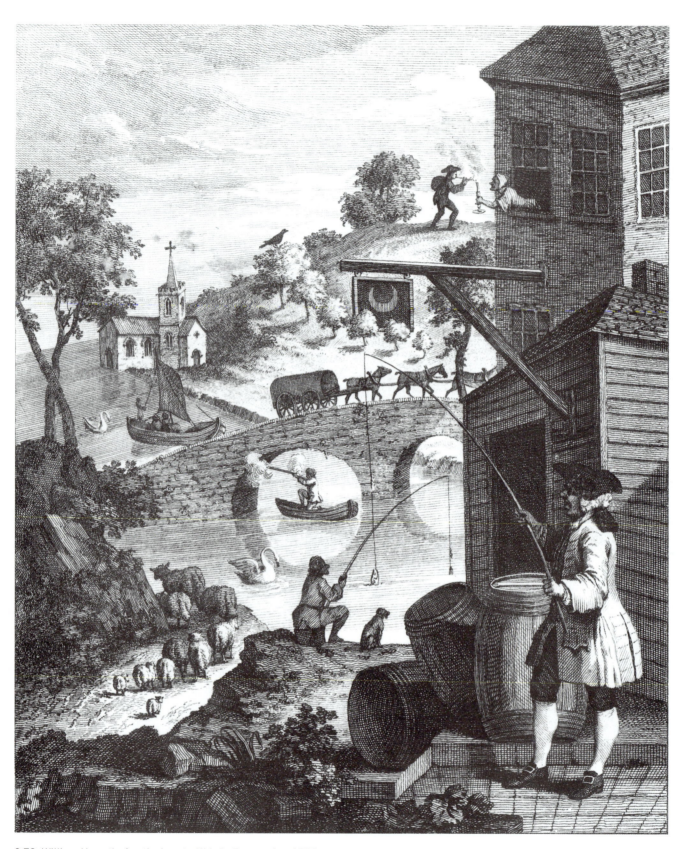

2.76 William Hogarth, frontispiece to Kirby's *Perspective*, 1753.
Engraving, 8¼ × 6¾ ins (20.96 × 17.15 cm).
Victoria and Albert Museum, London.

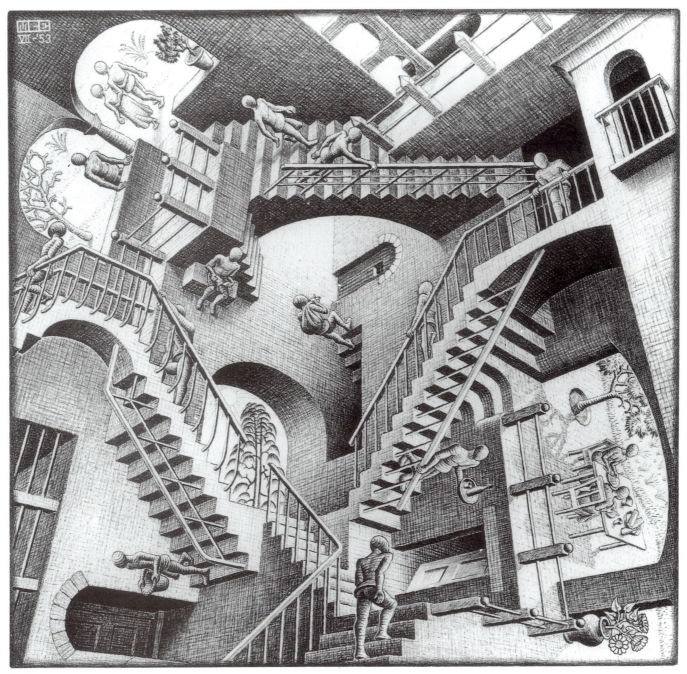

2.77 M. C. Escher, *Relativity*, 1953.
Lithograph, 10¾ × 11½ ins (27.3 × 29.2 cm).
Print on loan to Gemeentemuseum, The Hague, by the Escher Foundation.
© 1990 M. C. Escher Heirs/Cordon Art, Baarn, Netherlands.

The Dutch graphic artist M. C. Escher was fascinated with spatial illusions. In his *Relativity* (2.77), many surfaces serve three purposes at once—wall, ceiling, and floor—depending on the angle from which the figures approach them. The remarkable staircase to the right has figures walking both on the top and underside of its treads. Each segment is plausible unto itself but becomes spatially impossible when compared to adjoining areas. For Escher, his art was not a game but a serious inquiry into infinity—the point beyond which human concepts of space and time have no meaning.

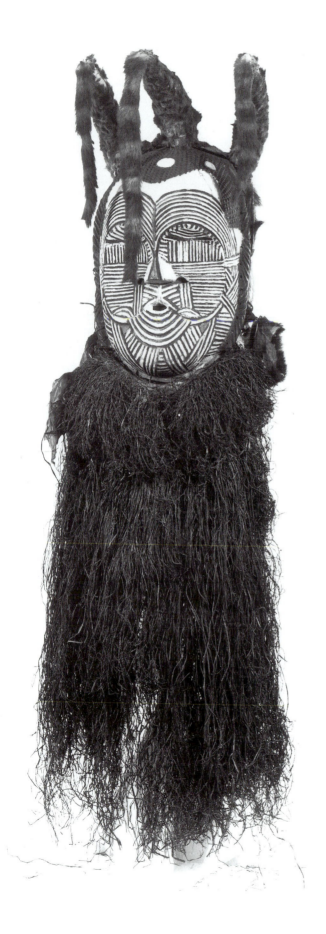

TEXTURE

The **texture** of a work of art is its surface quality—how it would feel if we touched it. From our experiences in the world, we are quite familiar with a great range of textural qualities: coarse, slimy, bristly, smooth, furry, matted, scratchy, wrinkled, and so on. Our hands are equipped with sensitive nerves for distinguishing textures, and we find sensual joy in feeling certain surfaces. Artists know this, and often use textures as a major influence on our response to a piece.

The sculptor Henry Moore encouraged people to touch his works. His *Reclining Figure* (**2.79**) makes us want to do so. Its highly polished wood surface reminds us visually of the smoothness of taut skin and invites caressing. Despite the abstraction of the form, the prominent grain in the elm wood accentuates the visual similarity to a human body by suggesting the curves of muscles.

Some textures are much less inviting, but nonetheless enhance the intended visual impact of a piece. The Batetela mask shown here (**2.78**) was designed for a shaman's use in exciting crowds with fear of the spirit world. Its several textures are in dramatic contrast to each other, from the hairy, unkempt quality of the beard, to the geometrically precise, incised lines defining the contours of the face, to the furry antennae flopping down over the face like the legs of a dangerous spider. In this context, all these textures become alarming yet fascinating. The effect of the mask in motion must have been truly terrifying.

Textures may toy with our curiosity, using it to lure us into spending time with a piece. Lucas Samaras's *Book 4* (**2.80**) presents us with sharp found objects we know would hurt us if we touched them. What is more, Samaras has placed them in menacing projections. But rather than totally avoiding such dangerous things, we tend to come as close as we dare out of a sense of adventure. The combination of all these sharp materials with an open book increases their perception as textures. Since a book is something we usually hold in our hands, turning the pages, we can readily "feel" these textures.

2.78 African Batetela mask. Wood, fur, and fiber, length 16½ ins (42 cm). British Museum, London.

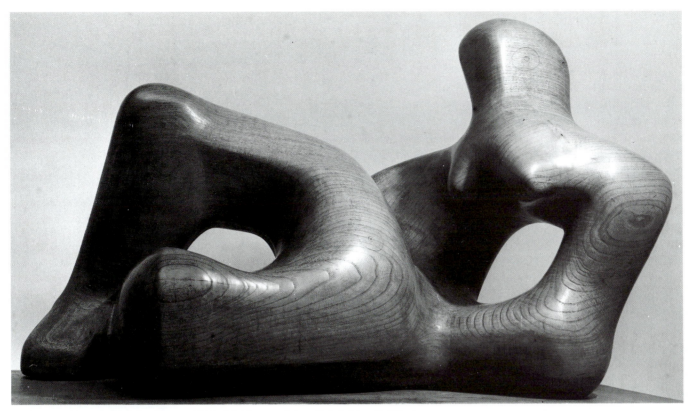

2.79 Henry Moore, *Reclining Figure*, 1935–36. Elm wood, length 3 ft 6 ins (1.07 m).
Wakefield Metropolitan District Council Art Gallery and Museums, Yorkshire, England.

2.80 Lucas Samaras, *Book 4*, 1962. Assemblage: partly opened book with pins, razor blade, scissors,
table knife, metal foil, piece of glass, and plastic rod, 5½ × 8⅞ × 11½ ins (14 × 22.5 × 29.2 cm).
Collection Museum of Modern Art, New York. Gift of Philip Johnson. Photograph © 1997 MOMA.

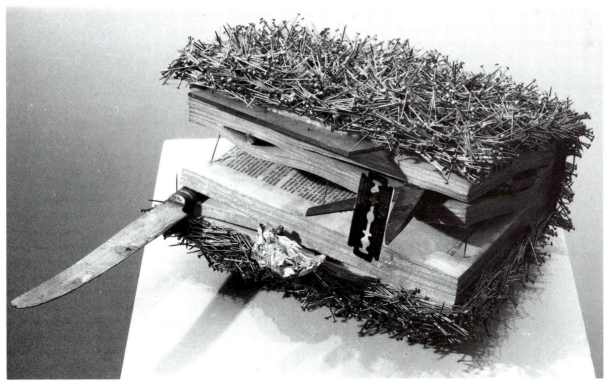

Actual Texture

The textures with which we are most familiar are those we can feel with our hands: **actual textures**. Everything has a surface texture, but some textures are more noticeable than others. The Danish rune stone (2.81) is carved as a low relief into rock so grainy that its roughness shows in the photograph. The over-and-under interlacing patterns that wrap around the Christ figure ask to be touched and followed with the fingers, almost bringing us into physical contact with the person who carved the stone.

To create an impressive, magical bust of the war-god Kukailimoku (2.82), a Hawaiian artist applied several materials with striking actual textures to a wicker frame. The feathers of tropical birds create a mysterious texture for the skin, pearl shells make a smooth and shining eye, and sharp dogs' teeth make an impressive array in the mouth. These textural materials may have been used partly because they were plentiful, but to the eyes of those from other cultures, they give a strange, inexplicable quality to the piece.

Some actual textures are created rather than used just as they are found. In her "rock books," such as the one shown in Figure 2.83, Michelle Stuart captures the "story of a place" by gathering rocks and dirt there

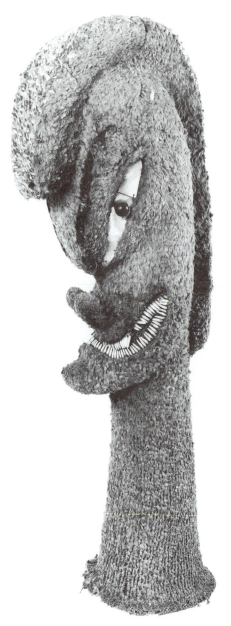

2.82 The war-god Kukailimoku, from Hawaii, before 1779. Feathers over wickerwork, pearl shells, and dog teeth, height 3 ft 4¾ ins (1.03 m). British Museum, London.

2.81 Rune Stone, Jelling, Denmark, 965–86 AD. Granite, height 8 ft (2.44 m).

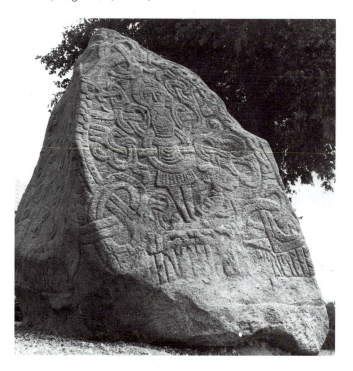

and pounding it into paper, rubbing its surface until it develops a gloss. A series of such "pages" made from diggings at the site are then bound into a "book." The book, in turn, is sealed with a found texture—a feather, a coarse-woven string, a bone. These assemblages bespeak touching the earth, but they do not invite much handling by the viewer because they appear fragile, precious, and even ancient.

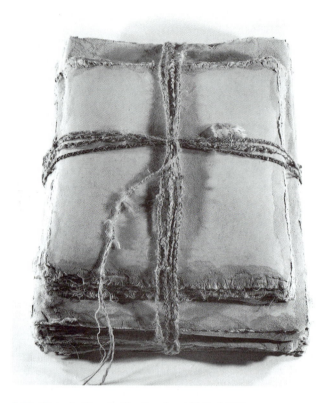

2.83 Michelle Stuart, *The Pen Argyl Myth*, 1977. Earth and feather from Pen Argyl Quarry, Pennsylvania, rag paper, 13½ × 10½ × 3½ ins (34.3 × 26.7 × 8.9 cm).

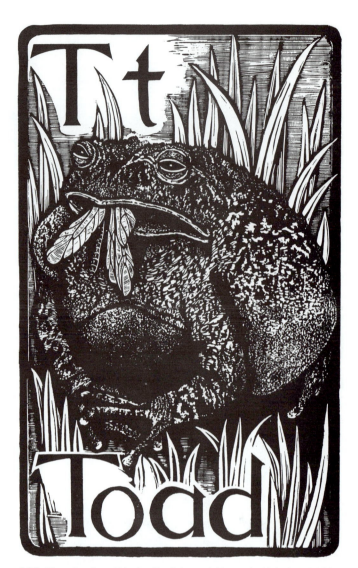

2.84 Mary Azarian, *T is for Toad*, from *A Farmer's Alphabet*, 1981. Two-color woodcut, 12¼ × 7½ ins (31.1 × 19 cm).

Simulated Texture

Two-dimensional works often create the visual sensations of textural qualities on a surface that would actually feel quite different if touched. If we touched a print of Mary Azarian's woodcut (**2.84**) from the alphabet she was commissioned to create for the Vermont public schools, we would feel only the slight coarseness of the paper and the ink across the surface. But visually, what we perceive is the relative smoothness of grass blades, the filmy delicacy of dragonfly wings, and the bumpiness of the toad's skin. None of these textures is described utterly realistically. For instance, the bumpiness is more hard-edged than the smooth, moist lumps on a real toad. Instead, Azarian uses a visual shorthand that reminds us of these natural textures, if we are familiar with them. These shorthand simulated textures also provide an interesting series of visual contrasts.

In comparison, certain artists have gone to great lengths to capture the visual effects of textures. One of the masters in this respect is Ingres. In his *Portrait of the Princesse de Broglie* (**2.85**), the facial skin and hair are rather stylized and simplified, in dramatic contrast to the extreme attention to detail in rendering the textures of the fabrics. The lush satiny dress fabric is so realistically painted that we can guess exactly how it feels. One clue is the way it reflects the light, a characteristic of smooth and shiny surfaces. We can see that the lace and gold-trimmed throw have very different textures, though they share with the satin the suppleness of fabric. And the information given to our eyes about the chair allows our fingers to imagine the play of the smooth surface and raised brocade across its plump contours.

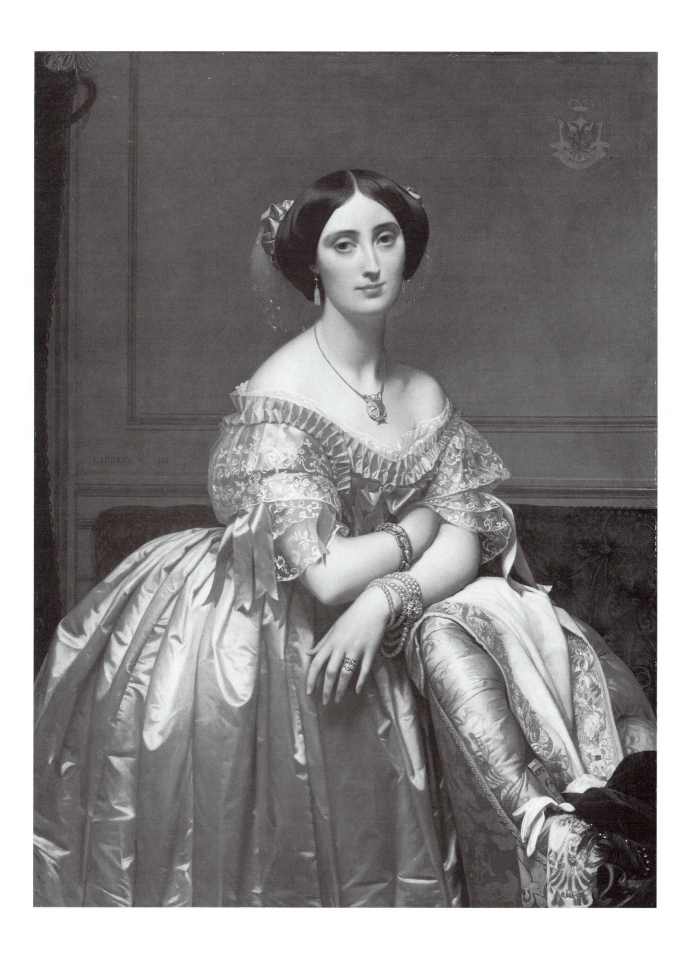

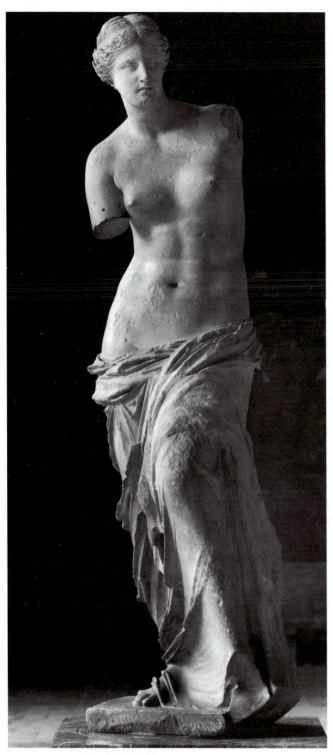

This same realism in simulated textural effects has occasionally been achieved in three-dimensional works. One of the hardest of materials—marble—has been lovingly sculpted to suggest the feel of human skin in the *Venus de Milo* (**2.86**) from the Hellenistic period. It looks not only soft but as though it would feel warm to the touch.

When a visual effect is so realistic that it totally fools our perceptions, it is called **trompe l'oeil** (literally, "deceive the eye"). We are fascinated with deception in art. There is probably little innate visual appeal in a golf bag. But the fact that Marilyn Levine has created a lifesized golf bag (**2.87**) from ceramics makes her piece utterly intriguing. She has carefully studied and captured precisely in the hardness of fired clay the

2.87 Marilyn Levine, *Two-toned Golf Bag*, 1980. Stoneware with nylon reinforcement, 35 × 10½ × 7 ins (89 × 27 × 18 cm).

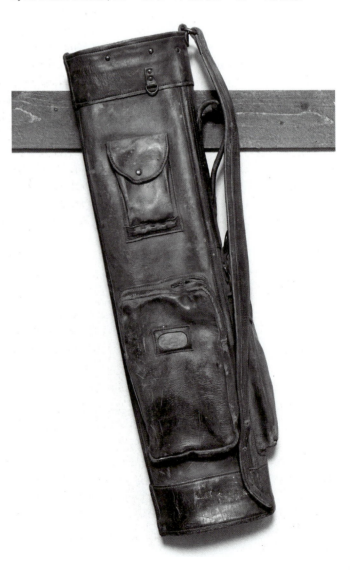

2.86 *Venus de Milo*, c. 150 BC. Marble, height 6 ft 10 ins (2.08 m). Louvre, Paris.

2.85 (opposite) Jean-Auguste-Dominique Ingres, *Portrait of the Princesse de Broglie*, 1853. Oil on canvas, 47¾ × 35¾ ins (121.3 × 90.8 cm). Metropolitan Museum of Art, New York. Robert Lehmann Collection 1975.

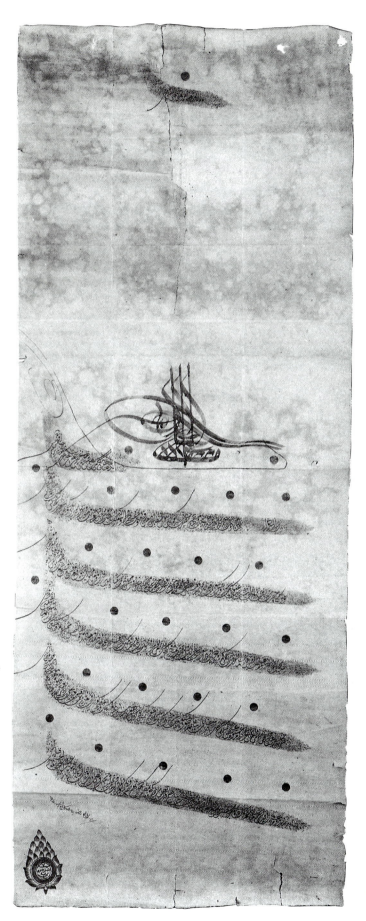

look of pliable worn leather and of metal. If we touched it, the actual feeling of the surface would be shockingly and humorously different from what our mind expects.

Texture-Like Effects

Certain works create a visual texture by repetition of elements of design. Imagine a forest seen from a distance. It has an all-over visual texture created by the repetition of tree forms that is quite different from the actual feeling of tree trunks and branches. But those of us who are familiar with trees and forests may not be aware of this all-over texture, for our familiarity with the particular blinds us to what we are actually perceiving. It is easier for us to perceive a texture-like effect in something unfamiliar, such as the Imperial Edict (*firman*) of Sultan Mustafa IV (**2.88**). Those who cannot read the Arabic scripts used for the imperial monogram and the edict that is written below it, can see them as nonobjective designs, each having its own distinct visual texture. Certainly the way that the calligrapher Mustafa Rakim presented the edict reflects his awareness that each line of characters forms a textured shape.

VALUE AND LIGHT

Another visual element that may escape our notice, but which is used quite consciously by artists, is **value**, the relative lightness or darkness of an area. Values are most easily perceived when color hues are subtracted. Black and white photographs of colored artworks translate hues into a range of grays from very dark to very light, as in this reproduction of Henri-Edmond Cross's watercolor *The Artist's Garden at St. Clair* (**2.89**). These value variations help us to understand the effects of lighting and distance despite the abstract quality of the painting. Here, the overhanging branches seem to create pools of shadow, beyond which values become very light in what appears to be strong daylight, fading to near-white in the distance. In general, as we saw in the section on space, perceived value contrasts are strongest in areas closest to the viewer.

2.88 Mustafa Rakim, *Firman*, early 19th century.
51 × 19⅝ ins (129.5 × 50 cm).

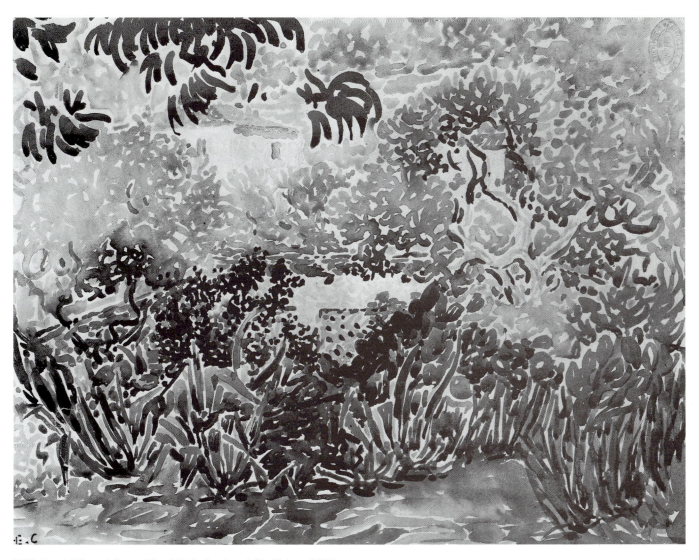

2.89 Henri-Edmond Cross, *The Artist's Garden at St. Clair*, c. 1908. Watercolor, 10½ × 14 ins (26.6 × 35.5 cm). Metropolitan Museum of Art, New York.

The gradations of value from very dark to very light can be represented by means of a **value scale**. The one shown in Figure **2.90** breaks down the variations into ten equal steps, with black at one end and white at the other. In a work such as *The Artist's Garden at St. Clair*, there are actually many more than ten values, but the value scale is a useful tool for seeing value gradations lined up sequentially.

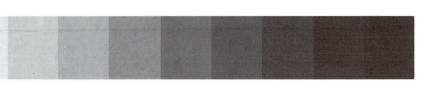

2.90 A 10-step value scale.

Local and Interpretive Values

The actual lights and shadows we see on real surfaces are called **local values**. Some photographers attempt by techniques of photographing and developing to capture on film the full range of local values, called a **full tonal range** in photography. Although Katherine Alling confines and twists feathers into interesting shapes in *Feathers #22* (2.92), she also emphasizes their visual reality, with all the local values created as they curve from light into shadow. She remarks:

> We generally don't look at a feather that carefully. We label it and that's it. One of the features of photography is that we examine an object more carefully as a visual thing. We don't just say "Feather" and let it go.[14]

Many artists have manipulated values for purposes other than reproducing visual realities. When they are not handled realistically, they may be called **interpretive values**. One technique is to reduce the degree to

2.92 Katherine Alling, *Feathers # 22*, 1984. Toned silver print, 12 × 9 ins (30.5 × 22.9 cm). Mansfield, Connecticut.

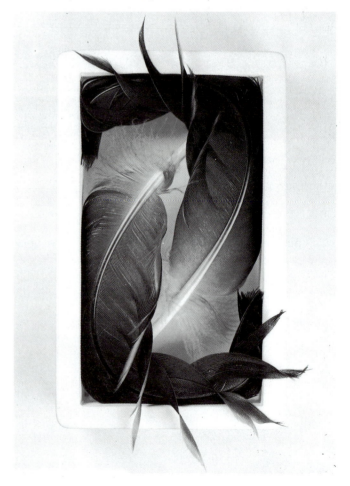

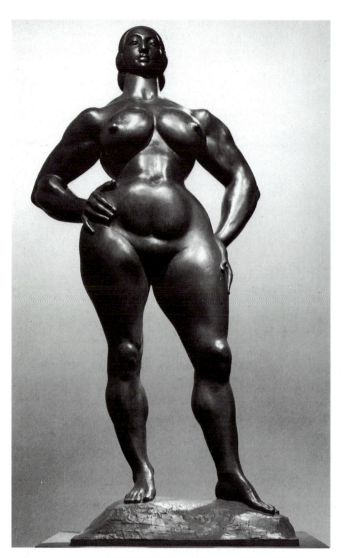

2.91 Gaston Lachaise, *Standing Woman*, 1932. Bronze (cast 1932), 88 × 41⅛ × 19⅛ ins (223.6 × 104.3 × 48.4 cm). Collection Museum of Modern Art, New York. Mrs. Simon Guggenheim Fund. Photograph © 1997 MOMA.

In addition to giving spatial clues, values also help us to perceive the modeling of forms. As light falls on a three-dimensional object, such as Gaston Lachaise's sculpture *Standing Woman* (2.91), the areas that light strikes most directly are the lightest, showing up as **highlights**. As contours curve away from the light source in space, the light dims, making the surface appear darker, until it approaches a true black in areas where light is fully blocked. The strong value contrasts on *Standing Woman* help us to grasp the extent to which the form swells out and draws back in space. In this photograph, strong lighting accentuates these contrasts; in more diffuse light, such as an overcast day, the ins and outs of the form would not be so apparent.

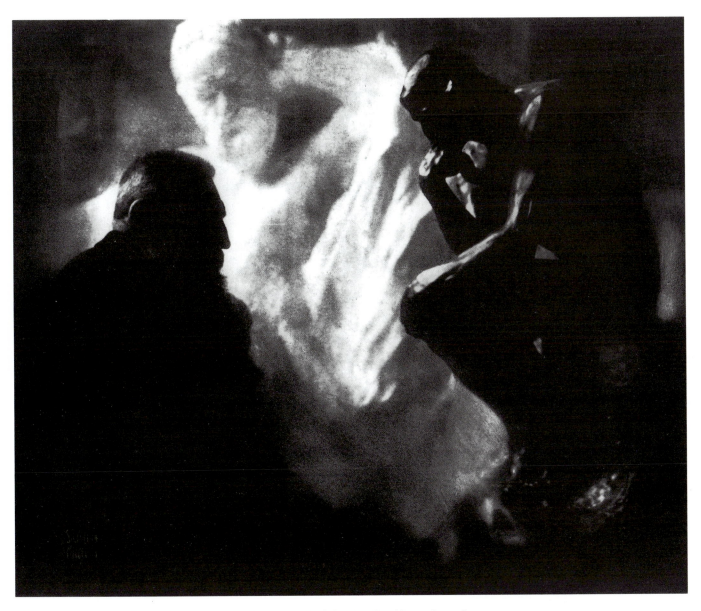

2.93 Edward Steichen. *Rodin: The Thinker*, 1902. Photograph. Collection The Gilman Paper Company.

which values gradually change, presenting them as more dramatic contrasts. To turn the sculptor Rodin's famous profile into a massive sculptural form, as if the man himself were a monument chipped from black stone, photographer Edward Steichen arranged for both Rodin and his sculpture *Le Penseur* ("The Thinker") to be in shadow, making them appear similarly strong (2.93). Their intense confrontation is set off by the white plaster figure of *Victor Hugo* brooding in the background. There are mid-grays in this photograph, but the main focus is on the stark contrast of the black forms to the highlights on *Le Penseur* and the light values of the *Hugo*. The drama of this approach is like

hitting chords on both ends of a piano keyboard at once, using none of the notes in between.

Another approach to interpretive value is to emphasize one area of the value scale: lights, darks, or mid-tones. Each carries a different emotional quality. Rembrandt used the dark end of the scale in his self-portrait (1.3), with the light of his face barely emerging from the shadows. Graphic designer Milton Glaser has chosen the light end of the scale to represent Monet on a poster (2.94). The choice is appropriate, for the artist emphasized the effects of light in his own work. Here he appears as if in midday light so strong that it has burned away all details except for those disappearing into the shadow under his hat. The fact that Glaser has added slight shadows to the right on Monet's hat and shoulder, an indication that the sun is slightly to the left of directly overhead, keeps the near abstraction within the realm of the nearly realistic.

In **high contrast** works, artists leave out all minor details, turning forms that usually include a range of grays into a dramatic contrast between black and white. The result may be an unrecognizable, seemingly nonobjective design. But in the case of the Guggenheim Museum poster (2.95), just enough information is left to allow us to fill in the missing edges of the building's famous spiraling form. Presented in high contrast, it is an intriguing abstraction that calls on us to bring our own knowledge to complete the picture.

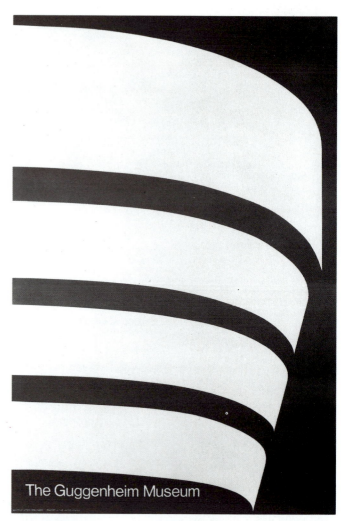

2.94 Milton Glaser, poster for the Monet Museum, Giverny, 1981.

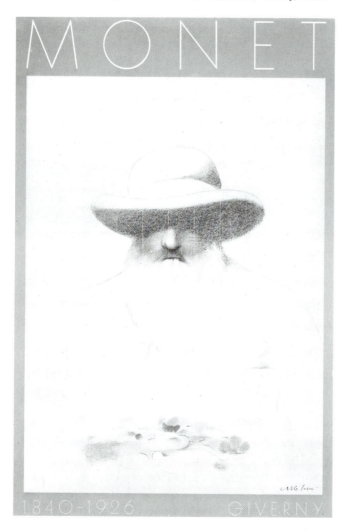

2.95 Malcolm Grear Designers, poster for the Solomon R. Guggenheim Museum, New York, 1970.

Lighting

The way a subject is lit—by the sun or by artificial lighting—will affect how we perceive it. In the Persian miniature painting to illustrate *The Concourse of the Birds* (2.96), as in most Persian miniatures, Habib Allah presents a uniformly lit scene with no shadows. This lighting represents no particular time of day, removing it from the realm of the real into the ideal, mystical setting of the parable, which symbolically illustrates the unity of individual souls with the divine. In the *Mantiq at-Tayr* thirty birds undertake a difficult journey in search of the Simurgh, king of the birds, only to discover that they are themselves *si murgh*, which means "thirty birds."

2.96 (opposite) Habib Allah, *The Concourse of the Birds*, 1609. Colors, gold, and silver on paper, 10 × 4½ ins (25.4 × 11.4 cm). Metropolitan Museum of Art, New York. Fletcher Fund, 1963.

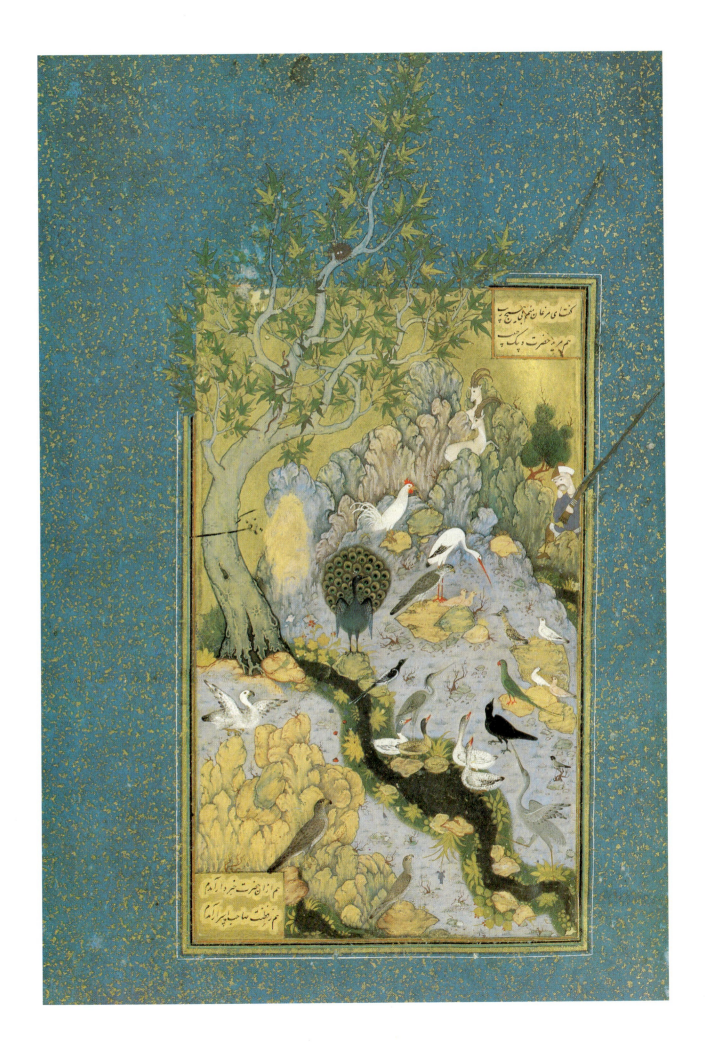

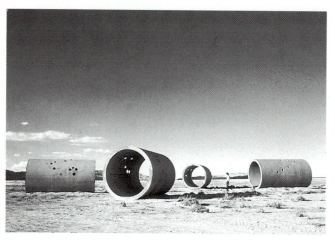

2.97 Nancy Holt, *Sun Tunnels*, 1973–76. Total length 86 ft (26.2 m), tunnels each 18 ft × 9 ft 4 ins (5.48 × 2.84 m). Great Basin, Northwest Utah desert, Utah.

2.98 (right) Nancy Holt, *Sun Tunnels* (detail). Sunset on summer solstice.

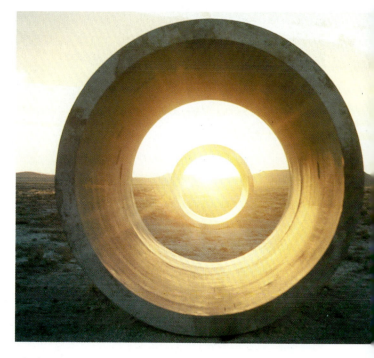

Many works do, however, contain some reference to the ever-changing reality of light. Three-dimensional pieces placed outside in a natural setting—as well as two-dimensional depictions of the natural world—will appear quite different when lit from the east at sunrise, overhead at noon, and from the west at sunset. The sun's angle changes during the year, also altering where the highlights and shadows fall. Moonlight brings a very different quality to a scene or piece of sculpture, softening edges and blurring distinctions between forms. And on cloudy days and during rain or snow the character of a piece or scene will be dramatically changed.

From antiquity, humans have used objects placed outside to track—and honor—the movements of the sun, moon, and stars. To do so reveals the predictabilities inherent in an otherwise uncertain existence. The sun will come up again tomorrow, though the point of its rising will have moved slightly. The solstices—the points on the horizon and calendar where this movement turns back on itself—have long had particular significance. A contemporary version of the ancient homage to the sun's apparent movements is Nancy Holt's *Sun Tunnels* (**2.97**). This consists of four enormous concrete tunnels placed on the Utah desert in such a way that the sun shines directly through two of them for ten days at the winter solstice and through the other two during the summer solstice. At other times, holes drilled into the pipes channel the light of sun, moon, or stars into their shaded centers to create the constellations Capricorn, Draco, Perseus, and

Columba. Looking directly through the appropriate pipe during a solstice (**2.98**) one sees a shining circle around a circle whose center is the sun. At other times, one sees encircled darkness studded with starlike points of light, a circular sunwashed openness beyond, and the dark circle of the opposite tunnel at its center.

The use of artificial lighting allows controlled rather than changing effects. Sculptors are very careful how their works are lit, for the shape, size, and position of shadows and highlights depend on the placement of lighting.

Even two-dimensional works can be enhanced or destroyed by lighting. Mark Rothko was extremely particular about the way his large luminous paintings (see 1.18) were illuminated when they were shown. He gave these instructions for a retrospective show of his work:

The light, whether natural or artificial, should not be too strong. The pictures have their own inner light and if there is too much light, the color in the picture is washed out and a distortion of their look occurs. The ideal situation would be to hang them in a normally lit room—that is the way they were painted. They should not be over lit or romanticized by spots; this results in distortion of their meaning. They should either be lighted from a great distance or indirectly, by casting lights at the ceiling or the floor. Above all, the entire picture should be evenly lighted and not strongly.[15]

During the Renaissance, European painters developed the technique of **chiaroscuro** (Italian for "light

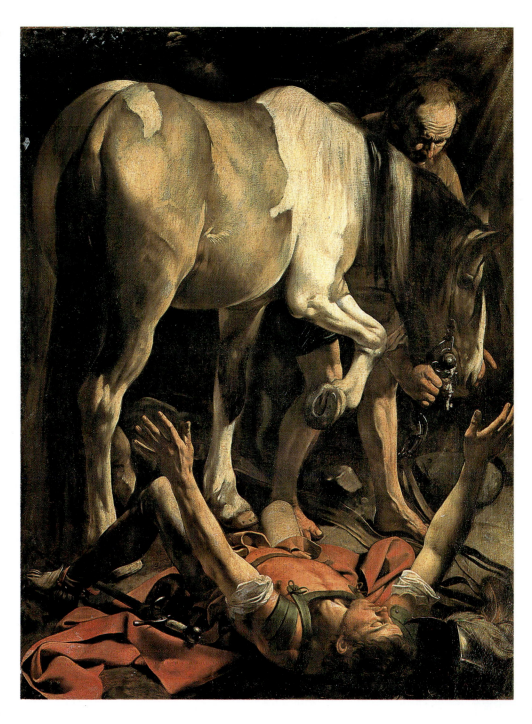

2.99 Caravaggio, *The Conversion of St. Paul*, 1600–2. Oil on canvas, 7 ft 6½ ins × 5 ft 9 ins (2.29 × 1.75 m). Cerasi Chapel, S. Maria del Popolo, Rome.

and shade")—the depiction in a two-dimensional work of the effects of light and shadow. Values are manipulated for their dramatic effect. In Caravaggio's *The Conversion of St. Paul* (**2.99**) Saul's body gleams with the reflection of the light of God which blinded him. The divine light is emphasized by the surrounding darkness. Rembrandt, the great master of chiaroscuro, portrays himself (1.3) as a softly illuminated form barely emerging from total shadow.

We are quite familiar with the use of artificial lighting to add drama to a city's skyline or friendly warmth and light to the interiors of our homes. Less familiar is the use of artificial colored lights to change the hues as well as the values in an area. A spectacularly theatrical use of colored neon lights appears at the Piazza d'Italia in New Orleans (**2.100**). A celebration of the contributions of Italian immigrants, it is like a stage setting for an opera. Flamboyantly sensual,

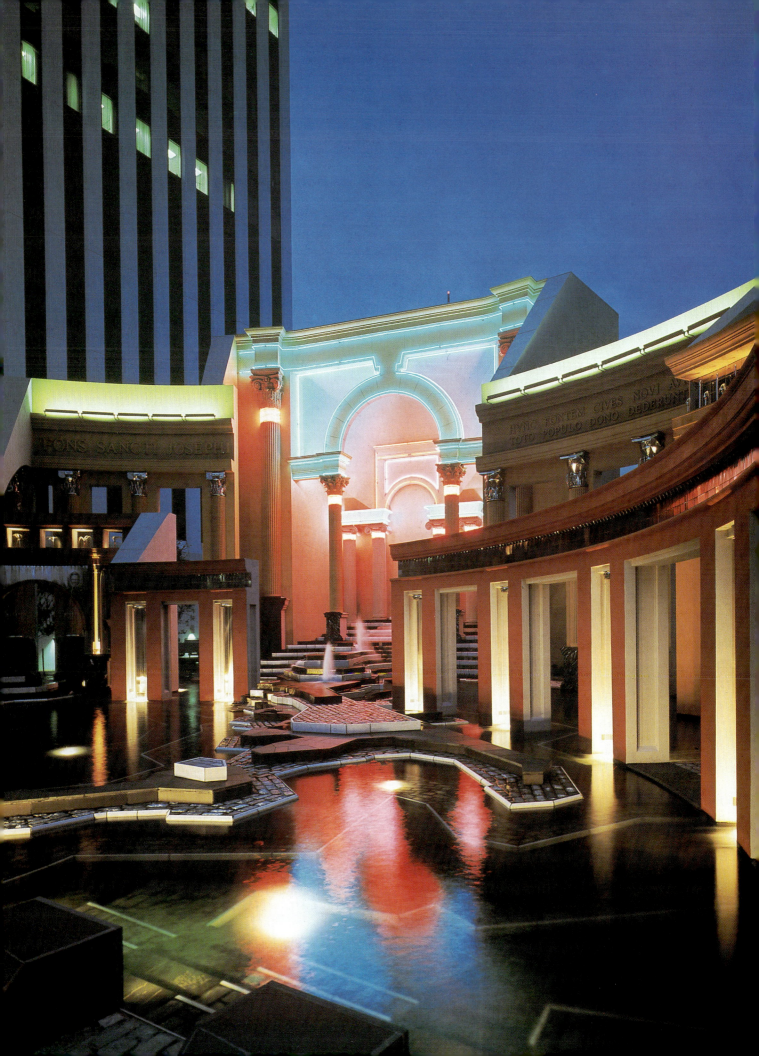

eclectic, and surprising in its architectural forms, it lures visitors to become part of the play. The neon lights throw a great range of colors across the fantastic architecture, for they mix where they overlap, enticing viewers to experience this multi-hued lighting playing across their own bodies.

Reflections

Another way in which light is used in art is by taking advantage of the fascinating effects of reflections off a smooth surface. Reflected light tends to capture our attention. The reflections of the surroundings on the highly polished interior of the *Double-Wall Bowl* (2.102) make us aware of this unfilled area. The reflections make this area surprisingly active and the high gloss adds to its sense of preciousness.

To depict such reflections convincingly in two-dimensional works takes great skill. Richard Estes has perfected the art of painting the reflections in artificial surfaces such as chrome and glass so realistically that they appear to be photographs. His *Double Self-Portrait* (2.101) is a complex tour de force, photorealistically displaying both the reflections in a restaurant's glass wall of the view across the street—including the artist, who is seen taking the photograph from which this painting was done—and the intermingled details of the interior of the restaurant seen through the same glass. In certain lighting situations, some glass will seem to hold reflections on its surface, but this glass allows both inside and reflected outside to be seen at once, as if the outer world were penetrating the interior. To add to the visual puzzle of figuring out what is inside and what is outside, there is a mirrored surface inside the restaurant, in which a second reflected image of the artist appears.

2.100 (opposite) Charles W. Moore and William Hersey, Piazza d'Italia, New Orleans, Louisiana, 1978.

2.101 Richard Estes, *Double Self-Portrait*, 1976. Oil on canvas, 24 × 36 ins (60.8 × 91.5 cm). Collection Museum of Modern Art, New York. Mr. and Mrs. Stuart M. Speiser Fund. Photograph © 1997 MOMA.

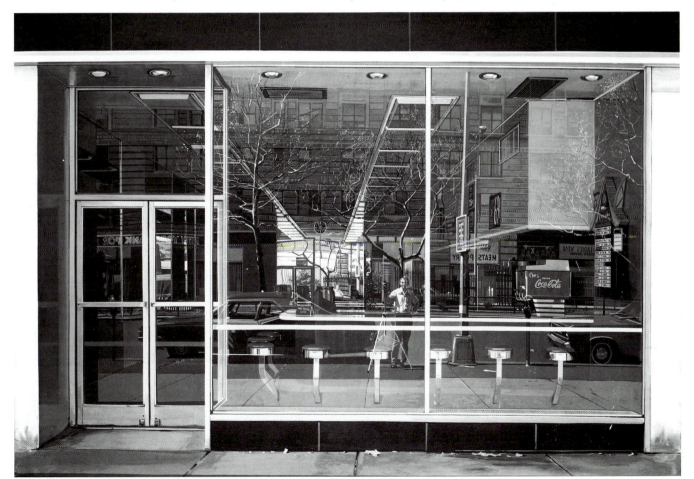

When we see an object reflected in water, it may seem to lose its grounded position on the earth and instead appear to be floating in space. Such reflections hold great fascination for us, for they draw us into a different world of spatial possibilities. When the water outside the Byodoin Temple (2.103) is as smooth as it is in this photograph, the temple and its reversed image become a totality apparently floating without support in space. The reversed image is visually exciting in itself as a symmetrical counterpart of the actual temple.

Light as a Medium

Light itself may be captured and controlled as an element of design. We humans have always been fascinated by looking at light. It has the power to bring us out of the darkness and to illuminate spaces, both outside and inside us. Artistic presentation of light is of ancient origin. The aesthetic care given to fashioning early clay lamps suggests the reverence and joy with which we regard light.

Since light is energy that tends to diffuse through space, it must be controlled in different ways from

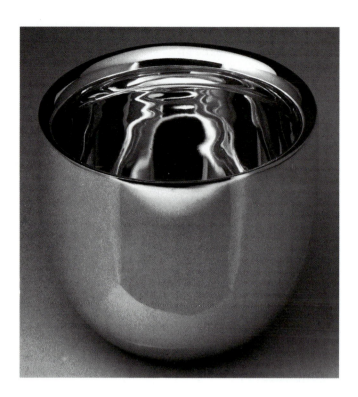

2.102 Labbar Hoagland, Alfonso Soto Soria, and Pedro Leites, *Double-Wall Bowl*, 1985. Silver, 8 × 5½ ins (20 × 14 cm). Manufactured by Tane Orfebres, Mexico.

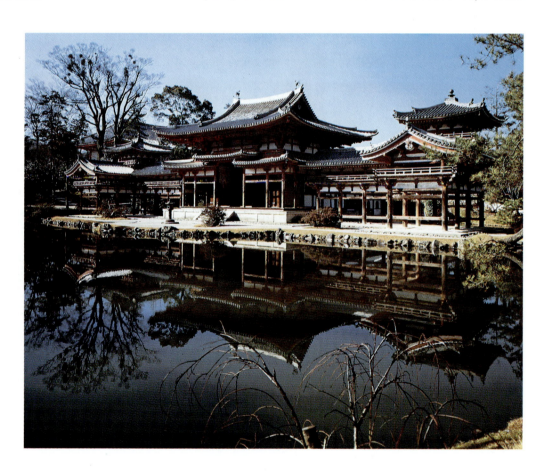

2.103 Hoodo (Phoenix Hall), Byodoin Temple, Uji, near Kyoto, Japan, 11th century.

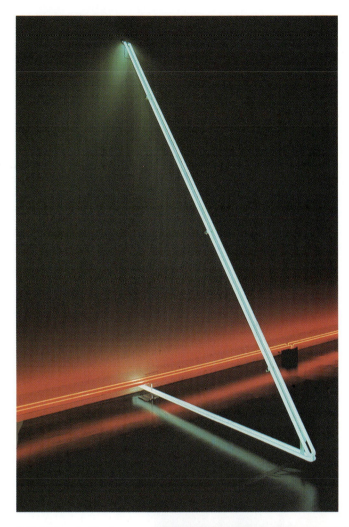

corporeal matter. From the familiarity of neon signs—such as the *EAT* restaurant sign—contemporary artists have derived the idea of using neon tubes to create lines of light in space, such as Stephen Antonakos's *Green Neon from Wall to Floor* (**2.104**). The invention of lasers suggested another art form: laser projections thrown against the night sky or a dark wall (**2.105**). Here no structure is needed to confine the light; it is shaped as a needle-thin beam.

Windows provide another way of controlling light for aesthetic purposes. The use of elaborate stone arches allowed great openings to be made in the walls of Gothic cathedrals for stained-glass windows that told Biblical stories and created a mystical atmosphere for worshippers within, like the breath of the divine. At Sainte-Chapelle (**2.106**), a chapel for the French kings, the interior is suffused with many jewel tones that color the sunlight coming through the intricate stained-glass panes, more brilliant than any flat-painted color could be. The architect Le Corbusier translated this effect into contemporary terms at his *Notre-Dame-du-Haut* (**2.107**), placing bits of stained glass within continually varying window openings. As the light bursts through each of these recesses in the thick walls, it creates a series of focal points in complex mathematical relationships to each other. Within the safe thickness of the walls, the light of God breaks through to touch each person physically.

2.104 (above) Stephen Antonakos, *Green Neon from Wall to Floor*, 1969–70. Neon tubing, 8 × 24 × 5 ft (2.4 × 7.3 × 1.5 m).

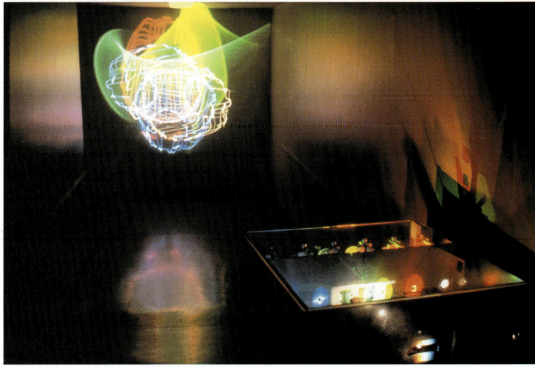

2.105 Laser deflection images, produced by Video/Laser III, 1987. Operated by Professor Lowell Cross at the University of Iowa.

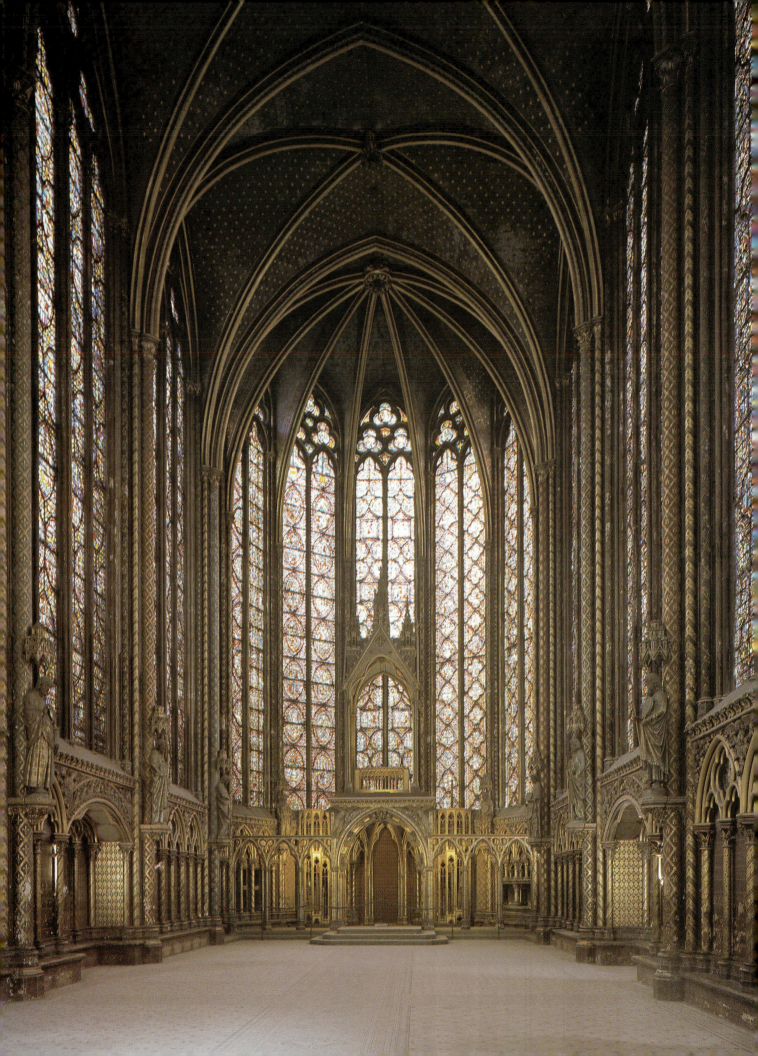

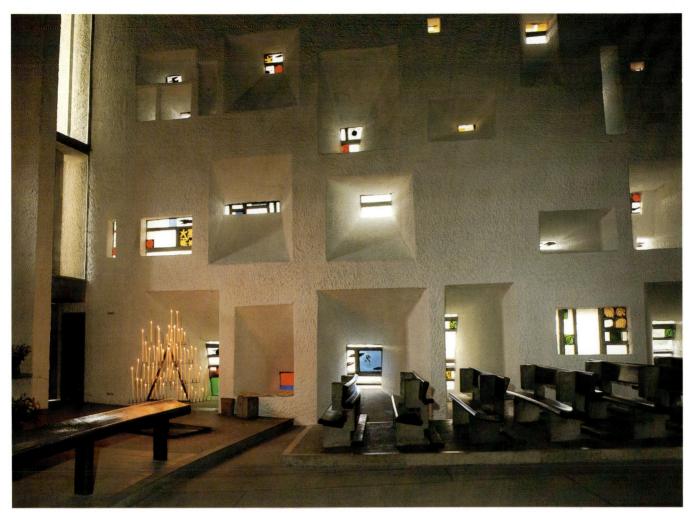

2.107 Le Corbusier, Interior of the chapel of Notre-Dame-du-Haut, Ronchamp, France, 1950–55.

COLOR

Color is an immediately obvious aspect of a work of art that clearly impresses itself on our consciousness. In describing any work that strikes a particular color note, we inevitably speak of it as "that red cube" or "one of Picasso's blue paintings." Less obvious are the subtle effects of colors on our visual receptors, emotional state, and our perceptions of space, though these effects are under study by scientists and used consciously by many artists. Color may even affect us spiritually, as the Russian nonobjective painter Wassily Kandinsky wrote:

2.106 (opposite) Sainte-Chapelle, Paris, 1243–48.

Color is a power which directly influences the soul. Color is the keyboard, the eyes are the hammers, the soul is the piano with many strings. The artist is the hand which plays, touching one key or another, to cause vibrations in the soul.[10]

A Vocabulary of Color

From Kandinsky's sublime perception we descend to the need to establish a vocabulary for speaking about the colors we perceive. The first point to understand is that what we perceive as the color of an object is actually the reflection of light of a certain wavelength off the surface, as this reflection is received by the retina of the eye and perceived by the brain. It does not "belong" to the object itself. The wavelengths that humans can see (only a tiny fraction of the great spectrum of electromagnetic radiation) are collectively

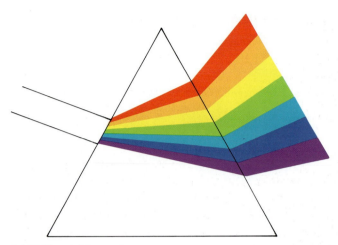

2.108 The visible spectrum.

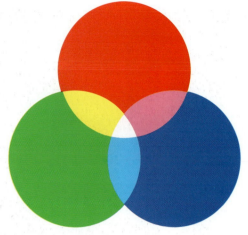

2.110 Primary and secondary hues in refracted lights.

referred to as the **visible spectrum**. As shown schematically in Figure **2.108**, the visible spectrum is the rainbow of colors we see when the white light of the sun passes through a prism that breaks up the wavelengths into seven graduating bands of color.

Centuries ago, Sir Isaac Newton proposed that the ends of this band of hues were so similar that they could be joined, pulling the band into a circular model of color relationships that we now call the **color wheel**. Newton's original proposal is shown in Figure **2.109**. The color wheel demonstrates theoretical relationships among **hues**, the wavelength properties by which we give colors names such as "red," "blue," and so on. In **refracted** (light or "additive") colors, there are theoretically three basic hues, from which all other

hues can be mixed (**2.110**). These basic hues are called **primary colors**. In refracted colors, the primaries are red, green, and blue-violet. If you examine a color television picture very closely, you will see that it is composed entirely of dots of these three hues. There is no yellow in television transmission. Yellow is one of the **secondary** hues in refracted light mixtures; it is created by mixing red and green light.

2.111 The traditional color wheel of pigment mixtures. Primary, secondary, and tertiary colors are numbered, respectively, 1, 2, and 3.

2.109 Newton's color wheel, from Isaac Newton, *Optice*, 1706. British Library, London.

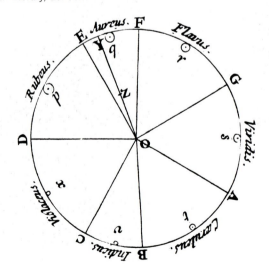

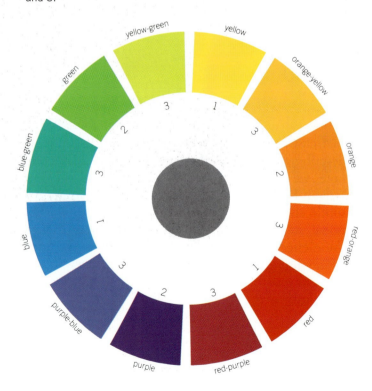

This information is hard for many of us to grasp, since the color wheel with which we are more familiar (2.111) shows the relationships between **reflected** hues. Also called "pigment" or "subtractive" hues, reflected hues are those that result when light is reflected from a pigmented surface that absorbs all wavelengths except those that we see. In this case, the primary hues according to traditional color theory are red, blue, and yellow; the secondaries that can be mixed from them are orange, green, and purple (2.112). If primary and secondary hues are mixed, they form another level of mixtures: **tertiary hues,** as shown in Figure 2.111. For example, red and purple mixed together make red-purple. Note that there is a circle of gray in the center of the color wheel. If pigments of hues lying opposite each other on the wheel—which are called **complementary hues**—are mixed in equal amounts, they will theoretically produce a neutral gray. Purple and yellow, for instance, are complementary to each other, as are blue-green and red-orange.

The problem with Newton's model of color relationships—in addition to the open question of whether the two ends of the spectrum can really be joined—is that it accounts for only one characteristic of color: hue. The colors we perceive also differ in two other ways: **value** and what is called **saturation** (also known as "chroma" or "intensity"). Value, as we have seen, is a measure of the relative lightness or darkness of a color. It can be conceived as a vertical pole with white at the top and black at the bottom, and increasingly darker grays in between. Value variations in reds, blues, and so on run a similar course from near-white

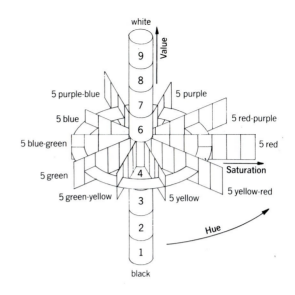

2.113 The color tree illustrating relationships in hue, saturation, and value, according to the color theorist Albert Munsell.

to near-black, with middle-value reds or blues lying at the middle of the pole. These value variations are shown as a three-dimensional model in Figure 2.113. To illustrate the effects of value changes in a hue, Georgia O'Keeffe's *Abstraction Blue* (2.114) can be seen as a beautiful study in value changes in several hues. At their darkest, the hues of the cloudlike forms are almost black, graduating to pastels that are almost as light as the shape dividing the center of the canvas. At either end of the value scale, different hues are almost indistinguishable from each other.

The three-dimensional model of color relationships (2.113) also illustrates differences in saturation, which is a measure of the relative brightness and purity of a color. The most highly saturated colors are those that are the pure hue with none of its complementary added. As more and more of its complementary is added—for instance, as we mix yellow with purple—the color becomes more and more subdued, until, at the center of the vertical axis on this model, it appears as a gray value. O'Keeffe worked with highly saturated, pure hues, though many are shown only in their lighter values to minimize jarring contrasts.

The three-dimensional models shown in Figure 2.113 and in Figure 2.115 were developed by the color theorist Albert Munsell. Munsell found that color relationships could best be explained with a system of five primaries—yellow, green, blue, purple, and red. Therefore, Munsell's complementary colors

2.112 Primary and secondary hues in reflected pigments.

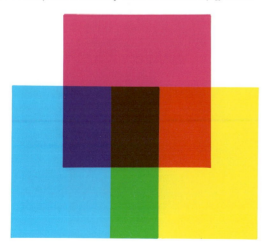

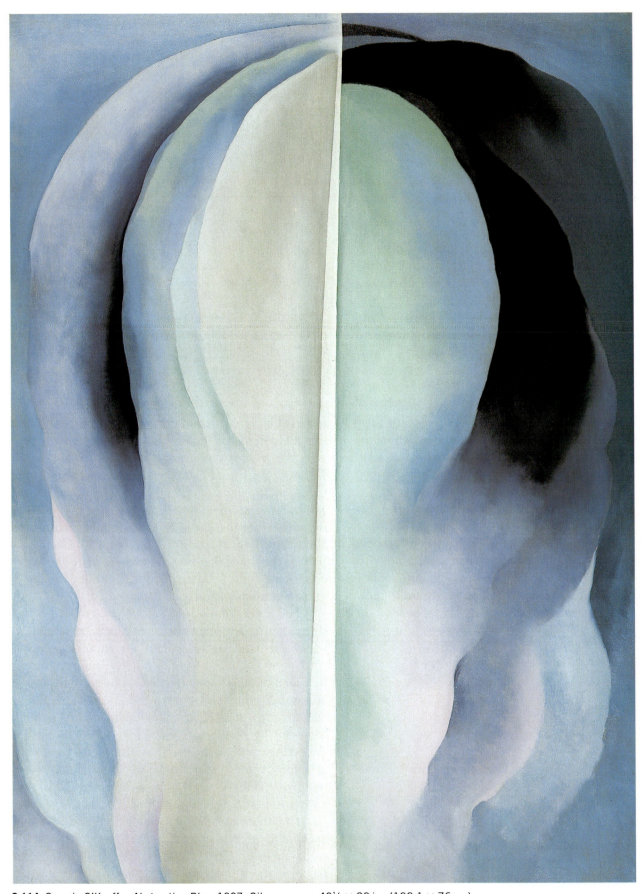

2.114 Georgia O'Keeffe, *Abstraction Blue*, 1927. Oil on canvas, 40¼ × 30 ins (102.1 × 76 cm).
Collection Museum of Modern Art, New York. Acquired through the Helen Acheson Bequest. Photograph © 1997 MOMA.

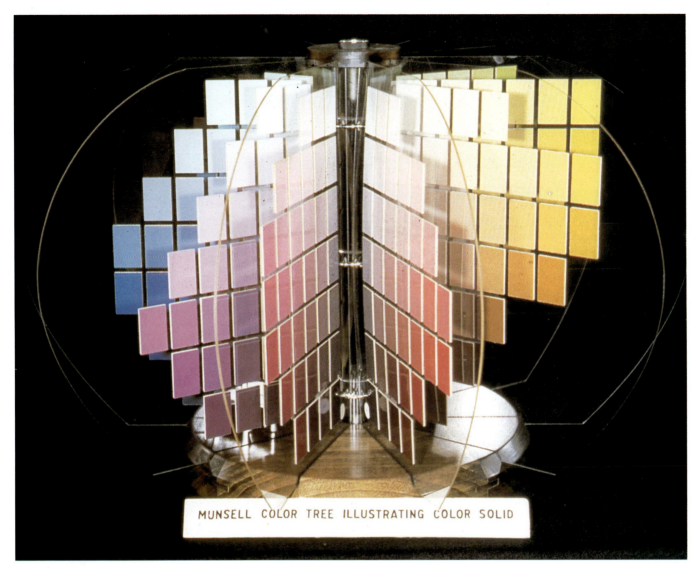

MUNSELL COLOR TREE ILLUSTRATING COLOR SOLID

2.115 The Munsell color tree.

do not exactly match those of the traditional color wheel shown in Figure 2.111. Munsell's system is now used as a commercial standard for naming and mixing pigments. His models show that the number of equal steps in saturation, from gray to most saturated, varies from one hue to another, red having the most possible steps and yellow the least. The Munsell color tree is therefore asymmetrical.

Natural and Applied Color

We are surrounded by color in the natural world. Our awareness of its subtleties depends partly on how open our eyes are and partly on where we live. Those who live in snowy areas may become sensitive to the varied hues that can be seen in the "whiteness" of snow, from blue and even green in its shadows to the grayness of "white" flakes seen falling against a pale sky.

Many artists doing three-dimensional work have featured the natural colors in materials rather than covering them with another color. The many hues that lie beneath the bark of wood are often prized by woodworkers. Semi-precious stones may be cut and polished to bring out their colors, and amethyst and citrine quartz crystal clusters are presented as art objects not only because of their unusual crystalline forms but also because of the natural beauty of their translucent colors. Isamu Noguchi dwells on the nat-

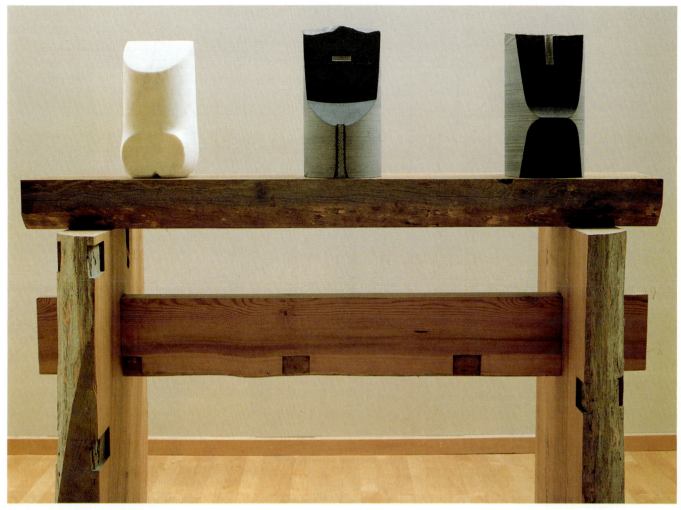

2.116 Isamu Noguchi, (from left to right) *Small Torso*, 1958–62, Greek marble, 13¾ ins (34.9 cm); *Core Piece # 1*, 1974, basalt, 14¼ ins (36 cm); *Core Piece # 2*, 1974, basalt, 15¼ ins (38.7 cm). Photo by Shigeo Anzai.

ural colors of marble, basalt, and wood in the sculptural composition shown in Figure **2.116**. He writes, "I attempt to respect nature, adding only my own rawness."[17]

Diametrically opposed to Noguchi's preference for a restrained use of natural colors is the view that color applied to materials intensifies the significance of a work. Many Classical Greek and Roman marble sculptures were originally painted to bring out the details. Medieval wooden sculptures were also painted, as was the Chinese statue of the Bodhisattva (an enlightened being), *Guanyin* (**2.117**). Guanyin, like other Chinese divinities, had both male and female qualities, and was at various times considered the Bod-

hisattva of Mercy and the traditional Chinese mother goddess. The gold suggests a rich and spiritual presence; the red and green excite the eye, in addition to carrying connotations of life, fertility, and good fortune. When colors that are complementary to one another, such as red and green, are juxtaposed, they intensify each other's brilliance. Here this effect is used only sparingly, for the garment is chiefly red trimmed with gold, with a green sash draped here and there like a pathway through the red and gold.

2.117 (opposite) *Guanyin*, Chinese, 11th to early 12th century. Polychromed wood, height 7 ft 11 ins (2.41 m). Nelson Gallery, Atkins Museum, Kansas City, Missouri.

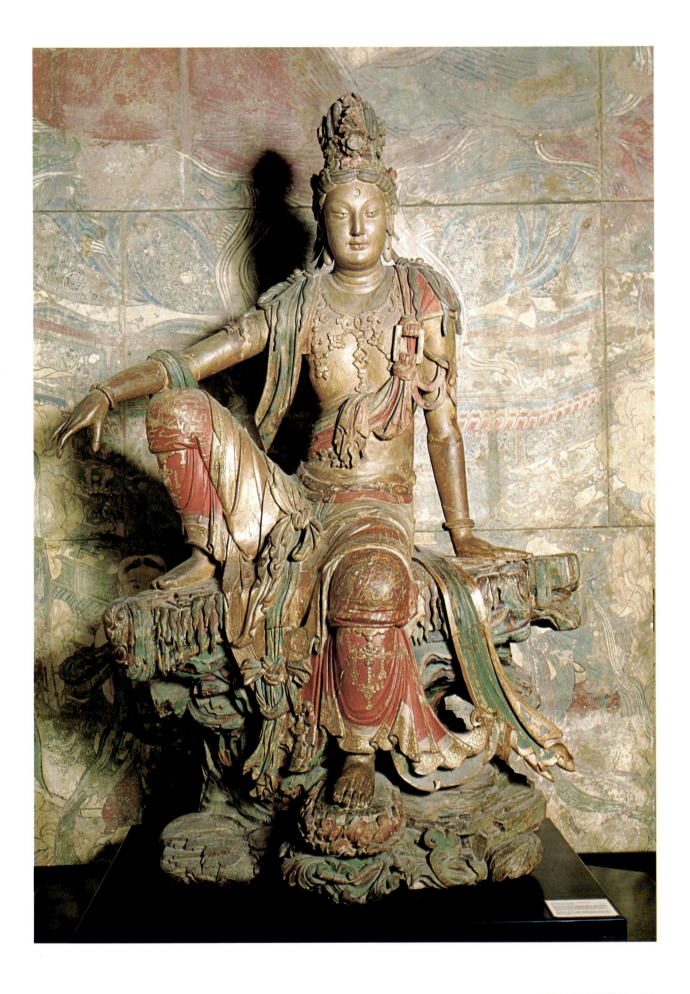

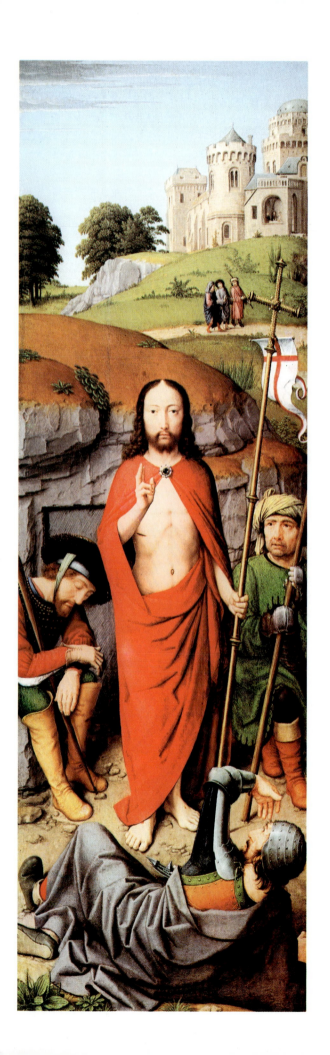

Local, Impressionistic, and Interpretive Color

Many of us are taught as children that objects in our world "are" predictable colors: an apple is red, an orange is orange, a tree has a brown trunk and green leaves, the sky is blue, and so on. These perceptions are called **local colors**. They are the color an object appears if seen from nearby under normal lighting. Often these ideas of what color an object "is" are used to guide color choices in painting. In Gerard David's *The Resurrection* (2.118), boulders are gray, dirt is brown, and grass is green. Although the values of forms in the distance are generally painted lighter than those in the foreground, the hues are still largely local colors. Christ risen from the tomb clearly dominates the composition, not only because of his central position and upright, frontal stance but also because of the intense red of his cloak, heightened by contrast with the greens that surround it.

A fixed mental model of the world can blind us to its subtle and shifting realities, however. The French Impressionists met with tremendous opposition when they trained their minds to perceive the actual colors and forms their eyes were seeing. When Monet painted haystacks, as in Figure 2.119, he discarded the idea that hay is yellow and presented what he actually saw in the cool light of morning. The surprising, scintillating color impressions tend to dematerialize the form. To capture visual truth as nearly as possible, Monet took his canvases outside to paint in natural lighting, from nature, rather than making sketches with color notations and then working inside. He returned again and again to the same field near his home, from summer into winter, painting the ever-changing effects of lighting on the same haystacks.

An **interpretive** use of color is different from either local or impressionistic color. Here color choices are guided by the artist's intent rather than by any external reality. Color is often used interpretively to set the emotional tone for a work. Picasso's *The Old Guitarist* (2.120) was painted during his "Blue Period" (1901–4). During these years, he used blues as the predominant colors in his paintings to express the pathos

2.118 (left) Gerard David, *The Resurrection*, c. 1500.
Oil on wood, 34 × 11 ins (86.4 × 27.9 cm).
Metropolitan Museum of Art, New York.
Robert Lehmann Collection, 1975.

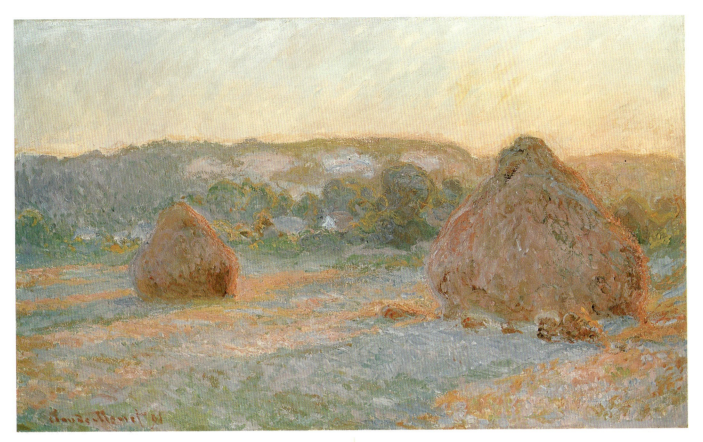

2.119 Claude Monet, *Stacks of Wheat (End of Summer)*, 1890-91. Oil on canvas, 23⅝ × 39⅜ ins (60 x 100 cm). Art Institute of Chicago, Chicago, Illinois. Gift of Arthur M. Wood in memory of Pauline Palmer Wood.

of poverty. In the West, blue is often associated with a feeling of melancholy. If Picasso had used other colors—such as the pinks of his "Pink Period" that followed—the tone of the painting would have been more jovial, but that was not his intent.

Emotional Effects of Color

Colors affect our moods, and we tend to surround ourselves with the psychological atmosphere we want through our choices of colors in clothing and interior design. Research into the effects of colors suggests that a certain pink has a calming effect on us, for instance, whereas red is stimulating. In addition to these physiological effects, we respond to our culture's color associations. In northern European cultures, white is a symbol of purity. But to the Sioux Indians, white symbolized wisdom and health; and in the Far East white is a symbol of death. As we see in Picasso's *The Old Guitarist* (2.120), blue is associated with sadness in Western cultures; it is also linked with serenity and humanity and is therefore the color often used symbolically for the robes of the Virgin Mary (15.19, 15.22, and 15.28).

While such knowledge is interesting and useful, it does not totally explain the way colors are used expressively in art, for color is only one aspect of the totality to which we respond in a work of art. As an illustration, let us look at three works, all of which feature red as their dominant color. Considered

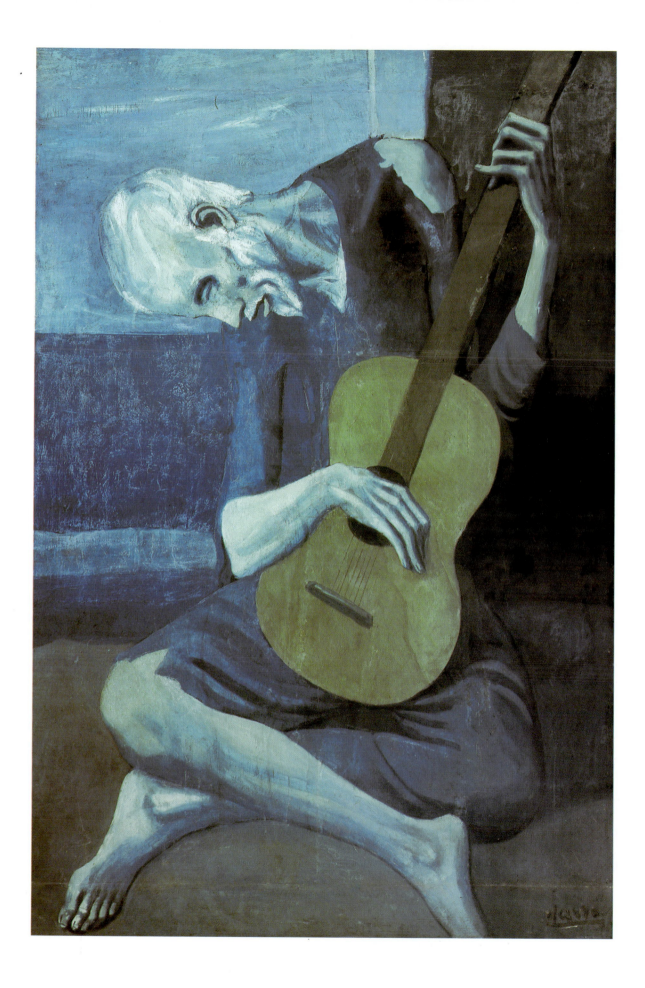

sensitively, each has a different emotional content. In Matisse's *The Red Studio* (**2.121**), the red is joyous and noisy, and the slight accents of other colors make the red seem boisterous. Matisse intentionally subordinated realism to expression in his use of color, explaining, "What I am after, above all, is expression ... I am unable to distinguish between the feeling I have for life and my way of expressing it."[18]

The red of Danny Perkins's *White Square* (**2.122**) is lush and sensual. This expressive color sensation is enhanced by the sensuous organic curves of the blown glass sculpture and the light passing through it. But even where red appears on a flat area above the white square, the color itself maintains its lusciousness.

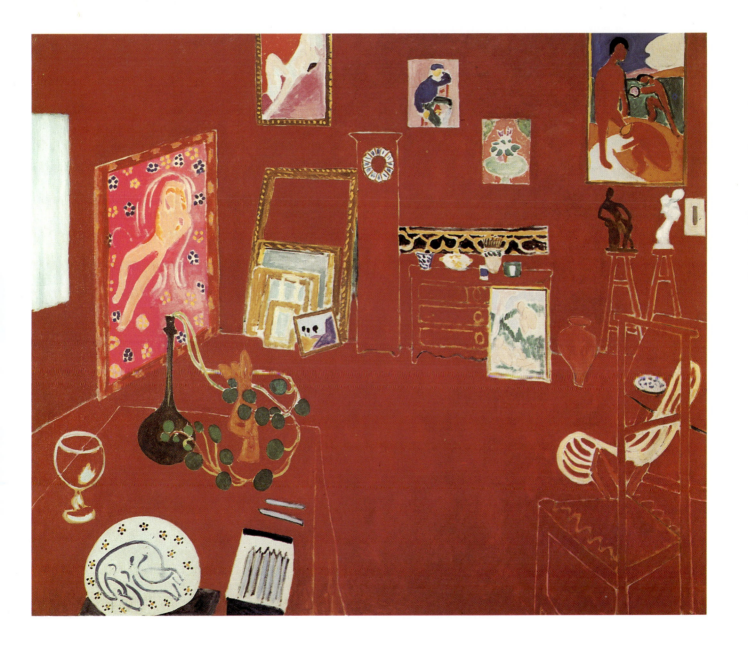

By contrast, in Josef Albers's *Homage to the Square: Board Call* (**2.124**), red has an almost cold and intellectual quality. Albers presents reds in such precisely geometrical gradations, with edges softened by the minimizing of contrast, that his work suggests itself as an object for quiet contemplation. These very different ways of handling the same hue attest to the genius of the artists: that they can make red do whatever they ask, by the way that they use it.

Warm and Cool Colors

In addition to—and perhaps linked with—our perceptions of colors as having certain emotional qualities, we also tend to associate degrees of heat or cold with them. Although scientific evidence is inconclusive, we do seem to respond to colors kinesthetically, as though they produced different color sensations in our bodies. Some of us intuitively dress in red to feel warmer and blue or green to feel cooler. Such choices of hues seem independent of value differences in the amount of light absorbed or reflected. In general, reds and yellows are considered **warm** colors, like those of fire; blues and greens are considered **cold**, like icy water. With this in mind, Pepsi spent US$500 million, including painting

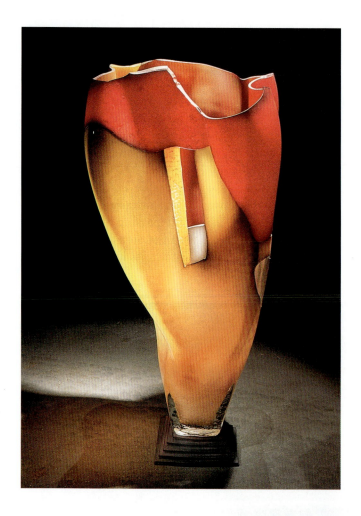

2.122 (above) Danny Perkins, *White Square*, 1994. Blown glass, oil paints, 42 × 16 × 16 ins (106.6 x 40.6 x 40.6 cm).

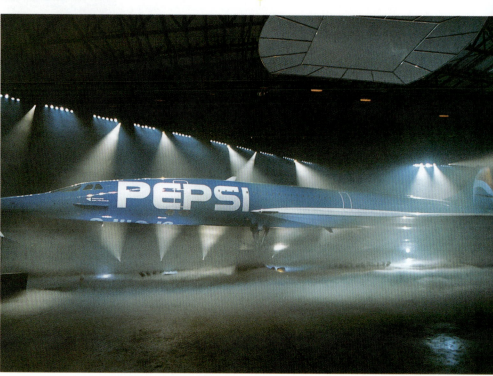

2.123 An Air France Concorde painted blue for Pepsi Corporation, Gatwick Airport, England, 1996.

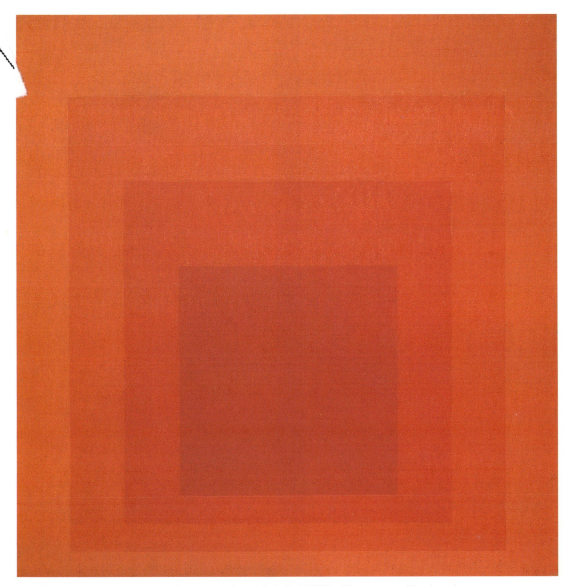

2.124 Josef Albers, *Homage to the Square: Board Call*, Fall 1967. Oil on composition board, 4 × 4 ft (1.22 × 1.22 m). Collection Museum of Modern Art, New York. The Sidney and Harriet Janis Collection.

a Concorde jet blue (**2.123**), to announce its new all-blue can in many countries around the globe in 1996. The drink is the same, but presenting it in a blue can instead of a red, white, and blue can, would, Pepsi claimed, "fundamentally alter the international soft drink atmosphere."[19]

Consider the visual "temperature" of three interiors. The silvery-blue paleness of Jim and Sandy Howell's living room (**2.125**) has a feeling so cool and airy that even the red of the wood stove does not seem to give off much warmth. The house is designed to draw in a tremendous amount of outside light through broad glass walls and a skylit core. This light is of great importance to Jim, a painter who works with very subtle variations of color and light (one of his paintings hangs on the wall). The warmth and brilliance of

the light that floods the house are balanced by the quiet coolness of the blues inside.

By contrast, the reds of the sitting room shown in Figure **2.126** create an extremely warm effect. But, as we have just seen, when reds, oranges, and yellows are used in small amounts as accents rather than whole environments, they may not create a sense of warmth. The red-purple of the chair and ottoman in Judy and Pat Coady's townhouse (**2.127**) does not change the overall coolness of the room. Rather, the pale pastel green of the door draws our attention to the cool qualities in the focal point: Marni Bakst's stained-glass panels. The amounts in which colors are used and the areas where our attention is focused have a strong effect on our response.

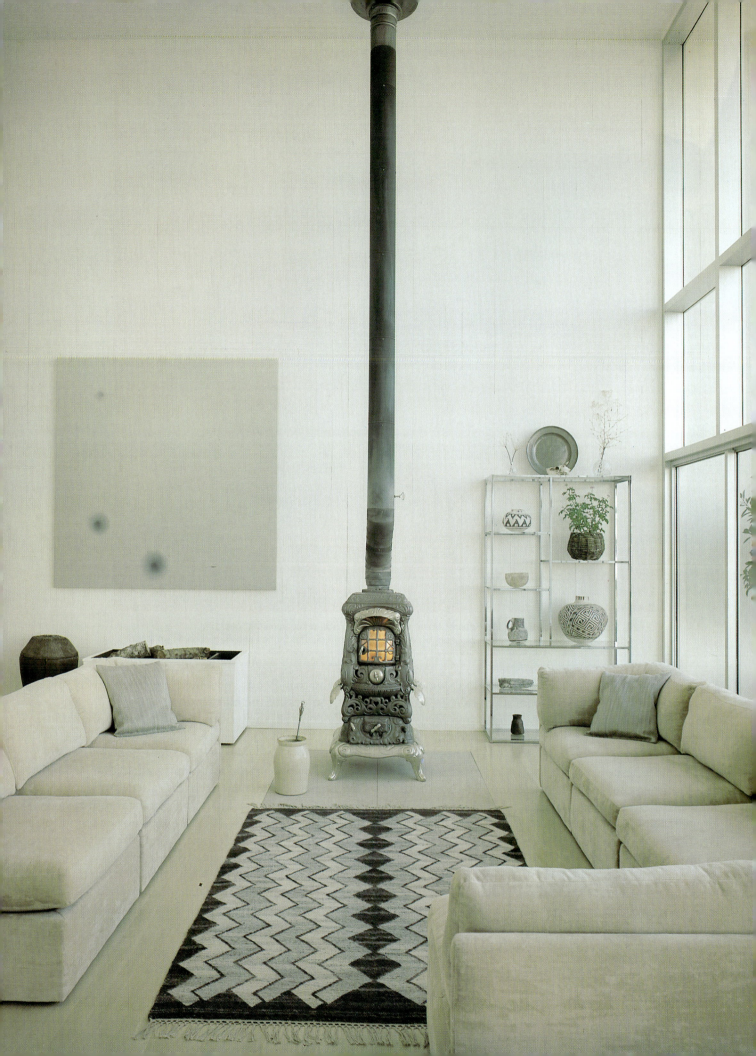

2.125 (opposite) Interior of Jim and Sandy Howell's home, Washington.

2.126 (right) David Hicks, sitting room of a house in Oxfordshire, England, 1970s. Courtesy of the artist.

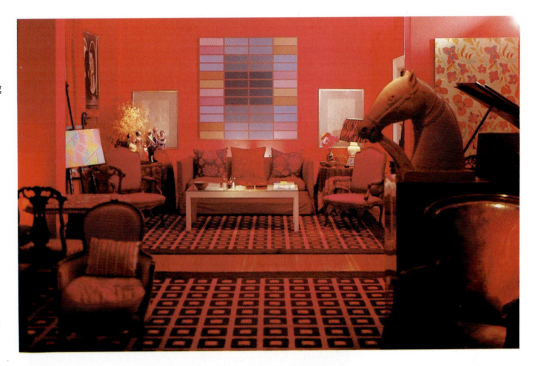

2.127 (below) Interior of Judy and Pat Coady's townhouse, with Marni Bakst stained-glass doors, column by Trent Whitington.

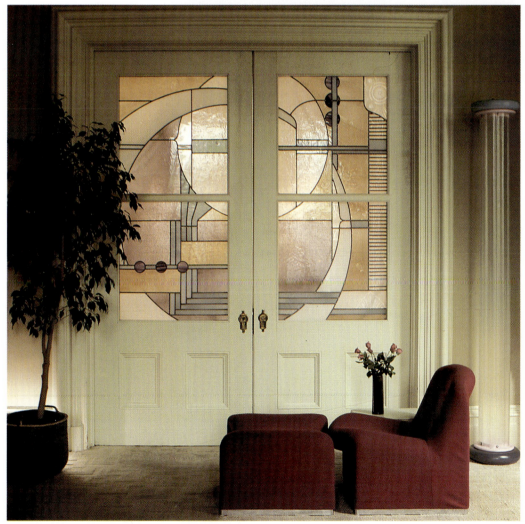

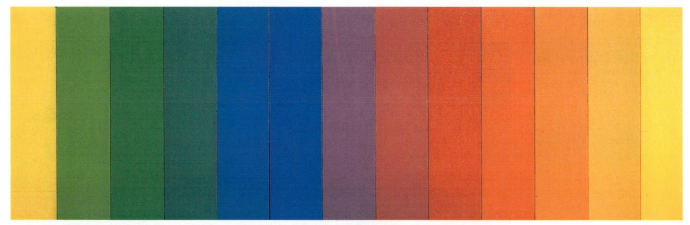

2.128 Ellsworth Kelly, *Spectrum III*, 1967. Oil on canvas in 13 parts, overall 33¼ × 108⅝ ins (84.3 × 275.7 cm). Collection Museum of Modern Art, New York. The Sidney and Harriet Janis Collection. Photograph © 1997 MOMA.

Advancing and Receding Colors

Because of the way our eyes see colors, warm colors tend to expand visually, seeming to come toward the viewer in space, while cool colors contract, seeming to draw back in space. But these effects do not exist in isolation. Look carefully at Ellsworth Kelly's *Spectrum III* (2.128). Because the same amount of color appears in each band, careful observation of our own reactions will give us some clues as to which colors seem visually larger and closer. Does the strip of colors seem to bow in or out at any point? Is this effect continuous, or does it change direction on any of the bands? Now try

blocking out the white of the page by placing four strips of some other color around the edges of the reproduction. Does the spatial effect of the colored bands change?

The only rule that is always true in dealing with the elusive subject of color effects is this: *All colors are affected by the colors around them.* Our perception of certain colors as closer or farther depends to a large extent on the colors to either side of them. Colors that are closer to the hue and value of the background will seem to lie on the same plane as the background; the more that colors differ in value and hue from the background, the more they will appear to come off or recede into it in

2.129 Color combinations.

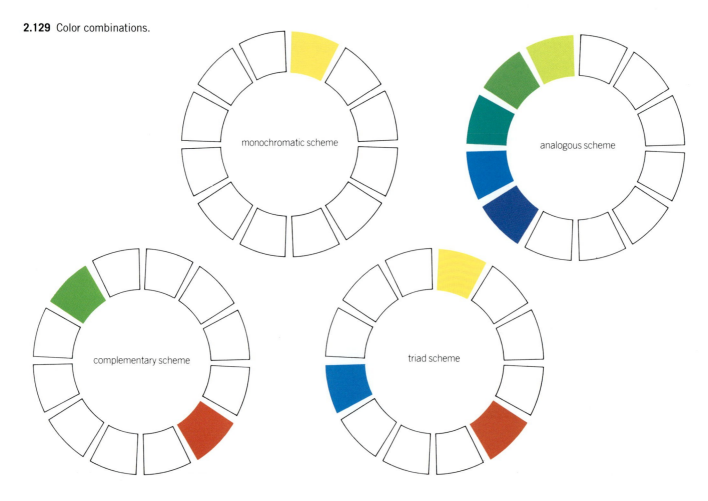

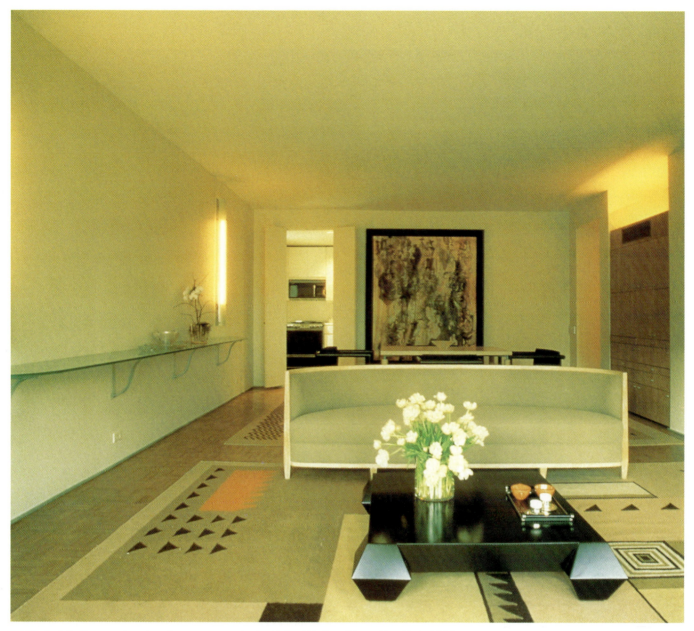

2.130 Andrée Putman, interior of an apartment in the United Nations Plaza, New York, 1985.

space, the direction depending on other spatial clues. The effect of contrast between individual colors and the background is complicated in the Ellsworth Kelly painting by the interactions between adjacent colored bands. If you look closely and for some time, you will begin to see that along many edges where colors meet, the light one appears lighter and the dark one darker. Colors affect each other optically by "subtracting" their own hue and value from that of their neighbor.

Color Combinations

Because colors affect each other, in our perception, theorists have noted that the distance between colors on a color wheel has a predictable effect on how harmonious they will be if placed together. Using the traditional color wheel, they have distinguished several common patterns of color combinations, as shown in Figure 2.129. These patterns apply to any sets of colors, and not just the ones shown as illustrations in the figure and the examples that follow. Such orderly relationships do not exhaust the possibilities but provide a basic framework for some designers' color choices.

When only one hue is used, perhaps in different values and saturations and perhaps with small amounts of other colors as accents, the color combination is said to be **monochromatic**. Andrée Putman's interior design for a New York apartment (**2.130**) focuses

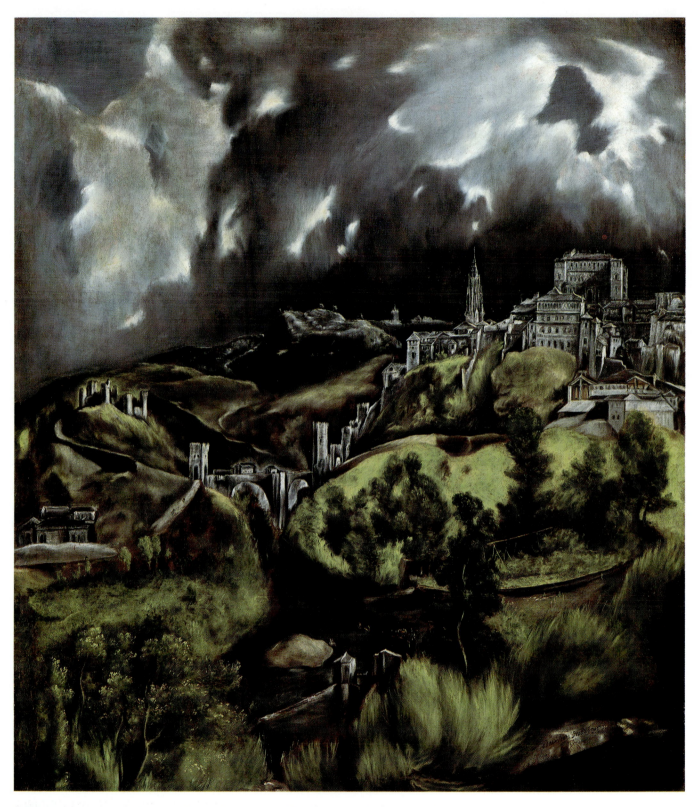

2.131 El Greco, *View of Toledo*, c. 1597. Oil on canvas, 3 ft 11¾ ins × 3 ft 6¾ ins (1.21 × 1.08 m).
Metropolitan Museum of Art, New York. Bequest of Mrs. H. O. Havemeyer, 1929. The H. O. Havemeyer Collection.

primarily on yellows, with neutral black. Values of one hue harmonize very closely with each other.

Another kind of close harmony occurs when **analogous** colors—hues lying next to each other on the color wheel—are used. Blue and green are analogous colors, with minimal contrasts. Blues and greens predominate in El Greco's *View of Toledo* (2.131), interspersed with neutral blacks, whites, and browns. Even the whites are bluish, and the browns are tinged with green.

In contrast with the peaceful coexistence possible between closely related hues, hues that lie opposite each other on the color wheel have a jarring or at least exciting effect on the eye when they are juxtaposed. These high-contrast combinations are called **complementary** color schemes. In the Chinese statue of Guanyin (2.117), the juxtaposition of red and green, which are complementary to each other, creates a sensation of vibrant life. Redon gave his *Orpheus* (2.47) an enhanced atmosphere of mystical space by juxtaposing purple and yellow where mountains meet sky, creating a sense of vibration between them. Milton

2.132 Milton Glaser, poster of Aretha Franklin.

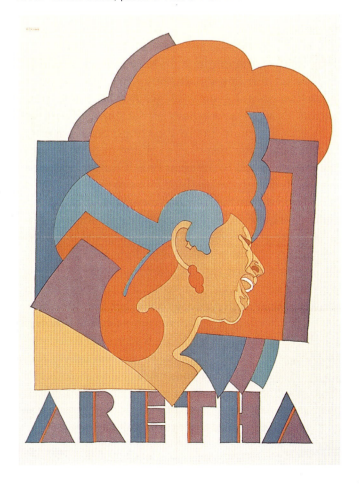

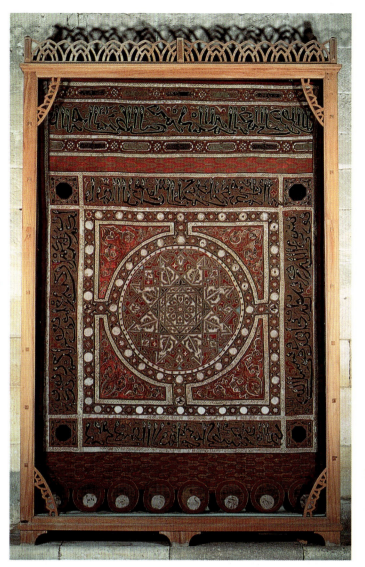

2.133 Banner of Las Navas de Tolosa, southern Spain, first half of the 13th century. Silk tapestry-weave with gilt parchment, 10 ft 9⅞ ins × 7 ft 2⅝ ins (3.3 × 2.2 m). Museo de Telas Medievales, Monastery of Santa María la Real de Las Huelgas, Burgos, Spain. Patrimonio Nacional.

Glaser's poster of Aretha Franklin (2.132) juxtaposes complementary blue-green and red at high saturation for a sizzling, almost jarring effect. But if complementary colors are used next to each other at low saturation or pale values, as in the subtle green in the Banner of Las Navas de Tolosa (2.133), the colors do not fight with each other. It is possible to capture the visual excitement of a complementary color combination without overstimulating the eye, if the artist wishes.

Another stimulating combination is a **triad** color scheme, in which three colors equally spaced around the color wheel are used together. The yellow, blue,

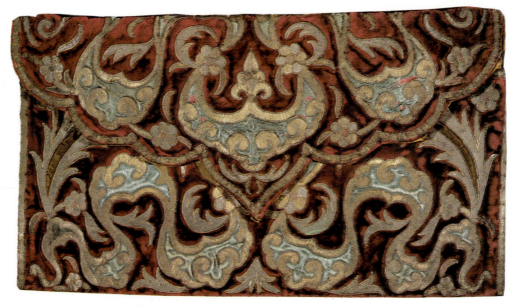

2.134 Embroidered envelope, Ottoman, 16th century. Velvet with silk, gold and silver wire, 7½ × 16⅛ ins (19 × 41 cm). Topkapi Sarayi Museum, Istanbul.

and red of the lovely Ottoman embroidered envelope (2.134)—a container for royal gifts, messages, and documents—are far enough apart on the color wheel to provide vigorous contrast for each other, but not so far apart that their hues clash.

Interaction of Color

The highly contrasting effects of complementary colors juxtaposed may be exactly what an artist desires. When highly saturated complementaries are used in the right amounts next to each other, the inter-action between the color sensations in our brain may create some extraordinary optical phenomena. The complementaries may seem to enhance each other's brilliance, the edges between them seem to vibrate, and ghost colors may appear where they meet. Op Art, a movement of the 1960s, used these phenomena extensively in nonobjective, hard-edged, geometrical works that create fascinating illusions in our percep-tual apparatus. In Op Artist Richard Anuszkiewicz's *Splendor of Red* (2.135), the juxtaposition of green and blue lines, and then blue lines alone, with a uniform red ground creates vivid optical illusions that tran-scend what has actually been painted. The red is the same throughout, but what we perceive is a diamond of very intense red popping forward from a less bril-liant red diamond against an even less brilliant red. That blue halo around the center diamond occurs solely in our perceptions; it has not been physically painted.

No one can yet state with certainty how these effects happen. Scientists have long tried to determine how we see colors, but only theories are yet available. Color perception seems to involve the one hundred million rods and six and a half million cones in the retina at the back of the eye. The rods and cones are specialized photoreceptive cells that glean information from light striking the retina and pass it along to the brain through a series of nerve fibers. In the brain, almost a third of the gray matter of the cerebral cortex is devoted to integrating the information from the two eyes.

We do not know quite how the brain perceives colors; we do not even know what triggers the infor-mation about different hues in the cones. There are light-sensitive pigments in the cones, but we are not certain how they respond to different wavelengths, which correspond to different hues. One of the current theories is that there are three kinds of pigments in the cones: one senses the long wavelengths (reds), one the middle-range wavelengths (greens), and one the short wavelengths (blue-violets). All other colors perceived are mixtures of these primaries in light mixing.

Be this as it may (for there are many other theories), it seems clear that color perception operates by com-parison of one colored area with another. For this reason, it is easily "fooled." Consider a simple case of contrast in value. If a medium gray value is seen next to a darker area, it appears light; if the same medium gray is seen against a lighter field, it appears dark. In Figure 2.136, the central line is actually the same value throughout, but the eye-brain mechanism does not see it that way.

Color perception is not like a camera; it is not a

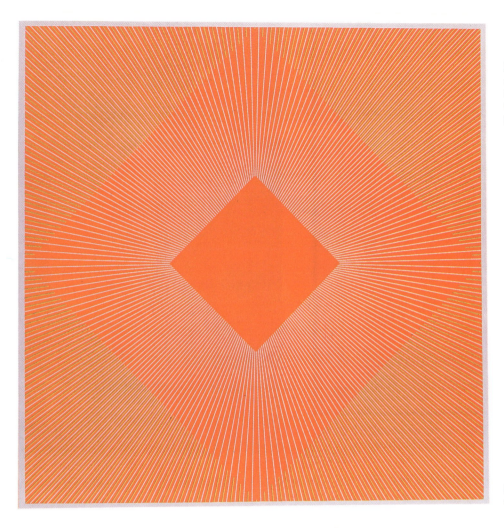

2.135 Richard Anuszkiewicz, *Splendor of Red*, 1965. Acrylic on canvas, 6 × 6 ft (1.83 × 1.83 m). Yale University Art Gallery, New Haven, Connecticut. Gift of Seymour H. Knox.

2.136 (below) Optical illusion from value contrast.

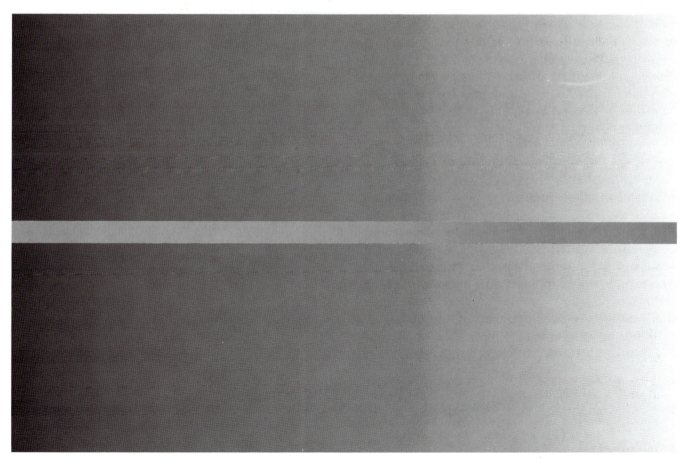

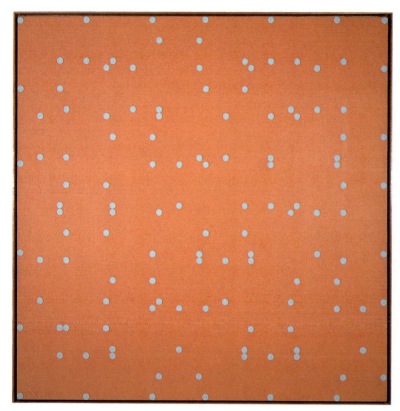

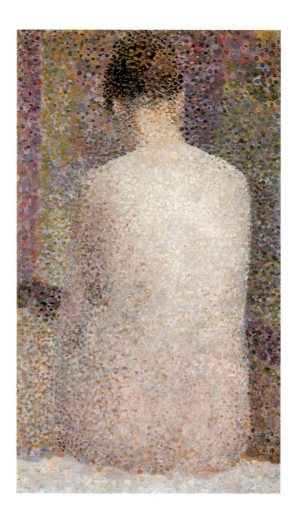

2.137 (above) Larry Poons, *Orange Crush*, 1963. Acrylic on canvas, 6 ft 8 ins × 6 ft 8 ins (2.03 × 2.03 m). Albright-Knox Art Gallery, Buffalo, New York. Gift of Seymour H. Knox, 1964.

2.138 (above right) Georges Seurat, *Seated Model*, 1887. Oil on board, 9½ × 6 ins (24 × 15.2 cm). Louvre, Paris.

simple registering of information from the outside world. If you were shown a green light in a dark room, you would be able to identify it as green by comparison with the surrounding blackness. But if that same green light were then presented amidst many other green lights, it would be very difficult to select which one had been shown to you first, for there would not be sufficient contrast to judge by.

In addition to effects of contrast, certain optical effects seem to happen when the photoreceptors are fatigued. If we look at one bright hue for a while—overstimulating those photoreceptors—and then look away, we will "see" its complementary hue briefly in an illusion of the same shape. If you stare at some of the blue-green circles in Larry Poons's *Orange Crush* (2.137) and then glance into the orange area, you are likely to perceive more brilliant illusory dots of orange there as after-images. Goethe, who in addition to being a great writer was also a major color theorist, proposed that this illusion arises from an inborn desire for wholeness:

> When the eye sees a color it is immediately excited, and it is its nature, spontaneously and of necessity, at once to produce another, which with the original color com-

prehends the whole chromatic scale. A single color excites, by a specific sensation, the tendency to universality.[20]

Whether the explanations are psychological or physiological, the unusual effects known to occur when colors are juxtaposed have led to some interesting artistic experiments. For instance, some artists and color theorists have tried to mix colors optically rather than physically. The Post-Impressionist painter Georges Seurat studied the science of color perception in depth and created a technique called **pointillism**. Using dots of primary and secondary colors in close juxtaposition, he coaxed the eye to mix other colors from them, as in his *Seated Model* (2.138). Seen from a distance, the dots tend to blend into colors other than those of the dots, such as flesh tones and their shadows. The effect suggests scintillating lights, rather than flat pigments.

A remarkable and effective contemporary approach to optical mixtures of colors was developed by Arthur Hoener. Working with the interactions among colors and the ground against which they are shown, he created optical color mixtures in the areas between colored figures. In his unique color theory, called **synergistic color mixing**, the primaries are orange, green, and

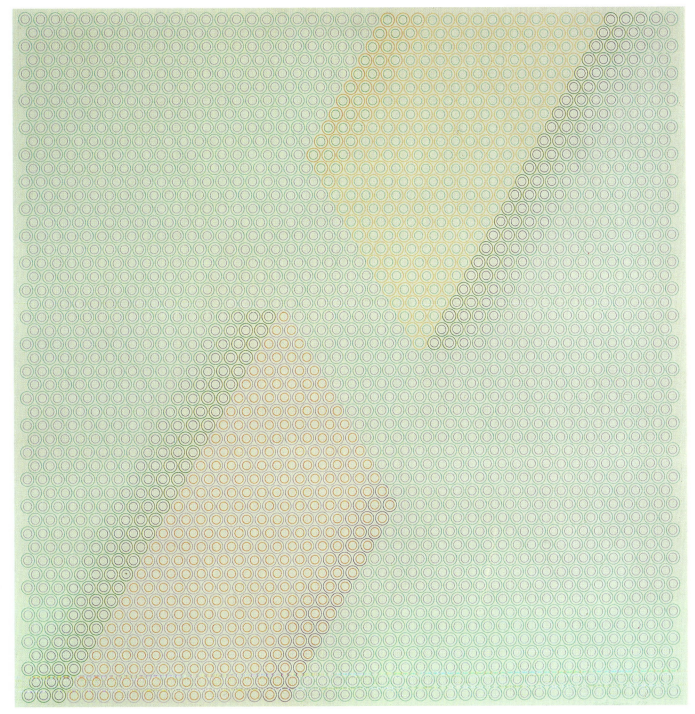

2.139 Arthur Hoener, *Tenuous*, 1974. Acrylic on canvas, 23½ × 23½ ins (59.7 × 59.7 cm). Collection of Mr. and Mrs. Walter Tower, Newton, Massachusetts.

violet. Violet and green mix optically to form blue, orange and green are mixed to produce yellow, and violet and orange mix to form red. Although these combinations are quite different from those of the traditional Newtonian color wheel shown in Figure 2.109, they do work surprisingly well. In Hoener's painting *Tenuous* (2.139), the "yellow" wedge you see is actually made from orange and green, and the "red" wedge is made from violet and orange. These color effects are most apparent if you look at the painting from a distance.

Color interaction effects also depend on the willingness of the viewer to perceive them. You are more likely to see them if you know to look for them or if you simply relax and allow your immediate experiences to register. Some people may use their brains to override their sensory experiences; if you know that no yellow has been physically painted in *Tenuous*, you may not perceive it as a visual reality. Some color interactions happen very quickly and are compellingly "real"; others are more subtle and take time to develop.

JOSEF ALBERS
on THE COMPLEXITY OF COLOR

Josef Albers (1888–1976) is widely considered the greatest twentieth-century teacher of the use of color in art, as well as being a great colorist himself. Albers created a great number of paintings called *Homage to the Square* (Figures 2.124 and **2.140**). In them he held the composition constant—nesting squares of certain proportions—but altered the color relationship in such a way that each painting has a unique effect.

The exercises Albers created for his students at Yale University forced them to recognize the startling optical changes that can be wrought by color interactions. In Figure **2.141**, which is a student solution to a problem given by Albers, two different colors (shown below) are made to look nearly identical by surrounding them with carefully selected colors. Albers did not begin by teaching the optics of color perception or theories of formal relationships between colors. He began by forcing his students to look carefully at colors, to pay attention to what they were actually seeing rather than what they thought they were seeing. He said:

"I like to recall a discovery of Gestalt psychology, that 80 if not 90 per cent of our perception is visual. This makes it clear that our sensory contact with the world is first of all visual, that is, through our eyes. And this contact is going on uninterruptedly all day long, as long as there is light and our eyes remain open.

Obviously, but also unfortunately, this continuous and most intensive connection with the surrounding world is not appropriately recognized in education, which remains predominantly auditory."[21]

"In visual perception a color is almost never seen as it really is—as it physically is. This fact makes color the most relative medium in art.

In order to use color effectively it is necessary to recognize that color deceives continually. The aim of such study is to develop—through experience—by trial and error—an eye for color."

"If one says 'Red' (the name of a color) and there are fifty people listening, it can be expected that there will be fifty reds in their minds. And one can be sure that all these reds will be very different.

Even when a certain color is specified which all listeners have seen innumerable times—such as the red of the Coca-Cola signs which is the same red all over the country—they will still think of many different reds.

Even if all the listeners have hundreds of reds in front of them from which to choose the Coca-Cola red, they will again select quite different colors. And no one can be sure that he has found the precise red shade.

And even if that round red Coca-Cola sign with the white name in the middle is actually shown so that everyone focuses on the same red, each will receive the same projection on his retina, but no one can be sure whether each has the same perception."

"We are able to hear a single tone. But we almost never (that is, without special devices) see a single color unconnected and unrelated to other colors. Colors present themselves in continuous flux, constantly related to changing neighbors and changing conditions."

"If one is not able to distinguish the difference between a higher tone and a lower tone, one probably should not make music.

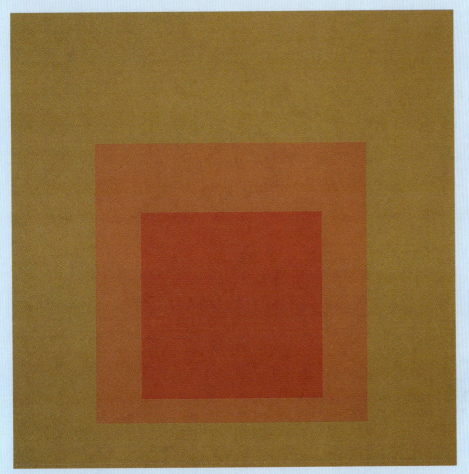

2.140 Joseph Albers, *Equivocal*. Silk-screened print, 11 × 11 ins (27.9 × 27.9 cm). From *Homage to the Square: Ten Works by Joseph Albers.* © 1962 Ives Sillman, New Haven, Connecticut. Collection of Margaret Hoener.

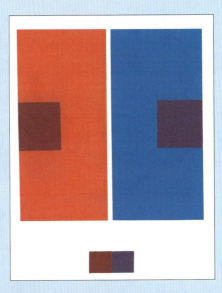

2.141 Two physically different colors can be made to appear nearly identical by careful choice of colored grounds.

If a parallel conclusion were to be applied to color, almost everyone would prove incompetent for its proper use. Very few are able to distinguish higher and lower light intensity between different hues. After some training one might easily agree on light relationship, that is, which of two colors is lighter and which is darker. However, there is rarely agreement on color intensity, that is, which among a number of reds is the reddest red."

"Usually, illustrations of harmonic color constellations which derived from authoritative systems look pleasant, beautiful, and thus convincing. But it should not be overlooked that they are usually presented in a most theoretical and least practical manner, because normally all harmony members appear in the same quantity and the same shape, as well as in the same number (just once) and sometimes even in similar light intensity.

When applied in practice, these harmony sets appear changed. In addition to quantity, form, and recurrence, wider aspects exert still more changing influences. These are changed and changing light—and, even worse, several simultaneous lights; reflections of lights and of colors; direction and sequence of reading; presentation in varying materials; constant or altering juxtaposition of related and unrelated objects. With these and other visual displacements, it should not be a surprise that the sympathetic effect of the original 'ideal' color combination often appears changed, lost, and reversed.

Good painting, good coloring, is comparable to good cooking. Even a good cooking recipe demands tasting and repeated tasting while it is being followed.

And the best tasting still depends on a cook with taste."[22]

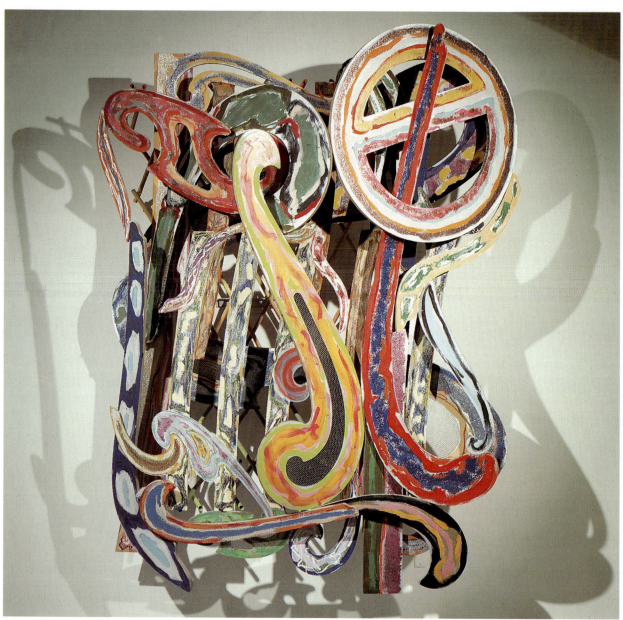

2.142 Frank Stella, *Katsura*, 1979. Oil and epoxy on aluminum, and wire mesh, 115 × 92 × 30 ins (292.1 × 233.7 × 76.2 cm). Collection Museum of Modern Art, New York. Acquired through the Mr. and Mrs. Victor Ganz, Mr. and Mrs. Donald H. Peters, and Mr. and Mrs. Charles Zadock Funds. Photograph © 1997 MOMA.

Limited and Open Palette

We leave the complex subject of color with a final measure of ways that artists use color: the range of colors used in a single work of art. An artist who works with an **open palette** draws from the full range of colors, as Frank Stella does in *Katsura* (**2.142**). His color choices seem completely unrestrained, in a composition held together by repetition of shapes such as French curves and other drafting tools. At the other extreme is the very **limited palette** used by Picasso in his *A Woman in White* (**2.143**). The painting is quite rich in color, however, despite the immediate impression of white. The hues Picasso uses are primarily reds and blues, in values so light that they approach white. In general, there is an obvious difference in emotional impact between the two approaches. A more open palette tends to be busy and exciting, especially when colors are used at full saturation. A more limited palette creates a far more subdued, tranquil emotional atmosphere. This is generally true even if those colors are red (2.124).

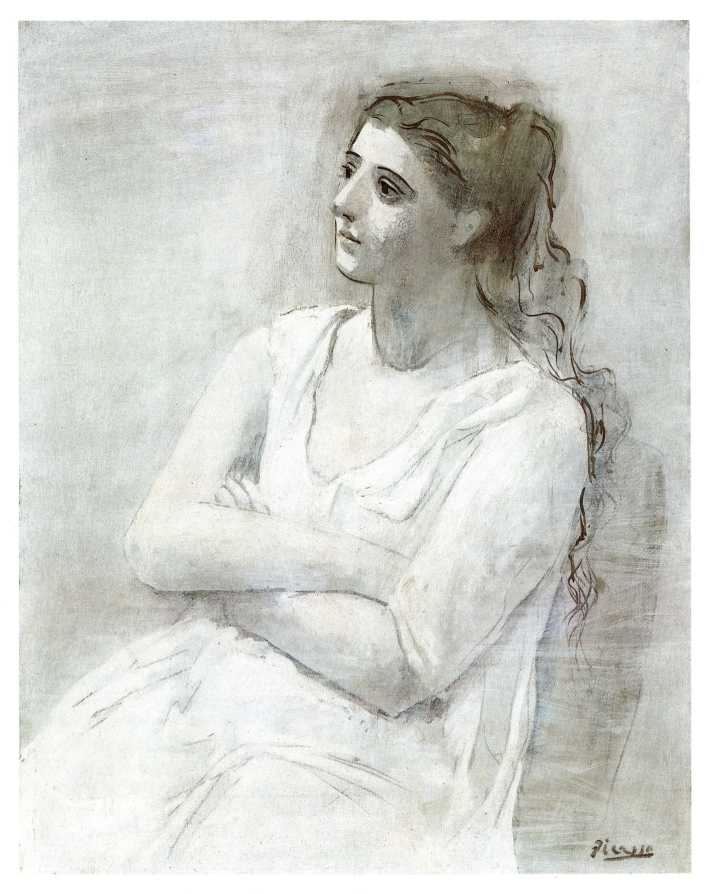

2.143 Pablo Picasso, *A Woman in White*, 1923. Oil on canvas, 39 × 30½ ins (99 × 77.5 cm). Metropolitan Museum of Art, New York. Rogers Fund 1951.

2.144 Trajan's Column, Rome, 113 AD. Marble, height 125 ft (38.1 m).

TIME

Thus far we have been exploring visual elements that exist in space: line, form and shape, texture, value and light, and color. But art exists in time as well as space, and time can be considered an element in itself. Ways in which artists work with time include manipulations of viewing time, actual movement, the illusion of movement, capturing a moment in time, using time as the subject of a work of art, and bringing attention to change through time.

Viewing Time

A certain amount of time is required for the viewing of any work of art. It is said that the average person spends only ten seconds looking at each work in a gallery or museum. This is not nearly long enough to really "see" it.

Some works have ways of calling us to spend more time with them. One way of doing so is to get us to walk all the way around a three-dimensional piece. The Roman Trajan's Column (2.144) does more than that: it lures us to walk around the column again and again, reading the story of Trajan's campaigns to expand the Roman Empire across the Danube. The low-relief narrative is carved in marble as a 625-foot-long (190-m) spiraling band that gets broader near the top to improve its visibility. Reading the 150 separate events thus chronicled, working out who and where the figures are and what they are doing, is time-consuming but was presumably possible for those who were familiar with the stories.

The Water Garden, Fort Worth (2.145), requires a different kind of exploration. The designers invite us

2.145 Philip Johnson and John Burgee, Water Garden, Fort Worth, Texas, 1974.

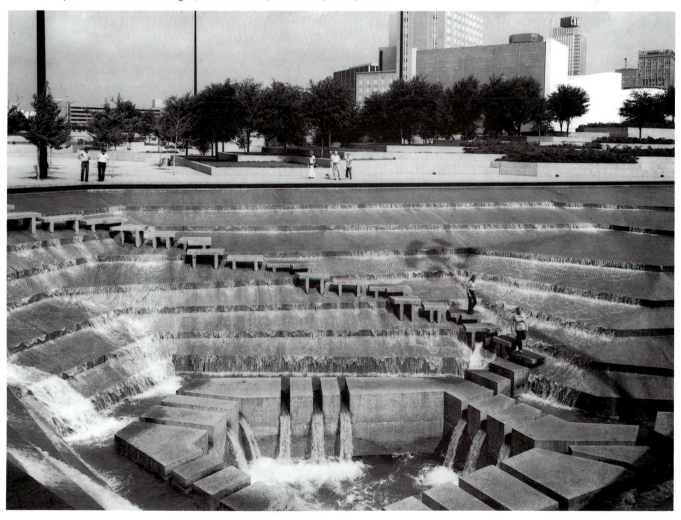

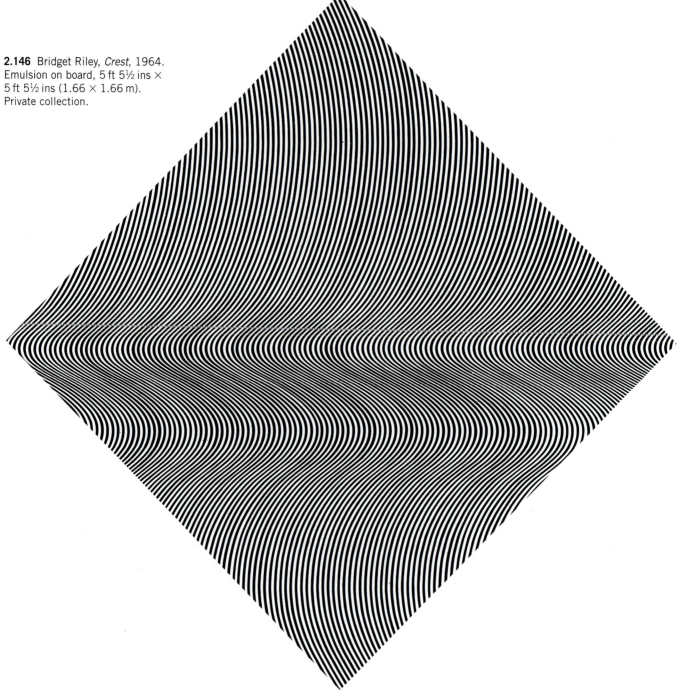

2.146 Bridget Riley, *Crest*, 1964. Emulsion on board, 5 ft 5½ ins × 5 ft 5½ ins (1.66 × 1.66 m). Private collection.

to walk not only around the perimeter of the artificial falls but also down through them to the pool at their center. The broad stepped slabs provide varying surfaces over which the patterns of the water change as it descends. The water is finally channeled into torrents as it gathers from the whole area and plunges into the pool. Many of us are fascinated by the patterns of moving water and will happily spend endless time watching them change.

An entirely different kind of viewing time is demanded by works of Op Art, whose reliance on the distortions introduced by visual fatigue requires that we look at them for a long time in order to experience their effects. In works that juxtapose bright complementary colors, effects such as vibrating edges and color halos appear as the retina tires of the contrast. In black and white Op Art, such as Bridget Riley's *Crest* (**2.146**), one's perception of mere black and white lines lasts only briefly. If you stare at it a bit longer, allowing the image to weave its hypnotic spell, continually changing optical phenomena will occur, including movement, wavy moiré patterns, and perhaps even the appearance of brilliant colors. Try focusing and unfocusing your eyes, shifting the ways you look at it, to see how many different effects you can experience.

AUGUSTE RODIN
on THE ILLUSION OF MOVEMENT

The sculptor Auguste Rodin (1840–1917) worked intently with naturally moving living models, creating vigorously realistic sculpture that flew in the face of prevailing French academic traditions. His marvelous *Monument to Balzac* (**2.147**), though commissioned by the Society of Men of Letters, was rejected by the Society because it did not coincide with their ideas of what a portrait should look like. Yet his genius in coaxing apparent life into cast metal and sculpted marble is now highly celebrated. The following are excerpts from conversations with his friend Paul Gsell, on the illusion of movement in sculpture:

"I have always sought to give some indication of movement. I have very rarely represented complete repose. I have always endeavored to express the inner feelings by the mobility of the muscles.

Art cannot exist without life. If a sculptor wishes to interpret joy, sorrow, any passion whatsoever, he will not be able to move us unless he first knows how to make the beings live which he evokes. For how could the joy or the sorrow of an inert object—of a block of stone—affect us? Now, the illusion of life is obtained in our art by good modeling and by movement. These two qualities are like the blood and the breath of all good work."

"Note, first, that *movement is the transition from one attitude to another*. . . . You remember how in Dante's Inferno a serpent, coiling itself about the body of one of the damned, changes into man as the man becomes reptile. The great poet describes this scene so ingeniously that in each of these two beings one follows the struggle between two natures which progressively invade and supplant each other.

It is, in short, a metamorphosis of this kind that the painter or the sculptor effects in giving movement to his personages. He represents the transition from one pose to another—he indicates how insensibly the first glides into the second. In his work we still see a part of what was and we discover a part of what is to be.

The sculptor compels, so to speak, the spectator to follow the development of an act in an individual. . . . Have you ever attentively examined instantaneous photographs of walking figures? What did you notice? If, in instantaneous photographs, the figures, though taken while moving, seem suddenly fixed in mid-air, it is because, all parts of the body being reproduced exactly at the same twentieth or fortieth of a second, there is no progressive development of movement as there is in art.

It is the artist who is truthful and it is photography which lies, for in reality time does not stop, and if the artist succeeds in producing the impression of a movement which takes several moments for accomplishment, his work is certainly much less conventional than the scientific image, where time is abruptly suspended."

"Note besides that painters and sculptors, when they unite different phases of an action in the same figure, do not act from reason or from artifice. They are naively expressing what they feel. Their minds and their hands are as if drawn in the direction of the movement, and they translate the development by instinct. Here, as everywhere in the domain of art, sincerity is the only rule."[23]

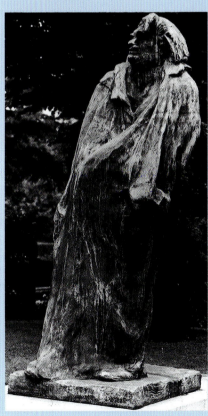

2.147 Auguste Rodin, *Monument to Balzac*, 1897. Bronze, 8 ft 10¼ ins × 3 ft 11½ ins × 4 ft 2½ ins (2.7 × 1.2 × 1.3 m). Musée Rodin, Paris.

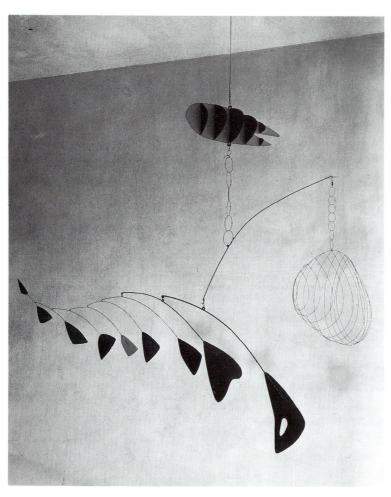

2.148 Alexander Calder, *Lobster Trap and Fish Tail*, 1939. Hanging mobile, painted steel wire and sheet aluminum, about 8 ft 6 ins high × 9 ft 6 ins diameter (2.6 × 2.9 m). Collection Museum of Modern Art, New York. Commissioned by the Advisory Committee for the stairwell of the Museum. Photograph © 1997 MOMA.

Actual Movement

Rather than requiring movement on the part of the viewer, some three-dimensional works move through space in time themselves. They are often called **kinetic sculpture**. Famous examples are the **mobiles** of Alexander Calder—constructions suspended by a system of wires so that their parts circle around the central point when pushed or moved by air currents. This aspect of the movement of a mobile such as *Lobster Trap and Fish Tail* (**2.148**) is partly predictable, but the ways in which the individually suspended parts turn around each other and on their own axes are unpredictable. Spatial relationships among the shapes will change continually, as long as the mobile is in motion.

The term kinetic sculpture is now also applied to works made of lights that flash on and off, so that they seem to be alive in time. Contemporary kinetic sculpture may be computer-animated at a high level of technical perfection. But perhaps because we have become so accustomed to the sophistication of computer-driven devices, we may find the bizarre revealed mechanics of Jean Tinguely's *Meta-Matic No. 9* (**2.149**) all the more whimsically appealing. The motor-driven arms of Tinguely's absurd machine clamor like a kitchen appliance as they create a series of scribbles on a small picture ground with colored pens. The product of this playful rattling busyness is a random drawing whose expressionistic quality is reflected in the form of the machine itself.

Where water is plentiful, as it is in Rome, it is sometimes used with great abandon. An entire river was diverted to feed the Water Organ of the Villa d'Este (**2.150**), a dynamic enviromental sculpture in which water is the medium. The intriguing effects of water in a fountain are organic and serendipitous, as pumps shoot jets into the air and then gravity draws the water back to earth, with wind tossing the spray. As the water falls onto rocks, it is churned and scattered again, continuously changing in form.

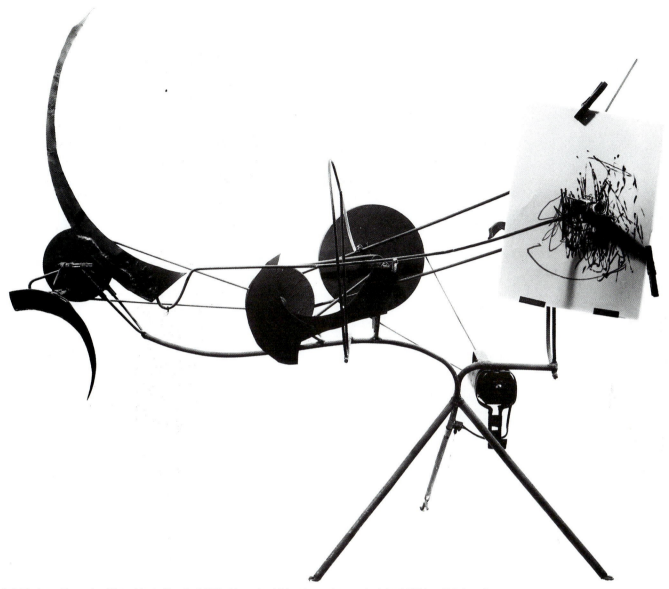

2.149 Jean Tinguely, *Meta-Matic No. 9*, 1959. Motorized kinetic sculpture, height 35½ ins (90.1 cm). Museum of Fine Arts, Houston, Texas. Purchased from funds by Dominique and John de Mevil.

Illusion of Movement

In two-dimensional works, movement obviously cannot happen in real time. It can only be suggested. How to do so was an intellectual and artistic challenge to the French artist Marcel Duchamp. He chose the device of showing a single figure in a sequence of motions, rather like stop-action photographs, for his famous and controversial *Nude Descending a Staircase* (**2.151**). Some scientists today feel that this is actually the way time moves: by little jerks, a series of barely different frames, rather than a continuously changing flow. So far we have no way of knowing which model of time is true. But when Duchamp painted *Nude Descending*, the European artists who called themselves

"Futurists" were insisting that modern art should reflect modern life, which is fast, fragmented, and in constant change. In their *Futurist Manifesto* of 1910, they asserted:

> The gesture which we would reproduce on canvas shall no longer be a fixed *moment* in universal dynamism. It shall simply be the *dynamic sensation* itself. Indeed, all things move, all things run, all things are rapidly changing. A profile is never motionless before our eyes, but it constantly appears and disappears. On account of the persistency of an image upon the retina, moving objects constantly multiply themselves; their form changes like rapid vibrations, in their mad career. Thus a running horse has not four legs, but twenty, and their movements are triangular.[24]

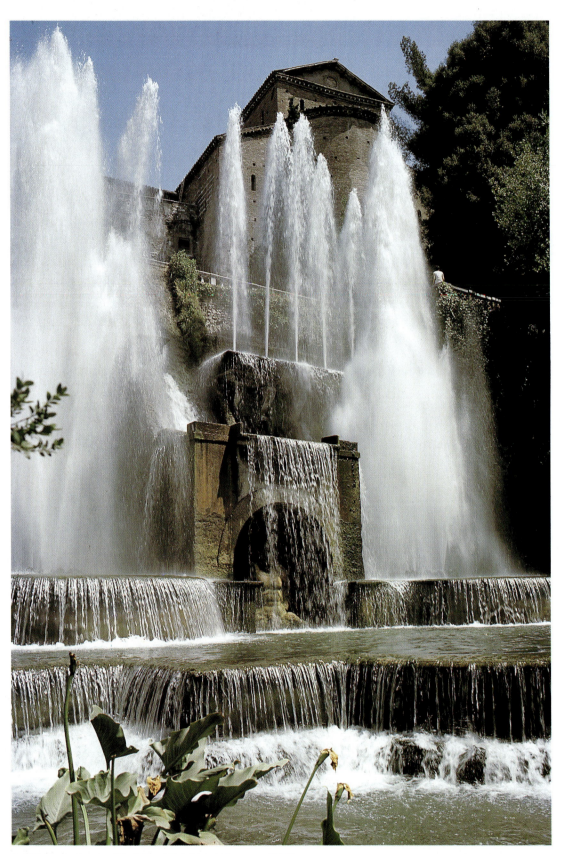

2.150 Water Organ, Villa d'Este, Tivoli, near Rome, c. 1550.

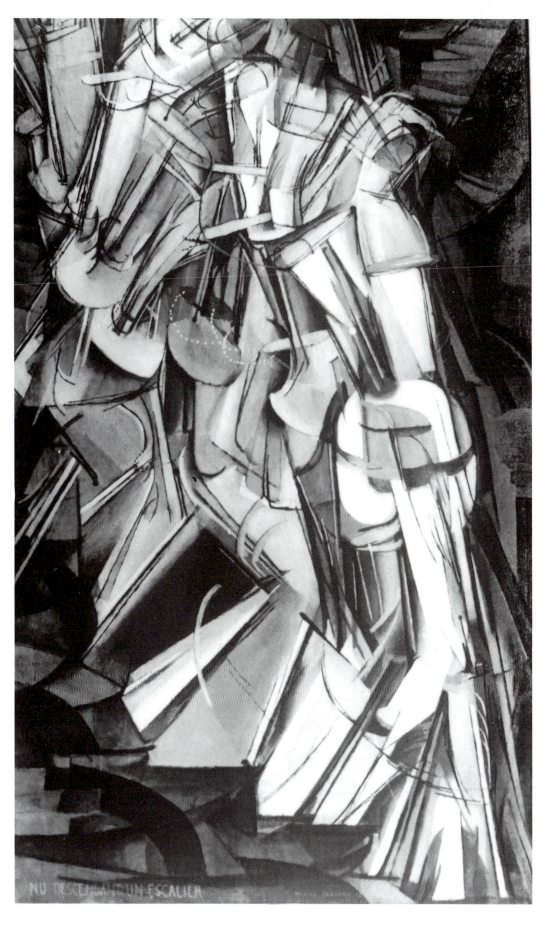

2.151 Marcel Duchamp, *Nude Descending a Staircase # 2*, 1912. Oil on canvas, 58 × 35 ins (147 × 89 cm). Philadelphia Museum of Art. Louise and Walter Arensberg Collection.

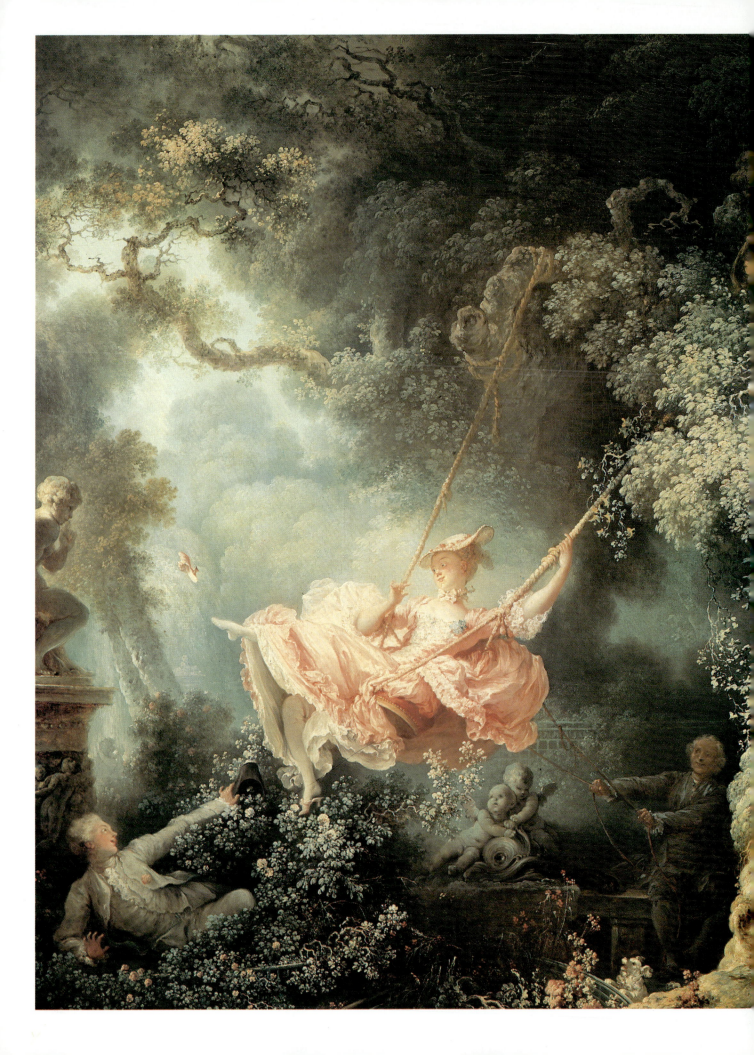

The Captured Moment

Although it is difficult to represent the passage of time in a single two-dimensional image, some images clearly refer to motion by capturing a moment of it in time. In Fragonard's *The Swing* (**2.152**), we see a young woman being swung by an obliging but naive old cleric at the behest of her hidden admirer, whose gaze she teasingly acknowledges by kicking off her shoe toward him. The sensuous swirling of her clothes, the dynamic positions of her limbs, and the curve of the ropes create a great sense of continuing motion in a fleeting, erotic moment.

With the invention of photography, some artists began selecting and framing their views of life as if seen through the lens of a camera. As we saw in discussing point of view, Degas did so to bring us into the intimacy of the ballet theatre (2.66). Considerably influenced by Degas, Toulouse-Lautrec used a photographic cropped effect to create a sense of motion in his *Equestrienne (At the Circus Fernando)* (**2.153**). This is what we could see if we were in the ring to the ringmaster's right, watching the horse almost from behind as it galloped around. We could not see much above the dancer's head without raising our glance, so the top of a clown standing on a stool is out of our sight, as is the left side of the clown to the left. Toulouse-Lautrec makes it clear that we are following the horse visually through time, of which only one moment is shown, and he gives the horse a large open area into which to move, increasing the impression of its movement.

In the early days of action photography, cameras were capable of capturing moving forms at speeds of up to 1/2500 of a second (in the case of the single-lens camera brought out in 1899 by Guido Sigriste). But they used a **focal plane shutter**, which was a curtain with a slit that travels across in front of the film to expose it. If the subject is moving rapidly or the

2.152 (opposite) Jean-Honoré Fragonard, *The Swing*, 1766. Oil on canvas, 32 × 35 ins (81.3 × 89 cm). The Wallace Collection, London.

2.153 (below) Henri de Toulouse-Lautrec, *Equestrienne (At the Circus Fernando)*, 1887-88. Oil on canvas, 3 ft 3⅜ ins × 5 ft 3⅜ ins (1 × 1.61 m). Art Institute of Chicago, Chicago, Illinois. Joseph Winterbotham Collection, 1925, no. 523.

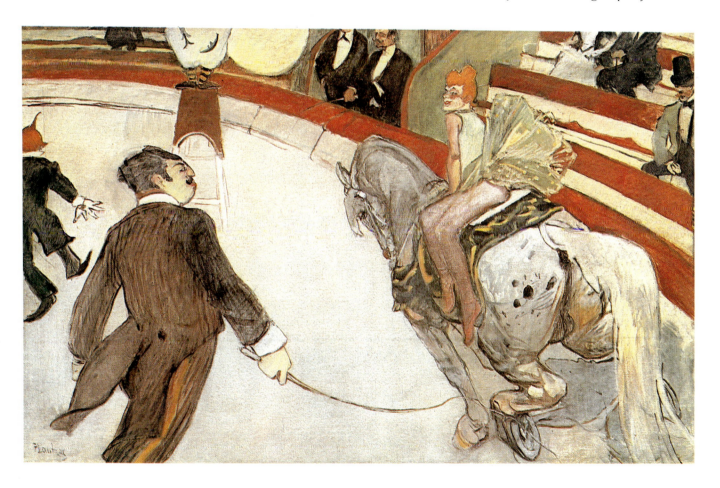

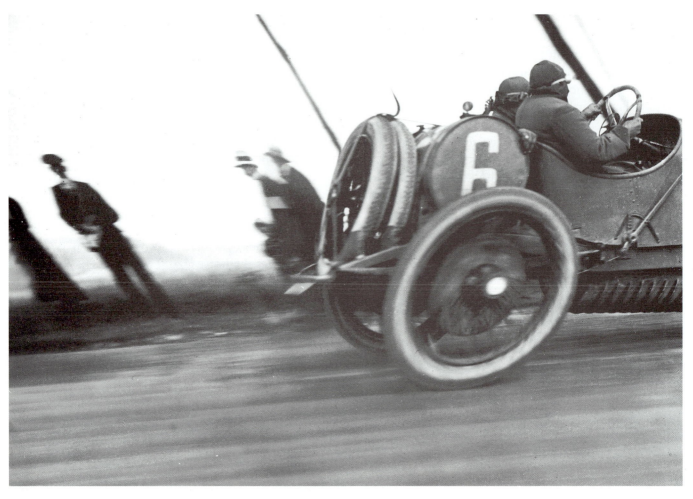

2.154 Jacques Henri Lartigue, *Grand Prix of the Automobile Club of France*, 1912. Photograph.

camera is being turned to follow the action, the image will be distorted in ways that give the impression of great speed, as in Lartigue's photograph of the Grand Prix (**2.154**). Unlike the Fragonard (2.152) and the Toulouse-Lautrec (2.153), this image does not show the area ahead of the action. This truncated space visually increases the sense of speed: the automobile is moving so fast that it has almost disappeared before the moment could be captured on film.

Not all captured moments deal with movement. Some references to moving time center on the ephemeral and precious nature of the present moment, which will never recur in exactly the same way. Juan Gonzales's exquisite pencil drawing *Sara's Garden* (**2.155**) shows us a fleeting glimpse of tiny dewdrops along fragile spider threads seemingly strung like cables to hold up lilies whose blossoms are at their peak. The work is executed so realistically that we can sense the fragility of the moment, fully expecting that

the slightest wind will break the gossamer threads, and the lilies will wither and die in the natural cycle of life. But here, captured, is the beauty of the moment.

Time as the Subject

Yet another way in which artists work with time is to make it the central subject of their piece. In uncertain times, such as the Hundred Years' War in France, artworks that addressed the orderly, predictable passage of time had a special significance. During that war, the three Limbourg brothers created for the Duke of Berry a remarkable Book of Hours—a private devotional book giving the Catholic prayers for each part of the day, from Matins to Compline, plus other liturgical

2.155 (opposite) Juan Gonzales, *Sara's Garden*, 1977. Graphite on paper, 22 × 18 ins (56 × 46 cm). Nancy Hoffman Gallery, New York.

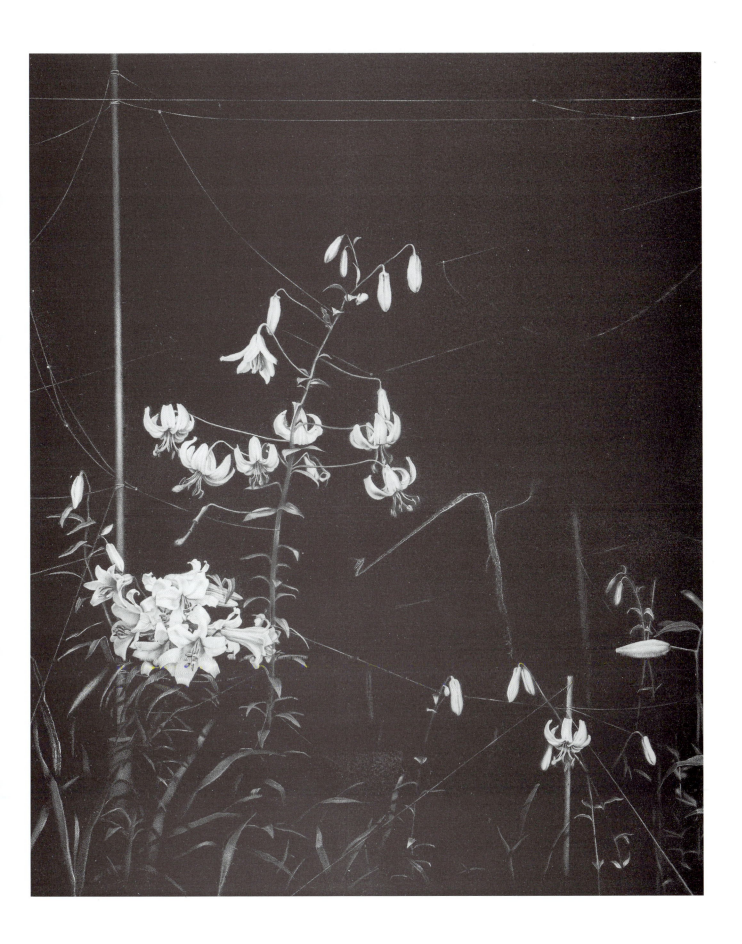

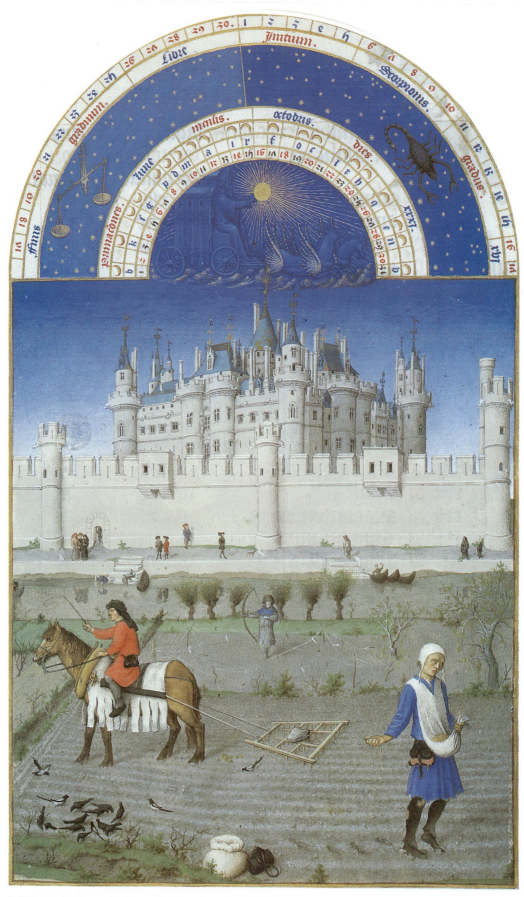

2.156 The Limbourg Brothers, *October*, from *Les Très Riches Heures du Duc de Berry*, 1413–16. Illuminated manuscript, 8½ × 5½ ins (21.6 × 14 cm). Musée Condé, Chantilly, France.

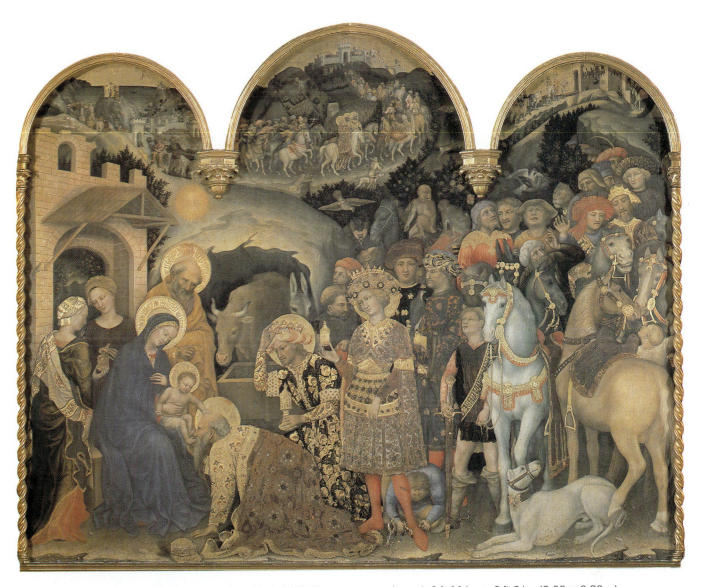

2.157 Gentile da Fabriano, *The Adoration of the Magi*, 1423. Tempera on wood panel, 9 ft 11 ins × 9 ft 3 ins (3.02 × 2.82 m). Galleria degli Uffizi, Florence.

duties and calendars for local feast days. Each month had a detailed miniature painting of what the peasants or aristocracy should be doing during the month. For October, shown here (**2.156**), the peasants are planting winter wheat. Above the scene are notations and symbols of the zodiac signs for the month—with images of Libra and Scorpio—and the reassurance that the chariot of the sun will be making its yearly rounds.

In addition to our desire for life's certainties, as time inevitably brings changes, we also like to be told stories about events happening *through* time. Works that tell a story using pictures rather than words are often called **narrative** works. Many were used to teach the illiterate the traditions of church or state; some are simply to entertain, such as Fragonard's *The Swing* (2.152).

While these paintings summarize a whole story in one image, others show progressive frames of action occurring through time, rather like a cartoon strip. In Gentile da Fabriano's *The Adoration of the Magi* (**2.157**) we see small scenes depicting the trip of the Magi to Bethlehem, culminating in the crowd spilling into the canvas for the moment in which the Three Kings actually kneel in adoration before the Christ child.

Time is such a subtle element in art that its manifestation may escape the notice or understanding of untrained viewers. Jackson Pollock's drip paintings (1.42) were subject to public scorn throughout his life, but he was deliberately working to avoid references to chronological time, as well as to objects. Time was actually one of his central subjects, but his emphasis was on the present moment, the immediate,

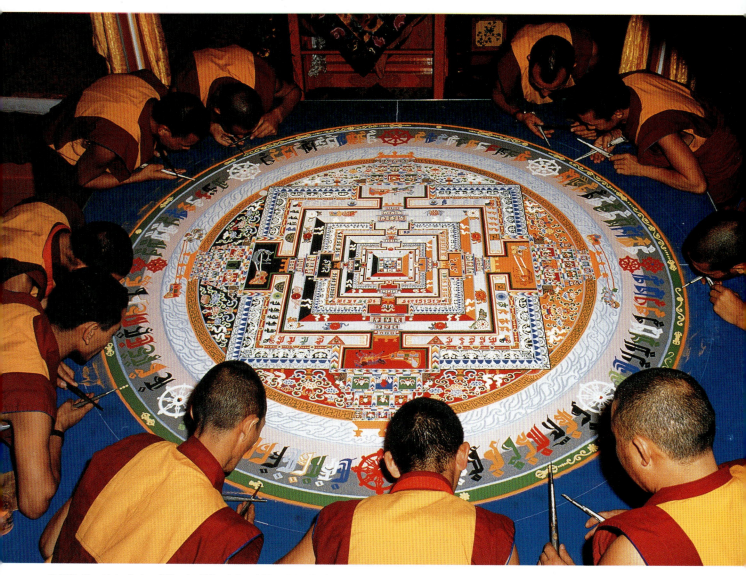

2.158 The Kalachakra (Wheel of Time) Sand Mandala. Grains of colored sand, constructed during a twelve-day ritual by monks from the Dalai Lama's Namgyal Monastery, Tibet.

spontaneous, and visible gesture of laying down the lines. He noted that "a reviewer wrote that my pictures didn't have any beginning or any end. He didn't mean it as a compliment, but it was."[25]

Ephemeral Time

Because most works of art involve lengthy time and/or investment, special care is often taken to make them as permanent as possible. In Chapter 15 we will look at extreme measures that have been employed in the attempt to prolong the lives of famous works of art. On the other hand, some sacred art is created as an act of worship and is then worshipfully abandoned.

Tibetan monks invoke the power of the deities by creating extremely elaborate mandalas—symmetric designs radiating from a center—of colored sands (**2.158**). It takes a group of monks a week or more of intense work to make the highly fragile design. Then, when the mandala is completed, the sands are regathered and poured into a river, with prayers for the healing of the water creatures.

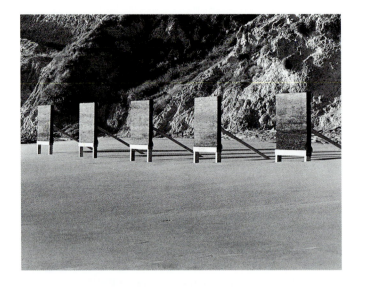

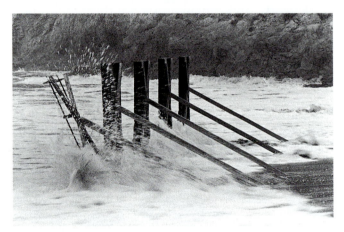

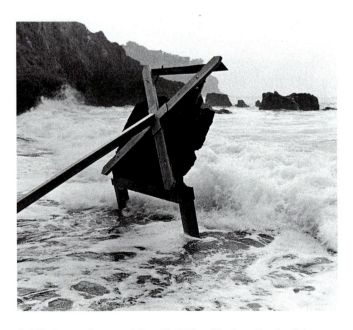

Change Through Time

All works of art themselves change through time. Usually they deteriorate gradually, some so slowly that the change is barely noticeable. But some are purposely fragile, so that witnessing their decay is part of the art experience itself. **Conceptual art** deals with ideas and immediate experience rather than with permanent form. Even clay, one of the most durable of media, can be handled conceptually as a temporary experience that changes through time, if the clay is not fired to hardness. George Geyer and Tom McMillin's installation, *"Surface Erosion," Laguna Beach* (**2.159**), was set up quickly when the tide was out and then inexorably destroyed by waves as the tide returned. To be touched by this work, one would have to stand close by, watching its disintegration until the forces of nature had again cleared the area of human efforts.

2.159 George Geyer and Tom McMillin, *"Surface Erosion," Laguna Beach*, California. Clay, wood, steel, water, and sand.

3
ORGANIZING PRINCIPLES OF DESIGN

The visual elements examined in Chapter 2 are manipulated by artists to form compositions that have a certain coherence, or **unity**. If these elements work well, they contribute to a whole that is greater than the sum of the parts. In trying to determine what holds an effective work together, theorists have distinguished a number of principles that seem to be involved. They include repetition, variety or contrast, rhythm, balance, compositional unity, emphasis,

economy, and proportion. Another subtle principle that artists use is the relationship of a work to its environment.

Not all of these principles are emphasized in a single work. And certain artists use them more intuitively than intellectually, using nonlinear thinking while sketching, planning, and manipulating design elements—until everything feels right. Nevertheless, the principles give us a basis for understanding the form of certain compositions. Often these formal considerations help to express the content of the work and can best be understood when the content as well as the form is taken into account.

3.1 Nathalie du Pasquier, Fabric, 1985. Silk. Manufactured by Memphis/Tino Cosmo, Italy.

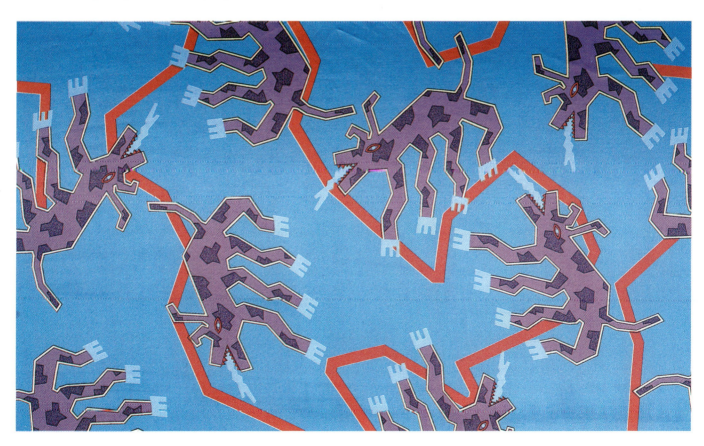

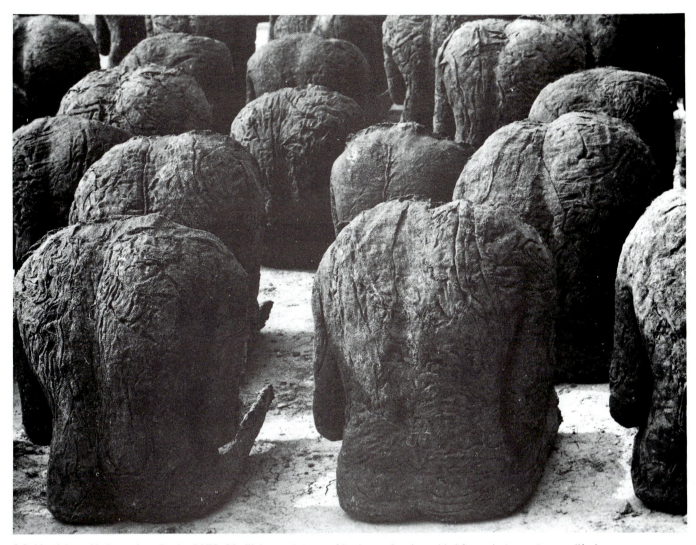

3.2 Magdalena Abakanowicz, *Backs*, 1978–81. Eighty sculptures of burlap and resin molded from plaster casts, over lifesize.

REPETITION

One of the basic ways that artists have unified their designs is to repeat a single design element, be it a kind of line, shape, form, texture, value, or color. As the viewer's eye travels from one part to another, it sees the similarities, and the brain, preferring order to chaos, readily groups them as like objects. Nathalie du Pasquier of the Milan-based Memphis design group presents imaginary animals as cut-out shapes tumbling across her fabric design (3.1). The turning of the same unique shape to many different positions makes the design lively and interesting, while its repetition holds the design together in the viewer's perception.

In three-dimensional work, repetition of a single design element can have a powerful effect. *Backs* (3.2), by Polish sculptor Magdalena Abakanowicz, has a disturbing emotional impact on viewers, not only because of the headless, limbless quality of the hunched-over, hollowed-out torsos, but also because there are so many of them. The artist explained: "I needed 80 to make my statement. At first I made six, but then I saw I must have 80 of them—to show a crowd, a tribe, or a herd, like animals."[1] She leaves their interpretation to viewers, preferring universal to specific references, but they clearly reflect human oppression, as experienced by one who grew up in a war-ravaged, enemy-occupied country.

The repeated figures in Abakanowicz's *Backs* and

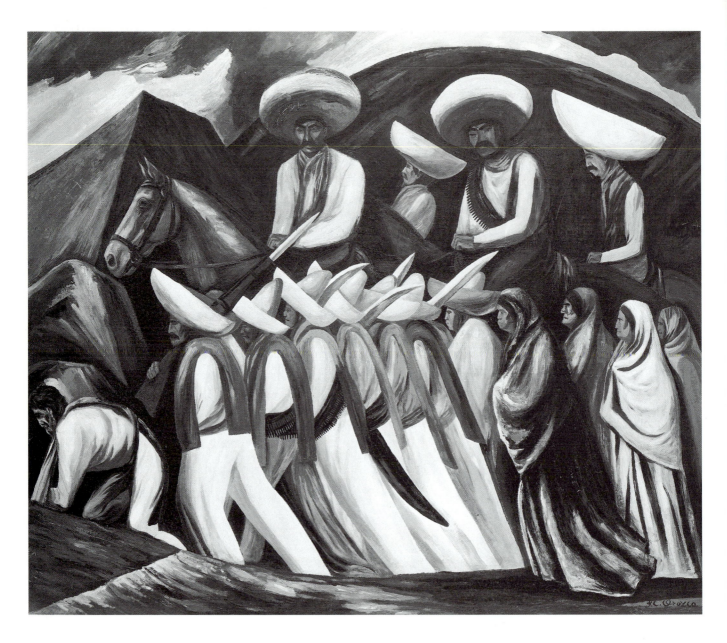

3.3 José Clemente Orozco, *Zapatistas*, 1931.
Oil on canvas, 45 × 55 ins (114.3 × 139.7 cm). Collection
Museum of Modern Art, New York. Anonymous donation.

3.4 (right) Repeated figures in *Zapatistas*.

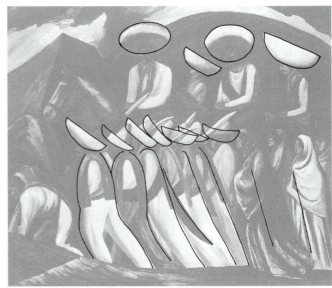

du Pasquier's fabric seem to stand alone, despite their
similarity. By contrast, in José Clemente Orozco's
Zapatistas (**3.3**), the similar figures in the peasant army
merge into a unified whole. As shown in the diagram
(**3.4**), our eye picks out the diagonals of the standing
figures and their hats as beats in a single flowing movement to the left, with bayonets as counterthrusts
pointing to the drum-like repeated beats of the large
hats above. We can see that even if one revolutionary
falls, the mass of the others still moves inexorably
forward.

3.5 Pablo Picasso, *Guernica* (detail), 1937. Oil on canvas, 11 ft 5½ ins × 25 ft 5¼ ins (3.49 × 7.75 m). Reina Sofia Museum of Modern Art, Madrid.

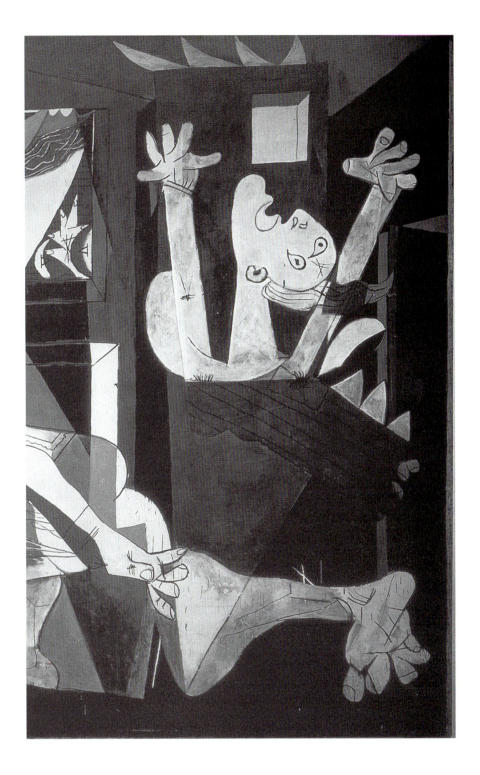

Many paintings use repetitions of some design quality to unify complex compositions. If you page through the illustrations in this book, you will find numerous examples—some obvious, some quite subtle. Jackson Pollock's drip paintings (1.42) have no unifying element except for the repetition of freely gestured lines of dripped and flung paint, but these in themselves create an all-over compositional effect. Picasso's *Guernica* (1.47) is unified partly by repetition of pointed shapes, such as flames and fingers of the figure on the far right (detail shown in **3.5**). Throughout the painting, sharp-pointed shapes appear again and again, not only for unity of design but also to create a sense of danger and fragmentation.

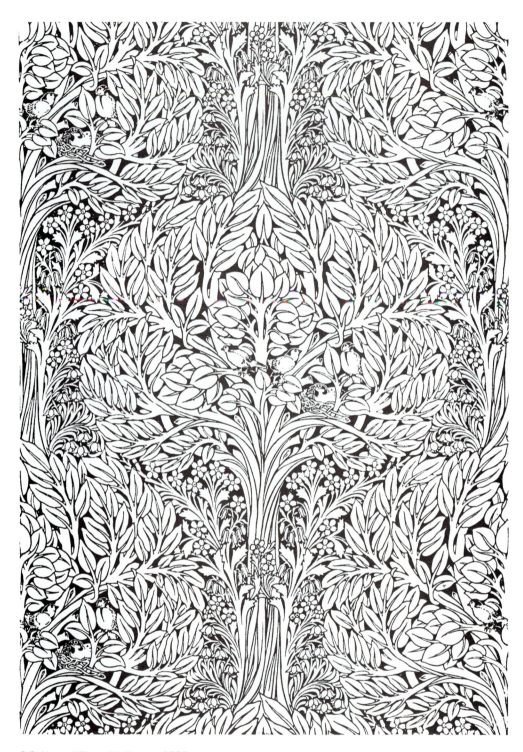

3.6 Henry Wilson, Wallpaper, 1898.

In purely decorative works, such as fabric and wallpaper designs, repetition of design elements is often used to build up an all-over **pattern**, a series of images that is repeated in an orderly way. When a whole wall is papered in Henry Wilson's wallpaper (**3.6**), one sees a pattern of interlocking stylized trees with flowers both separating and unifying them.

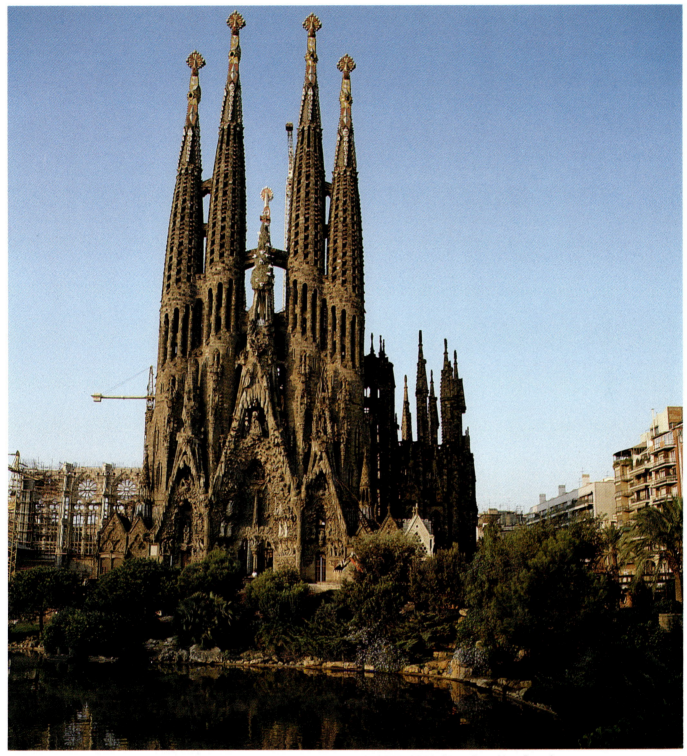

3.7 Antonio Gaudí, Church of the Holy Family (*Sagrada Familia*), Barcelona, 1883–1926. Photo from Mas, Barcelona.

VARIETY

The companion of repetition is **variety**: change rather than sameness through space and time. Variety often takes the form of subtle variations on the same theme: Du Pasquier's animals (3.1) vary in position and each of Abakanowicz's backs is slightly different (3.2). Antonio Gaudí's uncompleted church of the *Sagrada Familia* in Barcelona (3.7) is a fantastic conglomeration of many architectural styles. Yet it is held together visually by its spires, which vary in form but resemble each other in their tapering upward reach.

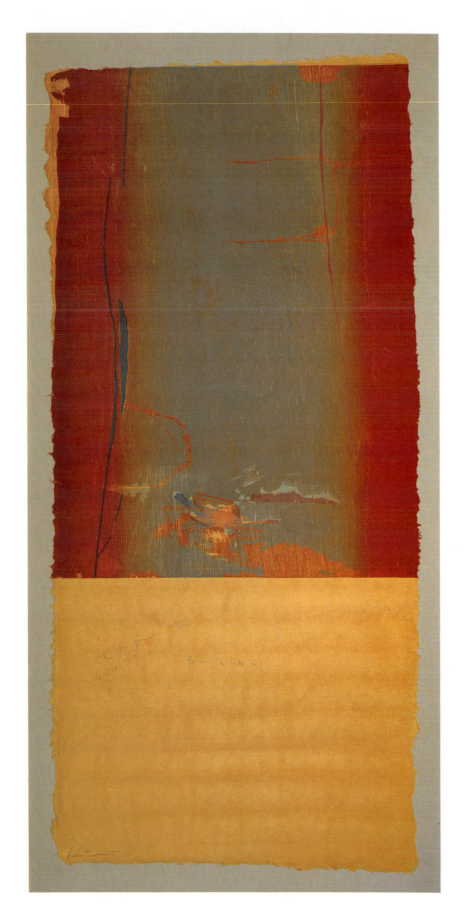

3.8 Helen Frankenthaler, *Essence Mulberry*, 1977. Woodcut, edition of 46, 40 × 18½ ins (101.6 × 46.9 cm).

Another way in which variety is expressed is through **transitions**, or gradual changes from one state to another. For example, one color may gradually blend into another, a line may change in character, or a form may dissolve into unfilled space. Helen Frankenthaler's woodcut *Essence Mulberry* (**3.8**) presents a beautiful transition from mulberry to a gray that echoes the gray of the ground. She also works with variety in the form of **contrast**—an abrupt change. Here the gradual vertical color change of the upper portion is played against the sudden horizontal of gold on the bottom. Frankenthaler is also working with contrasts in scale and shape, between the hard-edged geometry of the large golden rectangle and the soft-edged amorphous shapes above.

Contrast is often used to enhance our appreciation of both things being compared. The gold and the mulberry hues are so different that each brings out the other's richness by contrast. In a Balega mask (**3.9**) the rough, random fibers of the beard accentuate the smooth, fast lines of the head. The church of Taivallahti in Helsinki (**3.10**), excavated from rock as an underground space, calls us to appreciate both the organic roughness of the stone and the elegant refinement of the organ pipes, the earthiness of the walls and the light of the sky brought in beneath the great copper dome. Through a continuing series of contrasts, the stone church wakes up our perceptions and sharpens our awareness of each visual sensation.

Although it might seem logical that highly contrasting passages in a work would disorganize it, detracting from its unity, often the opposite is true. The roughness of the Balega mask beard keeps referring us to the smoothness of the face, tying the two together visually like an egg in a nest. In any work that makes us look from one passage to another and back, it is that act of comparing on the part of the viewer that is the unifying factor. Even if parts seem diametrically opposed to each other, they can be unified in the viewer's mind as two ends of the same continuum. Opposites have a certain unity, complementing each other like black and white, night and day, masculine and feminine.

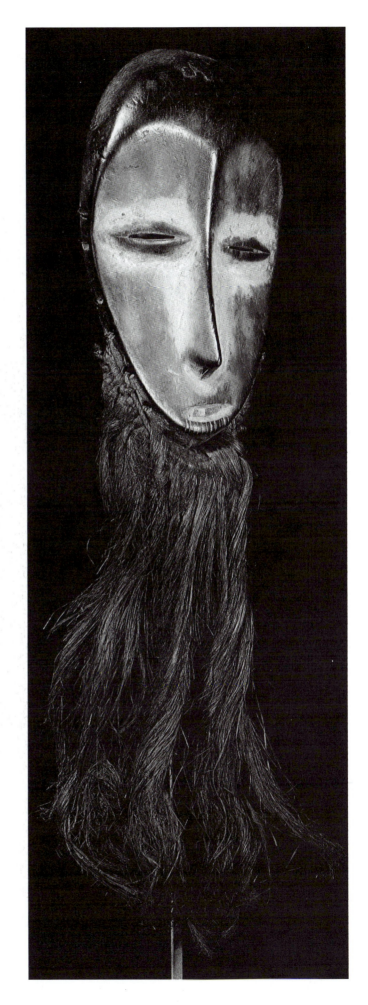

3.9 Balega mask, Africa. Wood with pigment and fiber, height 8 ins (20.3 cm). Private collection.

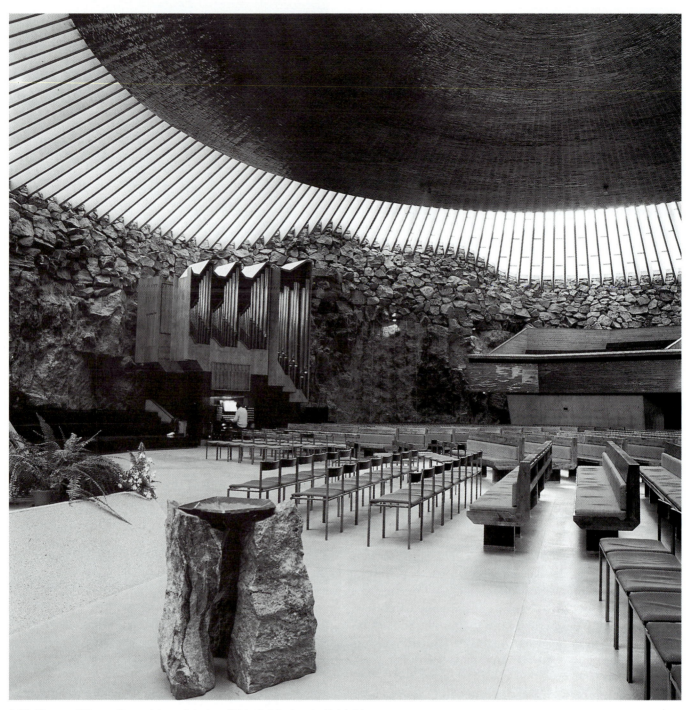

3.10 Timo and Tuomo Suomalainen, interior of Taivallahti church, Helsinki.

Artists may also use contrast to create a certain visual tension that adds excitement to a work. There is a fine point up to which things can fight with or pull away from each other as far as they possibly can but still without destroying the unity of the composition. Tintoretto seems to have found this point in his *Leda and the Swan* (**3.11**). As diagrammed in Figure **3.12**,

Leda and the observer form strong arcs actively pulling away from each other and twisting through space, accentuating Leda's movement toward her lover, Zeus, who has appeared in the form of a swan. Tintoretto worked out his compositions by posing small wax figures in boxes, as if on a stage. He then translated the three-dimensional scene to two dimensions by

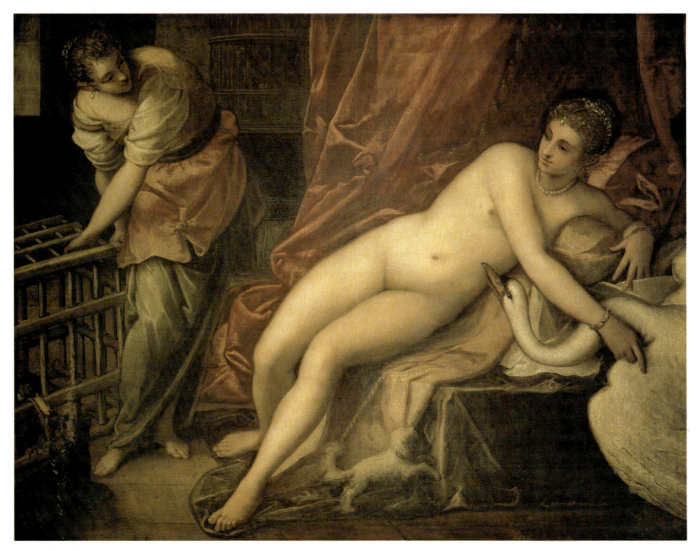

3.11 Jacopo Tintoretto, *Leda and the Swan*, c. 1570–75. Oil on canvas, 5 ft 3¾ ins × 7 ft 1¾ ins (1.62 × 2.18 m). Galleria degli Uffizi, Florence.

3.12 Compositional arcs in *Leda and the Swan*.

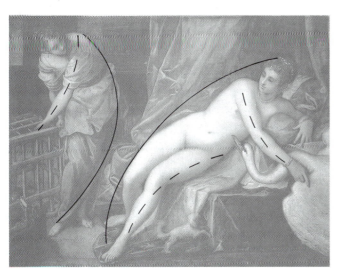

drawing the figures on a grid placed across the stage and then enlarging them from this grid to the scale of the painting. Not only has he depicted the figures pulling away from each other; each of the bodies is also twisted in a flowing serpentine movement called *serpentinata* in Italian, an exaggeration of the figure-posing used in High Renaissance art. First developed by Classical Greek sculptors, the technique involves twisting areas of the body in counterpoised opposition to each other. The twisting movement adds to the dramatic effect. Tintoretto was one of the so-called Mannerist painters, who exaggerated gestures for their theatrical impact.

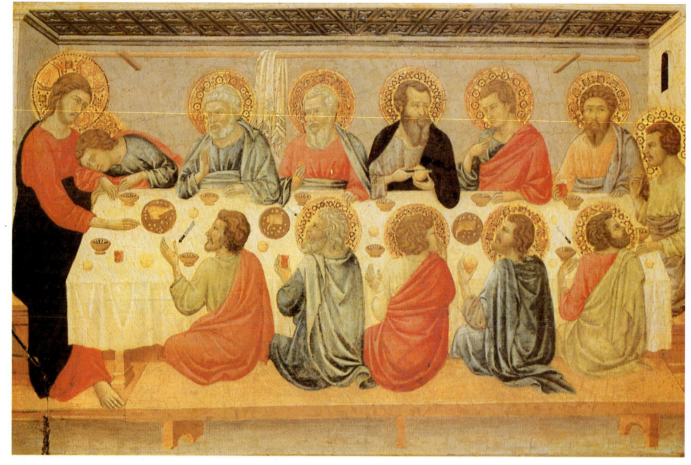

3.13 Ugolino di Nerio, *Last Supper*, c. 1322. Tempera and gold on wood, 13½ × 20¼ ins (34.3 × 51.4 cm). Metropolitan Museum of Art, New York. Robert Lehmann Collection, 1975.

RHYTHM

A third organizing principle found in many works is **rhythm**. Repetition and variety in design elements create patterns that are analogous to rhythms in music, from the predictable drumbeats of a marching band to the swirling rhythms of romantic symphonies to the offbeat intricacies of jazz timing. The same element— such as a line, form, or color—may be repeated visually through space, or groupings may be repeated so that the eye picks out recurring patterns, such as small-large-medium, small-large-medium. Such patterns, which may be easily perceived or complex and subtle, create repeated visual accents with spaces between them, like upbeats and downbeats, or waves and troughs.

Rhythm in a work satisfies the desire for order, for it brings a familiar sense of the pulsing of life. In the *Last Supper* altarpiece by the medieval artist Ugolino di Nerio (**3.13**), the rhythm formed by the repetition of the circles of the haloed heads of the disciples is as

regular as heartbeats. This easily perceived regularity is broken by the wider space separating Christ from the others, the grieving position of John the beloved, and the absence of a halo around the head of Judas. These dramatic elements are like crossbeats to the rhythms of the rest of the painting, another being produced by the alternating placement of reds.

Rhythms may flow continuously through time, without the measured pauses seen in Ugolino's *Last Supper*. In the Thonet rocking chair examined in the last chapter (2.16), the lines flow rhythmically through long curves, never stopping fully except at the delicate ends of the "tendrils." For the most part, the only changes we "hear" in the visual music of the chair are shifts in volume and speed, with slight crescendos through the center of the curves and slowing decrescendos as the lines change direction.

Painter Emily Carr sought to express the under-lying unity she experienced in nature, and she felt it as a "unity of movement." Citing van Gogh's paintings (1.21) as an inspiration in her discovery of this rhythmic unity, Carr explained:

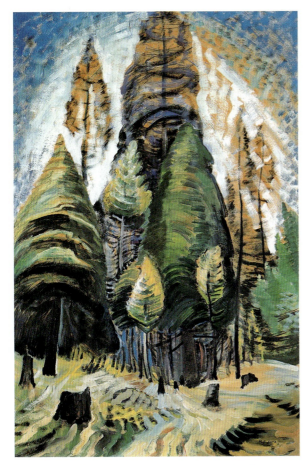

3.14 Emily Carr, *British Columbia Landscape*, c. 1934. Oil on wove paper, mounted on cardboard, 35¼ × 23¼ ins (90.2 X 60 cm). National Gallery of Canada. Gift of Douglas M. Duncan Collection.

I felt it in the woods but did not quite realize what I was feeling. Now it seems to me the first thing to seize on in your layout is the direction of your main movement, the sweep of the whole thing as a unit. One must be very careful about the transition of one curve of direction into the next, vary the length of the wave of space but keep it going, a pathway for the eye and the mind to travel through and into the thought. For long I have been trying to get these movements of the parts. Now I see there is only one movement. It sways and ripples. It may be slow or fast but it is only one movement sweeping out into space but always keeping going— rocks, sea, sky, one continuous movement.[2]

You can easily discern the rhythmic parts in Carr's *British Columbia Landscape* (**3.14**), but can you see this overall unity of movement to which she refers?

In freely stroked works, each line reflects the rhythm of the breath and movements of the artist. The Levha calligraphy by Sami Efendi (2.1) is created with single brush movements, precisely controlled for a free-flowing effect. The calligrapher cannot lift pen or brush before completing a stroke, for its subtly varying

width depends on the movement and angle of the writing implement. Traditional Chinese and Japanese painters were trained to use the whole arm to create brushstrokes. They practiced brush movements for years to develop the control and flexibility needed to create free-flowing lines that were also even and continuous. The wrist was used only in drawing very delicate lines.

The rhythm of certain works is like orchestral music, a complex interweaving of voices into a coherent progression in time. Remedios Varo's *Toward the Tower* (**3.15**) is full of dreamlike mysteries, but the artist holds these incongruous parts together visually like the music produced by an orchestra. The towers are like dull, booming bass notes, with the smaller rounded forms such as the nuns' heads and bicycle wheels as higher, faster counterpoints. With more nuns coming out of the towers and the birds inexplicably flying in and out of the peddler's pack, the music seems to be continuous, like a rondeau. Looking at it, one can almost beat out the timing of each of the parts and hear them fitting together into a symphony.

3.15 Remedios Varo, *Toward the Tower*, 1961. Photograph courtesy of Christie's, New York.

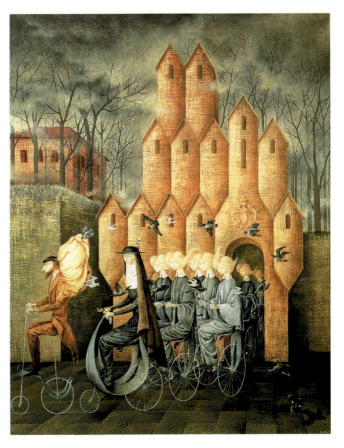

BALANCE

A fourth design principle is **balance**—the distribution of apparent visual weights so that they seem to offset one another. We subconsciously assign **visual weight** to parts of a work, and we tend to want the parts to be distributed through the work in such a way that they seem to balance each other. The sense of forms held in balance against the pull of gravity is psychologically pleasing; imbalances may give us an unsettled feeling, a reaction that is not usually the artist's desired effect.

The balancing of visual weights, read horizontally across a piece, is like a seesaw. As diagrammed in Figure 3.16, this kind of balancing of equal forces around a central point or axis is called **symmetrical** or **formal balance**. An example of absolutely symmetrical balance is the chest from the Haida culture of Queen

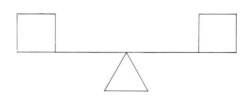

3.16 Symmetrical horizontal balance.

Charlotte Island off the northwest North American coast (**3.17**). If an imaginary vertical axis were drawn right through the center of the piece, the two halves of the central figure and the geometric animal motifs extending to the sides would be exact mirror images balancing each other. If a horizontal line were drawn through the center of the piece from left to right, the upper and lower halves would also consist of symmetrically balanced, though not identical, visual components.

3.17 Chest for clothes and jewelry of the Haida people of Queen Charlotte Island, off northwest coast of North America, 19th century. Wood inlaid with shells and animal tusks. British Museum, London.

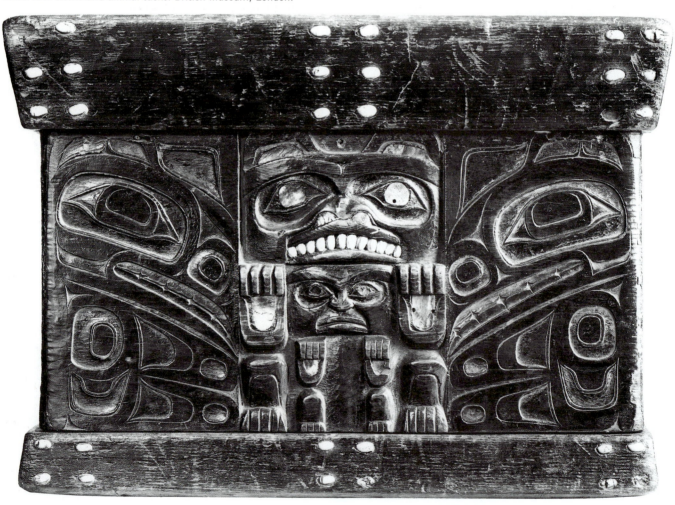

3.18 William Blake, *The Last Judgment*, 1808. Tempera, 19⅞ × 15¾ ins (50.3 × 40 cm). Petworth House, Sussex, England.

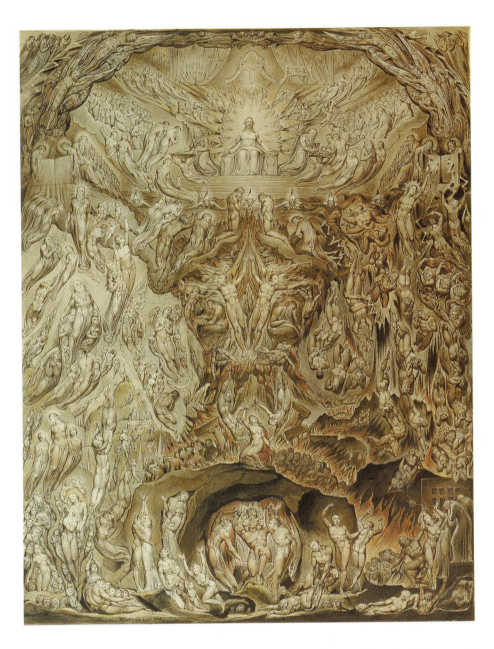

Symmetrical balance can occur even if images on each side of the vertical axis are not exactly the same. In Rodin's *Gates of Hell* (2.22), the symmetry of the panel frames gives it an underlying architectural structure, with a figure called "The Thinker" brooding in the middle of the vertical axis and "The Three Shades" arranged symmetrically to either side of the axis above him. The other writhing figures are not symmetrically balanced, yet the overall impression is one of symmetry. Compare this with William Blake's dramatic painting of *The Last Judgment* (3.18), where those who have erred are descending to the flames of hell on the right side, balanced by those blissfully ascending to the throne of God on the left side. The fact that the right side of the painting is darker than the left would unbalance the work. However, it is balanced by the symmetrical circular motion of the figures, as if radiating outward from the point between the two central beings blowing horns, and by the strong vertical axis created by the patterns of the figures rising through the center. The continuing movement of the figures reflects Blake's view that our fortunes are ever-shifting and that those who have sinned are not eternally damned.

Elements may also be symmetrically arranged around a central point in all directions, in which case the composition may be referred to as **radial balance**. In the Buddhist Wheel of Life (3.19), each circle

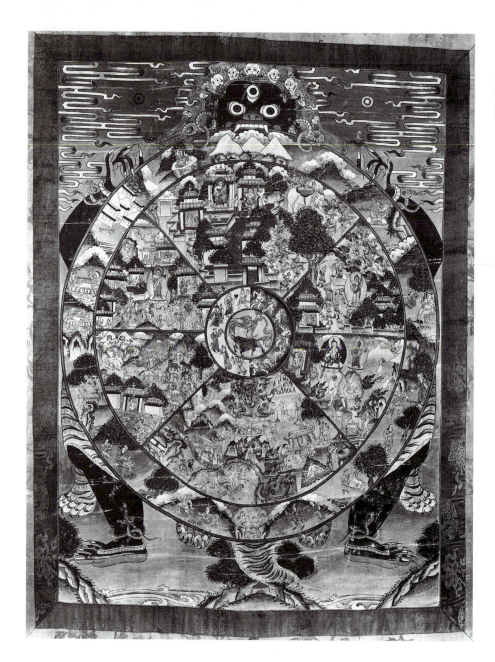

represents a different aspect of existence, with the whole wheel surrounded by the monster of death and impermanence. Note that even his parts are symmetrically arrayed around the center.

When the weights of dissimilar areas counterbalance each other, the result is called **asymmetrical** or **informal balance**. Expressed as a simple diagram

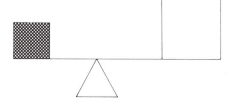

3.20 Asymmetrical horizontal balance.

(3.20), a large, light-colored area might be balanced by a small, dark-colored area, with the fulcrum off-center. Dark colors generally seem heavier than light ones, busily detailed areas heavier than unfilled ones, bright colors heavier than dull ones, large shapes heavier than small shapes, and objects far from the center heavier than those near the center.

Consider Thomas Gainsborough's *Mr. and Mrs. Andrews* (3.21). The painting is obviously asymmetrical, for both important figures are on the left side, with nothing but their lands to the right. The balancing point is established by the vertical thrust of the tree, well to the left of center. The pair carry considerable visual weight because they are visually interesting and detailed human figures, because they are looking

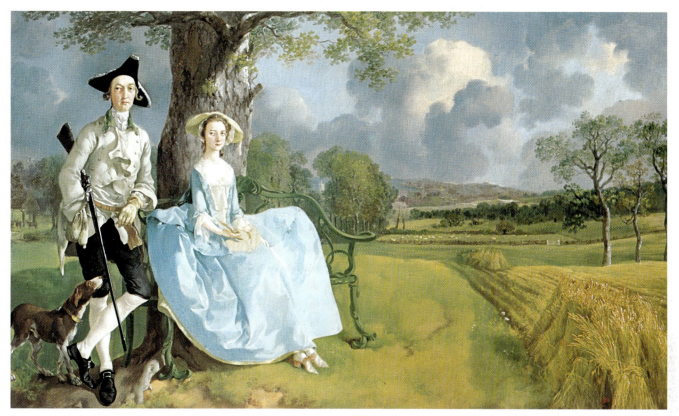

3.21 Thomas Gainsborough, *Mr. and Mrs. Andrews*, c. 1749. Oil on canvas, 27½ × 47 ins (69.8 × 119.4 cm). National Gallery, London.

at us and holding our attention, because they and the tree trunk are the largest and closest objects in the composition, and because their clothes are the brightest colors in the painting. The breadth of the fields to the right is not a wasted area in the composition, for Gainsborough needed a great expanse of less detailed space to balance his strong figures. Note that the fields recede into deep space. To a certain extent, Gainsborough is setting up a balance that extends into—as well as across—the picture plane. And those fields serve a purpose in the content as well as the form of the painting: they demonstrate the wealth of this couple, whose lands seem to stretch as far as the eye can see.

Sometimes artists violate the principle of balance intentionally to create tension in their works. Nancy Graves's *Trace* (**3.22**) is not visually "safe"; it appears to be extremely fragmented and precariously balanced, about to fall over in the direction in which the three slender "legs" are bent. Its three-point anchor in a heavy base actually makes the piece quite stable, but visually it seems to be dynamic and fragile. Contemporary aesthetics and materials allow an artist to push balance to limits never seen before.

3.22 Nancy Graves, *Trace*, 1979–80. Bronze, steel, patina, and paint, 8 ft 11 ins × 9 ft 8 ins × 4 ft 2 ins (2.71 × 2.92 × 1.27 m). Collection of Mr. and Mrs. Graham Gund, Boston, Massachusetts.

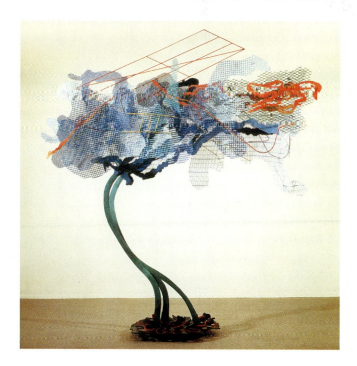

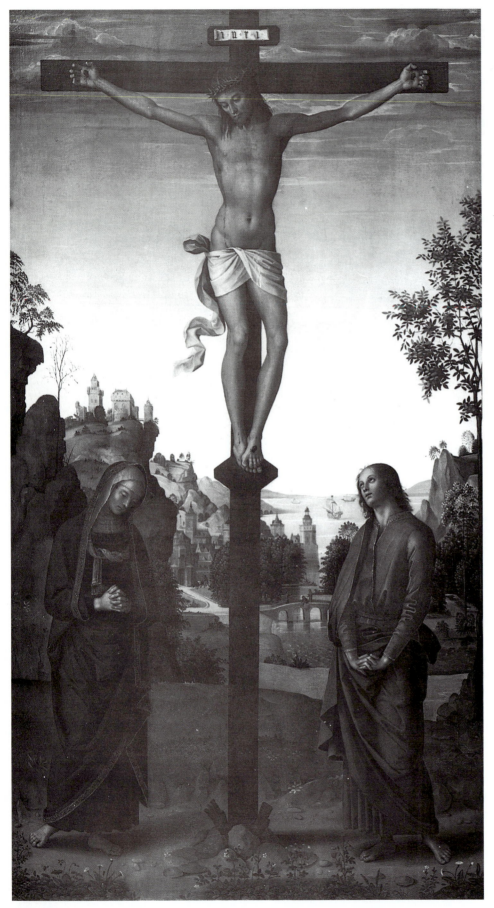

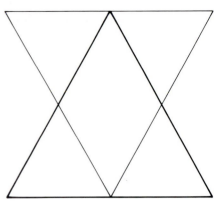

3.23 Double triangle composition.

3.25 Double triangle composition in *The Crucifixion with Saints*.

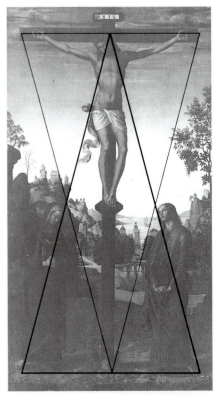

3.24 Pietro Vanucci, called Perugino, *The Crucifixion with Saints*, c. 1485. Oil, transferred from wood to canvas, middle panel 39⅞ × 22¼ ins (101.3 × 56.5 cm), side panels 37½ × 12 ins (95.2 × 30.5 cm). National Gallery of Art, Washington, D.C. Andrew W. Mellon Collection.

COMPOSITIONAL UNITY

Artists can also hold compositions together by creating strong attachments between elements within the work. They may physically touch each other, like the cut-out shapes forming Matisse's abstract *Snail* collage (2.41). They may be held together by the energy of opposition, like the magnetism of opposing arcs in Tintoretto's *Leda and the Swan* (3.11). Or the artist may have arranged the lines of the work—both actual and implied—in such a way that they lead the viewer's eye from one area to another, visually tying the work together.

A common formula for unifying compositional lines is the implied triangle. Standing on its base, a triangle is a highly stable shape. Christian sacred art has often used the solidity of a double triangle pattern, with a strong primary triangle counterbalanced and filled out by a weaker inverted secondary triangle, as in Figure **3.23**. The central panel of Perugino's *The Crucifixion with Saints* altarpiece (**3.24**) illustrates a complex series of these compositional triangles. As shown in Figure **3.25**, the major triangle is crowned by the head of Christ and bounded on its lower corners by the pointed feet of the mourners. A secondary inverted triangle is formed by the horizontal of the cross and implied lines joining it from the diagonal stakes pointing upwards at the base of the cross.

3.26 Implied triangles in *The Crucifixion with Saints*.

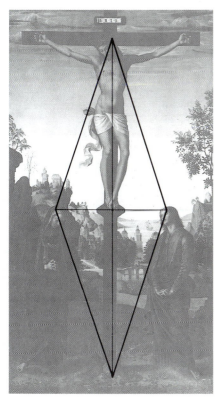

Another set of triangles is created by the eyelines among the figures, as diagrammed in Figure **3.26**. Jesus' head is inclined down toward Mary, whose downcast eyes lead us to a diagonal stake, which points us up to the face of John, whose gaze is directed up to Jesus' face. This circuit completes and reinitiates a diamond pattern that is divided into two triangles across the middle by the horizon. We can also read our way round and round each of these triangles. For instance, in the lower one, we read from Mary's gaze down to one stake, up through the other to John's head, and then across along the horizon back to Mary's face. Even the folds in the saints' robes contribute to the triangular patterns. Perugino carefully leads us through the composition, bringing us back again and again to the major figures and thus tying them together both in form and in emotional content. The balance and compositional unity of the work are entirely appropriate for an altarpiece forming the focal point of a symmetrically planned church. But it is not rigid. Notice, for instance, the off-center arrangement of the lake and hills in the background, placing John's head against water and sky and Mary's against rock. This interesting asymmetry is possible because the composition is so well unified by the triangular patterns in the foreground.

In two-dimensional works giving an impression of three-dimensional space, the order may attempt to unify the spatial planes of the composition. In Piero della Francesca's *Flagellation of Christ* (**3.27**) the artist has used very calculated means to unify three groups of figures at different angles in space. To the far left, in the middle ground, Pontius Pilate sits watching the whipping of Christ. Tied to a heroic Roman statue, Jesus is in the midst of the second group in the middle distance, slightly forward of Pilate. Three more unidentified but visually prominent figures are standing at the far right, in the extreme foreground. If we see them first, we read back along a diagonal from front right to back left to discover the other two groups. Piero has used architectural details to create a second diagonal from front left toward back right in the illusionary deep space of the picture plane. He has set up precisely rendered one-point perspective in which only the left side of the perspective lines are seen receding into the background. The two front-to-back diagonals are thus set in opposition to one another, linked where they cross in the figures to the left of Jesus. The two diagonals—the lines of humans and the architectural perspective line—are further tied together through the overlapping of the pillars by the human figures.

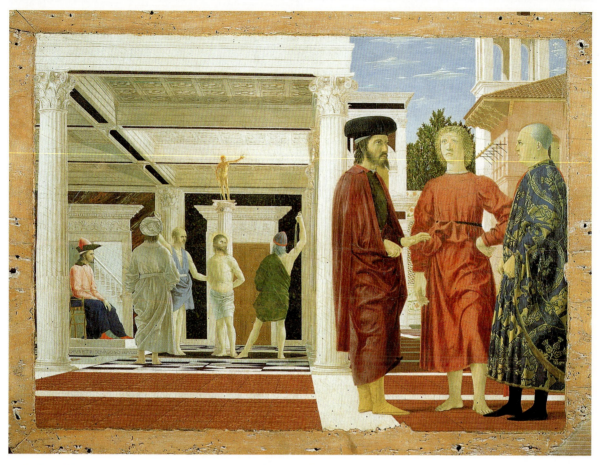

3.27 Piero della Francesca, *Flagellation of Christ*, c. 1455–60. Tempera on wood,
32¾ × 23½ ins (83.2 × 59.7 cm). Palazzo Ducale. Galleria Nazionale delle Marche, Urbino, Italy.

3.28 Pierre Auguste Renoir, *The Boating Party*, 1881. Oil on canvas, 4 ft 3 ins × 5 ft 8 ins (1.29 × 1.73 m).
Phillips Collection, Washington, D.C.

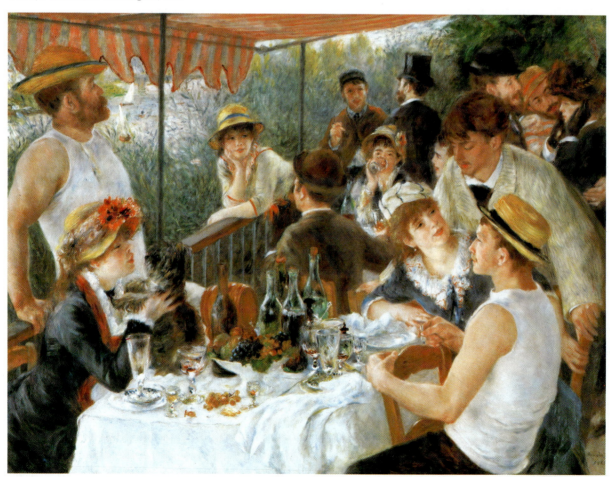

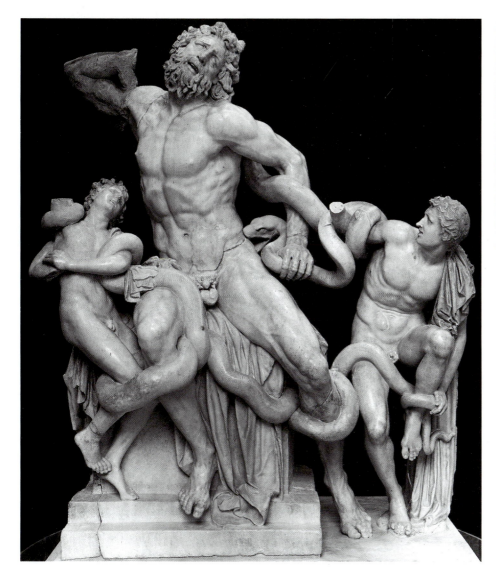

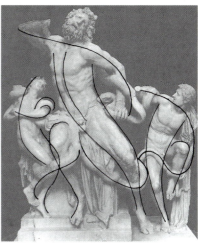

3.29 (left) Hagesandrus, Athenodorus, and Polydorus, *Laocoön*, 1st century AD. Marble, height 8 ft (2.44 m). Vatican Museums, Rome.

3.30 (above) Three-dimensional compositional lines in the *Laocoön*.

In later works, compositional unity is often achieved by less formulaic means. Renoir's Impressionist painting *The Boating Party* (**3.28**) uses a series of devices to unify the many individual figures. The first is the subject-matter: these people are relaxing together at a pleasure garden overlooking the Seine. They are unified into small groups because we see them talking to and looking at each other. The friends having lunch together in the foreground are not in conversation with each other—Aline Charigot, who was to become Renoir's wife, is paying more attention to her dog—but they are held together by being at the same table. The man standing and bending toward the table at the right brings the groups in the background into relationship with those seated at the table. The canopy over the whole group pulls them together visually, as does the bracketing of the figures by the two boatmen. Placed strategically at the right and left margins of the canvas, they stand out

from the others because of their large size and matching athletic clothes. Their gazes cross the canvas, encompassing the whole space.

Three dimensional works are often unified by compositional lines as well, though they cannot be fully appreciated in a two-dimensional photograph from a single point of view. The sculptors of the Hellenistic marble *Laocoön* group (**3.29**) wrapped a series of curving lines around the anguished figures of Laocoön and his sons. Most obvious are the lines of the sea serpents winding through the group. They were said to have sprung out of the sea to attack Laocoön, a Trojan priest, and his sons for defying Apollo or for warning that the Greeks' Trojan horse was a ruse. In addition to the serpents' horrifying way of connecting the figures, the lines of the three straining humans form a continuing series of related curves, as suggested two-dimensionally in Figure **3.30**. They are further tied together by the eyelines from the sons to the father.

EMPHASIS

A further organizing principle in many compositions is that of **emphasis**—the predominance of one area or element in a design. By its size, position, color, shape, texture, or surroundings, one part of a work may be isolated for special attention, giving a focus or dramatic climax to the work.

When awareness is drawn to a single place, it is called the **focal point** of the composition. In Leonardo da Vinci's *The Last Supper* (**3.31**), Christ is clearly the central focus of the work. The most obvious device used to emphasize him is his placement at the exact center of the painting. Leonardo has formally lined up the figures along one side of the table, opening the space in front of them so that they all face the audience, as it were, rather than using the arrangement favored by Ugolino (3.13). On this stage, Christ's central position is emphasized by the perspective lines, which all come to a point in or behind his head, as shown in Figure **3.32**. Or at least, so it now appears. As we shall see in Chapter 5, it is possible that the symmetry of the beams was boldly added by a later

restorer, replacing the original beams painted by Leonardo. In either case, the direction toward the center is established by the disciples, who are looking at Christ or pointing to him. Christ's head is also framed within the central window at the back of the room and by the arch over it.

Sacred architecture often develops a single focal point to center worshippers' attention on the forms used to represent divinity. In the small chapel (**3.33**) reconstructed at the Cloisters in New York from twelfth-century sources, the altar is clearly the focal point, with its candles, marble ciborium (canopy), and

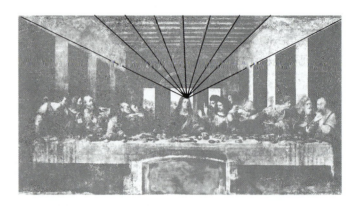

3.32 (above) Perspective composition in *The Last Supper*.

3.31 Leonardo da Vinci, *The Last Supper*, c. 1495–98. Mural painting, 15 ft 1⅛ ins × 28 ft 10¹/₁₂ ins (4.6 × 8.6 m). Refectory, Convent of Santa Maria delle Grazie, Milan.

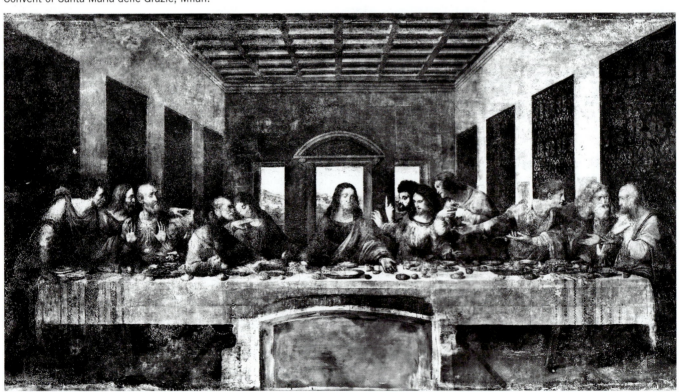

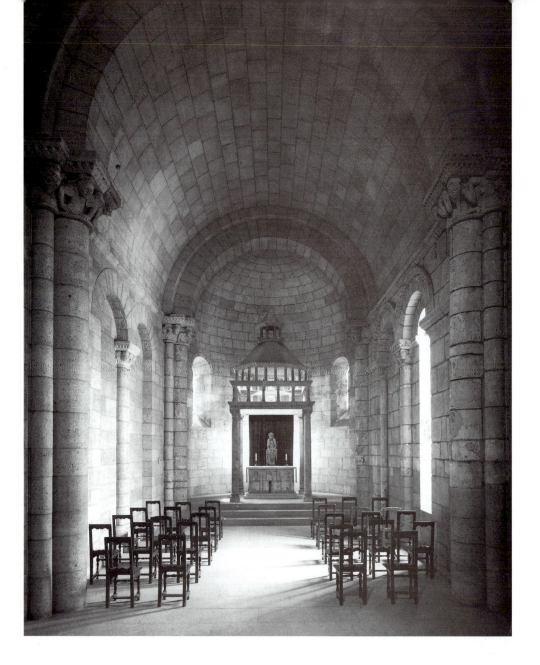

3.33 Chapel, from the church of Notre Dame du Bourg, Longon, Bordeaux, France, after 1126. Marble ciborium from the church of San Stefano, near Finao Romano, Rome, 12th century. Metropolitan Museum of Art, New York. Cloisters collection.

statue of the Madonna and Child. The altar is clearly the most visually interesting area of this simple chapel, and is further emphasized by the domed arch in the architecture, the windows to either side that highlight the area, the contrasting value of the curtain behind the statue, and the raised platform on which the altar rests. These devices also symbolize the sacredness of the spiritual, elevating it above the mundane.

Not all works of art have a focal point. In a wallpaper or fabric pattern, the same design motif may be repeated again and again with equal emphasis, scattering the attention in the interest of creating an overall effect. If the repeating unit has a particularly strong visual element, it may appear as accents within the larger pattern. Many pieces of sculpture also lack a single focal point, for the intention may be to lead the

viewer to examine the work from all angles, unlike two-dimensional images in which many elements must be unified across a single plane. Sometimes the entire sculpture becomes a focal point, as it were. Imagine how Brancusi's *Bird in Space* (1.34) would look if it were displayed by itself in a darkened room with a single spotlight gleaming off its polished bronze surface. In most museum settings, works are shown among many others rather than being emphasized by isolation in a dramatic setting. Altarpieces, for example, were originally intended as the focal points of symmetrical churches. Much of their emotional impact is lost when they are hung on the walls of museums, seen under uniform lighting, and flanked by other pieces to which they are visually unrelated.

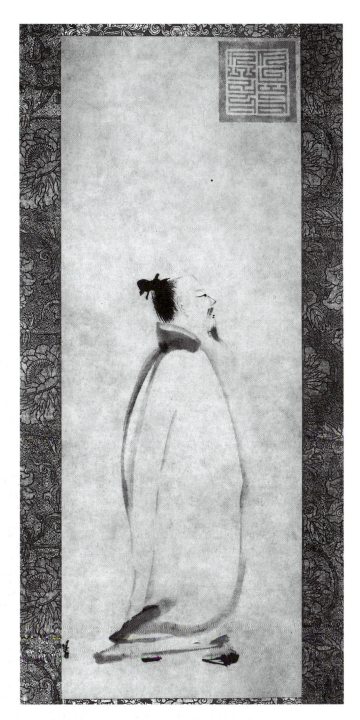

ECONOMY

The principle called **economy of means** refers to the ability of some artists to pare away all extraneous details, presenting only the minimum of information needed by the viewer. Economy is a hallmark of some contemporary design, and also of artists influenced by Zen Buddhism. In his portrait of the poet Li Bo (**3.34**), Liang Kai captured the man's spiritual essence as well as his voluminous form with a few quick brushstrokes. This was considered inspired art, possible only when the artist was in direct communion with the Absolute. Nevertheless, to develop the technique of the "spontaneous" brushstroke took many years of practice.

Economy is not limited to figurative art that suggests real forms by using a minimum of clues. The principle can also be applied to nonobjective art. In

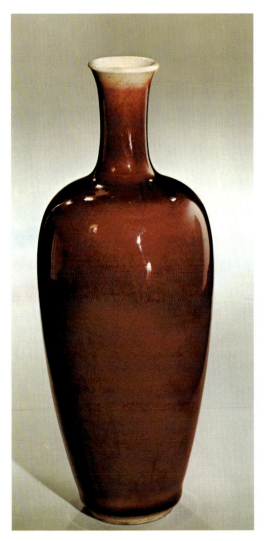

3.34 Liang Kai, *The Poet Li Bo*, 13th century. Ink on paper, 42⅞ × 13 ins (109 × 33 cm). National Museum, Tokyo.

3.35 Vase, Qing-de-zhen ware, China, Qing Dynasty, probably Kangxi period, 1662–1722. Porcelain, *sang de boeuf* glaze, height 7⅞ ins (20 cm). Metropolitan Museum of Art, New York. Bequest of Mary Clark Thompson, 1924.

contrast to the decorative approach of those who paint marble sculptures or cast salt cellars in the forms of the gods, it is possible to create objects of great beauty by severely limiting the design elements used. The elegant porcelain vase from Qing dynasty China (3.35) eschews any ornamentation in order to focus attention on the gracefulness of the form and the subtle crackles and color changes in the oxblood glaze. The intensity of the red gets our attention, but, in its simplicity, the vase becomes an object for quiet contemplation.

Isamu Noguchi, whose spare aesthetic is apparent in his unadorned rock sculptures (2.116) and his point-balancing cube (1.10), speaks of the difficulties of reducing art to the minimum:

> The absence of anything is very beautiful to me. That is to say, emptiness is very beautiful to me. And to desecrate that emptiness with anything takes nerve. So you might say, well, I'm not a lover of art. But I am, you know. I'm always in a quandary. Too much is not good. Too much of anything is not good. With my attitude, it makes it rather difficult to do anything at all. Nevertheless, I'm rather prolific.[3]

As in the Bauhaus dictum, "Less is more," it is possible to suggest very complex forms or ideas with very few visual clues. Graphic designers are challenged to do so when they are commissioned to create logos. A successful **logo** is a highly refined image that bespeaks the nature of an entire group or corporation with an absolute minimum of marks. The logo Peter Good designed for the Hartford Whalers hockey team (3.36) immediately suggests the tail of a sounding whale, completed by a fluid "W" for the Whalers and a

3.36 Peter Good, logo for the Hartford Whalers Hockey Club, 1979.

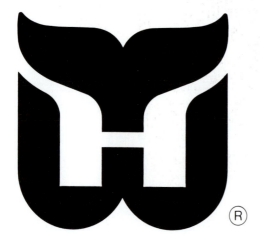

figure-ground reversed "H" for Hartford implied in the unfilled white space. Open to the surrounding space, the "H" has a dynamic flowing quality through the upper portion, with squared-off legs giving strength to the base. If you look very closely at the outer corners of the feet of the "H" you can see **light wells** there—tiny outward swells that counter the eye's tendency to round off the corners. The light wells actually make the lines of the "H" look straighter. The light pouring in through the opening seems to collect in these corners, creating vibrant effects and perhaps even colors in the eyes of some viewers. In what is actually only two simplified filled areas, this economic logo gives us the initials of the town and team, suggests the derivation of the Whalers name, and gives the impression of liveliness, strength, and speed.

PROPORTION

A further principle in composing artworks is that all parts should be in pleasing proportions to each other. From our experiences in the three-dimensional world, we have a learned sense of "correct" size relationships. In representations of the human figure, we expect the head, feet, arms, and fingers to be a certain size in relationship to the rest of the body. These expectations have been institutionalized in certain schools of art. In the art of China and Japan, for instance, one set of conventions for drawing the human figure was to make the standing body seven times the height of the head, the seated body three times the height of the head, the head itself twice the size of the open palm, and so on. These same schools taught proper proportions for representing on a panel the illusion of the vastness of landscapes, called *shanshui*, or "mountain-water" pictures in Chinese. According to one convention of proportions, if a mountain were shown ten feet (3.1 m) high, a tree should be one foot (30.5 cm) high, a house a tenth of a foot (3.05 cm) high, and a human the size of a pea.

In addition to these artistic conventions about proportion in figurative art, theories have been put forward suggesting that we have an innate abstract sense of ideal proportion. The Greeks formulated this idea of mathematical perfection as the **golden rectangle**: one in which the short side is to the longer side as the long side is to the sum of the two sides. This ratio works out

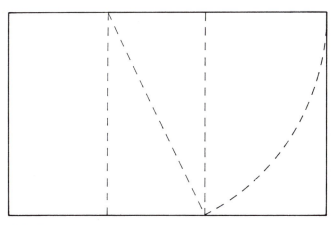

3.37 The Golden Rectangle.

3.38 Ictinus and Callicrates, Parthenon, Athens, 447–438 BC.

to approximately 1 to 1.618, as shown in Figure **3.37**. It is a now-familiar shape, for its proportions of length to height have been used for centuries as an approximate format for paintings.

Although the Greeks worked out the Golden Rectangle as a mathematical formula, they also recognized that our visual perception is not flawless and that it is influenced by our mental assumptions. Ictinus and Callicrates, the architects of the Parthenon (**3.38**), therefore used an astonishing series of "optical refinements" in the proportions of the building to make it appear perfectly regular and rectangular to the human eye.

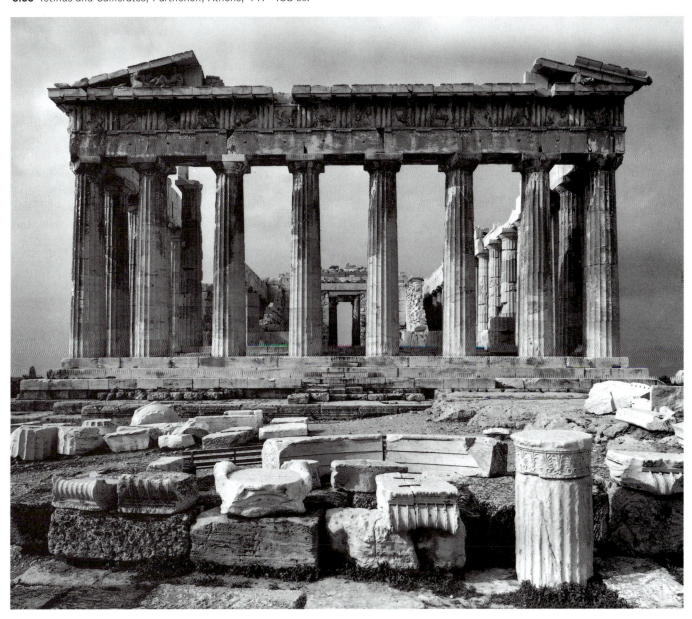

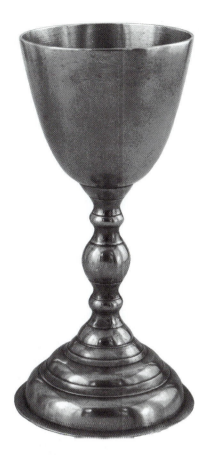

3.39 Timothy Brigden, chalice, late 18th or early 19th century. Pewter, height 8⅞ ins (22.5 cm). Metropolitan Museum of Art, New York. Gift of Joseph France, 1943.

Exact measurement of the Parthenon has revealed many apparently intentional deviations from regularity and rectangularity. Because the Greeks recognized that our visual apparatus perceives vertical lines as sloping and horizontal lines as sagging in the center, they corrected for these human errors in perception. The platform and steps actually curve upward. So does the **entablature** (the horizontal element above the columns), though to a lesser degree, presumably because it was farther from the viewer's eye. The columns and entablature also slope inward slightly to prevent their appearing to slope outward. At the corners, the columns are thickened slightly to counteract the optical thinning effect of their being silhouetted against the sky. The diameter of the columns bulges out by two-thirds of an inch (1.7 cm) part-way up to accommodate the human assumption that the columns will be slightly compressed by the weight they appear to bear (a subtle principle called **entasis**), and the illusion of regular spacing among the columns is created by spacing that is actually irregular. The result is what we perceive as the most perfectly proportioned building ever created.

Artists who are able to create satisfying proportions may thus be working with the actual visual "feel" of objects rather than mathematical precision. The lovely chalice by Timothy Brigden (**3.39**) is divided into three areas that are approximately—but not exactly—the same size: the cup, stem, and base. The base is actually slightly shorter in height than the cup and stem, but with its outward flare it would appear awkward if it were any higher. Brigden has also forsaken exact regularity in the area just below the bottom of the cup, making it straighter than the curves of the rest of the stem. It serves as a transition from the straighter lines of the cup to the undulations of the stem. If it had a more rounded curve, there would be "too many" curves. As it is, the chalice appears just right to the human eye.

Mathematical precision in proportions can actually be found in nature. The seeds in a sunflower head, the florets in a daisy, and the chambers in a nautilus shell (**3.40**) grow in spiraling increasing patterns in the mathematical relationship called a *Fibonacci series*. The ratio of the size of one unit to that of the following unit is 0.618 . . . (an infinite, irrational number); the size of any unit divided by the size of the preceding one is 1.618 . . ., the Greeks' **golden section**, on which the Golden Rectangle is based.

3.40 Diagrammatic section of a nautilus shell.

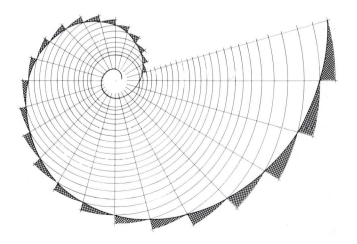

WASSILY KANDINSKY
on UNDERLYING HARMONY

The Russian nonobjective painter Wassily Kandinsky (1866–1944) began his adult career in the realm of principles, as a budding professor of law. But he gave that up for painting, and as a painter he worked to free himself from attempts to copy the world of outer appearances or abide by traditional ideas of aesthetic harmony (**3.41**). A mystic, he believed that expressions of a higher inner harmony could be presented through the pure language of colors and forms, with no references to the objective world. Excerpts from his book, *Concerning the Spiritual in Art*, follow:

"The need for coherence is the essential of harmony—whether founded on conventional discord or concord. The new harmony demands that the inner value of a picture should remain unified whatever the variations or contrasts of outward form or colour. The elements of the new art are to be found, therefore, in the inner and not the outer qualities of nature."

"The spectator is too ready to look for a meaning in a picture— i.e., some outward connection between its various parts. Our materialistic age has produced a type of spectator or 'connoisseur,' who is not content to put himself opposite a picture and let it say its own message. Instead of allowing the inner value of the picture to work, he worries himself in looking for 'closeness to nature,' or 'temperament,' or 'handling,' or 'tonality,' or 'perspective,' or what not. His eye does not probe the outer expression to arrive at the inner meaning.

In a conversation with an interesting person, we endeavour to get at his fundamental ideas and feelings. We do not bother about the words he uses, nor the spelling of those words, nor the breath necessary for speaking them, nor the movements of his tongue and lips, nor the psychological working on our brain, nor the physical sound in our ear, nor the physiological effect on our nerves. We realize that these things, though interesting and important, are not the main things of the moment, but that the meaning and idea is what concerns us. We should have the same feeling when confronted with a work of art. When this becomes general the artist will be able to dispense with natural form and colour and speak in purely artistic language."

"New principles do not fall from heaven, but are logically if indirectly connected with past and future. What is important to us is the momentary position of the principle and how best it can be used. It must not be employed forcibly. But if the artist tunes his soul to this note, the sound will ring in his work of itself.

The 'emancipation' of today must advance on the lines of the inner need. It is hampered at present by external form, and as that is thrown aside, there arises as the aim of composition— construction. The search for constructive form has produced Cubism, in which natural form is often forcibly subjected to geometrical construction . . .

The harmony of the new art demands a more subtle construction than this, something that appeals less to the eye and more to the soul. This 'concealed construction' may arise from an apparently fortuitous selection of forms on the canvas. Their external lack of cohesion is their internal harmony. This haphazard arrangement of forms may be the future of artistic harmony. Their fundamental relationship will finally be able to be expressed in mathematical form, but in terms irregular rather than regular."[4]

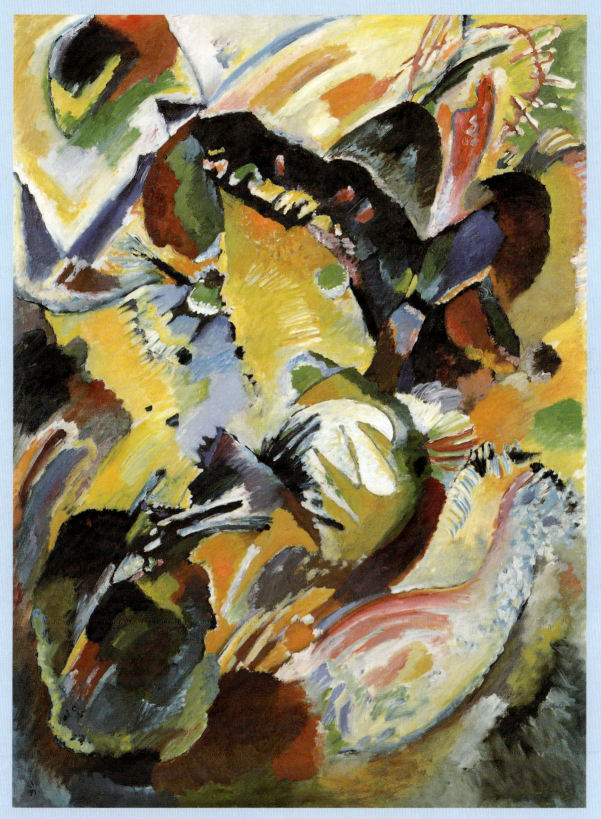

3.41 Wassily Kandinsky, *Panel for Edward R. Campbell, no. 2*, 1914. Oil on canvas, 5 ft 4⅛ ins × 4 ft ⅜ ins (1.63 × 1.23 m). Collection Museum of Modern Art, New York. Nelson A. Rockefeller Fund.

There are also proportional relationships that are entirely intuitive, based totally on the individual's innate sense of aesthetics. An extreme example is the perfection of the Zen rock garden in Ryoanji (3.42). The relationships of sand (raked in lines to represent the sea) to rocks (representing mountainous islands, like the islands of Japan), rock to rock within each grouping, and rock group to rock group are the result of a meditative attunement to the perfection of the universe, rather than obedience to any human system of perfection.

3.42 Rock garden of Ryoanji temple, Kyoto.
Courtesy Japan National Tourist Organisation, London.

RELATIONSHIP TO THE ENVIRONMENT

A final organizational principle which affects the harmony of a work of art is the relationship of the piece to its environment. When we see art on the pages of a book or on the walls of a museum, we cannot grasp this dimension, for it can be appreciated only within the living setting for the work.

Barnett Newman's *Voice of Fire* (1.40), whose purchase by the National Gallery of Canada raised a furor among those who considered it a waste of public funds, has been exhibited in various settings, including the United States pavilion at Expo '67. But now that it is in a commanding place in the Ottawa museum, visitors are often stunned by its impact. The eighteen-foot-high (5.9 m) painting has been hung by itself at the end of a tall gallery, dominating the space and the perception of the viewer.

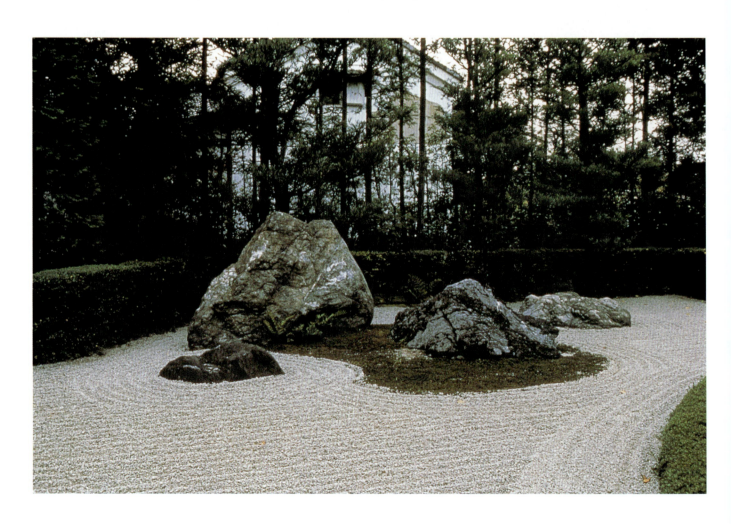

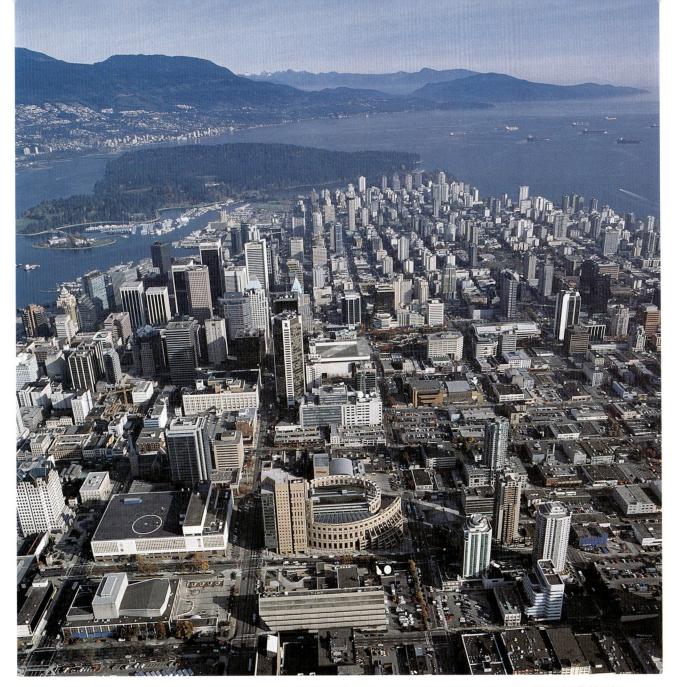

0.40 Moshe Safdie, Vancouver Library Square, Vancouver, British Columbia, opened May 1995, aerial view. Photo by T. Hursley.

In the case of Moshe Safdie's Vancouver Library Square (1.48), much of the controversy surrounding its commissioning involved its relationship to its environment. Critics said it was too dissimilar to the rest of downtown Vancouver's architecture to fit in properly. Moshe Safdie claims, "Basically I feel my real strength as an architect has to do with the fact that I can study a site, or discover a site for that matter, and get the most that one can extract out of it. Very often, great, inventive architecture has to do with someone reading the secrets of the place in a profound way."[5] Look at

the Library in its broadest context (3.43), including not only the cityscape but also the harbor and mountains beyond. The Library is in the foreground—a seven-story block surrounded by an elliptical wall and then an outer freestanding, sandstone colored, elliptical wall. On the right, this wall becomes a taller office tower, from whose windows the broader environment can be clearly viewed. Do you think the relationship between the urban and natural setting and the building has any kind of harmony? If not, is there some merit in the disharmony?

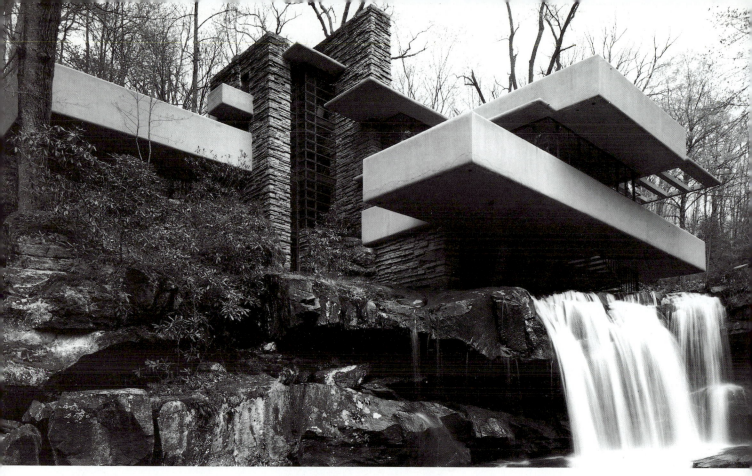

3.44 Frank Lloyd Wright, Kaufmann House ("Fallingwater"), 1936–39. Bear Run, Pennsylvania.

Artists must work within the limitations and features of the settings imposed by their commissions. Architect Frank Lloyd Wright, asked to build a house near a creek in Pennsylvania, chose to build it on top of the falls (**3.44**), "not simply to look at the waterfalls but to live with them." Preserving and capitalizing on the beauty of the waterfall, Wright cantilevered the decks of the house right out over it. The horizontal lines of the building mirror the slabs of rock below, echoing their pattern of linear, light-struck mass punctuated by deeply shadowed recesses. His ideal was what he called "organic architecture"—that which respects and merges with the natural environment. Wright wrote:

When organic architecture is properly carried out no landscape is ever outraged by it but is always developed by it. . . . Fallingwater is a great blessing—one of the great blessings to be experienced here on earth. I think nothing yet ever equalled the coordination, sympathetic expression of the great principle of repose where forest and stream and rock and all the elements of structure are combined so quietly that really you listen not to any noise whatsoever although the music of the stream is there. But you listen to Fallingwater the way you listen to the quiet of the country. . . .[6]

PART 2
TWO-DIMENSIONAL MEDIA AND METHODS

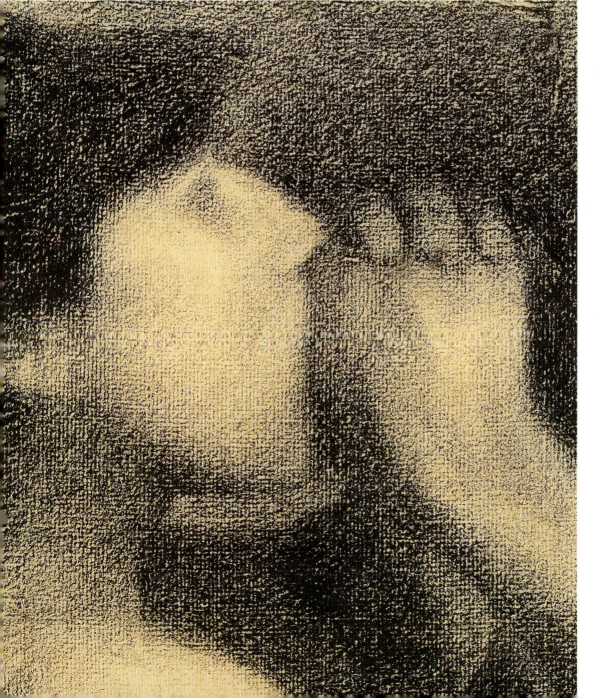

Since humans first approached their cave walls to scratch and paint images of the animals they hunted and spirits they sensed, flat surfaces have lured us to record our impressions of life. Across the millennia, we have appropriated everything from plaster walls to computer screens for this purpose.

Georges-Pierre Seurat, *L'Echo* (detail of fig. 4.11).

4

DRAWING

Understanding the technical aspects of art requires knowing what to look for. Each **medium**—the material with which the artist works, such as water-color, oil paint, or stone—has unique characteristics that can be seen in certain works, though some artists use their medium so skillfully that they transcend its limitations and can make it do anything they choose. In this chapter we will examine a variety of media that have been used in drawing.

APPROACHES TO DRAWING

Drawing is perhaps the most direct of all the arts. The marks the artist lays down in a drawing reflect the movements and skillfulness of the arm and hand. This aspect is somewhat different from the visual quality of the lines themselves. Aubrey Beardsley's Ali Baba (**4.1**) is composed of elegant flowing lines, but to get this free-flowing effect with pen and ink took tremendous manual control on Beardsley's part. Even the letters are elegantly controlled drawn lines.

Drawings are often created as illustrations, such as Beardsley's illustration for the book *The Forty Thieves.* Techniques of book printing are easily adapted to reproduction of drawn lines, and they resemble and complement the lines of letter forms, as in the Ali Baba cover.

Another way in which artists have often used drawing is in studying natural forms in preparation for rendering them in another medium. Artists do not typically paint or sculpt a human figure, for example, by starting at the head and working down, filling in all the details as they go along. Rather, they first analyze the general form, the underlying structure and relationships between parts. They study the figure in terms of volume, values, proportions, lines, and the dynamics of gestures. What they see they may then draw in a preliminary series of sketches—thinking on paper, as it

were. Before painting the Sistine Chapel ceiling (16.15–16.20), Michelangelo made numerous drawings to work out the musculature and gestures of the figures. The sketch page shown here (**4.2**) includes his working out of the famous arm of the Lord that we see infusing Adam with life in the celebrated *Creation of Adam* (16.20) portion of the ceiling. Michelangelo's technique in these drawings is alternately free and "sketchy," and tighter and more refined, with God's arm modeled in considerable detail.

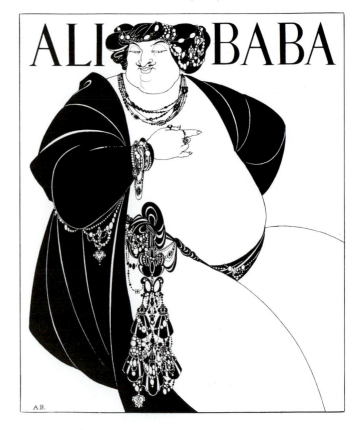

4.1 Aubrey Beardsley, cover design for *The Forty Thieves*, 1879. Pen and black ink, brush, and black chalk, 9⁷/₁₆ × 7¹³/₁₆ ins (24 × 19.7 cm). Fogg Art Museum, Harvard University, Cambridge, Massachusetts. Grenville L. Winthrop Bequest.

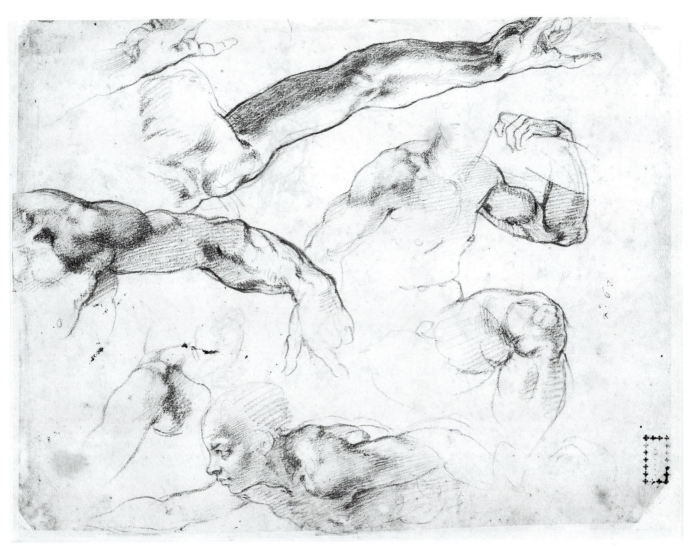

4.2 Michelangelo Buonarroti, preparatory drawings for *The Creation of Adam*, Sistine Chapel ceiling, 1511. Red chalk over black chalk, 8⅜ × 11 ins (21.3 × 27.9 cm). Teylers Museum, Haarlem, Netherlands.

A third way in which drawings may be used is in presentations, as models for future works. Claes Oldenburg's proposed colossal clothespin monument drawing (4.3) was a tongue-in-cheek entry in a competition for a Chicago memorial, 45 years after the fact, although he did actually erect a similar clothespin in Philadelphia in 1976. Such presentation drawings are now considered collectable works of art in their own right. Christo often sells his drawings of proposed earthworks to help finance his projects, such as *Running Fence* (2.8).

In today's broad aesthetic, all of these kinds of drawings—illustrations, sketches, and presentation drawings—are appreciated and hung as works of art. Many artists also create finished drawings as ends in themselves. The many media now at their disposal are

explored in the following sections. Those described are not an exhaustive list, some contemporary artists are drawing with new media such as felt-tip pens. Neither are these categories absolute. Chalks, crayons, charcoal, and pastels are quite similar, and pastel work is often classified as painting rather than drawing because it involves laying down masses of color rather than lines.

Note that most of the illustrations of drawings are of relatively recent works, for the medium on which most drawing is done—paper—has been readily available only since the early 1500s. At that time, increasing urbanization concentrated the population, and the manufacture of less expensive yard goods coupled with growing affluence led people to throw away clothes as they were worn, outgrown, or out of style.

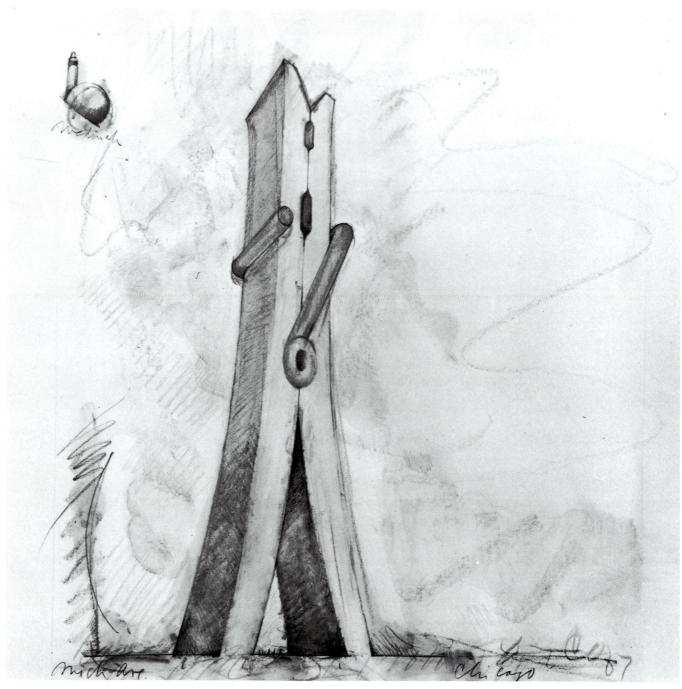

4.3 Claes Oldenburg, *Late Submission to the Chicago Tribune Competition of 1922: Clothespin (Version Two)*, 1967.
Pencil, crayon, and watercolor, 22 × 23¼ ins (55.9 × 60.3 cm). Des Moines Art Center.
Gift of Gardener Cowles by exchange and partial gift of Charles Cowles, New York, 1972.

Rag collectors moved through the cities buying the used fabric and selling it to paper manufacturers, enabling paper to be produced in greater quantities than in the past and bringing its price down. Today the best artist's papers are still made with rag; less expensive papers, made from wood pulp, yellow and deteriorate with time and don't hold up well under repeated working.

DRY MEDIA

Graphite Pencil

The pencils commonly used by artists are quite similar to those used as writing tools. They are simply thin rods of **graphite**—a soft form of carbon, mixed with clay, baked in a kiln and encased in wood or some other material as a holder. Though now commonplace, the graphite (or "lead") pencil was not widely used in drawing until the end of the eighteenth century, when techniques for varying the hardness of graphite were developed. Values range from silver-gray to black depending on the proportional relationship of clay to graphite. The hardest grades of graphite produce the palest, finest lines; the softer grades tend to produce darker, broader lines and to glide more smoothly across the paper. A lighter touch with a soft pencil can also be used to create paler values.

Artists may use many grades of graphite or varying techniques with a few grades to create a range of values in a single drawing. In Corot's *Cività Castellana* (**4.4**), soft grades of graphite have been used to create very black filled-in areas. For lighter gray values, Corot has used parallel lines of hatching. And on the right side of

4.4 Jean Baptiste Camille Corot, *Cività Castellana*, 1826. Graphite pencil on beige paper, 12¼ × 15⅜ ins (31 × 39 cm). Louvre, Paris.

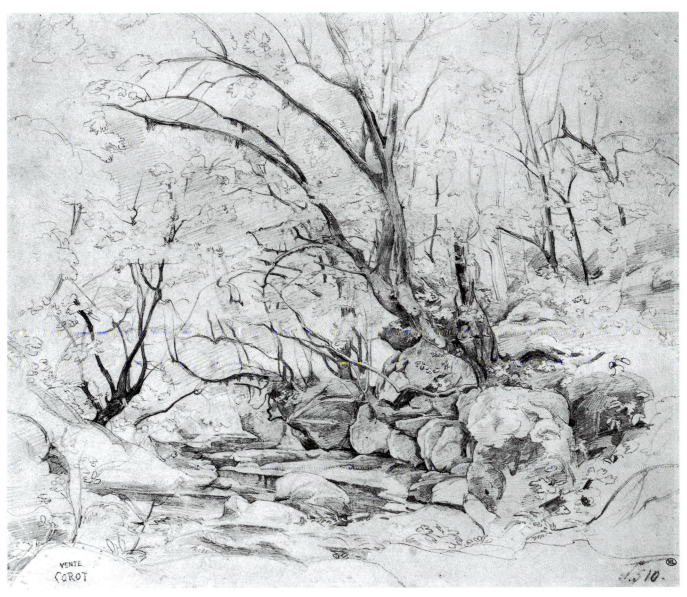

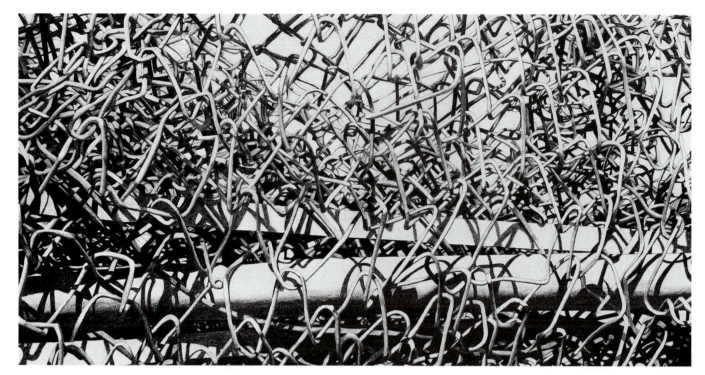

4.5 Stuart Caswell, *Chain Link Disaster*, 1972.
Pencil on paper, 22 × 28 ins (55.9 × 71.1 cm).
Minnesota Museum of Art, St. Paul, Minneapolis, Minnesota.

the drawing, he has used the side rather than the point of a pencil to lay down broad areas of graphite, which are then rubbed for an overall gray tone. These value gradations create contrasts that remind us of the continual variations between darks and lights in a deciduous forest. Corot has used a visual shorthand for trees, leaves, stream, and rocks, but gives enough information for us readily to perceive the representational scene.

Whereas graphite is laid down in quite a free fashion in Corot's drawing, it is used with great precision in Stuart Caswell's *Chain Link Disaster* (**4.5**). Whether real or imaginary, this view of mangled sections of chain link fencing is photorealistic in its precisely described values and interwoven, overlaid lines. Pencil drawings are more typically used as quick studies; this kind of tight rendering is extremely time-consuming.

Silverpoint

The advent of the graphite pencil greatly lessened the use of **silverpoint**, which had been popular in the fifteenth and sixteenth centuries. Silverpoint drawings are made with hard, finely pointed rods of silver in a holder. The paper is first coated with some medium, such as opaque white pigment or rabbitskin glue with bone dust, to prepare a rather abrasive surface that will scrape off and hold minute grains of the metal. The lines made as the silverpoint tool is run across this prepared ground are silver at first but soon oxidize to a darker, duller color with a special light-reflecting quality. Copper, gold, and lead have also been used in the same way. As shown in Roger van der Weyden's delicate silverpoint, *Head of the Virgin* (**4.6**), shadows and textures are usually built up using parallel lines.

Charcoal

In contrast to the tight, thin lines produced by silverpoint, **charcoal** is a medium that moves very freely across the paper, depositing broad, soft lines. Charcoal is made of charred wood or vine in sticks of varying width and hardness. The marks it makes are easily smudged. Though this possibility is often exploited by artists in toning an area, charcoal drawings are coated with a fixative when finished to prevent further accidental smudging.

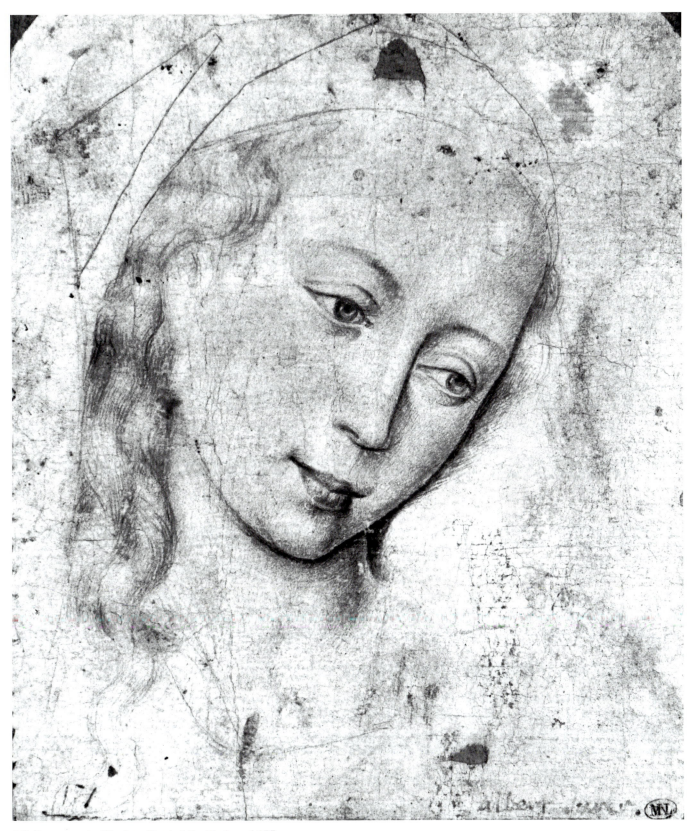

4.6 Roger van der Weyden, *Head of the Virgin*, c. 1455. Silverpoint. Louvre, Paris.

Käthe Kollwitz's uses of charcoal in her *Self-portrait with a Pencil* (**4.7**) demonstrate the great versatility of the medium. She has given a faint tone to the paper with a slight deposit of charcoal. The charcoal has also been used sideways with a light touch to create broad strokes across the chest. Laid down this way, the charcoal dust sits on the surface of the paper, allowing the grainy texture of the paper itself to show through. The side of a soft piece of charcoal has been worked into the paper with great strength along the arm, creating lines of a darker value whose boldness bespeaks the creative energy of the artist at work. The tip of the charcoal has been used to create lines describing the artist's features. And Kollwitz has used the tip of a harder, finer piece of charcoal to complete the upper contour of her head.

Because charcoal is such a soft and free medium, the tendency is to use it in a quick way, as Kollwitz has done. The spontaneity of the act of drawing is revealed and celebrated in this very natural use of the medium. But it is also possible to use charcoal in a more controlled manner. Richard Lytle's charcoal study, *Norfolk* (**4.8**), is a rare example of a very refined charcoal drawing in which the paper is left totally white in places. Whereas many charcoal drawings use only a range of mid-values, Lytle creates very rich blacks whose juxtaposition with true white makes them sing. He comments:

4.7 Käthe Kollwitz, *Self-portrait with a Pencil*, 1933.
Charcoal, 18¾ × 24⅞ ins (48 × 63 cm).
National Gallery of Art, Washington, D.C. Rosenwald Collection.

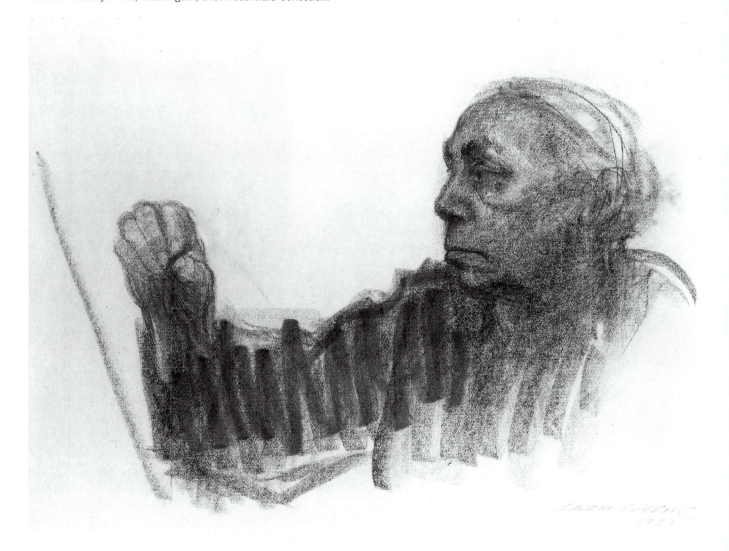

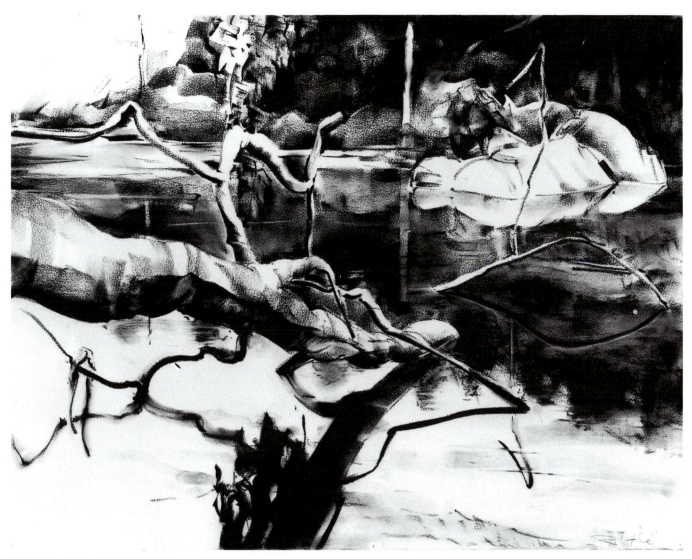

4.8 Richard Lytle, *Norfolk*, 1976.
Charcoal, 22½ × 30 ins (57.1 × 76.2 cm). Collection of the artist.

Most people use charcoal since it is a very forgiving medium. You can rub it off, in contrast to the immutability of ink. But I use charcoal with a mentality that was evolved through my work with ink. The imagery in this piece is slow in revealing itself, suggesting a bit of mystery, with the dark areas worked densely to a pure velvet black and the floating white areas developing volumes.[1]

Chalk

Chalk is a naturally occurring deposit of calcium carbonate and varying minerals, built up from fossil seashells. Powdered, mixed with a binder and compressed into sticks, it has long been used as a soft drawing medium. Renaissance, Baroque, and Rococo artists used white, red, and black chalks to work up and down the value scale on a tinted surface which served as a mid-tone. This technique is beautifully illustrated by the cartoon for *The Virgin and Child with St. Anne and St. John the Baptist* (**4.9**) by Leonardo da Vinci. A **cartoon** was a full-sized drawing done as a model for a painting. The lines from the cartoon were transferred to canvas or wall by pressing charcoal dust through holes pricked in the major line of the cartoon. But this cartoon is so striking in its own right that it is displayed by itself in a special dark room of the National Gallery in London, with lighting designed to keep the paper from deteriorating. To indicate volumes rounding in space, Leonardo used black chalk lines to separate the figures from the tone of the paper and then used dark tones within the figures to indicate

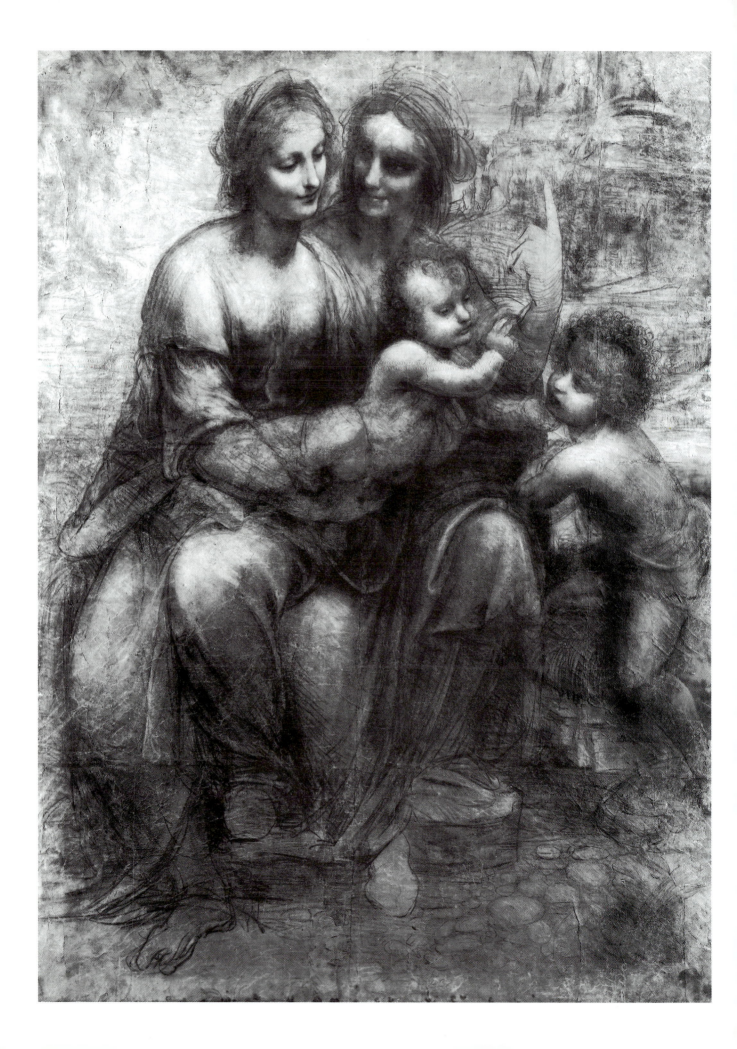

areas receding from the viewer in space. Areas that are to be seen as closest are lightened with white chalk. Notice how much flatter the areas that were not yet worked out—such as the upraised hand and the feet—appear without this use of values. Leonardo's very subtle value gradations were called **sfumato**, Italian for the smoky appearance that softens the lines of the contours and gives a mysterious hazy atmosphere to the image. He achieved the same effect in his paintings, such as *The Virgin of the Rocks* (15.23).

Pastel

Often confused with chalk, which is harder, **pastel** is a chalky stick made of powdered pigment plus filler bound with a small amount of gum or resin. When rubbed onto a rough-textured paper with enough "tooth" to hold the particles, it deposits masses of color. Pastel drawings are very fragile until treated with a fixative; if they are shaken before they are fixed, some of the powder will fall off. But an overabundance of fixative will deaden or spot the drawing, so the only way to assure the permanence of a pastel is to seal it under glass.

The word "pastel" is commonly associated with pale tones, and pale pastels are well suited for creating light and romantic images. In the hands of Degas, pastels became a brilliant medium, like paints, but with their own special powdery effect. *After the Bath* (**4.10**) is one of his many major works in pastel. Because pastels are so soft, most artists smudge and blend them on the paper; Degas handles them as lines of color that reveal the act of drawing. Degas was able to lay one coat of pigment on top of another without their blending, using a special fixative between layers. The formula for the fixative has since been lost, and it is now difficult to build up layers with pastels using contemporary fixatives without dulling the brightness of the colors. In

4.9 (opposite) Leonardo da Vinci, *The Virgin and Child with St. Anne and St. John the Baptist*, 1510. Black chalk heightened with white on paper, 4 ft 7¾ ins × 3 ft 5 ins (1.42 × 1.04 m). National Gallery, London.

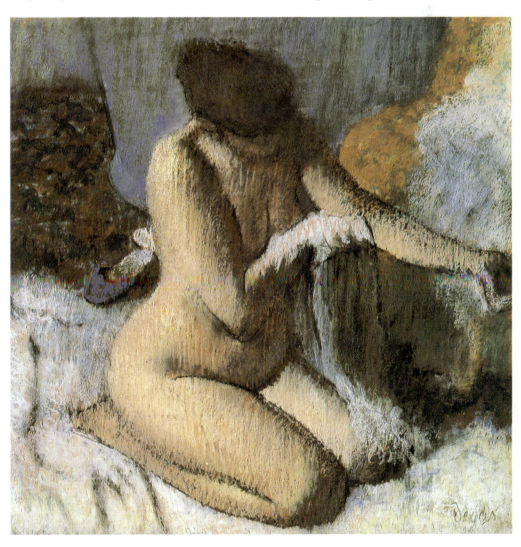

4.10 Edgar Degas, *After the Bath*, c. 1895–98. Pastel on paper, 27½ × 27½ ins (70 × 70 cm). Musée d'Orsay, Paris.

addition to his special fixative, Degas used pastels made with a high ratio of pigment to filler, juxtaposed at maximum strength so they intensify each other's brilliance.

Crayon

Several media carry the name "crayon." **Conté crayon**, named after the man who invented it in the eighteenth century, is a fine-textured grease-free stick made of powdered graphite and clay to which red ocher, soot, or blackstone has been added to give it a red, black, or brown color. Its somewhat powdery nature can be seen in *L'Echo* (**4.11**). Seurat drew with conté crayons on a handmade textured paper which broke up the conté crayon marks and thus developed a range of values. Artists find conté crayon a versatile drawing medium because it can be applied softly to create gently shaped areas, or the crayon can be sharpened to a point to create hard, crisp lines or shapes.

4.11 Georges-Pierre Seurat, *L'Echo*, 1883–84. Conté crayon, 12 × 9¼ ins (30.5 × 23.5 cm). Yale University Art Gallery, New Haven, Connecticut. Bequest of Edith M. Wetmore.

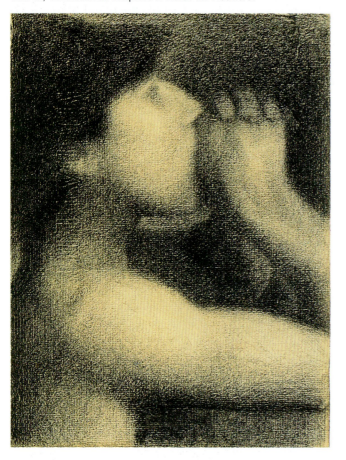

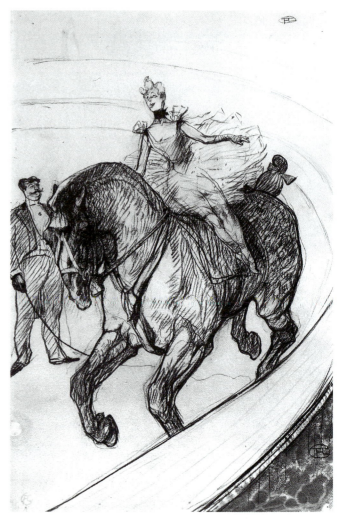

4.12 Henri de Toulouse-Lautrec, *L'Equestrienne*, 1899. Crayon, 19¼ × 12⅜ ins (48.9 × 31.4 cm). Museum of Art, Rhode Island School of Design, Providence, Rhode Island.

Children's crayons are made of pigmented wax. Oil-based crayons come in brighter colors than wax crayons and can be blended on the paper, rather like oil paints. Lithographic crayons are made of grease for use in lithographic printing, but have been adopted for drawing by contemporary artists who like the pleasing way they glide across the paper. Each has its unique qualities, but crayons in general tend to skip quickly across paper. This quickness—and the humor it brings out in the artist—is apparent in Toulouse-Lautrec's *Equestrienne* (**4.12**). To see how differently the mass of the horse is described when the artist is using drawn lines rather than painted masses of color, compare this crayon drawing with Toulouse-Lautrec's oil painting of a similar subject shown in Figure 2.153.

LIQUID MEDIA

Pen and Ink

The drawing media discussed so far are all **dry media**. It is also possible to draw lines with a **liquid medium**, usually ink. Today's drawing inks are made of pigment particles, shellac, and water. In traditional China, Japan, and Europe during the Middle Ages and Renaissance, ink was made from ground lampblack mixed into a weak glue. Ink is usually applied with pens made of steel, quills, reeds, or bamboo. Depending on the shape of its point, a pen may produce either lines of uniform width or lines that vary in width according to the direction and pressure of the pen.

Pen and ink drawings are difficult to execute, for the point of the pen may catch on the surface of the paper and splatter ink unpredictably. Today's technical pens can move more easily across the paper, like fine ballpoints, but it is still difficult to create so free-flowing a line as Picasso has used in his *Three Female Nudes Dancing* (**4.15**). If you follow the lines, you will see areas where the ink came out in spurts rather than a continuous flow, but the lines keep moving with utter assurance.

Whereas most ink drawings are dark lines on a white or toned surface, Hyman Bloom creates the texture and form of fish skeletons (**4.13**) by working in white ink against maroon paper. By varying the amount of white laid down in an area, Bloom creates a range of values that gives an in-and-out spatial quality that borders on both realism and fantasy.

Pen and ink is essentially a line medium; tone or shade is conveyed by the use of special techniques such as stippling (dots), scratching, **hatching**, or **cross-hatching** (see Bittleman's *Martyred Flowers*, 2.14). As an alternative, ink can be thinned with water or spirit and

4.13 Hyman Bloom, *Fish Skeletons*, c. 1956.
White ink on maroon paper, 16¾ × 22¾ ins (42.5 × 57.8 cm).
Collection of Mr. and Mrs. Ralph Werman.

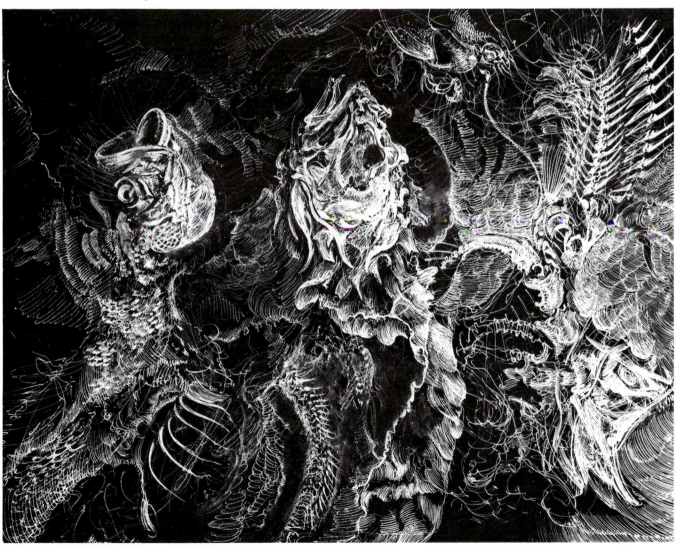

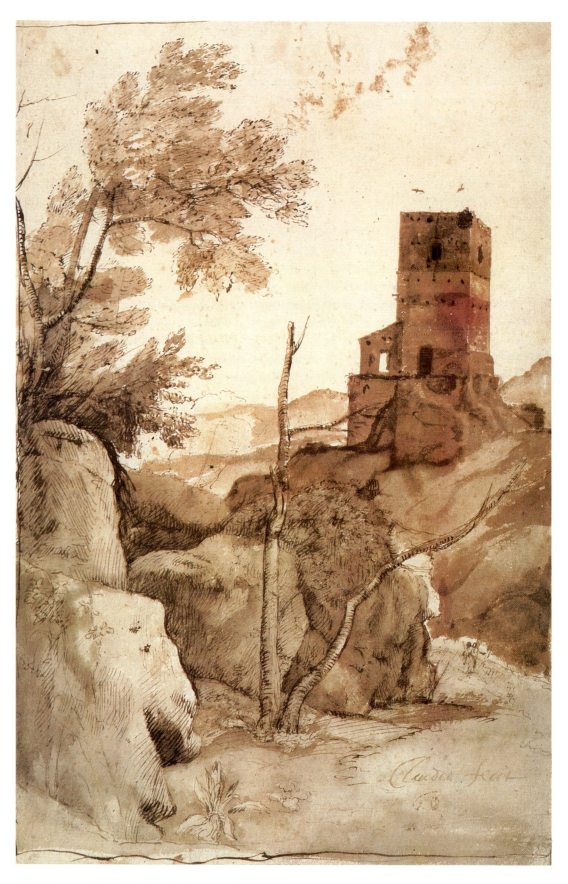

4.14 Claude Gellée, called Claude Lorraine, *Campagna Landscape*, 1660.
Pen and bister with wash, 12⅝ × 8½ ins (32 × 21.6 cm).
British Museum, London.

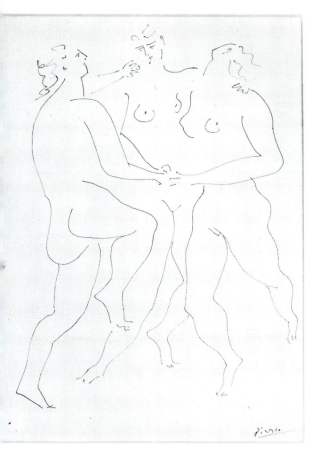

4.15 Pablo Picasso, *Three Female Nudes Dancing*, 1923. Pen and ink, 13⅞ × 10⅜ ins (35.2 × 26.3 cm). National Gallery of Canada, Ottawa, Ontario.

brushed on as a **wash** to suggest the tone. The wash can be applied to penned line which is still wet to soften and dilute it. If it is added to a dry drawing the original pen marks usually remain hard and dark.

In Claude Lorraine's *Campagna Landscape* (**4.14**), brown ink has been watered down and used to fill in varying brown tones, without overpowering the darker penned lines used to describe the trees and rocks. The tower, however, is described by a darker wash accented by drawn marks, and the distant hills are suggested by a very thin wash alone that almost blends into the light values of the sky.

Brush and Ink

The final step into liquid media that can still be classified as a "drawing" is the application of ink with a brush without any penned marks. Developed to a fine art by Oriental schools, this technique is used in a near-abstract manner by Rembrandt in his sketch of a sleeping girl (**4.16**). The action of making each wet stroke is clearly evident, including passages where the ink on the brush was spent and the white of the paper began to show through. Above the girl's head an area of the background is suggested with a brushed wash. Note the attention to the placement of the figure on the ground, a consideration that is particularly important when large areas of the ground are left unfilled and will be perceived as flat shapes in themselves. The wash tends to contradict such an interpretation, softening and pushing the largely unworked area back in space.

There is no limit to the tools artists can use to draw with and surfaces to draw on: anything that will make a mark and anything that can be marked on can be used. As we shall see in Chapter 9, which is devoted to computer graphics, computers offer a very powerful new medium capable of producing drawings unlike anything ever done with traditional media and methods.

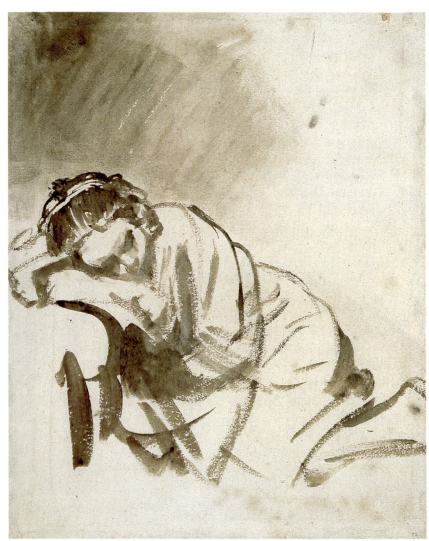

4.16 Rembrandt van Rijn, *Sleeping Girl*, c. 1660–69. Brush drawing in brown ink and wash, 9⅝ × 8 ins (24.5 × 20.3 cm). British Museum, London.

5
PAINTING

APPROACHES TO PAINTING

Painting is the process of coating a surface with colored areas by using a hand tool such as a brush or a palette knife. There is no absolute demarcation between drawing and painting. Some drawing techniques, such as pastel, can also be used to create areas of color, and a brush may be used for drawings, such as brush and ink drawings. There is a slight difference in approach, however: drawing is primarily linear mark-making. The media discussed in Chapter 4 are usually considered drawing media, while encaustic, fresco, tempera, oil, watercolor, gouache, and synthetics are considered paint media.

We now tend to associate the word "painting" with a flat, movable surface to which paint has been added, such as a canvas which can be hung on any wall, but paint was probably first applied directly to stationary surfaces such as the walls of caves and buildings. The women of West Africa still maintain a dramatic wall-painting tradition of unknown antiquity. They use their hands to paint liquid clays mixed with plant and mineral colors onto the mud and clay walls of their houses and shrines (**5.1**). Each rainy season these vibrant clay paintings dissolve and are then reapplied, usually by groups of women using patterns handed down from mother to daughter.

Over the years and around the world, many different technical solutions have been devised to allow the spreading of colored **pigments** (particles of color) across a surface. In general, painting is made possible by suspension of pigments in a liquid medium—a solvent such as water or linseed oil—plus a **binder** that makes the pigments adhere to a surface. The surface on which the paint (that is, pigment plus medium) is spread is called the **support**, be it a wall, a piece of wood, or a stretched canvas.

Through time, varying media have been developed to improve properties such as ease in working, drying time, permanence, or brilliance. The forms of painting thus evolved are often referred to as **media**, in reference to the varying vehicles that distinguish them. Each medium has its own strengths and difficulties. Most are still in current use, though sometimes only by a few artists who are willing to tolerate the technical difficulties for the sake of the special effects possible.

5.1 Silla Camara painting the wall of her family compound, Soninke village, Djajabinnit, Mauritania. Paste of ground white kaolin, water, and pigments collected from the Senegal River area.

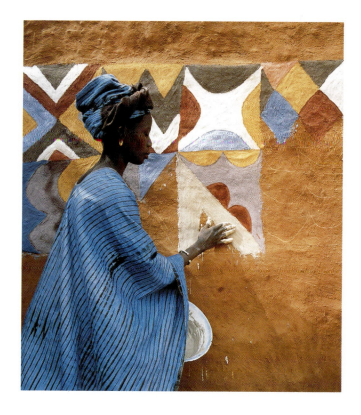

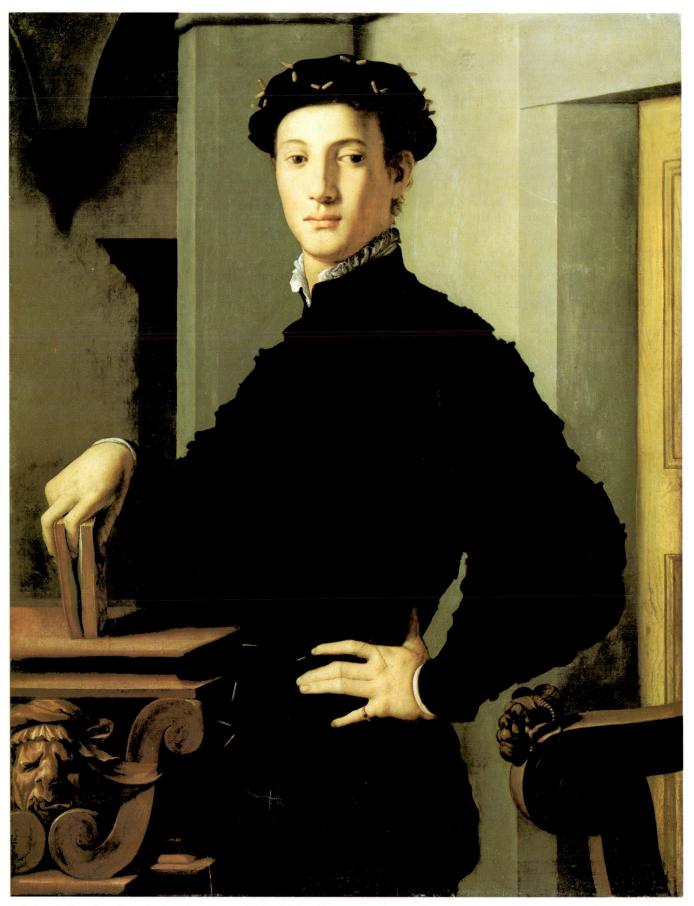

5.2 Angelo Bronzino, *Portrait of a Young Man*, c. 1550. Oil on wood panel, 37⅝ × 29½ ins (95.7 × 74.9 cm). Metropolitan Museum of Art, New York. H. O. Havemeyer Collection.

Approaches to painting have changed as well. In general, the older approach was to plan carefully and execute a painting in stages, beginning with drawing studies of the forms to be represented. Once the drawing satisfied the artist, it was transferred to a support and the forms were developed in a series of stages. In this **indirect** method, used for works such as Bronzino's *Portrait of a Young Man* (**5.2**), perfection in technique was a painstaking matter but was capable of representing subtleties such as the textures of wood and fur and the translucent appearance of skin. Such effects involved a process of sketching, **underpainting** to define the major forms and values, and then a series of overpaintings to tint and describe the forms.

Another approach—the **direct** ("alla prima") method—is to paint imagery directly on the support without staged underlayers. By this means the paint and the painter may reveal their presence. Oil paint, for instance, has a lush, creamy quality. Van Gogh laid down his paint with heavy **impasto** strokes that reflected the spontaneity of his gestures. His paintings (such as *The Starry Night*, 1.21) have appreciably three-dimensional surface textures. Oil paints now available also carry sensually rich colors. In Pierre Bonnard's

5.3 Pierre Bonnard, *Nude in a Bathtub*, 1941–46. Oil on canvas, 4 ft × 4 ft 11½ ins (1.22 × 1.51 m). Carnegie Museum of Art, Pittsburgh, Pennsylvania. The Sarah Mellon Scarfe Family.

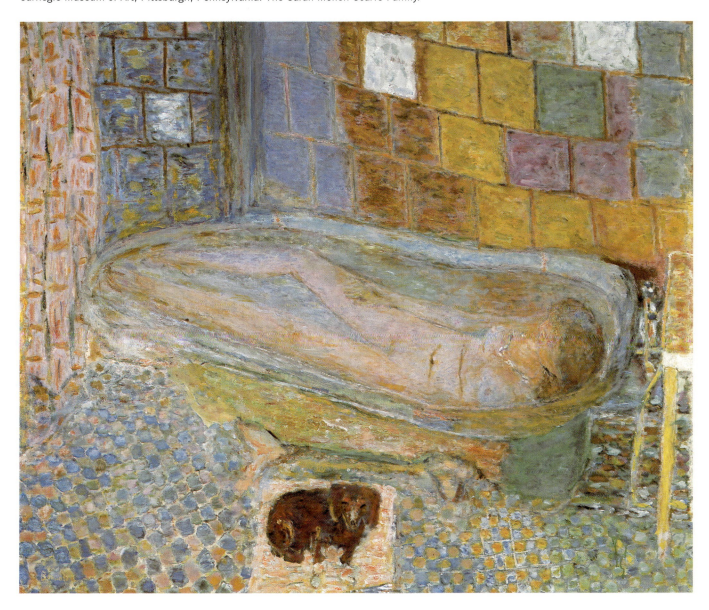

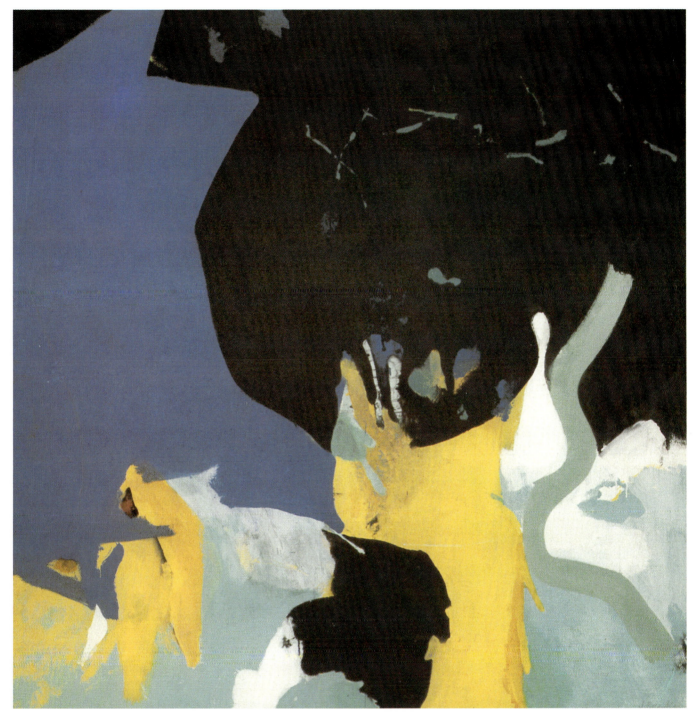

5.4 James Brooks, *Anteor*, 1981. Acrylic on canvas, 5 × 5 ft (1.52 × 1.52 m). Collection Exxon Corporation.

Nude in a Bathtub (**5.3**), the model's body is almost obscured by the way the dabs of paint juxtapose varied colors, breaking up the outlines of the forms. The colors are playful, sensual delights rather than reports of actual local colors; the shapes they "describe" are flattened, abstracted.

Contemporary direct painting does not necessarily call attention to the texture of the paint or the activities of the painter, and may not even be used to describe forms. Whereas canvases are usually treated with a glue solution to hold the paint on their surface and white-lead (**gesso**) to keep oils from rotting the canvas, certain nonobjective painters in the twentieth century worked on **unsized** canvases so that the paint would be absorbed, with no noticeable surface texture and no trace of the artist's hand. Their works (**5.4**) are created with an appreciation for the essential quality of pigment as pure, flat color.

LEONARDO DA VINCI
on CHIAROSCURO

Leonardo da Vinci (1452--1519) was one of the major figures of the Italian High Renaissance. His subtle *Mona Lisa* (**5.5**) is perhaps the world's most famous painting. The mysterious smile of his model has fascinated viewers for centuries. Speculations about the reason for her smile include these: (1) smiling with the left side of one's mouth only was considered a beautiful habit at the time, (2) the young woman was the mistress of the aging artist and was looking at him affectionately, (3) she was in pain from a pulled tooth, or (4) she was beginning to suffer from facial paralysis. It is said that Leonardo took four years to complete the painting and that it was his favorite. In his journals, he wrote that he had lute music played and books read to his model so that boredom would not spoil her smile.

Leonardo was an inventor, sculptor, and architect as well as a painter, and he had far-reaching curiosity about all natural phenomena. His intensive studies of human anatomy involved dissection of corpses, from which he created detailed drawings of musculature, bones, and joints. He also wrote extensively on art, anatomy, machinery, and natural history, but his voluminous writings were never published during his lifetime. His statements about the use of lights and darks in painting help us to understand why the boundaries of Mona Lisa's facial features are soft and undefined, though undoubtedly the darkened dirty state of the varnish now obscures the original colors of the painting:

"The first intention of the painter is to make a flat surface display a body as if modeled and separated from this plane, and he who most surpasses others in this skill deserves most praise. This accomplishment, with which the science of painting is crowned, arises from light and shade, or we may say *chiaroscuro*."

"Shadow is the privation of light. Shadows appear to me to be supremely necessary in perspective, since without them opaque and solid bodies will be ill defined. Those features that are located within their boundaries—and their boundaries themselves—will be ill defined if they do not end against a background of a color different from that of the body. In addition to this, these shadows are in themselves of varying degrees of darkness because they represent the loss of varying quantities of luminous rays, and these I term original shadows, because, being the first shadows, they clothe the bodies to which they are attached. From these original shadows there arise shadowy rays which are transmitted throughout the air, and these are of a quality corresponding to the variety of the original shadows from which they are derived. And on this account I will call these shadows derived shadows, because they have their origins in other shadows."

"Shadow shares the nature of universal things, which are all more powerful at their beginning and become enfeebled towards their end. When I speak about the beginning of every form and quality, discernible or indiscernible, I do not refer to things arising from small beginnings that become greatly enlarged over a period of time, as will happen with a great oak which has a modest start in a little acorn. Rather, I mean that the oak is strongest at the point at which it arises from the earth, that is to say, where it has its greatest thickness. Corresponding, darkness is the first degree of shadow and light is the last. Therefore, painter, make your shadow darker close to its origin, and at its end show it being transformed into light, that is to say, so that it appears to have no termination."

"That body will exhibit the greatest difference between its shadows and its lights that happens to be seen under the strongest light, like the light of the sun or the light of a fire at night. And this should be little used in painting because the works will remain harsh and disagreeable.

There will be little difference in the lights and shadows in that body which is situated in a moderate light, and this occurs at the onset of evening or when there is cloud, and such works are sweet and every kind of face acquires grace. Thus in all things extremes are blameworthy. Too much light makes for harshness; too much darkness does not allow us to see. The medium is best."[1]

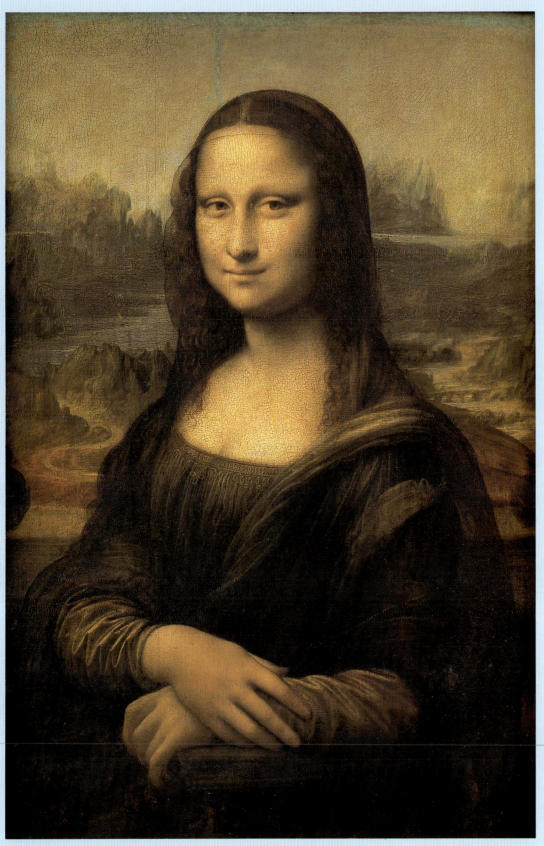

5.5 Leonardo da Vinci, *Mona Lisa*, c. 1503–6. Panel, 30¼ × 21 ins (76.8 × 53.3 cm). Louvre, Paris.

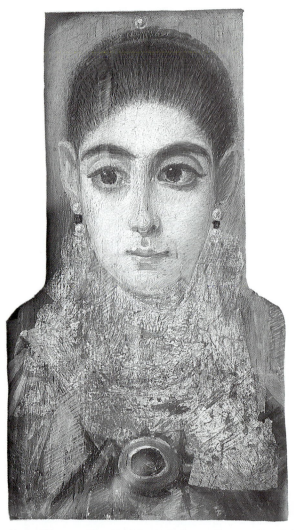

5.6 *Young Woman with a Gold Pectoral*, Egypto-Romano (Coptic), c. 100 AD. Encaustic, 16½ × 9½ ins (42 × 24 cm). Louvre, Paris.

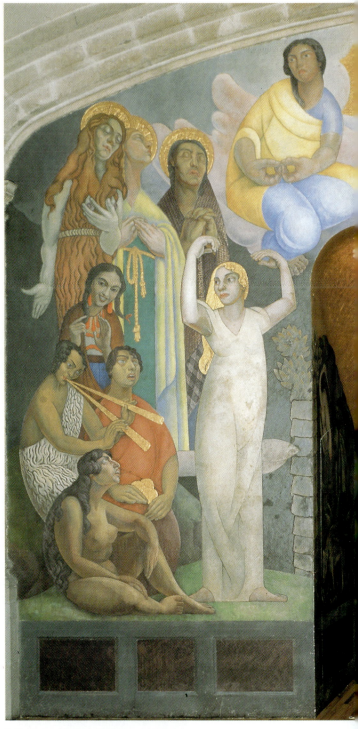

5.7 Diego Rivera, *Creation*, 1922–23. Encaustic and gold leaf, Anfiteatro Bolívar, National Preparatory School, Mexico City.

PAINT MEDIA

Encaustic

A very early method of painting that was used by the Greeks, Romans, and early Christians in Egypt, **encaustic** involves the mixing of pigments with wax. The wax must be kept hot as it is applied, to keep it liquid. Knowledge of the technique used to make such luminous works as *Young Woman with a Gold Pectoral* (**5.6**) was lost for many centuries, though temptingly described by writers such as Pliny. Leonardo da Vinci,

ever the experimenter, may have tried to revive the process in 1503, but his attempts failed. Early in the twentieth century, the Mexican muralist Diego Rivera studied books in Paris describing the techniques of the

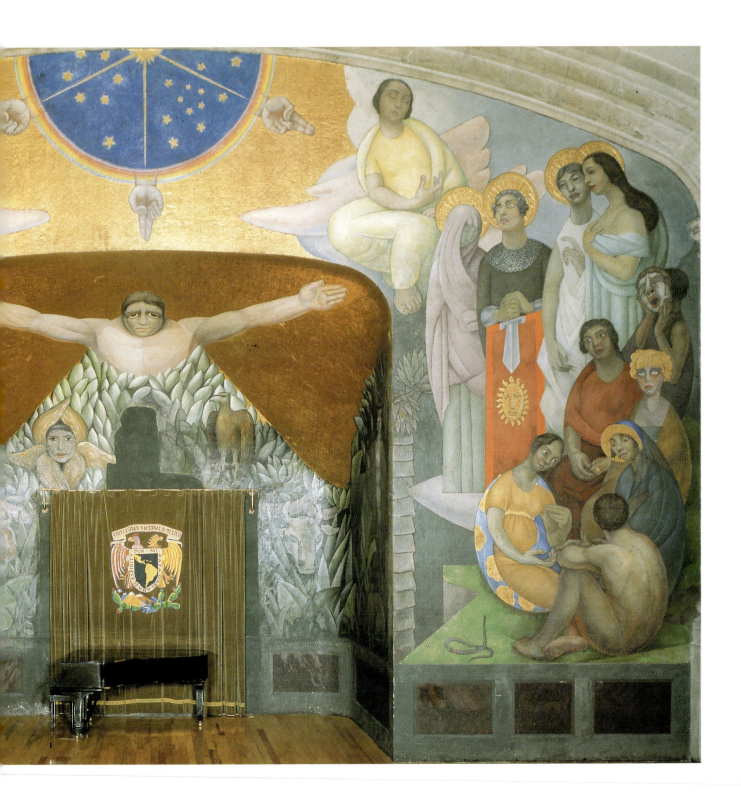

ancient Greeks, Romans, and Egyptians and experimented with combining hot wax and pigments. He was searching, he said, for "the traditional encaustic with its solidity, purity, depth, and richness of colors."[2]

Rivera mastered the difficult encaustic process sufficiently to use it for the first of his immense murals, *Creation* (**5.7**), and then switched to fresco for all his other major works.

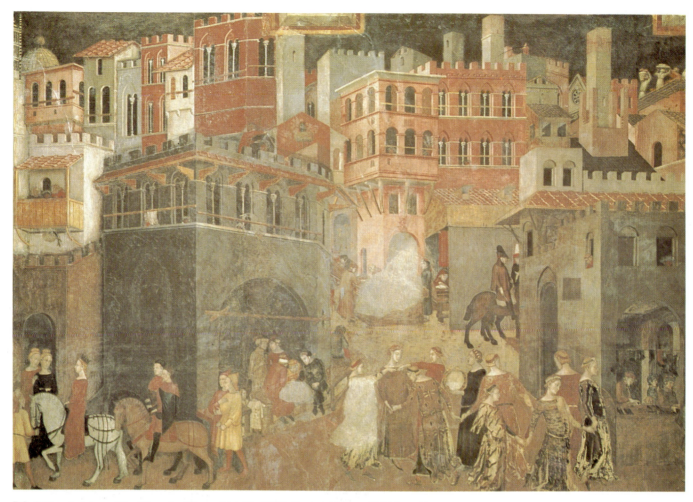

5.8 Ambrogio Lorenzetti, *Allegory of Peace* (detail), 1339. Fresco. Palazzo Pubblico, Siena, Italy.

Fresco

The **fresco** technique was developed by the ancient Mediterranean civilizations, refined to a supreme art by the Italian Renaissance painters, and used with great vigor by twentieth-century Mexican muralists. The word "fresco" means "fresh" in Italian, for traditional *buon fresco* paintings must be created quickly and spontaneously, and allow little room for error. They are wall paintings in which pigments in a water base are painted onto freshly applied plaster. The immediacy of this method is apparent in the lively feeling of the figures in Ambrogio Lorenzetti's *Allegory of Peace* (**5.8**). As indicated in Figure **5.9**, which is a reconstruction of the progress of Lorenzetti's fresco, the wall is first given two or three layers of plaster. Once the last of these is dry, the cartoon of the intended image may be traced or freely sketched by the artist onto the wall. Transparent paper is then used to make a copy of this cartoon; tiny holes are made along the lines of the copy with a perforating wheel. When the final layer of

plaster, the **intonaco**, is applied, a fine powder ("pounce") is tapped along the perforations of the tracing to transfer the sketch onto the wet wall. The

5.9 Layers in a fresco **1.** Masonry wall **2.** Underlayers of plaster **3.** Cartoon of image **4.** Fresh *intonaco* with pounced cartoon for the day's work **5.** Previously completed portion.

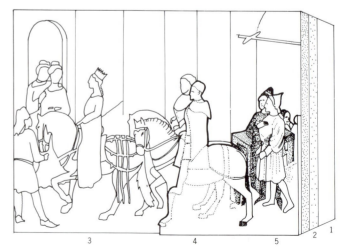

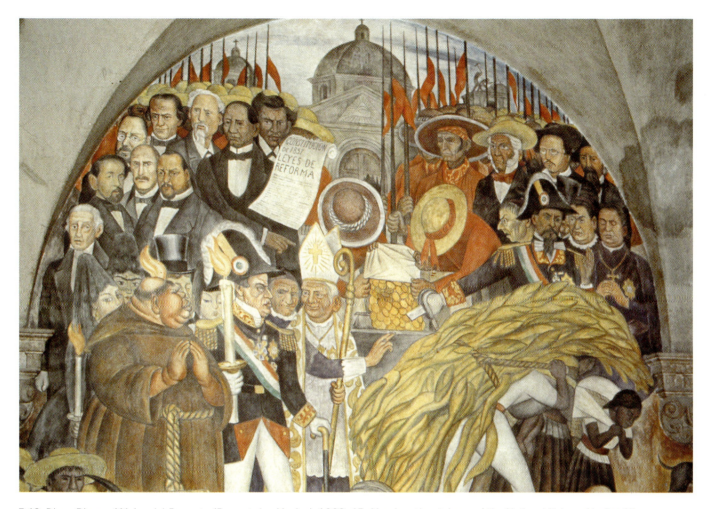

5.10 Diego Rivera, *México del Presente (Present-day Mexico)*, 1929–45. Mural on the stairway of the National Palace, Mexico City.

intonaco is applied over the underlying cartoon in sections small enough to be painted that day while the plaster is still damp, so that the paint is immediately absorbed into the plaster. If changes are made on the surface after the plaster is dry (*a secco*) they are more fragile. Once it is dry, *buon fresco* is as permanent as the plaster of the wall. Over the centuries, chunks of the plaster may fall away, as in *Allegory of Peace*, but fresco is by and large a very durable method of painting, so long as it is indoors. Outdoor frescos are vulnerable to air pollution and to wearing away by wind-blown particles.

Fresco is usually an intense collaborative effort involving a team of plasterers and assistants as well as the artist. For Diego Rivera's huge murals of Mexican political history (**5.10**), plasterers covered a wall with two coats of plaster, and then Rivera sketched with red chalk or charcoal directly on this rough "brown" coat. Assistants traced this sketch onto transparent paper and ran a perforating wheel over the copy. Very early in the morning, a third coat of plaster was applied to the part of the wall to be painted first that day, and the sketch was pounced with lampblack powder. Rivera had specified the area, following the lines of the shapes rather than a uniform square, so that all figures could be finished rather than trying to match colors another day.

Once the plaster had dried to the proper humidity, Rivera was awakened, usually about dawn. The plaster would remain sufficiently wet for six to twelve hours, depending on the weather, and his method was to paint the same area twice in one day. The first painting was to establish black modeling of the figures, the second to add colors. Even as he worked, usually sitting on a scaffolding, another team of plasterers was preparing a second section of the wall. Rivera would continue painting until evening, when there was no longer enough natural light to work by. Examining the day's work by the dim light, he often decided it was not quite right, and would instruct his assistants to remove it all. The same lengthy process would begin again the next morning.

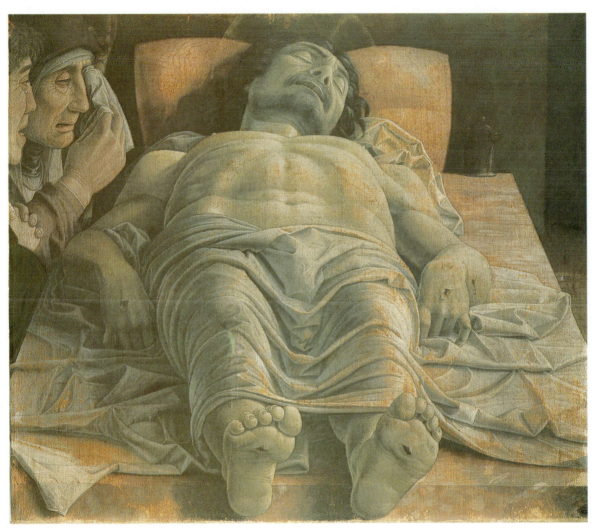

5.11 Andrea Mantegna, *Dead Christ*, after 1466. Tempera on canvas, 26¾ × 31⅞ ins (66.8 × 81 cm). Pinacoteca di Brera, Milan, Italy.

5.12 Layers in a tempera painting. **1.** Wood panel **2.** Gesso and perhaps linen reinforcement **3.** Underdrawing **4.** Gold leaf **5.** Underpainting **6.** Final tempera layers.

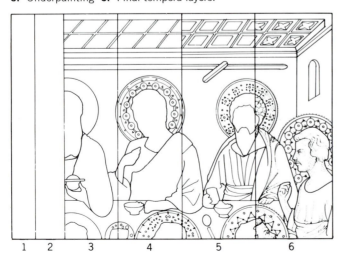

Tempera

Another old and very demanding painting technique involves the mixing in water of pigments with water-soluble egg yolk or some other glutinous material. The resulting **tempera** paint dries very quickly to a matt finish that will not crack, as can be seen in Andrea Mantegna's *Dead Christ* (**5.11**). Unlike later paints, tempera colors will not blend or spread well. The artist must painstakingly lay down tiny individual brush-strokes side by side, hatching or cross-hatching to cover an area with pigment (**5.13**). The painting of the final surface follows lengthy preparation procedures.

As diagrammed in Figure **5.12**, a simplified detail of Ugolino's tempera painting of the *Last Supper* (3.13),

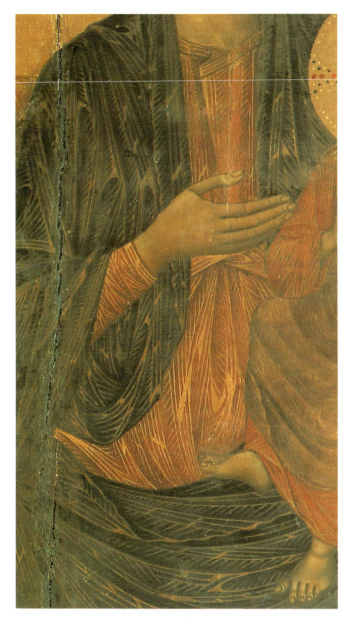

5.13 Cimabue, *Madonna Enthroned with Angels and Prophets* (detail of 2.75), c. 1280–85, showing handling of tempera paint. Tempera on wood, 12 ft 6 ins × 7 ft 4 ins (3.85 × 2.23 m). Galleria degli Uffizi, Florence.

leaves of gold are applied over the gilder's clay in layers, each of which is also burnished. As the gold leaf wears off, patches of the red gilder's clay underneath may show through.

Then comes underpainting. Most areas are first underpainted with a base tone of their local colors. But to keep flesh tones from appearing too flat, the painting guilds of the Middle Ages worked out a system of underpainting flesh passages with *terre verte* (green earth). In the final layers of the painting, the flesh areas are covered with pink pigment; the bits of green that show through make the complementary reds of the skin seem more vibrant. A faintly greenish cast that persists can often be seen in the finished work.

It is so difficult to create lively, fresh paintings with tempera that most artists eventually switched to oil paints. But a few contemporary artists still use this old medium quite skillfully, most notably Andrew Wyeth (**5.14**).

5.14 Andrew Wyeth, *The Virgin*, 1969. Tempera on canvas, 46 × 36 ins (116.8 × 91.4 cm). Brandywine River Museum, Chadds Ford, Pennsylvania.

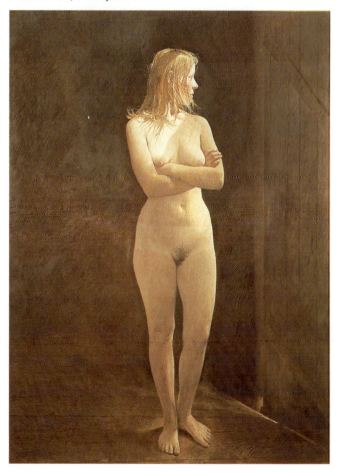

the support used—wood or canvas—is first coated with gesso. This is a fine white substance that gives the panel a smooth, brilliant, eggshell finish that accepts paint readily and has enough "tooth" to allow control of the brush. After the gesso dries, the cartoon of the drawing is scratched onto it. These scratched outlines can sometimes be seen beneath the paint in the finished work. If there are to be gold areas in the work, they are covered with a light coating of red gilder's clay, **burnished** (rubbed) to a gloss. Extremely thin

Oil

Tempera is a **lean medium**—a uniform thin film. By contrast, paint that uses oil as a binder for pigment is called **fat**. It can be piled up thickly and dries very slowly, allowing the artist to blend colors right on the canvas. The use of oil paints by artists began in the fifteenth century, opening great vistas to painters. Now they could simulate textures, portray the effects of light and shadow, model three-dimensional forms, add tiny bits of colors as highlights, and work from the darkest to the lightest tones without losing the brilliance of the pigments.

Vermeer's *Girl with a Pearl Earring* (**5.15**) is sparkling and lush in its use of color. The girl's garments are softly modeled, and her face glows with a fresh brilliance that can be seen now that the canvas has been cleaned and restored to what are considered its original colors (but see Box on page 232 for discussion of the controversies surrounding restorations). It is

5.15 Jan Vermeer, *Girl with a Pearl Earring*, c. 1665–66. Oil on canvas, 44.5 × 39 ins (113 × 99 cm). Stichting Vrienden van het Mauritshuis (no. 670), The Hague, Netherlands.

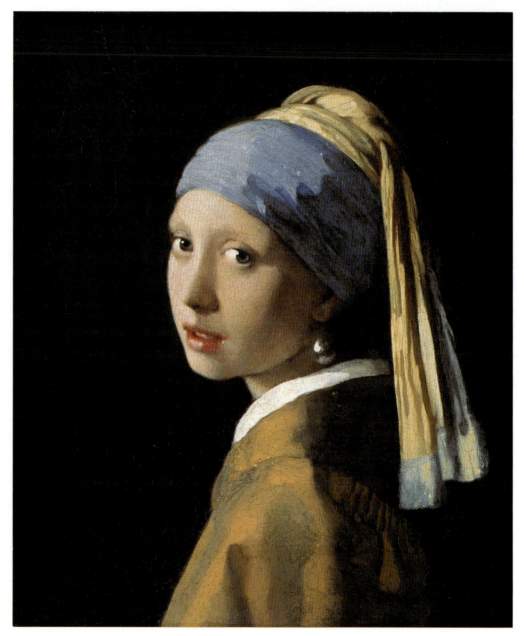

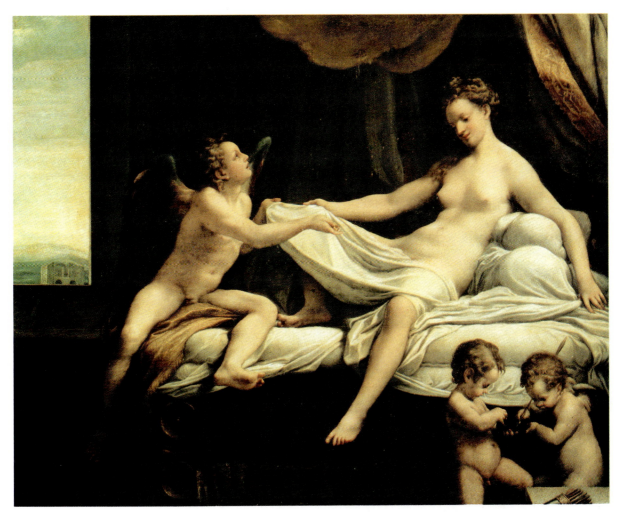

5.16 Antonio Correggio, *Danae*, c. 1532. Oil on canvas, 64½ × 29 ins (163.5 × 74 cm). Galleria Borghese, Rome.

known that Vermeer used costly ultramarine, made from the semi-precious stone lapis lazuli, as a blue-green pigment. He also created delightful highlights on the girl's lips, earring, and eyes by placing dots of light-reflecting paint on the surface of the painting.

Using oils, artists could work with optic realism, for, as they began to recognize, we do not necessarily see figures distinctly. Unless the air and light are very clear, colored areas may blend together visually. In Tintoretto's *Leda and the Swan* (3.11), which was painted entirely in oils, the attendant's dress merges into the dark tones of the background, as do Leda's left arm and hair, emphasizing her radiant torso as the central focus of the painting.

This radiance or luminosity is another special characteristic of traditional oil paintings. The flesh of Correggio's *Danae* (**5.16**) actually seems to glow. Even the shadows glow with life. These striking effects were

the result of underpainting and then overpainting with layers of **glazes** (films of pigments suspended in a transparent medium) to build up color tints and details of form. A very light passage, such as Danae's body, might be thickly underpainted with white and then glazed with skin tones; a dark passage such as the shadows of the room might be underpainted with brown and then glazed with thin layers of a darker gold-brown.

An unfinished painting by Leonardo da Vinci (**5.17**) allows us to see how he has blocked out certain areas by underpainting before building up details and optical effects with glazes. The painting appears much flatter than his completed works, such as *The Virgin of the Rocks* (15.23). Underpainting and then over-painting deepens the shadows of dark areas and also gives more tinting power to lighter and brighter pigments. Layers may also be used to create a more life-

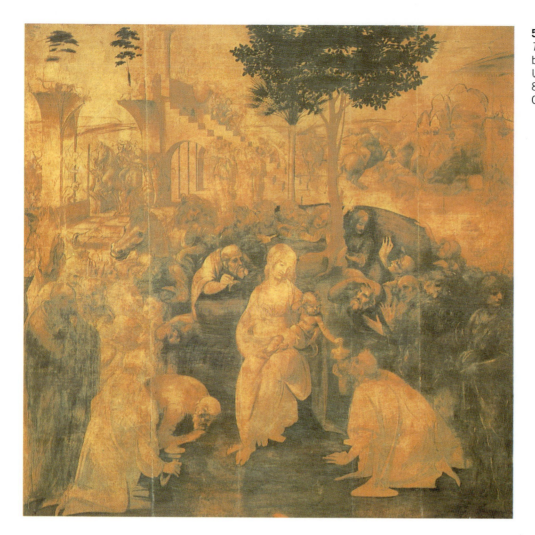

5.17 Leonardo da Vinci, *The Adoration of the Magi*, begun 1481 (unfinished). Underpainting on panel, 8 ft × 8 ft 1 in (2.44 × 2.46 m). Galleria degli Uffizi, Florence.

like color sensation, with green beneath red, for instance, to bring out its brilliance by complementary contrast.

Oil paint is itself luscious and can become part of the visual focus of a work. Hans Hofmann's *Rhapsody* (5.18) is a celebration of the sheer vitality and flexibility of the medium. Color passages are built one atop the other, by scumbling (brushing one opaque layer of paint on top of a dried lower layer in such a way that some of the undercolor still shows through) and heavy impasto strokes that leave such a thick deposit of the medium that the strokes of brush or palette knife are recorded as an actual texture on the surface. When layered wet, oil colors can be blended; if the underneath hue is to be kept the same, it is allowed to dry before the next layer is applied.

A layer of **sizing**, traditionally derived from animal skins, is typically given to canvas to reduce its absorption of the paint. A **ground**, white or tinted, of white

chalk, warm glue, and water ("glue gesso") or white pigment in linseed oil is often applied to the surface before painting, giving it a characteristic overall tone. The oil paint is applied in various methods: the artist may first draw important outlines on the support, or, in the direct or *alla prima* method, paint all the colors and details in a few sessions or a single session. In the indirect method, the artist works in steps, painting one color or object, letting it dry and then adding a glaze.

Highly saturated hues in prepared tubes of paint were a nineteenth-century innovation. Earlier oil paintings were built on a more subdued palette created from natural pigments, ground and mixed with oil by apprentices who devoted years to learning how to formulate paint.

5.18 (opposite) Hans Hofmann, *Rhapsody*, 1965. Oil on canvas, 7 ft ¼ in × 5 ft ½ in (2.14 × 1.54 m). Metropolitan Museum of Art, New York. Gift of Renate Hofmann, 1975.

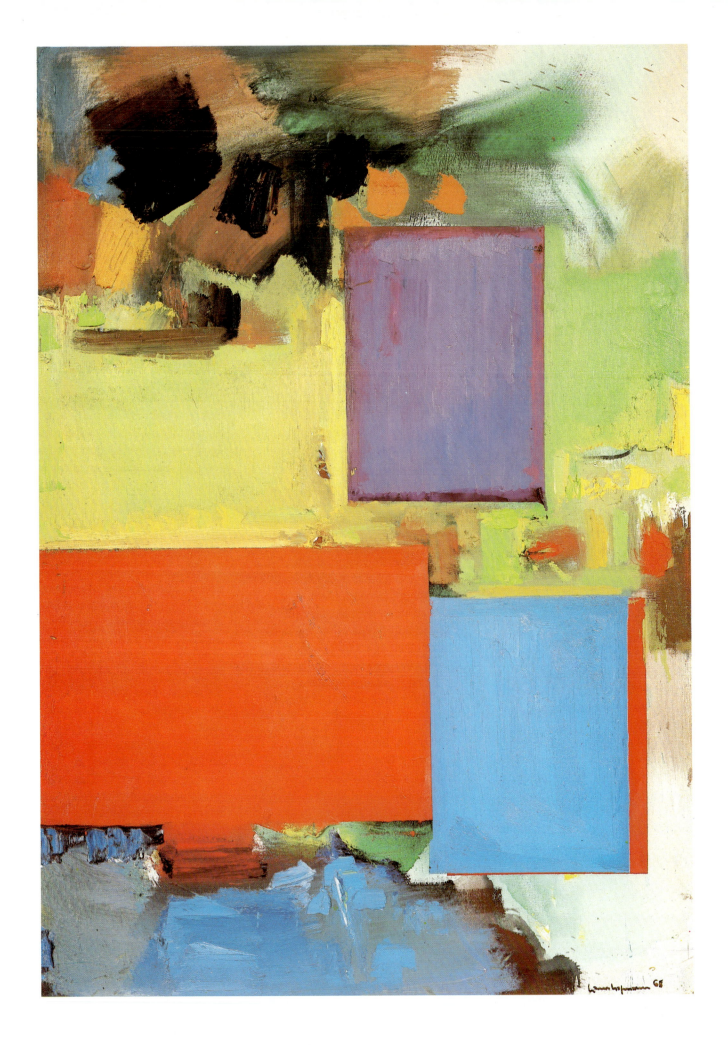

ART ISSUES
CLEANING AND RESTORING PAINTINGS

Over the centuries, great paintings are vulnerable to damage by aging processes, dampness, and filth. They may be further damaged by the methods used by restorers to attempt to clean and repair their surfaces. And attempts to repaint areas that are damaged are inevitably controversial, for restorers, no matter how skillful, do not have the rare talent and aesthetic judgment of the original masters.

Attempts to clean and restore great paintings are now undertaken with considerable caution. Restorer Pinin Brambilla Barcilon worked on a miniature scale for over twelve years trying to bring Leonardo da Vinci's *The Last Supper* (3.31) back to life as the master had originally painted it. Such restorations are now matters of high technology, including infrared and ultraviolet photographic analyses of what lies beneath the surface, and microscopic examination of paint chips to determine their layers. Even so, the restorer's task is quite daunting and, in some cases, nearly impossible.

The Last Supper is a restorer's nightmare. It is painted on a wall in the convent of Santa Maria delle Grazie, but it is not a fresco. Leonardo had apparently treated the wall as if it were a wood panel and painted it in tempera. Art historians speculate that this approach allowed Leonardo to work at his own pace and make corrections to the painting, whereas fresco cannot be handled in this way. But soon after its completion in 1497, the tempera began to decay and crumble off the damp refectory wall. To try to save the masterpiece,

it was repainted twice in the eighteenth century and three more times in the nineteenth century. It is thought that what then remained to be seen was only twenty per cent Leonardo's work; the rest was painted by restorers.

How can anyone, even working with the most sophisticated of means, now be sure what the original looked like? The surface of the mural has disintegrated into myriad delicate flakes, each no bigger than a grain of rice. No single pattern can be discerned in the layers of the flakes after the painting has been reworked with different painting approaches and additions of glues, waxes, and lacquers. Brambilla says:

"There are various strata of colors, and all sort of ditches and depressions beneath them. And there is an incredible variety of materials in the painting, meaning that a cleaning technique that might have worked in one section could be totally ineffective or even harmful a few centimeters away."[3]

Despite the treacherous difficulties, Brambilla claims that repainters' work is easily distinguished from Leonardo's original painting when each flake is examined under a microscope, cleaned, and then reattached to the wall. It has thus been determined that the roof beams as shown in Figure 3.31 are the work of a repainter; Leonardo's beams are actually in a different place, beneath the ceiling that was apparently added to the painting in the eighteenth century. The restored painting of the figures is also different, more three-dimensional

than earlier repaintings. Are we now seeing the true hand of Leonardo revealed afresh or the hand of the latest restorer at work?

The question of authenticity has brought great controversy into some restoration projects. Most notably, controversy raged throughout the major twentieth-century restoration of the Sistine Chapel ceiling in Rome (16.19). Opponents of the project particularly object to the newly brilliant but rather flat and simple colors, convinced that they are not those originally used by the artist. As we will see in Chapter 16, critics also assert that the new cleaning has removed delicate *a secco* overpaintings by which Michelangelo had finished the modeling of his figures and added details. Supporters of the restoration claim that Michelangelo worked only in the best *buon fresco* tradition, with very little *a secco* overpainting, so that nothing significant has been lost during the restoration, and that the newly cleaned fresco reveals Michelangelo's extraordinary use of color.

Even routine removal of aged varnish to clean the surface of paintings may engender controversy. Artists have traditionally used varnish on their paintings to protect the surface and keep the underlying image clean. The idea was that the varnish would be removed from time to time, again revealing the clean surface, which would then be revarnished. The varnish itself would get dirty and change color as it aged, usually turning yellow. Grays and greens then tend to look brown, and blues turn green. (It was not until the 1930s that artists had access to

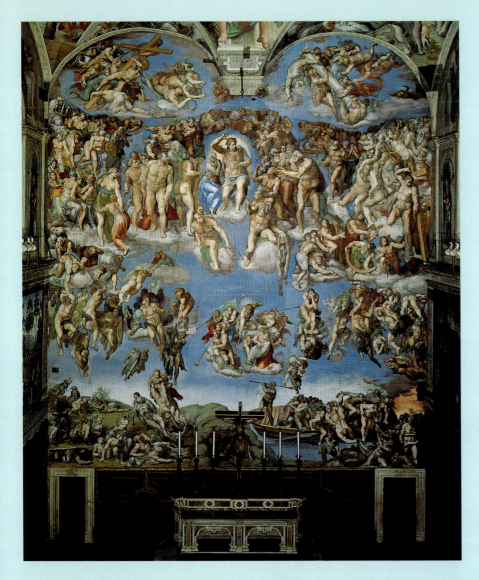

5.19 Michelangelo's *Last Judgment*, end wall of the Sistine Chapel, after latest restoration (completed c. 1994). Vatican City, Rome.

acrylic varnish, which dries clearer than glass.) Other materials have accumulated on top of the yellowing varnish. In addition to being darkened by the soot from the candles of the devout, church paintings in Italy and elsewhere were often rubbed with bacon rind before major holidays. To remove these coatings without harming the glazes of the painting itself is very difficult. Even water brushed lightly over the surface may dissolve glazes as well as varnish.

Leonardo's *Mona Lisa* is extremely dirty, as you can see in Figure 5.5, but it is otherwise in good condition and is only dusted lightly each year. Cleaning has been eschewed to avoid outraging a public who are accustomed to the painting as it is, with thick yellowed

varnishes. A clue to its original colors is revealed when Mona Lisa's frame is annually removed for dusting: a clear blue color can be seen on the untrimmed and unvarnished edges of Leonardo's painting of the sky. Elsewhere the built-up layers of varnish are reportedly a quarter of an inch (0.63 cm) thick. The Louvre's chief curator of paintings, Pierre Rosenberg, explains that the painting has not been cleaned because it was treated with reverence from the beginning and thus escaped harmful restorations. Now, he says, "We are not afraid of the job—it's a simple procedure—but of reactions nationally and internationally."[4] When other oil paintings by Leonardo have been

restored, it has been discovered that he worked with extraordinarily fine strokes, some as minute as 0.0013 of an inch (a thirtieth of a millimeter), and sometimes he blended areas with his fingers for a soft-focus *sfumato* effect.

Public reactions and technical difficulties in rejuvenating a masterwork are not the only problems in restoration. Aesthetics may be lost in the process. Art history Professor James Beck of Columbia University argues that, especially in the case of restoration of Michelangelo's huge *Last Judgment* fresco on the end wall of the Sistine Chapel, restorers have worked piece by piece and thus have lost the aesthetic harmony of the whole. Beck explains:

"The fundamental problem was that no viewing distance was possible. Seen at arm's length, the oversized details, segments, and fragments were overwhelming but fundamentally misleading."[5]

Even if they had tried to step back and look at the huge painting as a whole from a distance, as an artist must when working, the restorers' vision would have been blocked by the maze of scaffolds erected for the restoration. After four years of section-by-section work, the scaffolds were removed and the restoration unveiled. According to Beck, it was a "garish and disharmonious" mistake. No consistent light source remained, and the figures appear flat, with loss of the modeling effects of careful differences in value. Another loss, claims Beck, is Michelangelo's shifting use of outlines sometimes as borders and sometimes as shadows. Figure **5.19** shows the entire *Last Judgment* after its recent restoration, for comparison with Figure 1.41.

Watercolor

An extremely fluid and transparent medium—**watercolor**—is created when pigments are bound with a water-soluble binder such as gum, thinned with varying amounts of water, and applied to wet paper. The white of the paper is usually allowed to shine through the thinned pigment in some areas. Whereas the white usually appears as the background against which images have been worked, Richard Lytle brings the white into the foreground as the color of flower petals in his *Spring Thaw on Goose Pond* (**5.20**). Note how well watercolor adapts itself to portraying the transparency of water and sky here, with one tone blurring into another.

Although watercolor can be applied with a "dry brush" it is generally a very runny medium, so hard to control that Lytle's tight rendering is exceptional. Watercolor cannot be extensively corrected and reworked, unlike oil paint, so the artist is committed to each stroke, which must be made quickly, before the paper dries. This necessity becomes a virtue in the hands of artists such as Turner, whose *A Whale Aground* (**5.21**) uses the medium's liquid freedom of gesture and transparent airiness to the fullest. The heaviness of the whale is barely suggested by the shadowed area in this powerful and free abstraction.

A more traditional approach to watercolor is exemplified by Winslow Homer's *The Gulf Stream* (**5.22**). The paint looks very wet, as if freshly painted, but bleeding into the paper and blending of colors are carefully controlled, with the white of the paper revealed as a significant design element.

5.20 Richard Lytle, *Spring Thaw on Goose Pond*, 1986. Watercolor, 30 × 41½ ins (76.2 × 105.4 cm). Courtesy of the artist.

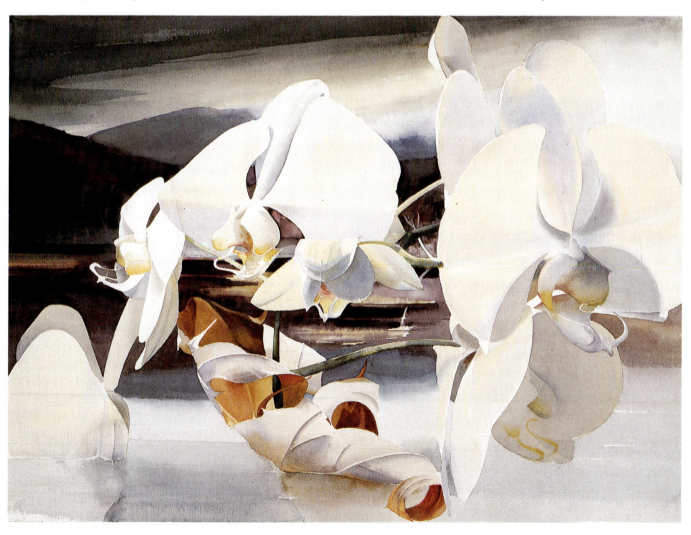

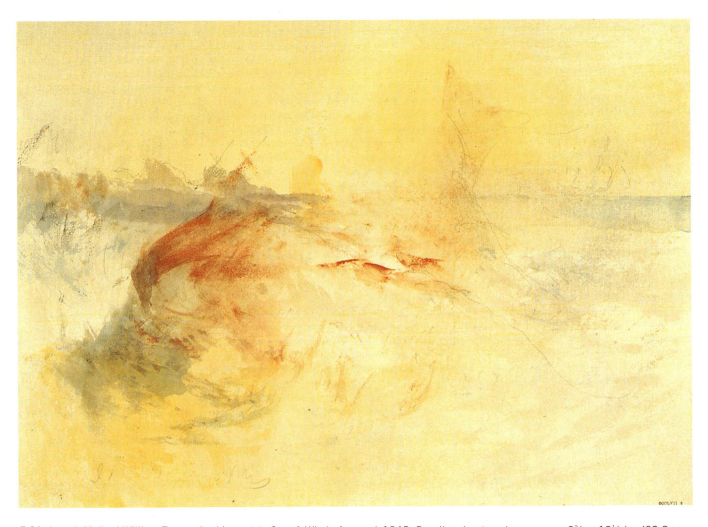

5.21 Joseph Mallord William Turner, *Looking out to Sea: A Whale Aground*, 1845. Pencil and watercolor on paper, 9⅜ × 13¼ ins (23.8 × 33.5 cm). Tate Gallery, London.

5.22 Winslow Homer, *The Gulf Stream*, 1899. Watercolor, 11⅜ × 20 ins (28.9 × 50.9 cm). Metropolitan Museum of Art, New York.

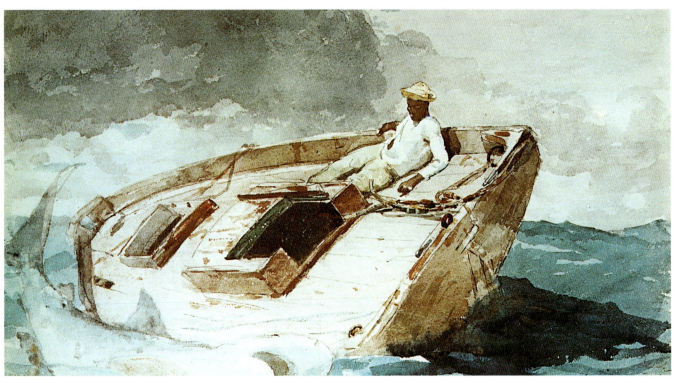

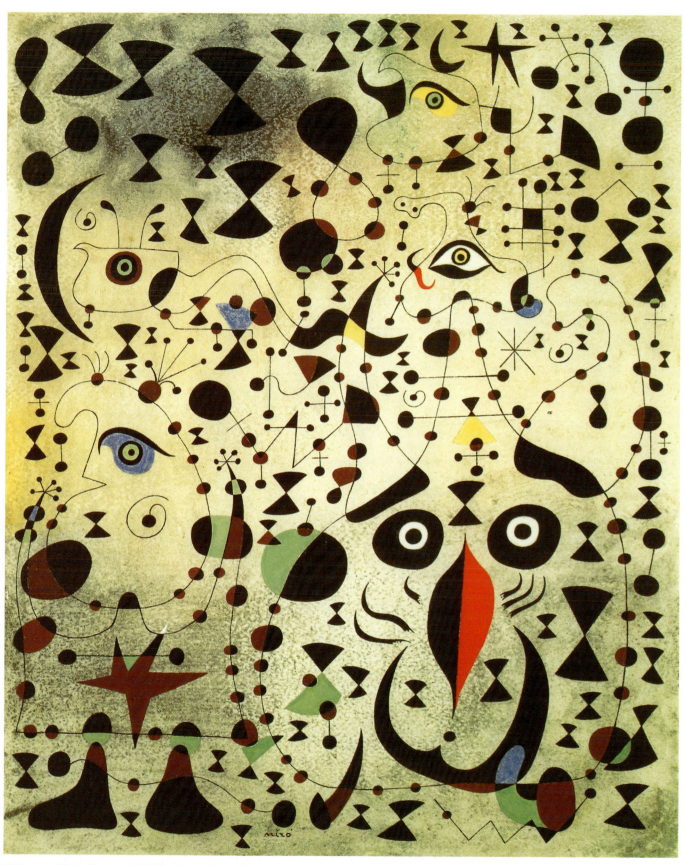

5.23 Joan Miró, *The Beautiful Bird Revealing the Unknown to a Pair of Lovers*, 1941. Gouache and oil wash on paper, 18 × 15 ins (45.7 × 38.1 cm). Collection Museum of Modern Art, New York. Acquired through the Lillie P. Bliss Bequest. Photograph © 1997 MOMA.

Gouache

In contrast to the transparency of watercolor, **gouache** is an opaque medium. It, too, is water-soluble, but in this case it is mixed with inert pigments such as Chinese zinc white or chalk for opacity, with gum arabic as the binder. This combination makes painting with gouache feel like spreading not quite melted butter, in contrast to painting with oils, which flow like melted butter. Some artists use opaque gouache passages to strengthen their otherwise transparent watercolors: some paintings referred to as "gouache" are actually watercolors painted over an opaque white ground.

Gouache cannot be piled up like oil paint, for it will crack if heavily built up. But it will stay opaque as it ages, rather than becoming more transparent as watercolor tends to do. This means that it can be worked over a colored ground and be counted upon to cover it thoroughly.

In Joan Miró's *The Beautiful Bird Revealing the Unknown to a Pair of Lovers* (**5.23**), the fantastic galaxy of lines and shapes sits atop a toned ground without any bleed-through of the underlying color. In Miró's hands, gouache was the instrument of a spatially flat other-worldly vision.

Gouache is quite flexible, however, and can also be used to create realistic illusions of depth and form. And whereas Miró painted dark over light, the artist using gouache can also paint light colors over dark without bleed-through. In Bill Martin's *Abalone Shells* (**5.24**), a tour de force of realistic gouache painting, light highlights sit atop darker areas.

Gouache dries very quickly by water evaporation, in contrast to oils that dry slowly by oxidation. Gouache is usually painted in immediate, spontaneous, direct ways; wet can so soon be painted over dry that blending of adjacent colors is difficult. The paint is also flat and non-reflective. Despite these characteristics of the medium, Bill Martin has painstakingly juxtaposed soft-edged areas of similar hues to create striking pearlescent illusions of glossy, light-reflecting surfaces. The opaque gouache gives the shells a convincing solidity: even the paint has the appearance of thickness. This is a special characteristic of gouache. Even though it cannot be built up deeply like oils, it forms a film of paint on a surface, unlike watercolor, which sinks into the paper.

5.24 Bill Martin, *Abalone Shells*, 1982. Gouache, 11⅞ × 15¾ ins (30.2 × 40 cm). Courtesy of the artist.

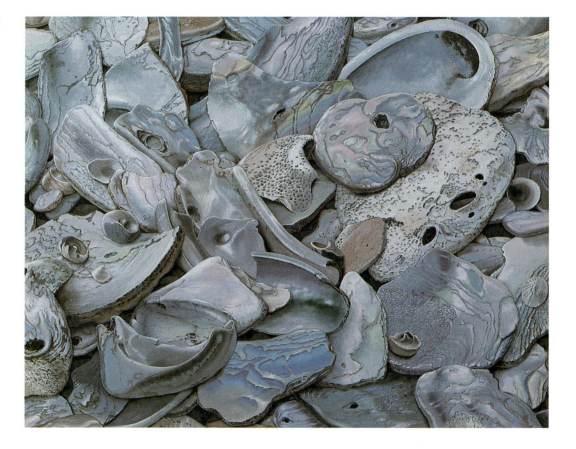

Synthetics

Several decades ago, **synthetic media** created chemically rather than derived from natural substances were introduced as part of the artist's tool kit. The form most used today—called **acrylic emulsion**, or **acrylics**—is a water-based medium that can be used straight from the tube with techniques similar to those of oil paints, thinned and blown out as a fine spray through an **airbrush**, or thinned right down to the consistency of watercolor. Acrylics dry quickly, and for this reason are preferred by some artists to oils. This property not only allows the artist to complete a

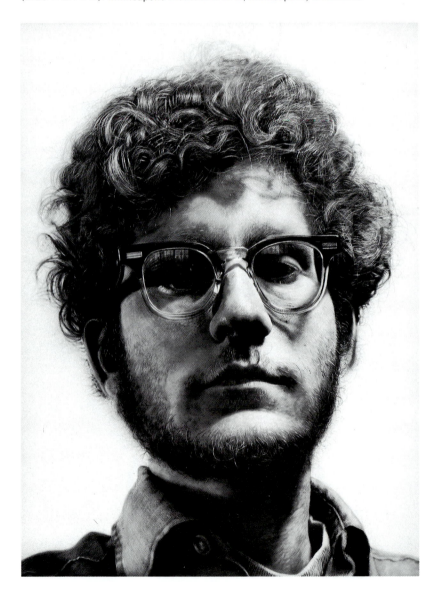

5.25 Chuck Close, *Frank*, 1968–69. Acrylic on canvas, 7 ft × 9 ft (2.13 × 2.74 m). Minneapolis Institute of Arts, Minneapolis, Minnesota.

painting quickly, but also makes it possible to create special effects, such as painting hard-edged shapes by laying a line of masking tape over previously painted, already dried areas. Even without tape, acrylic stops where the brush stops, unlike oil, which spreads slightly into the canvas. A retarder may be added to extend the period during which the acrylic paint is workable.

Very bright, pure colors can be formulated with synthetics; without the pigment, the medium itself would dry clearer than glass. The colors do not yellow with age, as oils tend to do. Acrylics are also permanent and fade-proof; in theory, even if the support rots away, the acrylic paint won't. Its molecular structure is similar to that of the superglues, so it has tremendous bonding power and can be used on many different grounds. Not all artists have switched from slow-drying oils to acrylics, however, for acrylics have a different feel and optical quality and are less easy to blend on the canvas. They do not have the sheen of oils, and whereas oils flow from the brush like softened butter, acrylics have a slight drag.

Airbrushing with acrylics can be used to create very even gradations in value. As used by some fantasy illustrators and commercial artists, these transitions are flawless rather than more realistically irregular. But by precisely controlling the gradations, Chuck Close is able to create photorealistic human heads of monumental proportions, such as his *Frank* (**5.25**), which is nine feet (2.75 m) tall. Close begins with a photograph which he blows up and transfers to the canvas by a grid system and then re-creates in minute detail, complete with facial blemishes and slightly fuzzy areas where the close-up photograph was out of focus.

Helen Frankenthaler's *Hint from Bassano* (**5.26**) demonstrates how synthetic paints behave when thinned to the consistency of very fluid watercolors. The paint can get so runny that Frankenthaler often works with her canvases on the floor rather than on an easel. Unlike watercolors, acrylics can be painted in

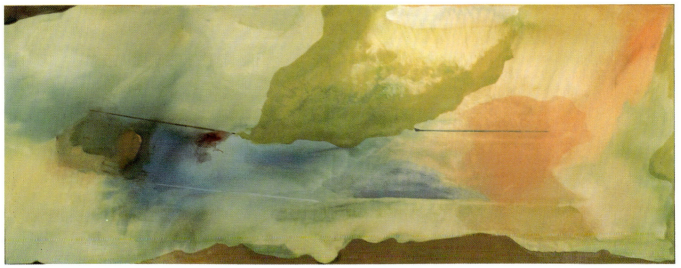

5.26 Helen Frankenthaler, *Hint from Bassano*, 1973. Acrylic on canvas, 7 ft 1 in × 18 ft 11¼ ins (2.16 × 5.77 m). Collection of Mr. and Mrs. David Mirvish, Toronto, Ontario.

layers, allowing the preservation of the hue of an underlayer rather than the blending that occurs when two watercolor hues are laid on top of each other wet. Frankenthaler's thinned acrylics sink into the unsized canvas and become part of that ground itself, rather than sitting on top of it. She had earlier used a similar technique with oils thinned with turpentine, but the turpentine left a halo where it spread into the canvas. The striking freshness of the results is a quality for which she aims:

A really good picture looks as if it's happened at once. It's an immediate image. For my own work, when a picture looks labored and overworked, and you can read in it—well, she did this and then she did that, and then she did that—there is something in it that has not got to do with beautiful art to me. And I usually throw those out, though I think very often it takes ten of those over-labored efforts to produce one really beautiful wrist motion that is synchronised with your head and heart, and you have it, and therefore it looks as if it were born in a minute.[6]

5.27 Layers in painting.

General method commonly used in Europe after the 1600s	Claude Monet	Helen Frankenthaler
Support: canvas or wood	Support: canvas	Support: raw, unsized canvas
Gesso	Pale gray, cream, or beige ground	
Oil paint, beginning with dark ground	Broad areas of local color using thin, opaque, scumbled oil paint	Acrylic paints thinned to watercolor consistency, sinking into and blending with the canvas
Glazes (thin layers of pigment in transparent medium, with lighter colors over the dark ground)	Layers of oil paint, brushed as a web of colors over the partially visible lower layers	
Varnish to protect the painting		

Collage

A relatively new art form, introduced in 1912 by Picasso, is **collage**. Though technically classified with paintings, a collage does not necessarily involve the application of paint to a surface. Rather, it is built up two-dimensionally, or as a relief, by selecting and gluing to a surface varying flat materials, such as the colored papers, leaf, and Polish stamp in *Connecticut Remembered* (**5.28**). For the artist, it is exciting to collect materials that are interesting in themselves—such as old documents and drawings—and then combine them into an effective whole. Having ready-made areas of colors, textures, and shapes that can be physically moved around allows a very experimental approach to design. One item compels the artist to lay another next to it. For the viewer, the excitement comes first in responding to the work as a whole and

5.28 Paul Zelanski, *Connecticut Remembered*, 1986.
Collage, 8 × 10 ins (20.3 × 25.4 cm). Courtesy of the artist.

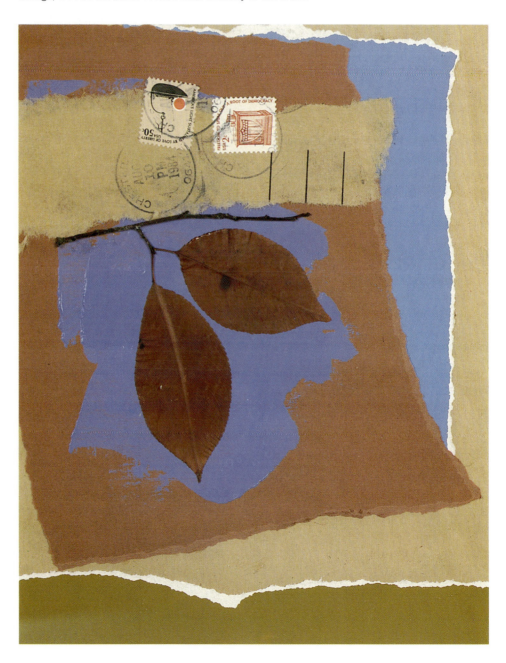

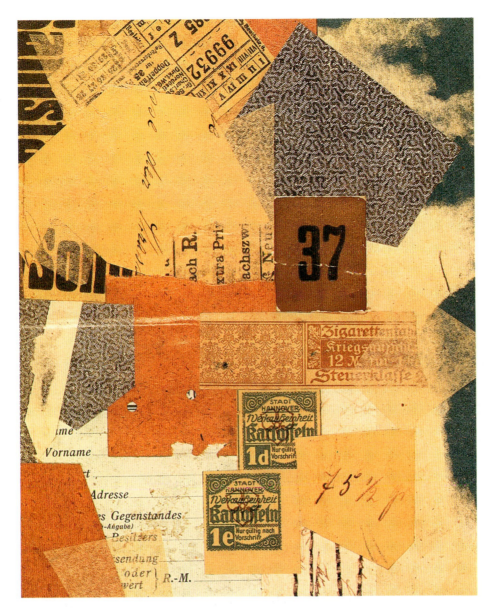

5.29 Kurt Schwitters, *Merz 19*, 1920.
Collage on paper, 7¼ × 5⅞ ins (18.4 × 14.7 cm).
Yale University Art Gallery, New Haven, Connecticut.

then trying to figure out the original identity of its parts. As in a successful recipe, one does not at first notice the different spices used as ingredients.

Kurt Schwitters, a master of collage, often used bits of paper with writing or printing that read first as abstract design elements and then, as one examines the work more closely, as cryptic clues to meaning. Schwitters was working in the period after World War I in Germany in which inflation was so great that stamps were overmarked from 5 marks to 5 million marks, and money was so worthless that houses were wallpapered with banknotes. But Schwitters has given these discarded fragments of a disordered life a kind of dignity by the way in which he has put them together.

In a successful collage, such as *Merz 19* (**5.29**) the fragments appear to be spontaneously laid down, but are actually chosen and juxtaposed very carefully. If one more thing were added to this collage, it would be too much; if one thing were subtracted, its visual unity would fall apart.

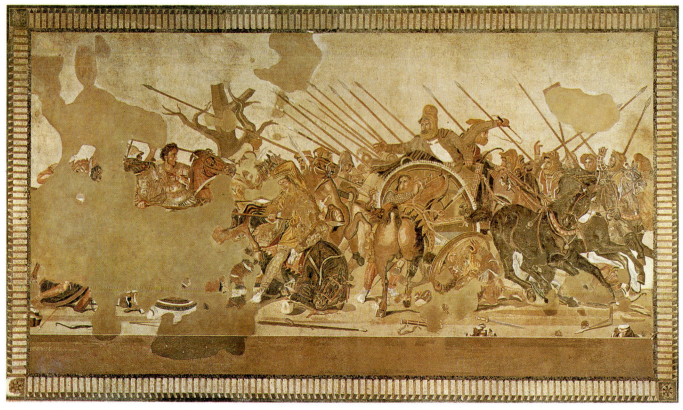

5.30 *The Battle of Issus*, 2nd to 1st century BC. Mosaic, 8 ft 11 ins × 16 ft 9½ ins (2.72 × 5.13 m). Museo Archeologico Nazionale, Naples.

5.31 *The Battle of Issus*, detail of Alexander the Great.

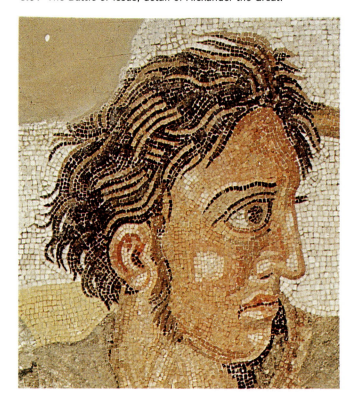

Mosaic

An ancient and long-lived technique for creating two-dimensional imagery, **mosaic** is composed of small pieces of colored ceramic tile, glass, pebbles, marble, or wood. These are embedded in cement along the surface of a wall, floor, or ceiling of a building. The subtleties possible with this process are illustrated by *The Battle of Issus* (**5.30**), an impressive Roman mosaic that was buried by the eruption of Vesuvius in A.D. 79 and not unearthed until the eighteenth century. The image is a lively depiction of Alexander the Great's defeat of the Persians (Alexander is bare-headed at left, with the Persian King Darius in retreat in his chariot). Its vigorous realism seems all the more surprising when we recognize that the colors are composed of small **tesserae**, cubes of natural stone that can more readily be distinguished in the detail (**5.31**). The hues are limited to black, white, yellow, and red, but stones of varying values in each hue have been used to suggest spatial modeling and to provide details for the forms.

Mosaics were common in the early civilizations of Sumeria, Greece, and Rome and were used to decorate early Christian and Byzantine churches until the fourteenth century, when the cheaper medium of fresco was introduced. But the technique has not been lost. Visionary architect Lluís Domènech i Montaner used it lavishly and playfully in the decoration of architectural structures such as pillars in his Palau de la Música Catalana in Barcelona (5.32). An exhilarating feast for the senses, the building borrows from the Byzantine, Moorish, and Gothic styles of Catalonia's past. The architect's exuberant use of the mosaics on the pillars almost negates their function. Pillars are usually convincingly solid visual evidence that they are holding up heavy structures. We don't expect them to appear so flowery and airy as these do. Here the tiles are much larger than in the Roman mosaic and no attempt is made to hide their identity as individual pieces.

5.32 Lluís Domènech i Montaner, balcony of the Palace of Catalan Music (Palau de la Música Catalana), Barcelona.

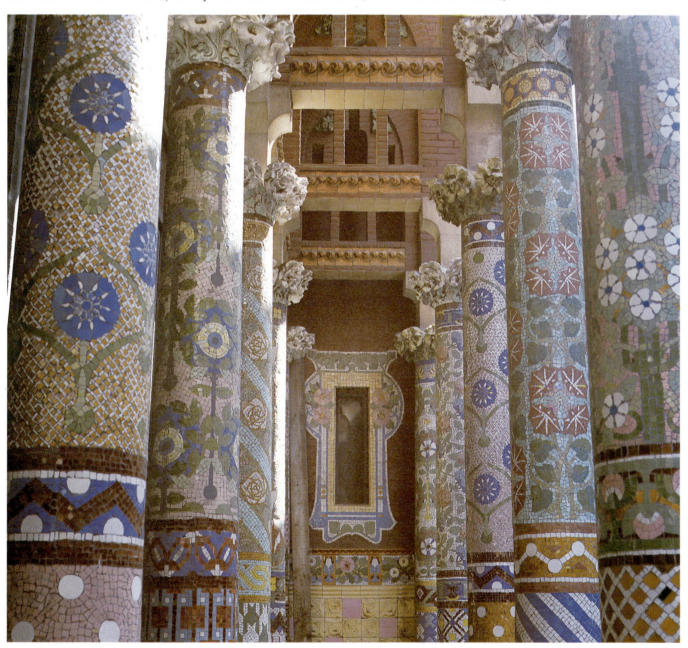

MIXED MEDIA

Art forms no longer fit neatly into the traditional categories. We live in a period of great experimentation with all media, and some artists are introducing media and art forms that have never existed before, such as computer graphics (see Chapter 9). Often media are mixed, crossing all previous boundaries. Robert Rauschenberg gleefully mixes media, combining fine art techniques such as painting and printmaking with a great variety of ready-made and partially altered bits of popular culture, in ways that suggest meaning, even if one cannot be quite sure what it is. His *Monogram* (**5.33**) features a stuffed ram within a tire mounted on a base of Abstract Expressionistic paintings. Rauschenberg says the point is to:

> begin with the possibilities of the material and then you let them do what they can do. So that the artist is really almost a bystander while he is working. The hierarchy of materials is completely broken down.[7]

5.33 Robert Rauschenberg, *Monogram*, 1959.
Stuffed ram, automobile tire, collage, and acrylic, 4 × 6 × 6 ft (1.22 × 1.83 × 1.83 m).
Moderna Museet, Stockholm.

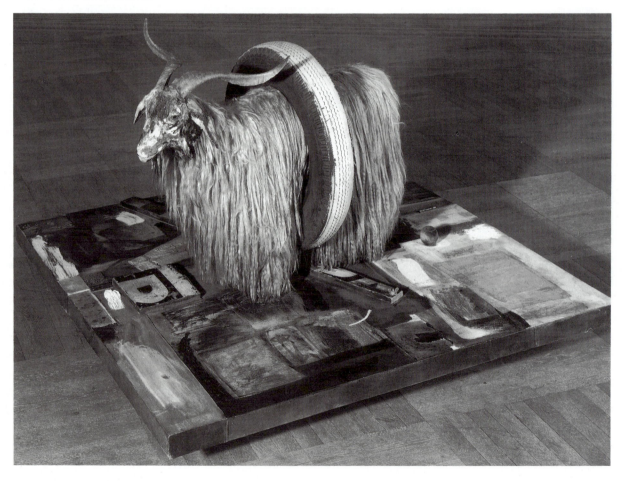

6

PRINTMAKING

Prints—images made by transference of ink from a worked surface onto a piece of paper, usually in multiples—were originally used as illustrations in books and other kinds of printed matter. Books, in turn, were largely dependent on the appearance of inexpensive, readily available paper. Aside from hand-illustrated, one-of-a-kind treasures (such as the Duc de Berry's Book of Hours, shown in Figure 2.156), books were illustrated with images printed from durable blocks of wood, metal plates, or stones worked by hand. Even after photomechanical methods of reproduction removed this need for prints, the print-making arts continued to be practiced, for prints became valued as artworks in themselves. Now artists can print a limited edition of an image and sell each one as an original.

Processes used for the creation of transferable images allow great variety in artistic styles. Some prints are similar to tightly rendered representational drawings. Antonio del Pollaiuolo's influential *Battle of the Ten Nude Men* (6.1) is a highly skilled example of this approach. All of the muscular human forms and foliage

6.1 Antonio del Pollaiuolo, *Battle of the Ten Nude Men*, c. 1460.
Engraving, 15⅛ × 23¼ ins (38.4 × 59 cm). Metropolitan Museum of Art, New York. Purchase 1917, Joseph Pulitzer Bequest.

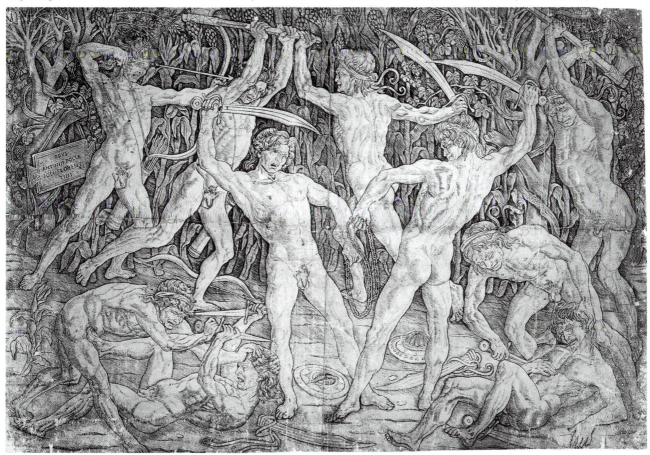

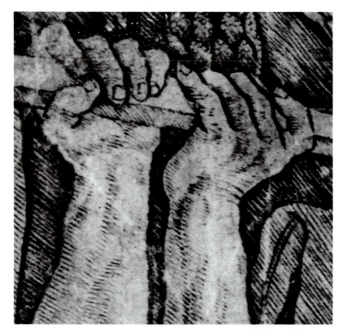

6.2 *Battle of the Ten Nude Men* (detail), c. 1460.

6.3 Hokusai, *Southerly Wind and Fine Weather*, late 1820s. Woodblock print, 10 × 14¾ ins (25.5 × 37.5 cm). British Museum, London.

in this line engraving are built up through a series of small lines, as shown in the detail view (**6.2**). The painstaking effort involved in making such a work is not immediately evident because of the great vigor of the image as a whole. Pollaiuolo's skill as an engraver apparently derived from his training as a goldsmith, but his genius in conceiving this dramatic composition of opposing lines far transcends mere manual skill.

A far freer approach to the block is apparent in Hokusai's *Southerly Wind and Fine Weather* (**6.3**), one of his famous views of Mt. Fuji. With stylized simplification of natural cloud and tree forms into flat shapes and a limited palette of hues, it creates an atmosphere all its own that expresses the respect of the Japanese people for their most-loved mountain. The color woodcut print was highly developed in Japan as a way of illustrating popular picture books. Hokusai, one of the greatest of the practitioners of the art, created tens of thousands of such prints, each of which was reproduced in multiples and usually sold very cheaply. These mass-produced **ukiyoe** woodcut prints were not considered fine art until pages from one of Hokusai's

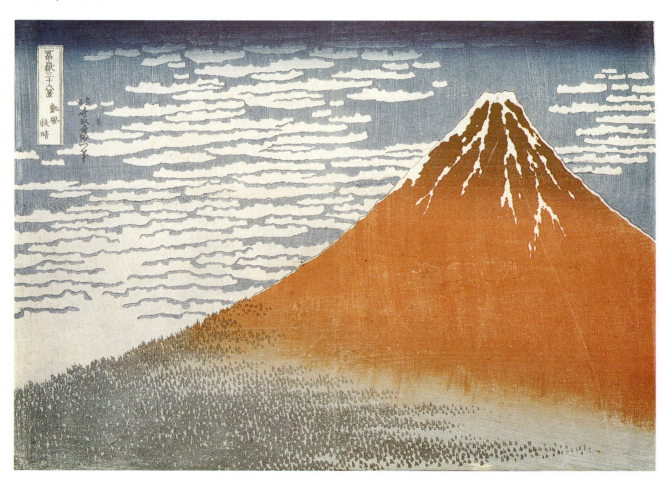

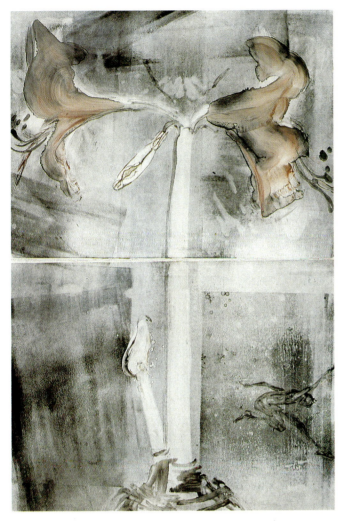

6.4 Mary Frank, *Untitled*, 1977. Monotype on two sheets, printed in color, 35½ × 23¹³⁄₁₆ ins (90.2 × 60.4 cm). Collection Museum of Modern Art, New York. Mrs. E. B. Parkinson Fund. Photograph © 1997 MOMA.

illustrated books turned up in Paris in 1856 as packing material for a shipment of valued porcelains.

Printmaking has usually been defined as a method for creating multiple identical copies of an image by repeatedly inking and printing a worked plate. An alternative introduced in the seventeenth century is **monotype**, a printmaking process in which the artist paints an image directly onto a sheet of metal or glass with printer's ink or paint and then presses paper onto it to transfer the image. Some ink or paint may be left on the surface, as a ghost of the image which can then be re-inked and reprinted. Each time the image may change slightly, so no two monotype prints will be exactly alike. And the fact that the artist is printing and improvising freely, perhaps even wiping off areas with turpentine and adding something else, rather than

scratching fixed lines, gives the monotype an entirely different quality from other prints, as is evident in Mary Frank's soft and fresh rendering of an amaryllis in bloom (**6.4**).

Another departure from traditional definitions of printmaking is the possibility of making an image that is transferred without any ink. Covers of some books are **blind embossed**, pressed against an uninked cut plate of metal to create an image that can only be seen when it is turned against the light to bring out the shadows in its indentations.

There are many ways of preparing a plate to be printed. Most can be grouped into four major categories: relief, intaglio, planographic, and stencil. Each is explored below.

PRINTMAKING PROCESSES

Relief

In a **relief** technique, a block of wood, metal, linoleum, or even a found object is carved so that lines and areas to be printed are raised above areas that will stay blank. A simplified diagram of the process is shown in Figure **6.5**.

The classic relief process is the **woodcut**. Typically, a drawing of the intended image is created on or transferred to a smooth block of soft wood—though some artists develop the image directly on the block, as they cut it. Everything that is to remain as an inked line or area is left intact; all other wood near the surface is carved away with a knife along the edges of lines. Gouges are used to remove large areas of wood. All cut-away areas will be shallower and will not pick up ink when it is applied to the surface with a roller. After the woodblock is inked, a sheet of paper is pressed onto it in such a way that it picks up, in reverse, the inked image.

Traditional European woodcuts used intricate lines of hatching and even cross-hatching to build up tones and textures, rather like ink drawings. Although it is much more difficult and indirect to carve wood

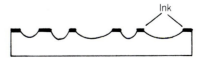

6.5 Cross-section of a relief block.

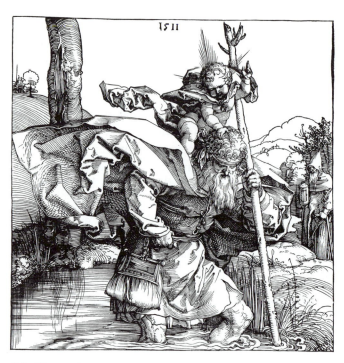

6.6 Albrecht Dürer, *Saint Christopher*, 1511. Woodcut.
Metropolitan Museum of Art, New York. Fletcher Fund 1919.

6.7 Antonio Frasconi, *Portrait of Woody Guthrie*, 1972.
Woodcut, 23½ × 38¾ ins (59.7 × 98.4 cm).
From Antonio Frasconi, *Frasconi—Against the Grain*
(New York, Macmillan Publishing, 1972).

away from lines than to draw them, this approach to the medium was handled with superb technical and aesthetic proficiency by Albrecht Dürer. Although Dürer was personally skillful at woodcutting, like many artists of the period he often prepared only the drawing, delegating the actual cutting of the block to some of the finest artisans of the time. Dürer's *Saint Christopher* (**6.6**) illustrates the range of tones and flowing lines these collaborators were able to coax out of the stiff, flat wood. Some were used as book illustrations; others were sold as single sheets so cheaply that the middle classes could afford to buy them.

Although the woodiness of the block is well hidden in Dürer's work, some contemporary artists have chosen to reveal the character of the wood. Different kinds of wood have very different grain patterns, which appear as lines in the printed areas. Wood from the beech tree and fruit trees—such as cherry, apple, or pear—is uniformly hard and even-grained. These woods are often used when the artist wants to create fine details that will stand up to hundreds of printings of the block and to avoid obvious grain lines. Certain species of pine, on the other hand, have wood that varies considerably in softness and hardness from

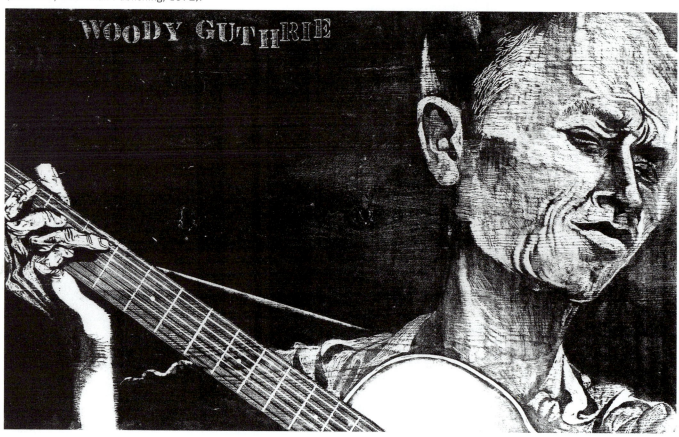

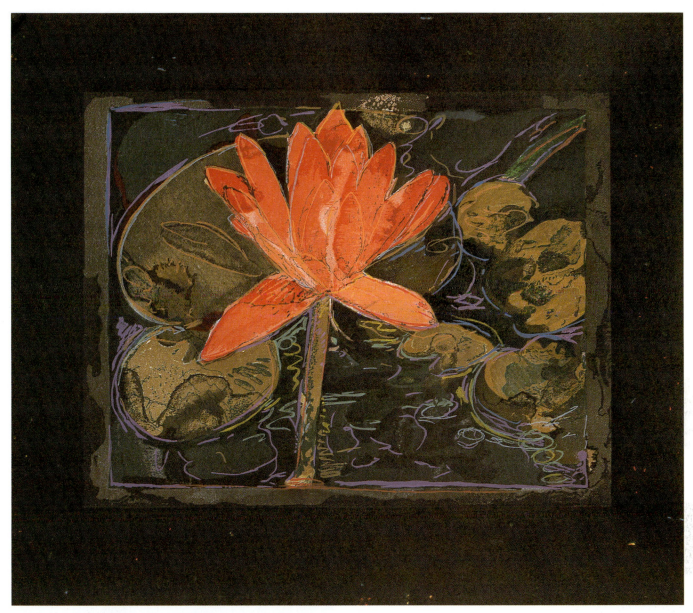

6.8 Joseph Raffael, *Matthew's Lily*, 1984. Twenty-eight-color woodcut, edition of 50, 32 × 37 ins (81.3 × 94 cm). Courtesy of the artist.

one ring to another, producing strong grain lines that the artist may choose to exaggerate in order to create visual textures in the print. The grain may be heightened by scraping a wire brush across it so that it will be sure to print. In Antonio Frasconi's *Portrait of Woody Guthrie* (**6.7**), the woody quality is a quiet visual pun that accentuates the rough-cut, homespun character of the folk guitarist. The grain—which can clearly be seen running horizontally through the work—is also used to indicate tones and textures, in a rather serendipitous fashion. Whites with bits of grain printed through them become optically grayer.

Woodcuts can also be executed in colors, as in Joseph Raffael's *Matthew's Lily* (**6.8**), in which the image is composed of twenty-eight colors. The traditional way of adding extra colors—developed to a precise art by the Japanese *ukiyoe* printmakers—is to cut a series of precisely matched blocks, each having only the area to be printed in a certain color raised as a printing surface. To match the blocks, a master or "key" block with the essential details is first cut and inked, and numerous reference prints are made from it. Areas that are to be printed in different colors are then indicated on these prints. These guides are glued face-down onto new blocks, one for each color, and everything except the intended colored areas is cut away. At the corners, beyond the edges of the print, registration guides are also cut to help in precise placement of the paper used for the final printing of the entire image. After all the blocks are cut, the same piece of paper is printed by each of the blocks, usually working from lighter to darker tones. The ink is somewhat transparent, and where two colors overlap they will blend. Interestingly, although Germany and Japan had little contact with each other until the mid-nineteenth century, their artists had devised very similar ways of printing color woodcuts from a series of blocks. The chief difference in the result was the more delicate values of the Japanese prints, which were made with water-soluble rather than oil-based inks. As an alternative to the use of separate blocks, some woodcuts were hand-tinted, one-by-one.

When the end-grain rather than a lengthwise slab of wood is cut, the process is called **wood engraving**. The cross-section of a tree trunk is less likely to splinter than a lengthwise plank and can be incised directly with burins and gravers.

As Figure **6.9** indicates, wood engraving tools are solid rather than having grooved cutting lips like woodcutting tools. The engraved lines become areas that do not print, and are therefore white in the print. Wood engravings are typically conceived as white lines cut directly, rather than black lines from which the wood to either side has been cut away. The difference in these two approaches becomes apparent by contrasting Dürer's classic woodcut style (6.6) with the wood engraving of Fritz Eichenberg (6.10). Ecclesiastes' beard, hair, and musculature are all described primarily with white lines within areas left black. Of wood engraving, Eichenberg says:

> I have made thousands of drawings for many purposes, I have made many etchings and lithographs, but nothing can compare to the excitement when again I hold in my hand a beautiful block of close-grained,

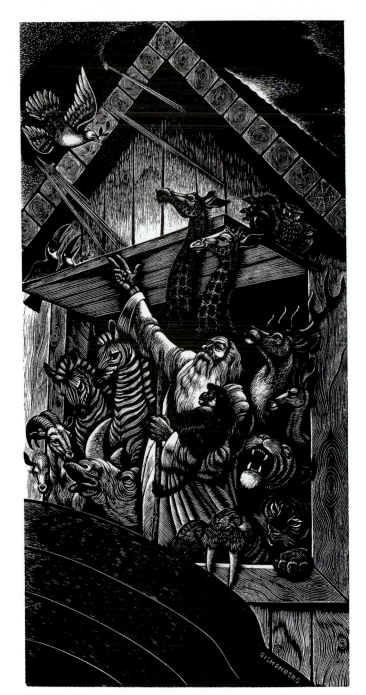

6.10 Fritz Eichenberg, *Ecclesiastes*, "*And in her mouth was an olive leaf*," 1945. Wood engraving, 12 × 6 ins (30.5 × 15.2 cm).

polished boxwood. I caress the silky surface before the burin touches it, digs in lightly, and then glides smoothly through the wood. A little curl rises from the groove in the path of the tool. I am in control, I am happy.

Wood engraving is a contemplative medium; it gives one time to think, to meditate, to listen to good music. As the graver cuts into the darkened surface, it creates light, order, beauty, out of a piece of a living thing, a tree perhaps much older than the artist himself. There are no shortcuts as the artist conjures out of a small square of wood a microcosm of life.[1]

6.9 (left) Wood engraving tools. (right) Wood cutting tools.

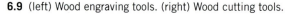

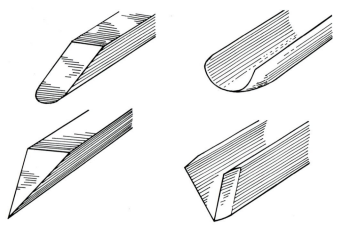

STEPHEN ALCORN
on THE CHALLENGE OF LINOCUTS

Stephen Alcorn is a contemporary printmaker and painter whose work is often commissioned for applied art uses such as book covers. He cites both Picasso (6.12) and his father, John Alcorn (see Figure 2.3), as his greatest inspirations:

"Although I am not particularly indebted stylistically to these pivotal influences in my life, fundamental aspects of their guiding philosophy have permeated my work and have left an indelible mark on the way I perceive the world around me. Curiously, I have felt compelled to seek ways of combining the sophistication and complexity of vision of the twentieth-century artist with the innocence, honesty, and naiveté of the most humble primitive. Over the years I have sought to develop this particular dichotomy, while striving to carry on the tradition of the turn-of-the-century [20th century] printmaker for whom there existed little, if any, distinction between the fine arts and the applied arts. In this regard I am particularly indebted to my father, who as a craftsman could not resist endowing each and every mark he made with a sense of purpose and beauty."[2]

" 'Black is noble,' proclaimed the great French artist Odilon Redon (2.47) almost a century ago. With that inspired conviction so simply stated fresh in my mind, I momentarily cast aside the complex color printmaking techniques I had been employing and returned to the directness and simplicity of the black and white linocut. I was attracted to linoleum by the uncompromising discipline it requires. It is not a flexible medium. The challenge that faces the artist who chooses to make linoleum cuts lies in bringing the surface of this versatile material to life. Since the linoleum block possesses no texture or grain of its own, whatever tonal gradations, ornamentations, or patterns that appear in the final print must be deliberately invented, in contrast to media such as charcoal or lithography, where the artist can hide a lack of structure in the drawing by creating facile atmospheric effects, or oils, where the possibilities for creating subtleties with transparent glazes are endless.

Linocut is a medium that requires the utmost economy of means by the artist, forcing one to distill one's images and successfully translate them into graphic textures, signs, and patterns that can effectively be cut. A print is in fact a 'mirror' image of the original drawing on the block. Consequently, the artist works in reverse, not only in the sense of one's orientation of left and right but in terms of the positive and negative elements as well, requiring considerable foresight on the part of the artist. Furthermore, what one cuts away cannot be put back, making this a most unforgiving medium.

Linoleum is a bold and healthy medium. It requires vigor, decisiveness, and solidity in drawing. And to experiment to find ways to enrich the initially barren uncut surface, to make it come to life, is very exciting."[3]

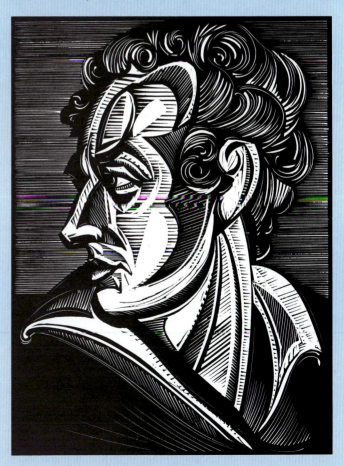

6.11 Stephen Alcorn, *Don Juan*, 1984.
Linocut, 12⅞ × 10 ins (33 × 25.2 cm).
From *The Bibliophile's Calendar*, Meriden-Stinehour Press, 1986.

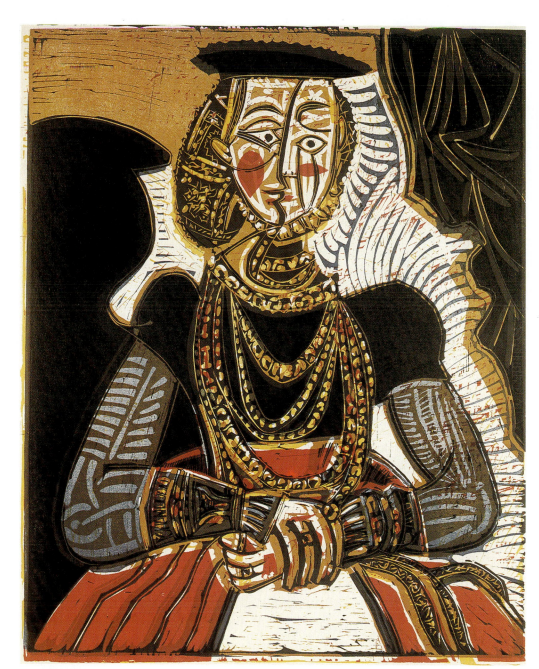

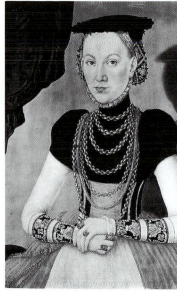

6.12 (left) Pablo Picasso, *Bust of a Woman after Cranach the Younger*, 1958. Color linocut, 25¼ × 21⅛ ins (64.1 × 53.7 cm).

6.13 (above) Lucas Cranach the Younger, *Portrait of a Woman*, 1564. Oil on wood, 32⅝ × 25⅛ ins (83 × 64 cm). Kunsthistorisches Museum, Vienna.

Wood engraving was adopted for printing illustrations in books and newspapers until it was replaced by photographic methods at the end of the nineteenth century. When illustrations were needed quickly for new stories, a team of wood engravers who had been trained to use the same style were given different parts of an image to cut, and then their blocks were bolted together and printed as a unit. The engraved blocks could be clamped into place at the same height as type and the two printed together to make illustrated texts.

In the twentieth century, linoleum blocks have been added to the printmaker's options. Linoleum cuts, commonly referred to as **linocuts**, lack the directional character of woodgrain. Lines can be cut equally smoothly and uniformly in any direction, and uncut areas can print in a strong solid black, as in Stephen Alcorn's *Don Juan* (**6.11**). When lines are made directly with a gouge, rather than being what is left after the surrounding wood is carved away, the image is often conceived as white lines within a black area, rather than vice versa. Lines tend to be free flowing and bold, reflecting the speed of the direct cuts. Although linoleum is easy to cut, it is also somewhat crumbly and cannot be used for ultra-fine lines. Linocuts have been eschewed by some serious artists because of their association with children's art, but using the medium well is actually quite difficult.

Some prints, such as wood and steel engravings, have historically been used as a means of reproducing works of art originally executed in other media. Picasso plays with this method in his color linocut *Bust of a Woman after Cranach the Younger* (**6.12**). It is loosely derived from Cranach's sixteenth-century painting, *Portrait of a Woman* (**6.13**). Note that the linocut image is the mirror opposite of the painting; Picasso apparently worked it with the same orientation as the painting, but when the sheet was pulled off the inked block, the image was reversed. Picasso's linocut version is also obviously much more direct and playful. For the multiple colors of his linocuts he developed the **reduction print** method of continually cutting away areas on a single block, inking the surface a different color at each stage rather than cutting a series of registered blocks.

Intaglio

The second major category of printmaking methods is **intaglio**, a term derived from the Italian word for engraving. As shown in Figure **6.14**, it is the exact opposite of relief techniques. In intaglio prints, the image is cut into the surface of a plate. Thin ink is applied to the plate with dabbers that force the ink into all the grooves. The plate is then wiped so that no ink remains on the surface, and a sheet of dampened paper is pressed onto the plate so that it picks up the ink that remains in the sunken areas. For special tonal effects or softening of the lines, the plate may first be rubbed lightly with a piece of gauze or muslin, lifting small amounts of ink from the incisions. To avoid missing any part of the image, a strong roller press—traditionally hand-operated but now mechanized—is used for intaglio prints. There is a slight sculpting of the paper as it is pressed in a damp state into the grooves of the plate.

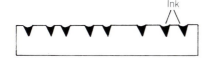

6.14 Cross-section of an intaglio plate.

The earliest intaglio process developed was **line engraving**. In this relatively direct method, the image is drawn on a plate of metal such as copper or copper faced with steel, thus deriving the workability of copper plus the durability of steel for printing multiple copies.

A **burin** is used to cut the lines. This is a bevelled steel rod with a sharpened point and a wooden handle. A similar tool is used for wood engraving, which is a relief process. But because line engraving is an intaglio process, the ink is forced into the v-shaped grooves cut by the burin, and these become the printed lines.

Line engravings, like wood engravings, were traditionally used for illustrations and reproductions of works of art before photography took over this function. The translation of an image from one medium to another is never precisely accurate. In the steel engraving (**6.15**) of Turner's oil painting *Snow Storm: Steamboat off a Harbor's Mouth* (**6.16**), the engraver has skillfully created a complete range of values from black to white, with many mid-tones, by engraving a tremendous number of tiny lines that vary in width, length, and proximity to other lines, as shown in the enlarged detail of waves (**6.17**). But even though the values and shapes are similar in the reproduction and the original, the two versions differ tremendously in attitude. The engraving is necessarily conceived in terms of precise lines; the painting is a swirling mass of free-moving brushstrokes, depicting the wild and ever-changing elements as almost obliterating the identity of the steamboat. Another obvious difference, of course, is that the painting is executed in color, whereas line engraving is traditionally a black-and-white medium.

A second major intaglio technique is **etching**. A copper, zinc, or steel plate is coated with a waxy, acid-resistant substance called a **resist**. The design is drawn through this coating with an etching needle, baring the surface of the metal. The plate is then bathed in an acid solution that bites grooves into the metal where the needle has cut through the resist. These grooves are then inked and printed as in engravings. Because the waxy resist offers little resistance to the etching needle, the lines in an etching can be quite freely drawn, as they are in Matisse's *Young Woman, Goldfish, and Checkered Cloth* (**6.18**).

Another unique characteristic of etchings is the possibility of varying tones by withdrawing the plate from the acid bath, "stopping out" certain areas with varnish to keep them from being etched any deeper

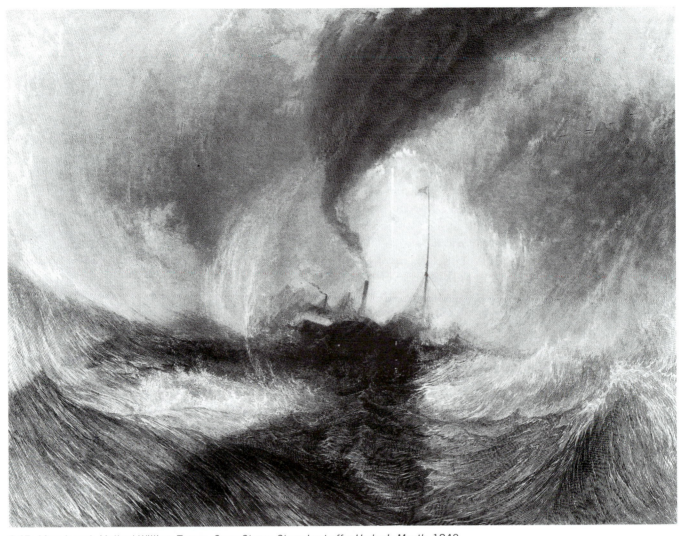

6.15 After Joseph Mallord William Turner, *Snow Storm: Steamboat off a Harbor's Mouth*, 1842. Steel engraving, 1891. British Museum, London.

6.16 Joseph Mallord William Turner,
Snow Storm: Steamboat off a Harbor's Mouth, 1842.
Oil on canvas, 36 × 48 ins (91.5 × 122 cm). Tate Gallery, London.

6.17 *Snow Storm*. Steel engraving (detail of 6.15).

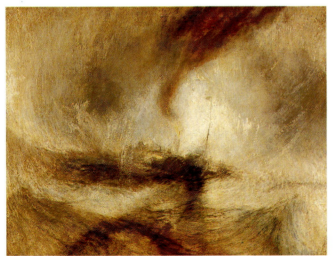

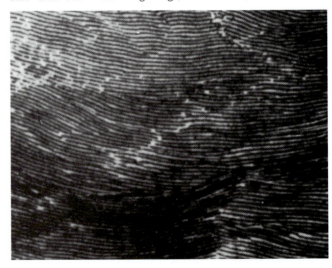

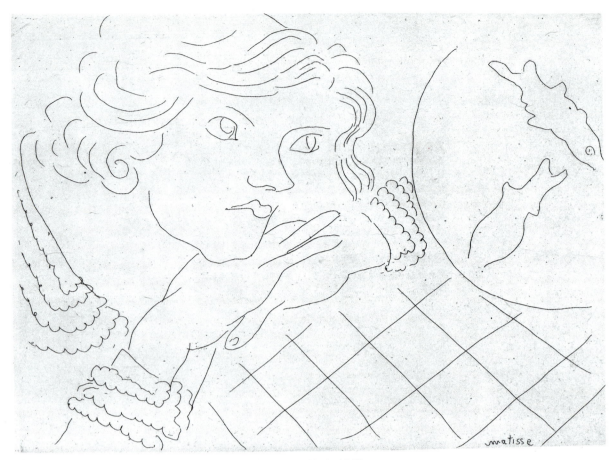

6.18 Henri Matisse, *Young Woman, Goldfish, and Checkered Cloth*, 1929.
Etching, printed in black, plate: 5 × 7⅙ ins (12.8 × 17.9 cm).
Collection Museum of Modern Art, New York. Stephen C. Clark Fund. Purchased.
Photograph © 1997 MOMA.

(and therefore printing darker) and then returning the plate to the bath for rebiting of the unstopped areas. If printed individually, each stage is called a **state**. Rembrandt, whose etchings helped to establish the process as a major art form, printed five states of his *Three Crosses*, of which three are illustrated here (6.19–21). The second state is printed on **vellum**, a fine parchment made of animal skin, rather than paper. The vellum blurs the lines, giving a softer, more paint-like quality to the composition. The fourth state reveals a tremendous amount of reworking. As the states proceed, the work becomes more abstract, with the masses milling below the crosses receding into the shadows (6.22–24).

In addition to being stopped out and rebitten, etching plates may also be altered directly with a **drypoint** tool—a sharp-pointed device for scratching lines directly into a copper plate. This is a way to work more value and textural variations into the basic

design. The long, dark, parallel lines in the later stages of Rembrandt's crucifixion etchings were obviously added after the original plate was cut.

Drypoint cutting can also be used by itself to scratch lines into a blank copper plate. When inked and printed, the plate yields what is called a **drypoint print**. Mary Cassatt's *The Caress* (6.25) is a lovely example of the directness and sensitivity of this process. The darkness of lines is directly determined by the depth to which they are cut. Drypoints also have a characteristic soft and furry line quality. This softening of the line is created by the burr of metal pushed up by the drypoint tool. The burr tends to hold ink when the plate is wiped. Because the burr does not hold up under repeated prints, editions of drypoints are usually small.

A fourth method of intaglio printing is called **mezzotint**. In this process, the copper plate is first scored with a rocking device, creating a burr across the

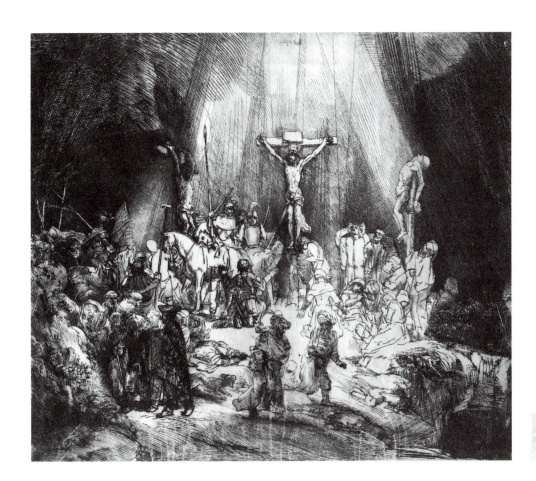

6.19 Rembrandt van Rijn, *The Three Crosses*, 1653. State II. Drypoint and burin etching, on vellum, 15⅛ × 17¾ ins (38.4 × 45 cm). Metropolitan Museum of Art, New York. Gift of Felix M. Warburg and his family.

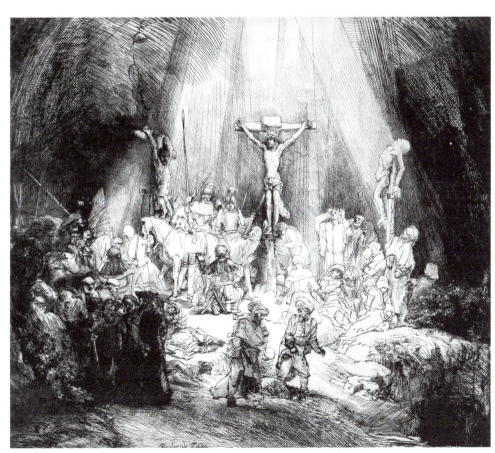

6.20 Rembrandt van Rijn, *The Three Crosses*, 1653. State III. Drypoint and burin etching, 15⅛ × 17¾ ins (38.4 × 45 cm). British Museum, London.

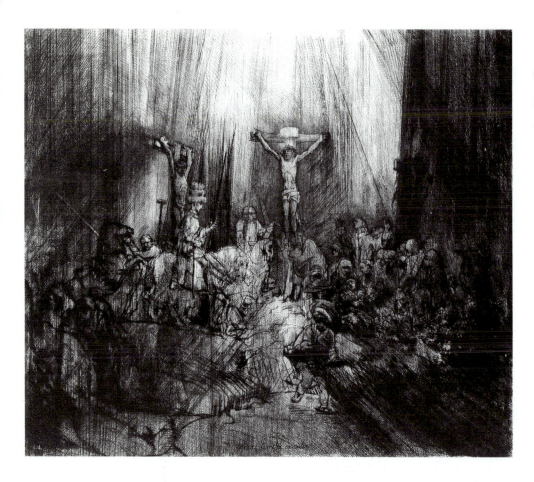

6.21 Rembrandt van Rijn, *The Three Crosses*, 1653. State IV. Drypoint and burin etching, 15⅛ × 17¾ ins (38.4 × 45 cm). British Museum, London.

6.22, 6.23, 6.24 *The Three Crosses*. States II, III, and IV.

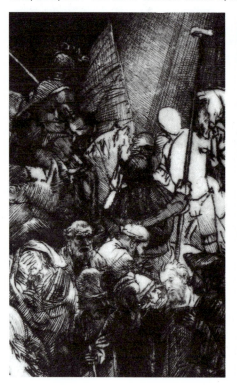

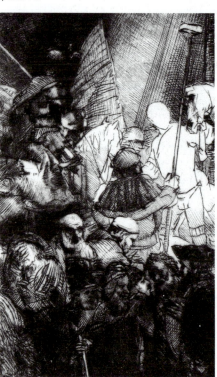

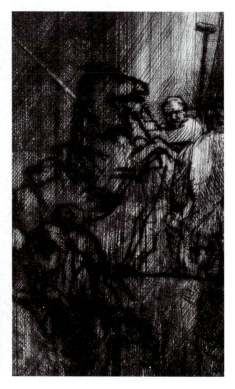

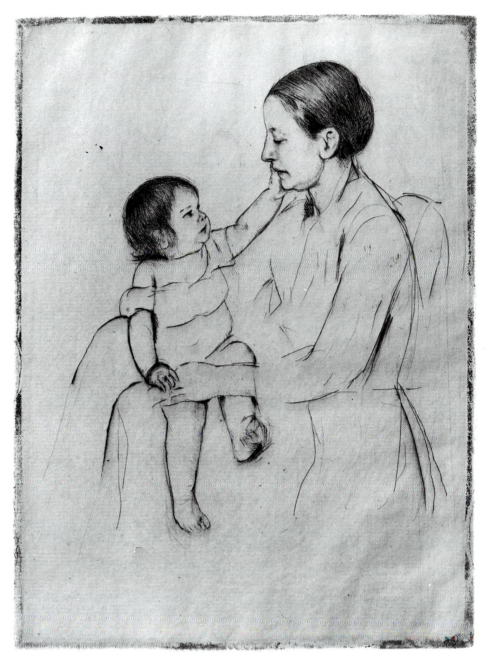

6.25 Mary Cassatt, *The Caress*, 1891. Drypoint, 7¹¹⁄₁₆ × 5¾ ins (20 × 15 cm). Metropolitan Museum of Art, New York. Gift of Arthur Sachs, 1916.

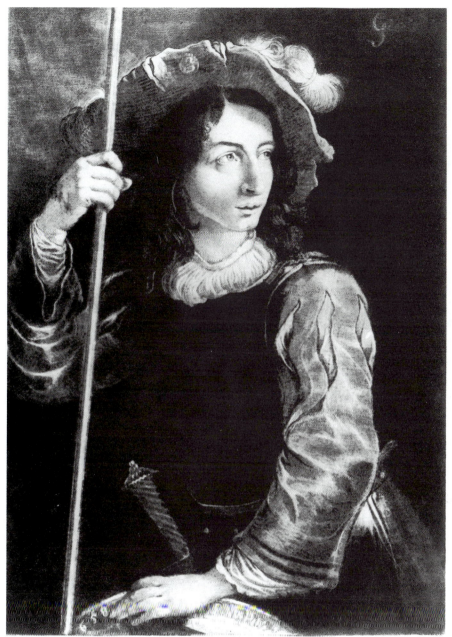

6.26 Prince Rupert, *The Standard Bearer*, 1658. Mezzotint. Metropolitan Museum of Art, New York. Harris Brisbane Fund, 1933.

whole surface. The burr is then smoothed and scraped to varying degrees to create variations in tone and texture. The lightest tones will appear in areas that are smoothed the most. Gradations from very dark to white are possible, and the print will have a rich velvet visual texture, as in Prince Rupert's *The Standard Bearer* (**6.26**).

Another intaglio printing method is called **aquatint**. Like mezzotints, aquatints are capable of creating toned areas rather than the lines to which line engraving, etching, and drypoint are limited. The aquatint process is like etching tones instead of lines. Transparent areas of ink that resemble a wash drawing are created by allowing acid to penetrate a porous covering of powdered resin. Where the surface of the copper or zinc plate is not protected by the resin particles, the acid etches pits in the metal, producing the grainy tones characteristic of aquatints, as in Anne Sobol-Wejmen's *Boyka Fable* (**6.27**).

In the traditional aquatint method, the whole surface is first dusted with the resin and then variations in tone are created by repeatedly stopping out areas with

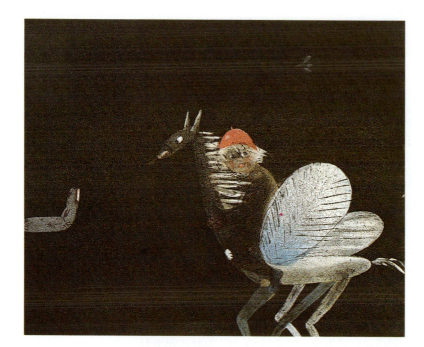

6.27 Anne Sobol-Wejmen, *Boyka Fable*, 1979. Aquatint, 9¼ × 11½ ins (23.5 × 29.2 cm). Collection Annette Zelanski.

varnish to vary the degree to which the acid bites into the plate. Linear details are usually added using line engraving or drypoint. A version of this process that allows more spontaneous, direct work on the plate is called **sugar aquatint**. In this method, the composition is painted onto the resin-coated plate with a sugar solution. The plate is then varnished and immersed in water. The water swells the sugar, which bursts the varnish in the painted areas and exposes the metal there. When the plate is bathed in acid, the previously painted areas will have the grainy aquatint texture, while the varnished areas will remain white.

Planographic

The major **planographic** or "surface" process of print-making is **lithography**. In lithography, prints are made from a perfectly flat surface rather than one that is raised (as in relief methods) or incised (as in intaglio). Adopted as an art medium in the late eighteenth century, the method is based on the observation that grease and water will not mix. A design is drawn on a slab of fine-grained limestone (or a metal or plastic plate) with a greasy substance, such as a litho crayon made of wax, soap, and lampblack. The stone is chemically treated to fix the grease and make the open areas more porous, and then it is dampened. When oily lithographic ink is spread across the surface, it is repelled by the wet areas but sticks to the greasy areas.

Lithography can easily reproduce both lines and tones. The dark areas in the prints pulled from a lithographic plate can be very lush, in contrast to darks that must be built up by lines. Artists find it a very free way to work, and one that mirrors the gestures of their drawings exactly. Although many lithographs are freely drawn, creating dark lines against the white ground of the paper, it is also possible to work in a *manière noire* ("black manner") by brushing a broad area of grease onto the plate and then scratching lines and tones into it. Frank Boyden explains how he used this time-consuming process to develop his exquisite lithograph, *Changes # IV* (**6.28**):

> What you see as the black image was brushed out on a stone with autographic ink—a very fine oil- or grease-based emulsion. The lines along the sides are where the brush dragged along. Then I went back into it. The salmon was done with etching needles. The gray of the raven was removed with a very sharp razor blade, like an Exacto knife, to expose the stone just a very little bit. To get those kinds of gradations took about five hours of work, just in that area. Fiddling, just scraping and scraping and scraping. Then the ribbed sorts of things were drawn back over that, with an etching tool and also a razor blade for just a little bit more contrast. You don't often see this kind of work, because it's a horrible drag. And *manière noire* is very difficult to print, because it's so difficult to hold the values.[4]

Like many contemporary lithographers, Boyden has his work printed by a fine-printing lithography house.

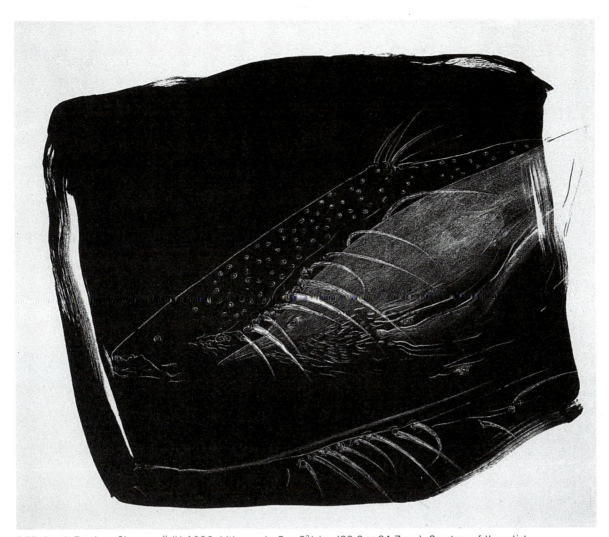

6.28 Frank Boyden, *Changes # IV*, 1986. Lithograph, 8 × 9¾ ins (20.3 × 24.7 cm). Courtesy of the artist.

6.29 James Rosenquist, *Iris Lake*, 1975. Nine-color lithograph, 36 × 52 ins (91.4 × 132 cm). Courtesy of the artist.

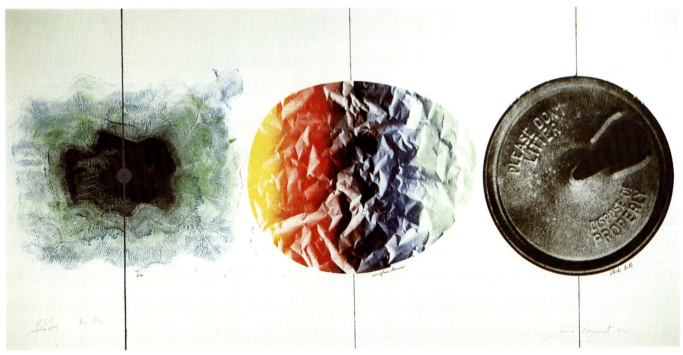

They work together to get a satisfactory print, on which the artist writes BAT, for *"bon à tirer"* ("good to pull"); all prints pulled are compared to that model in order to be approved for the edition.

Although fine lithographs are printed in limited editions, a great number of prints can be pulled from a single stone or plate, so modern versions of the lithographic process are widely used for commercial printing of everything from cigar labels to books. In **offset lithography**—the process used to print this book and most others today—illustrations are converted to systems of dots that give the effect of different tones. The dot patterns are created by photographing the image through a screen of crossed lines. You can see the dots if you examine one of the black-and-white illustrations in this book with a strong magnifying glass. Screened illustrations and typeset text are then transferred photochemically to plates for printing. Ink is picked up—"offset"—from the cylindrical plates onto a rubber roller and thence transferred to paper so that the final image is the same way around as that on the plate, rather than reversed, as it is in most art printing processes.

In both original works of art and commercial printing processes, lithography can also be adapted to multiply colored images. In prints that originate as lithographs, such as James Rosenquist's nine-color *Iris Lake* (**6.29**), a separate plate is made for each color. Each plate is marked so that it can be carefully aligned to match the others during printing. In commercial reproduction of colored images created by other processes, such as those in color in this book, *color separations* are done on a computerized *color scanner*. It reads a *transparency*—a flexible transparent photograph of the work—to translate the colors into mixtures of the four colors that will be used to print it on a *four-color press*: yellow, magenta (red), cyan (blue), and black. Each color is printed from a separate plate; the pages of this

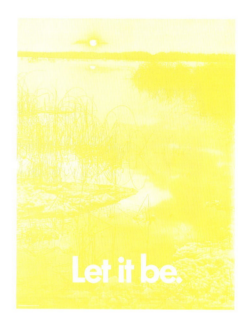

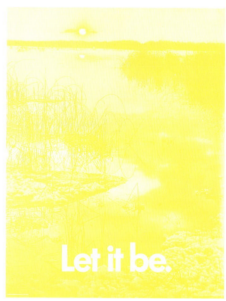

6.30 The color separation process. For this demonstration, the four colors are printed separately across the top row. In reality, one color is printed on top of another, as shown in the lower row. Color separations from a 1970 poster by graphic designer Peter Good, employing a photograph by Bill Ratcliffe. Printer: The Hennegan Company.

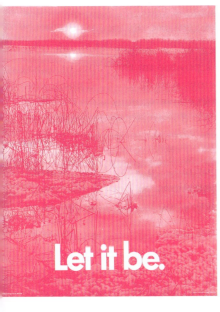

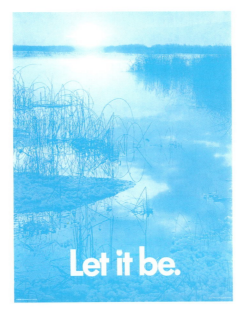

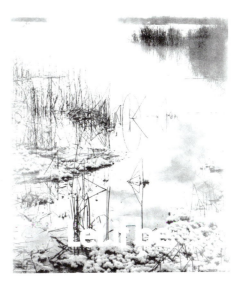

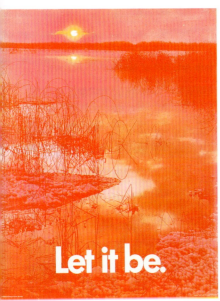

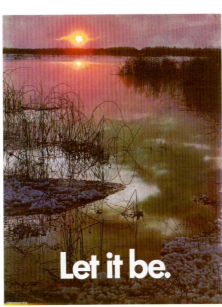

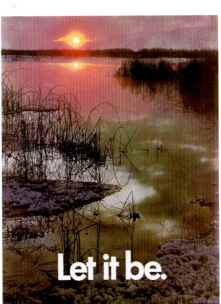

book that have color illustrations have received four precisely registered printings. Figure **6.30** illustrates the process and results of four-color printing. In highly specialized printing, additional passes may be used for purposes such as varnish, metallic inks, intensification of reds, or use of mixed inks specified by the designer.

Stencil

The fourth major printmaking process is *stenciling*— masking out areas that are not to be printed. The form of stenciling now most often used both by fine artists and commercial printers in this increasingly sophisticated medium is the **silkscreen** or **serigraph**. A fine silk or synthetic fiber screen stretched across a wooden frame is masked in places by a cut paper or plastic stencil or by lacquer, glue, or lithographic crayon. High-contrast photographs may also be transferred to

special film whose glue-like emulsion is adhered to the screen as a stencil. When ink is brushed across the screen with a squeegee, it passes through the unmasked areas to be deposited on the paper or other surface to be printed below. A multi-colored image can be created by use of successive screens with different colors and different masked areas. Precise registration (placement of successive screens) is necessary to prevent gaps or overlapping. But in his silkscreened, photo emulsion self-portraits (**6.31**), Andy Warhol allowed slight misregistrations to reveal the mass-production "non-art" derivation of the medium, as an exercise in Pop Art.

In addition to flat colored shapes, graduated tones can also be created in a silkscreen print by means of a photomechanical screen of dots. Andy Warhol deliberately enlarged the dots in his self-portraits to reveal this mechanical process.

6.31 Andy Warhol, *A Set of Six Self-portraits*, 1967.
Oil and silkscreen on canvas, each 22½ × 22½ ins (57.2 × 57.2 cm). San Francisco Museum of Modern Art. Gift of Michael D. Abrams.

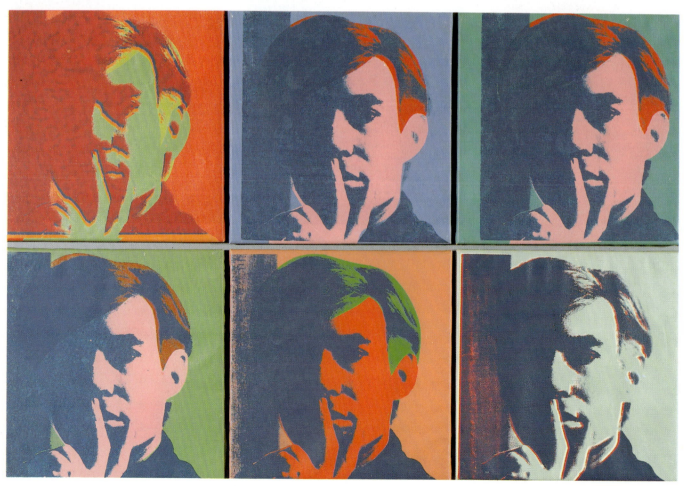

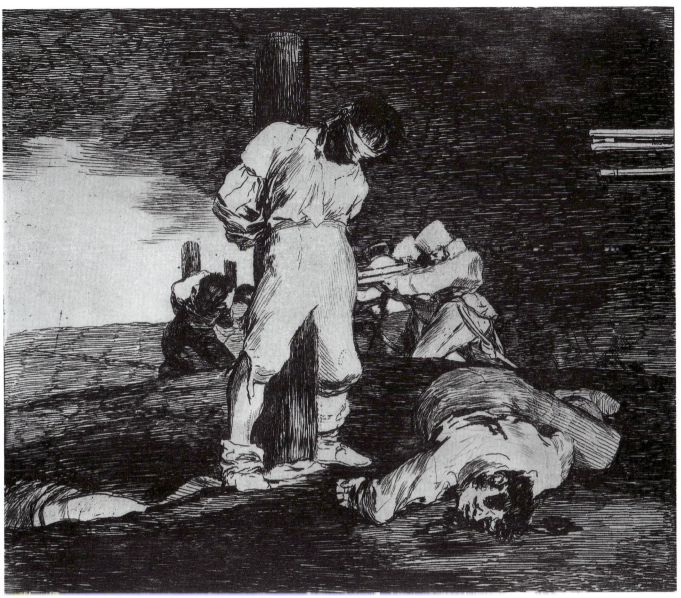

9.92 Francisco de Goya, *And There Is No Remedy*, Plate 15 from *Los Desastres de la Guerra*, 1808–20. Etching and aquatint. National Gallery of Art, Washington, D.C. Rosenwald Collection.

Paints used in silkscreens may be transparent or opaque. Colors can blend into each other through a *split fountain* technique, in which different paints are placed at different ends of the squeegee and blended where they overlap as they are pushed across the screen.

MIXED MEDIA

Although we have examined the major printmaking processes separately, in practice they are often mixed

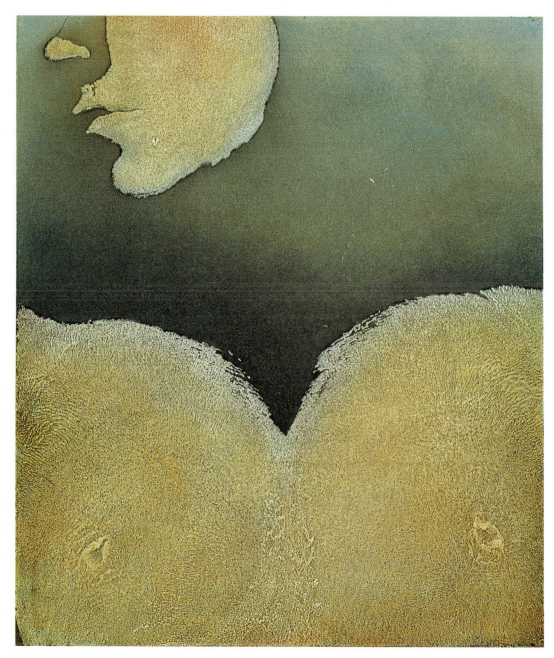

6.33 Janet Cummings Good, *Cerulean Sky*, 1990. Mixed media, 12 × 11 ins (30.5 × 27.9 cm).
Courtesy of the artist.

with each other. Relief, intaglio, planographic, and stencil plates can be alternately printed on the same surface. Francisco de Goya used both etching and aquatint in his *And There Is No Remedy* (**6.32**), for a combination of dark, scratchy etched lines and gray tones.

In today's wide-open experimentation, some artists are also combining printmaking with other media. Janet Cummings Good coats parts of her own body with gesso, presses herself against paper, and then works into the texture of the resulting monoprint with oil paint and drawing media (**6.33**). Sometimes

she cuts up the impression and reassembles the parts. She began these body prints after a period of doing very tight drawings of the body. Good reports:

I felt I had taken the realism of the body as far as I could. I wanted to get more personal, more expressive with the subject. I was unsatisfied with representing the surface. The irony is that the way to get beyond my fixation with surface was to deal with it even more directly and immediately, by literally placing my body on the surface of the paper.[5]

GRAPHIC DESIGN

The term "graphic designer" is a rather new label in the history of art. It is applied primarily to those who design two-dimensional images for commercial purposes, from advertisements, packaging, and corporate images to the pages of books. Their challenge is to catch the eye of an already optically saturated public, conveying information in a memorable way.

THE GRAPHIC DESIGNER AND VISUAL IDEAS

Graphic designers must have their fingers on the ever-changing public pulse, staying one step ahead of shifting tastes and interests. This does not necessarily mean that effective designs are always futuristic. For a logo for New York's Russian Tea Room (7.1), Milton Glaser has combined contemporary honed-down, hard-edged lines with a more lyrical, nostalgic, invented type style that is reminiscent of the Cyrillic alphabet, bespeaking the wealth of Czarist Russia. The gradually thinning lines around the border and the implied lines that run outward from the center on the corners give the center shape and letter forms greater impact by making them appear to project toward the viewer in space.

In line with the current public mood, many designers are packaging food in ways that make it appear more "natural." To market a new pasta sauce as

7.1 Milton Glaser, logo for the Russian Tea Room, from *Milton Glaser, Graphic Design*, Woodstock, New York: The Overlook Press, 1983.

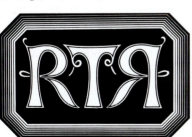

if it were homemade from an old family recipe using all natural ingredients, Duffy Design Group suggested bottling the sauce in traditional canning jars, complete with raised measurement marks along the side. The labels they designed for the jars (7.2) have the rustic appearance of hand-cut, hand-tinted woodcuts, adding to the homemade image. Through words and imagery, the designers elicit a certain feeling toward the product in the attitude of the consumer.

7.2 Charles Spencer Anderson, designer/illustrator, Duffy Design Group, packaging for Prince Foods' Classico pasta sauce.

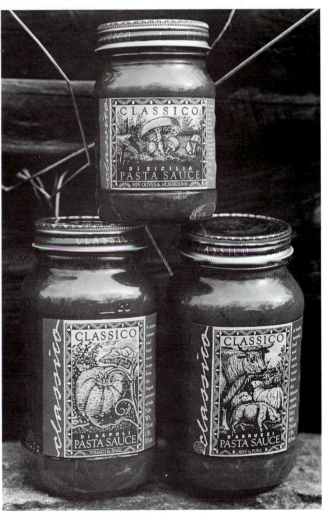

PETER GOOD
on THE ART OF GRAPHIC DESIGN

Peter Good is an internationally known graphic designer and illustrator. His graphic design studio, Cummings and Good, works on assignments for corporations, small businesses, and arts organizations. He is best known for his posters (**7.3**). Good observes:

"Things are constantly changing. How do you become a graphic designer? I think we need to begin by constantly being open to new ways of seeing things. Everything depends on context; everything is a reaction to what is in the present. The designer works to communicate another person's ideas. The artist is usually someone who has his own ideas.

If there's anything that can go in two directions [as art and as

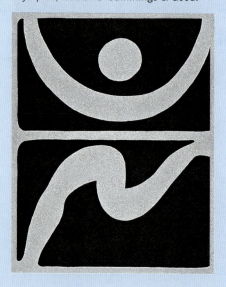

7.3 Peter Good, logo for the Special Olympics, 1995. © Cummings & Good.

commercial design], it's posters. They act like paintings—they're on a wall. But there is information on a poster—it has to perform a certain function. After the function is over and people put it on a wall as art, you no longer have the informational requirements."

"There are a few American designers who use ambiguity as Tomaszewski, the father of Polish posters, does. But the American culture is not receptive to that kind of imagery, that use of metaphor and levels of meaning. It's not as sophisticated. I face this all the time with clients. I say, 'Well, don't you see? Someone will think about it and will become engaged in it, and therefore it will be a stronger communication.' But people tend to think you have to be obvious in all cases. Sometimes the obvious can work, but other times ambiguity enhances the communication. You see that in European and other cultures. Perhaps they have more design education; perhaps it's because multilingual areas rely more on visual language.

On the other hand, something that works really well may seem obvious. Even though you never saw it before, it seems understandable, it seems right. It is real genius to take something that's right before our noses and to do something with it that works so well that everyone says, 'Oh, my God!'"

"The worst thing for a young designer is freedom, because the best design, the best art, comes from limitations. There are too many options. There are many different solutions to design problems, some more successful than others. If you start with the broadest possible range, you can't possibly explore all those possibilities. You have to make certain decisions to narrow the range, so you begin to explore the possibilities within a smaller realm, and then you narrow it further, until you get into a manageable form to deal with. But if you don't know that process of self-limitation—from experience or talent or whatever—this process becomes arbitrary. I see that happening with the possibilities opened up by computer graphics. If you have an area of land to explore—say, an acre of land—you can't possibly explore it in detail. But if you have a square foot, you can get down to molecules, down to very fine things.

I feel graphic designers work much better if they get involved with things that are not design. If you're doing something for a hospital, to go to the hospital and see the people and see what the real problems are. Otherwise you're working blind. Empathy is one of the greatest tools a designer has—to always put yourself in someone else's position."[1]

The graphic designer works with visual ideas. Paul Rand, considered one of the world's greatest and most influential designers, observes that:

> Graphic design is essentially about visual relationships—providing meaning to a mass of unrelated needs, ideas, words, and pictures. It is the designer's job to select and fit this material together—and make it interesting. The problem is not simple; its very complexity virtually dictates the solution—that is, the discovery of an image universally comprehensible, one that translates abstract ideas into concrete forms.[2]

Rand's catalog cover for a Picasso show (**7.4**) catches the eye with its two bold lines, which still look freshly painted today, and it uses handwritten information in Picasso's style at a time when everyone else was using uniform, machine-set type. Picasso's photograph ever so slightly overlaps the circular line at the chin, setting up a delightful three-dimensional spatial illusion. He appears to be looking out at us from inside the catalog, enticing us to open it. The individual elements seem simple and uncluttered, but putting them together so effectively takes great mastery of design.

7.4 Paul Rand, a proposed catalog cover.

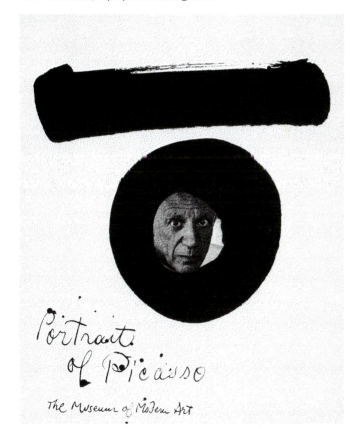

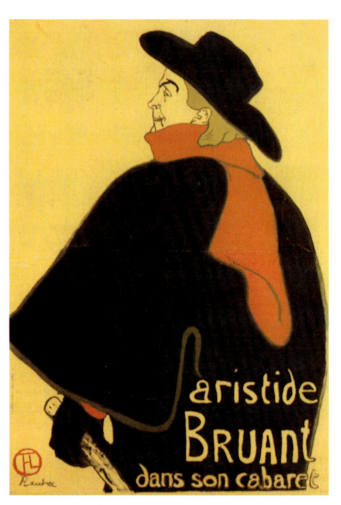

7.5 Henri de Toulouse-Lautrec, poster, *Aristide Bruant dans son cabaret*, 1893. Color lithograph, 54½ × 39 ins (138 × 99 cm). Metropolitan Museum of Art, New York. Harris Brisbane Dick Fund, 1932.

Graphic design is usually aimed directly at consumers, though there are often an art director and a marketing team between the designer and the end-user. But its commercialism has not kept some graphic design from being treated as fine art. Some is created by recognized artists who have distinguished themselves in other media, such as Toulouse-Lautrec, whose lithographed posters for dance halls and cabarets (**7.5**) raised the poster to an art form. They were so admired by collectors that they were stolen as fast as they were put up.

The poster, like most graphic design, was initially conceived as an ephemeral piece to be thrown away once its commercial purpose was finished. But posters are often so visually compelling that someone saves—or buys—them and hangs them as would be done with a painting. They have become a relatively inexpensive way to bring art into one's home. Whereas a few

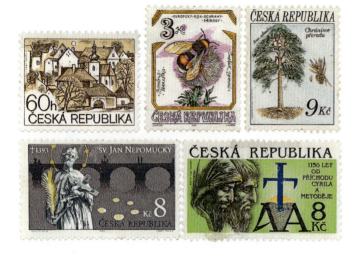

7.6 Selection of Czech postage stamps.

printing the Roman alphabet have been developed over the years. Most can be grouped into two large categories: **serif** and **sans serif** typefaces. A serif is a fine line that finishes the larger "stroke" used to make a letter form. Originally used in the Classical Roman alphabet on which modern letters are based, serifs tend to lead our eye through a word, tying it together visually, as well as giving elegant calligraphic flourishes to the individual letter-forms. Most books, including this one, are printed in one of the many serif typefaces. Many modern typefaces eliminate the serifs, however, for a more contemporary look. These sans serif ("without serif") type styles are often chosen when an upbeat, forward looking message is desired. Figure 7.7 illustrates the general difference between these two categories: Baskerville is a serif typeface originally

7.8 Albrecht Dürer, page from *Underweisung der Messung*, 1525. Victoria and Albert Museum, London.

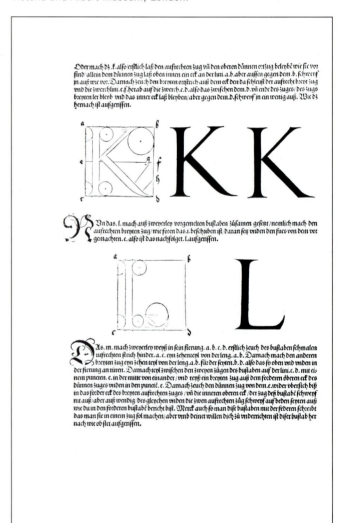

decades ago, those who couldn't afford original works of art hung reproductions of them in their homes, many people now display posters by renowned designers, such as Henryk Tomaszewski (2.48).

Another bit of throw-away art that has increasingly captured the public eye and the interest of graphic designers is the humble postage stamp. To make a fascinating and successful work of art on a small scrap of paper is a *tour de force.* Many countries now commission excellent commemorative art for their stamps as a matter of national pride, and collectors queue up to buy the latest works. Consider the different approaches to this challenge taken up by contemporary designers in the Czech Republic (7.6). What means have they used to catch the eye without confusing it?

TYPOGRAPHY

The two major ingredients of graphic design are letters and images. Typography is the art of designing, sizing, and combining letter forms on a printed page. The choices the graphic designer must make are subtle and complex. Hundreds of **typefaces** that can be used for

7.7 Baskerville (left) and Gill Sans (right) typefaces.

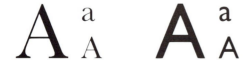

designed in the eighteenth century by John Baskerville, while Gill Sans is a twentieth-century sans serif typeface often used on modern English signs. Eric Gill based its proportions and shapes on the classic Roman letter forms, but made the rules for their creation so simple that even the least skilled signwriter could follow them perfectly.

When a typeface is designed, each letter is carefully constructed, with attention to the balance between stressed (thicker) and unstressed (thinner) portions. Albrecht Dürer, influential in so many of the visual arts, published in 1525 *Underweisung der Messung mit dem Zirckel und Richtscheyt* ("A Course in the Art of Measurement with Compass and Ruler"). This book included instructions for applying geometric principles to the construction of letter forms. In the page shown in Figure **7.8** Dürer relates each letter to a square, with a ratio of ten to one between the height and width of the letter strokes. Not only are his letters lovely; the page as a whole is beautifully designed,

with pleasing contrast between the scale of the text type and the display type, and enough white space around the printed text to allow it to breathe.

Typesetting has largely been turned over to computerized photocomposition processes rather than handsetting of metal type. But the art of the beautifully designed letter and page is being maintained by aficionados of fine printing. Hermann Zapf designed over fifty typefaces adapted to computer technologies, but with a poetic sense of the aesthetics of typography, as is evident in the alphabet sampler done in his own calligraphic hand (**7.9**), and in these remarks:

> Typography is fundamentally two-dimensional architecture. The harmony of single proportions, the grouping of lines of type, the judging of contrast and balance, the symmetry and dynamic tension of axial arrangement— all these are the shaping tools, so employed by the typographer in a given task as to bring the reader a text in its most appealing form. . . . The letters' indwelling wealth of form is a fresh, unending astonishment.[3]

7.9 Hermann Zapf, Alphabet with quotations, 1959. Ink. Mr. and Mrs Philip Hofer Collection. Houghton Library, Harvard University.

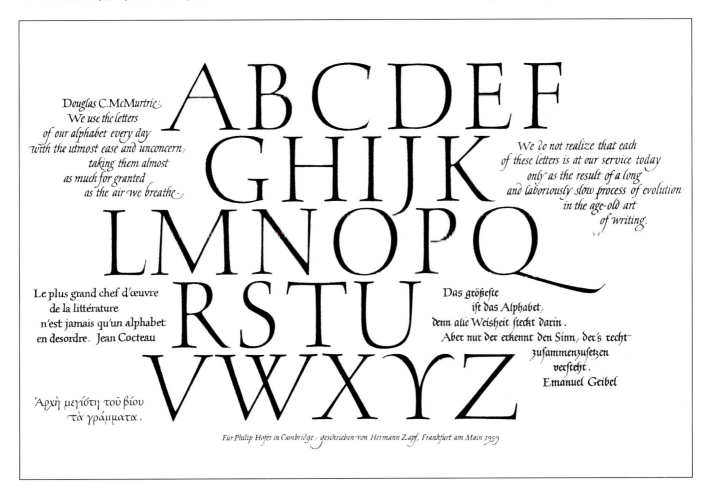

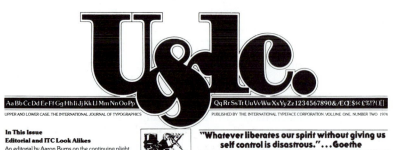

7.10 Herb Lubalin, cover for *U&lc*, 1974. Reprinted with permission from *U&lc* magazine, International Journal of Typographics, published by the International Typeface Corporation.

In addition to having unique characteristics if examined closely, each typeface creates a slightly different value when printed in blocks on a page. In Herb Lubalin's cover (**7.10**) for the typographic newsletter *U&lc* (Upper and Lower Case), each article in the right column is summarized in a different typeface, revealing noticeable differences in blackness and grayness. Lubalin, a highly resourceful graphic designer who often creates his own typefaces to make images of words and letters, has managed to integrate 59 different units of varying typefaces, seven illustrations, and 16 rules (lines) into a page that works well as a whole.

ILLUSTRATION

The other major ingredient in graphic design is illustration. Because graphic design is basically a functional art, illustrators must keep the character of what they are illustrating clearly before them. This need is especially true in advertising, where the intent is to portray the client's product as compellingly as possible. At one extreme, the illustration of the product may dominate the presentation. At the other extreme, an elegant and well-known product sometimes lends itself to considerable understatement, as in a refined Audi ad (**7.11**).

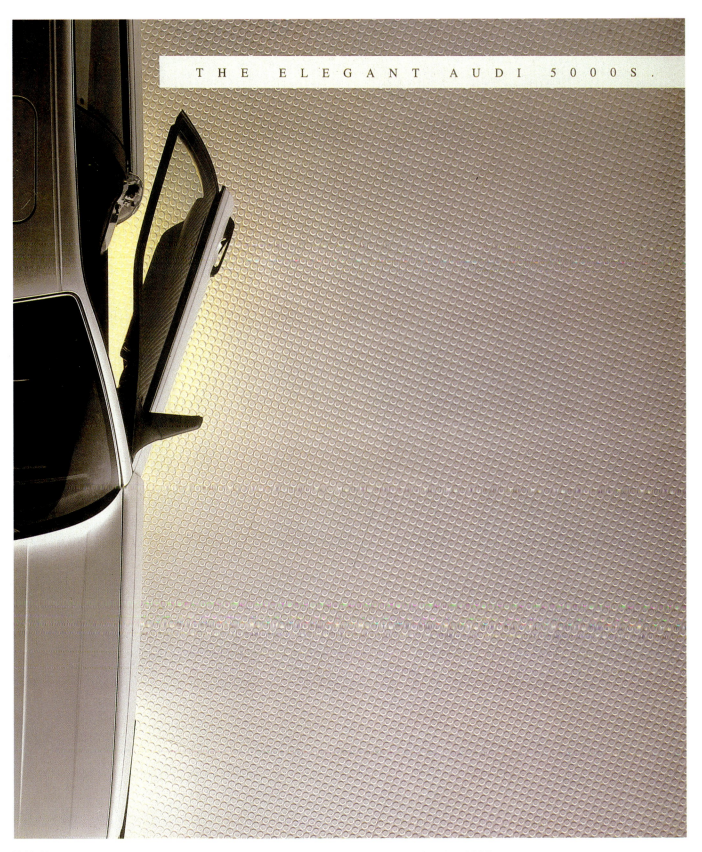

THE ELEGANT AUDI 5000S.

7.11 Barry Shepherd and Steve Ditko of SHR Communications, brochure for Audi of America, 1985.

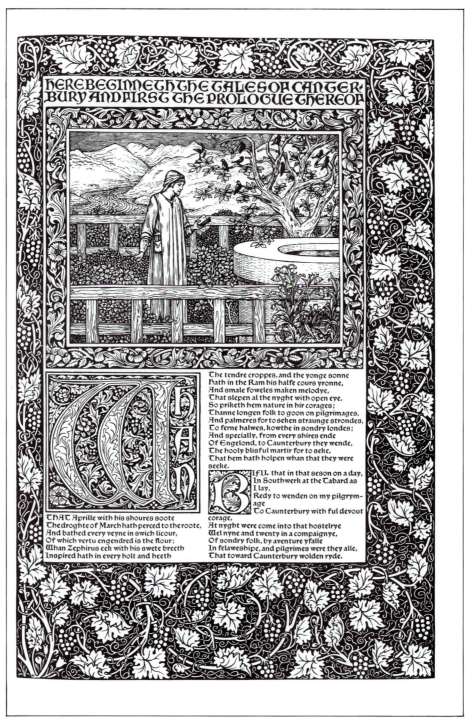

7.12 William Morris and Edward Burne-Jones, page from *Works of Geoffrey Chaucer*, Kelmscott Press, 1896. Victoria and Albert Museum, London.

Looking down, as if from the point of view of the gods, we are beckoned into the car by the slightly open door and the aureole of glowing light. Most of the brochure cover consists of unfilled space. By this extremely restrained use of color, image, and type, the designer suggests that the benefits of this product are so well known that they need not even be mentioned to genteel clients.

Any kind of image may be used, from photographs to woodcuts. The style of illustration and typography must be harmonious. To illustrate Chaucer's *Canterbury Tales*, William Morris created a special Gothic typeface, surrounded it with intricate borders, inset woodcuts of drawings by Edward Burne-Jones, and embellished the whole with large, illuminated capital letters, as shown in one of the 556 pages of the monumental book (**7.12**). In its brief life from 1891 to 1898, Morris's Kelmscott Press created 18,000 copies of 53 books, all handcrafted. Their quality and lavish decoration revived interest in fine printing as an art form, at the same time as commercial printing was becoming increasingly mechanized. Morris, who also designed wallpaper, furniture, stained glass, interiors, and industrial products, had a great love for the beautiful object, carefully made of the best materials available. He wrote:

> The picture-book is not, perhaps, absolutely necessary to man's life, but it gives us such endless pleasure, and is so intimately connected with the other absolutely necessary art of imaginative literature that it must remain one of the very worthiest things towards the production of which reasonable men should strive.[4]

Fine printing of illustrated works continues today, in limited editions prized by collectors. Barry Moser uses bold wood engravings and asymmetrical page layouts for *Alice's Adventures in Wonderland* (**7.13**). The illustration takes up most of the column and even breaks out of its own rectangle, spreading toward the "gutter" or central seam of the book. The head of the Mad Hatter is opposed to the strength of the white border, metaphorically illustrating the illogical frustrations and tensions built up in the story.

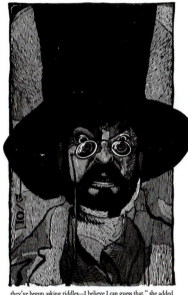

they've begun asking riddles—I believe I can guess that," she added aloud.

"Do you mean that you think you can find out the answer to it?" said the March Hare.

"Exactly so," said Alice.

"Then you should say what you mean," the March Hare went on.

"I do," Alice hastily replied; "at least—at least I mean what I say— that's the same thing, you know."

7.13 Barry Moser, The Mad Hatter, from *Alice's Adventures in Wonderland* (Pennyroyal Press, 1982). Wood engraving.

8
PHOTOGRAPHY, PHOTOCOPY, AND FILMMAKING

Although photography (the Greek word for "writing with light") and filmmaking are now so much a part of our visual world that we take them for granted, they are relatively recent inventions. From the time of the Renaissance, many artists had used the **camera obscura** to draw forms and linear perspective accurately. A camera obscura was a dark room or box with light entering through a tiny hole, perhaps focused by a lens. An inverted image from the world beyond would be thrown on the opposite wall or side, and its outlines could be traced on paper. But it was not until the first half of the nineteenth century that several researchers working independently of each other found ways to capture this image permanently.

Later in the nineteenth century, sequences of still pictures began to lead to "movies." By the mid-twentieth century, the technology of capturing moving images from the world had evolved to wireless television broadcasts and thence to video art.

PHOTOGRAPHY

One of the early developers of what became photography was William Henry Fox Talbot. Longing to be able to capture images from his travels and everyday life that he did not have the skill to draw, this English scientist experimented with various techniques.

One yielded what he called a *photogenic drawing*, or **photogram**, created by laying objects on paper coated with light-sensitive chemicals and then exposing it to light. The result is a negative, in which the objects appear light and the paper turns dark. Not only scientifically resourceful, Fox Talbot obviously also had an eye for design, as is evident in one of his early photogenic drawings (8.1).

At the same time that Fox Talbot was carrying on his experiments, several French researchers had been developing processes that worked along similar lines. After years of secret experimentation, Joseph-Nicéphore Niépce (an inventor) and Louis-Jacques-Mandé Daguerre (a painter of stage sets) began collaborating to produce the process that Daguerre named **daguerreotype** in 1837 after Niépce's death. The public was awed by the way in which actual images could be preserved in precisely accurate detail. The process was not yet perfect, of course. One problem was the lengthy time needed for exposures. Daguerre's picture of a Paris boulevard (8.2) makes it appear to be deserted except for a shoe-shiner and his customer. This strange effect occurred because although there were other people on the streets and sidewalks, they were moving too fast for their images to be recorded. In the excitement over the new invention, improvements appeared quickly, including the means of creating multiple copies of a single image, based on Fox Talbot's work with the negative.

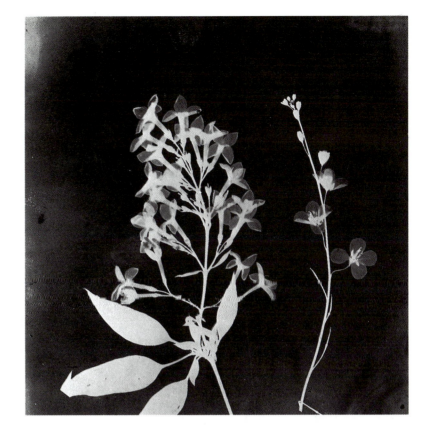

8.1 William Henry Fox Talbot, *Botanical Specimens*, 1839. Photogenic drawing. Metropolitan Museum of Art, New York. Harris Brisbane Dick Fund, 1936

8.2 Louis-Jacques-Mandé Daguerre, *A Parisian Boulevard*, 1839. Daguerreotype. Bayerische National-museum, Munich, Germany.

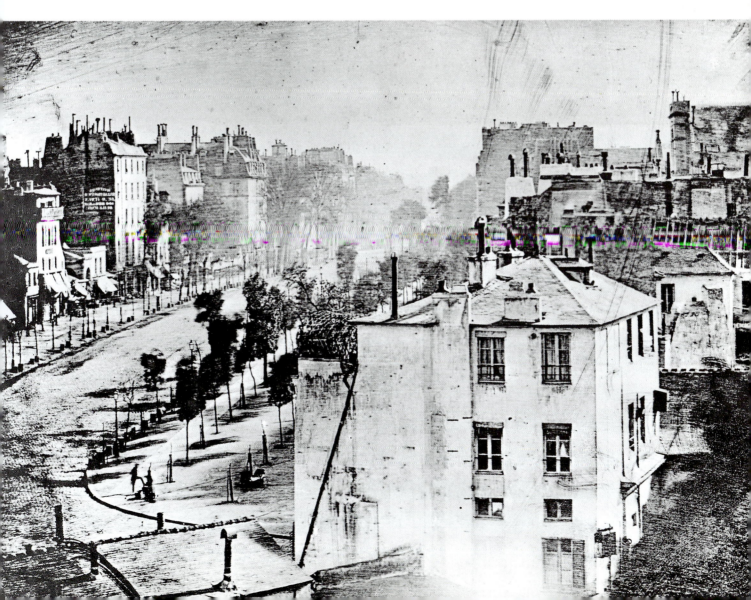

One of the exciting possibilities opened up by the invention of photography was that of having one's portrait captured for posterity. There had long been portrait painters, of course, but a perfect likeness was both rare and expensive. Many of the surviving early photographs are portraits, such as that of an Indian landowner (**8.3**), intricately hand-painted before the advent of color photography, with a false backdrop.

In the hands of some photographers, the portrait photograph became an opportunity to capture an essence or atmosphere rather than a superficial likeness of a person. One of the British gentlewomen who took up the new hobby of portrait photography was Julia Margaret Cameron. Her portraits appear out of focus, for during her long exposures (three to seven minutes) her subjects may have moved. Sharpness was not her intention anyway. Her *Iago* (**8.4**) illustrates the

8.4 Julia Margaret Cameron, *Iago*, 1867. Albumen print. National Museum of Photography, Film and Television, Bradford, England.

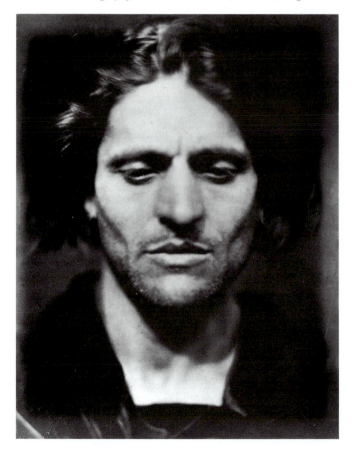

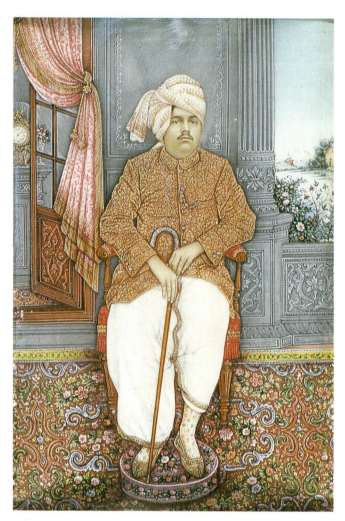

8.3 Anonymous, *Portrait of a Landowner*, India, c. 1900. Painted photograph. ARCOPA (Archival Centre of Photography as an Artform), Bombay, India.

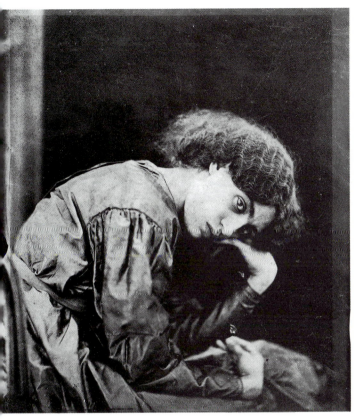

8.5 Dante Gabriel Rossetti, *Jane Morris*, 1865. Photograph. Victoria and Albert Museum, London.

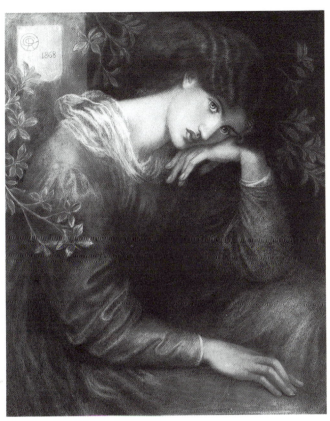

8.6 Dante Gabriel Rossetti, *Rêverie*, 1868. Colored chalk, 33 × 28 ins (83.8 × 71.1 cm). Private collection.

emotional and spiritual depth of her photographs. Although Iago was the villain of Shakespeare's *Othello*, we respond to this man as a complex and compelling human being, investing him with our own ideas about what he is feeling.

In addition to being enthusiastically embraced by the public as a new way of capturing images of the world, photography was adopted by many artists as a helpful tool for creating representational works in other media. As we have seen, painters such as Degas and Toulouse-Lautrec developed unusual perspectives and cropping of figures in response to the camera's-eye view of external experience. Then, as now, some artists also used photographs as the initial study from which to develop drawings or paintings. Rather than having William Morris's wife, Jane, pose through long sittings, Dante Gabriel Rossetti had her photographed as he posed her (**8.5**) and then developed his chalk drawing *Rêverie* (**8.6**) from the photograph. Note that he did not imitate it slavishly; the artist's license he took is obvious when the two images are compared. Even after

posing her himself, he changed her posture in the drawing, creating a pleasing circular flow of light across her neck, down her right arm, up her left arm, and back to the Classical styling of her face.

Whenever a new medium appears, artists often try to increase its acceptance by making its products approximate those created with earlier, familiar media. This was true in photography as well. At the turn of the century, the "Pictorialist" movement in photography sought, by elaborate printing techniques, to make photographs look like paintings, emphasizing the hand of the artist at work rather than the sheer duplicating ability of the camera. Edward Steichen used layered prints created with different chemicals to create the misty atmosphere of *Moonrise, Mamaroneck, New York* (**8.7**).

Although such painterly effects were dramatic, Steichen and Alfred Stieglitz, both leaders of the Pictorialist movement, also evolved strong interest in exploring the potentials that were unique to photography. One was the ability to capture a specific

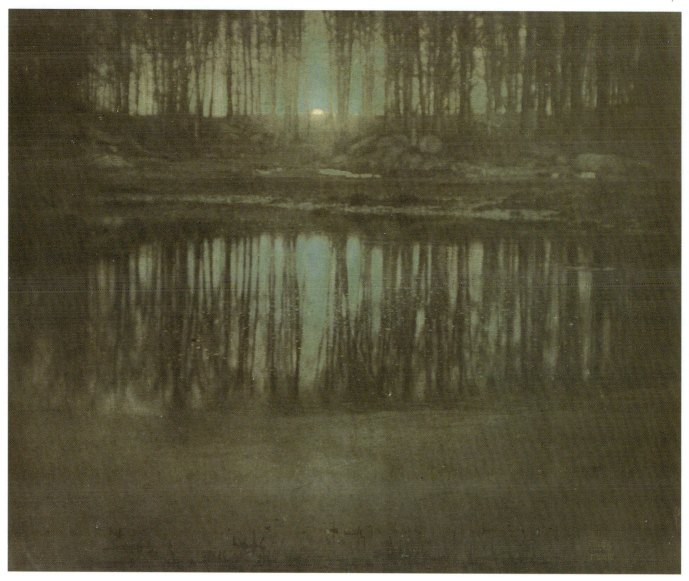

8.7 Edward Steichen, *Moonrise, Mamaroneck, New York*, 1904. Platinum, cyanotype, and ferroprussiate print, 15¹⁵⁄₁₆ × 19 ins (38.9 × 48.3 cm). Collection Museum of Modern Art, New York. Gift of the photographer.

moment in time. Stieglitz's *The Terminal* (8.8) is an ephemeral scene of a horse-drawn trolley being turned on a wintry morning. The steamy breath and body heat of the horses, the dusting of snow, and the man walking out of the picture in the background give a sense of immediacy to the image.

Willingness to abandon the search for beauty in favor of the straight *documentary* photograph made it possible for sympathetic photographers to share what they had seen of humanity. Documentary photographers—some of them hired by the Farm Security Administration in the United States—wakened public

concern for social welfare by recording the plight of the poor, from children working in mines and sweatshops to migrant workers living under wretched conditions. Dorothea Lange's photograph of a migrant mother and her children (8.9) was reproduced in thousands of newspapers and magazines across the country. According to Lange's field notes, this mother, who spoke to the heart of every mother, was "camped on the edge of a pea field where the crop had failed in a freeze. The tires had just been sold from the car to buy food. She was 32 years old with seven children." So effective was this memorable image in waking public

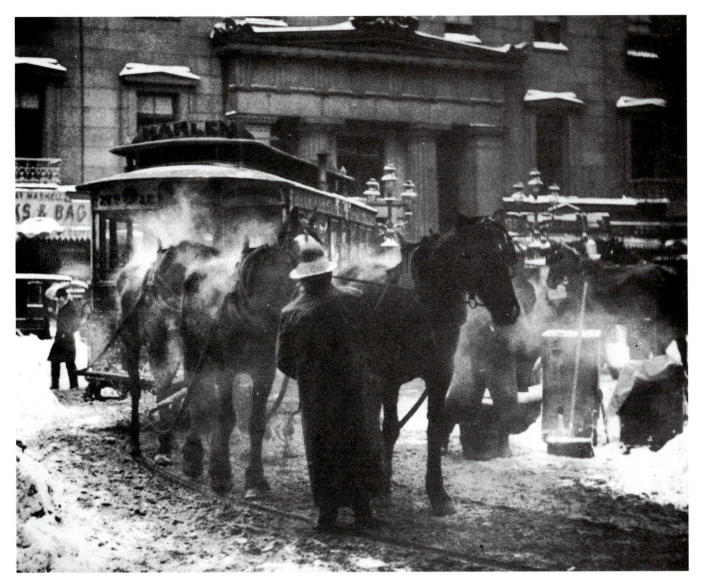

8.8 Alfred Stieglitz, *The Terminal*, 1915. Photograph.
Gernsheim Collection, Harry Ransom Humanities Research Center,
University of Texas at Austin, Texas.

sympathy and support for government welfare projects that the death of the mother decades later was publicly honored.

Documentary photographs are not necessarily so direct in their impact. Alex Webb has used a palette of pleasing blue and pinks for *Killed by the Army* (**8.10**) from his *Port-au-Prince* series of 1987, and has purposely underexposed the human figure and kept it in a corner. The viewer is initially drawn in by the colors, textures, shapes—and then comes the secondary realization that the man is dead. One is given no information about who he is or the reason for killing; with no

visible weapons, he seems a symbol of the multitudes of innocent, nameless, hidden victims of the Haitian government.

Sociological photo-reporting has not dwelt exclusively on scenes of human misery. Even among the poor, photographers have often captured moments of great integrity, ecstasy, or humor. Henri Cartier-Bresson specialized in images of everyday life around the world that are emotionally familiar to people from all cultures. His genius lies in his ability to catch the "decisive moment" when a naturally shifting scene of unposed people clicks into place as a strong

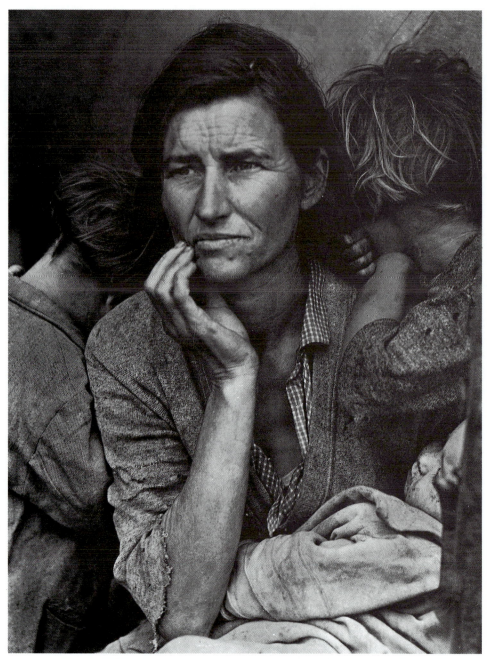

8.9 Dorothea Lange, *Migrant Mother, Nipomo, California*, 1936. Gelatin-silver print, 12½ × 9⅞ ins (31.75 × 24.9 cm). Collection Museum of Modern Art, New York. Purchased.

composition. In his *Sunday on the Banks of the Marne* (**8.11**), everything is placid and staid, from the calm surface of the water to the short, round forms of the well-fed torsos. The only action we sense is the business of eating, a central theme in these people's lives.

Photographs have also been used to preserve views of the earth's natural landscape that are continually threatened by the expansion of population and industry. In the United States, the work of the great landscape photographers, such as Ansel Adams, has played a major role in wilderness conservation efforts. Adams was a leader in the "f/64 Group," which used a small lens opening (such as f/64) in the interests of exceptional clarity, sharpness of detail, and depth of field (sharpness of detail at all distances from the viewer), as illustrated by Adams' *Clearing Winter Storm, Yosemite National Park* (**8.12**). Such arresting images resulted from planning at the photographing stage

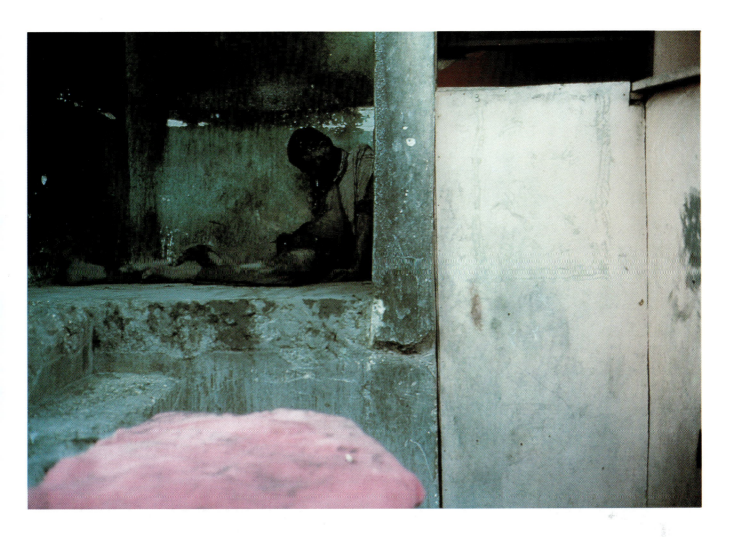

8.10 Alex Webb, *Killed by the Army*, from the *Port-au-Prince* series, 1987. Courtesy of the artist.

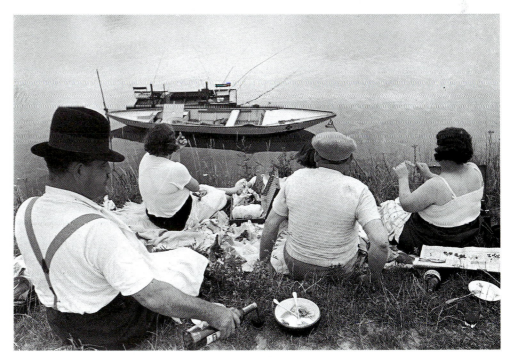

8.11 Henri Cartier-Bresson, *Sunday on the Banks of the Marne*, 1939. Gelatin-silver print, 9⅛ × 13¾ ins (23 × 34.9 cm).

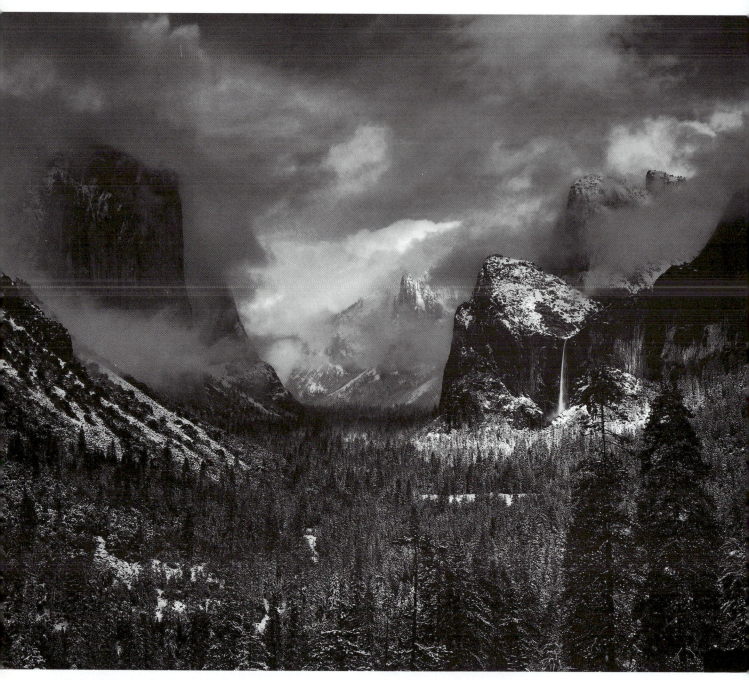

8.12 Ansel Adams, *Clearing Winter Storm, Yosemite National Park*, 1944. Photograph.

rather than manipulation in the darkroom. Adams' full tonal range, from lush blacks, through many grays, to pure whites, is also a hallmark of his work.

In addition to introducing armchair travelers to human and natural landscapes they have never seen, the eye of the camera has also been used to examine familiar objects in such a way that they became unexpected visual pleasures. Many variables can be juggled for the effect the photographer desires: lighting, type of camera and lens, point of view, exposure time, film, paper, and developing and printing options. Olivia Parker uses these options to create an unfamiliarly heightened sense of realism in her photographs of "familiar" objects. Trained as a painter, she composes her images carefully before photographing them,

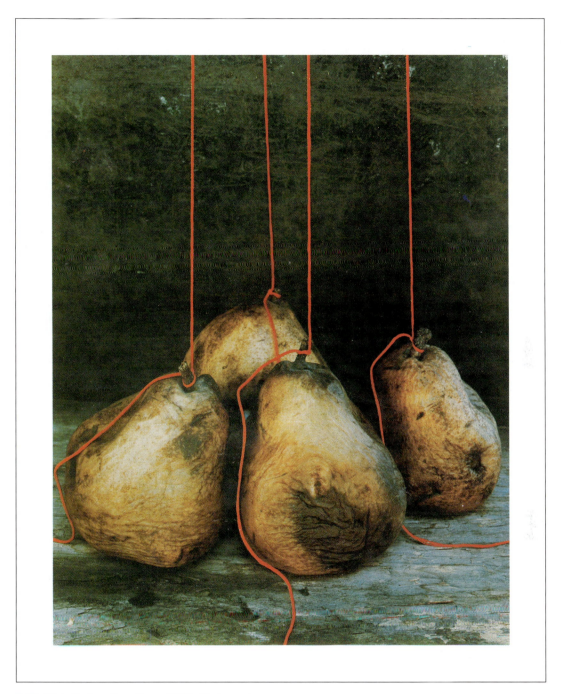

8.13 Olivia Parker, *Four Pears*, 1979. Photograph.

adding the near-fluorescent red strings to the shriveled fruits of *Four Pears* (**8.13**). Parker comments:

> Although we think of photography as more "real" than the other visual arts, it allows for transformation of objects in ways I find especially interesting. The substance of an object can be altered by removing it partway through an exposure. Light can change form and structure. Objects or figures can exist as shadows yielding only some of their information to a piece. Color can be the color of an object as we think of it, the color of light around an object or a new color caused by filtration, additional projected colored light or the peculiar way a certain film and print material see color.[1]

EDWARD WESTON
on PHOTOGRAPHY AS A WAY OF SEEING

Edward Weston (1886–1958), one of the great figures in American photography, initially created out-of-focus, dreamy portraits. But in the 1920s he began a movement he called "straight photography," in which objects were shot in sharp focus, with attention to their details. He particularly loved the "sculptural" forms of vegetables, rocks, trees, the human figure. For him photography was an intense way of seeing, as well as the technical expertise to capture what he saw. The following are excerpts from his daybooks:

"B. sat next to me again. As she sat with legs bent under (**8.14**), I saw the repeated curve of thigh and calf—the shin bone, knee and thigh lines forming shapes not unlike great seashells—the calf curved across the upper leg, the shell's opening.

These simplified forms I search for in the nude body are not easy to find, nor record when I do find them. There is that element of chance in the body assuming an important movement: then there is the difficulty in focussing close up with a sixteen-inch lens: and finally the possibility of movement in an exposure of from 20 sec. to 2 min.,—even the breathing will spoil a line . . . My after exhaustion is partly due to eyestrain and nerve strain. I do not weary so when doing still-life and can take my own sweet time."

[He imagines explaining himself to his friend, the painter Henrietta Shore:] "You see, Henrietta, with the Graflex I cannot possibly conceive my complete, final result in advance—as you can. I hold to a *definite attitude of approach*, but the camera can only record what is before it, so I must await and be able to grasp the right moment when it is presented on my ground glass. To a certain point I can, when doing still-life, feel my conception before I begin work, but in portraiture, figures, clouds—trying to record ever-changing movement and expression, everything depends upon my clear vision, my intuition at the important instant, which if lost can never be repeated. This is a great limitation and at the same time a fascinating problem in photography.

Imagine if you had to create in, at the most, a few seconds of time, without the possibility of previsioning, a complete work, supposed to have lasting value. Of course my technique is rapid, and serves me if coordinated at the time with my perception."

"Point Lobos! I saw it with different eyes yesterday than those of nearly fifteen years ago. And I worked, how I worked! I did not attempt the rocks, nor any general vista: I did do the cypress! No one has done them—to my knowledge—as I have, and will. Details, fragments of the trunk, the roots—dazzling records, technically superb, intensely visioned. . . . Amazing trees—those stark, bone-white, aged ones, storm-swept and twisted into the most amazing forms. This sounds all too picturesque—but wait—I have seen them with my eyes, at my best."

"I am the adventurer on a voyage of discovery, ready to receive fresh impressions, eager for fresh horizons, not in the spirit of a militant conqueror to impose myself or my ideas, but to identify myself in, and unify with, whatever I am able to recognize as significantly part of me: the 'me' of universal rhythms. Nature must not be recorded with a viewpoint colored by psychological headaches or heartaches. . . . [I want] an honest, direct, and reverent approach when granted the flash of revealment."

"I have been training my camera on a cantaloupe—a sculptural thing. I know I shall make some good negatives for I feel its form deeply. Then last eve green peppers in the market stopped me: they were amazing in every sense of the word —the three purchased. But a tragedy took place. Brett ate two of them!"[2]

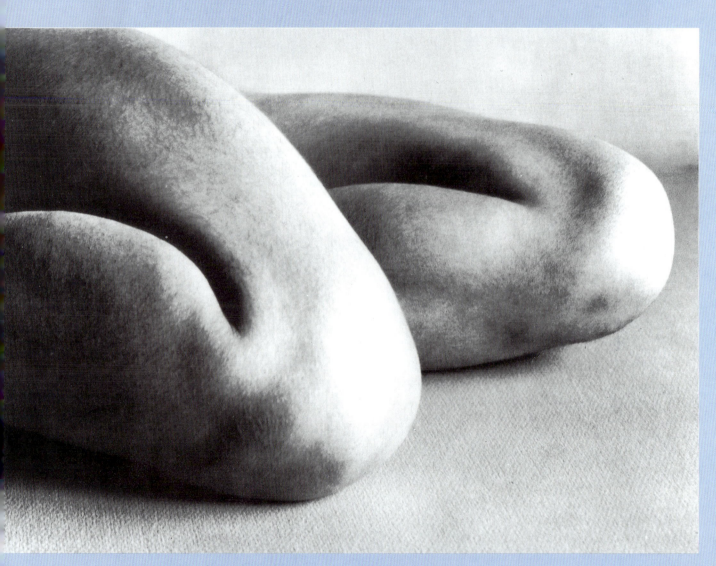

8.14 Edward Weston, *Knees*, 1927. Gelatin-silver print, 6¼ × 9³⁄₁₆ ins (15.9 × 23.4 cm).
San Francisco Museum of Modern Art, San Francisco, California. Albert M. Bender Collection. Bequest of Albert M. Bender.

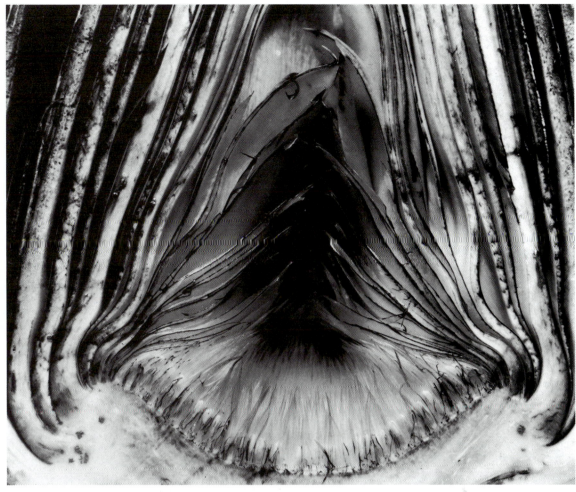

8.15 Edward Weston, *Artichoke Halved*, 1930. Photograph.

It is one of the wonders of photography that the camera can capture details that the eye does not perceive. Many of us have seen halved artichokes, but as photographed at close range by Edward Weston (8.15), this familiar object becomes a world unto itself, a sensual, evocative vision of secret recesses. One of the most influential members of the f/64 Group, Weston used a classic large-format 8 × 10 inch (20 × 25 cm) camera and did not enlarge his prints beyond that size, to avoid any distortion of the carefully previsualized image. Such photographs reveal the artist's love for the photographed object and inspire the same feeling in us.

The integrity of real objects, landscapes, and people is only one possible arena for the photograph. There are limitless ways of altering the realism of photography. Elizabeth Sunday uses reflective surfaces to elongate forms (8.16), to convey spiritual truths that

are not apparent in conventional photographs. Sunday explains:

> Using elongations allows me to go beyond the world of right angles into an inner place of emotions, where we live. We are so used to seeing the world as it appears in the material manifestation—in surfaces. I want to go behind and through that to someplace else.[3]

Sunday's photographs reveal a world in which everything is dynamic; nothing is as solid as it appears on the surface. In this lively, unseen world, whose truth is accepted as fact in modern physics, there are no sharp boundaries between humans and their environment.

Whereas we tend to treat photographs as precious objects, handling them carefully by the edges, some artists have violated this taboo to cut into their pristine surfaces, rearranging the pieces at will. An artist can also work directly on the surface of a photograph, as

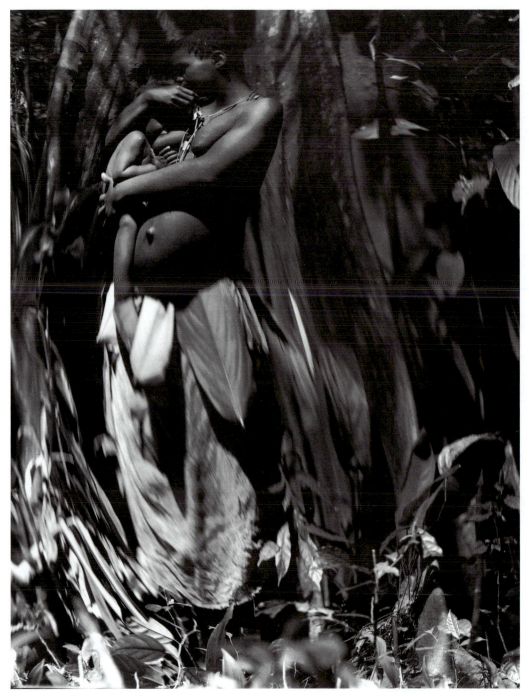

8.16 Elizabeth Sunday, *Life's Embrace*, 1989. Silver print, 40 × 30 ins (101.6 × 76.2 cm). Courtesy of the artist.

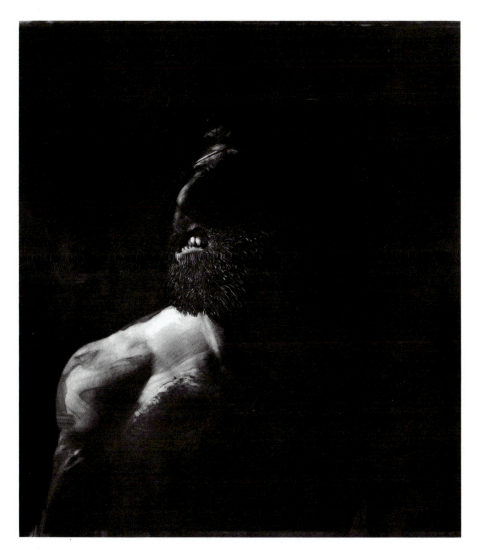

8.17 William E. Parker, *The Temperaments (Choleric II)*, from *Der Wilde Mann* series, 1985. Hand-colored black and white silver print—oil, aquamedia, wax crayon, graphite on Kodak Type N. polyfiber paper.
Frame 4 ft 1 in × 3 ft 9 ins (1.24 × 1.14 m), image 3 ft 8 ins × 3 ft 4 ins (1.12 × 1.01 m). Eileen Cohen Collection, Great Neck, New York.

William Parker has done in his "Wild Man" series (**8.17**). He photographs a person, makes a "grand-scale" photographic print from the negative, and then makes hand-colored alterations on the print with oil paint, wax crayon, pastels, and graphite sticks or powder. Why? In addition to the visual drama of such work, Parker says he wants to get beneath the emotionally vacant slickness of the Western male to reveal "a primal expressiveness, the energy that has been suppressed in the man who cannot express emotions."[4]

Computer manipulation of photographic images opens another new field of possibilities. Japanese designer Susumu Endo takes photographs of everyday objects and natural scenes and then works with a computer operator to digitize and then transform them into magical visions which challenge our understanding of spatial relationships. In *Space and Space Forest 91A* (**8.18**), a forest photograph changes in hues and values, and is turned into sharp-edged blocks which appear, disappear, and spill beyond their edges. In the center, the imagery becomes so visually dense that it creates an ambiguous series of shadows, as if it were a three-dimensional object. Endo says he seeks to "explore and create new space, to express the co-existence of normal space and the space beyond focus where different planes are fused together."[5]

Technological advances in cameras and films are increasing the range of images that can be captured and manipulated. Stephen Dalton, for example, has developed high-speed photography as an exquisite art to capture images that usually pass unnoticed by the naked eye. Although our visual perception mechanism is fairly good at judging size, form, distance, and color, it cannot see what is happening when things are moving quickly. Moving objects tend to be seen as blurs; the retina cannot pass information to the brain

or the brain interpret the information quickly enough to keep changing imagery in sharp focus. By contrast, the camera needs only to record an image; the brain of the viewer can interpret the arrested movement at leisure. Technological innovations such as high-speed electronic flash units now allow us to see what we could not see before.

Stephen Dalton's photograph in Figure 8.19 reveals the dropping of spores by a common horsetail plant. He has controlled values and composition in such a way that this seemingly commonplace occurrence becomes an elegant ballet; rather than appearing frozen in time, the cascading of the spores appears to be happening as we watch. Dalton insists that it is the observant eye of the artist that is most important in any form of photography:

> Clearly, equipment will not produce pictures on its own—the make and complexity of the camera have little to do with the final results and, more often than not, the simpler the equipment the better. . . . The beauty of the natural world can only be revealed to the eye and camera spending time in the field. Above all, it requires patience, light and an understanding of nature.[6]

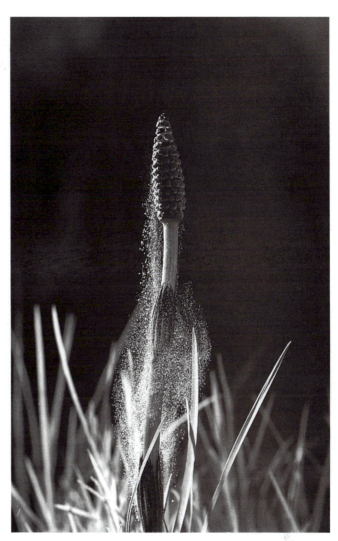

8.19 Stephen Dalton, *Spores Falling From the Common Horsetail*. Photograph. © Stephen Dalton.

8.18 Susumu Endo, *Space and Space Forest 91A*, 1991. Offset lithograph, 23½ × 23½ ins (60 × 60 cm). Courtesy of the artist.

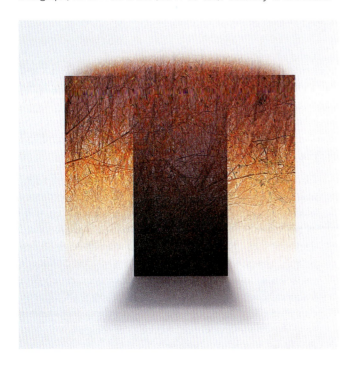

PHOTOCOPY AND FAX ART

Photocopying (also called "xeroxing," after an early trade name) is named after photography, though the process is based on a different technology. An original of some sort is exposed to a bright light; the light reflects off the white areas, is totally absorbed by the dark areas, and is reflected to varying degrees by gray and colored areas. In "indirect photocopying," this light image is focused by a lens onto an intermediate surface to form an image composed of electrical charges. These charges attract toner (photocopy ink) which is transferred onto copy paper. "Direct photocopying" digitizes the light image—including analysis

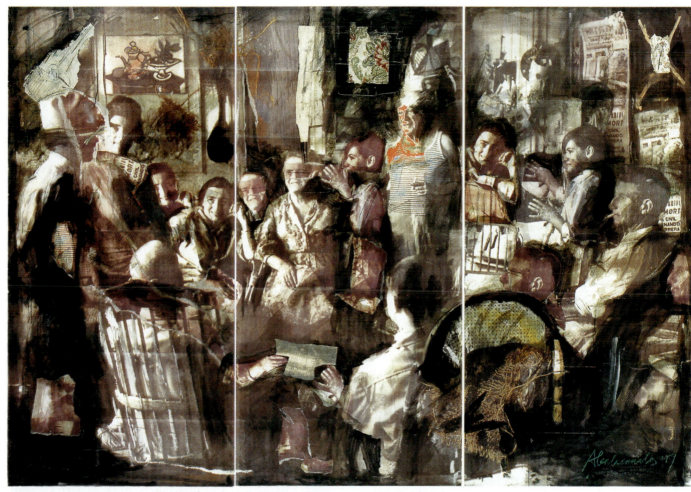

8.20 Alcalacanales, *La Corrida de Cannes*, 1989. Xerox art, 3 ft 5 ins × 7 ft (1.04 × 2.13 m). Courtesy Fernand N. Canales, Colección Museo Internacional de Electrografia, Universidad de Castilla.

of colors—and prints them at high resolution by lasers.

Like photography, photocopying technology was not originally created as an art process, but artists have been quick to discover and experiment with its possibilities. Anything that fits into the imaging area can be copied; it can be moved during the copying process, creating blurred results. Color xeroxes can be over-copied, with colors mixing where they lie atop each other. Xeroxed images can be worked on, cut up, assembled, re-xeroxed. Alcalacanales's *La Corrida de Cannes* (**8.20**) is a photocopy collage created from a family photograph, manipulated repeatedly with layers of colors and drawings building up textural and spatial effects.

Anything that can be photocopied can also be faxed—sent electronically by telephone to a facsimile-

receiving machine anywhere in the world. David Hockney, who gained fame and fortune as a painter and photographer, became very uncomfortable with the astronomical prices some paintings—including his own—now command, so he switched to xerox and fax art. He explains:

> On one hand, there is a movement towards unbelievable prices in art. On the other is a countermovement—fax art is essentially a Xerox copy, isn't it? What's it worth? Nothing. That makes the art world very nervous. They don't know what to do with it. But to me, that's what makes it great: you can send the exhibition anywhere. You don't really need much of a gallery. You can glue fax art on almost any wall. . . . You can give them away, or you can send them to Brazil or to Moscow—anywhere there's a telephone, fax machine, and a bit of paper.[7]

FILM

In photography a work usually consists of a single shot, but in a motion picture film a single frame is only one of a great number of consecutive shots. Viewed individually, each is like a still photograph, as in the sequences Eadweard Muybridge shot in the nineteenth century to analyze the components of animal and human motion. To photograph the movement of a horse galloping (to answer the question of whether all four feet were ever simultaneously off the ground) or a man turning cartwheels (with interference from a pigeon—8.21), Muybridge set up a line of 12 cameras whose shutters were tripped as the subject rushed by. Putting the images side by side in a strip suggested the idea of viewing them through the whirling toy called a *zoetrope*. This was a topless drum with slits around its sides through which a series of images seemed to merge in the viewer's perception as a continuous movement. The reason for this phenomenon is the *persistence of vision*. Our perceptual apparatus retains images for about a tenth of a second after they have disappeared. In a professionally made film, images are typically presented to us at the rate of 24 frames per second.

Late in the nineteenth century, French inventions made it possible to record successive movements on a single strip of film; George Eastman turned this strip into durable celluloid. By the end of the century, means of projecting these images onto a screen for public viewing had been developed. Thus was laid the base for the use of moving pictures as an art medium: **cinematography**.

Cinematography is broadly defined as the application of photography to moving images. As an art, it involves the technical considerations of photography—such as the control of lighting, color, camera angle, focal length, and composition for desired emotional and atmospheric effects. In addition, it involves relationships between shots and scenes, and between images and sound (which is carried on a separate track alongside the images). These choices are made by a team. In addition to the person behind

8.21 Eadweard Muybridge, *Headspring, a Flying Pigeon Interfering, June 26, 1885.* Victoria and Albert Museum, London.

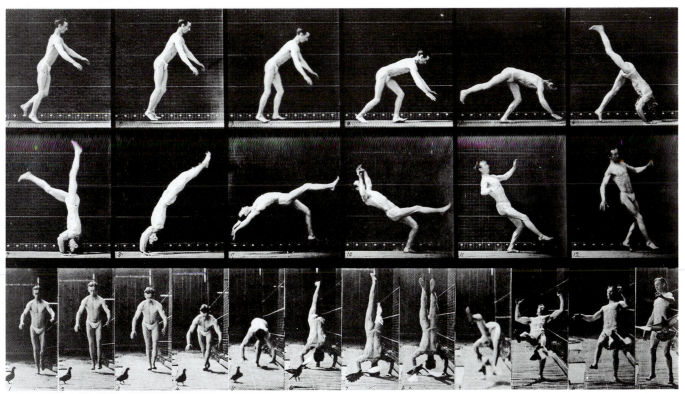

the camera, the team typically includes a director, a designer, a music director, a sound mixer, and an editor.

The ability to manipulate the elements of cinematography has been used to a certain degree in all films. When these manipulations make little or no attempt at the illusion of realism, films are often termed **Expressionist**. One of the most extreme examples is *The Cabinet of Doctor Caligari* (8.22), which came out of the German Expressionist movement prior to World War I. Everything in the film was stylized to evoke a mood of dread, the world seen through the eyes of a madman. The sets were painted in stark black and white, with delirious diagonal lines, distorted perspectives, and strange painted shadows. The spatial wrenching was mirrored by jerky, mechanical acting, portraying the nightmarish control of a sleepwalker's mind by the hypnotist Caligari.

The term *avant-garde* or *experimental* film has been applied to a great variety of works intended to make a philosophical or artistic statement with little regard for public taste. Some, such as *Un Chien andalou* by Salvador Dalí and Luis Buñuel, have even gone out of their way to shock. Conceived in rebellion against the art of "witty, elegant, and intellectualized Paris," as Dalí wrote in his *Secret Life of Salvador Dalí*, the film

8.22 Robert Wiene, *The Cabinet of Doctor Caligari*, Germany, 1919. Decla-Bioscop (Erich Pommer).

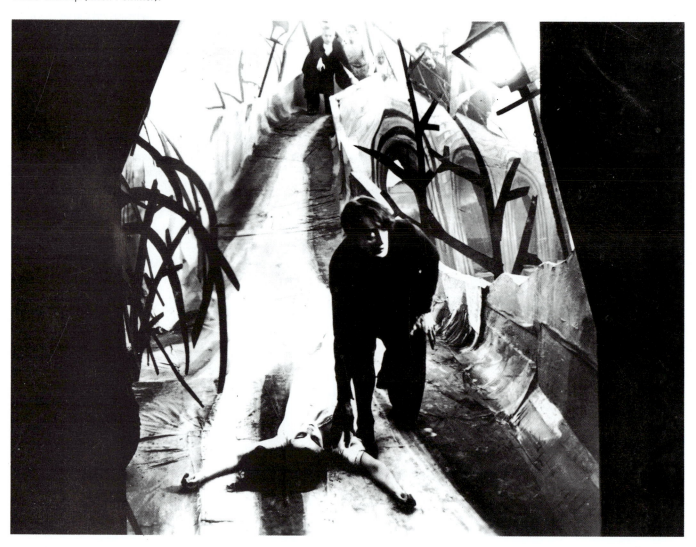

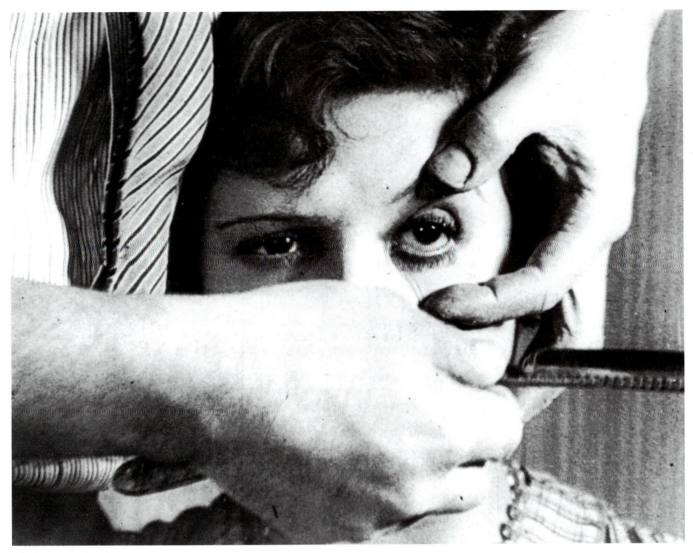

8.23 Luis Buñuel and Salvador Dalí, *Un Chien andalou (An Andalusian Dog)*, France, 1928.

begins with a close-up of a woman's eye about to be slit by a razor (**8.23**). This shot is followed by one of a cloud crossing the moon, and then a close-up of the slitting of the eye (actually that of a dead animal). It was the Russian director Sergei Eisenstein who had pioneered this technique of **montage**—the splicing together at editing stage of a variety of shots of brief duration to produce a complex visual statement. Although all the scenes in this film are composed of photographs of actual objects, they are as disorderly and yet as surrealistically vivid as images in dreams.

Even in more apparently realistic films, visual effects may be carefully manipulated to control the audience's response. Orson Welles' still-fresh *Citizen*

Kane (**8.24**) is the portrayal of the life of a powerful press magnate. This classic work is a showcase for cameraman Gregg Tolland's brilliant use of *deep-focus shots* (in which the viewer's eye can travel across subjects in many different spatial planes, all in focus), symbolic camera angles (such as the tilting of the image shown here to suggest the distorted nature of the politics in the film), *wide-angle shots* that make people standing near each other seem widely separated in space, and expressionistic use of dark and light values.

In *Rashomon* (**8.25**), the famous Japanese director Akira Kurosawa's training as a painter is evident in the careful compositions of figures and the elegance with

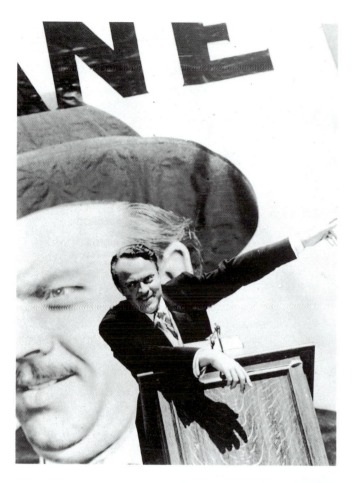

which the camera lingers over lights, shadows, textures, and visual rhythms. As in *Citizen Kane*, the enigmatic narrative proceeds by *flashbacks* to previous events, as four characters each retell the story of a woman's rape and her husband's murder in a different way, leaving the audience to draw their own conclusions.

Horror and thrill in contemporary movies are greatly exaggerated by computerized *special effects*. Devices such as scale models, painted backdrops, smoke, cloud tanks, laser beams, light flares, and computer-generated imagery are pieced together to create terrifying illusions of fiery diasters, alien invasions, air battles, explosions, and general devastation. Oddly, the "problem" now is that viewers have become so accustomed to such effects that they no longer find them thrilling. Furthermore, worldwide violence is documented daily. Producer Dean Devlin explains:

> At the time *Airport* [an earlier disaster film] came out, it worked because no one had yet captured a plane crash on video. Now, there are cameras everywhere. Riots, earthquakes, fires, tornadoes and floods are on the news every day. It's very hard to create a disaster that people haven't already seen.[8]

8.24 (above) Orson Welles, *Citizen Kane*, USA, 1941. RKO Pictures.

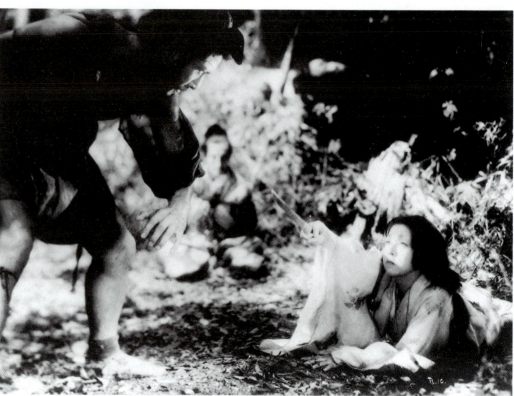

8.25 Akira Kurosawa, *Rashomon*, Japan, 1951. Daiei.

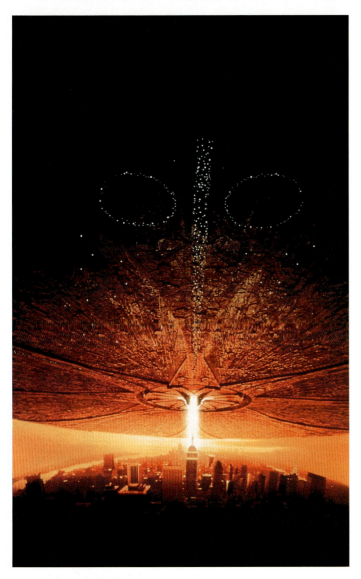

Nevertheless, working with some 250 special effects artists, Devlin created the "blockbuster" thriller movie *Independence Day*, in which monstrous alien spacecrafts hover over and attack every major city in the world. In the scene shown in Figure **8.26**, New York appears to be in flames because of dozens of smoke and fire special effects overlaid on a miniature backdrop of the Manhattan skyline in forced linear perspective. The Statue of Liberty is a five-foot-tall (1.52-m) model made of foam. The hovering alien spacecraft is also a scale model. Computer imaging is used to create effects such as reflections in the water, tying the separately filmed illusions together into a convincingly realistic scene of mass disaster.

A contrasting approach to filmmaking is the *documentary*—a true-to-life depiction of real people, rather than actors, living their own lives, without an imposed story line or fake shots. To create the beautiful 1922 film *Nanook of the North* (**8.27**), filmmaker Robert Flaherty lived with the vanishing native people of northern Canada for 16 months. He shared the hardships of their lives in order to record their everyday activities within a harsh natural environment. The vast arctic whiteness was a constant backdrop for the naturally unfolding narrative.

8.26 (above) Image from film *Independence Day* shown in *Cinefex*, no. 67, Sept. 1996, p. 72, bottom. Dean Devlin, Producer, Roland Emmerich, Director, and Volker Engel and Doug Smith, Special Effects Supervisors, *Independence Day*, 1996. 20th Century Fox Film Corp

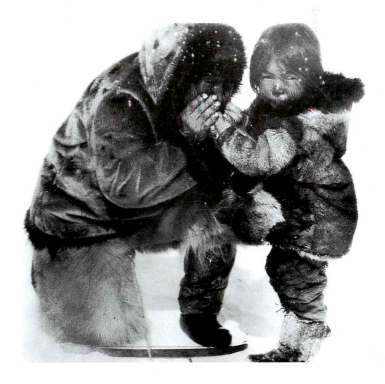

8.27 Robert Flaherty, *Nanook of the North*, USA, 1921. Revillon Frères. Collection Museum of Modern Art, New York, Film Stills Archive.

Finally, there is the film as a poetic image, mysterious and beautiful. The Russian filmmaker Andrei Tarkovsky's films, such as *Nostalgia* (**8.28**), have this quality. Tarkovsky spoke of the difficulty of staying true to the beauty of one's original inspiration when confronted by technical problems and the continual distractions of coordinating the efforts of so many people. He did not rely on editing to fix things; he specialized in *extended takes*, often incorporating entire 12-minute cans of film in the finished work. He did edit and join segments, but with keen awareness of the effect of editing on the viewer's sense of time in what is essentially a time-based art. He referred to film-making as "sculpting in time."

TELEVISION AND VIDEO

Television—a staple of the modern age—includes both live broadcasts and playbacks of videotaped sequences. In *live television*, **video** (visual) and audio signals are broadcast and read as images and sound on television sets far removed from the transmitter. There is little or no editing. In general, what the camera is recording at the time is what the viewers see. This immediacy can bring the emotional impact of distant events—such as the South Vietnamese policeman executing a Vietcong officer (**8.29**)—right into people's homes.

8.28 Andrei Tarkovsky, *Nostalgia*, Italy, 1982. Opera Film/Sovin Film/RAI.

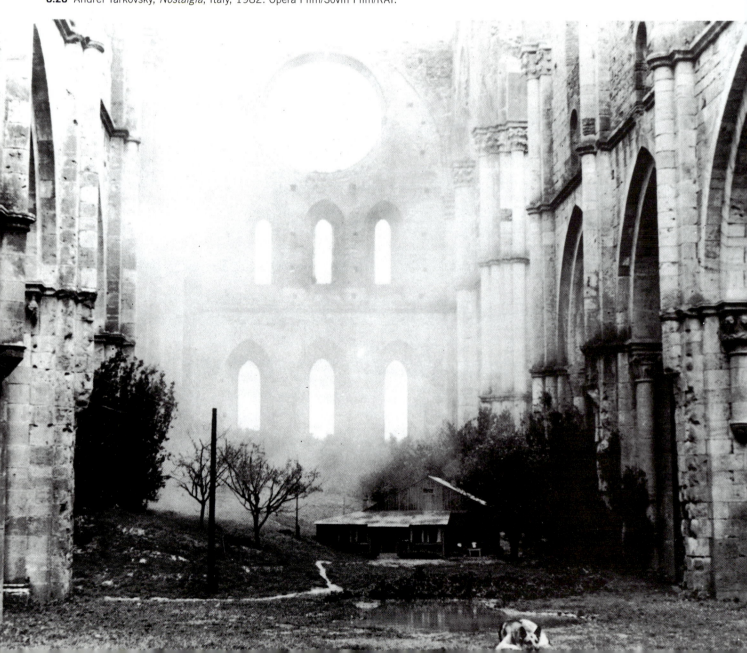

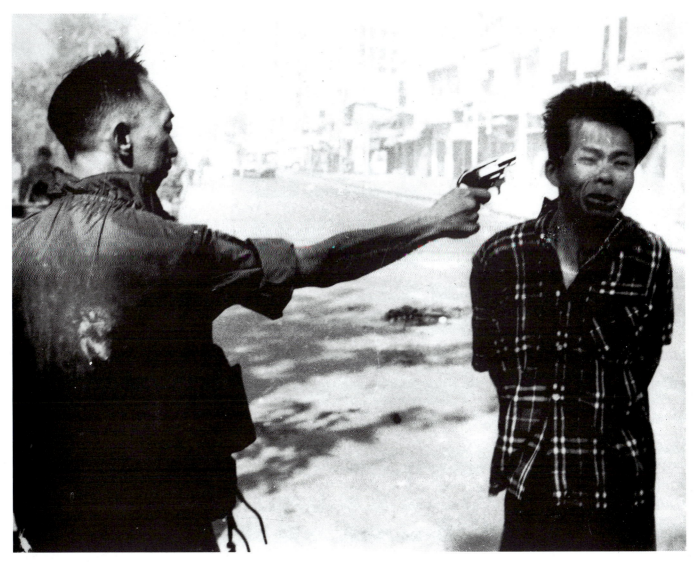

8.29 Eddie Adams, *Execution of a Vietcong officer by the South Vietnamese National Police Chief in Saigon*, 1968.

Television camera lenses relay the amounts of light in a scene to a tube that translates light into electric signals. An electron scanner reads the hundreds of lines of signals so rapidly that the entire image is completely read 30 times a second. These signals, along with audio signals, are transmitted through the air by electromagnetic waves, or bounced off communication satellites, and received by antennas, satellite dishes, or cables for transmission to television sets, where the signals are translated into the original pattern of light and sound. The persistence of human vision makes the separately transmitted signals seem to blend into continuous images.

Television signals can also be recorded on magnetic videotapes, which can then be read by video and audio heads in a videocassette player. Because a permanent recording is made, it can be edited electronically for special effects. Some of the most innovative video effects are being created for music videos broadcast over special music video cable television channels. Images captured by a video camera can be computer-analyzed, broken down into their components, and then visually altered in an ever-expanding variety of ways.

Use of montage and special effects in television has accustomed us to responding to very complex manipulations of time and space. When viewers were first exposed to split-screen images in televised baseball games, where close-ups of players on bases were shown at the same time as the pitcher winding up or the batter getting ready, they could not at first understand what they were seeing. Now, especially in music videos, multiple images dissolving into each other are

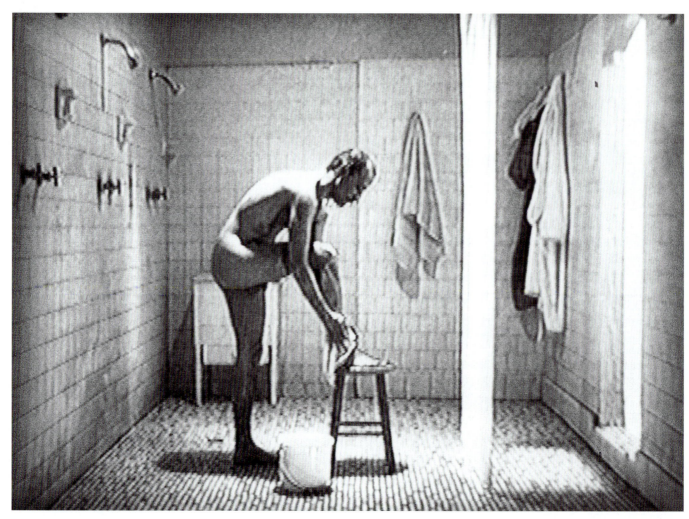

8.30 Bill Viola, "Interval" (detail) from *Buried Secrets*, a video/sound installation of five pieces. Photo by Kira Perov.

presented very rapidly to a visually sophisticated public, who are so familiar with the techniques that they can grasp the images and follow the sequences at speeds beyond conscious thought.

Since the 1960s, artists have also been experimenting with video as an expressive art form. Video art is collected and shown by museums and presented as installation pieces. Some seem intended primarily to show off technological brilliance; other video art uses the medium with an emphasis on the aesthetics of form and experience. Bill Viola, a master of this new medium, uses it to engage people bodily. He feels that Western culture has too long tended to separate the body from the mind. Viola says, "I want to talk to the body in order to reach the mind, . . . the forbidden zone of the deeper emotive energies."[9] To do so, he creates three-dimensional video environments which surround and fully engage the viewer.

In Viola's *Buried Secrets*, viewers physically enter a series of five rooms, each engulfing them in a different emotional journey through time. In one room, a work entitled "Interval" (**8.30**), one sees a man quietly bathing, in a sequence projected on one wall. It is periodically blacked out, as huge videos of elemental fury—resembling a terrific fire, a tumultuous storm, a frightening chase through rough bushes by night—are projected on the opposite wall. The frightening images and the roaring sound accompanying them interrupt ever more quickly, assaulting the viewer with ever more incoherent violence. By contrast, another room draws out time languidly, slowing a brief videotaped encounter between three women into a sensuous ten-minute exploration of their slightest gestures. Viola sees time as a major aesthetic element of video art, in which the medium becomes the servant of the artist's intention rather than an object in itself.

9

COMPUTER GRAPHICS

During the late twentieth century, computer graphics—visual imagery created with the aid of computers—has been rapidly moving from high-tech laboratories into artists' studios. Extremely sophisticated and realistic visual effects are now being widely created, existing only as binary digits in the memories of small machines and "cyberspace"—the global network of computer linkages through modern communication technologies. Rapidly evolving innovations in miniaturized memory, screens with extremely fine resolution and the capacity to display over sixteen million colors, high-resolution color printers and plotters that can produce a continuous range of values of the same hue, and highly sophisticated software are opening up previously unimaginable possibilities to artists. Some artists are treating the computer as a tool for handling conventional techniques very rapidly and perfectly. Other contemporary artists find that the computer is a new medium in itself, facilitating entirely new approaches to art.

THE COMPUTER AS A DRAWING MEDIUM

In the fast changing world of computers, some drawing programs allow artists to work rather conventionally, drawing by hand. However, they draw with an electronic stylus on a digitizing tablet that transfers their markings to a computer screen (9.1) The computer "knows" where to put the marks because the computer screen is divided into an invisible grid of points called **pixels**. The computer assigns mathematical references to points on the image, thus **digitizing** them so that they correspond to the numbered grid of pixels on the screen. Higher-resolution screens are those with more pixels. One can also move a "mouse" off-screen in order to give positional commands to a cursor on-screen.

These indirect methods of drawing require that the artist develops some unfamiliar eye-hand

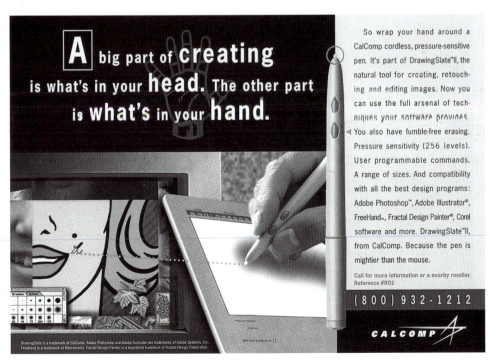

9.1 Reader service card no. 28, from *Adobe Magazine*, November 1996, p. 68.

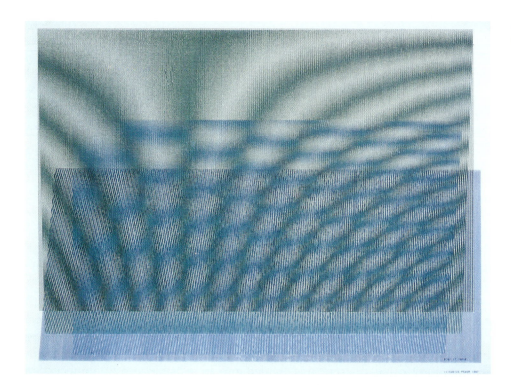

9.2 Eudice Feder, *Swarm*, 1988. Plotter drawing, ballpoint, felt-tip, ink, 30 × 25 ins (76.2 × 63.5 cm). Courtesy of the artist.

9.3 William Latham, *Ornamental Mutation* (third variation), 1992. Created at IBM UKSC. Courtesy of the artist/Computer Artworks.

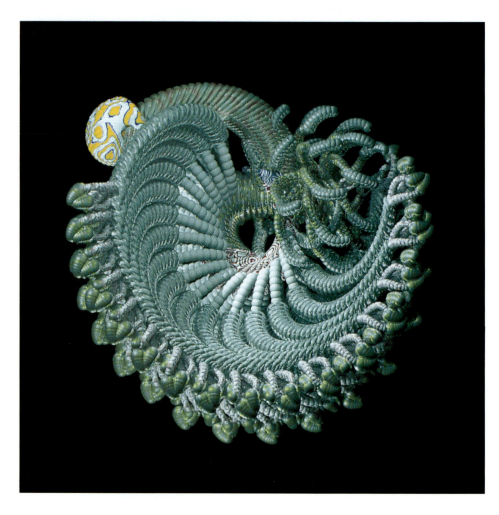

coordination skills, for the image appears on the screen as one draws it, rather than directly under the stylus or mouse. Additional "tools" on the computer screen allow the artist to do painterly things such as filling in, blending, or "spraying" colors.

A less direct method of building up computer images is to use mathematical formulas—programs—to communicate with the computer and printer. In this case, art is created solely by numbers, and it takes a lot of them just to draw a line. For example, a very simple program that tells a plotter to draw 25 random lines in color looks like this:

```
10  HGR:FOR Z = 1 TO 25: H1 = RND(1)*270:V1 = RND(1)*190
20  H2 = RND(1)*270:V2 = RND(1)*190. HCOLOR = INT(RND(1)*8)
30  HPLOT H1, V1 TO H2, V2
40  NEXT Z
```

Once the basic information is installed, the artist can manipulate it indefinitely, unlike a drawing done with any other medium. Images can be flipped, rotated, stretched, compressed, added to or subtracted from; lines can be widened or narrowed, and their texture and color altered ad infinitum. Intricate drawings become possible which no one would attempt by hand, such as Eudice Feder's *Swarm* (**9.2**). She has equipped her plotter with hand-drawing tools—ballpoint, felt-tip, and ink pens—but then given it information to create images that transcend anything ever done by human hand.

As illustrated by *Ornamental Mutation* (**9.3**), a computer can even be programmed to "know" how to create the impression of three-dimensional form on a two-dimensional surface, by using visual clues such as shading, overlapping, and scale change. Such work may require the combined skills of an artist and a computer programmer, or its technological aspect may be carried out by graphics software.

COMPUTER AS A PAINTING MEDIUM

The computer screen is divided into a grid of tiny cells. To use the computer as a medium for creating paintings, these cells are "colored" by electronic instructions, which have become so sophisticated that computer artists can now mimic hand-painted work, if they so choose. Many commercial programs are available that allow the artist to draw an image on a digitizing tablet which transfers it to the computer monitor as in computer drawing; areas can then be

"painted" on the screen by making choices from a "palette" of over sixteen million colors, in the case of high-end equipment.

Another starting point is to use a colored photograph as a source image which is electronically scanned as a **bitmap** reporting the predominant color of each small area (**9.4**). These areas can be reproduced with

9.4 Bitmap scanning. The scanner looks at the image square by square. If there is a lot of dark color in the square, it registers a black dot. If the square is mostly white, it registers nothing. The finer the imaginary grid of squares, the better the resolution and the better quality the bitmapped image. For a color halftone it scans three times, using red, green, and blue filters.

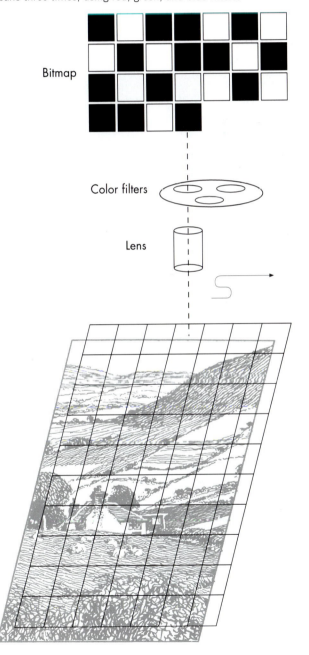

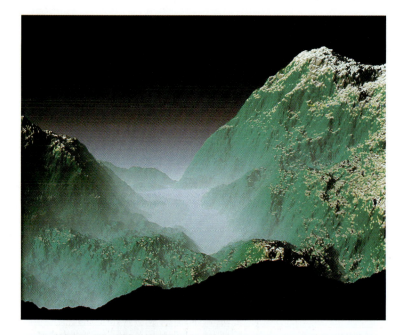

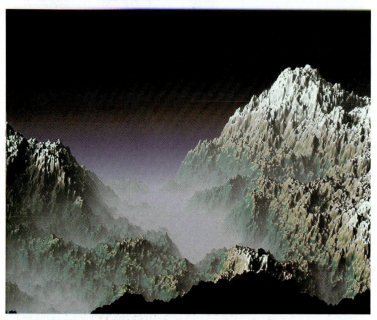

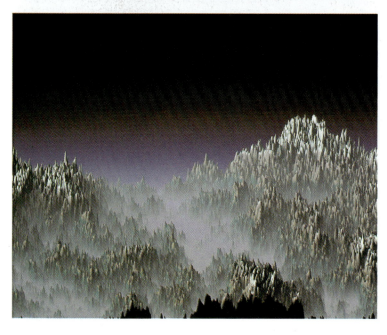

realistic color-matching, or the colors can be changed at will, including the option of limiting rather than extending the palette. Colors can be "painted" in with brushlike strokes of any size or direction. Edges can be "pushed" to exaggerate the contrast between colored areas, to develop three-dimensionality. The whole background can be "washed" with color, as if toning a canvas, and additional images can be overlaid. Three-dimensional illusions of forms can be created with realistic or skewed "lighting" effects and visually textured surfaces, even if the forms are unlike any ever seen on earth.

With **fractal geometry**, astonishingly realistic landscapes can be created arithmetically without reference to any known landscape. This mathematical modeling of complex and random patterns in nature was developed in the late 1970s by the mathematician Benoit Mandelbrot. He based his computer models on the concept of "self-similarity"—the observation that large natural forms consist of visually similar smaller forms. Richard Voss's fractal images, *Changing the Fractal Dimension* (**9.5**), demonstrate this logic: using the same program, Voss changed the fractal dimension of this computer-simulated landscape to be more and more attenuated, thus altering the roughness of the smallest details along with the large forms. Fractals have been taken up with great enthusiasm by many artists who are also mathematicians—or mathematicians who also have aesthetic sensibilities.

To create traditional painting-like results, artists may choose to print "hard copies" of their computer paintings, using film, plotters, or printers, onto art paper, canvas, or textiles.

Moral and legal issues arise. What state of this process is the work of art? Can it be freely duplicated by the artist? In traditional print media, a series of prints are pulled from one block and each print is numbered. If further editions are made from the same block, they must be marked as second or third editions. Otherwise, the block must be scored so that it cannot be re-used. If the art consists in programming a computer disk, must the program be erased after an edition is printed out or photographed from the electronics of the computer? Should the disk itself be sold? Can the purchaser make changes in it? Does the work exist as art only if it is seen

9.5 Richard Voss, *Changing the Fractal Dimension*, 1983. Cibachrome prints, each 10 × 14 ins (25.4 × 35.6 cm). Courtesy of the artist.

in real time on a computer monitor or video screen? These are new questions evoked by an entirely new set of artistic circumstances.

VIDEO GRAPHICS

Lively experimentation is also underway in the field of computer-generated video graphics. In these animated pieces, imagery is both generated and transformed digitally. The same processes are used as those described in computer drawing and painting, except that the potential for altering colors, reducing, enlarging, and rotating figures through space, and "photographing" them from differing focal lengths, all at great speed, is played out for the viewer in real time instead of creating a single image.

Science fiction and thriller movies now make great use of computer-generated special effects (8.26). The first feature-length movie incorporating computer-generated animation was *Tron* (**9.6**). The rapidity of computer calculations enabled the designers not only to design fantasy machines, but also to show them in realistic and continually shifting linear perspective as "light cycles" zoomed through illusionary space.

The same technologies are increasingly used to enhance the visual excitement of television commercials.

Computer graphics have also been used to create animated representations of forms in our natural world that no one has yet seen, but that can be deduced from scientific data. These are primarily created for scientific study, but some are aesthetically exciting as well. Melvin L. Prueitt, of the Los Alamos National Laboratory, where this kind of computer imagery is generated, speaks of the beauty of the unseen world:

> The universe is filled with beauty, most of it unseen and unsensed. What does an intense magnetic field look like as it churns and bubbles near a neutron star? . . . The narrow spectrum of our vision, our hearing, designed to detect the coordinated motions of molecules under restricted conditions, our sense of smell allowing us to detect only a few chemical compounds in the gaseous state, and our short-range sense of touch give us only a partial view of all there is. . . . Although science discovered myriad strange phenomena, we could not see them. . . . By computer graphics we begin to see what we have suspected for some time: that the foundations of the universe are filled with niches of loveliness.[1]

As the field of video graphics evolves, designers are also creating dynamic invented forms that tell their own visual stories of change through time and space, from varying "camera angles." They can be programmed for credible if unfamiliar "growth" and

9.6 Walt Disney Productions, *Tron*, 1982.

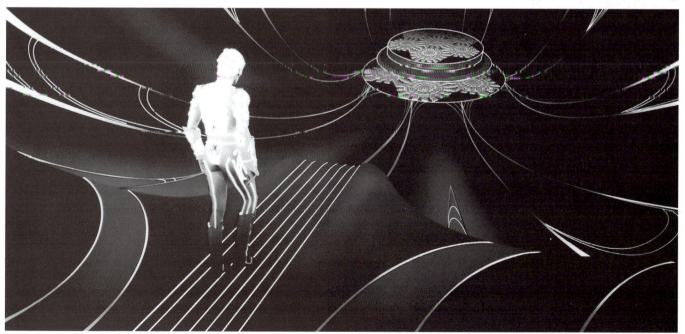

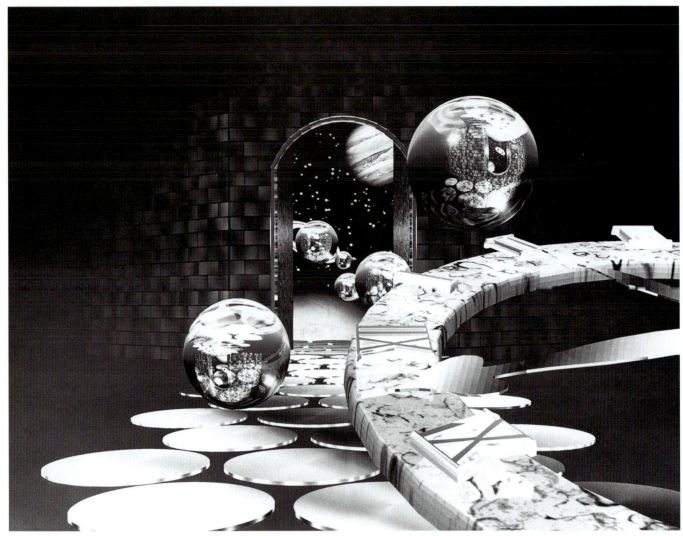

9.7 Hiroshi Yagi, *No. 27 Time Space Passage*, Yagi Studio.

movements, through space that need not bear any relationship to spatial realities (**9.7**).

VIRTUAL REALITY

The newest form of computer-generated experience is *virtual reality* systems in which the viewer also becomes participator in the action. This new technology allows architects to "walk through" buildings they have planned and examine what they will look like, before they exist in reality. Another art application is an extension of video games. One enters a fantasy world by donning a headset with a pair of miniature monitors and earphones inside or by putting one's head into a tunnel that blocks peripheral vision. Position sensors within the headgear track movements of the user's head, giving a different computerized visual display on the miniature screens depending on which way the user is looking. This gives one the strange illusion of being in a three-dimensional reality, but without one's own body. Disembodied, the user can move through this illusory virtual reality and even "hear" things in the virtual environment.

A "tactile input device," such as a glove with sensors, baton or "joystick" (**9.8**), transfers the movements of the participant's hand to the computer by fiber optics and a special tracking system. To make industrial mock-ups, the designer's hand may receive "sensory reaction" feedback to allow manipulation on the screen of "virtual solid objects" by a "virtual hand".

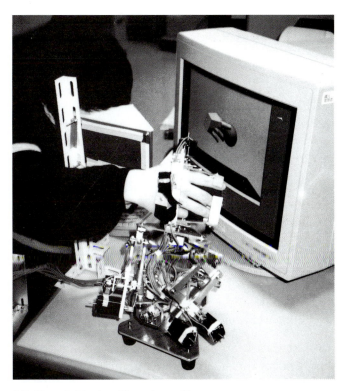

9.8 View of virtual reality system with pressure feedback for manipulation of virtual solid objects. Courtesy of the designer Hiroo Iwata.

9.9 Virtual reality radiotherapy. A researcher uses virtual reality to direct radiotherapy beams towards a cancer tumor in human lungs. With the aid of the headset, the researcher can see a three-dimensional view of the lungs and position multiple radiation beams. System under development at the Department of Computer Science, University of North Carolina. Photo by Peter Menzel.

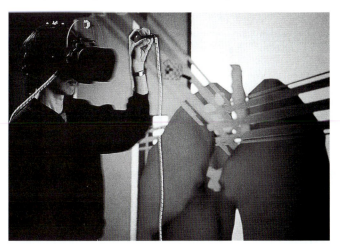

Both hand and object actually exist only as numbers but the designer can "feel" an object and alter it on the computer screen in approximation of crafting something by hand. Computer technology is evolving so rapidly that these experiences are becoming more and more "plausibly lifelike." They are now increasingly used in the design of automobile prototypes and architecture. Virtual reality systems are even used in selling real estate, in teaching doctors how to perform surgery, and in radiotherapy (**9.9**).

As virtual reality technology becomes less expensive and more accessible, it is being used not only for the creation of illusory three-dimensional art, but also for virtual access to the art collections of major museums. At the beginning of the twentieth century, universities had plaster casts of master sculptures for students to study. But these were not fully satisfactory, for they were big and easily broken, and soon became dusty. Nearly a century later, students can "enter" a pristine virtual room and examine "sculptures" within it from every angle, or "walk" through the intricacies of ancient rock temples.

THE COMPUTER AS A UNIQUE ART MEDIUM

As computer graphics engineering advances, the question arises: Is computer graphics a new art form that does not require artistic sensibilities? Will the ease of creating complex, rapidly changing, brightly colored images by computer change public tastes in art? Does computer art have any meaning, or is it just a display of technological brilliance?

Computers were not created as art media; they were mathematical tools designed to generate more mathematics. Those who have recently taken them up to create art are now beginning to explore issues of aesthetics and content in computer-generated art.

Much of the money and brilliance behind the computer graphics explosion initially came from engineering laboratories. Before "user-friendly" software, computers were largely the province of engineers. Coming from an art rather than an engineering background, pioneering computer artist Charles Csuri first labored in the 1960s to create images using stacks of punched cards fed into a giant mainframe in the electrical engineering department of Ohio State

University. In the 1980s, he continued his fervent experimentation at night in the California Institute of Technology's Jet Propulsion Laboratory. Early computer technologies were so unwieldy and arcane that few artists attempted to master them. When computer images were created by programming, creating art required use of mathematical formulas. Nowhere was there the traditional tactile connection between the artist and the artwork.

Nevertheless, Charles Csuri and a few others persisted, because they had sensed the untapped potential of computer graphics as a unique art medium. Once microprocessors were introduced in the late 1970s, followed by user-friendly software programs that eliminated the need for programming skills, the potential of computer graphics began to be tapped by increasing numbers of artists.

Harold Cohen, for instance, carried out experiments in programming a computer to think for itself, as it were, making decisions and drawing pictures that resemble natural forms. Cohen then hand-colored the ones that he liked (**9.10**).

One of the computer's unique qualities is that it permits major changes to be made very quickly once a program is established—the user can instantly change an image's position, shape, scale, colors, lighting effects, and surface texture, fragment it, duplicate it, destroy it, bring it back in a new virtual incarnation,

and at the same time preserve the original unchanged. Another unique quality of computer graphics is that the artist is indirectly creating with light. Csuri explored treating computer-mixed colors as transparent light in his *Wondrous Spring* (**9.11**). The delicacy and creativity of this image reveal the training and attitude of a visual artist. By contrast, much computer art looks alike, because people have let the machine dictate to them rather than vice versa. Csuri explains:

> Just because the computer can do perspective and beautiful shadows and shininess, or make things look like glass, you still need to have an esthetic sensibility; you need a sense of culture and history. Even though we have all this marvelous technology, the problems for the artist are still the same. You can very easily be seduced by some special effect, but that in and of itself doesn't do it. You have to have some way of communicating what you feel as a human being.[2]

Just as early art photographs tried to imitate paintings, a major thrust of computer graphics has been the attempt to imitate photographs. Digital representation of familiar objects from the real world is becoming stunningly accurate, but is representational art the highest goal of this new medium? Just because computers can alter images with great speed, is there necessarily aesthetic value in doing so? And once computer artists have struggled to create an image, will

9.10 Harold Cohen, *Untitled*, 1986. Oil on canvas, 100 × 67 ins (254 × 170.1 cm). Collection of Robert and Deborah Hendel.

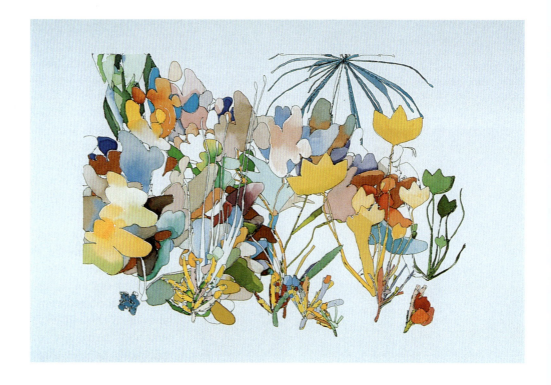

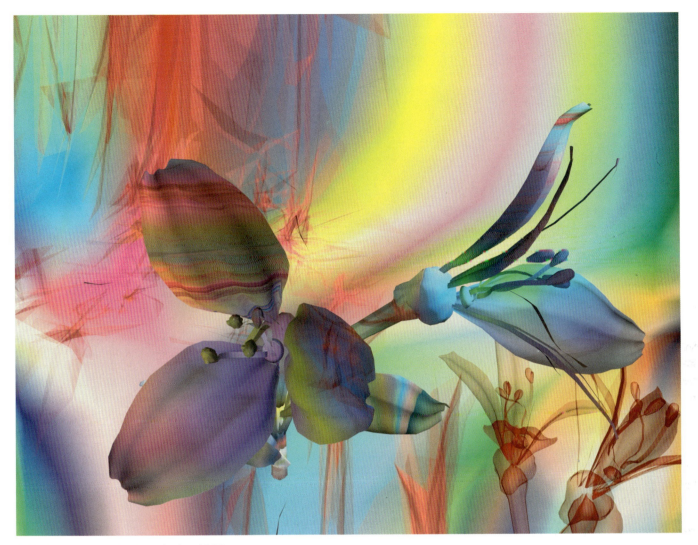

9.11 Charles Csuri, *Wondrous Spring*, 1992.

they have the discipline to examine it critically from an aesthetic point of view and reject it if it does not work well? Will they use a great variety of colors just because they are available, rather than being more selective? As computer video artist John Andrew Berton, Jr., observes:

> Objects created for a synthetic cinema piece generally represent a significant amount of creative effort, at least with today's technology. Thus an artist will often include objects in digital works simply because they are available, whether or not they carry meaning. Like all cinema artists, the digital animator must learn to throw away elements, occasionally, for aesthetic reasons, in spite of the work and technique that went into their creation. . . . The computer makes the viewer believe that an object exists, but the artist must make the viewer believe that the object's existence has meaning.[3]

ART IN CYBERSPACE

The newest frontier in art is the ether of cyberspace. With only a personal computer with graphics capability, a modem, and a telephone connection to the Internet, the international network of computer communications through telephone lines, a user can "upload" or "download" a wealth of digitized art. To "upload" is to enter material from your own computer onto the computer network for access by others; to "download" is to take material from the network and file it on your computer for your own use. This new world has its own rapidly evolving jargon, as well as a treasure of new possibilities in art.

Numerous artists now have their own "web site" (place) on the World Wide Web, the division of the

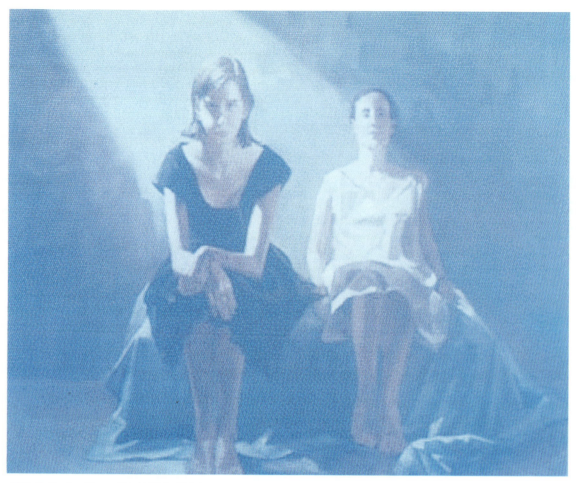

9.12 Katherine Myers, World Wide Web image.

Internet that displays graphics as well as text. If people find the "home page" of contemporary painter Katherine Myers while "surfing the net," they can view slides of her major works on their own computer screens (**9.12**). Many galleries and museums have digitized their collections for view on computer screens around the world through the Internet or CD-ROMs, or through interactive exhibits. With virtual reality, it may be possible to "walk" through a major museum and look at its art treasures from all angles without ever leaving home. In 1996, 125,000 people personally visited the National Museum of American Art in Washington, D.C., but each day of that year an average of 10,000 people "visited" its web site.

Seeing art on a computer screen is like seeing it reproduced in a book: one has no real idea of its size. Even if the size is written out, it takes a leap of the imagination to grasp the enormous size of Picasso's *Guernica* (1.47 and 16.1). To see that 25-foot-long (7.6-m) painting on a small screen is very different from experiencing the powerful impact of the original. One wonders also whether computer-literate genera-tions will become so accustomed to the brightness of computer colors that they will then be disappointed with the lower saturation of the original if they do see it?

Another issue concerns what is done with the art once it is downloaded. Art is legally copyrighted, but it is technically possible to download digitized images from cyberspace networks or CD-ROMs onto slides or printers and thus reproduce them. Once downloaded, images can also be altered at will. This is an opportunity for unlimited new learning experiences for art students. What happens, for instance, if you add colors to *Guernica*? If you wrap a two-dimensional image around a three-dimensional computer-generated "object"? If you change textures with the click of a mouse? At the same time, altering digitized artworks raises legal issues. Artists can download each other's art, change it a bit, and then claim that the new image is their own original work. How can ownership be protected? What does ownership of digitized images mean? Art in cyberspace thus creates a world of new possibilities and, at the same time, legal issues that have yet to be clearly defined.

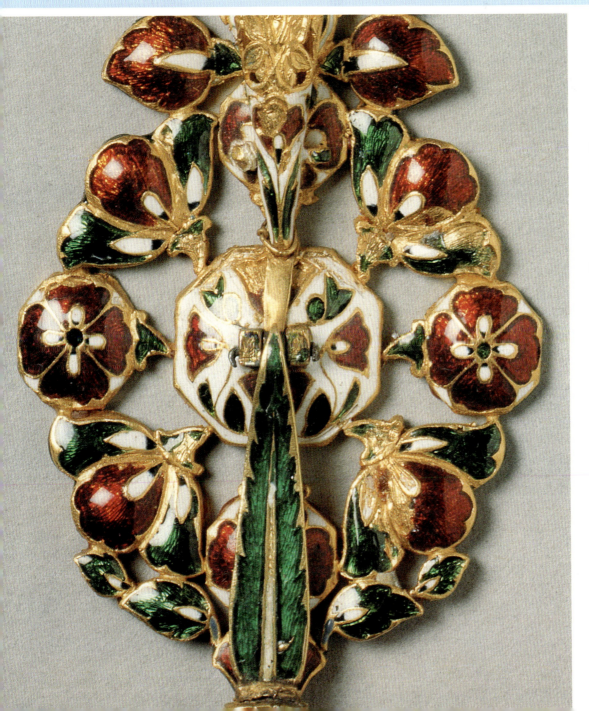

In our daily lives we are surrounded by works of three-dimensional art. Our clothes, buildings, gardens, cars, and functional objects all bear the designer's stamp, with varying artistic success, as do sculptural works whose main purpose is the aesthetic experience.

Mughal turban jewel, possibly from Jaipur, (detail of fig. 11.8).

10
SCULPTURE

The three-dimensional media are not just represented in isolation on our walls and television screens, but exist in the real world either as art objects or as our very surroundings. Our exploration of three-dimensional art begins with the fine art of sculpture.

There are four traditional ways of creating sculptures: carving hard materials, modeling soft materials, casting molten materials that will harden, and assembling materials that can be joined. Two other methods that fall somewhat outside these categories are shaping the earth into environmental works and creating sculptures that move through time and space.

CARVING

In the **subtractive** process of carving, the sculptor cuts away material from an existing piece of some hard material, such as wood, stone, or ivory. Often the original form of the material is totally altered in the process, but in Michelangelo's unfinished *"Atlas" Slave* (10.1), we can still see the rectangular block of stone from which he was extricating the form. "Atlas" seems almost to be struggling to free himself from the extra material. Indeed, Michelangelo, like many sculptors, felt that in carving away excess material he was releasing a form already existing inside the block. One of his poems includes these lines:

> The best of artists does not have a concept
> That the marble itself does not contain within it
> Within its surface, and only that is reached
> By the hand obeying the intellect.[1]

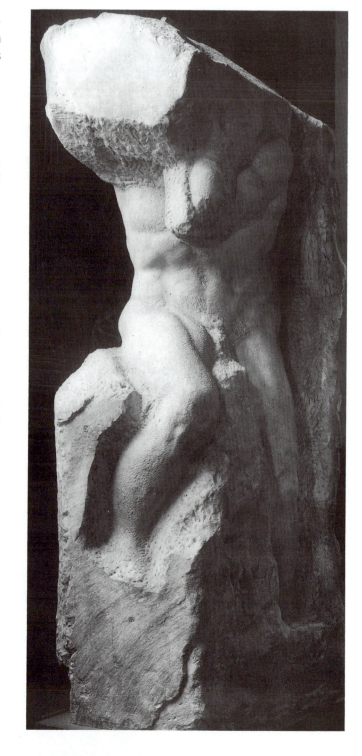

10.1 Michelangelo Buonarroti, *"Atlas" Slave*, c. 1513–20. Galleria dell'Accademia, Florence.

MICHELANGELO BUONARROTI
on MARBLE-QUARRYING

Michelangelo Buonarroti (1475–1564) was a true "Renaissance man"—sculptor, painter, architect, and poet. As a sculptor, he is best known for some of his earliest work, especially the colossal *David* (**10.2**) and the tender *Pietà* (15.22), both of which were executed when he was in his twenties. Whereas the *David* was carved from a huge block of marble that had been unsuccessfully begun by another sculptor, Michelangelo took personal responsibility for supervising the quarrying of other blocks of marble he was to use, as well as having them transported. In some cases he hired *scarpellini* (stonemasons) to do the initial rough carving of the forms. The following excerpts from his letters suggest some of the difficulties he faced in these processes:

March, 1518: "As the marbles [in the mountains of Seravezza] have turned out to be excellent for me and as those that are suitable for the work at St. Peter's are easy to quarry and nearer the coast than the others, that is, at a place called Corvara; and from this place no expense for a road is involved, except over the small stretch of marsh land near the coast. But for a choice of the marble for figures, which I need myself, the existing road will have to be widened for about two miles from Corvara to Seravezza and for about a mile of it or less an entirely new road will have to be made, that is, it must be cut into the mountains with pickaxes to where the said marbles have to be loaded."

April 2, 1518: "Commend me to His Magnificence and beg him to commend me to his agents in Pisa, so that they may do me the favor of finding barges to transport the marbles from Carrara. I went to Genoa and got four barges sent to the quayside to load them. The Carrarese bribed the masters of the said barges and are bent on balking me, so that I achieved nothing. . . ."

April 18, 1518: "These scarpellini whom I brought from Florence know nothing on earth about quarrying or about marble. They have already cost me more than a hundred and thirty ducats and haven't yet quarried me a chip of marble that's any use. . . . In trying to tame these mountains and to introduce the industry into these parts, I've undertaken to raise the dead."

December, 1523: "When I was in Rome with [Pope Julius], and when he had given me a commission for his Tomb, into which a thousand ducats' worth of marbles were to go, he had the money paid to me and sent me to Carrara to get them. I remained there eight months to have the marbles blocked out and I transported nearly all of them to the Piazza of St. Peter, but some of them remained at Ripa. Then, after I had completed the payment for the freight of the said marbles, I had no money left from what I had received for the said work, but I furnished the house I had in the Piazza of St. Peter with beds and household goods out of my own money, in anticipation of the Tomb, and I brought assistants from Florence, some of whom are still living, to work on it, and I paid them in advance out of my own money. At this point Pope Julius changed his mind and no longer wanted to go on with it."[2]

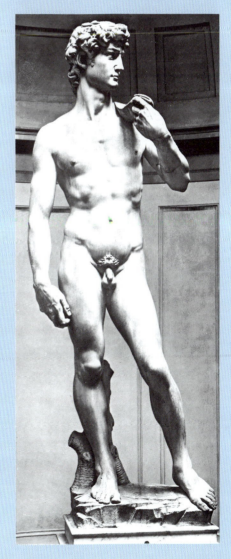

10.2 Michelangelo Buonarroti, *David*, 1501–4. Marble, height approx. 18 ft (5.5 m). Galleria dell'Accademia, Florence.

Tools from hammer and chisel to chainsaw can be used to "liberate" the form conceived in the block. Sculptors may begin with drawings and a small clay or plaster model, or **maquette**, of the intended work. The studio of the late Henry Moore (10.3) was filled with such maquettes. He explained to a visitor:

> Everything I do is intended to be big, and while I'm working on the models, for me they are lifesize. When I take one in my hand, I am seeing and feeling it as lifesize. . . . When I've got the model in my hand, I can be on all sides of it at once and see it from every point of view—as a sculptor has to do—instead of having to keep walking round it.[3]

Working at full scale, the artist then continually takes clues from the material itself as the form emerges. The form must fit within the bounds of the original block of stone or log of wood. Carvings often therefore have rather compact contours, to minimize the labor involved in removing excess material. A lengthy projection—such as an outstretched arm—requires a tremendous amount of labor in cutting away open space above and below it. Projections also present structural problems in materials with low **tensile strength**, such as stone. Tensile strength is the ability of the material to resist forces tending to tear it apart—such as gravity, which pulls at thin unsupported pieces.

10.3 Henry Moore, maquettes, Hoglands studio. Courtesy Henry Moore Foundation, Hertfordshire, England.

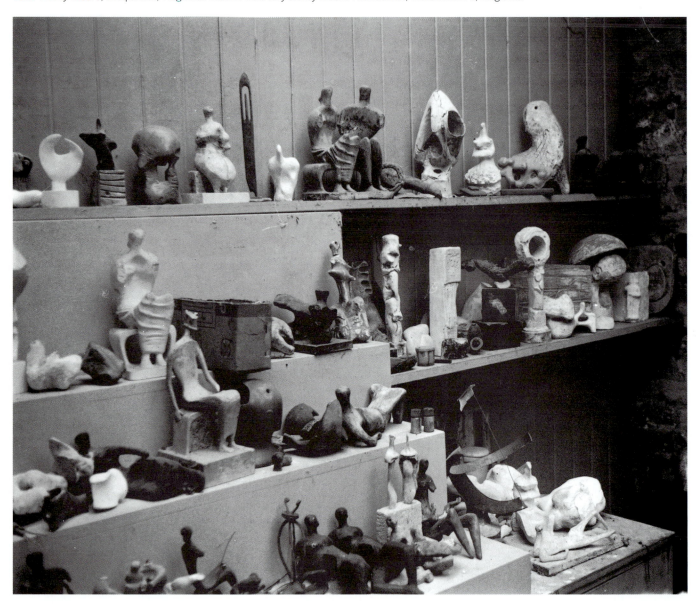

Often a support is integrated into the design, perhaps disguised as clothing or a tree-stump.

Wood is a highly personal medium, warm and organic to the touch, rhythmic in its unfolding growth patterns, and requiring respect for the natural direction of its grain. If wood is protected from weathering and insects, it can be very long-lived. Beautifully carved wood reliefs over 4000 years old survive from ancient Egypt.

In the subtractive process of carving away, taking away too much is disastrous. To keep track of where they are in the block, wood sculptors may draw the outline of the intended piece on it and first remove any excess material that clearly lies outside of the outline, perhaps with a handsaw or even a chain-saw. A medium-sized gouge struck by a mallet may then be used to start working in toward the final form. After this *roughing out* process approximates the desired final form, smaller gouges may be used to create fine details. For the finest of these, the gouge may be hand-driven rather than struck with a mallet. The sculptor continually reads and works the piece in the round, often referring to sketches of the desired appearance from many sides. Finer details are often sketched on the wood itself as the form emerges. Donna Forma carved *Ode to Life* (**10.4**) from a large pine tree trunk some four feet (1.22 m) in diameter, removing a tremendous amount of excess material. She notes:

> You have to visually imagine in your mind which are the furthest points out and then leave those and come in from them. In *Ode to Life*, I used just the basic chisel and mallet to come in to the form. A lot of people use a chain-saw when there is so much extra material, but I like using the chisel. It took a long time. It's always a problem no matter what size you work in—there's always that taking away the excess in order to show the form. Actually, you can't think of it as a problem, or you'll never do anything. From the very beginning, the whole time you are working on the form—it's just different steps. There are parts of it that are right out on the surface, whereas in other areas—such as under the bend of an arm—there is so much excess. But you are working all around the form so you're not just concentrating on one spot. Each person does it their own way—but I find that in working all around, it comes together better for me.[4]

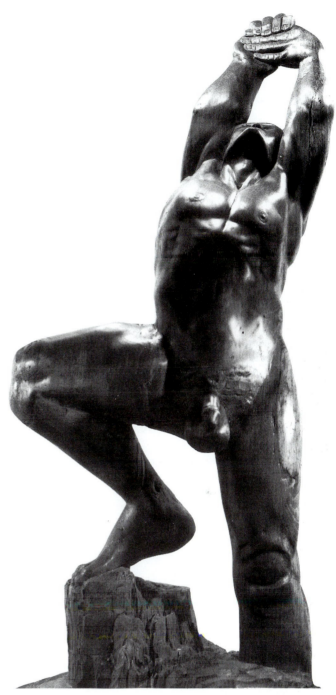

10.4 Donna Forma, *Ode to Life*, 1988. Pine, height 9 ft (2.27 m), original diameter of log 4 ft (1.22 m). Photo by Tom Forma.

LINDA HOWARD
on COMPUTER-AIDED SCULPTURE DESIGN

Florida-based sculptor Linda Howard (b. 1934) has been commissioned to create large-scale public sculptures that are installed in sites from Sydney, Australia, to Bogota, Columbia, to Fairbanks, Alaska. She assembles her sculptures from aluminum square tubing, welded into mathematically precise forms that nonetheless resemble natural growth patterns. Since this fabrication process is large-scale and demands precision of measuring and placement, Howard now uses a combination of two methods in designing and developing specifications for her pieces: maquette and computer-aided design.

"I first make a little model of styrene strips, perhaps five to ten inches [12.5–25 cm] tall. When I'm working on these small maquettes, I visualize them as being the completed size, and visualize myself as being about an inch [2.5 cm] tall. I never see them as small pieces; I always see them as big pieces. That's the way I think. I like the inside of pieces; I like being able to be inside, looking up, looking out.

Once the model is done, I put it on the computer as a wire-frame drawing. The three-dimensional volume of each square tube becomes four lines. You see it as if it were transparent, and all you are seeing is the edges. I don't see the drawing as solids, for I don't have access to a solids-modeling computer package.

In wire-frame, I can rotate the piece and look at it from different views. Seeing it in the wire frame gives you much more to look at than the solid maquette—the two-dimensional images of the three-dimensional model are very exciting, and they give you new ideas. I don't design new pieces on the computer from these wire-frame drawings, however. Because they are really three-dimensional pieces in three-dimensional space, I still really like a three-dimensional model in real space to work with. But I might see something on the computer that I then want to test out in actual 3-D.

In addition to their visual excitement, the wire-frame computer drawings give me all my shop dimensions, all the fabricating dimensions I need. It doesn't matter who is doing the fabrication—whether I'm cutting it myself or giving the specifications to someone else to cut. The computer provides the shop guide: all the lengths to cut, all the angles to cut.

The wire-frame model also reveals how organic these structures are, like the curving growth forms of nature. It happens because of the way I run out the mathematic progression. I nest things. Each point has its own center of radius and they spiral because they are not turning off a common core.

The computer-plotted drawings can even become works of art in their own right. For *Centerpeace* (**10.5**), in cooperation with the art department and engineering department of Bradley University, we did wire-frame computer images from different eye-level points of view. I did one from a central point of view, the way you would ordinarily look at the piece, another higher up, another higher up, and another down from the top. Then I mirror-imaged each one, and we are turning them into lithographs with watercolor backgrounds, named after the four seasons depending on how open or closed the piece felt from that viewpoint. It's a gorgeous sculpture, and the linear wire-frame drawings (**10.6**) are also beautiful in themselves."[5]

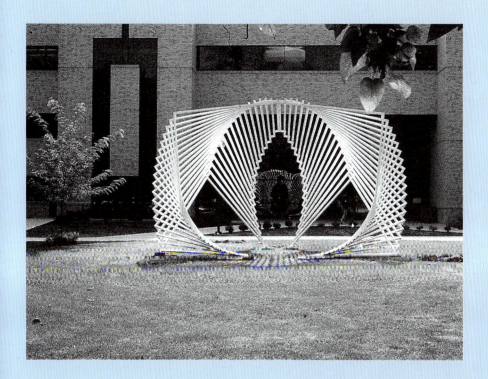

10.5 (left) Linda Howard, *Centerpeace*, 1991. Aluminum, 14 × 24 × 16 ft (4.3 × 7.3 × 4.6 m). Bradley University, Peoria, Illinois.

10.6 (below) Linda Howard, CAD wire-frame drawings.

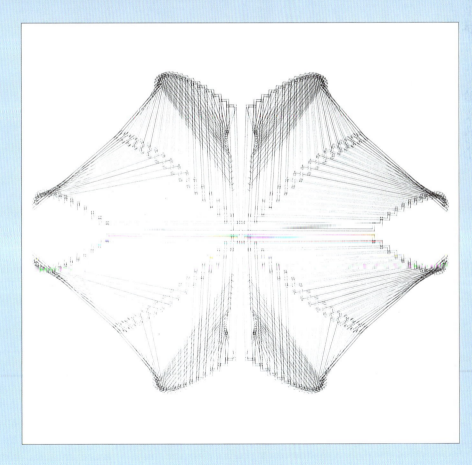

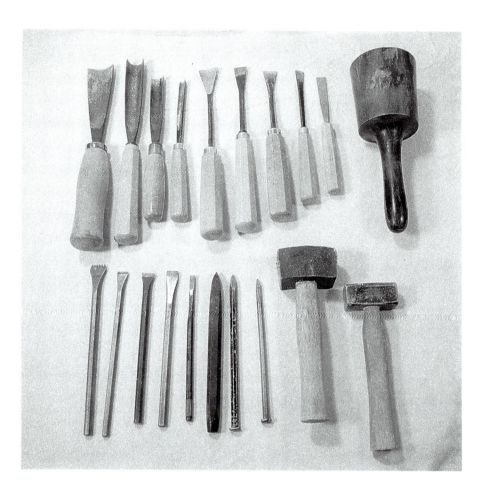

10.7 Wood-carving (above) and stone-carving (below) tools.

A number of tools (**10.7**) are used to give the piece a smooth finish, including a scraper with a beveled cutting edge that is drawn across the surface, revealing the grain, and compressing the fibers to make the surface glossy. If desired, the gloss is enhanced with a wax polish. Contemporary wood-carvers often **laminate**, or bond, many thin layers of wood together before carving them as a block, revealing striations of color on the surface.

Although stone offers much more resistance to the sculptor's chisel than does wood, its permanence, colors, and textures have long been prized for creating subtractive sculptures. Sometimes the original surface texture of the stone is retained. The twentieth-century *Head of a Woman* by Modigliani (**10.8**) is carved directly into a limestone block, celebrating its stony texture with a deliberately "primitive" technique. Some traditional marble sculptures have been carved mechanically, often by hired artisans, by transferring measurements from a maquette to a block of stone, but such a process is not responsive to the uniqueness of the individual block. The sculptor may live with a block of stone for a long time, allowing it to "speak" its own nature before approaching it with a preconceived image.

Stone may be carved and polished to resemble non-stone textures, such as the youthfully smooth, taut-muscled skin of Michelangelo's *David* (**10.2**). The nearly 18-foot-high (5.5 m) statue is famous not only for the beauty of its surface but also for its ability to suggest a highly lifelike, dynamic energy within the form. The contrapposto attitude (head and shoulders twisted one way, hips and legs another) of the Biblical shepherd suggests that what is frozen in stone is only a brief moment in time, in which David prepares his slingshot for the giant Goliath.

Marble from the quarries at Carrara, Italy, is highly prized for its exceptionally fine, durable, translucent white nature. Granite is hard and more difficult to carve; sandstones and limestones, widely used in northern European architectural sculptures, are more granular. However, all kinds of stone—from the roughest limestone to the finest marble—can be polished to a high sheen, enhancing the stone's color and

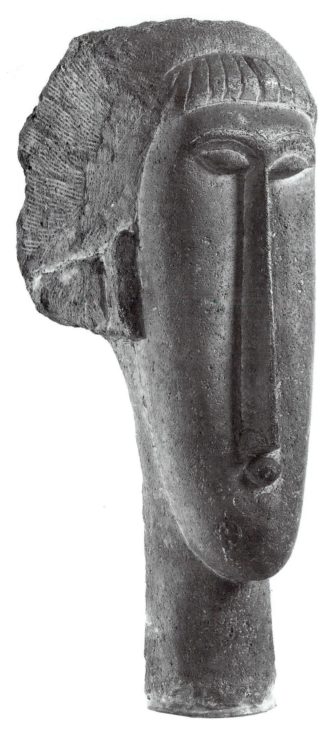

10.8 Amedeo Modigliani, *Head of a Woman*, c. 1901. Limestone, height 25¾ ins (65.4 cm). National Gallery of Art, Washington, D.C. Chester Dale Collection.

erasing the tool marks. After the lengthy process of carving the form, polishing the surface entails another series of steps with flat chisel, file, carborundum stone, wet sandpaper, or an abrasive sanding screen, and rubbing with a polishing agent that seals the surface and makes it glisten. As these steps are taken, previously hidden colors and deeper tones will often appear, but so also may weaknesses in the design, requiring some reshaping of the piece.

The Chinese vase of jade (**10.9**) is painstakingly carved from a single block of the extremely hard semi-precious stone. Jade is so hard and brittle that artists may grind it with a power diamond-tipped bur rather than cut it with hammered chisels, claws, points, and files. Whatever the material, stone-carving is a slow and patient art.

10.9 Magnolia vase, c. 1900. Jadeite, height 10½ ins (27 cm).

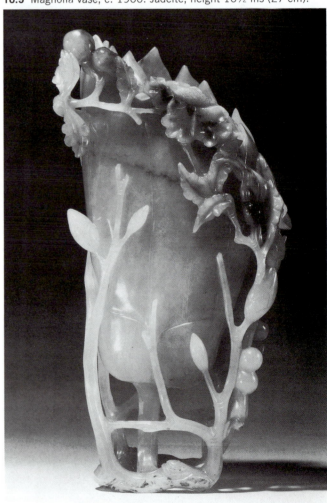

MODELING

At the other extreme from carving hard stone is **modeling**—the hand-shaping of soft, malleable materials. Some are so soft, in fact, that they cannot support their own weight and must be built over an **armature**, a simple skeleton of harder material, such as wood or wire. *Plaster* is typically built up over an armature by

10.10 Jean-Antoine Houdon, *Bust of a Young Girl*, c. 1779–80. Plaster, height 19½ ins (49.5 cm). Metropolitan Museum of Art, New York. Bequest of Bertha H. Busell, 1941.

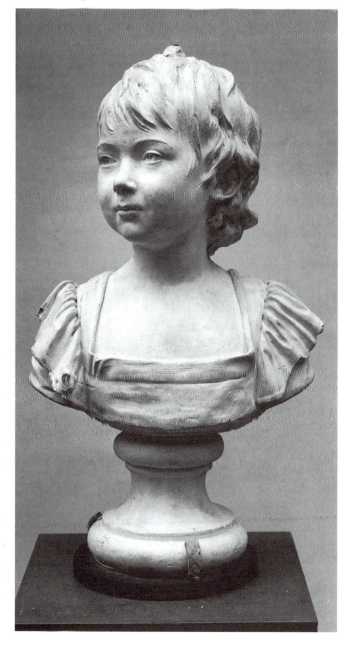

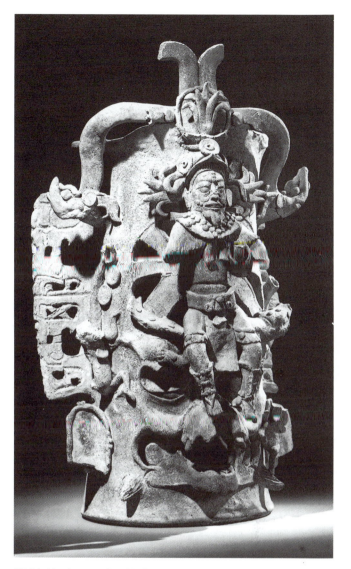

10.11 Urn incensario with figure seated on monster head, Tobasco, Mexico. Classic Maya, 250–900 AD. Unslipped buff earthenware, height 16⅛ ins (40,8 cm). Indianapolis Museum of Art, Indianapolis, Indiana. The Wally and Brenda Zollman Collection of Pre-Columbian Art. Photo by Justin Kerr.

strips of fabric that have been dipped in wet plaster of Paris. The final layer is plaster alone, spread with the hands or tools such as knife or spatula. Details—such as the modeling of the hair on Houdon's *Bust of a Young Girl* (**10.10**)—are then worked with a blade.

The use of *clay*—a fine-grained natural deposit—as a modeling medium was common in many ancient civilizations. Worked moist, it can be used to create quite fine details and then be fired to a hard, permanent state. It has more structural integrity than wet plaster, so it will hold slight projections, such as the serpent and elaborate headdress worked above the seated man in Figure **10.11**. The Classic Mayans of

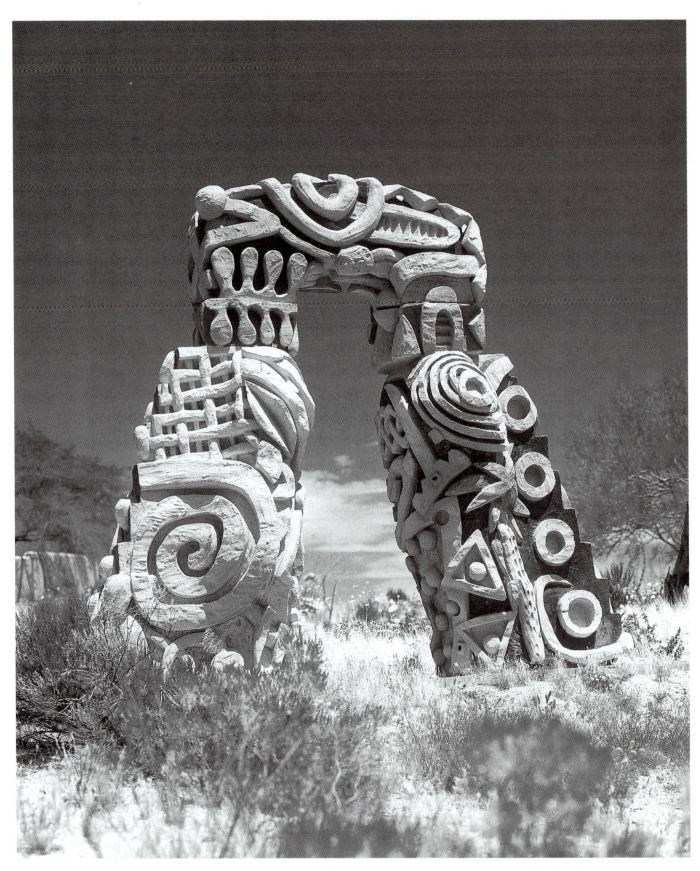

10.12 Arnold Zimmerman, arch for a private residence, Arizona.

Mesoamerica had highly developed clay-modeling skills, sometimes used in creating naturalistic details such as the leg musculature and footgear bindings. In clay modeling, the major form may be coaxed into shape by the fingers. Details may be added as lines incised into the form—as in the lines defining the man's eyes—or extra bits of clay attached to the piece with **slip** (a mixture of clay and water), as in his necklace, beard, and headdress.

Whereas freestanding clay pieces have traditionally been rather small, large kilns now allow huge constructions of clay to be fired. Even so, monumental clay sculptures are often constructed and fired in several pieces and then assembled, as can be seen in the joints of Arnold Zimmerman's great ceramic arch (**10.12**).

Wax is very easily shaped and reshaped when warm. It was used by the ancient Greeks for toy dolls and small religious statues and by the Romans to make death masks. But wax is vulnerable to melting when the weather is hot. It is therefore more often used to capture the fresh immediacy of hand-shaping and then the figure is cast in some more permanent material. An example is the bronze cast of Degas's wax model of a galloping horse (**10.13**). The dabs of wax Degas pressed on to build up the form are clearly preserved in the cast. Some collectors prize such evidence of the artist at work.

10.13 Edgar Degas, *Horse Galloping on Right Foot*, c. 1881. Bronze cast of wax model, height 11⅞ ins (30 cm). Metropolitan Museum of Art, New York. Bequest of Mrs. H. O. Havemayer, 1929.

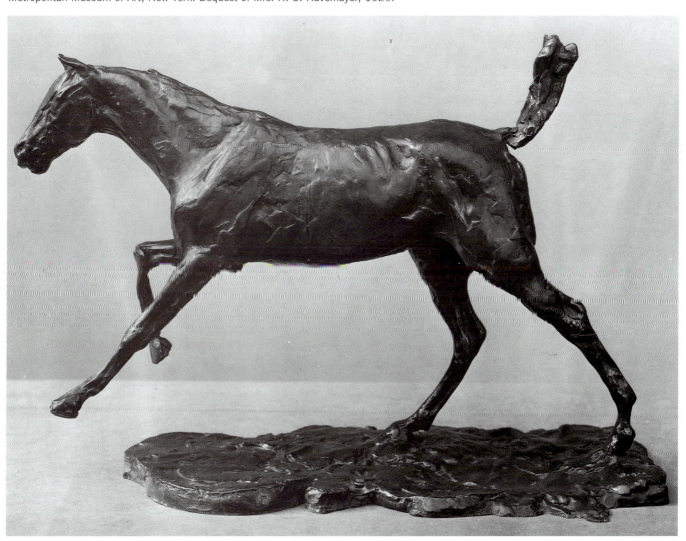

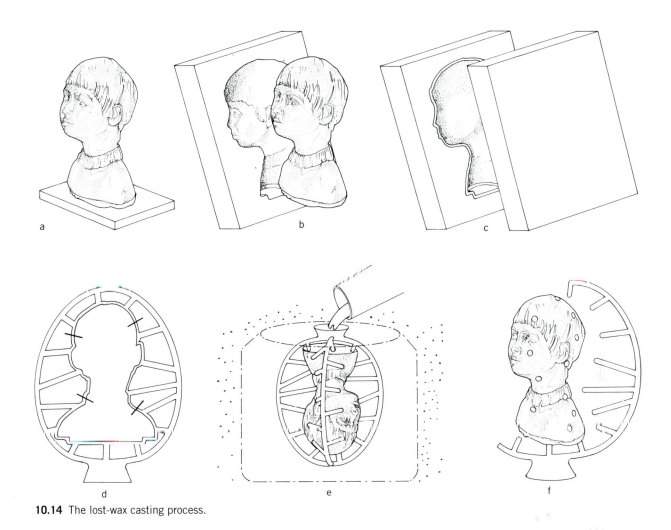

10.14 The lost-wax casting process.

CASTING

In **casting**, easily shaped materials are used to create a negative mold into which a molten material such as bronze or plastic is poured and then allowed to harden. When the mold is removed, anything that was concave in the mold is convex in the cast form, and vice versa. If the mold is salvageable, multiple copies can be made of the same form.

This process, for which the Bronze Age was named, was refined by the ancient Greeks. They developed the **lost-wax** process illustrated in Figure 10.14, which is still in use at contemporary foundries. A positive model (a) is used to make a negative mold (b), which is then coated with wax (c). The wax shell is filled with a core of some material such as plaster or clay (d). The mold is removed and metal rods are driven through the wax into the clay to hold the layers in place, as shown in Figure 10.15. Wax vents that allow the metal to be poured in and the gases to escape are fitted around the piece. This assembly is then coated with plaster—called the **investment**—and buried in sand (e). The investment and sand are unharmed when this assembly is heated, but the wax melts. It is drained off, leaving an opening between the core and the investment that is filled with molten bronze. When it has hardened, the extraneous investment, tubes, and core are removed (f) and the halves of the cast are reassembled. What remains is a perfect hollow replica in bronze of the original pattern. Solid casting of large pieces does not work well, and hollowness economizes on bronze and weight. Even cast

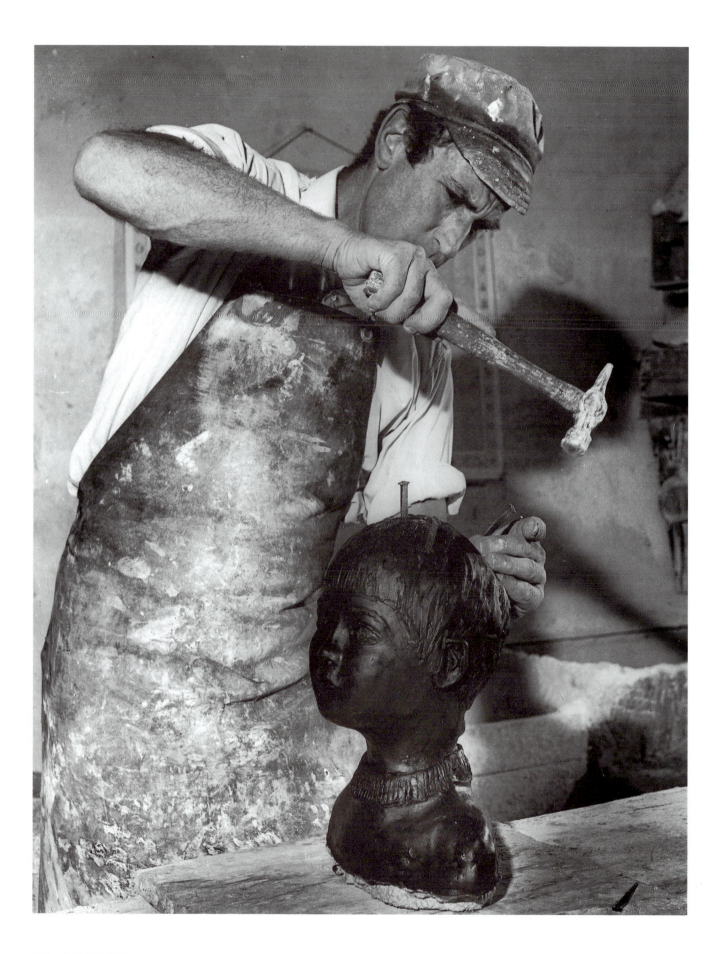

hollow, bronze is quite strong enough to support the open, extended forms of arms and legs.

Despite their complexity, casting processes are capable of reproducing very fine details. In the fifteenth- to eighteenth-century kingdom of Benin in western Africa, intricate bronze castings such as the *Altar of the Hand* (**10.16**), which celebrated the divine king (the figure whose large head symbolizes his intelligence and power), were made by highly skilled members of a respected professional guild under the direction of the king.

10.15 (opposite) Rods are driven into the wax replica to hold the outer investment in proper relationship to the core.

10.16 Anonymous, *Altar of the Hand*, Benin, Nigeria, 1550–1680. Bronze, height 17½ ins (44.4 cm). British Museum, London.

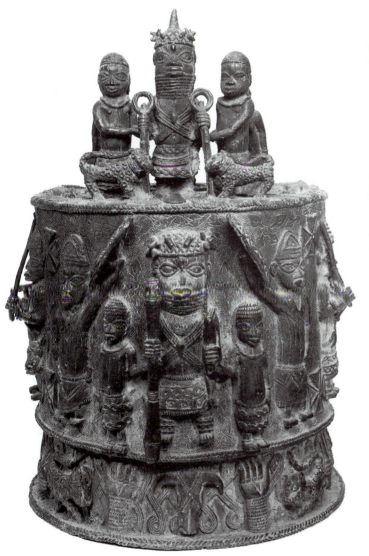

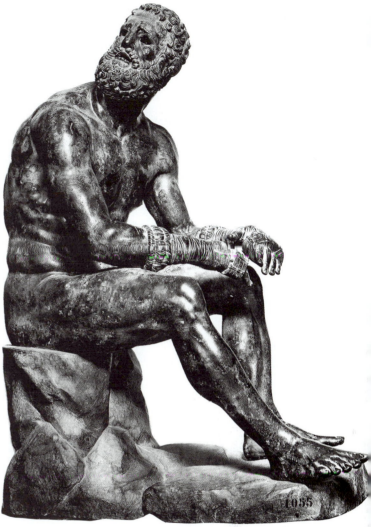

10.17 Apollonius, *Seated Boxer*, c. 50 BC. Bronze, height 4 ft 2 ins (1.27 m). Museo Nazionale Romano, Rome.

While the *Altar of the Hand* is quite stylized, casts are also capable of reproducing very naturalistic detail, such as the anatomical and psychological accuracy of the Greco-Roman *Seated Boxer* (**10.17**). His musculature is superbly defined, and yet this is not an heroic, idealized portraiture. In the boxer's hunched, tired posture, broken nose, scarred body, and sidelong glance we can infer exhaustion, defeat, battered pride, or introspection about the emptiness of victory.

BENVENUTO CELLINI
on A NEAR-DISASTROUS CASTING

The Florentine Renaissance artist Benvenuto Cellini (1500–71) was one of the world's greatest goldsmiths and also a bronze sculptor whose *Perseus with the Head of Medusa* (**10.18**) is considered an amazing *tour de force*. His casting techniques were difficult and unique to himself, and the fact that the *Perseus* came out intact seemed quite miraculous, considering the dramatic problems that arose. In his autobiography he describes the drama that unfolded after the waxed, clay-encased, air-vented, and drained mold was lowered into the pit of a specially built furnace:

"At last I called out heartily to set the furnace going. The logs of pine were heaped in, and my furnace worked so well that I was obliged to rush from side to side to keep it going. The labour was more than I could stand; yet I forced myself to strain every nerve and muscle. To increase my anxieties, the workshop took fire, and we were afraid lest the roof should fall upon our heads; while, from the garden, such a storm of wind and rain kept blowing in, that it perceptibly cooled the furnace.

Battling thus with all these untoward circumstances for several hours, and exerting myself beyond even the measure of my powerful constitution, I could at last bear up no longer, and a sudden fever, of the utmost possible intensity, attacked me. [In despair he announced to his helpers that he thought he was dying, left them with instructions for finishing the project, and went to bed, racked with fever.]

While I was thus terribly afflicted, I beheld the figure of a man enter my chamber, twisted in his body into the form of a capital S. He raised a lamentable, doleful voice, like one who announces their last hour to men condemned to die upon the scaffold, and spoke these words: 'O Benvenuto! your statue is spoiled, and there is no hope whatever of saving it.' . . . Jumping from my bed, I seized my clothes and began to dress. The maids, and my lad, and every one who came around to help me, got kicks or blows of the fist, while I kept crying out in lamentation, 'Before I die I will leave such witness to the world of what I can do as shall make a score of mortals marvel.'

[Cellini made his way back to the workshop, where he discovered work stopped because the metal had caked. He ordered hotter-burning oak wood to be fetched.] When the logs took fire, oh! how the cake began to stir beneath that awful heat. At the same time I kept stirring up the channels, and sent men upon the roof to stop the conflagration, which had gathered force from the increased combustion in the furnace; also I caused boards, carpets, and other hangings to be set up against the garden, in order to protect us from the violence of the rain. . . .

I then ordered half a pig of pewter to be brought and flung it into the middle of the cake inside the furnace. By this means, and by piling on wood and stirring now with pokers and now with iron rods, the curdled mass rapidly began to liquefy. . . .

All of a sudden an explosion took place attended by a tremendous flash of flame, as though a thunderbolt had formed and been discharged amongst us. I discovered that the cap of the furnace had blown up, and the bronze was bubbling over from its source beneath. So I had the mouths of my mold immediately opened, and at the same time drove in the two plugs which kept back the molten metal. But I noticed that it did not flow as rapidly as usual, the reason being probably that the fierce heat of the fire we kindled had consumed its base alloy. Accordingly I sent for all my pewter platters, porringers, and dishes, to the number of some two hundred pieces, and had a portion of them cast, one by one, into the channels, the rest into the furnace. This expedient succeeded, and everyone could now perceive that my bronze was in most perfect liquefaction, and my mold was filling. . . . Seeing my work finished, I fell upon my knees, and with all my heart gave thanks to God."[6]

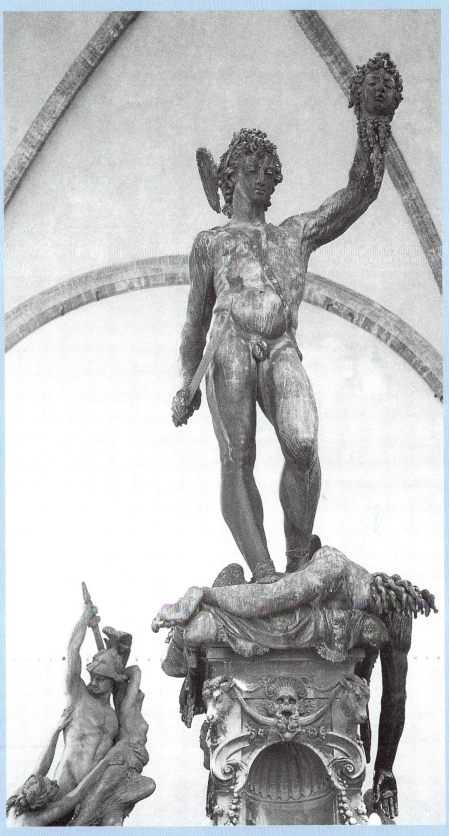

10.18 Benvenuto Cellini, *Perseus with the Head of Medusa*, 1554. Bronze, 18 ft (5.4 m) high. Loggia dei Lanzi, Florence.

ASSEMBLING

Another approach to sculpture is to fashion or collect pieces of varying materials and then somehow attach them to each other to form an aesthetically unified whole. Some works are assembled from **found objects**, such as the cast-off metal parts assembled by Richard Stankiewicz into *City Bird* (**10.19**). He was a pioneer in the creation of "junk sculpture," in which industrially manufactured goods that have been thrown away are given new life, new figurative identities. There is a certain poignancy in these homely creations, but also a sense of fun. Stankiewicz spoke of his joy when, in 1951, he first discovered in the yard behind his New York studio:

> a great number of rusty metal objects which seemed so beautiful by themselves that I set them aside as objects to look at . . . things that were so decayed and corroded that you couldn't identify them, and of course, it was only a step of the imagination to combine various things together and make compositions from them . . . [Found objects are] more provocative than invented effects. Also visual puns, mechanical analogies, and organic resemblances in machinery provide a large and evocative vocabulary for sculpture.[7]

When a sculpture is obviously constructed of bits of found objects (not limited to the mechanical discards used in junk sculpture), it may be referred to by the French term, **assemblage**. Lucas Samaras's *Book 4* (2.80) is assembled from a book, pins, a razor blade, scissors, a table knife, foil, glass, and a plastic rod.

Louise Nevelson assembled large frontal sculptures of bits of turned wood, encased in a series of boxes. In her *Black Wall* (**10.20**), fragments are unified visually by the repetition of the box forms and the uniform black paint. Within this coherent framework, we are invited to explore the differences in form between the wood turnings and the varying ways they relate to each other.

In addition to unifying an assembled work visually, the artist must deal with the mechanical problems of physically joining the pieces so that they will not fall apart. Metal may be welded or bolted; a wooden piece may be held together with glue, nails, and screws. Nevelson has chosen to hide these joining techniques, whereas William King openly reveals the bolts uniting the sheets of aluminum in *Collegium* (**10.21**). In fact, the bolt heads are presented as part of the design interest in these tall-walking college figures.

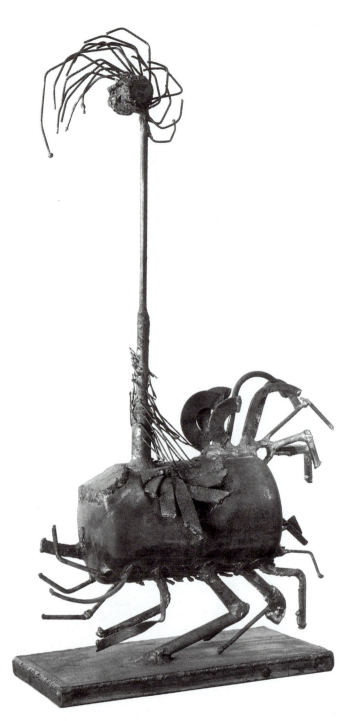

10.19 Richard Stankiewicz, *City Bird*, 1957. Iron and steel, 27⅛ × 12¼ × 7¼ ins (68.8 × 31.1 × 18.4 cm). Collection of Museum of Modern Art, New York. Philip Johnson Fund. Photograph © 1997 MOMA.

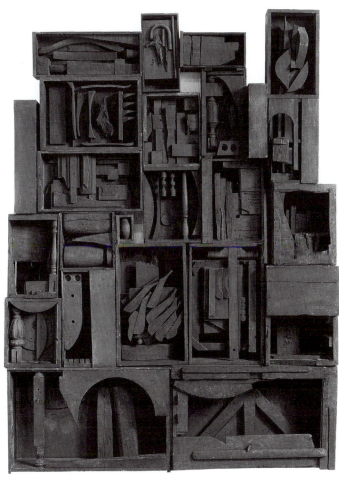

10.20 Louise Nevelson, *Black Wall*, 1959.
Wood painted black, height 9 ft 4 ins (2.84 m).
Tate Gallery, London. Courtesy of the Trustees.

When an assembled piece seems to lack structural or aesthetic unity, the effect may be intentional. A certain disunity—according to Classical principles of design—is an intentional choice of freedom to allow new things to happen in sculpture. This trend is particularly evident in contemporary assembled works and installation pieces. Judy Pfaff, creator of the installation *3D* (**10.22**), explains:

I want the latitude of shifting thoughts in regard to materials, colors, and references. I can't be bound by how they "should" relate to one another. By going after a certain speed traditionally reserved for painters, I'm reaching for a crossing over of ideas and a weaving of thinking and making . . .

What's happening now in sculpture seems really wide open and generous . . . taking all sorts of permission and running with it, full out.[8]

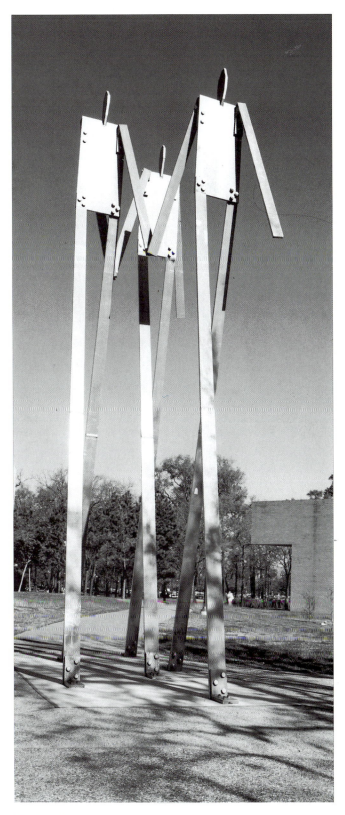

10.21 William King, *Collegium*, 1984.
Cast and plate aluminum, height 32 ft (9.75 m).
Installation at University of Houston, Texas, 1984.

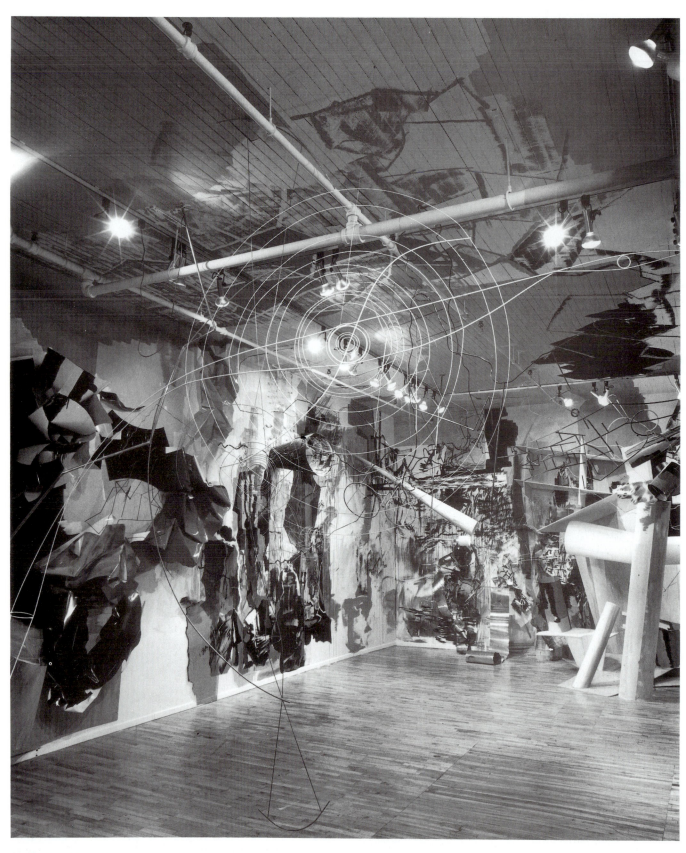

10.22 Judy Pfaff, *3D*, 1983. Installation piece made of mixed media, occupying a room 22 × 35 ft (6.7 × 10.7 m). Photo by D. James Lee. Courtesy of the artist.

EARTHWORKS

Rather than sculpting materials taken from the earth, some artists have used the earth's surface itself as their medium. This is an ancient form of art, found in certain cultures around the world, in which the earth is sculpted into serpentine mounds, spirals, and mazes. Most spectacular are the lines on the desert floor of the Nasca Valley in Peru, sculpted by scraping aside the surface to reveal lighter materials beneath, forming huge drawings such as one of a hummingbird (10.23). Perhaps using only strings for measurement, its creators kept its outline surprisingly regular over a vast space—450 feet (137 m) in length. Its superhuman scale has led many observers to speculate that it was meant to be seen from the air, or was even designed by visitors from outer space. However, even though the figure cannot be viewed as a whole from the surface of the desert, it can be seen from the foothills of the Andes. If it is not spaceship art, then what is it? A pilgrimage route? An astronomical calendar? Stylized paths to waterholes? We do not understand; we can only admire.

Contemporary earthworks have something of the same aura of mystery about them. Robert Smithson's *Spiral Jetty* (10.24) is an immense spiral of 6000 tons (more than 6 million kg) of basalt and limestone laid into the primordial red water of Great Salt Lake. He said it was a concrete expression of the "gyrating space" he experienced at the site.

The tools of contemporary earthwork artists have become those of the earth-mover, from shovels to bulldozers and dynamite, perhaps with the addition of structurally reinforcing materials, such as the concrete framing Michael Heizer used to strengthen the earth mound of his *City Complex One* (2.35).

10.23 Aerial view of hummingbird, Nasca Plain, Nasca, southwestern Peru, c. 200–600 AD. Wingspan 200 ft (60.9 m), total length 450 ft (137.1 m). Weathering and the scraping aside of stones revealed lighter clay and calcite beneath.

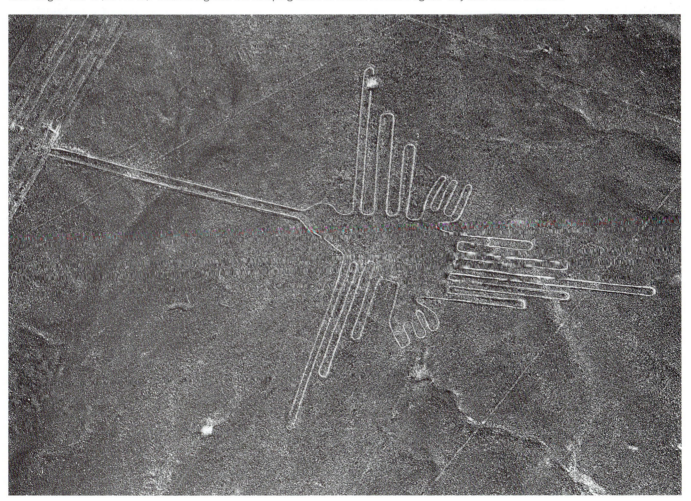

Despite the huge amounts of rock and earth that are displaced and rearranged to create earthworks, their existence is often strangely ephemeral. *Spiral Jetty* was inundated by the rising water of the lake for twenty years but then re-emerged in a transformed state, covered with salt. Heizer's huge gashes in the earth's surface have filled in again as a result of erosion. Some earthworks now exist as art only in photographs taken when they were new. But permanency is not necessarily a goal of earth artists. Although their medium is the landscape, their subject-matter is often mental concepts. Their writings and conversations often tend to be more cerebral than earth-centered. Heizer said he didn't come to the Nevada mesa because of the landscape:

> I didn't come here for context. I came here for materials—for gravel and for sand and for water, which you need to make concrete, and because the land was cheap. The desert is a flat and totally theatrical space. There is no landscape.[9]

Robert Smithson encouraged nature to participate in *Spiral Jetty*: He knew that brine shrimp would gather around the construction, giving it a lovely magenta color. But his approach to earthwork was not naturalistic. He explained:

> I'm not just presenting materials, there's a kind of transformation that takes place. So that it's not a return to nature; it's like a subsuming of physical properties, and then gathering them into some kind of coherence, and this coherence can be quite a wilderness that is quite fascinating at the same time. Just like the actual wilderness, but in this case it becomes abstract, and it becomes a kind of entity that points to a lot of different possibilities.[10]

10.24 Robert Smithson, *Spiral Jetty*, 1970. Great Salt Lake, Utah, 1500 × 15 ft (457 × 4.6 m).

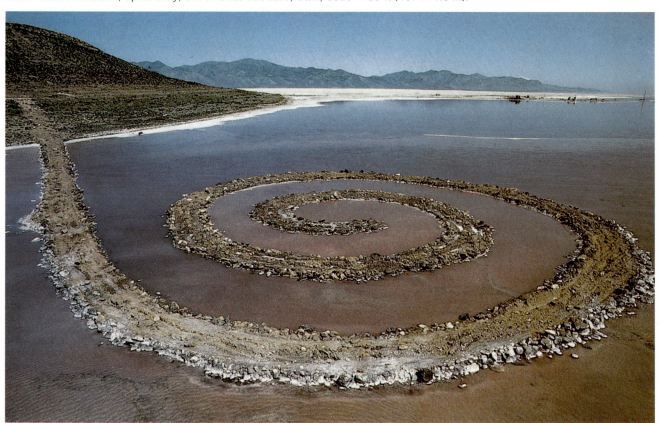

The appreciation of fine handmade objects is undergoing a renaissance. This trend may be a reaction to our highly industrialized surroundings, a reassertion of the value of what is made by human hands. Many craftspeople make no attempt to hide their tracks, for the sense of the individual at work may be more highly prized than machinelike perfection and sameness. Even though some craft objects are created in multiples on a semi-production basis, they may still reflect the human touch.

In general, crafts also tend to celebrate the materials from which they are made. The wood, clay, or fiber has been chosen and worked lovingly. This appreciation for natural colors and textures is contagious. To fill one's home with handcrafted functional items is to turn everyday activities—such as eating and storing food—into sensual experiences of beauty. We feel that these objects have been made slowly, with care, and they can evoke the same unhurried appreciation in us.

The major craft media are clay, metal, wood, glass, and fibers. All have been in use since antiquity, and many of the traditional methods are still employed. At the same time, many craft artists are experimenting with new techniques, materials, and approaches, sometimes to the point of using craft techniques to create nonfunctional works of art.

CLAY

The ancient craft of making objects from clay is called **ceramics**. In traditional cultures such as rural India, most villages have at least one working ceramist creating functional pieces for everyday use.

Clays are found across the globe, but only those clays that are easily shaped and capable of being hardened by heat without cracking or warping are suitable for ceramics. Sometimes several different kinds of clay

are mixed to form a *clay body* that has a combination of desirable properties. The most common clay bodies are **earthenware** (porous clays such as terracotta), **stoneware** (clays that become impermeable when fired at high temperatures), and **porcelain** (a very smooth-textured clay, translucent when fired, and with an extremely smooth, glossy surface).

Clay can be worked by freeform hand modeling, as in **pinching** a small pot out of a lump of clay (11.1). Three traditional methods of building up clay into

11.1 Maria Martínez pinching a pot.

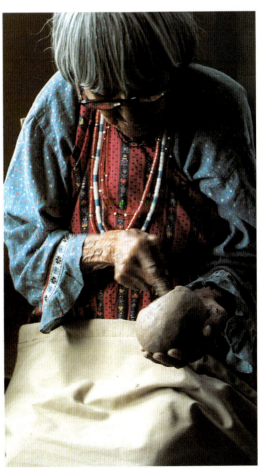

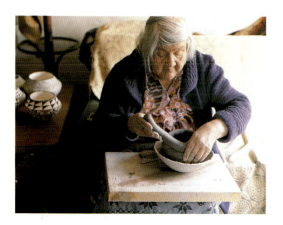

11.2 Lucy Lewis coiling a seed pot .

larger walled vessels have been in use for thousands of years. **Slab building**, used for straight-sided pieces, involves rolling out flat sheets of clay for sides and bottom. The joints are sealed with a rope of clay or with slip, a slurry of clay and water.

In **coil building** (11.2), the potter rolls out ropes of clay and curls them in spiraling layers on top of a base, welding the bottom layer to the base and joining the coils to each other. Scraping and patting of the outside may be used to obliterate the in-and-out coiled structure. To build up a tall pot, the lower area must be allowed to dry and harden somewhat so that it will support the upper layers. For a narrow-necked piece, the upper layers are gradually diminished and then perhaps pulled out again. The potter must work all around the piece if it is to be uniformly rounded, so it may be placed on a hand-turned base. This method is widely used by Native Americans.

The third major method is **wheel-throwing** (11.3). The potter's wheel, found in the ruins of ancient Greece, China, and other early civilizations, is a flat disk attached by a shaft to a large flywheel. This lower wheel is kicked by the potter or driven by a motor to make the upper wheel turn. The continuous turning of the wheel allows the potter to pull the pot upward, symmetrically. After *wedging* (repeatedly slamming the clay onto a hard surface, cutting and folding it, and throwing it again, to remove air pockets and create an even consistency), the clay is centered on the wheel with the hands while the wheel is being rapidly turned. Working with both moistened hands, the potter then shapes the inside and outside of the pot at the same time by finger pressure applied in just the right places as the wheel is rotating. For a symmetrical

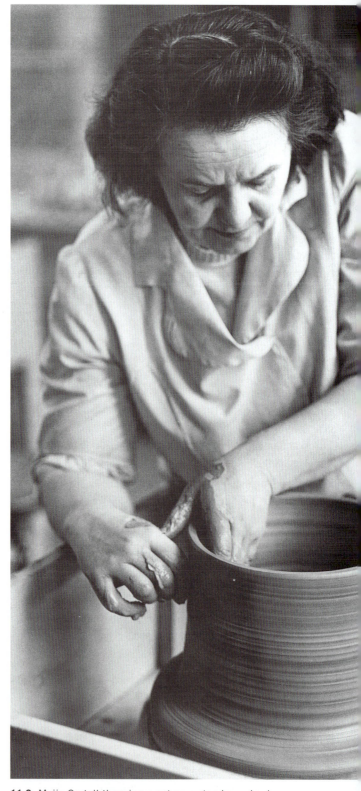

11.3 Maija Grotell throwing a pot on a stand-up wheel. Photo courtesy of Department of Special Collections, Syracuse University Library, Syracuse, New York.

form with walls of even thickness, the potter's hands must be disciplined to apply perfectly even pressure.

After any of these building techniques—slab, coil, or wheel-throwing—the pot is typically **glazed** (painted with a material that turns glassy when heated) and **fired** (baked in a kiln or open fire) for permanence and water resistance.

Facility with such techniques allowed ancient artisans to create vessels that were as beautiful as they were functional. The elegantly proportioned wheel-thrown amphora from Athens (11.4) is of the type used to hold the prize of sacred olive oil for the winners of the Panathenic festivals. The foot runners,

11.4 Attributed to Euphiletos painter, black-figured prize amphora, Athens, c. 530 BC. Height 24½ ins (62.2 cm). Metropolitan Museum of Art, New York. Rogers Fund 1914.

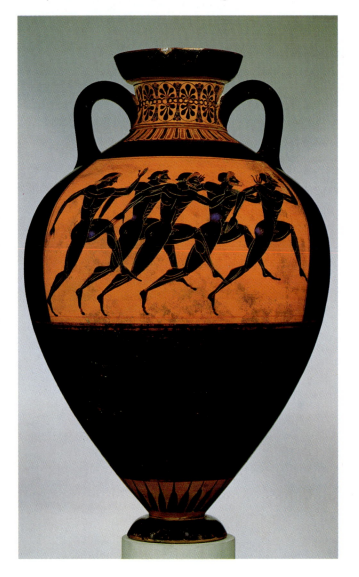

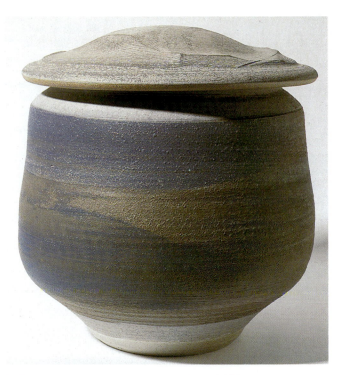

11.5 Karen Karnes, stoneware pot with lid, 1982.

whose lines carry the eye around the width of the jar, were painted in black and white onto a ground of slip which turned red-orange when fired.

Some contemporary potters have eschewed elaborate ornamentation to bring out the beauty of the natural clays and earth-toned glazes. Karen Karnes' pots (11.5) are noted for their simple strength of form and the subtle glazes that emphasize rather than hide the grainy texture of the stoneware.

Another contemporary direction is the use of ceramic techniques for artistic expression rather than the creation of functional pieces. Clay is prized as a very plastic medium for nonfunctional sculpture, although clay processes are not easily mastered. Many variables come into play at every stage, requiring great skill and knowledge if the piece is not to be ruined during the firing stages. Fired clay can withstand decay over thousands of years, but clay is sometimes built up without firing to create purposely temporary conceptual pieces (2.159).

PAULA WINOKUR
on WORKING IN CLAY

Paula Winokur (b. 1935) has been working in clay for over 35 years. At mid-century, like most other ceramists, she was creating functional pottery. She has continually evolved along with this rapidly evolving medium, and has for some time been using clay to express ideas sculpturally. Many of her recent works conceived as fireplace mantels or arches (**11.6**) are in major museums and private collections.

"In college I majored in both painting and ceramics, which was a strange combination at that time. When my husband Bob [also a renowned ceramist] and I moved to a farm in Massachusetts in 1964, I really began to find out about working with clay, because we started doing production pottery [making multiples of the same objects]. That in itself was like going to graduate school, because we made a lot of mistakes and learned a lot.

There is a certain satisfaction in making the same forms over and over again. I used to make fifty cups at a time, which really isn't that much. A good Japanese thrower will make hundreds of something in one day. You would set a goal of how many of what you were going to make in the day, and you would do it, and it was a business.

Simply functional pottery was the accepted mode in the early fifties until Peter Voulkos and that California crew started shaking things up. The material used to be associated with pots and figurines. People didn't think of it as a fine arts material. That's what I grew up with: you made pots, and you made them for use. Now there has been tremendous interest in the material and all of its potentials as a sculptural medium that can be used to describe all sorts of things— political statements, aesthetic statements, one's internal musings. I think what I've done in the past few years is combine my original interest as a painter with what I'm doing in clay, although I'm not using it as a painter—I'm using it more as a sculptor. The things that have happened in the clay world have allowed people the flexibility and opportunity to do whatever they want with it.

Now in my work I'm trying to explore my ideas and use the clay as a vehicle for those ideas. The mantels say something about precipices; as a society, as a species, we are always on the edge, ready to fall off. When I visited Mesa Verde in southwestern Colorado, the peculiar window openings and niches in the canyon walls and the precarious cliff ledges were of great interest to me. The spirit of the Anasazi, the ancient

ones, surrounds the place. I was fascinated by the shapes and forms, some left for hundreds of years, some eroded by time and some arranged by the caretakers. Somehow this is information that I continue to use. I believe that for the most part my work is about memory . . . of places which exist and yet do not exist.

Production pottery was physically demanding; many potters have backaches. Doing unique pieces is also very physical. We make our own clay body. We buy bags of a particular clay, a particular feldspar, silica, and grog, and mix all these things together. That's time-consuming and labor-intensive. At this point, I train students to help me do it. I don't trust just anybody to make my clay body, because in my unglazed porcelain pieces, the clay is the whole thing. If something goes wrong, I can't hide it with glaze.

For these big pieces, I wedge maybe 200 pounds [91 kg] of clay at once and then lay out the slabs, let them stiffen, and put them together. Once I understood that you don't have to make something of clay as a single piece, that you could use many parts and put them together, then scale became no problem for me. The big archways are four or five sections on each side, constructed and fired separately, and then put together

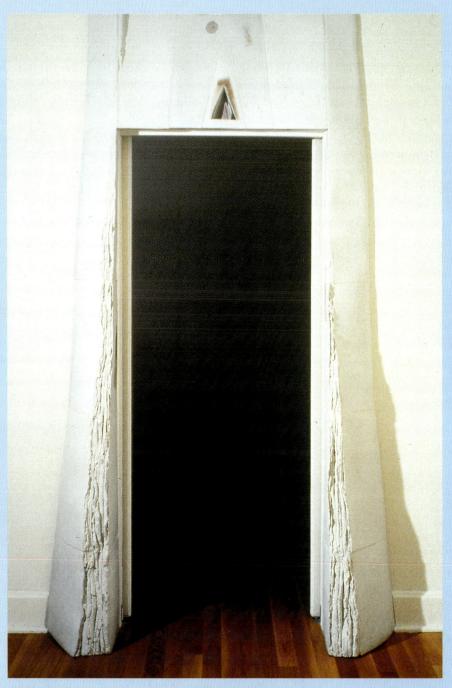

11.6 Paula Winokur, *Entry I: Sakkara*, 1986. Porcelain,
102 × 53 × 10 ins (259 × 135 × 25 cm). Courtesy of the artist.

with grout over an internal structure of pipe that holds it all together. I usually start by making a cardboard template of the different sections. Then if something should break, I can just remake that section. It does happen: I was carrying one piece of one of the fireplaces to the kiln to fire it. I hit it against the side of the table and it went 'Kronchh!' and just fell apart.

Despite years of experience, sometimes I still lose things in firing, or sometimes I don't like the way something looks. Clay does have that element of risk, and you wonder why you keep doing this. But I've been committed to this particular material a long time. A lot of people look at someone throwing and say, 'Oh, I can do that,' and then they sit down at the wheel and realize that to be a really good thrower takes years of practice."[1]

METAL

Like clays, many metals are quite amenable to being shaped. Those used for handcrafted objects have included copper, brass, nickel, pewter, iron, and the precious metals gold, silver, and platinum. They vary in **malleability** (the capacity for being shaped by physical pressure, such as hammering), **ductility** (the ability to be drawn out into wire), and hardness. Gold is the most ductile and malleable and is of course prized for its untarnishing color and luster. It is often drawn into wires and shaped into jewelry. The Mughal turban jewel in Figure 11.8 is crafted of gold and further ornamented with enamel, a glass-like, jewel-toned coating that can be fused to metal by heating.

At the opposite extreme, iron and steel (an alloy of iron and other materials) are the hardest of the common metals and among the least malleable. But they are somewhat ductile and when heated are malleable enough to be **forged** (hammered over an anvil), stretched, and twisted into forms such as Joseph Brandom's kitchen utensils and rack (11.7). These combine the sought-after feeling of old-fashioned blacksmithing technology with a light, clean, contemporary design. Note that some of the hammering marks are retained, for the desired handcrafted appearance. If a metalsmith chooses to erase all hammer marks, bulges, and wrinkles from a piece, it can be **planished** smooth with a flattening hammer. As metal is worked, it may also need to be continually **annealed**, or heated to make it more malleable, because many metals harden when they are hammered.

Iron that is worked in a heated state with hand tools is called **wrought iron**, in contrast to *cast iron*, in which molten iron is poured into molds. Szabó's extra-

11.7 Joseph L. Brandom, utensils and rack, 1982.
Stainless steel, rack length 39 ins (99 cm).

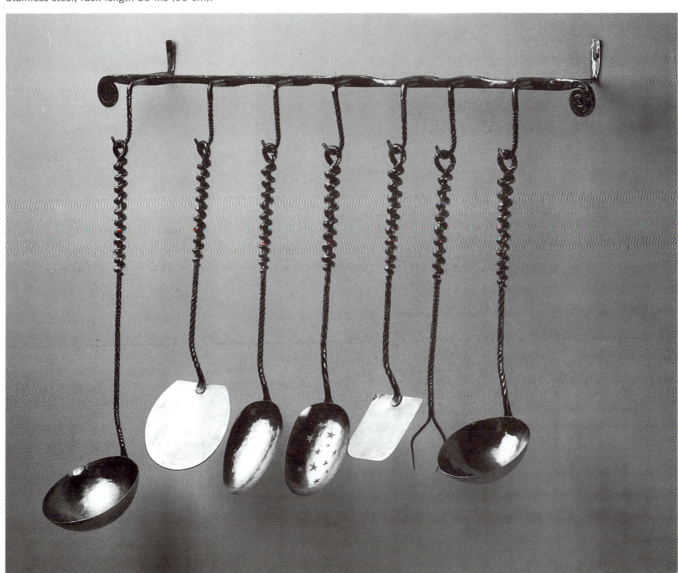

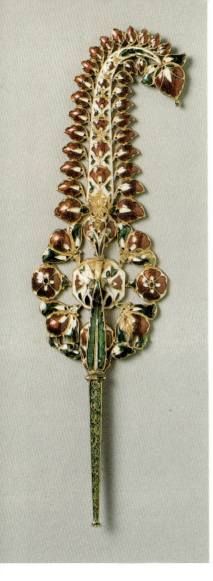

11.8 (left) Mughal turban jewel, possibly from Jaipur, c. 1750. Enameled gold, 6¾ × 1⅞ ins (17.3 × 5 cm). Victoria and Albert Museum, London, IM 47–1922. Courtesy of the Trustees of the V&A.

11.9 (below) Szabó, clock, c. 1924. Wrought iron.

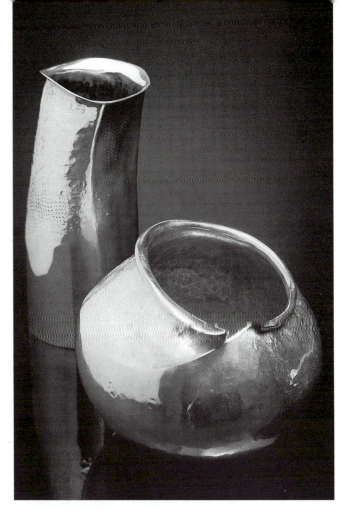

11.10 Douglas Steakley, raised vessels. Copper, (left) height 8 ins (20 cm), (right) height 5 ins (13 cm).

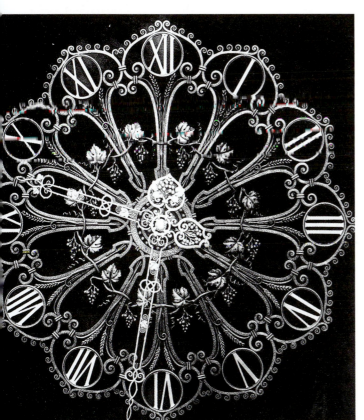

ordinarily crafted wrought-iron clock (**11.9**)—a product of the early twentieth-century rebirth of art metalwork in France—achieves the delicate filigree usually seen only in jewelry fashioned from fine wires. Such decorative details may be created by drawing out, hammering over varied forming stakes, punching, splitting, bending, incising, or repoussé (hammering punches against a sheet of metal from the back to create a low-relief pattern). Individually worked pieces of iron can be riveted, screwed, bolted, brazed, or torch-welded together, but purists prefer the traditional hammered weld, with pieces heated to the point at which they will fuse.

Metal can even be coaxed into hollow vessel forms by *raising* (hammering a flat sheet over a stake to raise the sides and work them inward). Douglas Steakley's raised copper vessels (**11.10**) have been purposely textured with marks of punch and hammer to accentuate their handcrafted appearance and add subtle textural interest to their asymmetrically curving surfaces.

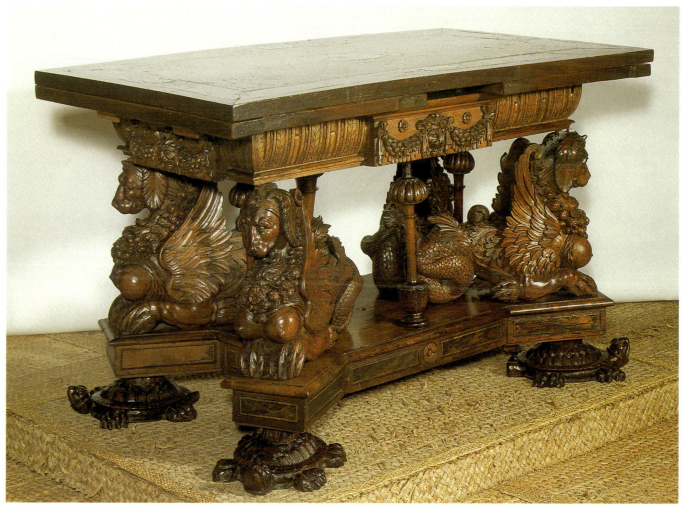

11.11 "Sea dog" table, mid-16th century, based on designs by Jean-Jacques Androuet du Cerceau. Walnut. Hardwick Hall, Derbyshire, England.

WOOD

Because trees grow in most parts of the world, and because wood is sturdy and fairly easily shaped by saw, chisel, lathe, file, and sanding devices, it has been pressed into service by artisans of most cultures. Its warmth to the touch, smoothness when sanded and polished, rich natural colors, and lively growth patterns give it a highly sensual appeal. It has been used to fashion everything from picture frames and furniture to kitchen utensils, toys, and musical instruments. Many handcrafted wooden objects are now valued as collectors' items, from jewelry boxes with ebony inlays to folk-art pieces made of soft woods such as pine and spruce. These soft woods are not necessarily the easiest to work, for they may splinter. Medium-hard woods include birch, butternut, cherry, pear, and apple; the durable, fine-grained hardwoods include walnut, oak, maple, hickory, teak, ebony, and rosewood.

Wood can be worked into extremely ornate forms, such as the sixteenth-century walnut "sea dog" table (11.11) in the Withdrawing Room of Hardwick Hall in England. It may have been a royal gift to Hardwick Hall's original owner, Elizabeth, Countess of Shrewsbury. This extreme elaboration of a table's function is based on the designs of Jean-Jacques Androuet du Cerceau, French designer of architecture and fantastic ornamentation.

Some contemporary crafters of wood take a much simpler approach to the medium, allowing it to express the more natural linear qualities of trunk and branch. The large refectory table (11.12), designed by Fred Baier and Chris Rose for limited production by Professional Woodworkers, has the lithe grace of a bridge. The curve of the oak slab transforms its heaviness into a dynamic lightness, accentuated by the growing and diminishing lengths of the many cross-members. Although trees grow in relatively straight lines, their wood can be bent into curves when steamed, as in the slab here and the bentwood Thonet chair shown earlier (2.16).

Those who use milled lumber—such as the uniform boards and poles from which the refectory table is built—typically look for clear wood, with no cracks or knots where branches grew out of the main trunk. But some woodworkers purposely seek out and emphasize "defects" in wood for their design interest. **Burls**—woody hemispherical knobs that grow on the trunks of certain trees—have curling linear patterns that are often used to advantage in **veneers** (thin overlays of fine woods placed over other woods) and in handcrafted bowls. The art of Mark Lindquist's wood bowl (11.13) is less a matter of imposing a design on it than of careful selection of the burl and respectful minimal working to bring out the natural beauty of its sinuous curves.

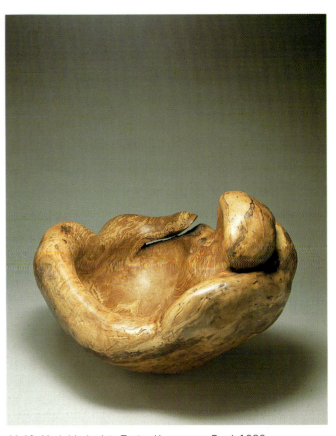

11.13 Mark Lindquist, *Toutes Uncommon Bowl*, 1980. Spalted yellow birch burl, length 32 ins (81.2 cm). Collection of Duncan and Mary McGowan.

11.12 Fred Baier and Chris Rose, Refectory table, 1985. Oak, length 23 ft (7.1 m). Professional Woodworkers Ltd., U.K.

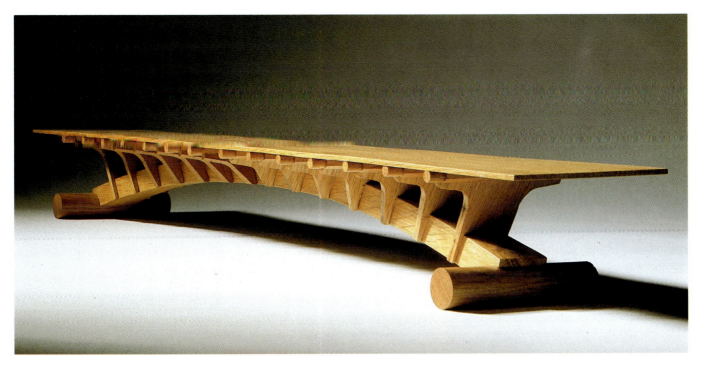

GEORGE NAKASHIMA
on A FEELING FOR WOOD

George Nakashima (1904–90) was a designer and craftsman of the highest order. Trained as an architect, he began designing handcrafted wood furniture in the 1930s and developed a deep appreciation for the nature of wood from a Japanese woodworker in an internment camp during World War II. When his family was released from the camp, they moved to New Hope, Pennsylvania, where Nakashima established a furniture-making business. His work has many distinctive characteristics, including revealed joinery, architectural bases, and slabs of solid wood (rather than veneers) in which the natural edges are valued. His largest piece is the *Altar for Peace* (**11.14**), installed in the Cathedral of St. John the Divine in New York City as a shrine where people from around the world can pray and meditate. The following excerpts from his writings reveal his attitudes toward his material:

"It is not always . . . easy to find the best expression of a piece of wood, and sometimes I will keep an extraordinary piece for decades before deciding what to do with it. This process of selection and usage is the creative act . . . of the woodworker. It is this point of personal involvement with personal decision that might be called the essence of the craft. There is always an individuality that distinguishes craftsman-made furniture from mass-produced pieces. There is life there, and it is at odds with the lifelessness of high technology and mass production."

"In commercial lumber, knots and other imperfections are scorned. Only unblemished lumber will command upper-bracket prices . . . . Lesser grades of wood have more extensive figuring and many knots and other defects. They are less expensive and, in fact, logs of 'poor' quality may sometimes be had free of charge. To me, however, it is not the economy but the quality of this wood, the 'uniqueness' imparted by the imperfections, that makes these pieces appealing. Some of my most interesting work has come from logs that seemed hopeless to others. They have inspired a creative act and a close relationship with nature.

I search for the pieces with huge knots or with gaping cavities. I am drawn to the root section, which has been underground and has an exceptional quality, offset by one potential problem: roots often swallow up stones by growing around them. The root of a great tree such as a giant redwood is almost a natural treasure lying underground. It must be dug from the earth carefully, often by hand with machinery doing only the heaviest part of the work. Some roots can remain in the ground for a century and still be usable."

"Searching out the unusual specimens is an adventure. Deciding how to cut them is a challenge. The thickness and direction of the cut will determine the product that comes from them. I often meditate on a piece for many years before making a final decision. Sometimes a dialogue with a client will inspire the cut of a piece."

"Sadly, many of the world's great trees end up as nothing but a common object, cut into paper-thin veneers or parcels of thin wood for novelty boxes or something similar. Part of my destiny has been to intercept this process and give some trees a fitting and noble purpose, helping them to live again in my work."

"As materials and resources become more and more limited around the world, products of beauty and utility will almost have to become more efficient as man confronts the dwindling reserves of nature. . . . Back in our woods, in New Hope, I continue to make casual objects, objects as simple as a tea bowl. I pursue the path of low technology, away from the murderous syndrome of 'progress.' The fight for beauty has occupied my lifetime, and I have sought to create beauty in a world where little of it seems to exist. My efforts are small points of light within a large light that is still possible and can grow to a great illumination."[2]

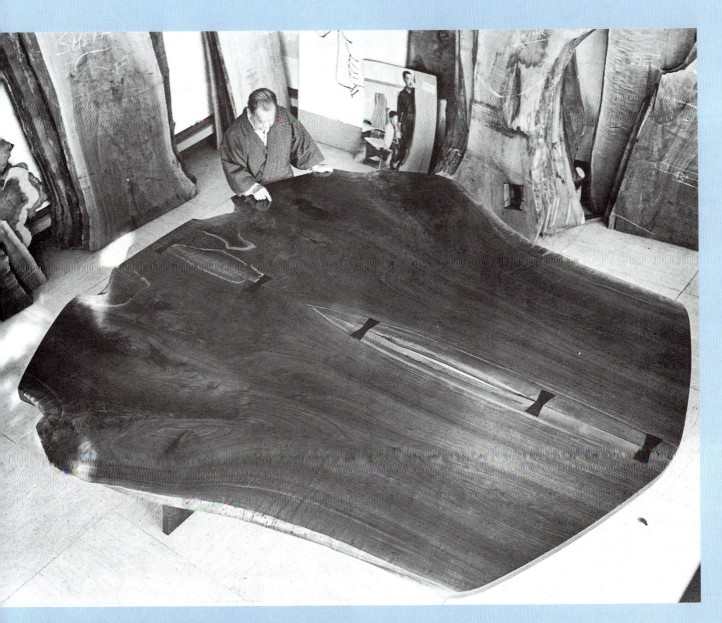

11.14 George Nakashima, *Altar for Peace*, made for the Cathedral of St. John the Divine, photographed in his New Hope, Pennsylvania, studio, 1986.

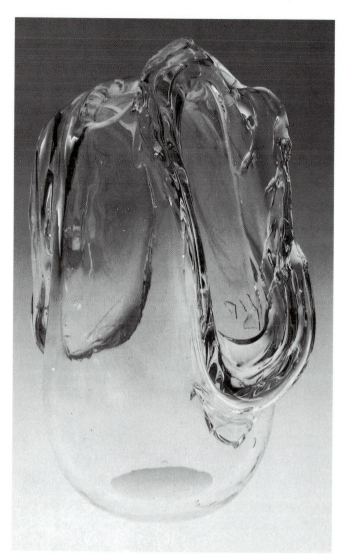

GLASS

For all its fragile, transparent beauty, glass is made by the surprisingly simple process of melting sand with lime and soda. The technique has been in use for at least 3500 years for creating luxury versions of functional objects.

One of the most common ways of making glass vessels is to scoop up a glob of molten glass with a long metal blowpipe and blow it into a bubble while shaping its form with hand tools. The liquidity of the glass before it hardens is captured in Harvey Littleton's freely blown and draped glass vase (11.15). Littleton was a pioneer in the twentieth-century "studio glass" movement, in which fine artists have learned the craft of glassblowing, expanding the medium far beyond traditional concepts of what can be done in glass.

Before the twentieth century, glass production had been done by skilled glassblowers using techniques

11.15 Harvey Littleton, vase, 1963. Hand-blown clear glass, 9¾ × 7½ × 4⅞ ins (24.8 × 19 × 12.4 cm). Collection Museum of Modern Art, New York. Greta Daniel Design Fund. Photograph © 1997 MOMA.

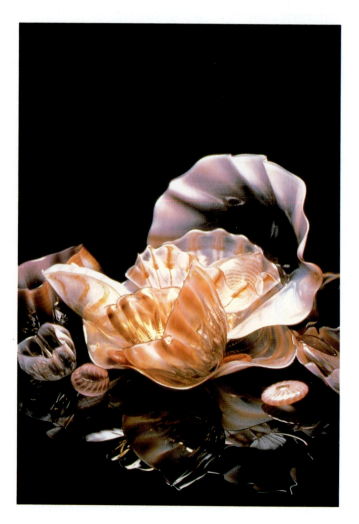

11.16 (right) Dale Chihuly, *No. 2 Sea Form Series*, 1984. Width 3 ft 8 ins (1.12 m). Courtesy of Foster/White Gallery, Seattle, Washington.

11.17 (opposite) René Lalique, glass vase, c. 1905–10. Cast glass, height 6 ins (15.2 cm). Private collection, Miami, Florida.

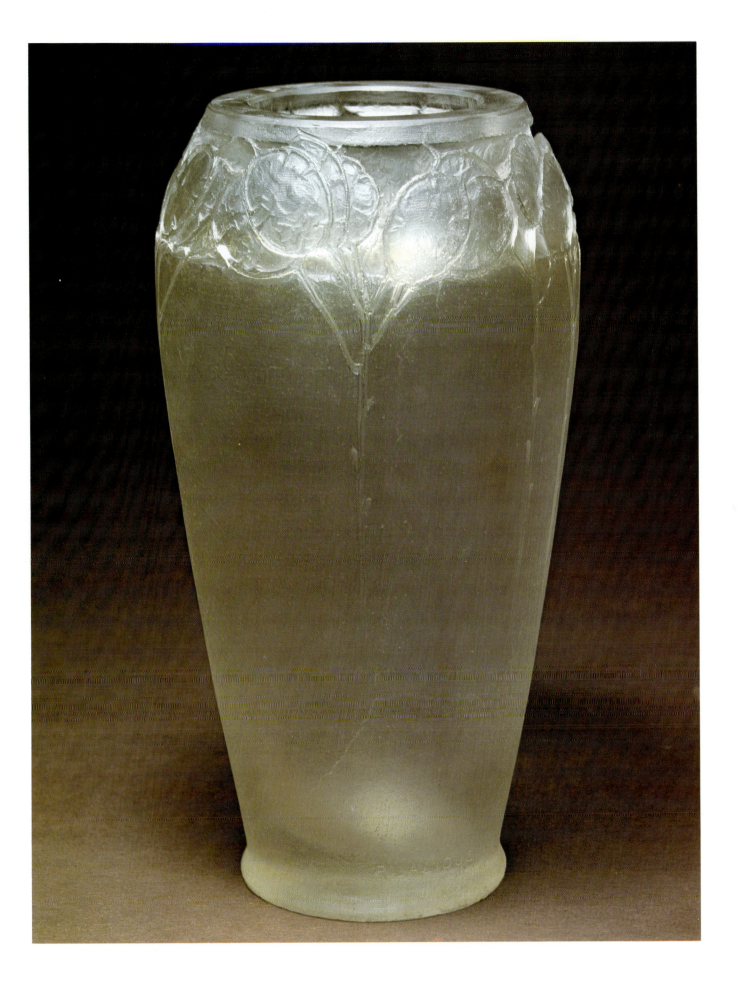

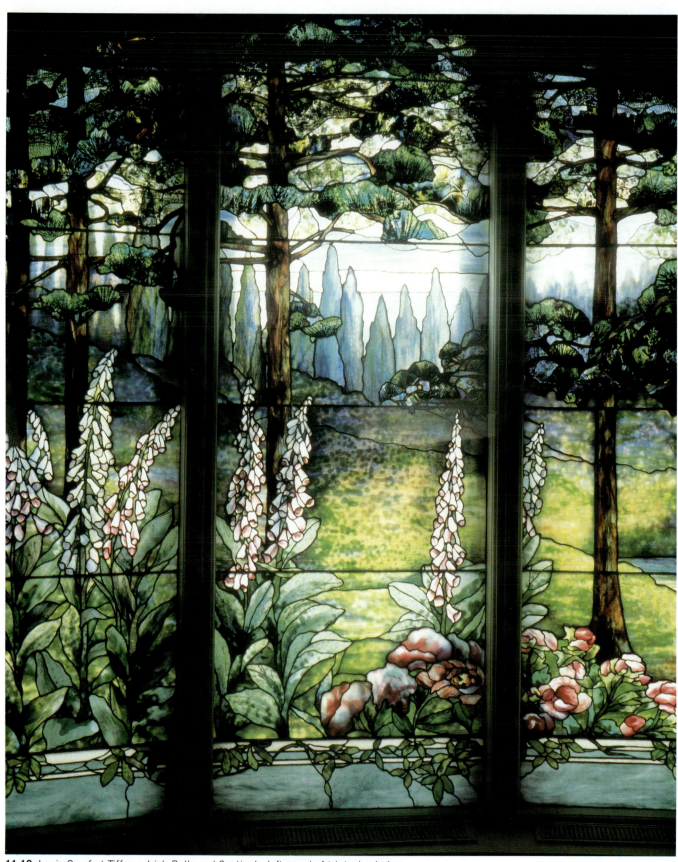

11.18 Louis Comfort Tiffany, *Irish Bells and Sentinels*, left panel of triptych window,
St. James Country Club outside Perryopolis, Pennsylvania. Width 6 ft 8 ins (2.03 m).

thousands of years old. But industrial techniques were developed that gradually ended the demand for glass-blowers. Even in those art glass studios that remained, the process was broken down into a series of steps handled by different specialists.

By the 1920s and 1930s there were only a few traditional glass craftsmen left. Given the rigors of the profession, it is not difficult to imagine why it was largely abandoned. Maurice Marinot, one of the last great artists in France, described what it was to work with such a hot medium:

> To be a glassmaker is to blow the substance to transparency into the blind furnace and to reblow it with tools of his art—his lips; to work in the heat, sweating with fever, the eyes full of tears, the hands seared and burnt.[3]

Nevertheless, glass was an enchanting medium with great aesthetic potentials—brilliance, light reflection and refraction, bubbles, iridescence, gem-like colors, extreme malleability when hot. Picking up from Marinot, Harvey Littleton (who had been a ceramist) and a few other artists and technicians held workshops in 1962 to create glass techniques that could be used by individual artists rather than factories, and a new type of glass that was cheap, durable, and easy to melt. The participants were so excited by their discoveries of what could be done with glass that they kept the furnace busy from 5:30 in the morning until midnight.

From this new start, studio glass has become a very dynamic feature of the contemporary art scene. Dale Chihuly is a major figure in today's rapidly evolving art glass field. Many of his pieces take off from traditional ways of forming glass as containers but exuberantly transcend functionality. His *No. 2 Sea Form Series* (11.16) is a dynamic sculptural play of flowing, organic forms, lines, and colors, heightened by the translucent qualities of the glass.

Glass can also be cast. The lost-wax ("cire perdue") process produces one-of-a-kind pieces. René Lalique, one of the great names in glass design, began his studies of the possibilities of glass with the lost-wax casting process. Pieces such as his glass vase shown in Figure 11.17 are prized by collectors not only for their subtle design and the beauty of the glass but also because they retain the human touch: the thumbprints of the modeler, which can be seen in the flowers. Lalique soon abandoned these unique, handcrafted pieces and turned to mass production of beautifully designed glass tableware, vases, bottles, boxes, jewelry, lamps, and panels for luxury cars, trains, and ocean liners.

In addition to blown and cast vessels, glass is also blown or poured into sheets to make two- or three-dimensional works that both admit and transform light, as in lampshades or cathedral windows. **Antique glass**, prized for its metal oxide brilliance and its "imperfections" such as bubbles and warps, is blown by a glassblower as a cylinder, cut lengthwise, and heated until it lies flat. For **stained glass**, chemical colorants are heated with the base glass in a kiln until they fuse. **Opalescent glass**, developed by Louis Tiffany and John La Farge, incorporates soda ash for opacity; the glassmaker swirls bright color oxides through the molten glass as it is poured out into a sheet. To create designs of different colors, pieces of stained glass are cut and then joined by means of soldered lead channeling, copper foil, glue, or heat fusing. Tiffany's virtuosity with glass is especially evident in his windows (11.18). They are mosaics of his custom-made glass, thousands of pieces cut and pieced together with dark lead strips—which also serve a design function as outlines defining the shapes. But unlike medieval stained-glass windows, the colors within the shapes are not solid; rather, they are mottled and swirled and juxtaposed to create lush and dynamic interplays of colors. Tiffany refused to paint on the glass, for to do so would inhibit the brilliance of the light effects.

FIBERS

Another ancient craft that is presently undergoing a great resurgence of interest is *fiber art*. This broad category includes everything made of threadlike materials, usually woven or tied into larger wholes. Many of these works are conceived with the functional purpose of maintaining warmth, such as the **tapestries** created in many ancient cultures. In Gothic Europe, tapestries were designed to take the chill off the cold masonry walls of castles and cathedrals during medieval Europe's mini-Ice Age. In these heavy, handwoven textiles, pictures were woven directly into the fabric. A cartoon of the desired image was drawn on the *warp*, the lengthwise threads strung on the loom. As the crosswise *weft* threads of varied colors were woven loosely over and under the warp and then pressed downward, complicated pictures emerged, as in the

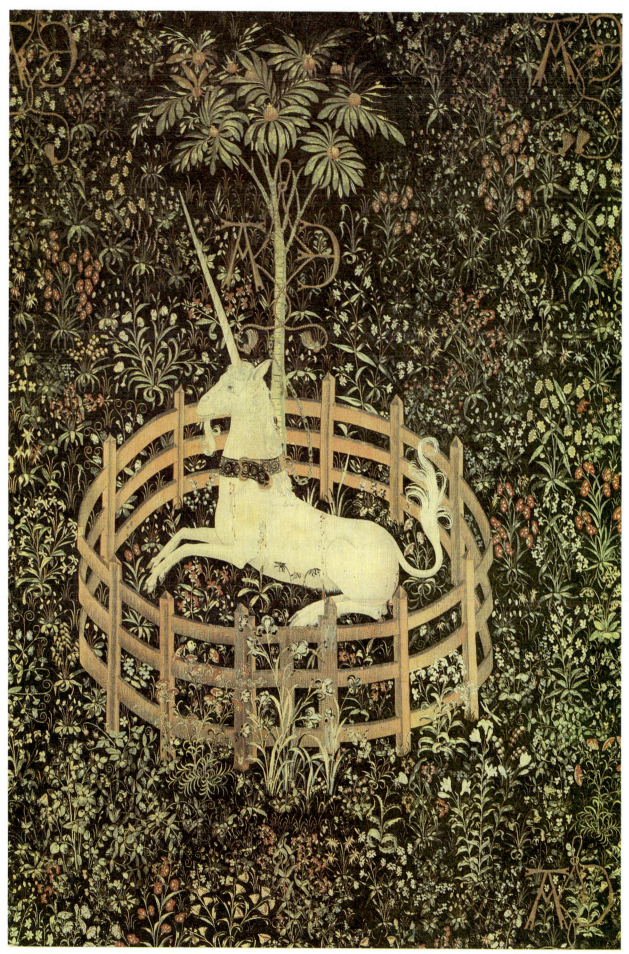

11.19 *The Unicorn in Captivity*, from the *Unicorn Tapestries*, c. 1500. Silk and wool, silver and silver-gilt threads, 12 ft 1 in ×
8 ft 3 ins (3.68 × 2.51 m). Metropolitan Museum of Art, New York. Cloisters Collection, gift of John D. Rockefeller, Jr., 1937.

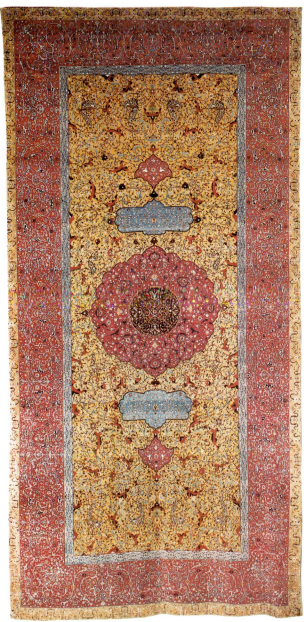

11.20 Carpet from Tabriz, Iran, Safavid period, 16th century. Wool pile on cotton and silk, 26 ft 6 ins × 13 ft 7 ins (8.07 × 4.14 m). Metropolitan Museum of Art, New York. Gift of Samuel H. Kress Foundation, 1946.

lovely *Unicorn Tapestries*, of which the last is shown in *The Unicorn in Captivity* (**11.19**). In the courtly medieval world, these time-consuming works were far more expensive than paintings.

Another prized fiber art is the weaving of Oriental rugs in the Near and Far East (**11.20**). Despite their intricate beauty, the original Persian rugs were used by nomadic peoples to cover the sand within their tents and to wrap their possessions when traveling. They were nonetheless treasured family possessions, and in the sixteenth century, Europeans began collecting them as works of art. In everyday use, they can last a hundred years, and the older sun-mellowed ones are much sought after. The highest-quality rugs are made from the wool of sheep grazed at high altitudes. The wool is knotted at densities ranging from 60 to 600 knots per square inch (2.5 cm^2).

Baskets woven of pliable materials are a form of fiber art used by many traditional cultures. A contemporary basketmaker, Susye Billy of the native Pomo people in California, the creator of the lovely tight-woven basket in Figure **11.21**, speaks of the reasons for working traditionally but also of the difficulty of doing so today:

> I feel that the generations before me tried all the different materials and found these to be the best materials, and so I'm pretty strict on that. The materials that we use are the willow. And then we use three main colored fibers: the white material is a sage grass root, and I use the bulrush root for the black fiber, and I use the new shoots of the redbud, and that gives a reddish-brown color. Of course, we have to dig all our own materials. They can't be bought anywhere and it's very hard today to find the places where the materials grow and to be able to gather them. The way that rivers have been dammed up, the way that the waters run different now, wipe out the roots and things that used to grow along the sides of the rivers. And a lot of the willows have been cut down along the roads, where they've put in roads that used to be just dirt roads . . . . You have to be very determined to be a basket weaver today.[4]

11.21 Susye Billy, Basket, 1973–85. Edged in redwood, single willow rod foundation, height 1¾ × diameter 4¾ ins (4.4 × 12 cm). Lost and Found Tradition Collection, Natural History Museum of Los Angeles County. The Collection is a gift of the American Car Corporation, now Primerica.

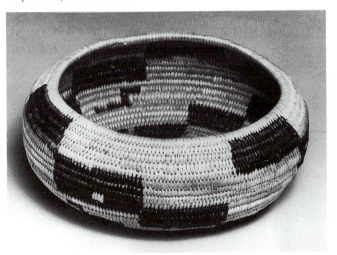

NORMA MINKOWITZ
on THE INTERFACE BETWEEN ART AND CRAFT

Norma Minkowitz's early work was in more or less functional fiber arts, such as pillows in reverse appliqué revealing layer upon layer of fabric, and clothing that was just barely wearable, with great attention to texture and line and shape. Then in 1983 she crocheted around a shoe, removed the shoe, and discovered that she had created a transparent form. Since then she has been exploring the possibilities of these open crocheted sculptures, stiffened into hard but transparent forms, which often make statements about containment. Minkowitz emphasizes that they are sculptures. At the same time, they have the intimacy of craft. She comments:

"This organic growth and shaping became possible from having a soft material become a hard material. It's very repetitious and time-consuming to create your own material, your own fiber, your own canvas. But through the medium of crochet the process becomes part of the content, and structure and surface are achieved at the same time. I am also motivated and excited by the intimate relationship that I have with the object I am creating, which is generally small and easy to hold on my lap. I sit in a quiet corner, alone with my thoughts and my work. At a time when many artists collaborate and have technicians to do part of their work (which is often monumental in size), I feel content with and more attracted to the oneness I feel with my work."

"The medium that I use is very important in my work, but yet the work isn't about the technique. I think in a successful art form there has to be a reason for the process used. The reason for my technique is that it becomes a really fragile but yet structured form which allows me to show an interior space. It's seeing within something, and the inside becomes ambiguous—Is it a shelter? Is it a trap? Is it someplace to be safe or someplace to be stifled or controlled? Many of my pieces show the feeling of being absorbed into the earth, bringing up universal themes of man's fear of death and dying and mortality. I try to impose meaning on my work because I feel that art is an extension of oneself and that, without a message or a meaningful reason for the choice of medium, it cannot be art."

"This piece (**11.22**) has a hand inside. Is the hand reaching out or is it being drawn down into this box, never to come out again? I could make the hand more obvious by darkening it, but I like having it be something that feels like it's there but yet it's not there. It almost has the feeling of a flower, a gentle flower. The floating red layer in the center was very hard to do because I had to crochet that part inside after the shell was stiff; my knuckles kept bleeding because the stiffened fiber is very rough."

"I think most artists, whether they are painters or sculptors or woodworkers or people working in fiber, are combining so many techniques and materials now that the line is very fine between what is craft and what is fine art. There is craftsmanship in a marble sculpture, and there is fine art in a fiber sculpture. It's no longer what material you are using—it's what you are saying with your work and what it means. If you see a beautiful wooden salad bowl, it's less of a statement in regard to expressive emotion and more of a statement about technique, craftsmanship, form, and function. But if you see something in fiber or wood that is purely sculptural and says something to you in a unique way, then it's an art form. If a piece motivates feelings and makes different people react in a different way, then the work is saying something intellectual and that's what makes it art. Art is something that is poetic; it reveals imagery that has not been done before and inspires a new way of seeing."[5]

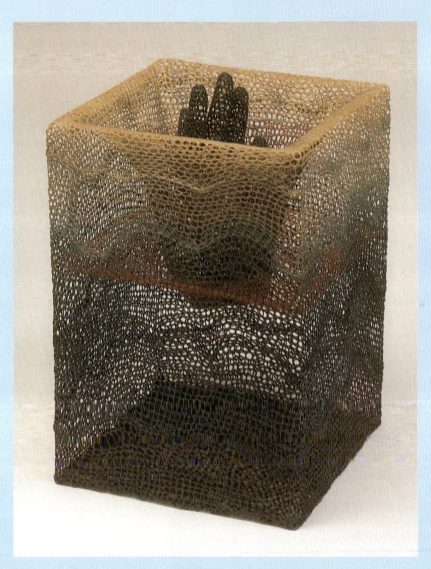

11.22 Norma Minkowitz, *Lotus*, 1989.
Open crocheted sculpture, 15½ × 12 × 12 ins (39.4 × 30.5 × 30.5 cm).
Photo by Bobby Hansson. Courtesy of the artist.

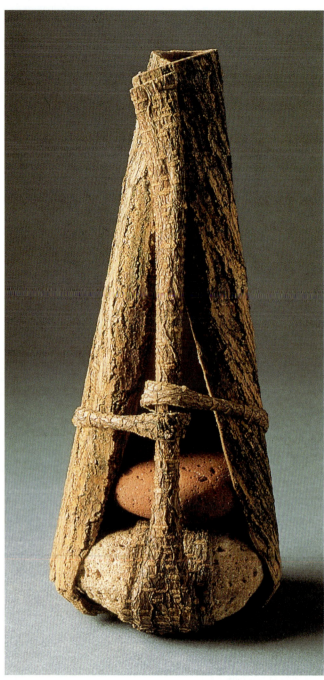

that are not intended to hold anything (see Box and 11.22). Traditional basketry techniques and fascination with the nature of tree bark led to Dorothy Gill Barnes' *North Beach Rocks* (11.23). Fresh mulberry bark that she wrapped around stones tightened to enclose them and also took on their shape as it dried. Like Barnes, many contemporary fiber artists are women creating nontraditional, nonfunctional container forms suggestive of inner feminine mysteries—enfolding, enclosing, protecting what lies deep within their embrace.

Quilting was traditionally a way of sewing fabric scraps into colorful, durable blankets that are also reminders of one's family history. The technique has now been adapted for nonfunctional wall hangings which are never to be used on a bed. Sandra Sider's

11.24 Sandra Sider, *Focus on the Belvedere*, 1990. Cyanotype chemicals, cotton fabric, fabric paint, photography, painting, machine piecing and stitching, 27 × 38 ins (68.6 × 96.5 cm). Photo by Roberto Sandoval. Courtesy of the artist.

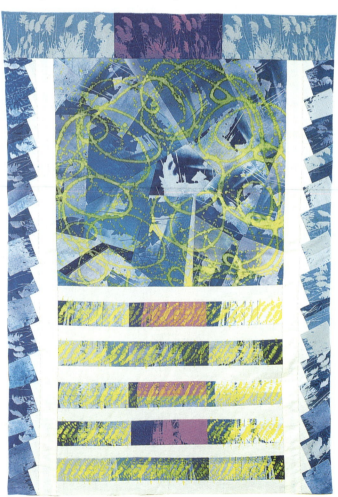

11.23 Dorothy Gill Barnes, *North Beach Rocks*, 1995. Mulberry bark, rocks, wrapped, 9½ × 5 × 5 ins (24.1 × 12.7 × 12.7 cm). The "rocks" are red and yellow bricks washed and rounded by the Lake Erie surf. Collection of Daphne Farago. Photo by Doug Martin.

In addition to carrying on the traditional fiber arts, contemporary artists are also experimenting with nonfunctional "paintings" and sculptures of fibers ranging from cloth and yarns to wire gauze, hog gut, and vines. Basketry and crocheting have been borrowed by fiber artist Norma Minkowitz to create vessel-like forms

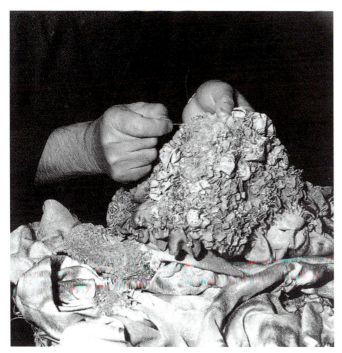

11.25 Itchiku Kubota cutting threads on an Itchiku Tsujigahana kimono. Exhibit catalog, *Homage to Nature: Landscape Kimonos by Itchiku Kubota*, Canadian Museum of Civilization, Hull, Quebec, and the National Museum of Natural History, Smithsonian Institution, Washington, D.C. Exhibit made possible by a gift from Sasakawa Foundation.

Focus on the Belvedere (**11.24**) combines traditional quilt piecing techniques with painting on the fabric and printing it with photographic processes. The ideas and techniques she says she was working with in this art quilt are clearly from the world of art for art's sake:

> Photographic processes in my art inspire creative efforts that involve an interplay between light and shadow, an exploration of the graphic relationships of text and image, and experimentation with the visual and emotional impact of color.[6]

Handmade fiber works often involve lengthy, painstaking hand labor. Itchiku Kubota has revived and adapted an ancient, time-consuming Japanese method of preparing silk fabric for kimonos. The silk is gathered into myriad tiny lumps with thread and then painted and dyed selectively, with some of the lumps covered by vinyl thread to resist the dyes. The artist must remember all details of the intended design, for it cannot be seen during the process. Silk cannot absorb much dye at one time, so the fabric is repeatedly dipped in dye baths and then rinsed again and again. After dyeing, it is dried while stretched on short bamboo sticks to prevent shrinking. Tiny scissors are used in pulling and cutting away the threads wrapped around the lumps (**11.25**); without precision, the silk itself may be cut. The exquisite results can be seen in the subtle color blending of the landscape kimono in Figure **11.26**.

Although many of the fiber arts have evolved from handwork done on someone's lap, some contemporary fiber pieces are of tremendous size and weight. Fiber installations may be so large that scaffolding must be used to erect them.

11.26 Itchiku Kubota, *Ohn (Mount Fuji), Tender, Cool Dawn.* Kimono. Unnumbered page from exhibit catalog, *Homage to Nature: Landscape Kimonos by Itchiku Kubota.*

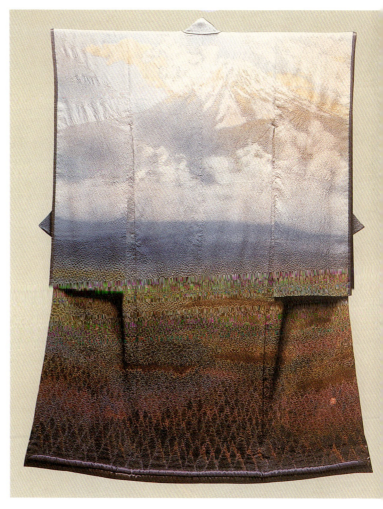

12
PRODUCT AND
CLOTHING DESIGN

In contrast to the unique nature of each handcrafted item, contemporary product design and clothing design usually involve mass production. But especially for more affluent consumers, artistic sensibilities are often guiding these designs.

INDUSTRIAL DESIGN

Industrial design used to be equated with dreary functionality in appearance. But in the past few decades contemporary designers have taken a new look at the familiar goods used in homes and offices, from furniture and toasters to computers. The result in many cases is a marriage of function and the aesthetics of color, surface texture, line, space, and form.

12.1 Eric Chan, toaster prototype. Courtesy of the artist.

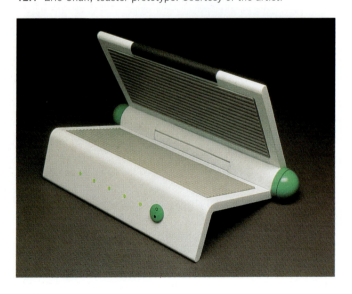

The basic designs of many mass-produced objects were conceived some time ago, to accommodate technologies then available. As the innards of electrical appliances change, so can their exterior forms. With miniaturized components, telephones can and do take any form or size. Eric Chan has totally redesigned the toaster, with easy-to-clean nonstick flat surfaces and no place for crumbs to accumulate (12.1). As he points out, "Because the hot electric metal coils are hidden within the ceramic-base fiberboard, the threat of electrocution and burned fingers is no longer a problem." New technologies can liberate design, Chan feels:

> Today's climate provides a challenge to explore meaning and feeling rather than just packaging a set of mechanical or electrical components in the most efficient form for mechanical and marketing purposes. I believe my task is to mediate the balance between people and object, poetry and logic, and technology and nature.[1]

New design houses are flourishing in many countries, some of which provide governmental support for their designers as national resources. For example, Vignelli Associates has offices in New York, Paris, and Milan and provides many firms with designs for graphics, consumer products, furniture, and interiors. Owners Lella and Massimo Vignelli, in conjunction with David Law—a designer of two-dimensional graphics, packaging, exhibits, furniture, products, interiors, and environmental works—designed the handsome dinnerware shown in Figure 12.2. They

12.2 (opposite) Lella and Massimo Vignelli and David Law, dinner set, 1984. Stoneware, large plate, diameter 10¾ ins (27.3 cm). Manufactured by Sasaki Crystal, Japan.

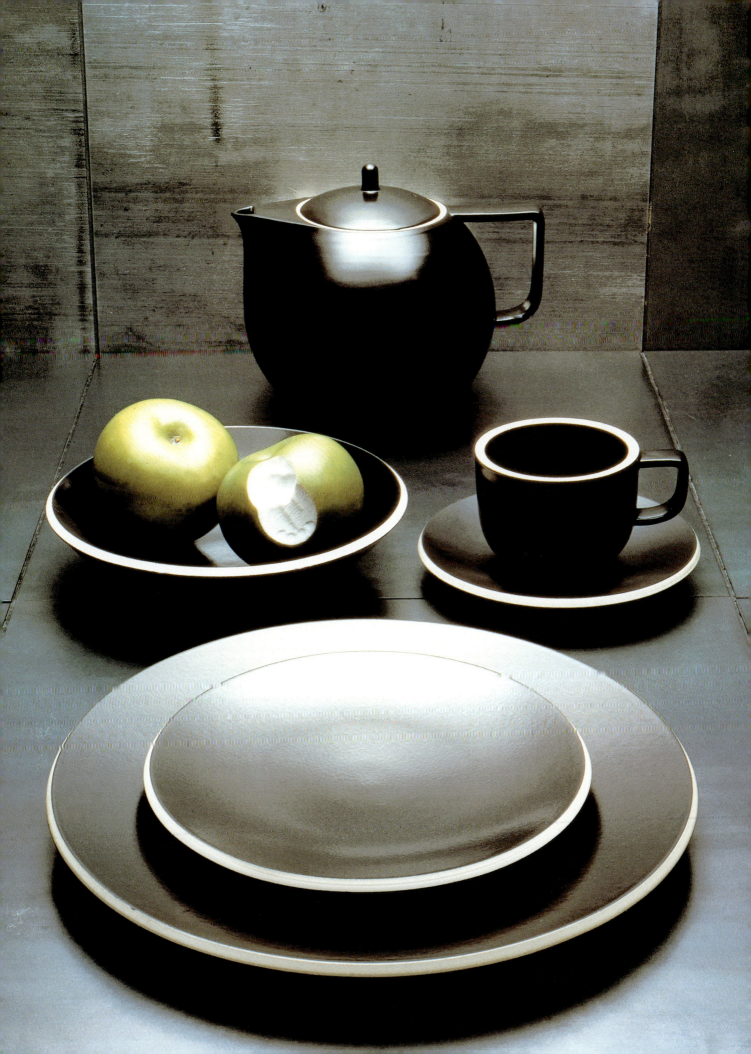

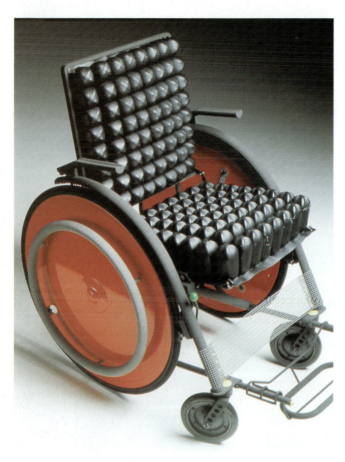

12.3 Kazuo Kawasaki, wheelchair. Lightweight titanium frame, aluminum honeycomb wheels. Courtesy of eX-Design, Inc., Japan.

gave great attention to the subtly pebbled "organic" texture of the dishes, the dramatic contrast between the black expanses and the wide, white beveled edges, and the sensuously rounded profile of the teapot. It is functional as well as pleasing to the eye, with an easy-to-grasp open handle, good balance in the hand, and a practical spout for pouring hot liquid.

Ergonomics is the new science of designing for efficient and comfortable interaction between a product and the human body. It attempts to cut down on awkwardness and fatigue in common home and workplace tasks. One offshoot of this new trend is designs that allow physically handicapped people to be as independent as possible.

Kazuo Kawasaki, who was himself paralyzed by a car accident, has redesigned the wheelchair to make it not only more comfortable and energy efficient, with huge wheels, lightweight titanium frames, and contoured seats but also more fun to look at (12.3). There is no reason for those who live independently in wheelchairs to stay with the drab colors of hospital wheelchairs; why not bright colors?

Although many contemporary products are the result of technological innovations in materials and industrial processes, paradoxically, some aspects of high technology make it possible to mass produce the look of the old and handcrafted. For example, the development of miniature, low voltage, halogen lights has allowed designers to eliminate the fuss of wires and fittings in a lamp and to use relatively flammable materials near the light source. Hiroshi Morishima's table lamp (12.4) has a gentle, handcrafted look, with the light glowing through the soft, random texture of handmade Japanese paper.

Up-tempo furniture design is combined with social justice in the expressive one-of-a-kind pieces of YA/YA (Young Aspirations/Young Artists). They are formerly problem students from a black vocational high school in New Orleans, inspired and supported by painter Jana Napoli. She encouraged them to paint thrift-shop chairs and chifforobes in their own exuberant styles. The chifforobes were conceived as "powerful boxes of hope and fear," painted outside with dreams and inside with hidden fears (12.5). The students work up to 30 hours a week after school

12.4 (opposite) Hiroshi Morishima, *Wagami Andon*, 1985. Lamp encircled in a cone of Japanese handmade paper, 29½ × 21½ ins (75 × 55 cm). Manufactured by Time Space Art Inc., Japan.

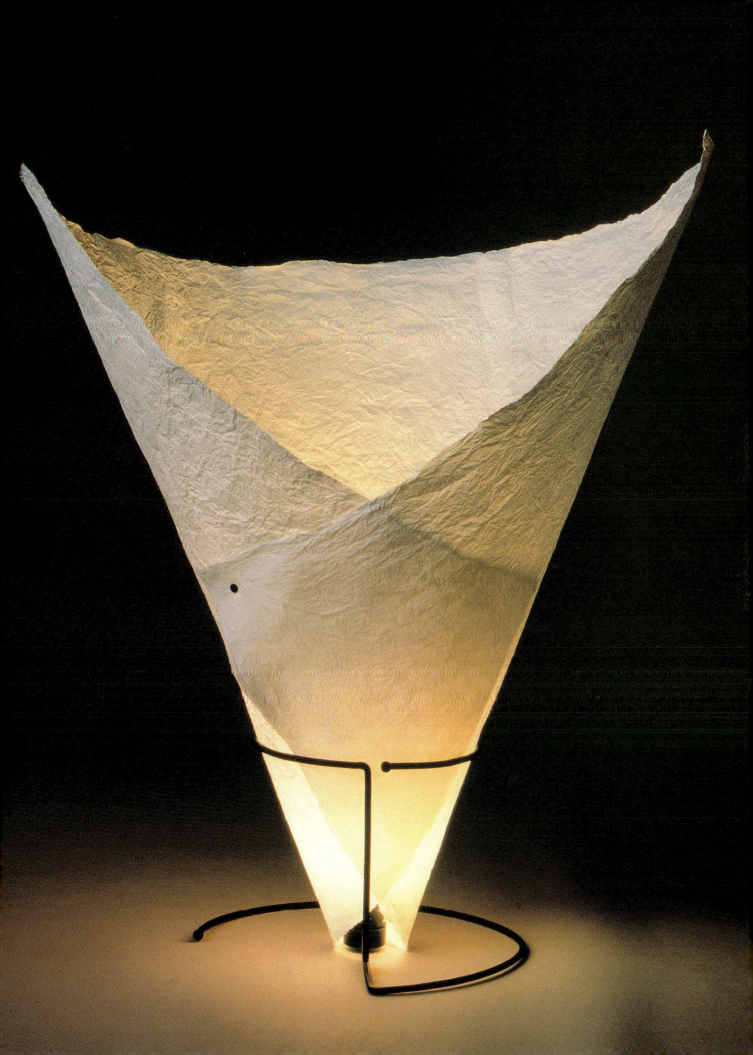

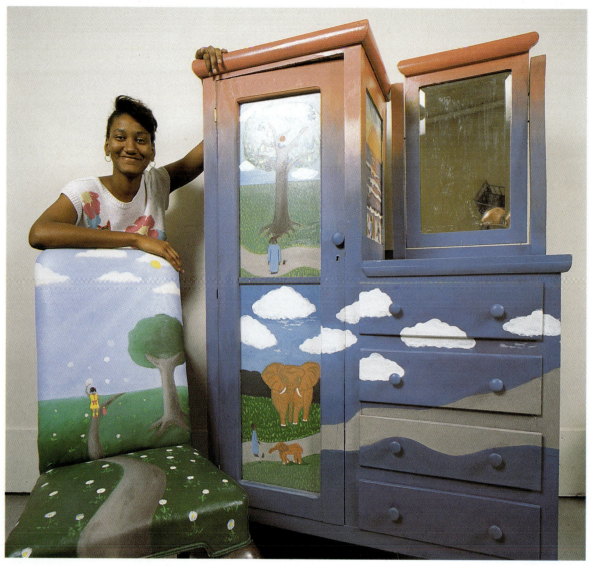

12.5 YA/YA artist Darlene Francis with her chair and chifforobe. Courtesy of Young Aspirations/Young Artists Inc., New York.

and on weekends, turning out lively, complex statements that are eagerly sought by collectors in several countries, at prices that are helping the artists save for college.

CLOTHING DESIGN

Those who design clothes sculpt in fibers, with the human body as a supporting armature. In addition to their aesthetic qualities, our clothes carry symbolic connotations that transcend the sheer function of protecting our bodies from the weather. Naked, we are all much the same. Clothed, we make symbolic statements about our wealth, status, lifestyle, sex role, personality, and taste.

The art of dressing often connotes class rank. Traditionally, the working classes have usually dressed for convenience, with simple sturdy fabrics and designs allowing free movement. Farther up the social scale, wealth and leisure may be demonstrated by a more ornamental than functional approach to design. In addition to demonstrating that the wearer was not involved in manual work, fashions for women have at times turned them into visual display cases. As

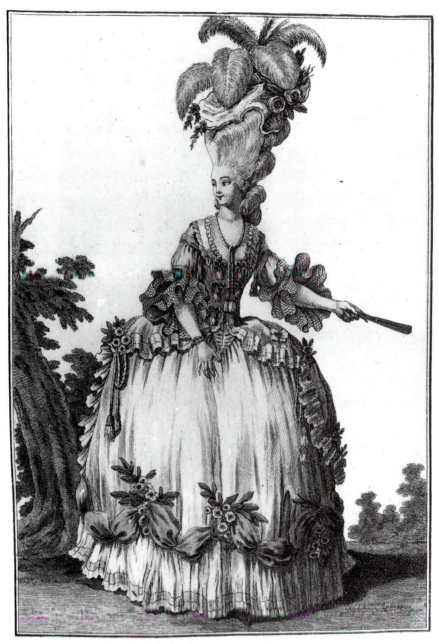

12.6 Voisard after Desrais, *A Lady of Fashion,* c. 1770.
Colored engraving.

indicated in the engraving by Voisard (**12.6**), high-born French women of the 1770s were almost immobilized by immense side paniers, tight-waisted corsets, frilly sleeves, and towering hats and hairstyles that took hours to put together and needed to be moved very carefully, if at all. Even to be carried in a sedan chair, women so dressed had to kneel on the floor to make room for the height of their headdresses. The hairstyles took so long to construct that they were maintained for a month or two, with the aid of lard and

whiting. Sleeping with them was as hazardous as it was uncomfortable, for mice liked to nibble on them; the solution, a mouse-resistant nightcap, added to the great weight of the contraption.

As well as being calculated to impress others with one's wealth and position, fashions have been used to accentuate one's gender image. Males may dress in ways that flaunt and exaggerate their masculine traits, such as the immense padded shoulders, decorated codpiece, and barely covered legs of Henry VIII's costume

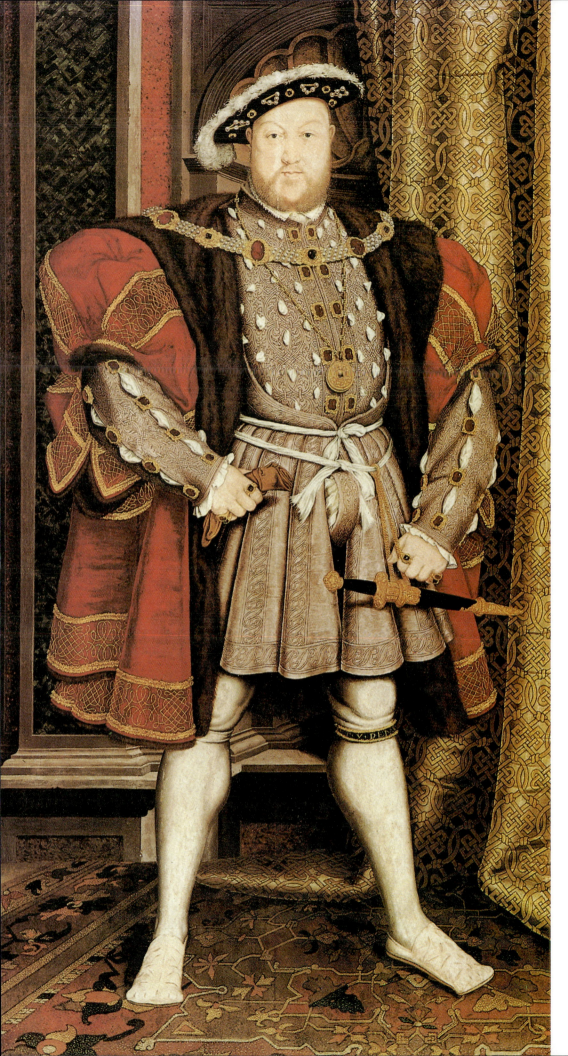

12.7 After Hans Holbein the Younger, *Henry VIII*, 1537. Oil on canvas, 7 ft 8 ins × 4 ft 5 ins (2.34 × 1.35 m). Walker Art Gallery, Liverpool, England.

(12.7). Not only do the artificially broad shoulders emphasize his masculinity; they also bespeak the great political power of the monarch.

Flamboyance in male attire has been rare in Western societies during the twentieth century, with the conservative business suit widely accepted as a uniform. But some cultures drape men with gorgeous fabrics, such as those shown in Figure 12.8, still the choice of clothing for some of African descent.

As we become more liberated from traditional social role expectations, we are freer to dress as individuals. Early in the twentieth century, women's emancipation from stricter Victorian standards opened the way for greater freedom in their clothing. The *Delphos* dress of pleated silk by Fortuny (12.9) allowed the natural curves of the body to show, without exaggeration or coyness. Its graceful lines—still in demand—were inspired by the draped garments of Classical Greece. The pleats travel well and are in fact best maintained by twisting the dress into a knot.

As in the other arts, the world of contemporary high fashion is a mélange of different styles. Its variety is personified by the exuberantly unconventional output of Japanese designer Issey Miyake. His garments range from marvelously loose and flowing pieces that allow and encourage free movement of the

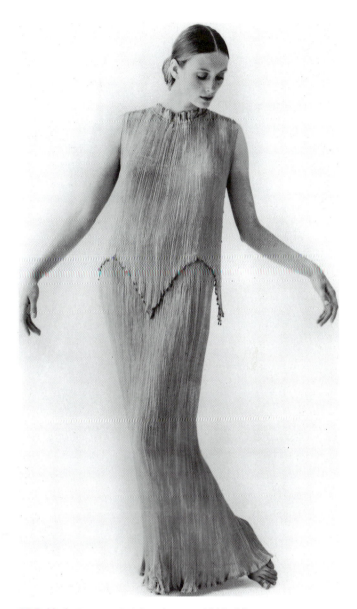

12.9 Maria Fortuny, *Delphos dress*, c. 1912. Silk.

12.8 Traditional dress from Nigeria, Africa.

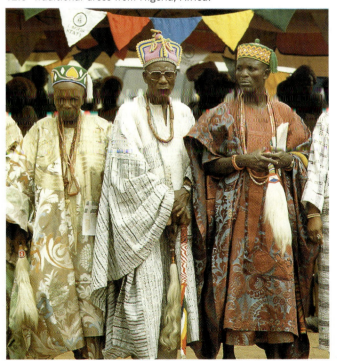

body to the open basketwork "coat" (12.10). Its cane framework resembles samurai armor, revealing and contrasting with the sensuality of the body. Even Miyake's fabrics are his own invention. To support his broad credo—"Anything can be clothing"—he takes his inspiration for fabrics from everyday images— "leaves, trees, bark, sky, air. Anything. A noodle." Miyake drapes the fabrics over himself to see what they will do. He says:

> Fabric is like the grain in wood. You can't go against it. I close my eyes and let the fabric tell me what to do.[2]

Ever pushing at the boundaries established for fashion by social convention and lack of imagination, Miyake observes that the Japanese word for clothing—*fuku*—

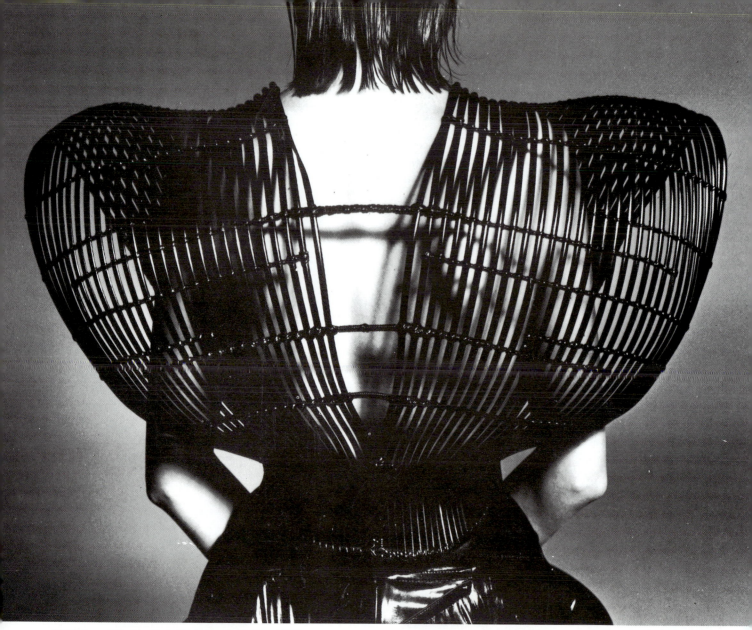

12.10 Issey Miyake, *Body Sculpture in Rattan*, 1982.

also means happiness: "People ask me what I do . . . I say I make happiness." The wearer of such a garment must have something of the same blithe spirit, a sense of independence and self-confidence. Designed for lithe and sensual movement, the clothes only "work" on a person who moves freely within them.

Some garments—such as those by Issey Miyake—are considered wearable art by collectors. High-quality Chinese and Japanese kimonos are hung as paintings, even though they are also very comfortably functional with their deep-cut arms and loose fit. Indeed, kimono designers old and new have treated this traditional garment as a broad surface for two-

dimensional art, such as the intricate embroidered patterns of silk and gold threads worked across the Chinese woman's coat (12.11).

In some cultures elaborate handmade garments are among a family's treasures passed down from one generation to the next and worn on special ceremonial occasions. There are also some contemporary attempts to maintain or revive the old labor-intensive costume-making arts as symbols of a cultural heritage. Cheryl Samuel visited museums from Leningrad to Toronto to study the 11 remaining old-style Kotlean robes woven 200 years ago by natives of the northwest coast of North America, in order to produce a twelfth one

(**12.12**). She found that the people had used their basketweaving techniques to twine the robes, working each row from left to right and knotting the weft strands into a fringe on both sides. After each of the concentric geometric patterns was completed, the black weft yarns were left hanging as tassels. When a dancer wearing one of these robes moves, the whole garment sways with the body, and the motion of the dance is accentuated by the swinging of the tassels. Because of Samuel's interest in the Kotlean robes, many people in the northwestern Canadian coastal communities have begun to create the traditional weavings again.

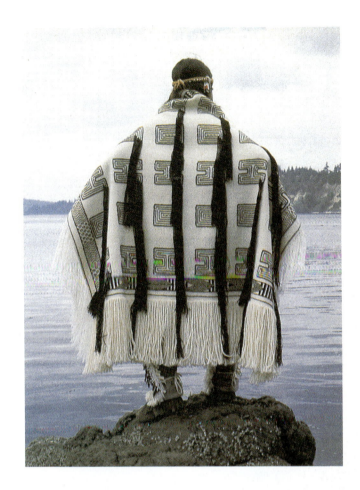

12.11 (below) Woman's coat, North or Northwest China, c. 1850–1900. Wool broadcloth, satin borders, embroidered in polychrome silks and gilt threads, length 29½ ins (75 cm). Metropolitan Museum of Art, New York. Gift of Dorothy A. Gordon and Virginia A. White, in memory of Madge Ashley, 1973.

12.12 (right) Cheryl Samuel, Kotlean robe, 1986. Handwoven wool. From Adams and Cheryl Samuel, *The Raven's Tail*, University of British Columbia Press, 1987.

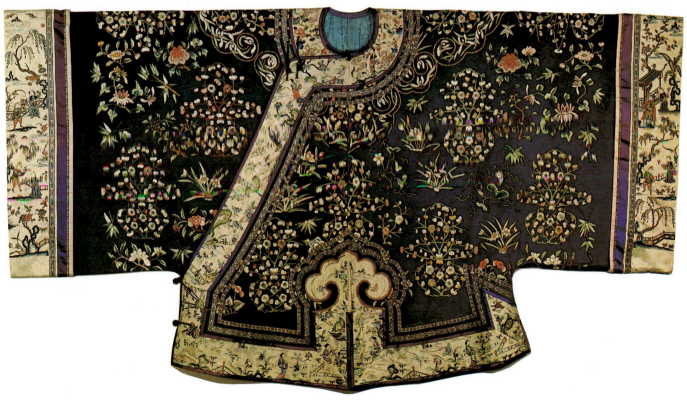

13
ARCHITECTURE

Architecture is similar to the other visual arts in aesthetic terms. Visually, buildings are developed from the same elements and principles of design as are other art forms. For example, architects work with form, texture, line, space, and color, using principles such as repetition, variety, and emphasis to unify the results visually. They are in effect designing large, three-dimensional works of art which have both external and internal contours. The insides and outsides of architecture each have their own aesthetic impact, as can be seen in the inner and outer views of an unusual round stone barn built by the Shaker spiritual community during the nineteenth century (**13.1** and **13.2**). Seen from outside, the stone exterior settles firmly into the land; seen from inside, the radiating wooden structures designed for cows and hay have a

13.1 Round Stone Dairy Barn, Hancock Shaker Village, Pittsfield, Massachusetts, 1826. Height 21 ft (6.4 m), diameter 270 ft (82.3 m).

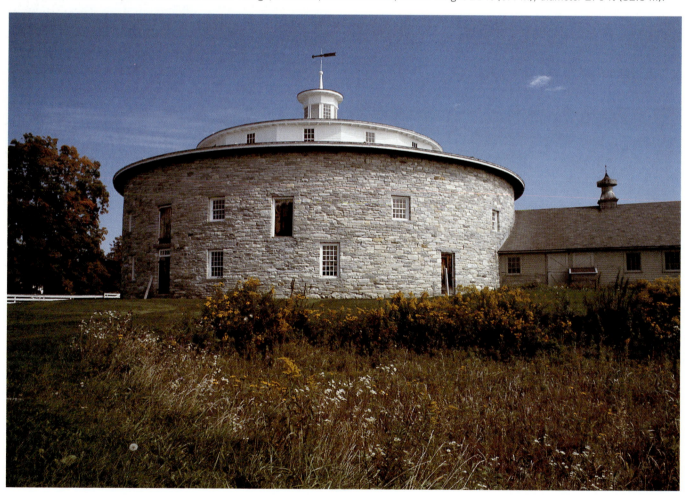

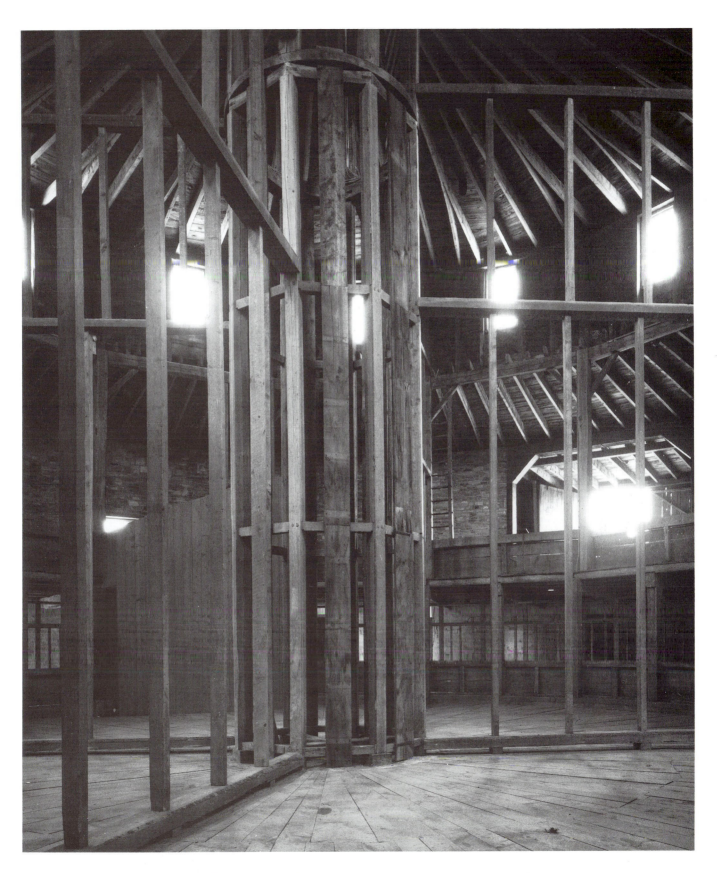

13.2 Interior of the Round Stone Dairy Barn, Pittsfield, Massachusetts.

surprising beauty and uplifting effect. Good three-dimensional functional works often demonstrate that what is elegantly logical and purposeful can also be visually beautiful.

Despite its aesthetic links to other visual arts, architecture is a much less direct medium of artistic expression. Professor Richard Swibold, architect and professor of art and architecture, observes:

> The architect's is not a one-on-one relationship between conception, design, detailing and construction, the way a painter's or sculptor's is. Once the architect has the idea—assuming all the other relationships with the client and community agencies and codes are acceptable—then the work is turned over to a contractor to build it. So the architect is cut off, unlike the painter or the sculptor, from that final artistic act of doing it himself. The work is performed usually by people he is never even going to meet. He might go to the construction site once a week to supervise and to look at problems and to evaluate quality work, but for the most part, all these craftsmen—sometimes hundreds or thousands on a really big project—are people he'll never have any personal contact with. So his artistic expression is the result of being able to communicate through drawings and details and written specifications and selecting materials. It relies on that ability to communicate specific intentions—and there are always misunderstandings. Therefore the completed work is almost always a compromise. It's not the pure result of a painter with his idea, his brilliance, completing it with the final brushstroke.[1]

The architect is an artist, but also a social servant. The designer of a house must think of the comfort and happiness of its inhabitants; the designer of university buildings must consider the teaching and learning environment from the point of view of teachers and students. Buildings must not fall down; roofs must not leak. Architects must undergo lengthy, specialized training; their creations must satisfy zoning regulations, building codes, planning committees. Projects must be commissioned and paid for by a client, satisfying the programmatic needs and tastes of the client; they must attempt to accommodate diverse and often contradicting social values. They are executed by contractors and developers, who in today's industrial societies are usually governed by short-range financial considerations.

Architecture must also concern itself with unique functional and structural considerations. These are explored in the pages that follow.

13.3 Kanna hut, Shiv Sadan, Uttar Pradesh, India.

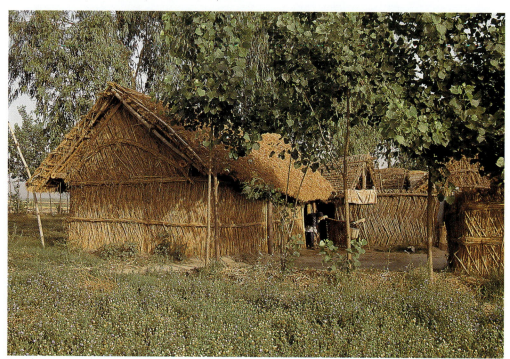

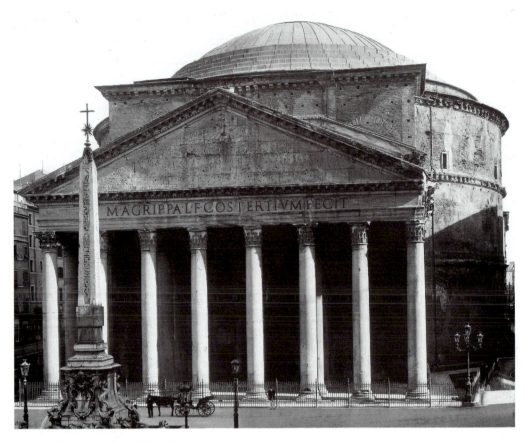

13.4 Pantheon, Rome, c. 118–28 AD.

FUNCTION

For comfort in living, we humans have always sought some kind of shelter from the elements. Not only have we clothed our bodies; we have also tried to create miniature environments that are warmer or cooler than our natural setting and that will provide shelter from the elements for ourselves and our possessions.

In the countryside along the Ganges River in India, the local canes and grasses are cleverly woven and bound together into comfortable dwellings that can be erected in two or three days (13.3). Although they may last only four or five years, they keep the rain out, keep inhabitants cooler in summer and warmer in winter, cost nothing, are minimally disruptive to the natural site, and are easily replaced when they fall apart or are swept away by floods. They are even lovely to look at, with their rhythmic repetition of woven lines.

In most cultures, however, there has been a desire to create larger and more permanent structures. Those designed for group assemblies—such as places of worship, houses of government, and commercial institutions—have required more elaborate technologies in order to stretch roofs over larger interior spaces and protect structures from wind, snow loads, earthquakes, and the like.

Where precipitation is infrequent, such as desert climates, buildings are often flat-roofed. In relatively warm but rainy climates, shallow domes or slightly pitched roofs are sufficient to shed rain. These were used in designing the Pantheon, an enormous second-century temple to the gods in Rome (13.4). The great circular **rotunda** is roofed by a hemispherical dome; the **portico** (column-supported porch) is covered by a slightly pitched roof from an earlier temple. When this kind of architecture was attempted farther north in Russia, it collapsed under the weight of snow. A snow-shedding solution devised in the twelfth century was the "onion" dome (actually intended to look like a

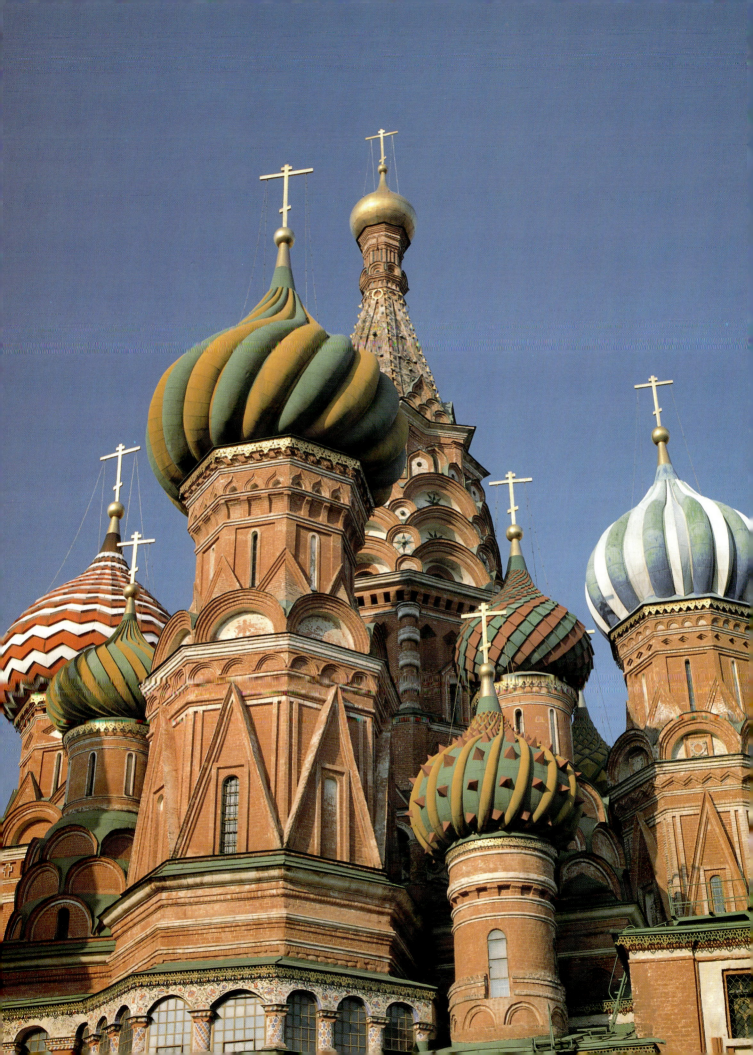

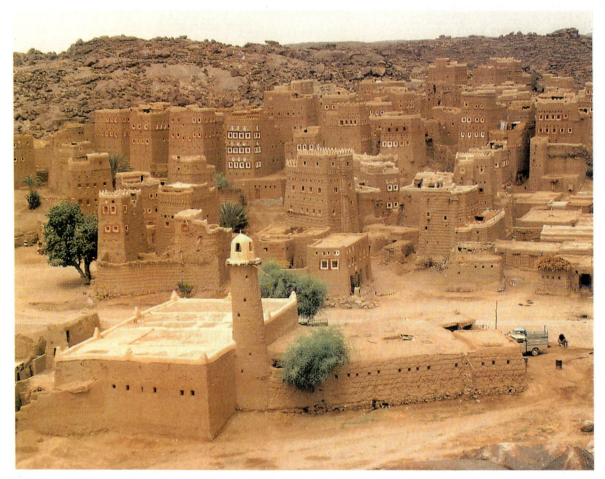

13.6 Suq al-Ainau, Barat region of the Yemen Arab Republic.

candle flame), which was used in fantastic varieties in St. Basil's Cathedral in Moscow (**13.5**).

Where environments are hot, people have often designed structures that are dark and cool inside, such as the thick-walled structures of Suq al-Ainau in Yemen (**13.6**) made of packed-mud bricks. In such cases, dark interiors are preferable to the heat. In temperate climates, structures may be more open to the outside air and light, as in the Wayfarers' Chapel by Frank Lloyd Wright (Jr.) in Palos Verdes, California (**13.7**). His illustrious father, the architect Frank Lloyd Wright, was highly enthusiastic about such uses of plate glass. In 1955, he wrote:

> By means of glass, open reaches of the ground may enter into the building and the building interior may reach out and associate with these vistas of the ground.

13.5 (opposite) Barma and Posnik, St. Basil's Cathedral, Moscow, 1555–61.

Perhaps more important than all beside, it is by way of glass that sunlit space as a reality becomes the most useful servant of the human spirit. Free living in air and sunlight aids cleanliness of form and idea.[2]

In cold climates, heating the interior for comfort creates new design considerations. Because heat rises rather than spreading out horizontally, buildings need to be more vertical, and their skins must keep cold out and heat in. With increasing concern about our impact on the environment, architects in cool climates are searching for better ways to capture the natural heat of the sun and prevent heat from leaking out of buildings. Ton Alberts' energy-efficient bank complex in Amsterdam (**13.8**) incorporates special design features such as solar energy panels on its ten towers, cutting energy use to only 25 percent of that normally used by buildings of the same size. The complex also features "flowforms," sculptures which channel and purify rainwater to water the plants in the building.

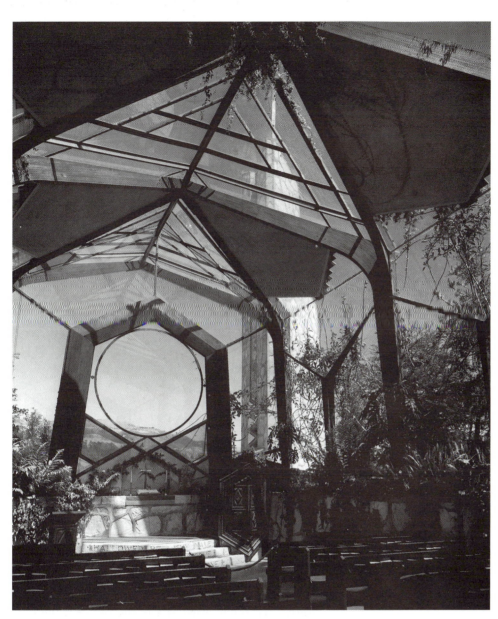

13.7 (left) Frank Lloyd Wright (Jr.),
Wayfarers' Chapel, Palos Verdes,
California, 1951.

13.8 (below) A. (Ton) Alberts and Van
Huut Architects, ten-building bank
complex, Amsterdam, Holland.

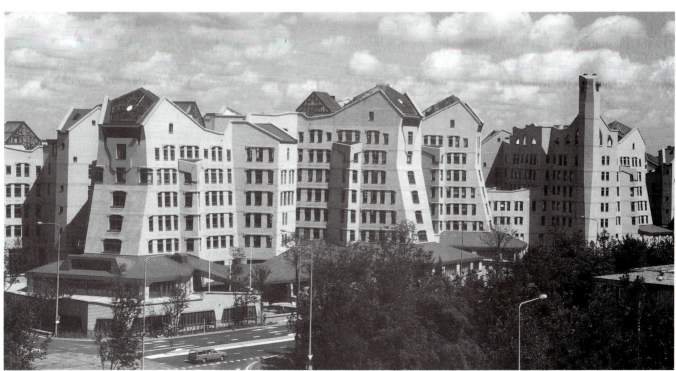

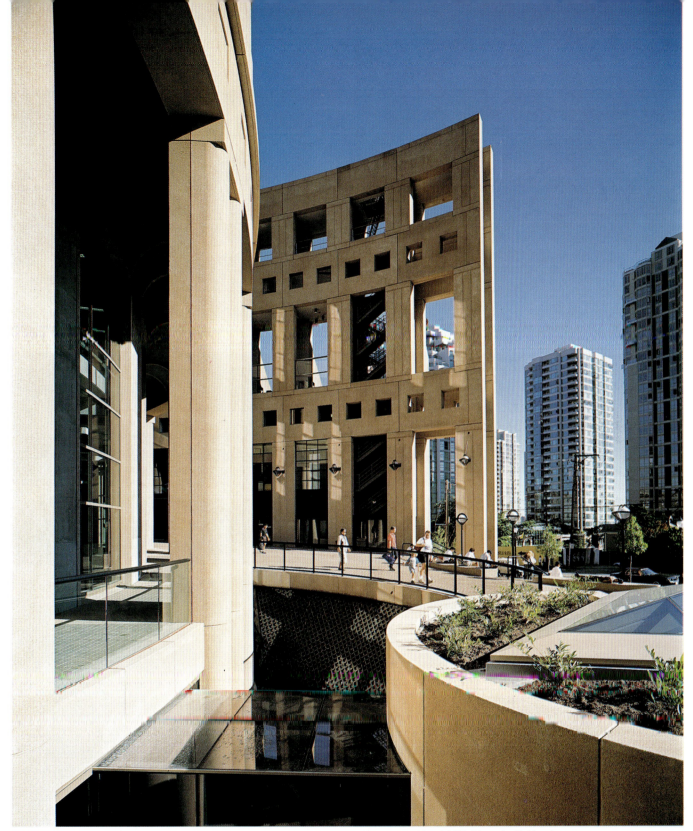

13.9 Moshe Safdie, Vancouver Library Square, Vancouver, British Columbia, opened May 1995. Photo by T. Hursley.

Architecture modulates people's movements as well as their climate, organizing their activities three-dimensionally. Ton Alberts's bank complex is designed with a curving interior walkway; in Moshe Safdie's Vancouver Library Square (**13.9**), pedestrians' movements are channeled through ramps, staircases, catwalks, and through the open gallery between the central library block and the outer structure.

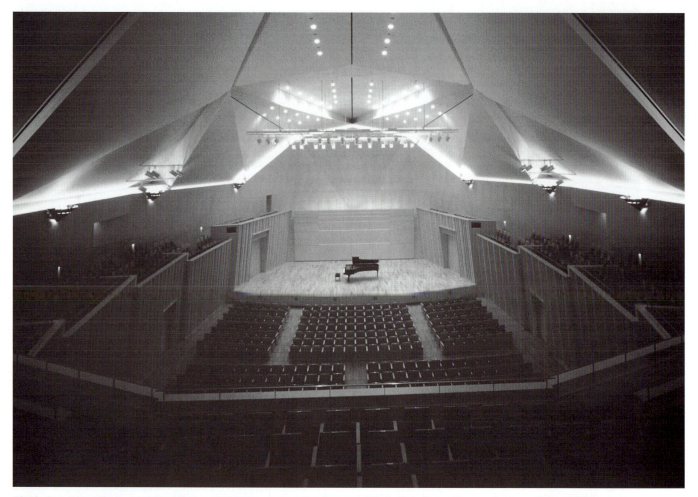

13.10 Fumihiko Maki, architect, interior of Kirishima International Concert Hall, Aira, Kagoshima prefecture, Japan, 1994. The leaf-shaped design has proved to be acoustically outstanding. It also unifies the stage with the rest of the auditorium, creating a satisfying bond between performers and their audience.

Sound as well as movement is modulated by building structures. **Acoustics**—the science of sound—becomes a major consideration in large open spaces. Sounds bounce off hard surfaces and reverberate within an enclosed space. To prevent this effect, soft materials may be used to help absorb sounds. In concert halls, acoustics are a major consideration in the design process. The Kirishima International Concert Hall in southern Japan (**13.10**) is shaped like a leaf, with an intimate relationship between the stage and the audience. Within this form, sound seems to expand. Triangular panels on the ceiling are designed to "smooth" the sound quality.

Architecture's functionality is not only physical but also psychological. Sacred structures, for example, create a devotional atmosphere based on the community's concept of the sacred. Christian cathedrals built in Europe during Gothic times, such as the one at Chartres (**13.11**), attempted to elevate worshippers above the difficulties of mundane existence. Their height was designed to lift one's awareness to the heavens, considered the abode of a distant, awe-inspiring God. Much of the community's resources were channeled into these great building projects, creating structures that tower far above the surrounding houses.

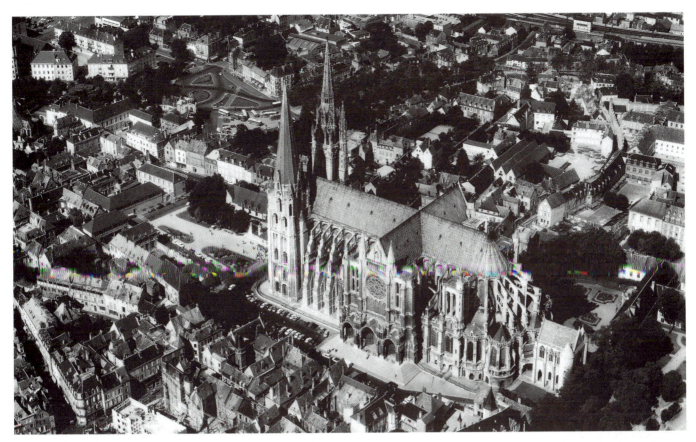

13.11 Chartres Cathedral, Chartres, France, constructed 1194–1220.

13.12 Ideal relationships of rooms within a house based on compass directions, according to Vastushastra.

Northwest	North	Northeast
Granary and cow shed	Treasury	Worship room
Dining room	Courtyard	Bathroom
Wardrobe, tools	Bedrooms	Kitchen
Southwest	South	Southeast

(West — left side, East — right side)

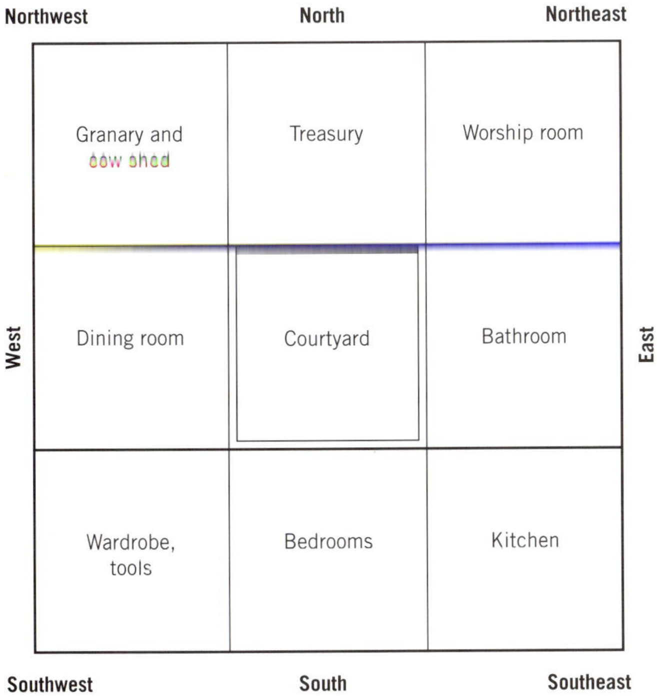

For thousands of years, Hindu Indian architects and artisans have been guided by laws of architecture referred to as Vastushastra. They are said to have been divinely given by Vishkarma, architect of the cosmos, and recorded by ancient sages. If these laws are applied in building, they will reportedly promote truth, beauty, harmony, peace, prosperity, and the health of the inhabitants. In Vastushastra, every detail—including geography of the land, placement of doors and drains, and the best time for building—is governed by cosmic relationships to planetary bodies, via compass directions (**13.12**). Some of India's great temples were built according to these elaborate guidelines. Plagued by mental and social problems prevalent in the world, some modern Indians are again attempting to build their homes according to Vastushastra as a way of restoring inner peace.

STRUCTURE

Architectural innovations have usually involved new materials or new ways of putting them together. Stone has been used since ancient times because of its great **compressive strength**—the ability to support pressure without breaking. In India, temples have been carved out of "living" rock as caves or as freestanding structures (**13.13**). The process is like subtractive sculpture—the boulder or mountain is treated as a giant block, and everything not needed is cut away. Metaphysically, their creation is thought to be a divinely inspired act that parallels the process by which material substance is created from ether. The resulting stonework is visually quite lively, expressing its infusion with the divine.

Stone and other materials with a certain compressive strength, such as bricks, have more often been used for what is termed **bearing wall construction**. One stone or flat block is stacked atop another in such a way that the wall thus formed will not topple; a roof may be placed over the walls by laying logs across the top. Earth that has adequate clay content to hold it together has often been shaped into blocks and then built up in this way. Using this technology, the Yemen packed-mud houses (**13.6**) could rise many stories high. Where wood is more plentiful than clayey soil, people have often flattened and notched the sides of logs and built them up as log cabins. Often some kind of mortar is used between the pieces of a bearing-wall construction building to hold the pieces together and fill the cracks. However, the mortarless stones of the famous sixteenth-century mountaintop Incan sanctuary, Machu Picchu (**13.14**), were so perfectly

13.13 The Dharmaraja Rath and other rock-cut temples, Mahabalipuram, India, 625–74 AD.

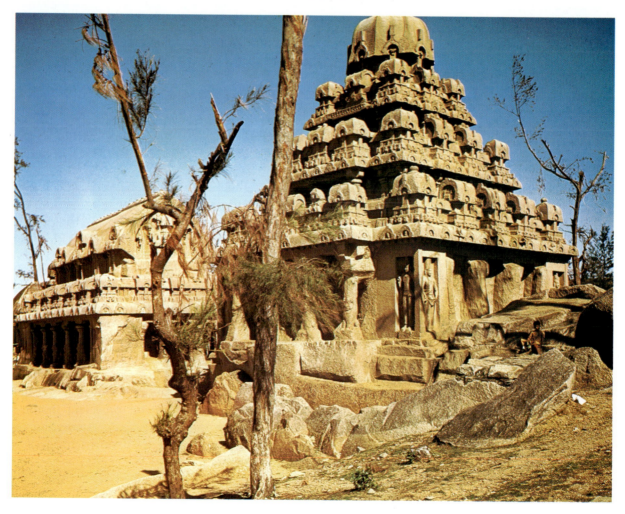

cut and fitted together that centuries later in many places a knife cannot be slipped between them.

One of the limitations of bearing-wall construction is that walls must be very solid, creating imposing separations between living spaces. A more open form of construction is allowed with **post and lintel construction** (13.15) which uses strong columns (posts) to support beams (lintels) across which the roofing materials are laid. The horizontal lintel helps to stabilize the posts as well, and the space beneath can serve as an opening, whether door, window, or room. Stone buildings made by this system may be held together by gravity; wooden post and lintel arrangements require some means of notching or bolting the horizontal and vertical parts together.

The Classical Greek architects became so confident in their development of post and lintel construction that they could use graceful refinements solely for the sake of visual proportion, such as posts that tapered toward the top. Sometimes they even used columns carved as goddesses bearing the lintels on their heads, as in the Erechtheum in Athens (13.16). The structures originally designed for wooden temples (partly to keep water from seeping into pillars and

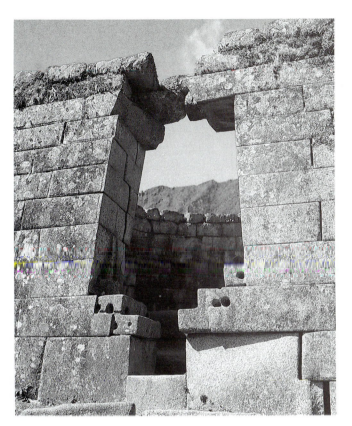

13.14 Stonework detail, Machu Picchu, Peru, c. 1500.

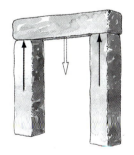

13.15 Post-and-lintel construction.

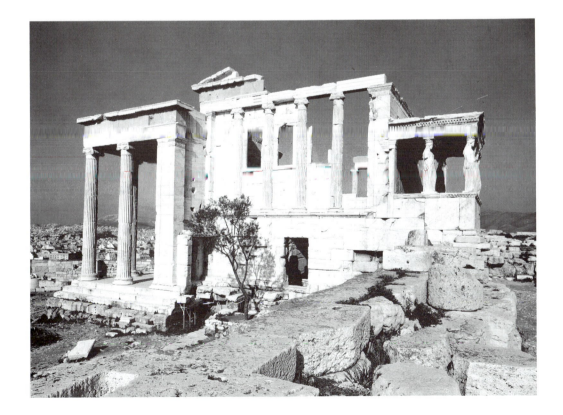

13.16 Erechtheum, Athens, 421–405 BC.

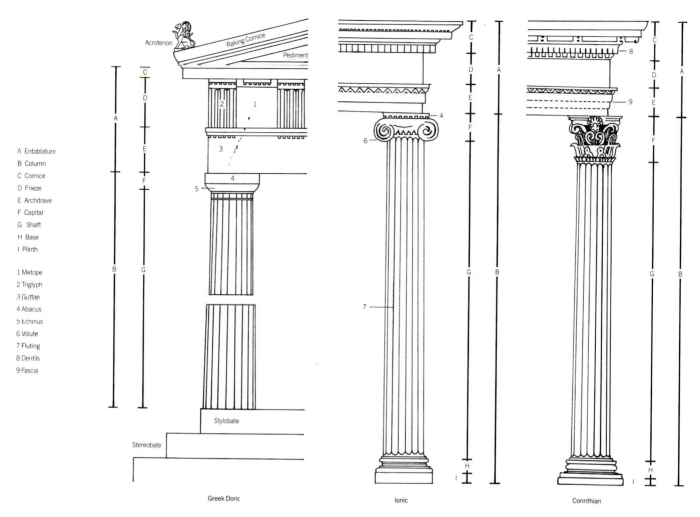

A Entablature
B Column
C Cornice
D Frieze
E Architrave
F Capital
G Shaft
H Base
I Plinth

1 Metope
2 Triglyph
3 Guttae
4 Abacus
5 Echinus
6 Volute
7 Fluting
8 Dentils
9 Fascia

Acroterion · Raking Cornice · Pediment · Stylobate · Stereobate · Greek Doric · Ionic · Corinthian

13.17 The Greek orders.

foundation) were translated into stone as elaborate sequences of parts known as the "Greek orders" (**13.17**). These started with a solid masonry foundation that spreads out the weight of the structure and keeps the building from settling. Upon this sat the **stylobate**, or base. Atop this were columns, carved vertically with lines to conduct rainwater downward, and topped by a **capital** on which the lintel rested. Next came the **entablature** (the elaborated lintel), and atop that, the **pediment**, the slightly pitched triangular roof support at the end of the temple. The simplest style in the Greek orders was the **Doric**. It is thought that it was derived from the flat clay patty and tile that were used atop wooden columns to protect them from rain. More elaborate versions were the scrolled **Ionic** and the **Corinthian**, which had capitals carved to look like

acanthus leaves pressed outward by the weight of the lintel.

A major development that appeared in Roman architecture was the **arch** (**13.18**). Crafted of stone by master stonemasons, arches were made of **voussoirs**. These are wedged-shaped stones cut to taper toward the inside of the curve. They are propped up with scaffolding until the **keystone** at the top is set in place. The counterpressure they then exert on each other supports the arch, and weight is transferred downward onto the posts. The Romans used the arch to construct an elaborate system of aqueducts, much of which still stands (**13.19**). They also developed ways of combining arches to span broad interior spaces. These three-dimensional arches were widely used in Roman, Byzantine, Romanesque, and Gothic architecture

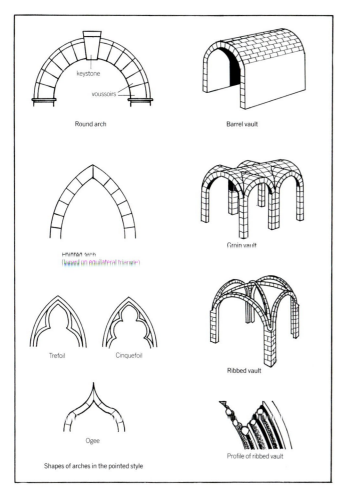

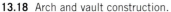

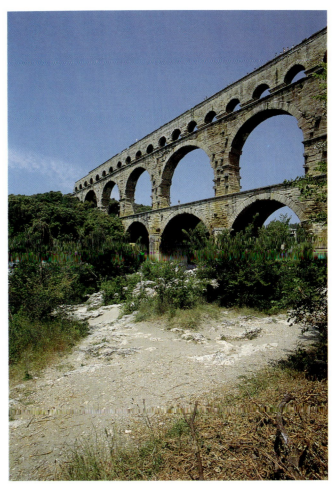

13.18 Arch and vault construction.

13.19 The Pont du Gard, Nîmes, France.

(styles that are explored historically in Chapter 15). They constituted the low tensile strength of stone, which makes it difficult to span a broad area with a single stone beam without its breaking of its own weight; in post and lintel construction the beam must be supported at frequent intervals by posts.

The desire to open greater areas as public spaces without obstructive columns led to elaborations of arch technology. Tunnel-like **barrel vaults** were made of rows of round arches, **groin vaults** were made of intersecting barrel vaults, and **pointed arches** intersected in a sharp angle. Gothic cathedral architects perfected systems of **ribbed vaulting** that carried most of the weight of an arch, allowing lighter materials to be used for the areas between. Seen from within, these cathedrals were symphonies of soaring arched lines and spaces, rhythmically repeated above and to either side of a long central hall, or nave (13.20).

Because arched vaults transferred pressure not just downward but also outward, the vertical structure had to be either very thick or else firmly braced to keep the sides from being pushed apart. To avoid overly massive walls, a Gothic solution was to engineer systems that gradually transferred lateral pressure to **flying buttresses** (13.21–22) external to the interior space. Figure 13.21 is an overhead view of some of the flying buttresses surrounding Notre Dame Cathedral. It reveals the slender ribs and vaults outside the building, braced against solid masonry piers. Note that each of the piers is capped with a spire that makes it appear less bulky.

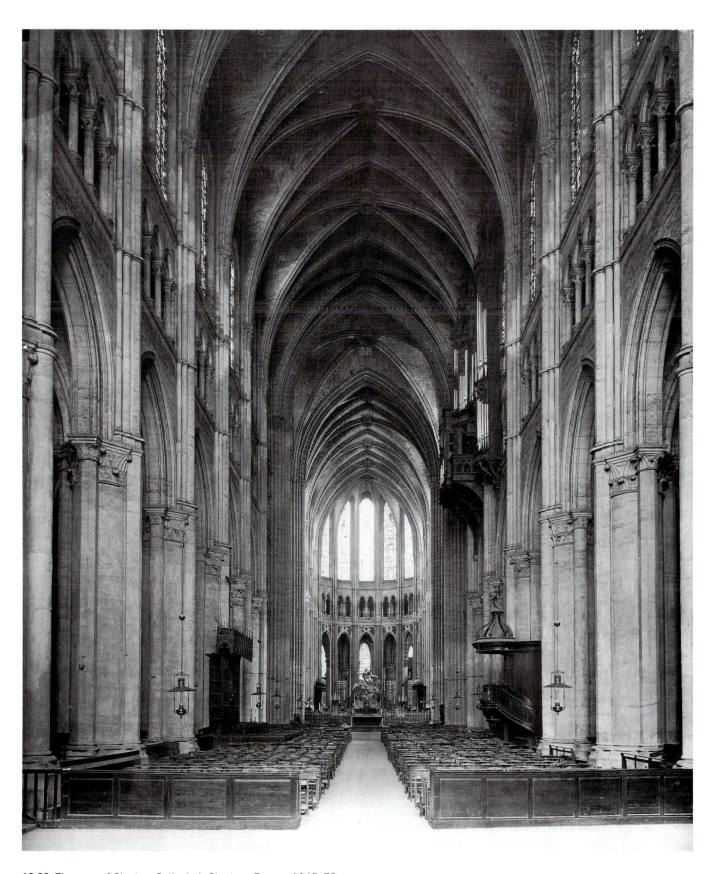

13.20 The nave of Chartres Cathedral, Chartres, France, 1145–70.

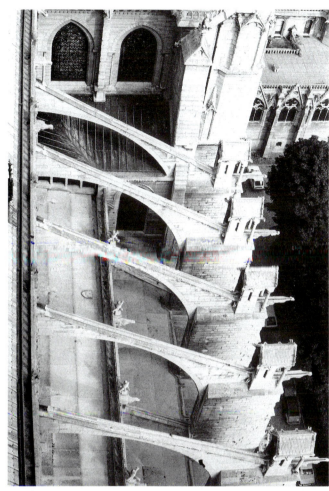

13.21 Flying buttresses on the side of Notre Dame Cathedral, Paris, 1163–1250.

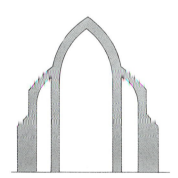

13.22 Flying buttresses.

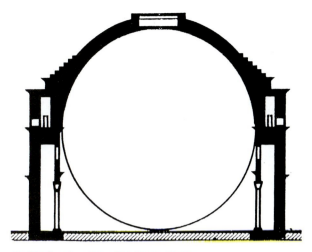

13.23 Section of the Pantheon, Rome.

When an arch is rotated through 360 degrees, the result is a **dome**. The immense and impressive dome of the Pantheon in Rome (also known as the Santa Maria Rotunda since it was converted into a Christian church in the seventh century) was for its time a marvel of engineering and building skills, with **coffers** (sunken panels) used to diminish the weight of the massive concrete roof, and a great oculus—"the eye of heaven"—for natural illumination (**13.26** on page 382). Even today, we do not fully understand the structural principles that have allowed the second-century temple to remain intact to the present. But it is known that the concrete mixture the Romans invented hardened into a highly coherent rigid structure, that the width of the drum (the vertical walls) is equal to the height of the dome above, as indicated in Figure **13.23** (so we can suspect some kind of intricate mathematical balance), and that an impressive series of arches is embedded in the concrete walls of the drum to help support the dome and counteract any possible outward-spreading pressure of the dome. In Byzantine architecture, the lateral thrust of the dome was frequently transferred to a lower-ceilinged surrounding aisle, as seen in this cross-section of a Byzantine church (**13.27** on page 383).

HASSAN FATHY
on INDIGENOUS ARCHITECTURAL INGENUITY

The Egyptian architect, Hassan Fathy (1900–89), attempted to solve his country's needs for rural housing for the poor by working with materials and technologies already at hand. Given the opportunity to design an entire relocated village for 7000 peasants, New Gourna, Fathy hired two masons from Aswan to carry out the most challenging aspect of building: roofing. Using nothing but adzes and their bare hands to set in mud bricks baked with extra straw for lightness, they quickly created marvelous vaulted roofs (**13.24–13.25**) in only a day and a half per room. In his book *Architecture for the Poor*, Fathy described the great skill with which they worked, despite the material simplicity of their means:

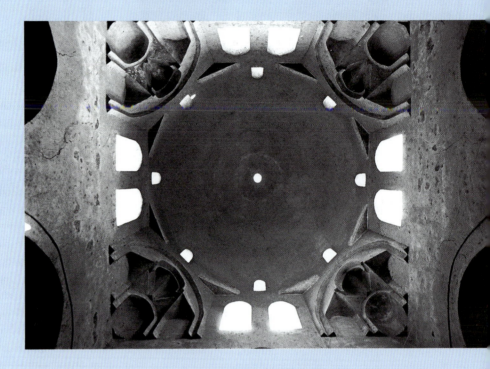

"The masons laid a couple of planks across the side walls, got up on them, took up handfuls of mud, and roughly outlined an arch by plastering the mud onto the end wall. They used no measure or instrument, but by eye alone traced a perfect parabola, with its ends upon the side walls.

Next, one at each side, they began to lay the bricks. The first brick was stood on its end on the side wall, the grooved face flat against the mud plaster of the end wall, and hammered well into this plaster. Then the mason took some mud and against the foot of this brick made a little wedge-shaped packing, so that the next course would lean slightly towards the end wall instead of standing up straight. In order to break the line of the joints between the bricks the second course started with a half-brick, on the top end of which stood a whole brick. If the joints are in a straight line, the strength of the vault is reduced and it may collapse. As they built each completed course, the masons were careful to insert dry packing such as stones or broken pottery in the gaps between the bricks. It is most important that no mud mortar be put between the ends of the bricks in each course, for mud can shrink by up to 37 per cent in volume, and such shrinkage will seriously distort the parabola, so that the vault may collapse . . .

At this stage the nascent vault was six brick-thicknesses long at the bottom and only one brick-thickness long at the top, so that it appeared to be leaning at a considerable angle against the end wall. Thus is presented an inclined face to lay the succeeding courses

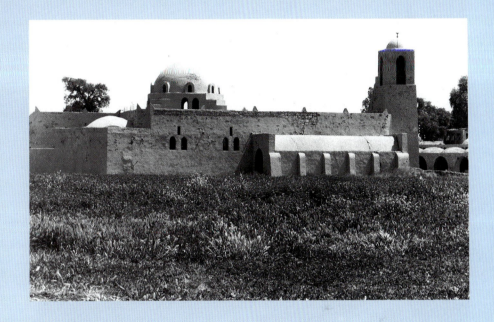

13.24 (left) and **13.25** Hassan Fathy, architect, Mosque in New Gourna, Egypt. Interior (left), looking up into the dome. Courtesy of the Aga Khan Award for Architecture, Geneva.

upon, so that the bricks would have plenty of support.

Thus the whole vault could be built straight out in the air, with no support or centering, with no instrument, with no drawn plan; there were just two masons standing on a plank and a boy underneath tossing up the bricks, which the masons caught dexterously in the air, then casually placed on the mud and tapped home with their adzes. It was so unbelievably simple. They worked rapidly and unconcernedly, with never a thought that what they were doing was quite

a remarkable work of engineering, for these masons were working according to the laws of statics and the science of the resistance of materials with extraordinary intuitive understanding. Indeed, to span three meters in mud brick is as great a technical feat as spanning thirty meters in concrete.

Engineers and architects concerned with cheap ways of building for the masses had devised all sorts of complicated methods for constructing vaults and domes. Their problem was to keep the components in place until the

structure was completed, and their solutions had ranged from odd-shaped bricks like bits of three-dimensional jigsaw puzzles, through every variety of scaffolding, to the extreme expedient of blowing up a large balloon in the shape of the required dome and spraying concrete onto that. But my builders needed nothing but an adze and a pair of hands."[3]

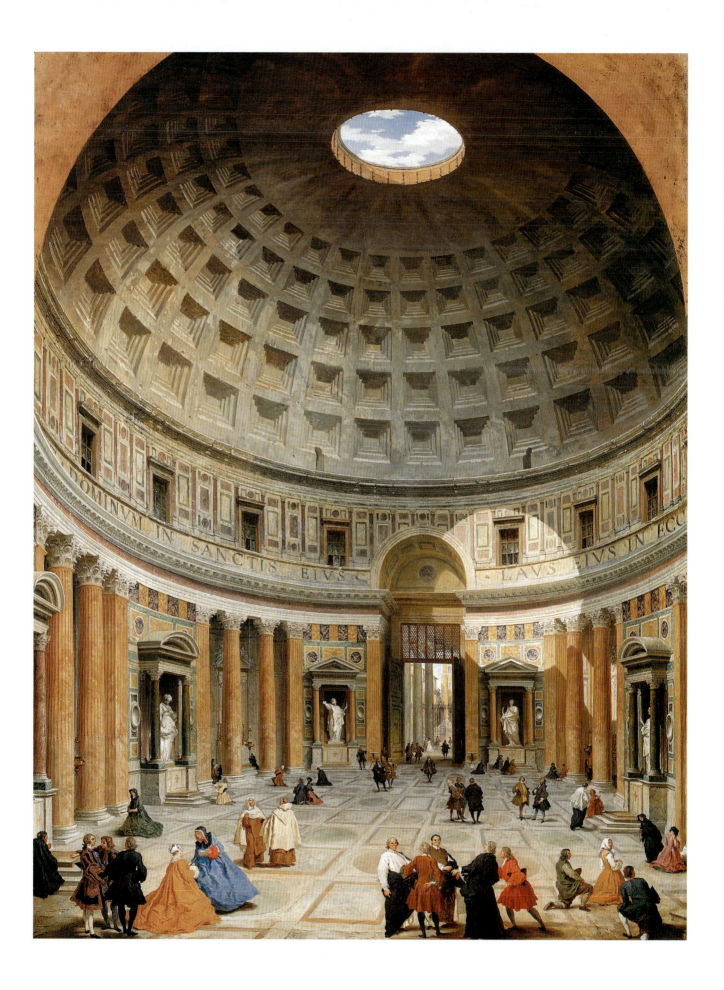

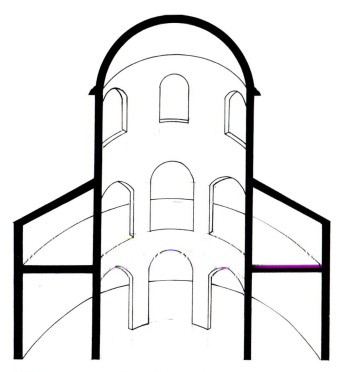

13.27 Cross-section of Byzantine church.

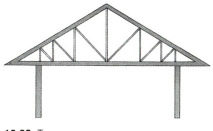

13.28 Truss.

Another approach is **frame construction**. In wood-framed buildings, pieces of wood are attached at right angles to each other and braced at the top with triangular **trusses** (such as the one shown in **13.28**). Initially, heavy weight-bearing timbers were used for posts and space-spanning floor and ceiling beams in such structures. But the development of mass-produced nails and sturdy but relatively lightweight milled boards in 2 × 4-inch (10-cm) widths allowed the invention, in the early nineteenth century, of **balloon-frame construction** (**13.29**). In such a frame, the thin vertical, horizontal, and diagonal roofing boards are closely spaced and nailed together. Stresses are borne by the multi-part frame as a whole rather than by individual posts and beams. The "skin" placed over the frame, such as windows and clapboards, plays no structural role. This system is still predominant in the building of individual houses in areas such as the United States, where wood is fairly plentiful.

In the nineteenth century, industrialization revo-

lutionized architecture. It was found that iron had great tensile strength, with relatively little weight, and could be wrought or cast into columns, beams, trusses, and arches which could be quickly joined into huge skeletons with nothing but glass between the bones. This technology permitted new uses for architecture, and there followed a spate of building great arcades for new kinds of public gatherings, such as trade expositions. The most celebrated of these early iron-skeleton buildings was Joseph Paxton's Crystal Palace (2.63). Built in London for the Great Exhibition of 1851, it was the world's largest building, covering an area of 770,000 square feet (71,535 sq m). All of its parts were prefabricated, in standardized repeating units. The entire thing was put up by 2000 workers in three months, and then dismantled after the six-month exhibition. The bits were re-used to build a similar, even larger structure (which accidently burned down in 1936). The "palace" was cleverly engineered not only for speed of construction but also for such functional considerations as shedding of water. The structural columns and beams doubled as a rainwater-conducting system; the structure was entirely watertight.

13.29 Balloon-frame construction.

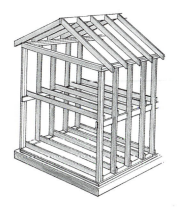

13.26 (opposite) Giovanni Paolo Pannini, *Interior of the Pantheon*, c. 1740. Oil on canvas, 4 ft 2½ in (1.28 m) high; 3 ft 3 in (0.99 m) wide. National Gallery of Art, Washington, D.C. Samuel H. Kress Collection.

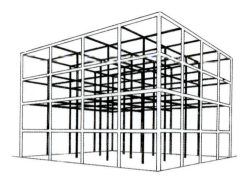

13.30 Steel-frame skyscraper.

The metal skeleton method was developed into steel-frame skyscrapers (**13.30**). As in downtown Dallas (**13.31**), the urban landscape of many cities was transformed during the twentieth century into clusters of these structures. With real estate extremely expensive in urban areas, the only economically feasible direction for expansion was upward. Vertical expansion became possible only through the development of steel and steel-reinforced concrete frameworks capable of supporting tremendous loads, and of elevators to lift people through the numerous floors. With these frameworks, walls became non-load-bearing curtains and could be made entirely of glass. Interiors also became broad-spanned open spaces within which partitioning could be arranged and moved about according to changing interior needs, rather than needing to support the upper structure.

The steel and concrete framework was mated with an austere approach to design which evolved in the 1920s—the so-called **International Modern Style**. Buildings were constructed along purely functional lines, with largely glass exterior walls, flat roofs, a lack of ornamentation except for horizontal bands defining floors, and symmetrical modular grids. The visual effect of these structures is that of space-filled volume

13.31 The Dallas skyline.

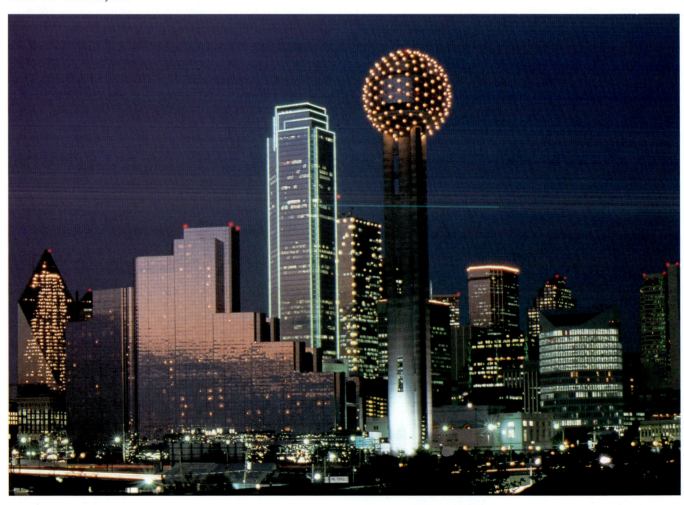

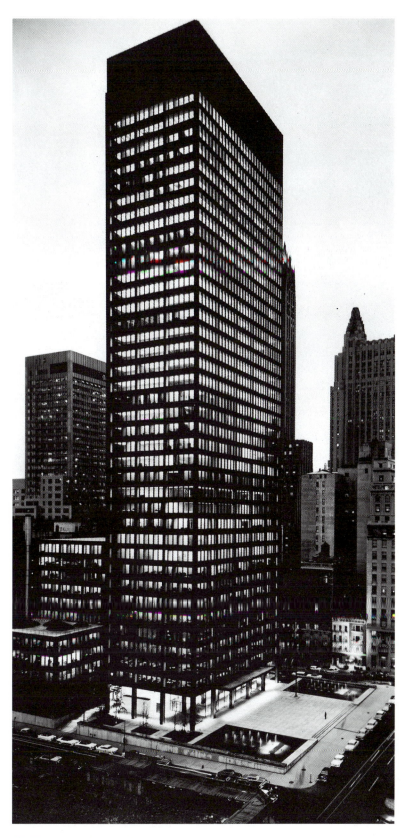

13.32 Ludwig Mies van der Rohe and Philip Johnson, Seagram Building, New York, 1956–58.

rather than the solid mass associated with earlier architectural forms.

The style was hailed as fresh and honest architecture for the machine age. It was even thought that the new approach to design would liberate humanity itself. The Swiss architect Le Corbusier wrote enthusiastically about the emancipating potential of a new tobacco factory:

> The sheer facades of the building, bright glass and gray metal, rise up . . . against the sky. . . . Everything is open to the outside. And this is of enormous significance to all those who are working, on all eight floors *inside.* The Van Nelle tobacco factory in Rotterdam, a creation of the modern age, has removed all the former connotations of despair from the word 'proletarian.'[4]

Mies van der Rohe and Philip Johnson's Seagram Building (**13.32**) in New York is a classic example of the now familiar International Style and perhaps its most successful product, with its elegant bronze details and perfect proportions. A large open area has been left beyond the sidewalk for a broad walkway and fountains, allowing a sense of spaciousness and graciousness in the heart of the crowded urban scene. Many large cities now require that skyscrapers be set back from the sidewalk to allow sun to penetrate into the canyons between tall buildings.

Philip Johnson also applied the International Style to the project of designing his own house—a rectangular metal-framed house with glass infill panels (**13.33**). The structure and walls of the house are actually almost invisible; what one sees from within and without are the surrounding trees and vegetation, the pond with fantasy pavilion below, and the valley in the distance. Most of us must use opaque walls and curtained windows to insure our treasured privacy; Johnson's personal life and private paradise are shielded from the curious by a high, dry-stone wall along the road.

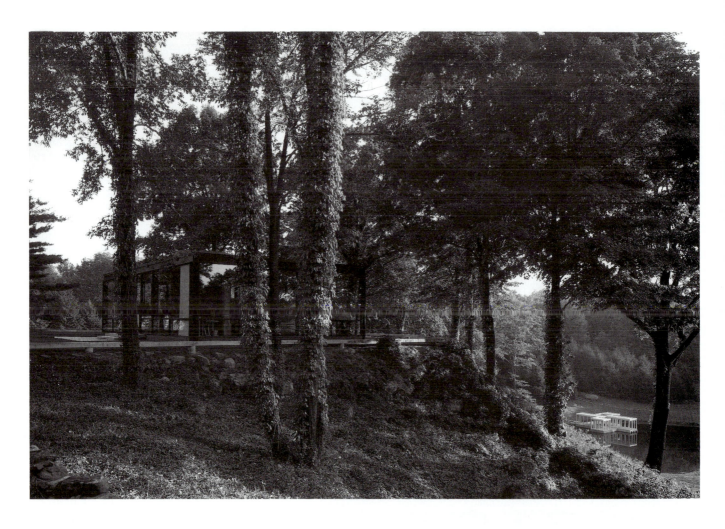

13.33 (above) Philip Johnson, Johnson House, New Canaan, Connecticut, 1949. Ezra Stoller © Esto.

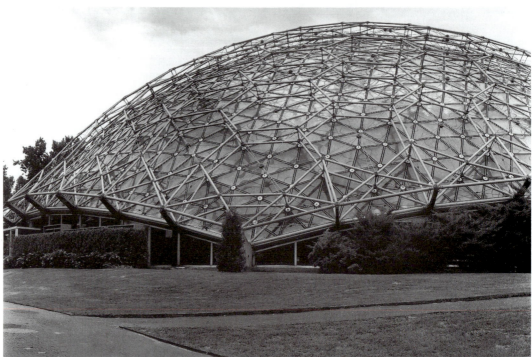

13.34 (right) R. Buckminster Fuller, United States Pavilion, Expo '67 geodesic dome. Photogaph © Wayne Andrews/Esto.

Another unique use of metal to frame a structure with non-bearing walls was developed by the pioneering genius of R. Buckminster Fuller. His brilliant investigations into natural structures led him to develop buildings on entirely different principles from any seen before. He explained:

> I often hear it said that architects build buildings out of materials. I point out to architectural students that they do not do that at all. That kind of definition dates back to the era of men's thinking of matter as solid. I tell architectural students that what they do is to organize the assemblage of visible modular structures out of sub-visible modular structures. Nature itself, at the chemical level, does the prime structuring. If the patterning attempted by the architect is not inherently associative within the local regenerative dynamics of chemical structure, his buildings will collapse. The principles governing structure not only prescribe what man can put together, but they are operative at the molecular level, at the atomic level, and at the nuclear level. They are also operative in each of man's life cells and throughout principles of structure in the starry heavens. They are universal, they are purely mathematical, weightless [5]

Fuller's **geodesic dome** is a very lightweight but sturdy metal framework in which the bracing strength of triangles is organized into a dome that needs no other support. Such a dome can top a structure or can be the entire structure itself, as in the United States Pavilion for the 1967 World's Fair (**13.34**). Any flat sheet material such as wood, metal, plastic, or glass can be cut into triangles and attached to the frame as a weatherproof skin.

Reinforced concrete—concrete that is internally strengthened with metal rods or mesh—has been widely used in twentieth-century architecture. In a post-and-lintel arrangement, reinforced concrete beams can be **cantilevered** (**13.35**)—projected beyond supporting posts—if anchored into those posts. Frank Lloyd Wright's Fallingwater (3.44) cantilevers large terraces out over the falls. In addition to flat slabs, reinforced concrete can also be used to create articulated freeform structures unlike any seen before. Italian post-war architectural engineer Pierre Luigi Nervi demonstrated that precast, reinforced concrete sections could be used in ways that were beautiful as well as functional. He applied this aesthetic sensitivity even to aircraft hangars (**13.36**). The famous Sydney Opera House (**13.37**), designed by Danish architect Jorn Utzon, features roof forms resembling ships' sails which cover a complex of separate concert halls and restaurants.

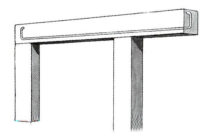

13.35 Cantilever of steel-reinforced concrete.

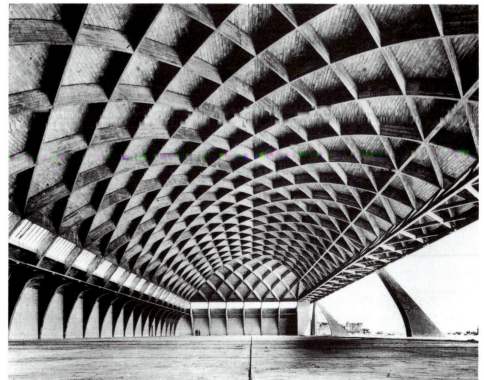

13.36 Pierre Luigi Nervi, aircraft hangar at Orbello, Italy, 1939–40.

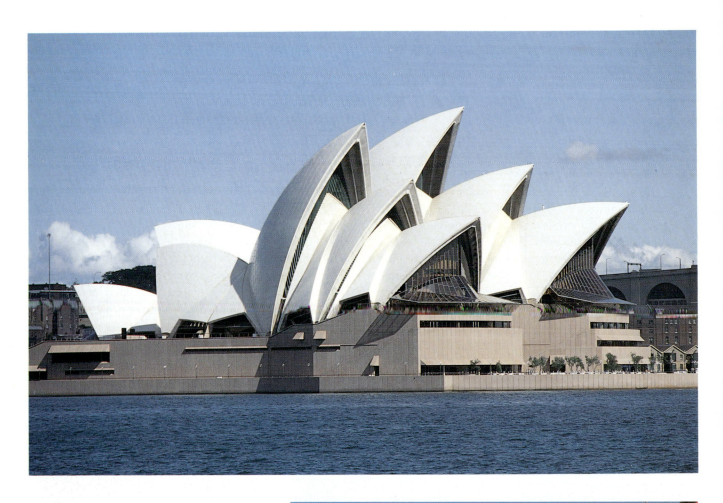

13.37 Jorn Utzon, Sydney Opera House, Australia, 1956–73.

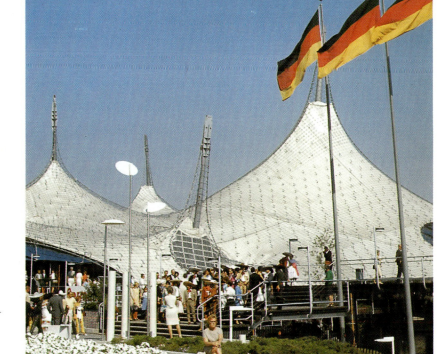

13.38 Drawing of suspended structure.

13.39 Frei Otto, German Pavilion, Montreal, 1967.

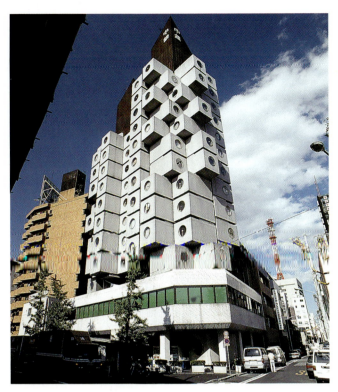

13.40 Kisho Kurokawa, Nakagin Capsule Building, Tokyo, 1972.

Whereas such structures have to support tremendous **compressive** (downward-pressing) loads without buckling, the German architect Frei Otto envisioned extremely light structures (**13.38**) where the primary stress would be **tensile** (pulling). Cables are strung under tension among a few anchored masts to support lightweight curving fabric membranes, as in the German Pavilion in Montreal (**13.39**). Such structures can be easily altered or moved, as needs change; they lack the monumentality and permanence long assumed necessary in public buildings.

There have also been attempts to use modern factory production-line technologies to pre-package structures and thus cut down on their cost. A common approach is **modular construction**. Using standard dimensions with electrical and plumbing connections sandwiched into the walls, buildings can be quickly assembled on-site from factory-made components. In an extreme example of this technology, Kisho Kurokawa created the Nakagin Capsule Building in Tokyo (**13.40**) from a series of stackable prefabricated rooms, each a complete dwelling. Each capsule is only 8 × 12 feet (2.43 × 3.65 m), but includes a bathroom, double bed, desk with typewriter, chair, tape deck, clock radio, storage space, kitchen, and a heating,

ventilation, and air conditioning unit. The capsules form a "community" connected to a central water, oxygen, and power supply.

Now that many building technologies are available to support architects' visions, there has been a backlash against strictly functional industrial construction and against the repetitive use of look-alike glass boxes. In what is called **post-modern** architecture, buildings tend to be more expressive and individual, and, some say, less elitist. There is no one look that defines them all. Some are sensual and decorative, some refer back to historical styles, some are lively and playful. Philip Johnson's shift from International Style

13.41 Philip Johnson and John Burgee, AT&T Building, New York, 1978–84.

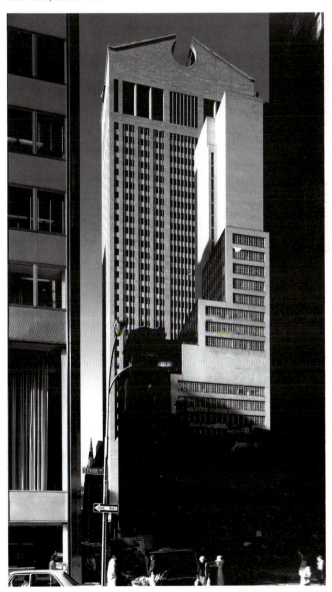

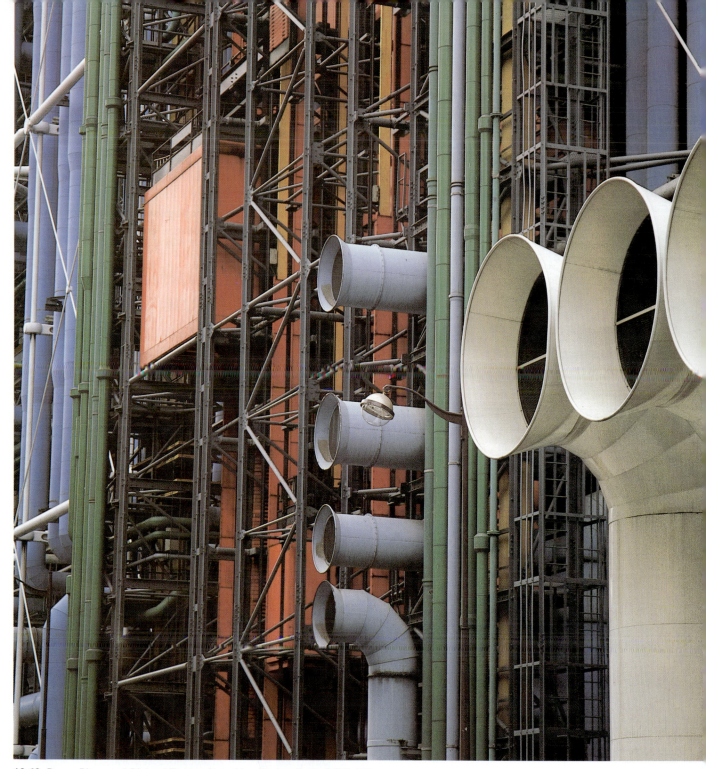

13.42 Renzo Piano and Richard Rogers, Pompidou Center, Paris, 1971–78.

buildings to a pastiche of historical references in the American Telephone and Telegraph Building (13.41) is an example of this change. Many critics object that post-modern architecture is neither structurally inventive nor aesthetically serious.

A more industrial, high-tech approach to architecture persists, though in forms that have broken out of the International Style mold. One of the most extreme examples of **high-tech revival** is the Pompidou Center in Paris (13.42) designed by Renzo Piano and Richard Rogers. Designed to house a modern art museum, a public library, exhibition space, and an audio-visual center, it is conceived as an upbeat public gathering place rather than an austere cultural center. Rogers explains its oil refinery appearance: "We wanted it to be fun and easy to read."[6] He and Piano put its mechanical services and functional supports on the outside and color coded them. Water pipes were

painted green, electrical ducts yellow, and air conditioning pipes blue. To carry people from one floor to another, they also put the elevator on the outside—a large glass caterpillar that slinks its way up the building and offers a superb view across Paris. Although some critics have condemned the ugliness and high cost of heating and cooling this "building turned inside-out," it is indeed popular with the people. Some 30,000 Parisians and tourists visit it every day, more than go to the Eiffel Tower and the Louvre put together.

New architectural trends have always had their critics. At the end of the nineteenth century, when the Eiffel Tower was being built, artists who did not like it expressed their distaste by sitting in cafés with their backs to the tower. Architects, artists, and writers wrote a petition against the tower, considering it decadent as well as threatening to their own established prestige. At the turn of the twentieth century and now

near the dawn of the twenty-first century, styles have been rapidly changing in an accelerated search for novelty and instant impact. Examples of **deconstructionist** architecture seem deliberately anarchical, with explosive arrangements of colliding asymmetrical forms. They are symptomatic of the contemporary breakdown of social structures and the lack of equilibrium in the world. They are meeting with opposition wherever they arise. Resistance to a proposed deconstructionist addition to the Victoria and Albert Museum in London (**13.43**) has been fierce. The former editor of *The Times* of London referred to it as "a disaster for the Victoria and Albert Museum in particular and for civilization in general. What is deconstructionism? It is the tearing down of the old [Enlightenment] culture of scholarship, truth, beauty, reason and order."[7] Others support the creative energy of change, wherever it may lead.

13.43 Daniel Liebeskind, model for the addition to the Victoria and Albert Museum, London. Photo by Agence France-Presse.

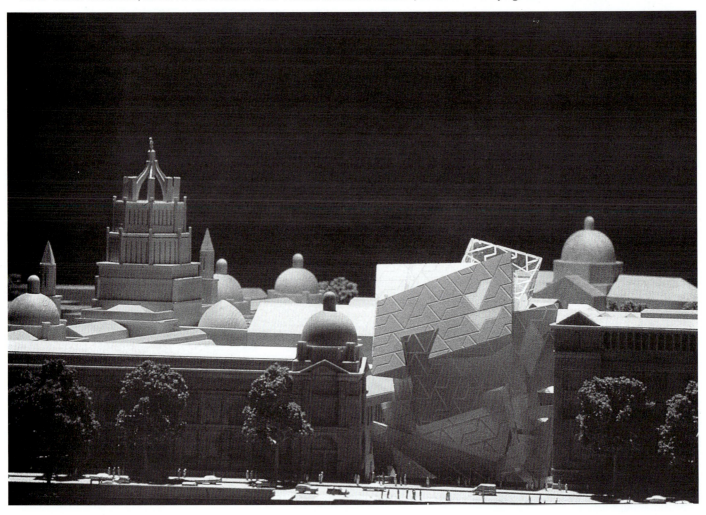

ALVAR AALTO
on HUMANIZING ARCHITECTURE

At a time when the impersonal technology of the International Style was predominant, Finnish architect Alvar Aalto (1898–1976) earned global recognition for the warmth and personality of his buildings. They ranged from family homes to total industrial complexes, complete with housing for employees. Aalto was deeply influenced by the architectural traditions of his native Finland, but his designs were highly original. Though extremely varied, they all tended to soften the mechanistic aspects of modern architecture in favor of honoring human needs and using organic materials. His methods of solving architectural problems were a combination of empirical research, original but logical thought, and sheer intuition (**13.44**). Aalto carried on his own research into the special needs of very weak bedridden patients at a sanatorium.

"The experiment showed the room must be different from an ordinary room. This difference can be explained thus. The ordinary room is a room for a vertical person; a patient's room is a room for a horizontal human being, and colors, lighting, heating, and so on must be designed with that in mind.

Practically, this fact means that the ceiling should be darker, with an especially selected color suitable to be the only view of the reclining patient for weeks and weeks. The artificial light cannot come from an ordinary ceiling fixture, but the principal center of light should be beyond the angle of vision of the patient . . . Ceiling radiators were used but in a way which threw the heat mainly at the foot of the bed so that the head of the patient was outside the direct heat rays. The location of the windows and doors likewise took into account the patient's position . . .

These are only a few illustrations from an experimental room at the sanatorium, and they are here mentioned merely as examples of architectural methods, which always are a combination of technical, physical, and psychological phenomena, never any one of them alone. Technical functionalism is correct only if enlarged to cover even the psychophysical field. That is the only way to humanize architecture."[8]

"When I have to resolve an architectural problem I find myself, first of all and without exception, halted by the thought of its realization. What is needed is a sort of '3 a.m. courage,' probably due to the difficulties arising from the weighty importance of the different elements at the moment of conception. The social, human, technical and economic requirements which present themselves side-by-side with the psychological factors and concern each individual and each group, their rhythm and internal friction, are so numerous that they form an entanglement, not lending itself to the methods of rational resolution. The resultant complexity prevents the basic architectural idea from taking shape.

In such cases I work in a completely irrational way. For a while I forget the whole entanglement of problems, clear it from my mind, and occupy myself with something which can best be described as abstract art. I start designing, allowing myself to be guided purely by instinct—and, suddenly, the basic concept is there, a point of departure which gathers together the different, often contradictory, elements which I named above, and puts them in harmony . . .

Whilst designing the library for the town of Viipuri, . . . I spent a long time making childlike drawings representing an imaginary mountain with different shapes on its sides. . . . Visually these drawings had nothing to do with architecture but from their apparent childishness there arose a combination of plans and sections whose interweaving it is difficult to know how to describe . . . . I believe that a great number of my colleagues will recognise in all that I have written the familiar characteristics of their own struggles with the problems of architecture . . . . I believe, rather, am convinced, that at their outset architecture and the other arts have the very same point of departure, which is indeed abstract, but is at the same time influenced by all the knowledge and feelings that have accumulated within us . . .

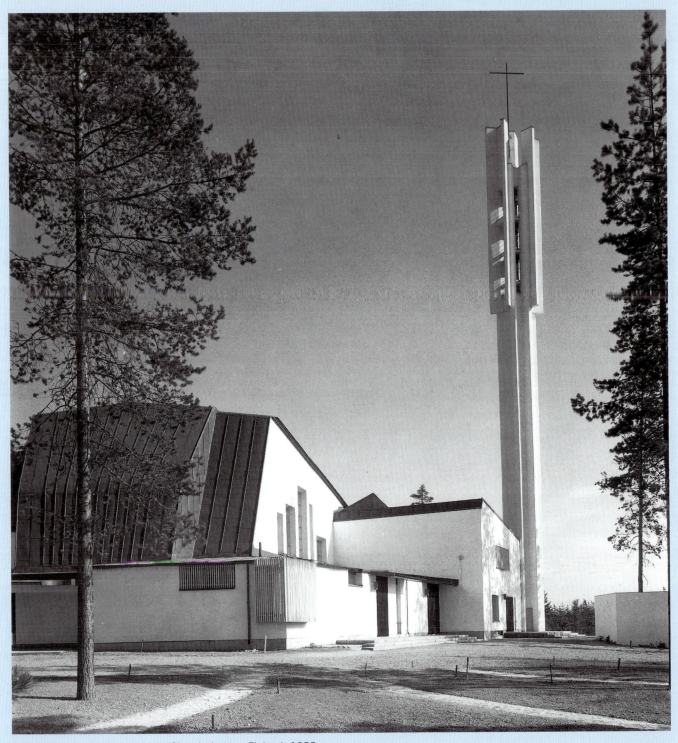

13.44 Alvar Aalto, Vuoksenniska Church, Imatra, Finland, 1958.

Architecture and its detailing are a sort of *biology* and their birth probably takes place in very complicated circumstances. One could compare architecture to the full grown salmon. It is not born full grown, it is not even born in the sea where it swims but far off, where the rivers narrow and divide into tributaries and mountain streams, beneath the first drops of water dripping from the glaciers. It is like the first stimuli of architecture, which arise as far from practicality and the finished result as the first impulses of our feelings and instinctive life can be from the everyday toil of our daily bread which binds us, each to the other."[9]

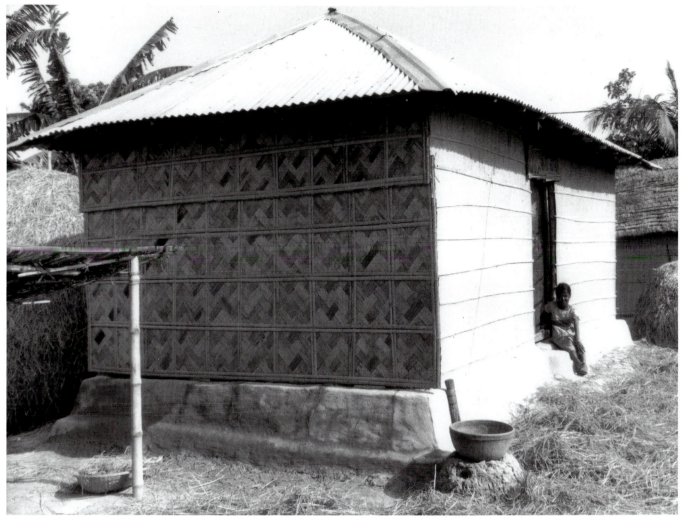

13.45 The Grameen Bank Housing Programme, Bangladesh. Courtesy the Aga Khan Award for Architecture, Geneva.

While architects and their critics are arguing about the creative potential of new ideas in architecture, some attention is also being paid to developing better housing for the poor and minimizing damage to the environment by the application of new technologies. The Aga Khan, leader of the world's 20 million Ismaili Muslims, has established an international architectural award for building projects that use local materials and satisfy true human needs. One recent recipient is the Grameen Bank Housing Programme in Bangladesh (**13.45**). These simple, sturdy, and clean homes combine the old and the new: bamboo supports and siding, corrugated iron roofs, prefabricated concrete floors, and reinforced concrete posts. Tens of thousands of them have been built by and for residents, with the help of small bank loans.

The Aga Khan speaks of the universal desire for good architecture:

> I can think of no human art form which exercises such a permanent influence over our lives. We must demand from our respective national decision-makers, our architects, our planners and our landscape architects an environment in which we live and work harmoniously and to the fullest.[10]

DESIGNED SETTINGS

Even those of us with the most meager of resources tend to make some attempt to organize and design our living environment to suit our sense of order, comfort, and beauty. This chapter will examine aesthetic and functional aspects of interior and environmental design, and conclude with a look at overtly staged settings for the performing arts.

INTERIOR DESIGN

Once a building is erected, there is the issue of selecting and organizing its contents—furniture, fabrics, art objects, functional objects, and personal possessions. In some cases, functionality of furnishings is

14.1 The old Reading Room, British Library, London, 1826–47.

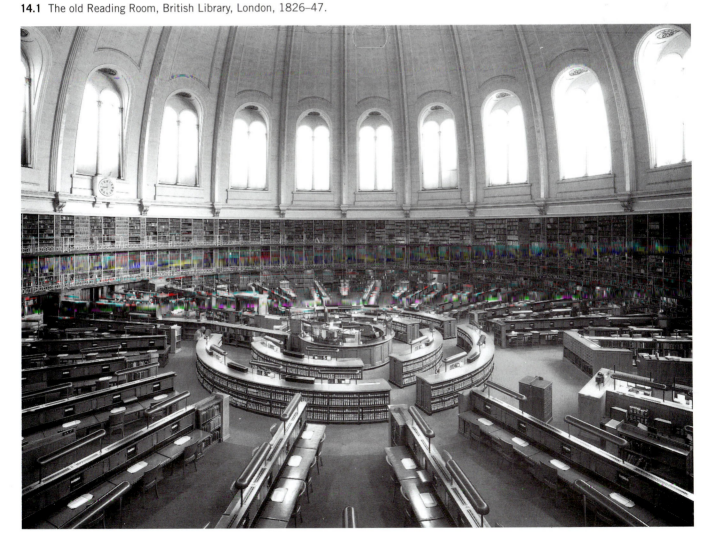

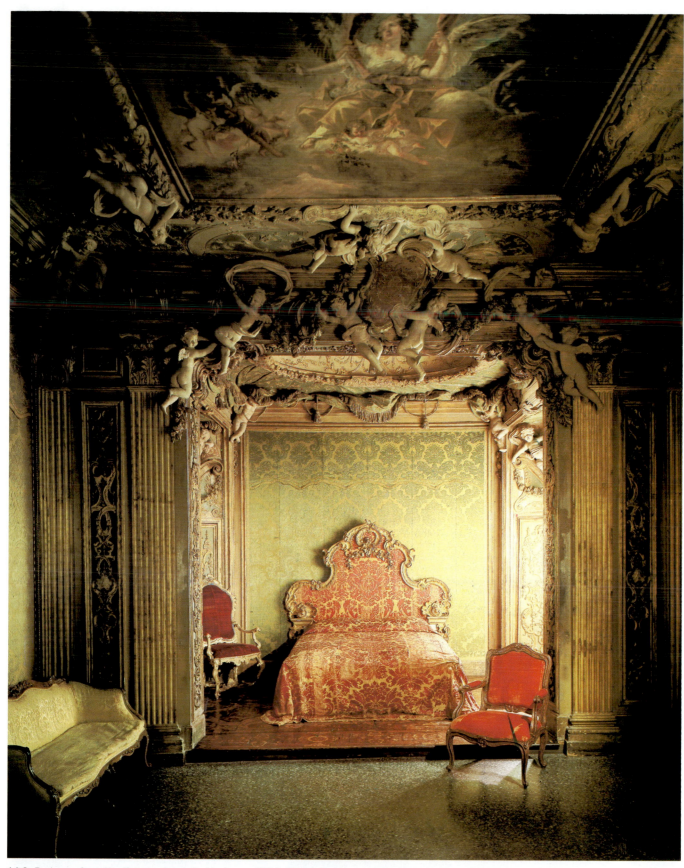

14.2 Bedroom from the Palazzo Sagredo, Venice, c. 1718. Wood, stucco, marble, glass, height 13 ft (4 m).
Painted ceiling by Gaspare Diziani, *Dawn*, c. 1755–60. Metropolitan Museum of Art, New York. Rogers Fund 1906.

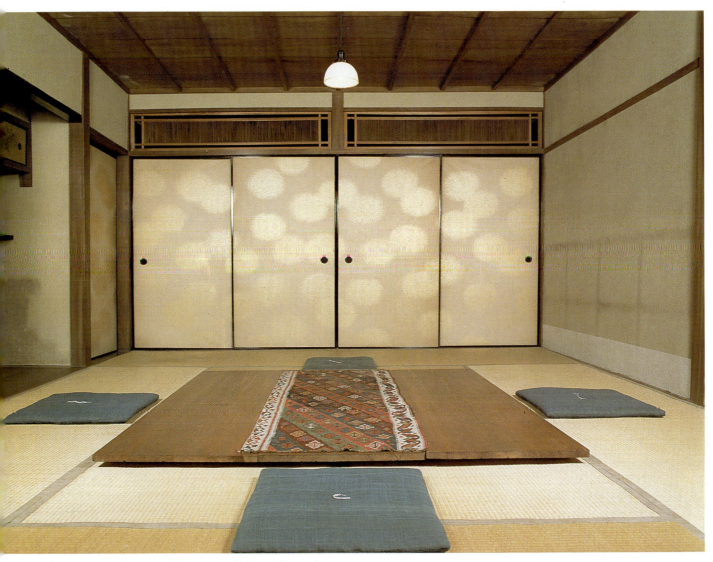

14.3 *Zashiki* or main parlor of a merchant's house, Kyoto, Japan.

the prime consideration. The old Reading Room of the British Library, London (14.1), is a businesslike arrangement of lighted reading tables fanning out like spokes from the central hub—shelves of reference volumes and an information desk. Chairs are upright, with no arms. All space is dedicated to task-solving equipment, with aisles left for convenient traffic flow. This is obviously not a place designed for comfort or conversation, but it efficiently carries out the function of providing reading spaces for a great number of people, with the elegance of a truly functional design.

By contrast, in our homes we tend to try to surround ourselves with things we consider beautiful or interesting, and furnishings designed to make our lives more comfortable. An extreme example of the opulent extremes to which this endeavor has been taken is the bedroom from Palazzo Sagredo in Venice (14.2), now preserved *in toto* in the Metropolitan Museum of Art in New York. The bedroom belonged to Zaccaria Sagredo, a major patron of the Venetian artists of the Late Baroque period. Every surface is richly ornamented, from the painting on the ceiling and the stucco cherubs to the magnificent brocade covering the bed and its headboard. The reds and golds increase the impression of sumptuous, almost royal wealth. The room has the appearance of a stage setting, with the bed raised on a platform, enclosed by an archway, and theatrically illuminated.

At the other extreme is the Japanese tradition that the home is not a place to display material abundance,

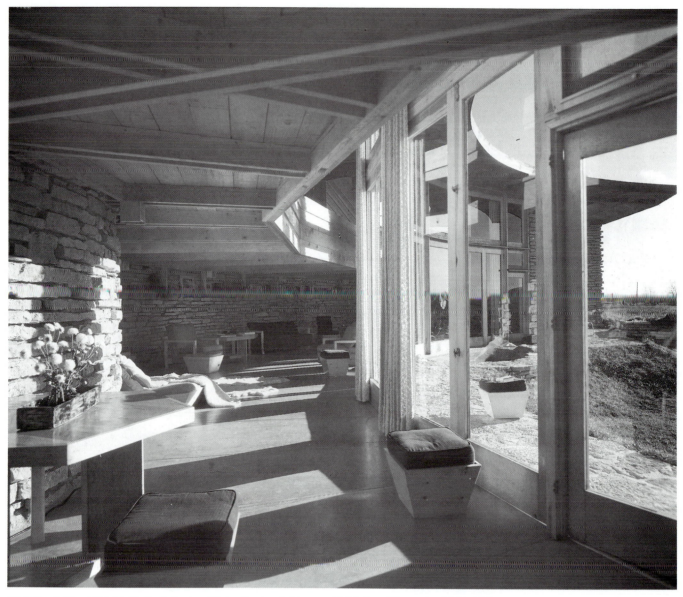

14.4 Frank Lloyd Wright, Herbert Jacobs, "Solar Hemicycle" house, Middleton, Wisconsin, 1944. Living room. Photo by Ezra Stoller, Esto, 1950.

though it may be a setting for appreciating the beauty of a few carefully selected possessions. The main parlor in a Kyoto merchant's home (14.3), lovingly restored along traditional lines by the son, is almost entirely bare of furnishings. The simple cushions and table are low to the *tatami* (mat)-covered floor, and all other possessions are stored out of sight. The only exception is the single painting within the **tokonoma** alcove to the left. This spare aesthetic turns a relatively small space into a quietly spacious sanctuary, a haven from the busyness and crowds of the streets. In the absence of visual noise, inhabitants can develop a heightened awareness of, and appreciation for, the

exquisite experiences of the moment. Instead of being submerged in a symphony, in this space one listens keenly to single notes—the scent of a flower, the texture of a cup, the sound of a voice. Kojiro Yoshida, the son, named his family's treasured home Mumeisha: "the hall for casting light on the unnamable things of the present."

Interior design necessarily involves a relationship with the architecture of the place. Frank Lloyd Wright often designed the interior furnishings as well as the architectural structure of houses. Typically, he attempted to relate the inside and the outside as a single whole, characterized by use of natural materials.

His "Solar Hemicycle" house built in Wisconsin (**14.4**) curves to embrace the sun, drawing it into a cavelike interior in which wood and stone are featured as organic surfaces which match the stone and wood used on the outside. A circular pool at the far end of the patio lies half inside, half outside the glass wall of the house. The simple wooden furniture was also designed by Wright specifically for the house. He insisted:

> Furnishings should be consistent in design and construction, and used with style as an extension in the sense of the building which they "furnish." Wherever possible all should be natural. The sure reward for maintaining these simple features of architectural integrity is great serenity.[1]

In contrast to the cozy, natural quality of Wright's house interiors, business environments may be carefully calculated to make a favorable impression on potential clients as well as employees and to facilitate and symbolize the division of labor. In the renovation of a former shopping mall as the corporate offices of Canberra Industries, a specialized electronics firm, the wide-open expanses were divided by movable partitions into a variety of workspaces. An open plan of mini-offices with low walls that allowed co-workers easy access to each other was used for most clerical and managerial employees, with a few private offices around the edges for corporate officers and conference spaces. Shown in Figure **14.5** is a low-ceilinged area used as a waiting "room" for visitors, backed by the president's receptionist and the offices of the president and senior administrators. Modern nonobjective works of art on the walls announce that this is a forward-looking company with good taste. Subdued lighting over couches and an area rug set them off from the brightly lit business areas beyond, without

14.5 Glenn Gregg, architect, Virginia Linburg, interior designer, Virginia McKernan, art consulting design, Executive Offices, Canberra Industries, Meriden, Connecticut, 1984.

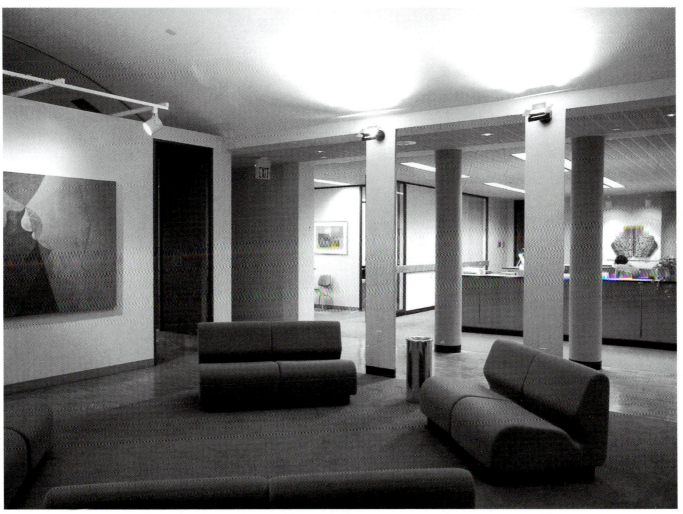

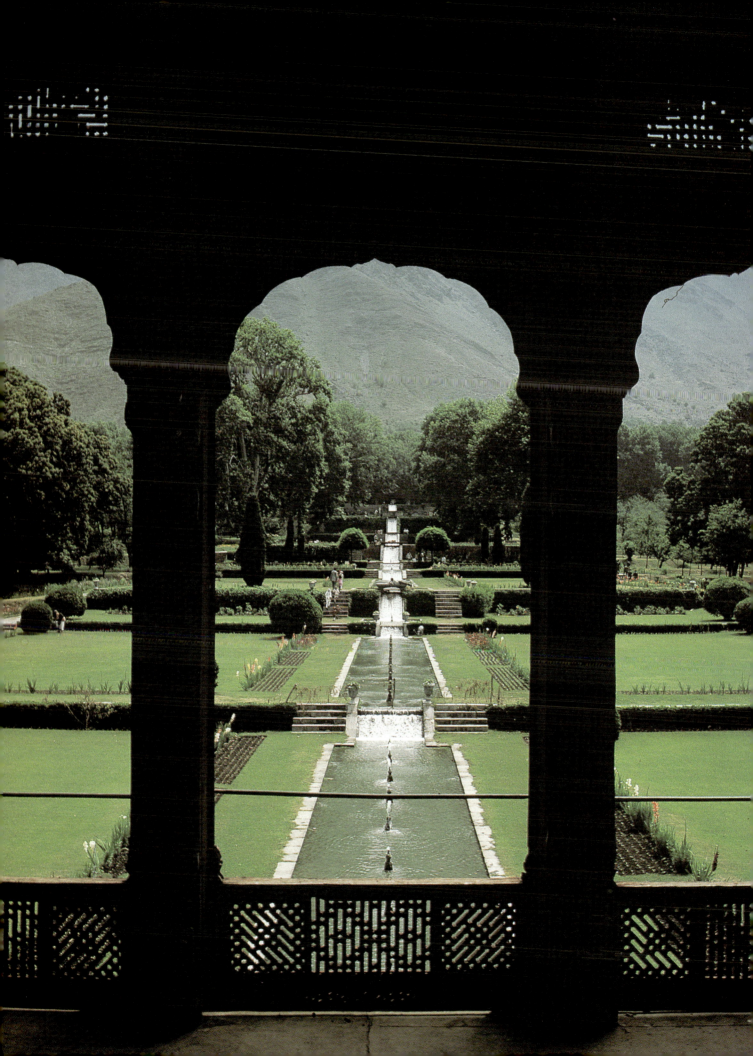

isolating them from view of the flow of business activity.

Lighting is itself a major new area of environmental concern. If all homes and businesses in the United States alone changed to existing energy-efficient lighting technologies, such as fluorescent bulbs and the introduction of daylight, there would be a saving of over $30 billion in electrical bills per year and elimination of the need for the energy produced by 120 power plants the size of Chernobyl. Such energy-saving techniques can also enhance the quality of lighting, which plays a major role in the aesthetics and comfort of interior design.

ENVIRONMENTAL DESIGN

Beyond our homes and public buildings, we humans have also longed to shape our immediate outdoor environment. Traces of gardens have been found in the ruins of the earliest civilizations. In arid countries, water and lush plantings have been especially prized. On the Indian plains, for example, few wildflowers can survive the fierce sun, but cultivated gardens were mentioned in early Buddhist and Hindu texts. During the great Mughal period of the sixteenth and seventeenth centuries, the emperors had magnificent formal gardens built around their mountain retreats in Kashmir. One of the most beautiful, Nishat Bagh (14.6), was built by Asaf Khan, Prime Minister to the emperor Jahangir and brother of his wife. When the emperor saw its lovely green terraces, the sparkling play of water over its stone water ladders, and its views of the lake and mountains beyond, he strongly recommended that Asaf Khan give it to him. Asaf Khan demurred, and the emperor in anger cut off the irrigation supply, without which the garden was deprived of much of its soul-soothing beauty. The water was eventually restored, and the garden again became a serenely refreshing oasis.

Every natural environment has its own underlying structure and harmony, both aesthetic and functional. Development has often obliterated these natural environments and resulted in unplanned, disharmonious concentrations of buildings. As urban centers become

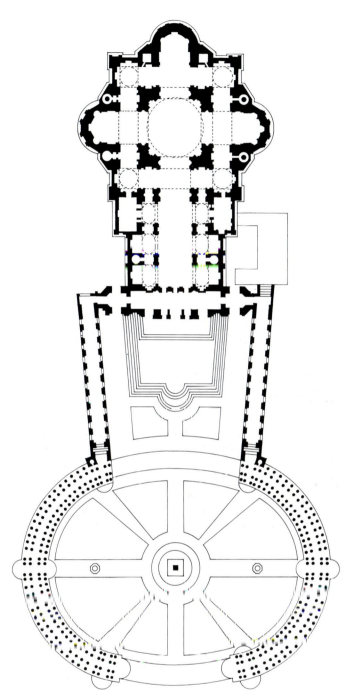

14.7 GianLorenzo Bernini, plan of the Piazza of St. Peter's, Rome, begun 1656.

14.6 (opposite) Nishat Bagh, India, 17th century. View from the pavilion along the main axis of the garden.

intolerable, the wealthy abandon them to live on their fringes, somewhat closer to nature. Then, as suburban developments proliferate, the inner cities often decay, both architecturally and socially. However, the urban concentration of living spaces is a reasonable strategy for distribution of human beings across the earth. Cities allow preservation of tracts of undeveloped land

and also energy-efficient systems of transportation. Urban planning is thus being revived to help create cities in which people like to live.

Urban planning is not a new science. Rather, it seems to have been practiced quite effectively in some times and places to create vibrant environments for the multiplicities of human activities. From ancient times, one feature of well-planned cities has been the provision for public gathering spaces. Within cities crowded with busy people on the move, plazas and public squares offer a different pace.

In seventeenth-century Rome, a need was felt for a great open public space to accommodate crowds approaching St. Peter's, the monumental central structure of the Roman Catholic Church. The desired

14.8 Nathan Phillips Square, Toronto, Ontario.

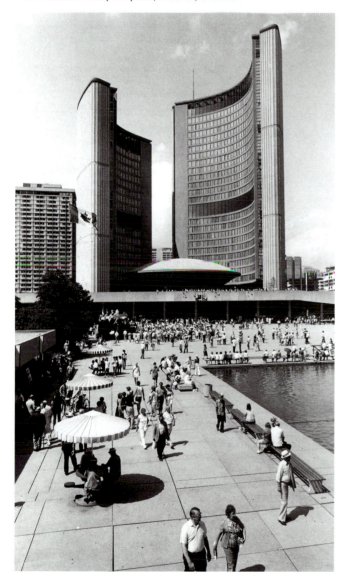

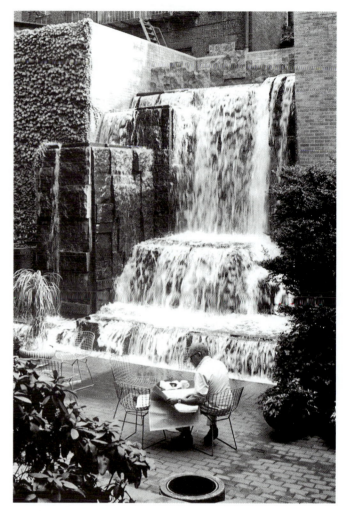

14.9 Hideo Sasaki, Greenacre Park, New York, 1979.

piazza (14.7) was designed by Gianlorenzo Bernini, who in addition to being a great painter and sculptor (1.13) was also an architect. He planned a huge oval area open at one end and embraced by enormous Tuscan columns lined up to form two giant colonnades, like the arms of the Church welcoming the people. The project was so expensive that it almost bankrupted the Vatican.

The success of open urban spaces can be measured by whether people choose to congregate there. By this criterion, Nathan Phillips Square (14.8) in Toronto is overwhelmingly successful. Beyond the embrace of the twin towers of City Hall, a multi-level public space is booked every day with entertainers, from rock concerts to drum majorettes performing their routines, and the area is always thronged with people.

Municipalities have also made provisions for their occupants to benefit from natural settings without having to leave the city, by creating city parks. Some are extensive green belts; some are tiny areas with plantings and benches. In the heart of mid-town Manhattan, the Greenacre Foundation used the space between two buildings for a "vest-pocket" park featuring an artificial waterfall, tables and chairs, and trees to provide shade (14.9). To step off the street into the ambiance of this place is a psychological and aesthetic respite from the high-pressure atmosphere of commercial New York. The sound of the waterfall drowns out street noises and its cooling spray adds to the soothing quality of the park.

At the grassroots level, some groups are bringing life to the walls of ghettos and otherwise unappetizing cityscapes by painting **murals**. Some are celebrations of ethnic pride; others are humorous illusions, such as *Isle of California* (14.10). It was painted by the Los Angeles Fine Arts Squad after a minor earthquake, as a teasing, surrealistically three-dimensional take-off on a Californian fear: the freeways collapsing into the ocean.

On a broader scale, many people now feel a need to protect the beauty and environmental functions of the natural environment. Lawrence Halprin's sketch for *Sea Ranch* (14.11), a planned community on the Californian coast, set up a series of restrictions that kept houses and roads hidden from view. In landscape design, he specified use of native materials, forbidding

14.10 Victor Henderson and Terry Schoonhoven (known as the Los Angeles Fine Arts Squad), *Isle of California*, 1972. Enamel mural, 42 × 65 ft (13 × 20 m). Los Angeles, California.

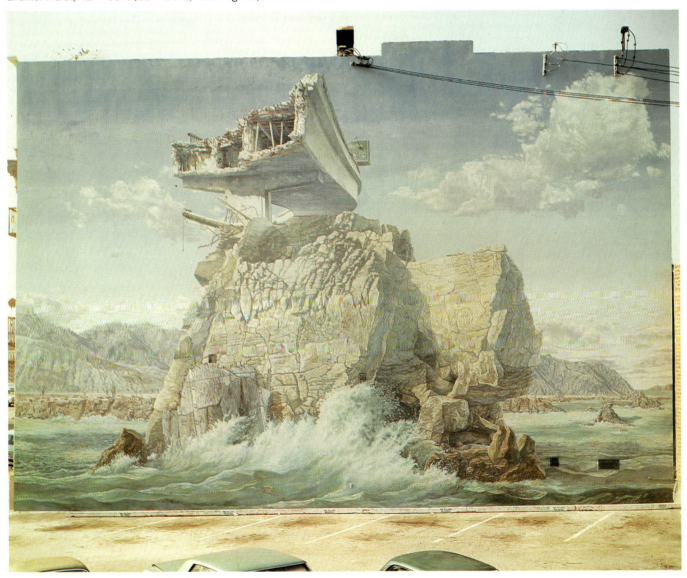

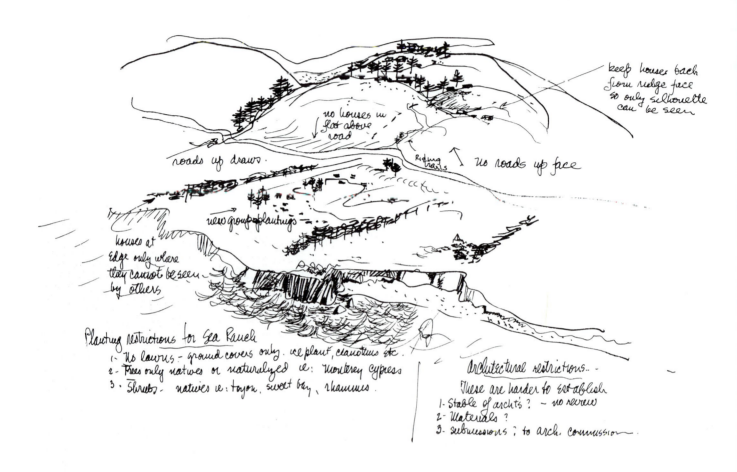

The following handwritten notes appear on the sketch:

keep houses back from ridge face so only silhouette can be seen

no houses in flat above road

roads up draws.

Riding trails

no roads up face

new group plantings

houses at edge only where they cannot be seen by others

Planting restrictions for Sea Ranch
1- No lawns - ground covers only. ice plant, ceanothus etc.
2- Trees only natives or naturalized ie: Monterey cypress
3- Shrubs - natives ie: toyon, sweet bay, rhamnus.

Architectural restrictions -
These are harder to establish
1- Stable of arch'ts ? - no review
2- Materials ?
3- submissions ; to arch. commission

14.11 Lawrence Halprin, environmental specifications for *Sea Ranch*, 1963. Notebook sketch.

attempts to create artificial grassy lawns, in the interests of preserving water and the original character of the dramatic setting. These are moral judgments about how our control of the environment affects the quality of our lives, as well as the ecological characteristics of the land.

In both urban and rural environments, there are now efforts to mitigate the aesthetic and environmental damage done by human habitation. Many artists are involved in projects such as sewage treatment and landscaping of garbage landfills, to make them both ecologically and visually successful.

Patricia Johanson "biologically restored" a formerly stagnant lagoon in Dallas (**14.12**) by reintroducing indigenous species of plants, turtles, and fish, and creating bridges and walkways with large plantlike sculptures. Not only do children like her Fair Park; birds are also returning to it. She asserts:

The reason we [artists] have to participate is that we can do something that's very visual, very poetic; we have the power to sway people to our point of view.[2]

In trying to deduce some general aesthetic principles common to all those cities around the world that are invigorating or pleasant rather than disagreeable, Lawrence Halprin came to the conclusion that good city planning—or happenstance—respects both the old and the new and provides a creative, vibrant environment for the multiplicities of human activities:

The provocative city results from many different kinds of interrelated activities where people have an opportunity to participate in elegant, carefully designed art and spontaneous, non-designed elements juxtaposed into what might be called a folk idiom, a series of unplanned relationships … those chance occurrences and happenings which are so vital to be aware of—the strange and beautiful which no fixed, preconceived order can produce. A city is a complex series of events.[3]

14.12 Patricia Johanson, *Pteris Multifida*, Fair Park Lagoon, Dallas, Texas. Photo courtesy of the artist.

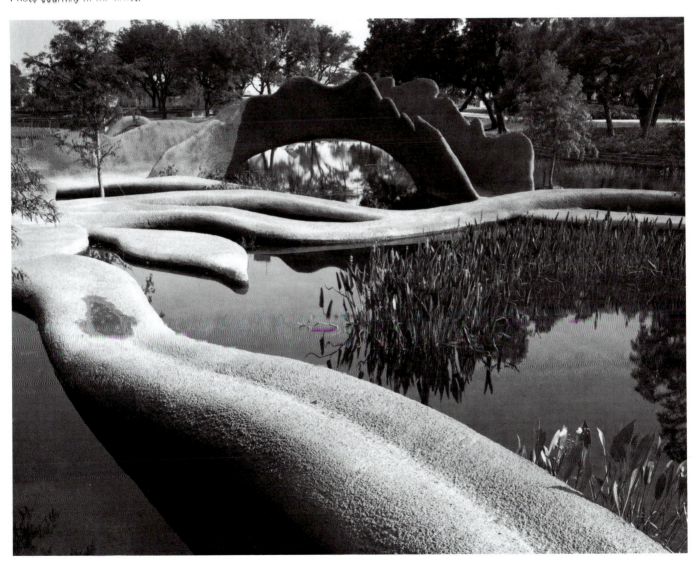

JOHN LYLE
on SUSTAINABLE ENVIRONMENTAL DESIGN

In the encounter between industrial civilization and the natural environment, the land has suffered extensive abuses. Many scientists are concerned that we may have so spoiled our own planetary home that soon we will be unable to live in it. Concerned artists are therefore taking up the challenge of creating more harmonious relationships between human development and the natural environment.

John Lyle, Professor of Landscape Architecture at California State Polytechnic University, has created at that institution a model project for sustainable community development. The land itself is carefully used as a medium for recycling "wastes"—for consciously working with the subtle flows of energy, water, and nutrients through a natural landscape, in the midst of human habitation. Solar heating, fish ponds, horticulture, and agroforestry are incorporated into the landscape and environmental architecture (**14.13**). Old tires are used to create hillside terraces, electric buggies and bicycles are used for transportation, the clay soil is improved by the addition of organic matter, and a compost heap accompanies the buildings where students live. At this Center for Regenerative Studies, the students themselves grow food and manage the flow of nutrients, water, and waste through their environment.

Professor Lyle contrasts this approach to that of conventional landscape design, which concerns itself only with visual form:

"Ecosystematic order, while enormously complex in its infinite detail, is relatively simple in concept. In essence, ecosystems are defined by three modes of order, all of which we reshape when we design a landscape.

The first is structural order, which describes the composition of living and nonliving elements: rocks, soil, plant, and animal species. In natural ecosystems, structure is usually consistent in that each species inhabits a particular niche and maintains ongoing interactions with certain other species.

The second mode of ecosystem order is the functional system, the flows of energy and materials that distribute the necessities of life to all the species included in the structure. When we include ecosystem functions in the design process, we deal with energy and with flows of water and nutrients and other substances which, in amounts that are too large or too small, cause serious disruption in the environment.

The third mode of ecosystem order is comprised of locational patterns and is the only one often consciously observed in landscape design. The shape, character, and cover of the landscape vary in space, creating ranges of conditions that differ in their ability to support different species and communities and different human activities.

In natural landscapes, these three basic modes of ecosystematic order combine to generate form. In the designed landscape, form is a somewhat different matter. Ecological order is as much there as in a natural landscape, but it meets and merges with human activity and with aesthetic order as perceived by the human mind. We can know nature only through perception and intellect. Where the merging is harmonious, where ecological and

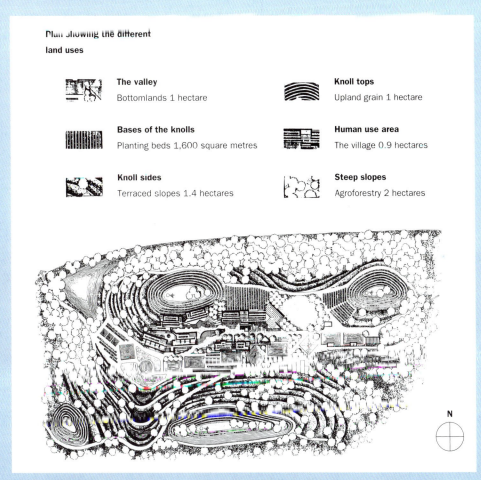

Plan showing the different
land uses

The valley
Bottomlands 1 hectare

Bases of the knolls
Planting beds 1,600 square metres

Knoll sides
Terraced slopes 1.4 hectares

Knoll tops
Upland grain 1 hectare

Human use area
The village 0.9 hectares

Steep slopes
Agroforestry 2 hectares

14.13 Site plan by John Lyle and Ronald Izumita, Center for Regenerative Studies, Pomona, California.

aesthetic order are in congruence, we have a human ecosystem. Such a landscape has deep form, because underlying its surface and giving it deeper substance is this cohesive fundamental order. Such deep form stands in contrast to shallow form, which has only the surface perceptual order and lacks the solidity of coherent process beneath the surface."[4]

VISUAL ASPECTS OF THE PERFORMING ARTS

While environmental designers use plants, water, earth, stone, paving materials, and screening devices to create pleasant settings for our daily lives, designers connected with the performing arts create artificial settings for make-believe. In the ancient Greek theater, actors initially performed from a flat space at the foot of a hill, with the audience seated on the hillside. There was no scenery. This simple way of separating the imaginary space of the performance from the real space of the audience was later formalized with tiered seating rising up a hillside in a semicircle around a wooden platform (**14.14**). Actors entered and exited from a small building called a **skene**, from which we get the words "scene" and **proscenium** (in front of the *skene*).

To enhance the illusionary setting for theatrical performances, the area designated as a stage became more elaborate, with fabricated scenery designed to give the illusion of deep space. The chief way of creating this spatial illusion was the use of **forced perspective**, an exaggeration of the speed at which parallel lines converge toward a vanishing point. Shortly after perspective drawings were adopted by Renaissance artists, the device was transferred to the stage. At the Teatro Olimpico in Vicenza, designed by Andrea Palladio, completed by his pupil Vincenzo Scamozzi in 1585 and still standing, three elaborate arches opened onto illusionary city streets with their

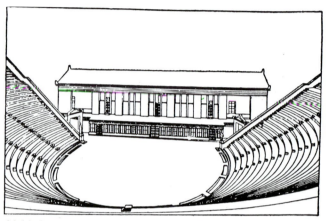

14.14 Reconstruction drawing of the Hellenistic theater at Ephesus, Turkey, c. 280 BC, rebuilt c. 150 BC.

14.15 Andrea Palladio and Vincenzo Scamozzi, interior of the Teatro Olimpico, Vicenza, Italy, 1580–84.

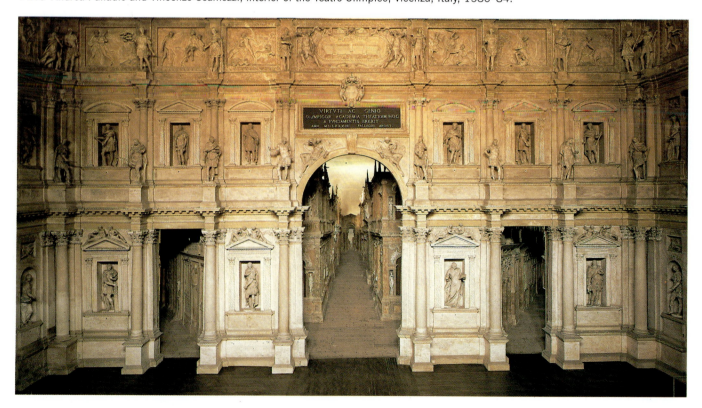

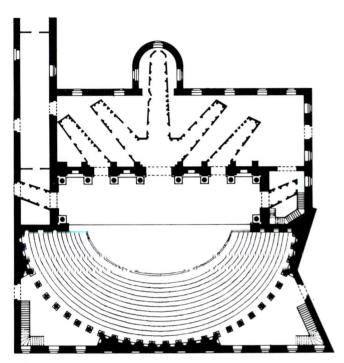

14.16 Plan of the Teatro Olimpico.

In some traditional African cultures, layers of cloth and wooden masks are similarly used to transform the bearer into a representation of a deceased ancestor, god or goddess. The spirits are thought to be close to the living, but invisible, and to have an active interest in intervening in earthly affairs. Dead ancestors, for example, may still be considered the owners of family property and must be consulted about its use. They influence the weather and the crops, so people must stay in their good graces. Their presence-made-visible is a powerful influence on the behaviors of the living. In the Yoruba language, the word *iron*, which means "theatrical performance," also means "vision." It signifies levels of reality that humans cannot usually see but which they can envision with the mind's eye, inspired by stories and masquerades. When the masqueraders dance, the layers upon layers of cloth whirl about like patterns of energy, dissolving the impression of solidity and physical boundaries.

14.17 Costume of a *kaivakuku* (taboo adviser) from Waima, Papua New Guinea, c. 1900. Bark cloth.

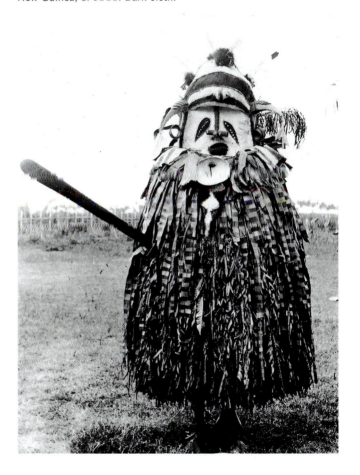

floors raked upwards and rows of models of wooden houses built in forced perspective. All of this elaborate scenery, shown in a frontal view in Figure 14.15 and in the plan in Figure 14.16, was intended to give the illusion of streets intersecting in a public square. Actors were confined to the acting space in front of the scenery; if they were to move up the streets, the falseness of their scale would become apparent.

Shortly after Scamozzi finished the Teatro Olimpico, he invented the form most familiar to us today, in which the entire stage is framed by a single **proscenium arch**. This arch is used to hide all the mechanics of the stage setting, such as the tops of painted sets, light banks, and pulleys that allow actors to "fly." Within the recessed space of the stage, some of the latest innovations involve computer technologies.

Another major illusionary device used in performing arts is costuming. Even when there is no stage, when performers and audience share the same space, performers may assume roles by wearing masks and costumes that hide their everyday identity. The Papuan costume shown in Figure 14.17 transforms ordinary people into spirits attending boys' initiation ceremonies. Such rituals express the beliefs of a culture and are vital to its sense of identity and continuity.

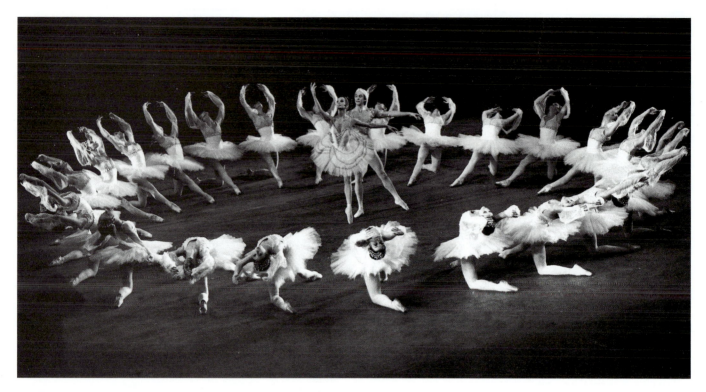

14.18 Scene from *La Bayadère*, Royal Ballet Company, London, 1978. Choreographed by Marius Petipa. Produced by Rudolf Nureyev.

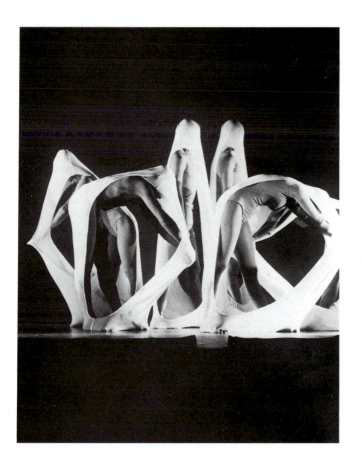

In some performing arts, the bodies of performers are deliberately turned into design elements—elongated lines, opposing or harmonizing forms—like parts of a painting or sculpture that changes through time. This is true in classical ballet; in this scene from *La Bayadère* (14.18), the corps forms a low circle around the central characters, like a splash radiating outward from the action in the middle. Dramatic high-contrast lighting is used to make the dancers appear as points of light within a dark and otherwise empty space. In Alwin Nikolais' modern dance choreography, all reference to the body as human is deleted. Dancers in his *Sanctum* (14.19) move within webs of stretchy fabric, creating an eerie grotto of fantasy forms.

The body is used as symbolic mask and gesture by Japanese *kabuki* actors. They wear highly stylized make-up over a white base, transforming their own faces into visages suggesting their roles. They offer their bodies as armatures for costumes weighing up to 50 pounds (23 kg), requiring frequent adjustments by stage attendants who wear black and are therefore not

14.19 Alwin Nikolais, *Sanctum*, Nikolais Dance Theater, New York, 1976.

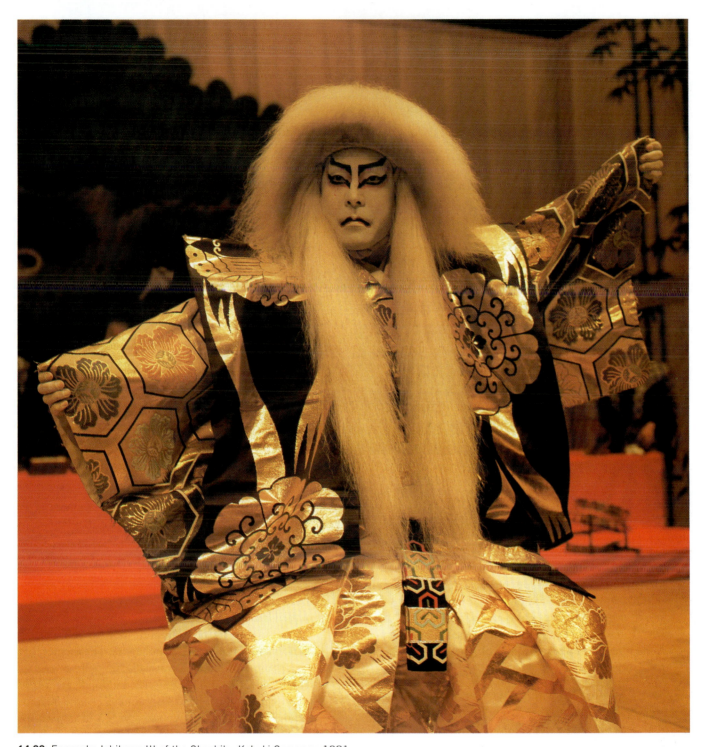

14.20 Ennosuke Ichikawa III of the Shochiku Kabuki Company, 1981.

considered visible. These highly trained actors, whose apprenticeships begin at the age of six or seven, assume stylized gestures, freezing momentarily like statues in melodramatic poses (**14.20**) that carry clear meaning for those familiar with *kabuki* conventions.

Men play all parts; women were banned in 1629 as part of an attempt by the rulers to restrict the popularity of this art form.

In puppetry, all is illusion. Figures can be as fantastic as the puppeteer's imagination allows, and

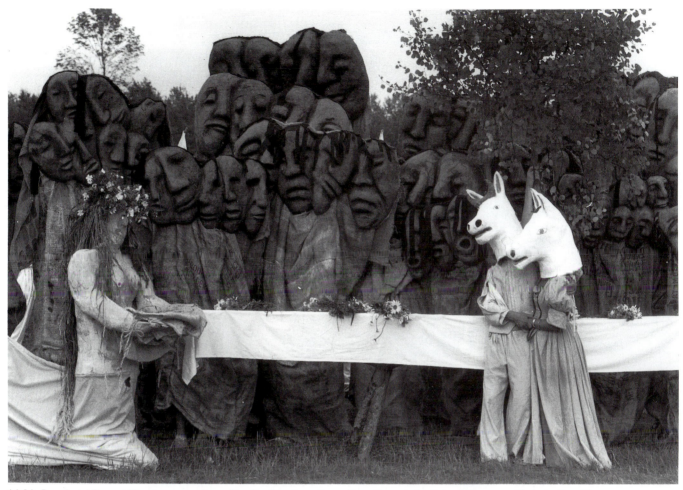

14.21 Bread and Puppet Theater, scene from *Passion Play for a Young Tree*. Puppets by Peter Schumann. Photo by Ron Simon.

designed to hide the hands or bodies that move them. Sculptor Peter Schumann, founder of the Bread and Puppet Theater, sees puppetry as:

> … an extension of sculpture. A professional sculptor doesn't have much to do but decorate libraries or schools. But to take sculpture into the streets, to tell a story with it, to make music and dances for it—that's what interests me…. A puppet may be a hand only, or it may be a complicated body of many heads, hands, rods and fabric.[5]

Many elaborate systems have been devised for remote control of marionettes and puppets, but in the Bread and Puppet Theater's *Passion Play for a Young Tree* (**14.21**), they are life-sized and worn by humans who walk around in them. The figures in the background are "crowd puppets," groups of heads with burlap drapes designed to create a crowd effect with only six to ten people beneath them. In the play, a poplar tree is subjected to a series of trials suggesting those preceding Jesus' crucifixion; after its "death," the broken tree is taken to a pine forest by washerwomen, laid on the ground, and tenderly covered with a sheet. The tree then flies up into the treetops, resurrected and covered with flowers. Shown here is a version of the Last Supper. Elka Schumann, one of the puppeteers, explains the intent:

> Bread and Puppet, one of the oldest alternative theaters in the United States, is not a children's puppet theater, but we like to include children, both in the performances and certainly in our audiences. The themes that we choose for shows are usually of quite a serious nature, dealing with issues that we think are really important to all people, like the nuclear arms race or ecological destruction. We use a very wide variety of puppets, including some very small cut-outs or hand puppets but mostly large or huge puppets that can be manipulated and require big groups of people to run them. Many of our performances are designed to be done outside, in a community or with a community. The Passion Play was a very simple format with no speaking in it. The audience followed the scenes from one beautiful spot to another. By moving with the show, the audience became, in a way, part of the story.[6]

ART IN TIME

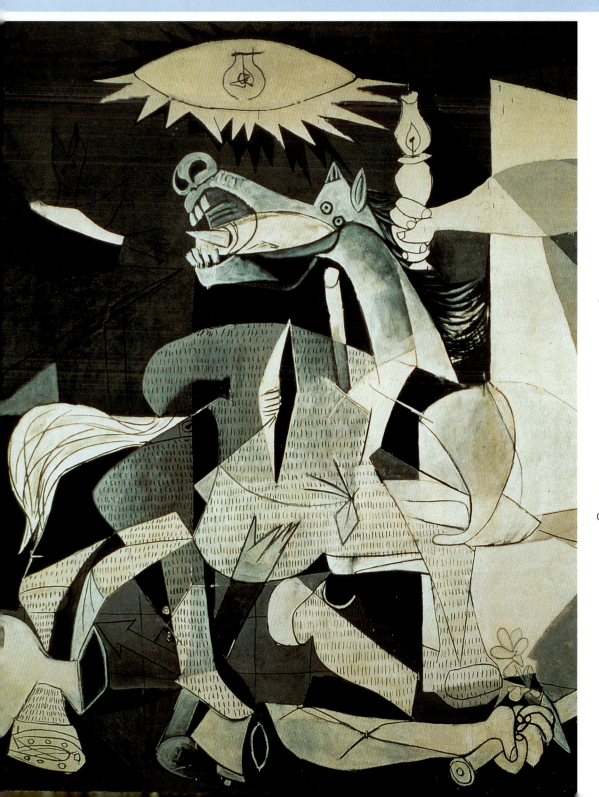

Change is the one sure constant in art. Over time, art movements typically go as far as they can in one direction and then some artists veer off to explore other approaches. Each work of art also has its own history, with its final appearance the result of many choices made as it evolved from an abstract idea into physical form.

Pablo Picasso, *Guernica* (detail of fig. 16.1).

15
HISTORICAL STYLES IN WESTERN ART

Works of art may express something of the person who created them. They may also reflect the views and artistic conventions of the society at the time. Approaches to art have often carried enough similarities among varying artists who were working at the same time, in the same place, for us to be able to categorize them as stylistic movements. These movements lasted a long time at first, since societies were isolated from each other and information passed very slowly from one to the next. Then, as commerce between areas became more common, innovations in one area were more rapidly reflected elsewhere.

Today styles come and go with such speed that the twentieth century alone was characterized by a great number of artistic movements. Contemporary societies are also far less uniform, supporting a plurality of lifestyles and life views. When the major patrons for art were the state and church, and when the academies dictated whose work was approved and shown, their views dominated what was done. Many stylistic movements now coexist, and many artists are doing unique work that does not fit into any group designation.

In this chapter we will trace the chain of the major art styles from earliest times to the present. Although we have examined art from all cultures throughout this book, in this chapter we will limit our focus to the evolution of European and North American art for the sake of clarity. The art of each culture has similarly evolved through many styles, partly through internal innovations and partly through contact with other cultures. Western art has often been influenced by that of non-Western societies—Rembrandt, for instance, was a collector of Near Eastern art, and Picasso was strongly affected by African sculpture. As communications shrink our globe, techniques and approaches to art are increasingly cross-pollinating. Many of the works in Western art discussed earlier are drawn into this discussion and are placed in context on the timelines on the following pages:

page 415 30,000 B.C.–500 A.D Prehistoric to Roman
page 427 500–1500 A.D. Early Christian to Gothic
page 440 1425–1640 Early Renaissance to Southern Baroque
page 446 1500–1800 Northern Renaissance to Rococo
page 452 1750–1950 Neoclassicism to Surrealism
page 473 1915–2000 At the Turn of the Twenty-First Century

The accompanying maps show the key artistic centers and the location of important buildings in the periods covered. The timeline on pages 416-417 covers movements from prehistory to the present and is illustrated with key works of art from this chapter.

Although our society tends to equate the passage of time with progress, some art historians feel that the art of certain periods in our past has never been surpassed. Note, too, that many of the historical groupings of artists are rather artificial constructs that were developed after the fact; others were actual groups of artists working together with a shared vision. Some of these are still called by the derogatory terms given to them by their detractors.

30,000 BC–500 AD Prehistoric to Roman		Events	Works of art
30,000	c. 30,000–10,000 Paleolithic c. 20,000–6000 Mesolithic c. 8000–3000 Neolithic c. 4000 Sumerian civilization emerges in Mesopotamia	c. 20,000 toolmaking c. 9000 domestication of animals c. 4000 cuneiform script developed in Mesopotamia	c. 30,000–25,000 *Venus of Willendorf*, Lower Austria (*15.2*) c. 15,000–10,000 "Hall of Bulls," Lascaux, France (*15.1*)
3000	c. 3000–1000 Cycladic culture, Aegean c. 2780–1085 kingdoms of Ancient Egypt c. 2000–1100 Minoan civilization, Crete c. 1760–612 Assyrian Empire, Mesopotamia c. 1600–1100 Mycenaean civilization, Greece	c. 3000 hieroglyphic writing, Egypt c. 3000–2000 use of bronze tools/weapons, Sumer c. 2000 "Book of the Dead" first papyrus book c. 1725 horse-drawn wheeled vehicles, Egypt c. 1200 beginning of Jewish religion	2700 Panel of Hesira, Saqqara, Egypt (*15.6*) 2700–2600 Statuettes from Abu Temple, Tell Asmar, Iraq (*15.4*) 2500 Cycladic figure, Amorgos, Greece (*15.3*) c. 1450 *Senmut with Princess Nefrua*, Thebes, Egypt (*2.30*)
1000	c. 800–650 Geometric period, Greece c. 700–480 Archaic period, Greece c. 500–400 Classical period, Greece c. 500–150 Hellenistic period, Greece 509–31 Roman Republic	c. 900 ideographic writing, China. c. 800 Homer's *The Iliad* c. 700 first Olympic Games 550–480 Gautama Buddha, founder of Buddhism c. 336–323 conquests of Alexander the Great	8th cent. Dipylon vase, Athens, Greece (*15.7*) 540–515 Kouros, Anavross, Greece (*15.8*) c. 530 Amphora, Greece (*11.4*) c. 450–400 *Spear Bearer*, Greece (*2.31*) 448–405 Acropolis, Athens, Greece (*15.9*) 447–438 Parthenon, Athens, Greece (*3.38*) 421–405 Erechtheum, Athens, Greece (*13.16*) c. 190 *Victory of Samothrace*, Greece (*15.10*) c. 20 *Augustus of Primaporta*, Rome (*15.11*)
0	31 BC–500 AD Roman Empire c. 400 Byzantine Empire begins	c. 30 crucifixion of Jesus Christ 79 Pompeii and Herculaneum destroyed 98–117 Roman Empire at greatest extent	1st cent. AD *Laocoön*, Rhodes, found in Rome (*3.29*) 113 Trajan's Column, Rome (*2.144*) 118–28 Pantheon, Rome (*13.4*) 220–30 Sarcophagus, Rome (*2.21*) 312–15 Arch of Constantine, Rome (*1.39*)

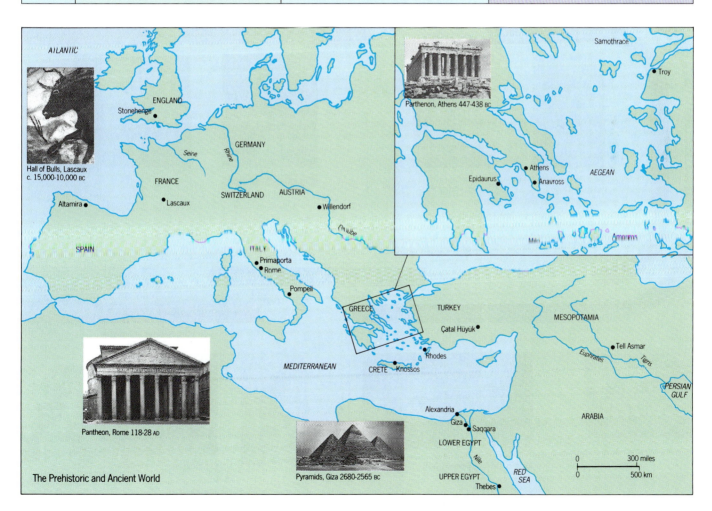

The Prehistoric and Ancient World

Hall of Bulls, Lascaux c. 15,000–10,000 BC

Parthenon, Athens 447–438 BC

Pantheon, Rome 118-28 AD

Pyramids, Giza 2680–2565 BC

TIMELINE

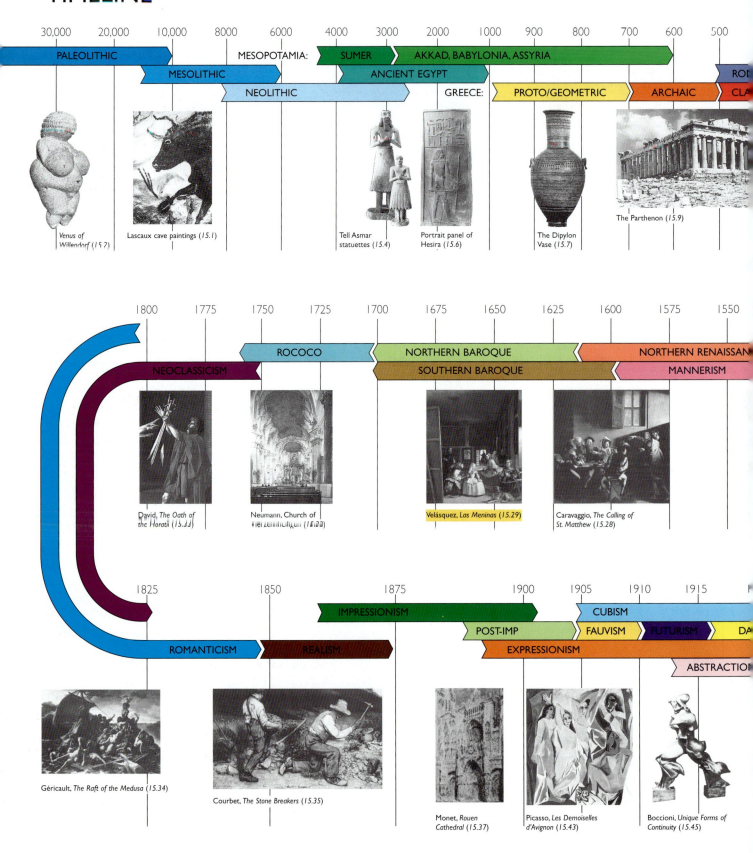

| 30,000 | 20,000 | 10,000 | 8000 | 6000 | 4000 | 3000 | 2000 | 1000 | 900 | 800 | 700 | 600 | 500 |

PALEOLITHIC

MESOPOTAMIA: **SUMER** **AKKAD, BABYLONIA, ASSYRIA**

MESOLITHIC

ANCIENT EGYPT

NEOLITHIC

GREECE: **PROTO/GEOMETRIC** **ARCHAIC** **CLA** **RO**

Venus of Willendorf (15.2)

Lascaux cave paintings (15.1)

Tell Asmar statuettes (15.4)

Portrait panel of Hesira (15.6)

The Dipylon Vase (15.7)

The Parthenon (15.9)

| 1800 | 1775 | 1750 | 1725 | 1700 | 1675 | 1650 | 1625 | 1600 | 1575 | 1550 |

ROCOCO **NORTHERN BAROQUE** **NORTHERN RENAISSAN**

NEOCLASSICISM **SOUTHERN BAROQUE** **MANNERISM**

David, *The Oath of the Horatii* (15.33)

Neumann, Church of Vierzehnheiligen (15.32)

Velásquez, *Las Meninas* (15.29)

Caravaggio, *The Calling of St. Matthew* (15.28)

| 1825 | 1850 | 1875 | 1900 | 1905 | 1910 | 1915 |

IMPRESSIONISM **CUBISM**

POST-IMP **FAUVISM** **FUTURISM** **DA**

ROMANTICISM **REALISM** **EXPRESSIONISM**

ABSTRACTION

Géricault, *The Raft of the Medusa* (15.34)

Courbet, *The Stone Breakers* (15.35)

Monet, *Rouen Cathedral* (15.37)

Picasso, *Les Demoiselles d'Avignon* (15.43)

Boccioni, *Unique Forms of Continuity* (15.45)

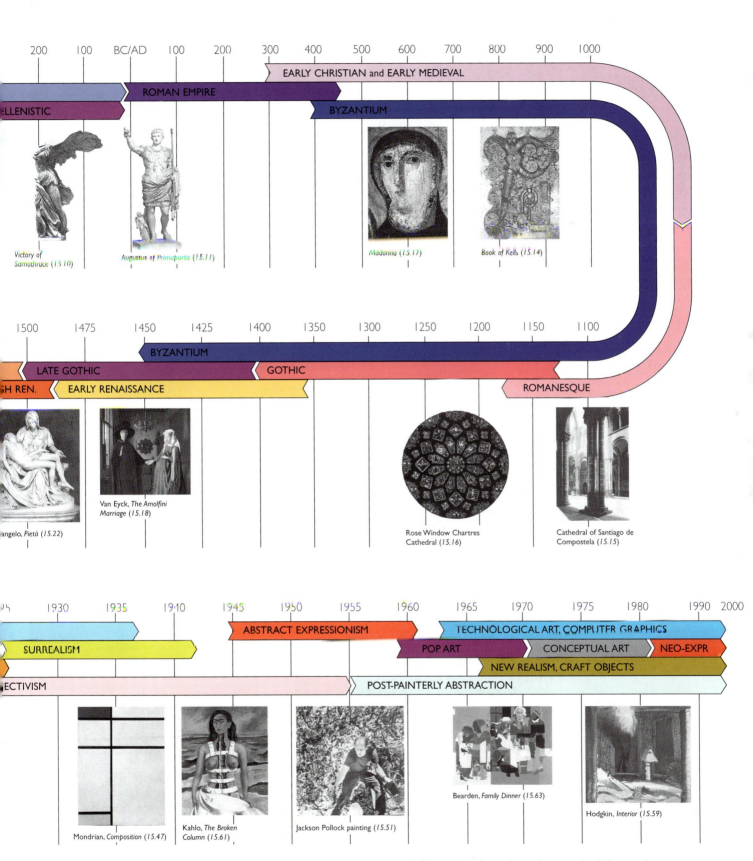

200 100 BC/AD 100 200 300 400 500 600 700 800 900 1000

EARLY CHRISTIAN and EARLY MEDIEVAL

ROMAN EMPIRE

ELLENISTIC

BYZANTIUM

Victory of
Samothrace (15.10)

Augustus of Primaporta (15.11)

Madonna (15.17)

Book of Kells (15.14)

1500 1475 1450 1425 1400 1350 1300 1250 1200 1150 1100

BYZANTIUM

LATE GOTHIC

GOTHIC

GH REN.

EARLY RENAISSANCE

ROMANESQUE

angelo, Pietà (15.22)

Van Eyck, The Arnolfini
Marriage (15.18)

Rose Window Chartres
Cathedral (15.16)

Cathedral of Santiago de
Compostela (15.15)

5 1930 1935 1940 1945 1950 1955 1960 1965 1970 1975 1980 1990 2000

ABSTRACT EXPRESSIONISM

TECHNOLOGICAL ART, COMPUTER GRAPHICS

SURREALISM

POP ART

CONCEPTUAL ART

NEO-EXPR

NEW REALISM, CRAFT OBJECTS

ECTIVISM

POST-PAINTERLY ABSTRACTION

Mondrian, Composition (15.47)

Kahlo, The Broken
Column (15.61)

Jackson Pollock painting (15.51)

Bearden, Family Dinner (15.63)

Hodgkin, Interior (15.59)

Differential timescales have been used, resulting in the relative compression of earlier periods. This apparent bias in favor of recency should be noted, although it is difficult to avoid: for if this Timeline represented all periods on the timescale used for the twentieth century, it would measure 315 feet (96 meters) in length.

THE BEGINNINGS OF WESTERN ART

Prehistoric

Very few traces remain of the lives of our earliest ancestors. We do know, however, that by 30,000 B.C. *Homo sapiens* was creating works we now regard as paintings and sculptures. Of the latter, the most famous is the tiny female figure found at Willendorf in Austria (**15.2**). Often referred to as the "Venus of Willendorf," she is only 4½ inches (11.5 cm) tall, small enough to fit comfortably in one's hand. Archeologists think she, like other similar figures from the same period, was probably a fertility image, judging from the exaggeration of her reproductive areas to the exclusion of facial features, or an image of the Creator as Mother. Somebody carved her of limestone and painted her red, just as the people painted their bodies with red ocher.

In addition to other small, stylized stone carvings of humans and animals, early peoples incised and painted remarkably realistic animals on the roofs and walls of caves. The most famous of the cave paintings were found in Lascaux, France (**15.1**), by children exploring an extensive cave beneath an uprooted tree. There are hundreds of paintings covering a series of chambers, with large figures of bulls, deer, horses, bison, and ibexes. They were apparently created by many artists over many years, using fur, feathers, moss, sticks, or fingers to outline the creatures with pigments from natural minerals. These outlines were then colored in with powders perhaps blown through tubes of bone. Some of these cave paintings are so vividly wrought that archeologists at first thought they were fakes, but now their authenticity has been verified, and the ones at Lascaux have been dated to about 15,000 B.C.

In 1994, cave explorers in the Ardèche Valley in France crawled through a hole and discovered a great gallery of 300 such cave paintings, some of which seem to be over 30,000 years old—the oldest known

15.1 Main hall ("Hall of Bulls"), Lascaux, France, c. 15,000–10,000 BC.

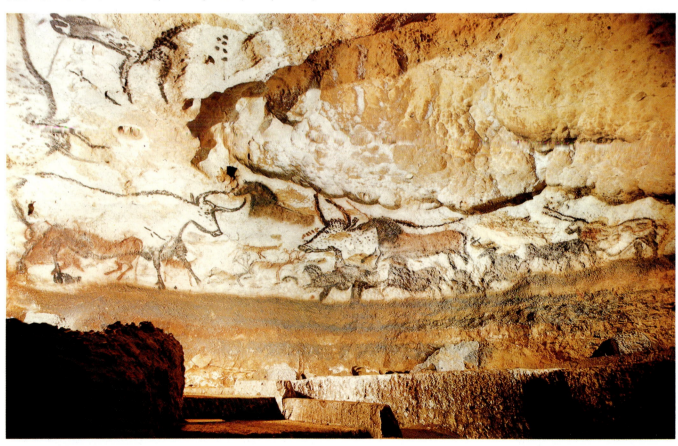

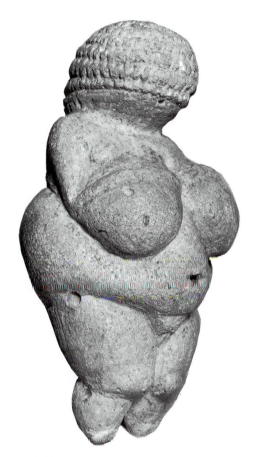

Aegean

One of the earliest known Western civilizations was a seafaring culture centered in the Aegean Sea around Crete and islands to its north, known as the Cyclades. It was in the Cyclades that the art objects most often found in the ruins of these civilizations seem to have originated. Like the figure shown in **15.3**, they were small, stylized female figurines with folded arms, carved out of marble with hard obsidian blades and rubbed to a smooth surface. Remaining bits of paint suggest that they once had painted eyes and jewelry. The fact that they will not stand upright suggests that they were conceived as lying down; usually they have been found in tombs, perhaps as partners for the dead or as homage to the mother goddess. This translation of living, fully round forms into abstracted, nearly flat geometric shapes did not begin to reappear in Western art until the late nineteenth century.

15.2 *Venus of Willendorf*, Lower Austria, c. 30,000–25,000 BC. Limestone, height 4½ ins (11.5 cm). Natural History Museum, Vienna.

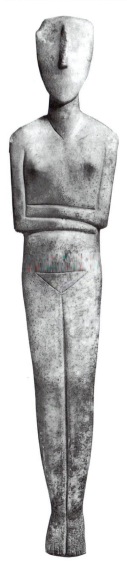

15.3 Cycladic figure from Amorgos, c. 2500–1100 BC. Marble, height 30 ins (76.2 cm). Ashmolean Museum, Oxford.

paintings in the world. Despite their age, they employ sophisticated artistic techniques to represent perspective and movement.

The Lascaux caves, like others in which prehistoric paintings have been discovered, were tortuous underground water channels up to 4000 feet (1300 m) long, and the painted areas were far removed from the cave mouths where the people lived. They would have been very dark, illuminated only by small stone lamps, and very quiet, creating an atmosphere of otherworldly strangeness appropriate for the magical purposes for which some scholars think the paintings were created. Although we have no way of knowing for sure, one common theory is that the images were painted to insure success in the hunt, their surprising representational accuracy being a valuable aid in invoking the spirit of the animal ahead of time and ritually killing it. Those animals depicted as pregnant might have been magically encouraged to be fruitful.

Near Eastern

The other earliest settled civilizations in the West were in Mesopotamia, on the plains between the Tigris and Euphrates rivers in what is now Iraq. The first of these organized urban communities were in Sumer, where each of many cities was protected by a local god or goddess, served and represented by human rulers. Much of the Sumerians' art was devoted to ritual religious themes, such as presentations of gifts to the gods. Some of the low-relief stone carvings and impressions made in clay or wax by cylindrical seals are lively and realistic. The statues placed around the inner walls in a temple devoted to Abu, god of vegetation (15.4), are more simply conceived as dignified,

stylized cylindrical forms in an attitude of worship. The largest figure represents Abu. All are carved in rather soft gypsum marble, with painted hair and beards and inset eyes of black limestone or lapis lazuli against shells.

Egyptian

In isolation from the Mesopotamian civilization, an elaborate culture was developing in Egypt that spanned about 2000 years. At first the arts of Egypt focused almost exclusively on the hereafter, particularly on insuring eternal life for deceased rulers. Great pyramids, such as those at Giza (15.5), were erected to house the mummies, statues, and belongings of

15.4 Statuettes from the Abu Temple, Tell Asmar, c. 2700–2600 BC. Marble, height of tallest figure 30 ins (76.2 cm). Iraq Museum, Baghdad.

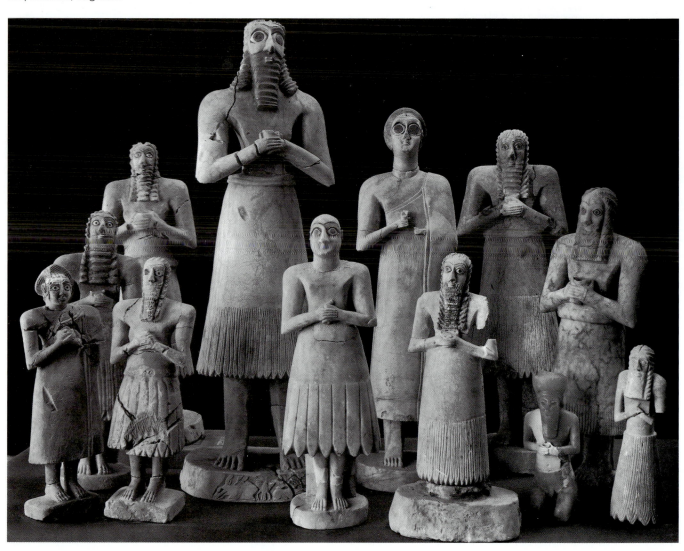

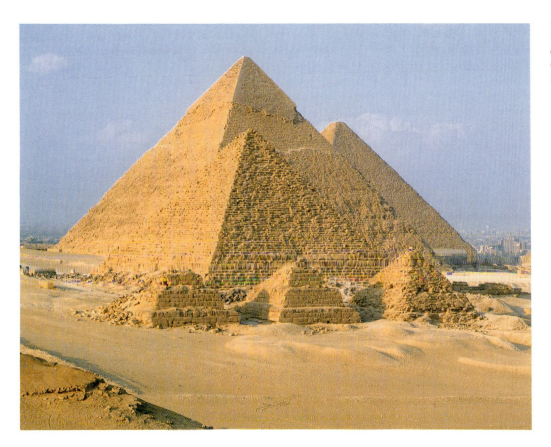

15.5 The Pyramids of Mycerinus (c. 2470 BC), Chefren (c. 2500 BC), and Cheops (c. 2530 BC), Giza, Egypt.

15.6 Portrait panel of Hesira, from Saqqara, c. 2700 BC. Wood, height 4 ft 7½ ins (1.41 m). Egyptian Museum, Cairo.

kings. The pyramid form was intended as an image of the rays of the sun, a stairway on which the king could ascend to heaven. We still don't really know how these monumental structures were built, though many theories have been explored.

Egyptian paintings and sculptures, such as the block form of the Chancellor Senmut with Princess Nefrua as a child shown in Figure 2.30, often combined considerable artistic skill with rigid stylistic conventions. Sculptures were quite obviously rectangular, paintings and exquisite low reliefs of the human form (15.6) usually showed the head in profile, the torso in frontal position, and the legs in profile, leading to some anatomically impossible positioning. Such conventions were not designed to please mortals; they were ways of insuring that a statue would be a suitable dwelling place for the spirit, or that a painting gave as much information as possible. But as the New Kingdom evolved, with Egypt becoming the strongest entity in the Mediterranean area and Akhenaton declaring himself the son of a single god, the god of the sun, art became somewhat more earthly and less stylized. After Akhenaton's time, Egyptian art reverted to earlier stylized conventions.

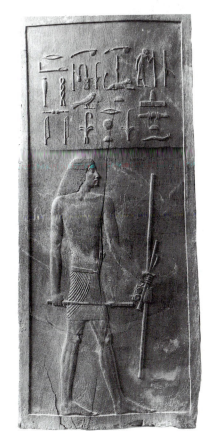

ART OF ANCIENT CULTURES

Greek

From the sixth to second centuries B.C., a remarkable civilization arose in Greece which is still regarded as one of the highest models for the arts. Even before this time, potters of the **Geometric period** were creating two-handled amphoras and other vessels of symmetrical beauty, worked with elaborate geometric patterns. The lovely wheelthrown Dipylon Vase (**15.7**), so named for the cemetery in Athens in which it was found, was of a type used to mark graves. Almost 5 feet (1.5 m) high, it had to be built in separate sections, which were then joined. In addition to the Greek fret pattern later used on buildings and bands of other

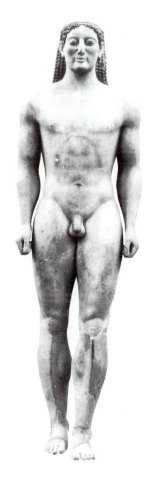

15.8 Kouros, c. 540–515 BC.
Marble, height approx. 6 ft 4 ins (1.92 m).
National Archeological Museum, Athens.

15.7 The Dipylon Vase, Attic Geometric amphora, 8th century BC. Height 4 ft 11 ins (1.5 m). National Archeological Museum, Athens.

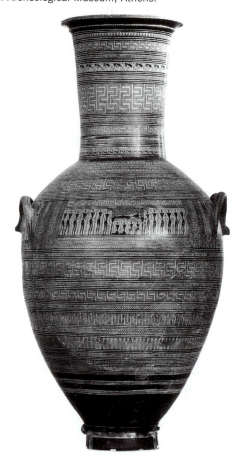

geometrically symmetric motifs, the amphora is decorated with a frieze of mourning human figures reduced to a visual shorthand.

The **Archaic period** in Greece (approximately 700 to 480 B.C.) brought inquiry into the natural structure of the human body. The Kouros ("young male") statues (**15.8**) show great attention to anatomy, and the figures are fully freed from the block of marble from which they were carved, in contrast to the block-like Egyptian statues.

The Golden Age of Athens—the heart of the **Classical Period**—lasted for only part of the fifth century B.C., but its emphasis on rationality, idealized beauty of form, and avoidance of extraneous ornamentation have never been equaled. It was during this period that Pericles signaled his victory in Athens by rebuilding the Acropolis high above the city, with the Parthenon (**15.9** and 3.38) as its focal point. In sculp-

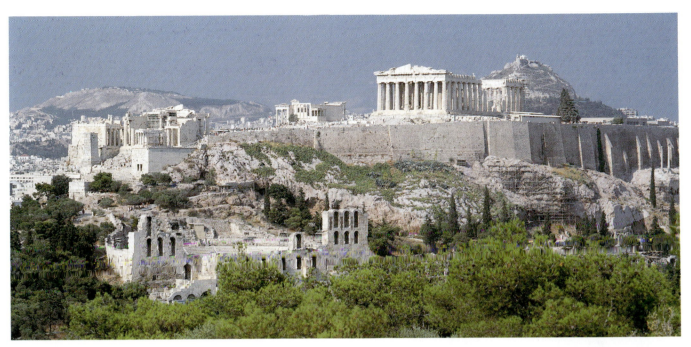

15.9 The Acropolis and Parthenon, Athens, 448–405 BC.
View from the west.

ture, artists abandoned the contrived Egyptian poses for more naturalistic ones, as in the *Spear Bearer* (2.31). This sculpture turns the body in a dynamic, spiral twist known as contrapposto in which the head and shoulders face a different way from the hips and legs.

After the elegant restraint of the Classical period, the **Hellenistic period** was marked by greater emotionalism. During this period, dating from the death of Alexander the Great in 323 B.C. and spanning about 300 years, the power of the Greek city-states declined but Greek culture continued to spread and was adopted by the newly dominant Romans. One of the greatest works of this period was the life-filled, wind-blown *Victory of Samothrace* (15.10), a marble sculpture erected by the people of the little island of Samothrace to celebrate a victory at sea. The emotional drama of her form also characterizes the Hellenistic mosaic of *The Battle of Issus* (5.30). The more natural, informal style of the Hellenistic period can also be sensed in the warm body of the *Venus de Milo* (2.86), and its predilection for "human interest" is reflected in the late Hellenistic bronze of the *Seated Boxer* (10.17).

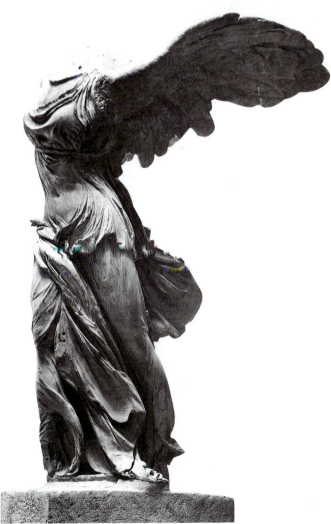

15.10 *Victory of Samothrace*, c. 190 BC.
Marble, height 8 ft (2.44 m). Louvre, Paris.

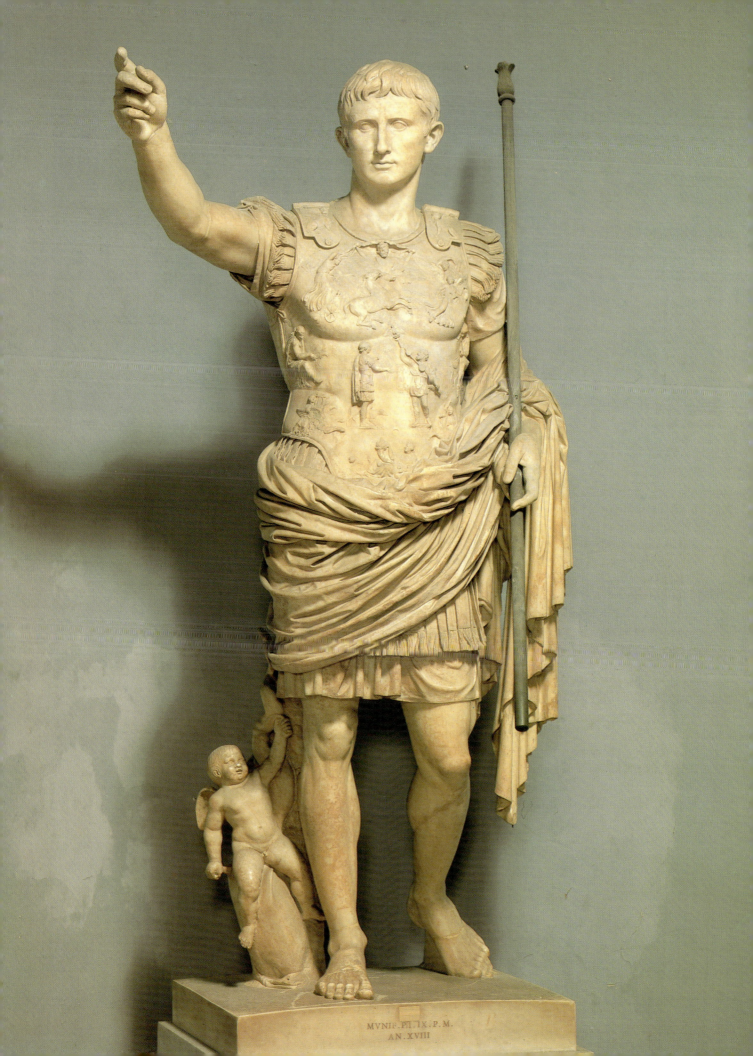

MVNIF·PI·IX·P·M·
AN·XVIII

Roman

Whereas the Greeks developed a culture of ideas, the Romans built a military empire that eventually controlled southern and western Europe and much of North Africa and the Near East. As people of varied cultural background, those living within the Roman Empire did not have a single artistic style, nor did the Romans themselves develop significantly new styles in art. In general, they copied the much-admired Greek art, to the point of using copies of Greek statues with sockets in their necks so that heads of Romans could be attached. Copies of Greek nude statues were also draped with Roman clothing, as in the statue of Augustus (15.11), which is thought to be based on the Greek *Spear Bearer* (2.31).

Many Roman sculptures were celebrations of the secular might of the emperors. Augustus's cuirass is covered with symbols of victory. As part of their empire-building, the Romans erected many public buildings, larger than those of Greece, on a scale facilitated by the introduction of concrete and space-spanning arches, vaults, and domes. It was the Romans who introduced nonfunctional architectural monuments, such as the Arch of Constantine (1.39) and Trajan's Column (2.144). Funerary art of the times included busts made from death masks and sarcophagi, such as the one featuring high reliefs of Dionysos and the Seasons (2.21), for honored corpses once the practice of cremation was abandoned.

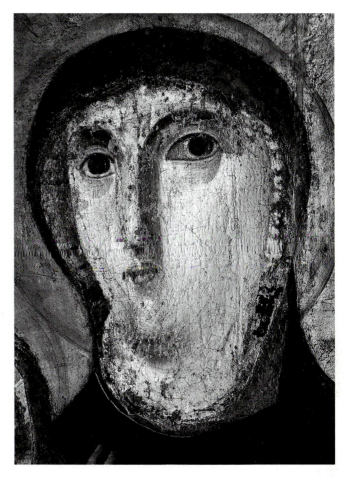

15.12 *Madonna* (detail), 6th–7th century AD.
Encaustic on wood.
Santa Francesca Romana, Rome.

Early Christian and Byzantine

In the first centuries after Christ's death, Christians were persecuted as threats to the state, so they kept what little sacred art they created secret and symbolic. Most of it consisted of burial pieces for those of the faith buried in the catacombs beneath Rome.

When the Emperor Constantine embraced Christianity in 313 as the official religion of the Roman Empire and made Constantinople its second capital, Christian art began to flower. This was particularly so in the eastern half of the Empire as barbarian groups inundated the Western Empire in the fifth century. In the eastern **Byzantine** culture, which lasted 1000 years, all art was religious and created anonymously by the devout. Icons, inspired paintings of Christ, the Virgin Mary, and the saints, were revered for their mystical wonder-working powers. The elongation of figures was stylistically distinctive (**15.12**). Elaborate mosaics (**15.13**), rendered in a stylized, spiritually expressive manner, covered the ceilings and walls of churches with Christian stories. The vast domed church of Hagia Sophia (2.50), built in Constantinople by the Emperor Justinian as the greatest of all Christian churches, was so large for its structure that it had to be rebuilt and buttressed after the dome collapsed.

15.11 (opposite) *Augustus of Primaporta*, c. 20 BC.
Marble, height 6 ft 8 ins (2.03 m).
Vatican Museums, Rome.

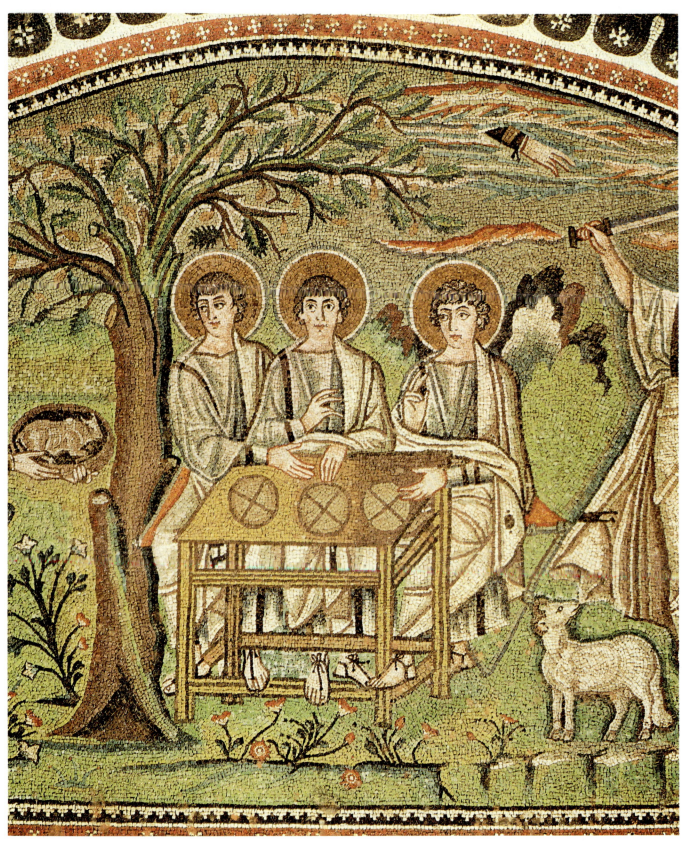

15.13 *Abraham's Hospitality and the Sacrifice of Isaac*, c. 547 AD.
Wall mosaic. San Vitale, Ravenna, Italy.

500–1500 AD Early Christian to Gothic		Events	Works of art
500	c. 400–1453 Byzantine Empire c. 622–900 Islamic Empire	c. 500 Fall of Rome c. 570–632 Mohammad, founder of Islam 652 Koran written down c. 700 porcelain invented in China	6th–7th cent. *Madonna*, Rome, Italy (*15.12*) 532–37 Hagia Sophia, Istanbul (*2.51*) c. 547 *Sacrifice of Isaac*, Ravenna, Italy (*15.13*)
750	Feudalism in Europe to 900 c. 952–1056 Ottonian Empire	c. 750 "Beowulf" epic written c. 800 Charlemagne crowned Emperor of Western (Holy) Roman Empire c. 800–1000 growth of monasticism 868 first printed book in China	9th century *Book of Kells*, Ireland (*15.14*)
1000	c. 1050–1200 Romanesque period c. 1200–1400 Early Gothic	1096–1204 Crusades c. 1100 rise of universities in Spain, France, England c. 1200–50 Marco Polo travels to China and India	c. 1077–1124 Cathedral of Santiago de Compostela, Spain (*15.15*) 1145–70 Chartres Cathedral, France (*13.20*) 1163–1250 Notre Dame, Paris (*13.21*) 1243–48 Sainte-Chapelle, Paris (*2.116*)
1250	c. 1300 Beginning of Renaissance c. 1400–1500 Late Gothic	c. 1250 Arabic numerals introduced in Europe c. 1350 Black Death in Europe 1446–50 Gutenburg prints using movable type 1492 Columbus voyages to America	c. 1280–85 Cimabue, *Madonna Enthroned with Angels*, Florence (*2.75*) 1305–6 Giotto, *The Lamentation*, Padua (*15.17*) 1339 Lorenzetti, *Allegory of Peace*, Siena (*5.8*) 1413–16 Limbourg Brothers, *Les Très Riches Heures*, France (*2.156*) 1423 Da Fabriano, *The Adoration of the Magi*, Florence (*2.157*)

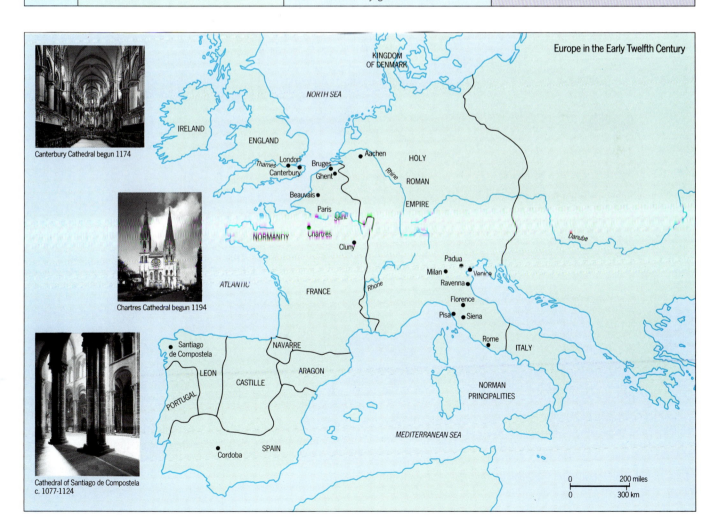

Canterbury Cathedral begun 1174

Chartres Cathedral begun 1194

Cathedral of Santiago de Compostela
c. 1077–1124

Europe in the Early Twelfth Century

KINGDOM OF DENMARK

NORTH SEA

IRELAND

ENGLAND

Thames
London
Canterbury
Bruges
Ghent
Aachen
HOLY
ROMAN
EMPIRE
Rhine
Beauvais
Paris
Seine
NORMANDY
Chartres
Cluny

ATLANTIC

FRANCE

Rhone

Padua
Milan
Venice
Ravenna
Florence
Pisa
Siena
Rome
ITALY

Danube

Santiago de Compostela

NAVARRE

LEON
ARAGON

CASTILLE

PORTUGAL

Cordoba
SPAIN

NORMAN PRINCIPALITIES

MEDITERRANEAN SEA

0   200 miles
0   300 km

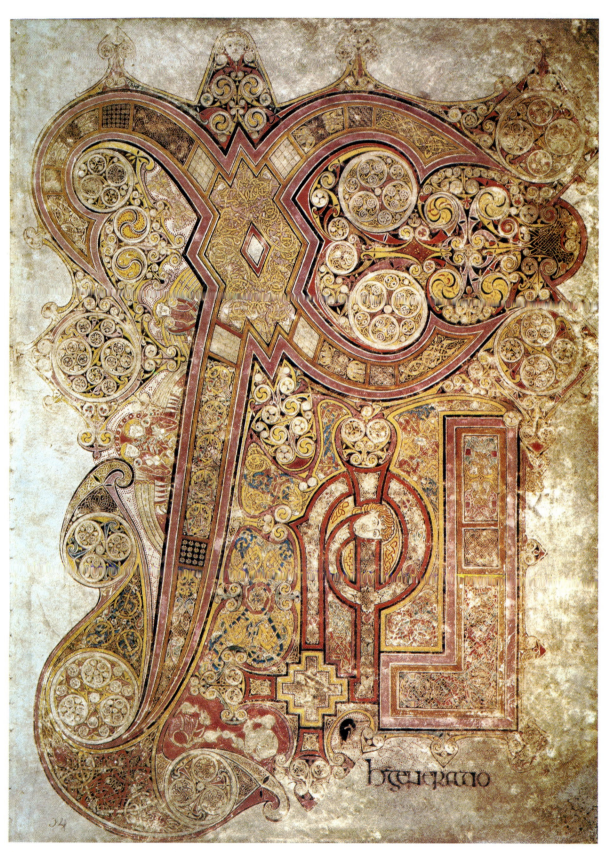

15.14 Incarnation initial from the *Book of Kells* (fol. 34), early 9th century AD.
Vellum, 13 × 10 ins (33 × 25 cm). Trinity College Library, Dublin.

MEDIEVAL ART

Early Medieval

Meanwhile, western Europe was in the throes of the Dark Ages. Learning, spirituality, and art were kept alive in the monasteries and convents. A stunningly beautiful new development under these circumstances was the appearance of elaborate illuminated manuscripts. These unique, handmade copies of sacred

15.15 Interior of the Cathedral of Santiago de Compostela, Spain, c. 1077–1124.

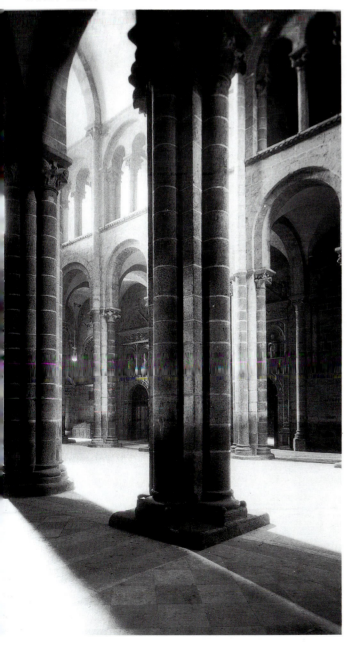

texts, such as the Gospels, became especially ornamental in Ireland and the northern islands of Britain, where Christian fervor was allied with ancient traditions of interlaced and spiraling spiritual motifs. In the hands of the monks of the Iona community off the coast of Scotland, capital letters became extraordinarily ornate. In the *Book of Kells*, which they created, there are over 2000 illuminated capitals used at the beginning of Gospel passages. The one shown here (**15.14**) fills an entire page with intricate traceries surrounding the *Chi-Rho* monogram that begins St. Matthew's story of the birth of Christ.

Romanesque

In the middle of the eleventh century, Europe entered a new period of intense creative activity centered on the Christian Church. Life was still uncertain, and the Roman culture that had once dominated the area was still widely considered the height of the arts. Nevertheless, a new, distinctive aesthetic began to emerge. It was later called **Romanesque** because of its supposed borrowings from Classical Rome, but it had its own form, expressed primarily through architecture. The great longing for churches was answered with a sacred architecture characterized by rounded arches, thick walls and columns, and relief carvings in stone (3.33). The desire for repentance inculcated by the Church led many people to undertake long pilgrimages to certain churches, most notably the Romanesque Cathedral of Santiago de Compostela in Spain (**15.15**). These heavy structures admit only indirect lighting in most areas, lending Romanesque interiors a massive, blocky, almost fortress-like atmosphere.

Gothic

In the middle of the twelfth century, European art and architecture began to undergo an even more profound change. As burgeoning cities shifted the concentration of power from feudal rural areas, spirits seemed to lift, and with them soared the ethereal vertical heights of the new **Gothic** cathedrals. This way of building had a clear beginning in the directions given by Abbot Suger for the first Gothic cathedral: that space be used to symbolize the mystery of God, that God is mystically revealed in light, and that perfect harmony between parts is the basis of beauty. The pointed arch, ribbed vault, and flying buttress allowed architects to replace the heavy appearance of Romanesque structures with more slender and vertical architectural details, such as those at Chartres Cathedral (13.11). The new technology also allowed much larger windows, and these were often filled with intricate stained-glass designs and pictures of gemlike brilliance. They were created from cut pieces of colored glass, some of which were also painted for fine details, joined with lead strips, and reinforced with a framework of iron bands. The great rose window in Chartres Cathedral (15.16) is over 42 feet (13 m) in diameter; it offers an illuminated view of the Virgin Mary surrounded by angels, archangels, doves representing the Gospels and the Holy Spirit, and then outer circles of Old Testament figures.

In painting, artists began using the two-dimensional surface as a frame within which to create the illusion of three-dimensional depth. Although it was difficult to do so in the demanding medium of fresco, Giotto's *The Lamentation* (15.17) illustrates a revolu-

15.16 Rose window, north transept, Chartres Cathedral, Chartres, France, c. 1230. Stained glass, diameter 42 ft 8 ins (13 m).

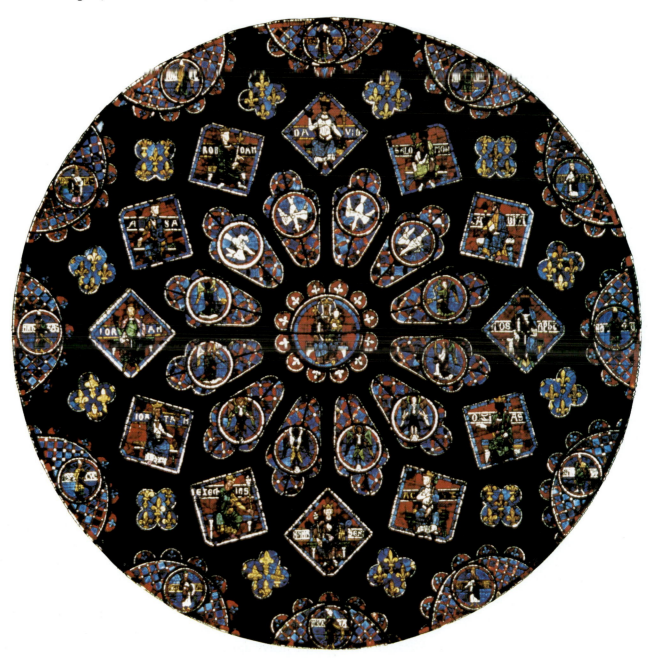

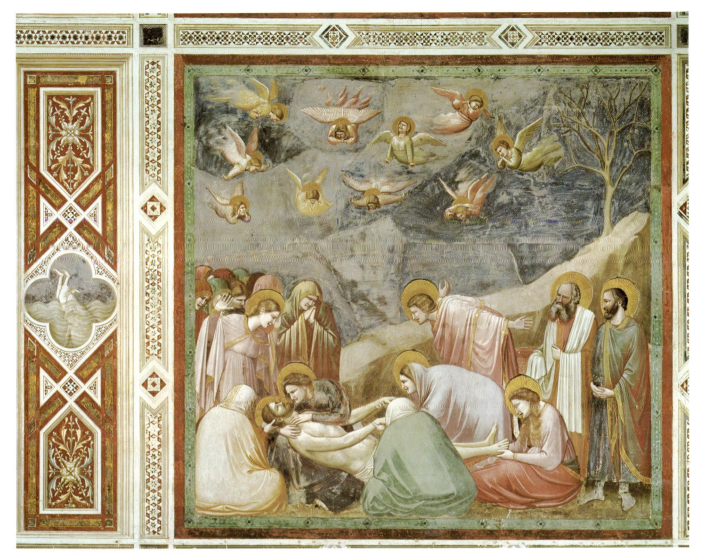

15.17 Giotto, *The Lamentation*, 1305–6.
Fresco, 7 ft 7 ins × 6 ft 7½ ins (2.31 × 2.02 m).
Arena Chapel, Padua, Italy.

tionary approach to the modeling of forms and the new effort to give figures an appearance of being alive and mobile, rather than frozen in static postures. These figures are also imbued with individualized human emotions, from the fierce grief of Mary to the pitiful sorrow of Mary Magdalene, to the philosophical acceptance of the two disciples to the right. Giotto was a great Florentine artist whom many consider the originator of the movement that led to the Renaissance.

In contrast to Romanesque relief carvings, Gothic sculptures integrated into cathedrals were more three-dimensionally separate from their supports.

Late Gothic

Although Gothic art appeared in countries throughout Europe, it waxed and waned at different times at different places, complicating our later efforts to piece together a coherent picture of art history. In north-western Europe, an increasingly expressive and naturalistic successor to the Gothic style lived on until about 1500. Painting was developed to new heights by artists of the Flemish school using the new medium of oil rather than tempera. The van Eyck brothers were early masters of the medium and used it to create the illusion of three-dimensional figures in deep space,

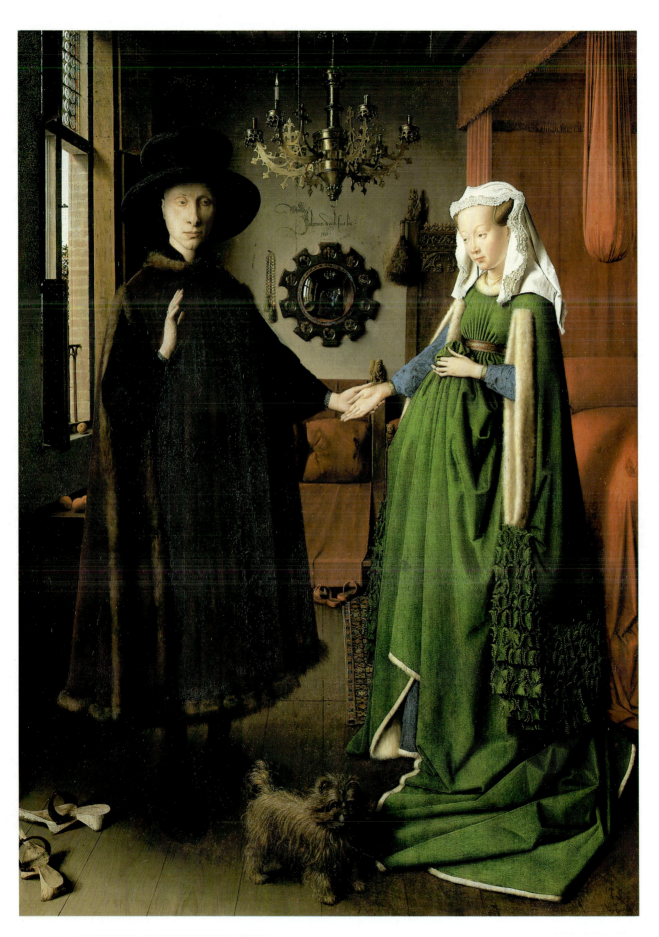

with fine details and the luminous appearance possible only with skillful use of oils. Jan van Eyck's *The Marriage of Giovanni Arnolfini and Giovanna Cenami* (**15.18**) is studded with traditional symbols from the Gothic period—such as the dog indicating faithfulness in marriage, the single candle in the chandelier symbolizing Christ's sacred presence in the marriage ceremony, and the couple's shoes on the floor, reminders of God's commandment to Moses to take off his shoes when he was on holy ground. Yet the textures of metal, furs, fabrics, and wood are rendered with a realism never before achieved in any medium.

15.18 (opposite) Jan van Eyck, *The Marriage of Giovanni Arnolfini and Giovanna Cenami*, 1434. Oil on oak panel, 32¼ × 23½ ins (81.8 × 59.7 cm). National Gallery, London.

15.19 Fra Angelico, *Annunciation*, c. 1440–45. Fresco, San Marco, Florence, Italy.

RENAISSANCE ART
Early Renaissance in Italy

Meanwhile, in fifteenth-century Italy a major shift was underway from the metaphysics of the Middle Ages to a rebirth, or **Renaissance**, of interest in the Classical styles of ancient Greece and Rome. Classical sculptures and architecture were carefully studied for their principles of harmony and symmetry. To these were added a new understanding of perspective based on rediscovery of Euclidian geometry from Classical Greece. The careful use of linear perspective contributes to the sense of spaciousness in Fra Angelico's *Annunciation* (**15.19**), one of many frescoes he painted for a Dominican convent in Florence. A gentle and conservative monk, Fra Angelico retained many

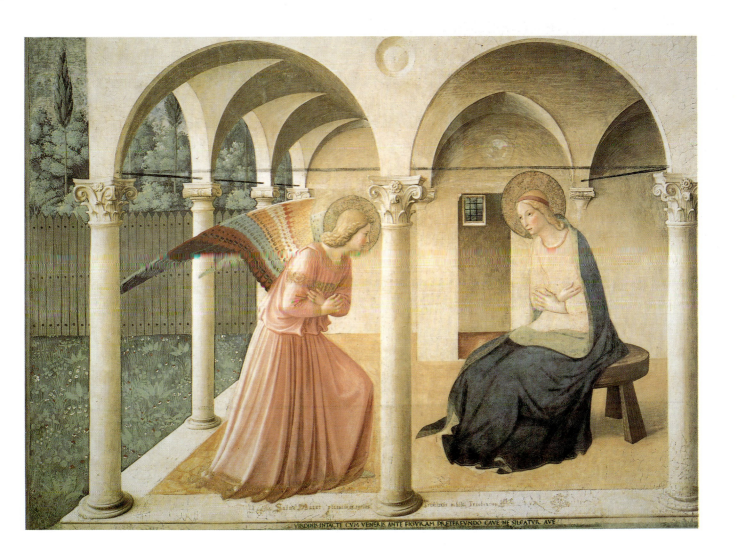

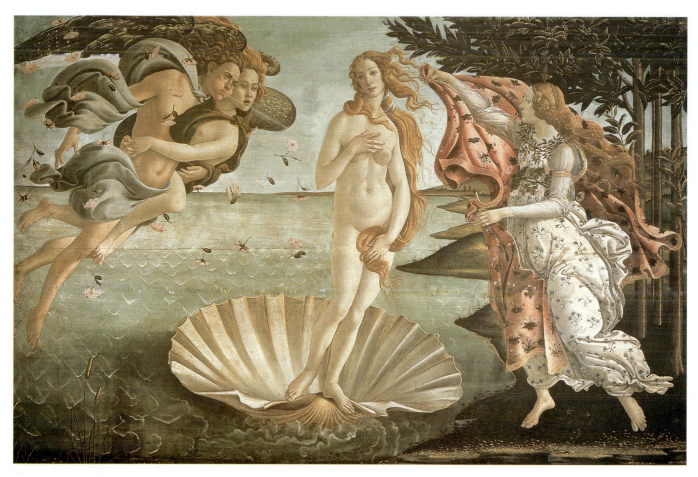

15.20 Sandro Botticelli, *The Birth of Venus*, c. 1482. Tempera on canvas, 5 ft 8 ins × 9 ft 1 in (1.75 × 2.78 m). Galleria degli Uffizi, Florence.

Gothic traits—such as bright pigmentation and the use of the flowery garden as a symbol of Mary's virginity—while incorporating some of the new devices such as perspective rendering and more realistic depiction of anatomy and fabric draping.

The work of the Florentine painter Sandro Botticelli, such as *The Birth of Venus* (**15.20**), likewise shows certain ties with Gothic traditions, such as a more two-than three-dimensional approach to figure drawing. But Botticelli's lyrical evocation of the idealized beauty of the human body and of harmonious configurations of forms is clearly innovative, with Classical origins apparent in its style as well as its mythological subject-matter.

The Early Renaissance also marked a rebirth of logic, though still in the service of the Church. In contrast to the devotional quality of Gothic arts, the Renaissance artist and art historian Lorenzo Ghiberti held that artists should be trained in grammar, geometry, philosophy, medicine, astronomy, perspective, history, anatomy, design theory, and arithmetic. Of his splendid gold-covered *Gates of Paradise* (**15.21**), paneled with ten scenes from the Old Testament, some incorporating scores of figures, he wrote that he "endeavored to imitate nature as much as possible, . . . with buildings drawn to the same proportions as they would appear to the eye and so true that, if you stand far off, they appear to be in relief."[1] The doors are actually modeled in low relief, but the illusion is that of very deep space.

15.21 (opposite) Lorenzo Ghiberti, *Gates of Paradise*, 1424–52. Gilt bronze, height 17 ft (5.2 m). Baptistery, Florence, Italy.

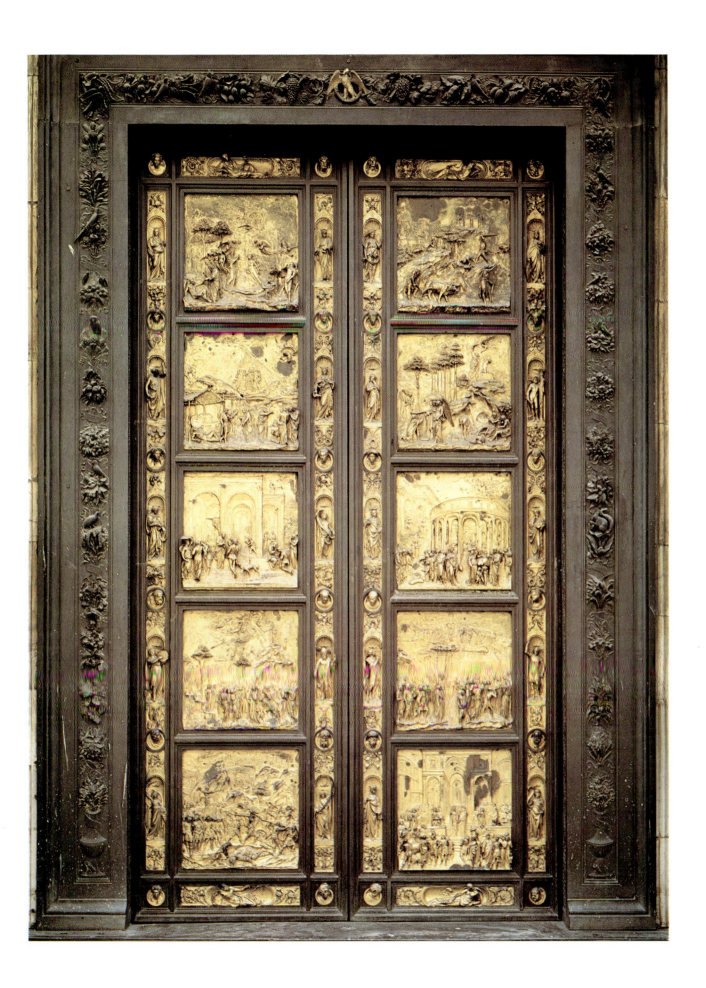

High Renaissance in Italy

During the brief period in Italy now known as the **High Renaissance**, roughly 1490 to 1520, a number of artists centered in Rome created some of the best-loved works of Western art. This great outpouring was freed from the stylized conventions of earlier sacred art, and informed by but not held to Classical traditions. The work of Michelangelo was passionately individualistic, glorifying the divine in the individual. After hundreds of years, people are still deeply moved by Michelangelo's *Pietà* (**15.22**), sculpted when he was only 24 years old. He regarded the human body as the prison of the soul, noble on the surface and divinely yearning within, and experienced sculpting as liberating a living form from inert stone. In addition to his anatomically and emotionally powerful sculptures, he also painted the vast Sistine Chapel ceiling (16.15), in an agonizingly awkward upward-looking position. Perhaps the extreme example of the Renaissance ideal of human freedom, Michelangelo refused to be enslaved by tradition or other people's standards, recognizing only his own divinely inspired genius and his longing for beauty as his guides.

Leonardo da Vinci applied his inventive genius to many fields, including art, and was thus the epitome of the "Renaissance man." His searching mind led him to engineering, mathematics, music, poetry, architecture, and natural science, as well as painting and sculpture. He continually studied animals, plants, human anatomy, the movement of water, and the play of light and shadow for a fuller understanding of the natural world. In art, his beautifully observed figure drawings are still consulted by artists as guides to the depiction of human anatomy. He used chiaroscuro effects not only to round his forms in space but also to enhance the emotional qualities of his paintings and guide the viewer's eye. In his compelling *The Virgin of the Rocks* (**15.23**), light glimmers on the flesh of the sacred figures and beckons in the mysterious distance.

15.22 Michelangelo Buonarroti, *Pietà*, 1499. Carrara marble, height 5 ft 9 ins (1.75 m). St. Peter's, Rome.

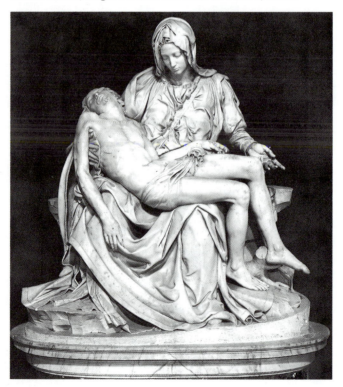

15.23 (opposite) Leonardo da Vinci, *The Virgin of the Rocks*, c. 1485. Oil on panel, 6 ft 2⅝ ins × 3 ft 11¼ ins (1.89 × 1.2 m). Louvre, Paris.

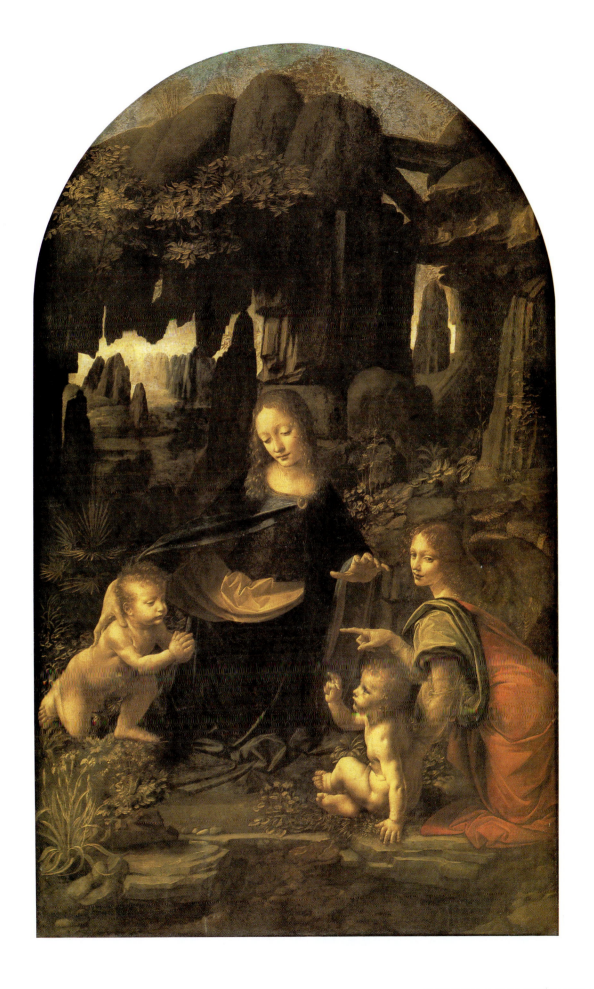

ART ISSUES
PROTECTING FAMOUS ARTWORKS

When tourists from around the world visit the Louvre in Paris, seeing Leonardo's *Mona Lisa* at first hand is the most essential experience the majority of them are seeking (5.5 and **15.24**). But nowadays the object of their pilgrimage can be viewed only in a humidity-proof box through a protective shield of bulletproof glass. What they see is mostly their own reflection in the glass, trying to see past it to the famous smile. All around are signs indicating that they must not photograph the painting, which they can barely see. Within its hermetically sealed box, the painting is quite dirty, for the museum curators dare not remove its yellowed varnish lest there be a public outcry. A twenty-four-hour alarm system is always on alert to prevent damage or theft.

With all these protective measures, what is left of the intimate encounter between the viewer and the famous artworks? The *Mona Lisa* can barely be seen; it has become a sacred icon of sorts. Museum officials have taken extreme measures to protect the painting precisely because it is so famous.

The bulletproof shield is to protect the painting from physical attack. In 1956, a Bolivian tourist threw a rock at it, damaging the left elbow. The ban on photographs is to prevent flashes of bright light,

which could turn the varnish even yellower and change the pigments. The climate-control case keeps the painting at 68 degrees Fahrenheit, with 50 to 55 per cent humidity maintained by boxes of silica gel below, to help preserve the poplar wood panel on which Leonardo painted his famous image. Behind the panel, a series of slats has been added to check its expansion and contraction. Already there is a fine crack descending from the top into the forehead. Monitoring the health of the painting is a precise science, carried out with a sense of sacred duty.

Paintings are designed to be seen only from the front, so they can be mounted behind glass shields if necessary. To protect sculptures from human damage requires measures that distance the public even further. Famous statues are often cordoned off. After Michelangelo's touching *Pietà* (15.22) was attacked in 1972 by someone who was out of his senses, a bulletproof glass shield was also placed around it. Without such a shield, the foot of Michelangelo's great statue of *David* (10.2) was attacked in 1991 by a mentally ill person wielding a hammer. He explained that a woman in a painting by Veronese told him to strike the *David*. In a moment of sheer madness, the painstakingly and perfectly sculpted end of a toe

was reduced to a pile of marble chips and dust.

As powerful nations have looted precious art treasures from countries they have conquered as part of the spoils of war, another issue has arisen. There they may remain in captivity, long after the wars have been resolved, with the rationale by the conquering country that they are "protecting" the art. The British Museum, for instance, still houses Classical Greek reliefs that were taken from the Parthenon in Athens (3.38) in the early nineteenth century by the British nobleman Lord Elgin with the agreement of the Ottoman authorities then in control of Greece. This removal may arguably have protected the reliefs from damage during the Greek war of independence, but that strife ended long ago. Despite repeated protests from the Greek government, the reliefs are still lodged in the British Museum. The same thing has happened in many parts of the world, including the United States, where Native Americans want the return of artifacts that were "collected" by archeologists and anthropologists and now reside in distant museums.

The other side of the arguments about protection and seclusion from the public is that masterworks are irreplaceable and can perhaps never be restored to

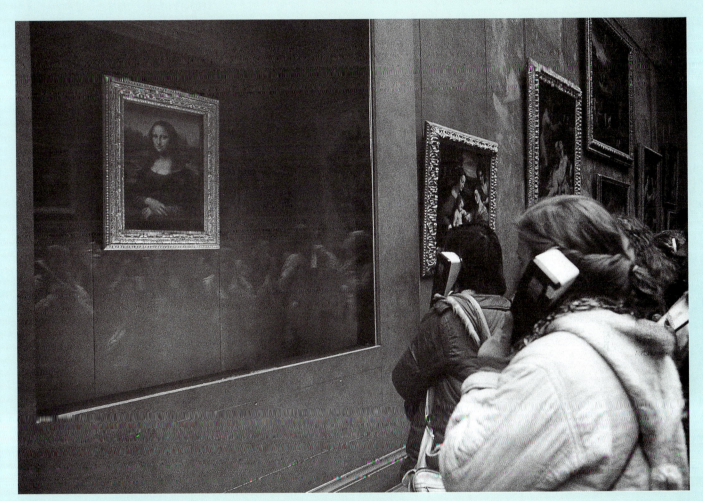

15.24 Visitors viewing Leonardo da Vinci's *Mona Lisa* through bulletproof glass.

their original condition once they are damaged. Masters such as Michelangelo and Leonardo are rare in human history. But to truly protect their works for posterity would require fully sealing them off from the public in climate-controlled, tamper-proof archives.

Herein lie the difficulties. What balance should be struck between the desire of people to see famous works of art and the desire to preserve them as long as possible? Who has the right to see them? In 1995, the Reina Sofia Museum of Modern Art in Madrid chose to remove the protective glass shield with which it had covered Picasso's *Guernica* (1.47). Now the great work can be fully seen again, but it is again vulnerable to the unpredictable passions of the viewing public.

1425–1640	Early Renaissance to Southern Baroque	Events	Works of art
1425	Renaissance begins in Italy	1416–25 Brunelleschi reinvents linear perspective 1431 Joan of Arc burned at the stake 1434–94 de Medici dynasty in Florence c. 1450 printing press invented 1453 Turks enter Constantinople; end of Byzantine Empire	1424–52 Ghiberti, *Gates of Paradise*, Florence (*15.21*) c. 1440–45 Fra Angelico, *Annunciation*, Florence (*15.19*) c. 1460 Del Pollaiuolo, *Battle of the Ten Nude Men*, Florence (*6.1*) c. 1482 Botticelli, *The Birth of Venus*, Florence (*15.20*)
1485	c. 1490–1520 High Renaissance c. 1500–1600 Northern Renaissance c. 1525 Mannerism begins	Opening of European trade routes 1520–22 Magellan sails round the world 1543 Copernicus refutes geocentric view of universe	c. 1485 Da Vinci, *The Virgin of the Rocks*, Milan (*15.23*) c. 1495–98 Da Vinci, *The Last Supper*, Milan (*3.31*) 1499 Michelangelo, *Pietà*, Rome (*15.22*) 1501–4 Michelangelo, *David*, Florence (*10.2*) 1509–11 Raphael, *The School of Athens*, Rome (*15.25*) 1508–12 Michelangelo, Sistine Chapel ceiling, Rome (*16.15*) c. 1532 Correggio, *Danae*, Rome (*5.16*) c. 1550 Bronzino, *Portrait of a Young Man*, Florence (*5.2*) 1554 Cellini, *Perseus with the Head of Medusa*, Florence (*10.18*) 1592–94 Tintoretto, *The Last Supper*, Venice (*15.26*)
1595	Baroque period Colonial period in North America	1607–19 Kepler establishes planetary systems 1620 Puritans land in New England	1596 Caravaggio, *The Calling of St. Matthew*, Rome (*15.28*) 1656 Velázquez, *The Maids of Honor*, Spain (*15.29*) 1656 Bernini, Piazza of St. Peter's, Rome (*14.7*)

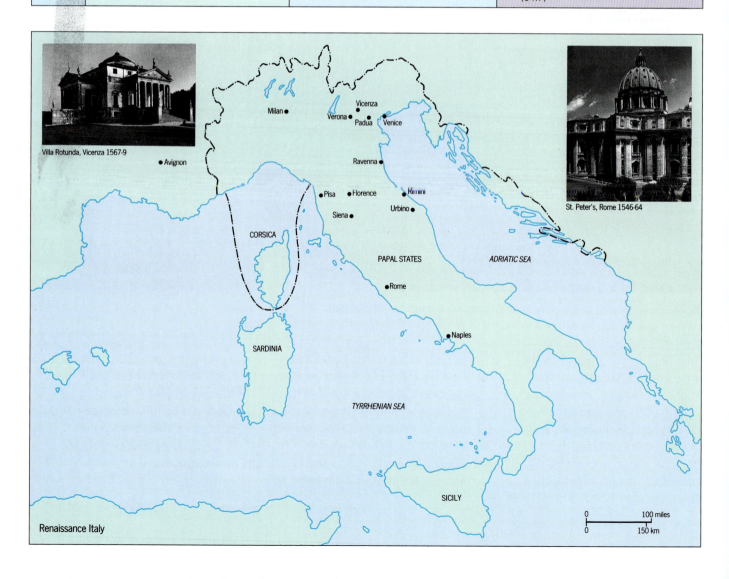

Villa Rotunda, Vicenza 1567-9

St. Peter's, Rome 1546-64

Milan
Verona Vicenza
Padua Venice
Avignon
Ravenna
Pisa Florence Rimini
Siena Urbino
CORSICA
PAPAL STATES
ADRIATIC SEA
Rome
SARDINIA
Naples
TYRRHENIAN SEA
SICILY

0 100 miles
0 150 km

Renaissance Italy

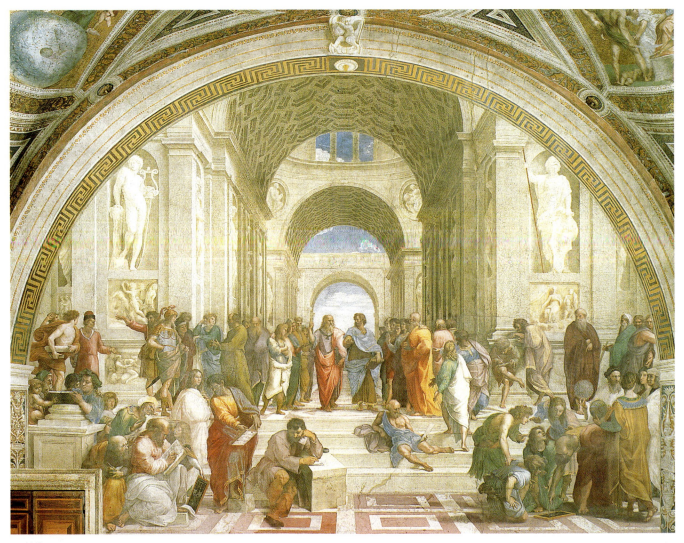

15.25 Raphael, *The School of Athens*, 1509–11.
Fresco, 26 × 18 ft (7.9 × 5.5 m).
Stanza della Segnatura, Vatican Palace, Rome.

It was Leonardo who also developed sfumato modulations in oil painting to soften contours and create hazy atmospheric effects. Ever experimenting, he completed few works. His famous *The Last Supper* (3.31) was done in tempera with a ground of pitch and mastic that he had invented—and which soon began to break down, requiring a series of restorations.

The artist whose work most clearly characterizes the High Renaissance was Raphael. In contrast to Michelangelo's passion and Leonardo's inventiveness, Raphael's work emphasizes Classical harmony, reason, and idealism. His *The School of Athens* fresco (**15.25**) stands as a symbol of the humanistic High Renaissance appreciation of learning. The central figures are Plato and Aristotle, flanked by other ancient philosophers, mathematicians, scientists, and their students, including Pythagoras writing at the lower left and Euclid demonstrating a theorem at the lower right. This serenely balanced composition covers a 26-foot (8-m) span at the Vatican Palace in Rome. Raphael further developed the triangular composition associated with Leonardo, and it was thereafter used extensively in depictions of the Madonna and the Holy Family.

Mannerism

In opposition to the humane balance and order of High Renaissance works such as *The School of Athens*, many Italian artists from 1525 to 1600 developed a more self-consciously sophisticated approach called **Mannerism** by their detractors. Bronzino's work (5.2) is one example of the cool, sometimes almost sinister quality of elegance that some artists sought; Correggio (5.16) explored the refinements that technical perfection could lend to sensuality. A comparison of Tintoretto's version of *The Last Supper* (**15.26**) with that of Leonardo (3.31) reveals the great aesthetic distance between the Renaissance ideals of harmony and logic and the inventive theatricality of Tintoretto's Mannerism. As in his *Leda and the Swan* (3.11), bodies turn in agitated gestures to tell a story of the infusion of the divine spirit into the bread and wine as if the narrative were being expertly enacted on a stage. In sculpture, Mannerism is most obviously exemplified by the sensuous work of Benvenuto Cellini (10.18).

Northern Renaissance

Beyond the Alps, the explosion of creativity in Italy at first had little effect on artists still following Late Gothic traditions, until 1520, when distinctively northern and Protestant versions of the new trends appeared briefly and vigorously in Germany. At one extreme was the dramatic intensity of Matthias Grünewald's work, such as *The Isenheim Altarpiece*, with its agonizing central *Crucifixion* panel, and exuberant *Resurrection* panel (**15.27**).

While only the individualistic aspects of the Italian Renaissance seem to come forth in Grünewald's work, Albrecht Dürer was so impressed by the disciplined, rational approach of the art he studied in Venice that he intentionally modeled himself as a humanistic scholar and wrote extensively to convince his compatriots of the value of Renaissance approaches to art. He was very influential because his skillful woodcuts (6.6) and engravings were widely distributed.

15.26 Jacopo Tintoretto, *The Last Supper*, 1592–94. Oil on canvas, 12 × 18 ft (3.65 × 5.5 m). San Giorgio Maggiore, Venice, Italy.

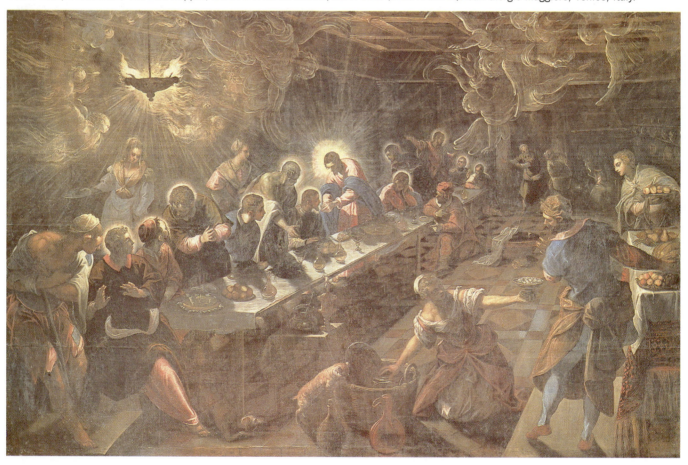

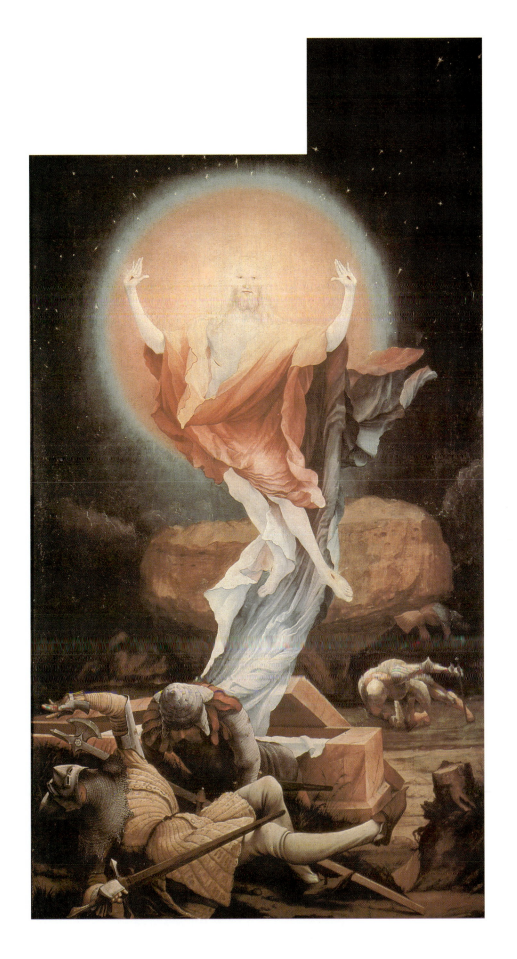

15.27 Matthias Grünewald,
The Resurrection, from
The Isenheim Altarpiece, c. 1510–15.
Oil on panel, 8 ft 10 ins × 4 ft 8 ins
(2.7 × 1.4 m). Musée Unterlinden,
Colmar, France.

BAROQUE ART

Southern Baroque

Throughout Europe, the seventeenth century was a period in which the new middle classes joined the Church and nobility as patrons of the arts. Art became more realistic and emotional, speaking directly to viewers in sensuous, exuberant forms. In Catholic Italy, the tempestuous Caravaggio opened this **Baroque** period with his earthy focus on real people, an entirely new concept for religious paintings. In his *The Calling of St. Matthew* (**15.28**), he dresses Matthew and his companions in contemporary clothes and has them counting the day's takings when Christ appears, recognizing his spiritual beauty in the midst of familiar everyday life rather than in a formal, idealized setting.

The same unposed, naturalistic quality appears in the works of Velázquez, even when his subjects were the Spanish royal family. His famous *Las Meninas* (**15.29**) is not a formal family portrait but a domestic scene of the young Princess Margarita with her attendants; the king and queen are seemingly reflected in a mirror at the end of the room. Is Velázquez, who has painted himself before the canvas, looking at them? Does the mirror reflect part of the canvas instead? The artist's fascination with the effects of light is evident not only in these compositional ambiguities but also in the subtle variations of light and shadow throughout the work. For his highly skilled, suggestive brushwork, the later French Impressionists regarded Velázquez as the best of the painters of the past.

In sculpture, Bernini created ornate new forms for everything from fountains to building façades. His *The Ecstasy of St. Teresa* (1.13) reflects the actively emotional quality of the Baroque period, in contrast to the cool intellectualism of Mannerism. Swirling and diagonal lines create complex circular paths through the piece, which differs from the serenity of Classical draping, and Bernini dares to give St. Teresa a facial expression of supreme ecstasy whose sexual quality is hardly even ambiguous. Bernini's approach was soon copied by artists throughout Europe.

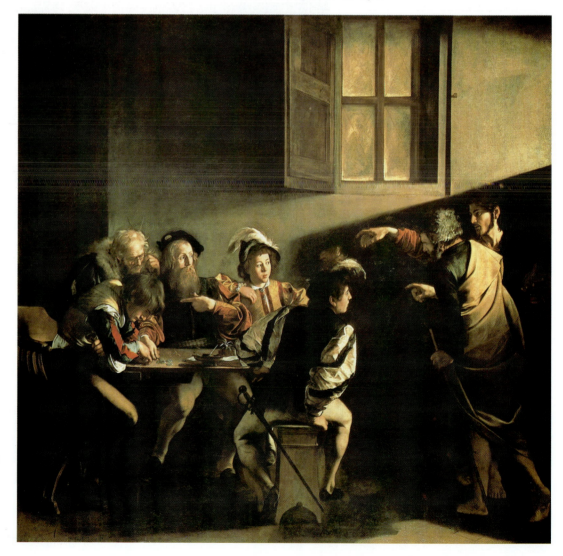

15.28 Michelangelo Merisi da Caravaggio, *The Calling of St. Matthew*, 1596. Oil on canvas, 11 ft 1 in × 11 ft 5 ins (3.37 × 3.47 m). S. Luigi dei Francesi, Rome.

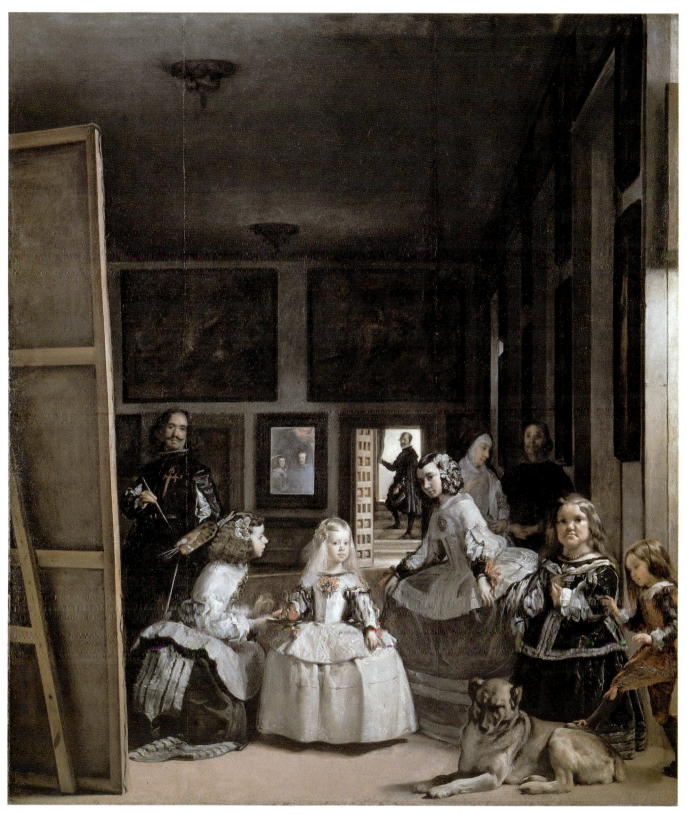

15.29 Diego Velázquez, *Las Meninas (The Maids of Honor)*, 1656.
Oil on canvas, 10 ft 5 ins × 9 ft (3.18 × 2.76 m).
Reina Sofia Museum of Modern Art, Madrid.

1500–1800	Northern Renaissance to Rococo	Events	Works of art
1500	c. 1500–1600 Northern Renaissance	1517 Reformation begins 1521 Luther translates Bible into German, pub. 1534 1545–64 Catholic Counter-Reformation 1566 iconclastic destruction in Netherlands Spread of Humanism, availability of books increases	1508 Dürer, *Head of an Apostle*, Nuremburg, Germany (*2.13*) c. 1510 Bosch, *The Carrying of the Cross*, Ghent, Netherlands (*2.69*) c. 1510–15 Grünewald, *The Resurrection*, Germany (*15.27*) 1511 Dürer, *Saint Christopher*, Nuremburg, Germany (*6.6*) c. 1540 Hans Holbein, *Jane Small*, Basel, Switzerland (*2.73*) 1565 Bruegel, *Hunters in the Snow*, Antwerp, Netherlands (*2.59*)
1600	Northern Baroque	1611 first authorized version of the Bible 1663 reorganization of the French Academy 1672 Bellori writes *Lives of Modern Artists*	c. 1626 Rubens, *The Assumption of the Virgin*, Antwerp, Netherlands (*15.30*) c. 1635 Rubens, *Landscape with Rainbow*, Antwerp, Netherlands (*1.26*) 1660 Claude Lorrain, *Campagna Landscape*, France (*4.14*) c. 1660 Rembrandt, *Self-Portrait*, Amsterdam, Netherands (*1.3*) 1660–69 Rembrandt, *Sleeping Girl*, Amsterdam, Netherlands (*4.16*) c. 1665-70 Vermeer, *The Art of Painting*, Amsterdam, Netherlands (*2.37*) 1669–85 Palace of Versailles, France (*1.9*) 1675-1710 Wren, St. Paul's Cathedral, London (*15.31*)
1700	Rococo style	c. 1710–95 rise of Prussia 1789 French Revolution 1792 Paine, *The Rights of Man*	1743–1772 Neumann, Vierzehnheiligen Church, Germany (*15.32*)

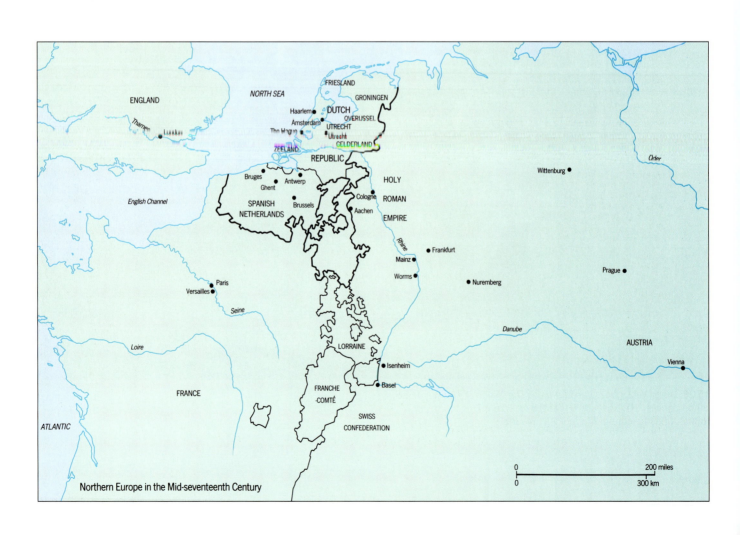

Northern Europe in the Mid-seventeenth Century

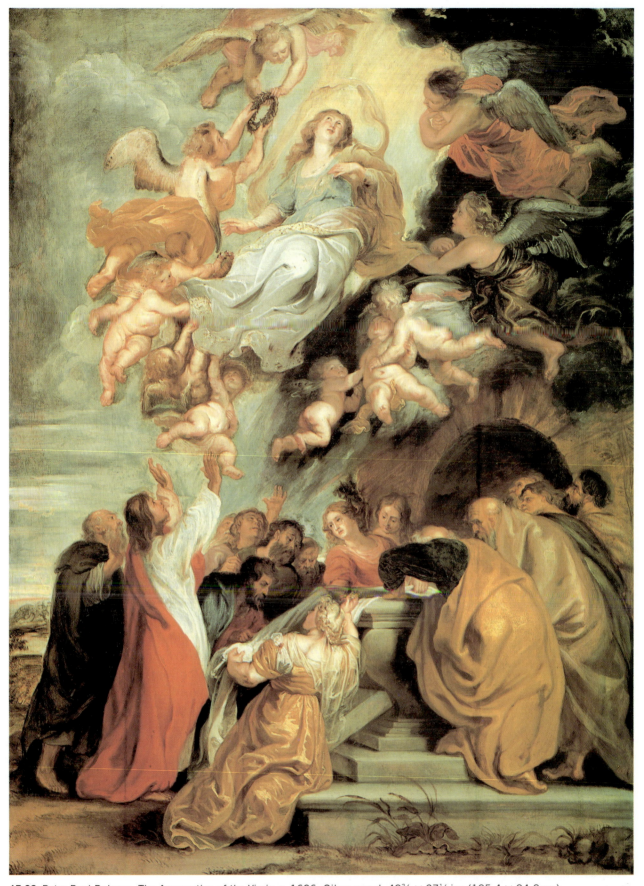

15.30 Peter Paul Rubens, *The Assumption of the Virgin*, c. 1626. Oil on panel, 49⅜ × 37⅛ ins (125.4 × 94.2 cm). National Gallery of Art, Washington, D.C. Samuel H. Kress Collection.

Northern Baroque

The Baroque style in northern Europe found other forms. One of its greatest exponents was Peter Paul Rubens of Antwerp. His *The Assumption of the Virgin* (15.30) represents plump, rounded figures in an appreciative, joyful way, with flowing movement and warm colors. This was spirituality in the flesh. His typically large, swirling paintings are quite recognizable in style, even though Rubens employed a workshop of assistants to do much of the work on his 3000 signed paintings, a common practice at the time.

In the Netherlands, where a Protestant culture drew its strength from a sober and prosperous middle class which rejected the influence of Rome, Rembrandt emerged as one of the greatest artists of all time. Influenced by the work of Rubens—as well as that of many other artists, including those of non-European cultures—he made use of Baroque devices for leading the eye through undulating three-dimensional space. Highly spiritual, he brought the psychological impact of religious themes directly through to the viewer with subtlety and deep human understanding. His self-portraits (such as 1.3) and treatments of religious subjects, such as *The Three Crosses* (6.19–24), are the work of one who feels life profoundly, as well as of a master of the visual arts.

In architecture, the Baroque period was characterized by grand effects and exuberant, swelling forms. This tendency was combined with a certain Classical restraint by Christopher Wren in his rebuilding of St. Paul's Cathedral (15.31) in London. He planned the structure from the bottom up, while it was under construction, and the clearly Baroque dome and towers are wedded to more Classical lower levels inspired by the Italian Renaissance architect Palladio.

Rococo

In the late Baroque—or **Rococo**—period in central Europe (the first half of the eighteenth century), formal restraint was abandoned. In France, painters such as Antoine Watteau and Jean Honoré Fragonard (2.152) honored the whims of the aristocracy (led by Louis XV, who called for a more lighthearted art) with dreamy scenes of carefree and beautiful people in a natural paradise. These visions were rendered with delicate, swirling lines and pastel colors in a style considered so frilly by the French revolutionaries who overthrew the aristocracy that they dubbed it "Rococo," a frivolous concoction of shells. Today the Rococo style is considered to have rather more substance—an intentional freeing of art from academic rules of composition in favor of exuberant, dancing lines and gentle coloring.

Architecture also became unabashedly ornate and fantastic. The most extraordinary of the German Rococo churches is Balthasar Neumann's pilgrimage church of Vierzehnheiligen (15.32). Everything seems to be in constant motion. There are few straight lines; curling motifs developed in France swirl endlessly, and the ceiling is treated to create a floating

15.31 Christopher Wren, St. Paul's Cathedral, London, 1675–1710.

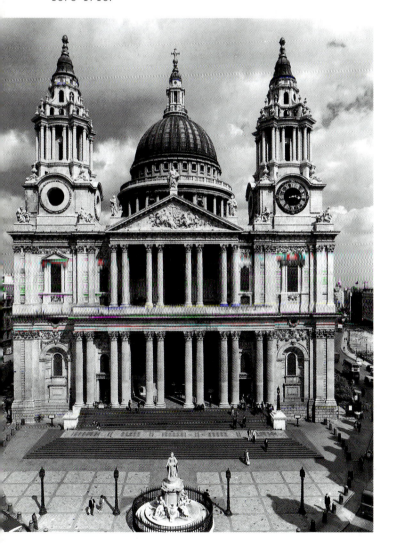

15.32 (opposite) Balthasar Neumann, Vierzehnheiligen Church, near Staffelstein, Germany, 1743–72.

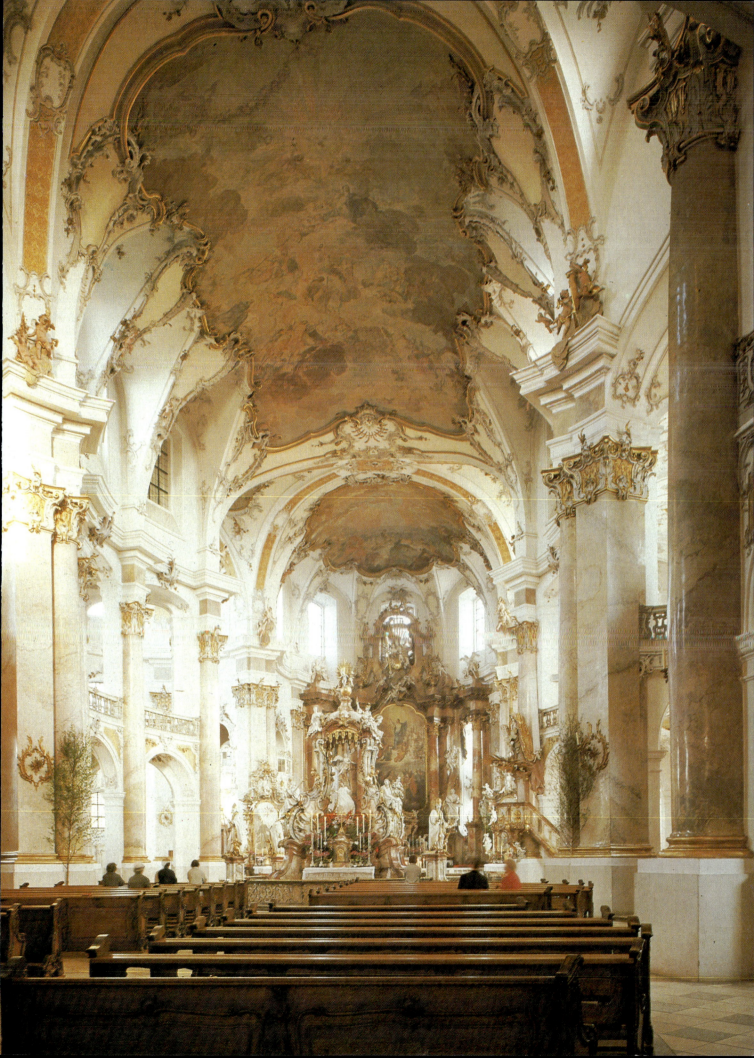

illusion of boundless space. The gaiety expressed here is a far cry from the heavy, still atmosphere of Romanesque churches or the soaring, vertical thrusts of the Gothic cathedrals—yet all are conducive to certain kinds of spiritual experiences and appropriate for their times.

EIGHTEENTH- AND EARLY NINETEENTH-CENTURY ART

Neoclassicism

In the swings of action and reaction that increasingly characterized art history, the late eighteenth century brought another return to the aesthetics of ancient Greece and Rome. As a reaction to Baroque and particularly Rococo styles, and as an expression of the Enlightenment, artists such as Jean-Antoine Houdon sought a quiet, informal dignity (10.10). Archeologists' discoveries of Classical cities such as Pompeii gave architects models to follow in their return to noble, restrained buildings. Winckelmann's highly influential *Thoughts on the Imitation of Greek Works of Art* (1755) held that "The only way to become great . . . is by imitation of the ancients. . . . [Art] should aim at noble simplicity and calm grandeur."[2]

Neoclassical painters tried to re-create the style of Classical sculptures, since little was known of ancient painting. Using his art to encourage reformist patriotism and stoicism during the French Revolution, Jacques-Louis David re-created a story of heroic self-sacrifice from Republican Rome in his *The Oath of the Horatii* (15.33). Its severity and clarity are clear departures from the works of the recent past.

15.33 Jacques-Louis David, *The Oath of the Horatii*, 1784–85. Oil on canvas, approx 14 × 11 ft (4.3 × 3.7 m). Louvre, Paris.

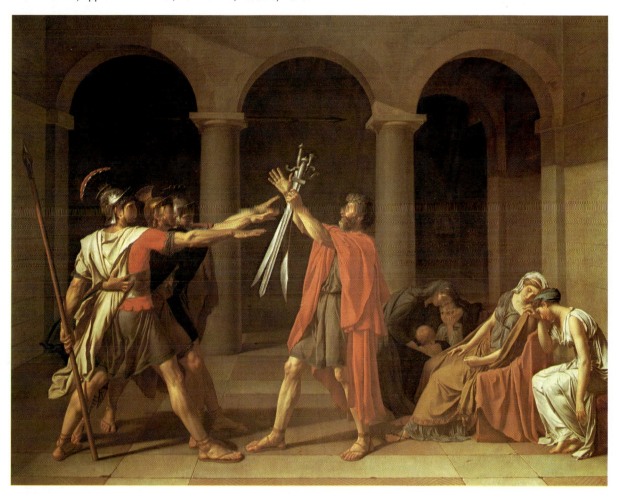

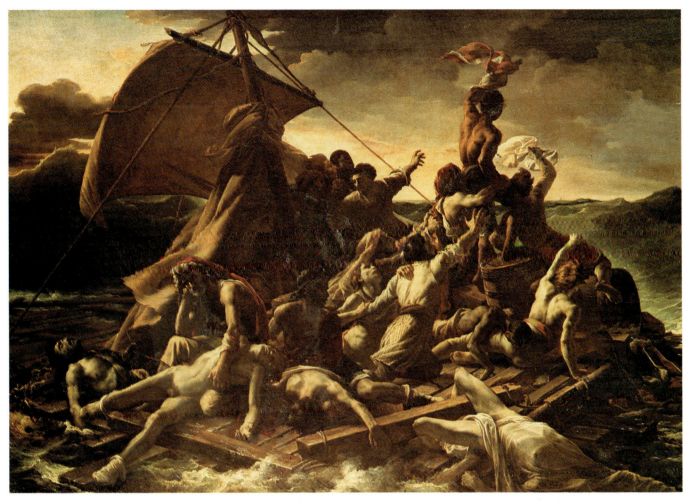

15.34 Théodore Géricault, *The Raft of the Medusa*, 1818–19.
Oil on canvas, 16 × 23 ft (4.9 × 7 m). Louvre, Paris.

Romanticism

Throughout the history of Western art certain artists have focused more on emotion and imagination than on the logic and harmony of Classicism. This perennial tendency surfaced in the **Romantic** movement in the early decades of the nineteenth century. In contrast to the austere Neoclassical attempts to be impersonal, Romantic artists openly expressed their own feelings. In their landscape paintings, newly elevated to a position as significant as figure paintings, they portrayed the natural world as an extension of their own sensibilities, which ranged from the peacefulness of John Constable's rural scenes to the turbulence of Turner's seascapes (5.21). Turner discovered the emotional impact of pure color and pushed it to the point where it almost became the subject-matter.

Théodore Géricault's *The Raft of the Medusa* (15.34) illustrates the emphasis on sensation and passion in content and dynamism in composition that characterized the French version of Romanticism. The huge painting, which implies criticism of the social status quo, depicts the 13-day ordeal of the few passengers who survived the sinking of a government ship. They were left adrift on a crude raft by the captain and crew. Emotions of despair, suffering, and hope are built into a strong double-triangle composition charged with energy.

The mystical prints and paintings of William Blake (3.18) carried something of the passionate emotional content of the Romantic movement, although Blake had his own unique visionary agenda. In architecture, Romanticism was expressed through nostalgia for Gothic structures, eclecticism, and exoticism.

1750–1950 Neoclassicism to Surrealism	Events	Works of art
1750 Neoclassicism, France	1775–83 American Revolution 1789 French Revolution	c. 1779–80 Houdon, *Bust of a Young Girl*, France (*10.10*) 1784 David, *The Oath of the Horatii*, France (*15.33*)
1800 Romanticism, France and England	1804–14 Napoleonic Empire 1814 first steam engine 1815–50 industrialization of England 1837 invention of telegraph 1839 invention of photography (Daguerre) 1848 revolutionary uprisings in Europe	1808 Blake, *The Last Judgment*, England (*3.18*) 1818–19 Géricault, *The Raft of the Medusa*, France (*15.34*) 1842 Ingres, *Two Nudes*, France (*2.39*) 1845 Turner, *Looking out to Sea*, England (*5.21*)
1850 Realism c. 1875–1900 Impressionism 1880–1900 Post-Impressionism	1859 Darwin, *Origin of Species* 1861–65 American Civil War 1876 Bell patents telephone 1894 Edison invents motion picture	1849 Courbet, *The Stone Breakers*, France (*15.35*) 1863 Manet, *Le Déjeuner sur l'herbe*, France (*15.36*) c. 1878 Degas, *Dancer with a Bouquet*, France (*2.66*) 1881 Renoir, *The Boating Party*, France (*3.28*) 1884–86 Seurat, *La Grande Jatte*, France (*15.40*) 1892 Monet, *Rouen Cathedral*, France (*15.37*) 1889 Van Gogh, *The Starry Night*, France (*1.21*) 1892 Gauguin, *The Spirit of the Dead Watching*, Tahiti (*15.39*) 1895–98 Cézanne, *Still-Life with Apples*, France (*15.38*)
1900 c. 1900–20 Expressionism Fauvism begins 1905 c. 1907–14 Cubism Futurism begins 1910 c. 1916–22 Dada Surrealism begins 1924	1903 Wright Brothers' first flight Rise of women's suffrage movement 1914–18 World War I 1928 first sound movie produced 1939–45 World War II	1880–1917 Rodin, *The Gates of Hell*, France (*1.46*) 1911 Matisse, *The Red Studio*, France (*2.121*) 1911 Braque, *The Portuguese*, France (*15.44*) 1913 Boccioni, *Unique Forms of Continuity in Space*, Italy (*15.45*) 1917 Duchamp, *The Fountain*, France (*15.48*) 1931 Dalí, *The Persistence of Memory*, France (*15.49*) 1936–39 Wright, Kaufmann House, Pennsylvania (*3.44*) 1937 Picasso, *Guernica*, Spain (*1.47*) 1939–40 Nervi, aircraft hangar, Ortbello, Italy (*13.36*)

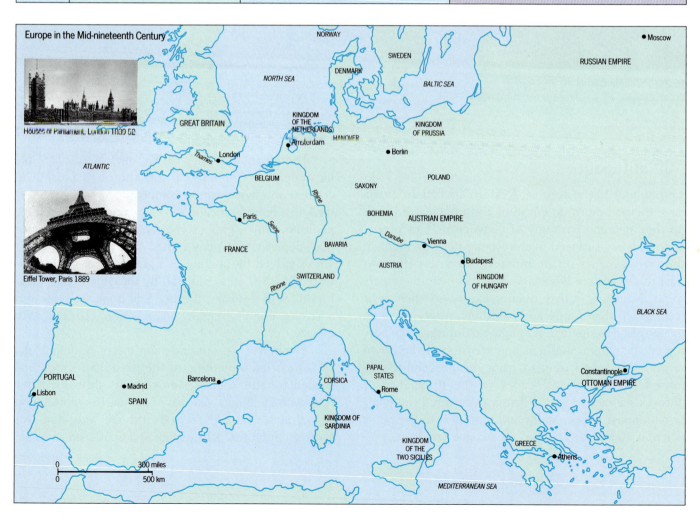

Europe in the Mid-nineteenth Century

Houses of Parliament, London 1839–52

Eiffel Tower, Paris 1889

LATER NINETEENTH-CENTURY ART

Realism

At odds with the idealized content of both Neoclassicism and Romanticism (for instance, Géricault's survivors are not gaunt and covered with sores), another approach to art began to appear as a recognizable movement in France from about 1850 to 1875. It was the work and theories of Gustave Courbet that led this rebellion against the "grand manner." In paintings such as *The Stone Breakers* (15.35), Courbet sought to present real people without artifice rather than idealized or heroic scenes drawn from the artist's imagination. It was his choice of subject-matter—everyday contemporary life—as much as his attempt to portray it truthfully that represented a sharp break with the past. Courbet eschewed historical, mythological, or abstract subjects ("Show me an angel and I'll paint one"), insisting on painting only what he could see, exactly as he saw it, without artistic conventions. In his "Open Letter to a Group of Prospective Students" (1861), Courbet gave a clear definition of **Realism**:

Painting is essentially a *concrete* art, and can consist only of the representation of things both *real* and *existing* ... Imagination in art consists in finding the most complete expression for an existing thing, but never in imagining or creating this object itself ... Beauty as given by nature is superior to all the conventions of the artist.[3]

Impressionism

Realism was not considered good art by the academic juries who controlled most of the purchasing of art in France. They also rejected the work of Edouard Manet, whose *Le Déjeuner sur l'herbe* (15.36) shocked even those who visited the counter-exhibition held in 1863 by many angry artists whose work had been refused by the official Salon. Manet used a Classical composition borrowed, in heavy disguise, from Raphael, but in such a manner as to obscure its meaning. In a complex way, he was denying the use of paintings to teach or arouse emotions; paintings, he asserted, can exist for the sheer beauty of colors, light, patterns, and the brushstrokes on the surface of the canvas.

Manet's **Naturalism** was closely followed by a group of artists who were dubbed **Impressionists**.

15.35 Gustave Courbet, *The Stone Breakers*, 1849. Oil on canvas, 5 ft 3 ins × 8 ft 6 ins (1.6 × 2.6 m). Formerly Gemäldegalerie, Dresden (destroyed 1945).

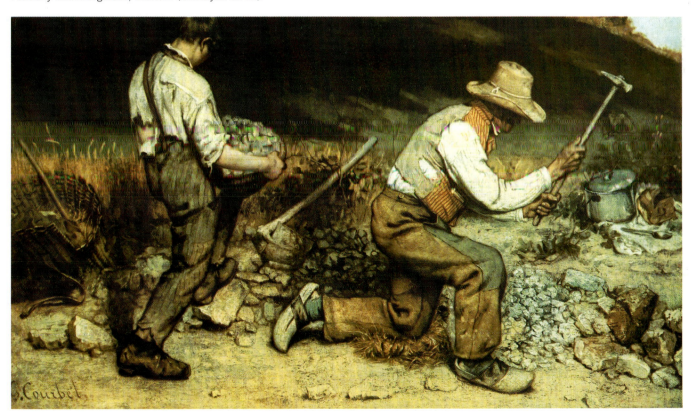

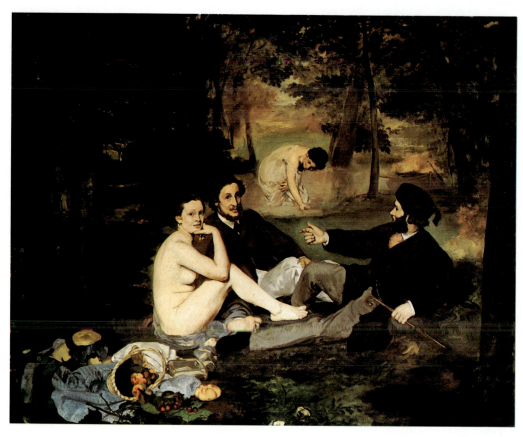

15.36 Edouard Manet, *Le Déjeuner sur l'herbe (The Picnic)*, 1863. Oil on canvas, 6 ft 10 ins × 8 ft 8 ins (2.08 × 2.65 m). Louvre, Paris.

15.37 Claude Monet, *Rouen Cathedral*, 1892. Oil on canvas, 39¼ × 25⅞ ins (99.3 × 65.7 cm). Metropolitan Museum of Art, New York. Theodore M. Davis Collection, 1915.

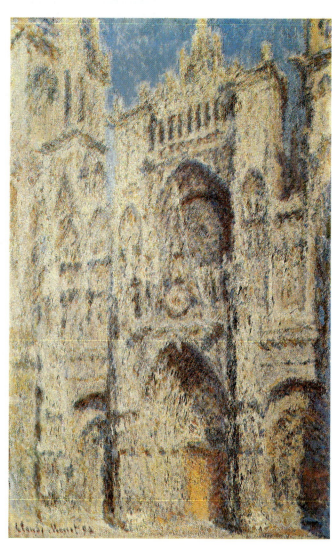

Some of them rejected not only story-telling and meaning but even realistic depiction of objects, seeking instead to capture the ephemeral impressions of light reflecting off surfaces under different atmospheric conditions. If anything, their dabs of unblended colors broke down images into montages of light, as in Monet's *Rouen Cathedral* (15.37). Whereas Realists often worked from photographs of everyday scenes, these Impressionists painted outside in order to observe and record the effects of natural lighting.

Others who are often grouped with the Impressionists—such as Degas (2.66, 4.10)—tried to capture the fleeting action or transient moments rather than focusing solely on the changing effect of light. Renoir (3.28) is also grouped with the Impressionists, but the style of his later works—luminous but blended use of color to describe lush, three-dimensional forms—varied considerably from the increasingly abstract brushstrokes of Monet. Renoir wrote:

> I had wrung impressionism dry, and I finally came to the conclusion that I knew neither how to paint nor how to draw. . . . Light plays too great a part outdoors; you have no time to work out the composition; you can't see what you are doing. . . . If the painter works directly from nature, he ultimately looks for nothing but momentary effects; he does not try to compose, and soon he gets monotonous.[4]

Post-Impressionism

In some art historians' ways of categorizing styles, the late works of Degas and Renoir are included in a group of paintings known as **Post-Impressionist**. In a narrower definition of this style, however, the major Post-Impressionists were Cézanne, Seurat, van Gogh, and Gauguin. What unites them is their movement beyond what they conceived as the limitations of Impressionism and their highly personal explorations of the art of painting. Van Gogh (1.21) distorted lines and forms to express essence; Gauguin (**15.39**) intentionally rejected a "civilized" style. In Cézanne, by contrast, there was a return to careful composition in an intense search for artistic perfection. But Cézanne did not return to the past; rather, he was perhaps the pioneering figure in modern painting. Rejecting both the messiness of Impressionism and the conventions of linear perspective used since the Renaissance to give the illusion of form and space, Cézanne tried to reinvent two-dimensional art from scratch. He built up spatial layers, geometric forms, and rhythms with colors, lines, and shapes alone (see 2.40), with careful attention to orderly relationships between forms across the picture plane. Even in his clearly representational works, such as *Still-Life with Apples* (**15.38**), he concentrated on meeting aesthetic goals such as balance, intensity of color, and the *feeling of depth*, even if doing so meant distorting the outlines of objects.

15.38 Paul Cézanne, *Still-Life with Apples*, 1895–98.
Oil on canvas, 27 × 36½ ins (68.6 × 92.7 cm).
Collection Museum of Modern Art, New York. Lillie P. Bliss Collection.

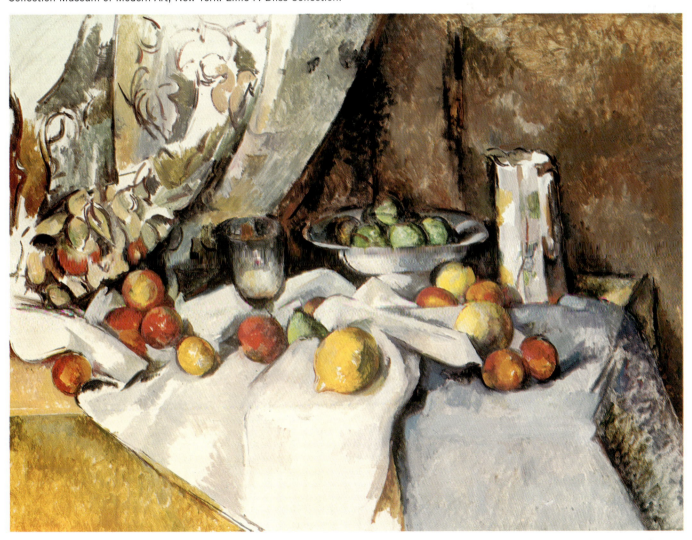

PAUL GAUGUIN
on CROSS-CULTURAL BORROWINGS

Contacts between cultures often bring new influences into art. In the middle of the nineteenth century, European artists began to discover the advanced arts of China and Japan and to take lessons from them. At the turn of the century, Picasso discovered African sculpture in a French museum as a great "revelation," and he became an avid collector of such works, as well as being influenced by them. Paul Gauguin, the French Post-Impressionist painter (1848–1903), has documented his fascination with Oceanic cultures, which deeply affected not only the style but also the content of his work.

Gauguin had what he called "a terrible itching for the unknown."[5] Leaving the security of his job as a stockbroker, he traveled widely, living as an impoverished artist. His journals and letters are full of disdain for European culture and idealistic impressions of the materially simpler Oceanic cultures in which he eventually tried to realize his dreams—to "escape to the woods of a South Sea Island and live there in ecstasy and peace."[6] But even in Tahiti and the Marquesas, he did not find inner peace, and he openly acknowledged that, while his paintings seemed to be about Oceanic subjects, they were his own inventions. "My artistic center is in my head; I am

not a painter who works from nature," he wrote in 1892. "With me, everything happens in my wild imagination."[7] The ideas behind his *The Spirit of the Dead Watching* (**15.39**) are those of a European wondering about something he does not fully understand. The paintings thus evoke in the viewer as well a sense of mystery:

"A young native girl lies on her belly, showing a portion of her frightened face. She lies on a bed covered with a blue *pareo* and a light chrome-yellow sheet. As it stands, it is a slightly indecent study of a nude, and yet I wish to make a chaste picture of it, and imbue it with the native feeling, character, and tradition.

The *pareo* being closely linked with the life of a Tahitian, I use it as a bedspread. The sheet, of bark-cloth, must be yellow, because, in this color, it arouses something unexpected for the spectator, and because it suggests lamplight. I need a background of terror, purple is clearly indicated.

I see only fear. What kind of fear? The *tupapau* (Spirit of the Dead) is clearly indicated. For the natives it is a constant dread. Once I have found my *tupapau* I attach myself completely to it, and make it the motif of my picture. The nude takes second place.

What can a spirit be, for a Maori? She knows neither theater or novels, and when she thinks of someone dead, she thinks necessarily of someone she has seen. My spirit can only be an ordinary little woman.

The title has two meanings, either she thinks of the spirit; or, the spirit thinks of her. The Soul of a living person linked to the spirit of the dead. Night and Day."[8]

As well as being intrigued by the Oceanic people and landscapes, Gauguin had great admiration for their design traditions. His own increasing use of large areas of relatively flat colors and abstracted shapes is probably influenced by the traditional approaches to design in the cultures he adopted. He wrote:

"We do not seem to suspect in Europe that there exists, both among the Maoris of New Zealand and the Marquesans, a very advanced decorative art. In the Marquesan especially there is an unparalleled sense of decoration. Give him a subject even of the most ungainly geometrical forms and he will succeed in keeping the whole harmonious and in leaving no displeasing or incongruous empty spaces.

Today, even for gold, you can no longer find any of those beautiful

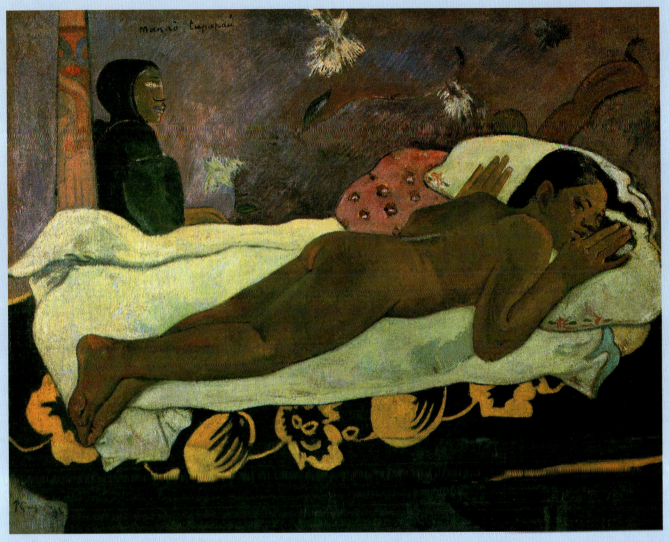

15.39 Paul Gauguin, *The Spirit of the Dead Watching*, 1892. Oil on canvas, 38¾ × 36¼ ins (98.4 × 92 cm). Albright-Knox Art Gallery, Buffalo. A. Conger Goodyear Collection.

objects in bone, rock, iron-wood which they used to make. The police have stolen it all and sold it to amateur collectors; yet the Administration has never for an instant dreamed of establishing a museum in Tahiti, as it could so easily do, for all this Oceanic art.

None of these people who consider themselves learned has ever for an instant suspected the value of the Marquesan artists. Dowdy from head to foot, with their superannuated finery, vulgar hips, tumble-down corsets, imitation jewelry, elbows that threaten you or look like sausages, they are enough to spoil any holiday in this country. But they are white—and their stomachs stick out!

The Marquesan art has disappeared, thanks to the missionaries. The missionaries have considered that sculpture and decoration were fetishism and offensive to the God of the Christians.

That is the whole story, and the unhappy people have yielded."[9]

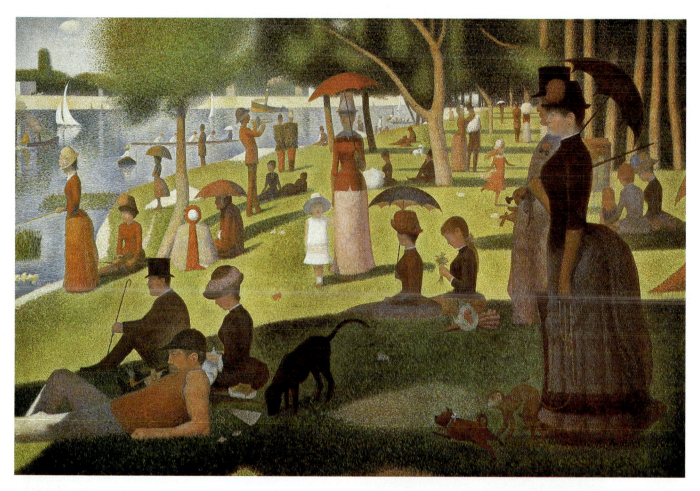

15.40 Georges Seurat, *A Sunday Afternoon on La Grande Jatte*, 1884–86. Oil on canvas, 6 ft 9 ins × 10 ft ⅜ in (2.07 × 3.08 m). Art Institute of Chicago, Chicago, Illinois. Helen Birch Bartlett Memorial Collection, 1926, no. 224.

Seurat's approach to painting was highly analytical. His **Pointilliste** technique of juxtaposing dots of unblended colors (to be blended optically)—as in his ground-breaking painting *A Sunday Afternoon on the Island of La Grande Jatte* (**15.40**)—is superficially similar to the unblended brushstrokes of the Impressionists. But his tiny vibrant dots of pigment are meticulously applied and calculated to define shapes rather than allow them to disintegrate under the effects of light. Under Seurat's systematic analysis, forms become precise, almost flat geometric shapes, carefully organized in space. Seurat's clearly delineated shapes and painstakingly applied dots of pigment contribute to a timeless sense of order that is in sharp contrast to the immediacy and spontaneity of Monet's paintings.

TWENTIETH-CENTURY ART
Expressionism

As artists began departing from academic standards to do their own experimenting into the nature of reality and how it could be expressed in art, some inevitably turned their attention inward. Art used as a vehicle for the portrayal of inner psychological states has been called **Expressionism**. This tendency was already evident in the late works of van Gogh (1.21), for whom trees and sky writhed in sympathetic resonance with his intense inner torments. The Norwegian Edvard Munch abandoned any attempt at objective reporting of external realities in his *The Scream* (**15.41**). The terror he feels inside becomes visible as wave upon wave of undulating colored bands, filling the environment. Prior to World War I, German artists in groups called *Die Brücke* ("The Bridge") and *Der Blaue Reiter* ("The Blue Rider") became Expressionists, usually portraying states such as anxiety or anger rather than the hopeful sweetness and materialistic complacency they

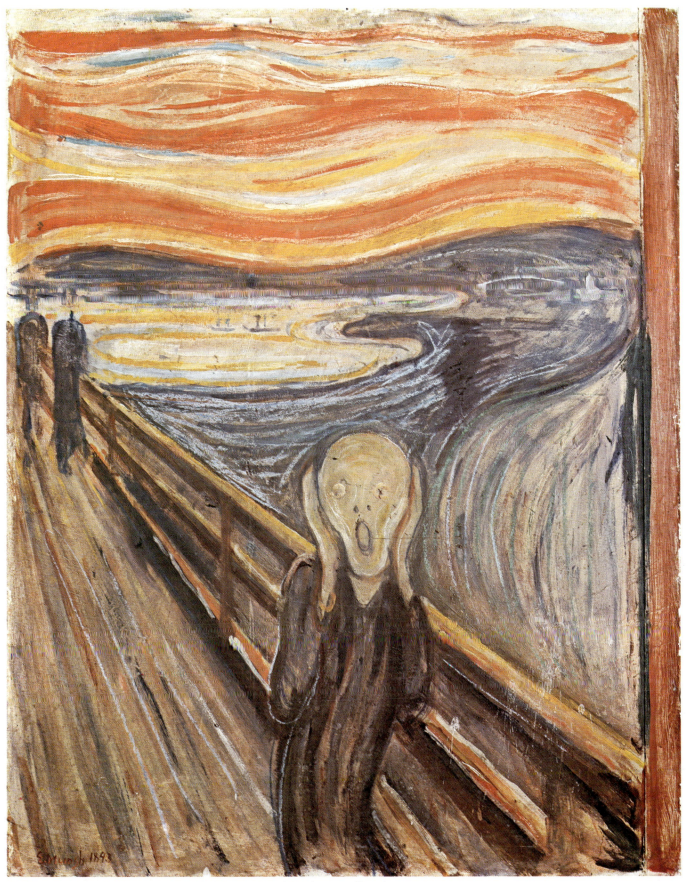

15.41 Edvard Munch, *The Scream*, 1893. Oil, pastel, and casein on cardboard, 36 × 29 ins (91.4 × 73.6 cm). National Gallery, Oslo.

perceived in French Impressionism. German Expressionism encompassed many of the arts, including filmmaking, with works such as *The Cabinet of Doctor Caligari* (8.22).

Fauvism

Meanwhile in France a group of artists led by Matisse held an exhibition in 1905 of works so revolutionary that the artists were called *les Fauves* ("the wild beasts"). They had abandoned any attempt at descriptive, naturalistic use of color and, in some cases, form. Instead they used these elements of design as ends in themselves or expressions of the essence of things, freed from strict associations with the observable world. André Derain's *The Pool of London* (15.42) illustrates the use of semi-realistic forms with free choice of colors; Matisse's *The Red Studio* (2.121) uses color even more

freely, with forms translated into flat shapes and painted with seemingly childlike abandon. Matisse had serious and orderly intentions, however. He rejected the "jerky surface" of Impressionist paintings, complaining:

> The splitting up of color brought the splitting up of form and contour. . . . Everything is reduced to a mere sensation of the retina, but one which destroys all tranquility of surface and contour. Objects are differentiated only by the luminosity that is given them.[10]

By contrast, Matisse sought to create the sensations of space and form by using color purely and simply rather than in dabbed spots. Moreover, he felt that color, like other elements of design, should serve the expressive purposes of the artist. Matisse's seminal experiments in modern art continued, but the **Fauve** group disbanded after three years.

15.42 André Derain, *The Pool of London*, 1906.
Oil on canvas, 25⅞ × 39 ins (65.7 × 99 cm). Tate Gallery, London.

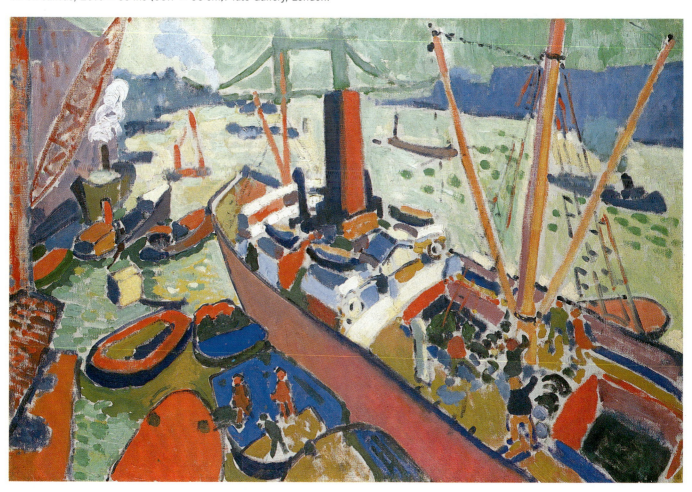

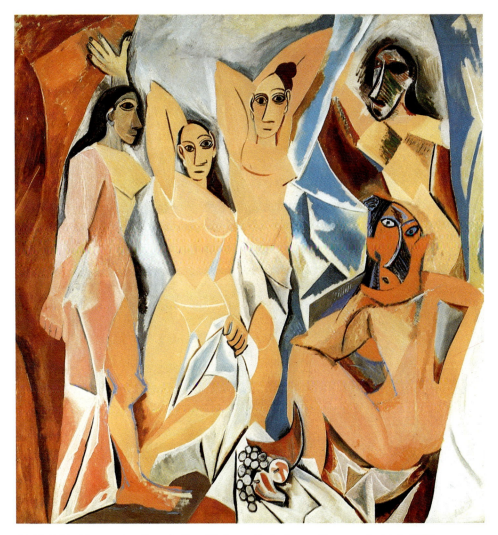

15.43 Pablo Picasso, *Les Demoiselles d'Avignon*, Paris, begun May, reworked July 1907. Oil on canvas, 8 ft × 7 ft 8 ins (2.44 × 2.34 m). Collection Museum of Modern Art, New York. Acquired through the Lillie P. Bliss Bequest.

Cubism

The next significant steps in modern art were taken by Pablo Picasso and Georges Braque. Some of Picasso's early paintings, such as *The Old Guitarist* (2.120), were delicately representational. But in 1907 he abruptly switched directions. Heavily influenced by the geometric forms of Cézanne and the stylization of African sculpture, Picasso created in *Les Demoiselles d'Avignon* (15.43) a work considered so ugly that people tried to attack it physically when it was first shown in the United States. What he had begun to do in this work evolved into a movement in which a subject was fragmented into geometric planes that simultaneously revealed more than one side at once, as though the artist were walking around a three-dimensional form and reporting the view from many angles. The ancient Egyptians had stylistic conventions for doing somewhat the same thing, but, under the angular analysis of **Cubism**, the subject sometimes becomes almost totally lost from view, as in Braque's *The Portuguese* (15.44).

Of this highly intellectual approach to art, Braque wrote, "The senses deform, the mind forms. Work to perfect the mind. There is no certitude but in what the mind conceives."[11] And Picasso asserted, "Nature and art, being two different things, cannot be the same thing. Through art we express our conception of what nature is not."[12]

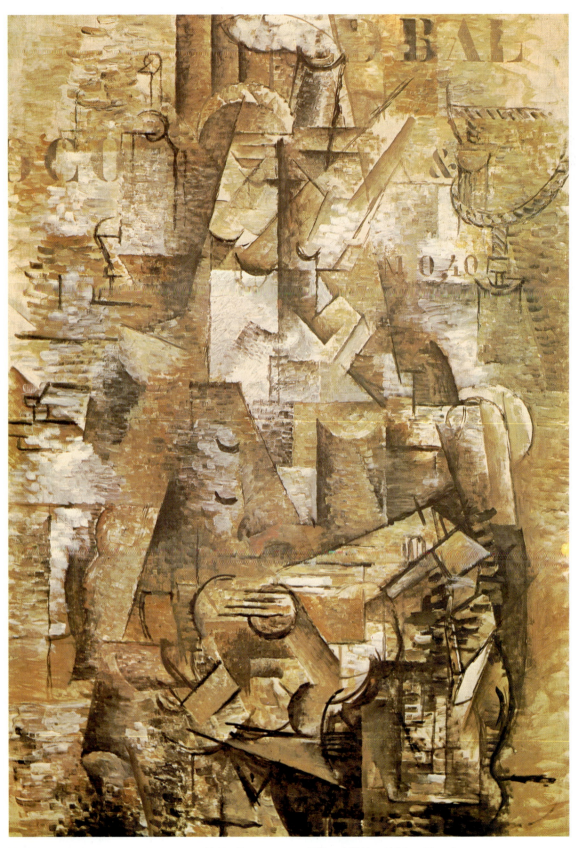

15.44 Georges Braque, *The Portuguese*, 1911. Oil on canvas, 45⅞ × 31⅞ ins (116 × 81 cm). Kunstmuseum, Basel.

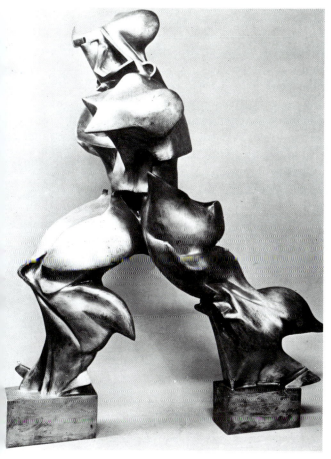

Futurism

In Italy, the sweeping changes of an industrializing civilization were answered by a call for revolution in the arts. In 1910 a group of artists set forth a passionate statement they called the *Manifesto of the Futurist Painters*. It contained these conclusions:

> Destroy the cult of the past, the obsession with the ancients, pedantry and academic formalism....
> Elevate all attempts at originality, however daring, however violent....
> Regard art critics as useless and dangerous....
> Rebel against the tyranny of words "harmony" and "good taste"....
> Support and glory in our day-to-day world, a world which is going to be continually and splendidly transformed by victorious Science.[13]

The principal aesthetic attempt of the **Futurists** was to capture in art the vigor, speed, and militant pride they felt characterized modern life. In paintings, this meant portraying successive movements over time, as Duchamp had done in the "dynamic cubism" of *Nude Descending a Staircase* (2.151). In sculpture, Umberto Boccioni tried to express not form but action in works such as *Unique Forms of Continuity in Space* (**15.45**).

15.45 Umberto Boccioni, *Unique Forms of Continuity in Space*, 1913. Bronze (cast 1931), 43⅞ × 34⅞ × 15¾ ins (111.2 × 88.5 × 40 cm). Collection Museum of Modern Art, New York. Acquired through the Lillie P. Bliss Bequest.

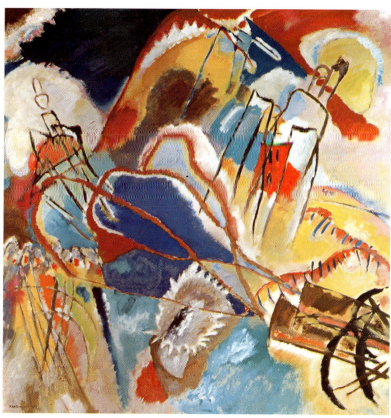

15.46 Wassily Kandinsky, *Improvisation no. 30 (Cannons)*, 1913. Oil on canvas, 3 ft 7¼ × 3 ft 7¼ ins (1.10 × 1.10 m). Art Institute of Chicago, Chicago, Illinois. Arthur Jerome Eddy Memorial Collection, 1931, no. 511.

Abstract and Nonobjective Art

In the same year that Boccioni's *Unique Forms* was completed, the Russian-born painter Wassily Kandinsky created another of the abstract paintings he had been working on for several years: *Improvisation No. 30* (**15.46**). In the intellectual ferment that followed the freeing of art from meaning, naturalistic representation, and academic aesthetic standards, Kandinsky's piece reflected the penultimate stages of movement away from art that tries to represent forms from the outer world. In Kandinsky's painting, bare references to the phenomenal world are retained only to keep art from descending to mere pattern-making; he uses colors and barely recognizable forms (here, cannons and tall buildings) to lead the viewer into a world of nonmaterial spiritual realities.

Piet Mondrian used the process of **abstraction** to strip natural forms to their aesthetic essence, as in his abstract paintings of trees (1.28-30). But he—as well as generations of later twentieth-century artists—soon abandoned all references to natural forms, creating purely **nonobjective** art. Works such as *Composition in Blue, Yellow, and Black* (**15.47**) and *Fox Trot A* (2.10) were so different from traditional paintings that Mondrian offered many written explanations of the theories behind nonobjective art. No longer were paintings self-evident; one needed an intellectual understanding of the artist's intention. Mondrian held that because paintings are created on a flat surface, they should honor that flatness rather than trying to give it the illusion of three-dimensionality. Furthermore, line and color are the essence of art, and to be seen most clearly they should be separated from forms to which each person brings personal associations. To display line and color nonobjectively, Mondrian chose the "universal" or "neutral" form of the rectangle.

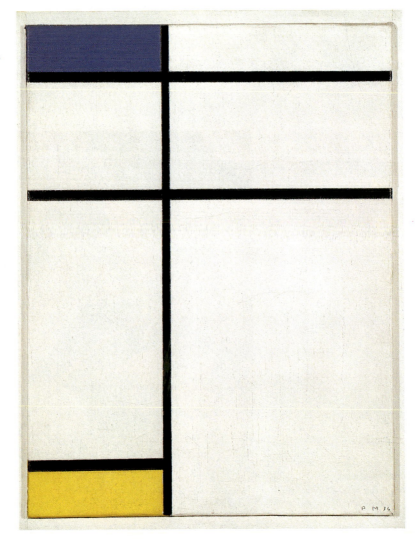

15.47 Piet Mondrian, *Composition in Blue, Yellow, and Black*, 1936. Oil on canvas, 17 × 13 ins (43.2 × 33 cm). Kunstmuseum, Basel, Emannuel Hoffman Foundation.

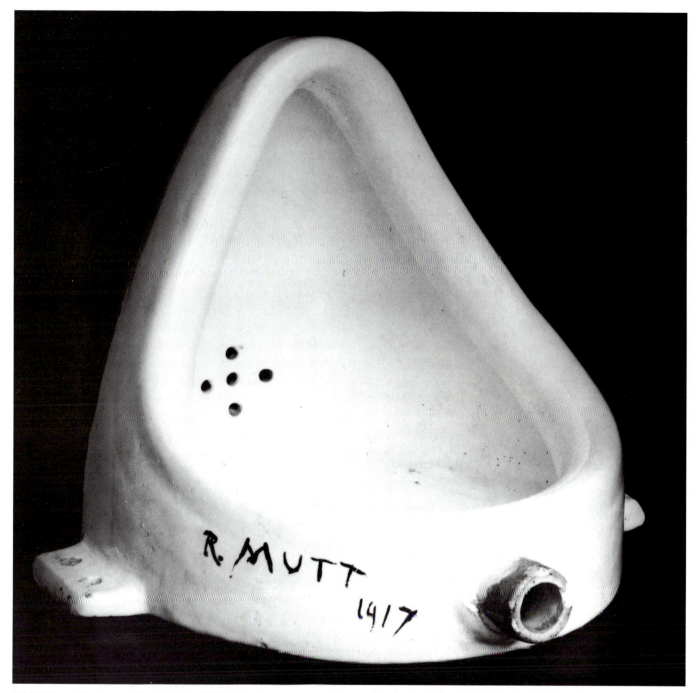

15.48 Marcel Duchamp, *The Fountain*, 1917. Ready-made, porcelain urinal on its back, inscribed on upper edge. Sidney Janis Gallery.

Dada

In contrast with the sublime rationality of Mondrian's theories and paintings, a group of rebellious artists and authors in Zürich launched in 1916 an anti-rational, anti-aesthetic movement called **Dada**, babytalk which they claimed meant nothing. The members of this highly influential movement had decided that humans were so unjust to each other that they did not deserve art, so they set out to destroy it. The ironically humorous, intentionally uncensored output of the group included offbeat art forms with titles such as "rubbish constructions," "rayographs," "exquisite corpses," and "ready-made objects."

Marcel Duchamp's *The Fountain* (**15.48**) is one of the more infamous examples of Dadaist "art." It consists solely of a men's urinal, purchased from the Mott Works Company and presented lying on its back, otherwise unaltered except for the crude signature Duchamp painted on the front, "R. Mutt, 1917." This "work" defies not only logical analysis but also the traditional minimal expectation that art is something physically created by the artist. The anarchistic Duchamp claimed that it is simply the act of choice that defines the artist. In a tongue-in-cheek defence of the art of "R. Mutt," which was banned from an exhibition, an anonymous article apparently written by Duchamp insisted:

> Now Mr Mutt's fountain is not immoral, that is absurd, no more than a bathtub is immoral. It is a fixture that you see every day in plumbers' show windows.
>
> Whether Mr Mutt with his own hands made the fountain or not has no importance. He CHOSE it. He took an ordinary article of life, placed it so that its useful significance disappeared under the new title and point of view—created a new thought for that object.[14]

Surrealism

Many of the Dadaist artists became part of the next major twentieth-century movement: **Surrealism**, in which the source of images is the subconscious. Rather than abandoning forms, surrealists render them with the illogic of dreams. Based on the theories of Freud, this approach spanned the period between World Wars I and II, for the most part, though surrealistic elements had appeared throughout the history of art and still do. One of the most famous Surrealist artists is Salvador Dalí, whose 1928 movie *Un Chien andalou* (8.23) was like a bad dream in itself. Expressed in a static painting rather than a time sequence, Surrealism often relies on unusual perspectives and symbols to express the apparently realistic but logically impossible contents of dreams. In Dalí's *The Persistence of Memory* (**15.49**), there is a haunting sense of loneliness and of time become meaningless. Melting watches, light-struck cliffs, and unrecognizable forms are meticulously described, as if in a vivid hallucination.

15.49 Salvador Dalí, *The Persistence of Memory*, 1931.
Oil on canvas, 9½ × 13 ins (24.1 × 33 cm).
Collection Museum of Modern Art, New York. Anonymous donation.

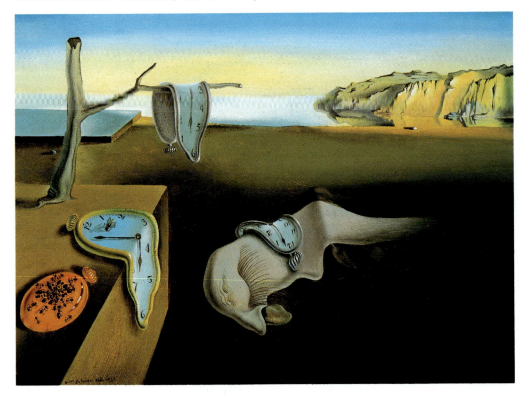

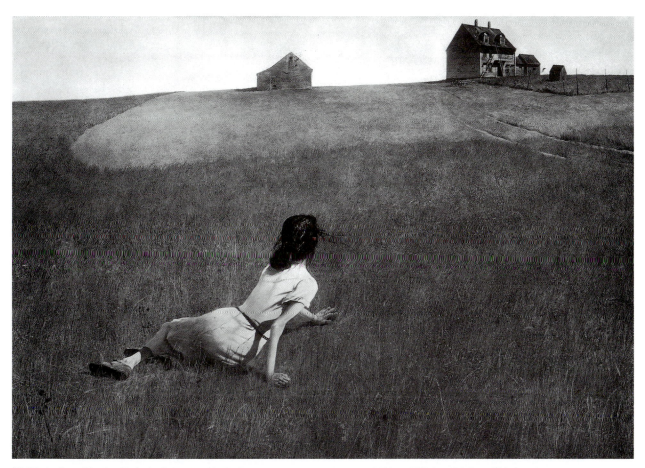

15.50 Andrew Wyeth, *Christina's World*, 1948. Tempera on gessoed panel, 32¼ × 47¾ ins (81.9 × 121.3 cm). Collection Museum of Modern Art, New York. Purchase.

Traditional Realism

While all these modern art styles were cropping up, many artists continued to work in a variety of traditionally realistic, representational styles. The United States particularly had an historical fondness for realistic art, and even after industrialization brought the country into the forefront of international commerce many artists retained a distinctive appreciation for naturalistic representation of life in their homeland. The emerging artform of photography was dominated in the United States by those who wanted to remain true to their subjects, as well as their medium, such as Alfred Stieglitz (8.8), Dorothea Lange (8.9), and Ansel Adams (8.12). A number of painters who had been drawn to abstract movements in Europe returned to more realistic work, such as the perennially popular Andrew Wyeth. With meticulous tempera technique, he focuses on quietly meaningful rural scenes, such as

the world of a small Maine island community as seen by a young woman with polio in *Christina's World* (15.50). The dreamlike content, symmetrical composition, and unusual point of view bespeak a modern approach to design, coupled with relatively representational imagery.

Abstract Expressionism

A parallel development at the opposite pole from traditional realism established New York as the leading center of modern art in the West. After World War II, the term **Abstract Expressionist** was applied to those of the New York school who rejected traditional European painting styles and instead emphasized the spontaneously expressive gesture and all-over composition, with all areas of the canvas equally important. One of the major figures in this movement was Jackson Pollock. He engaged in what was known as **Action**

Painting, throwing or dripping paint with whole-body motions onto a long sheet of canvas on the floor (15.51). Pollock did not feel that his movements were random; rather, his experience was that they were directed by the psychic forces within himself. To him, his paintings were a direct and fresh expression of the inner life that impels all artists. The frenetic, interlacing lines that he laid down have a restless energy, which leads the viewer around and through, again and again, to no conclusion—perhaps an apt metaphor for the pace and meaninglessness of contemporary urban life. The subjective, "painterly" approach of expressing oneself through freely applied paint was also used by other mid-century New York artists, including Hans Hofmann (5.18), Willem de Kooning, and to a certain extent Mark Rothko (1.18), and is still present in the brushwork of James Brooks (5.4), among others.

15.51 Jackson Pollock painting. Photo by Hans Namuth.

Post-Painterly Abstraction

As the New York school evolved, many artists developed more controlled nonobjective styles that had in common the attempt to remove the evidence of their presence, allowing their work to stand by itself as a stimulus to which the viewer can react. Barnett Newman explains these efforts in spiritual terms:

> The present painter is concerned not with his own feelings or with the mystery of his own personality but with the penetration into the world mystery. To that extent his art is concerned with the sublime. It is a religious art which through symbols will catch the basic truth of life. . . . The artist tries to wrest truth from the void.[15]

To engage the viewer in a direct experience of truth without using imagery, the Post-Painterly Abstractionists tended to focus on color and color relationships. The *Abstract Imagists* (or Chromatic

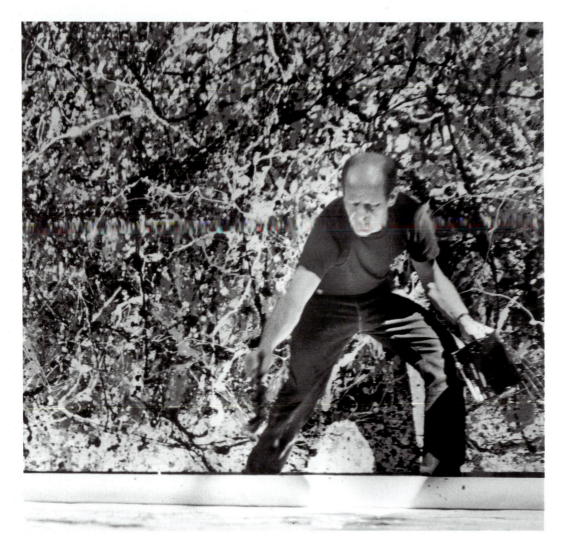

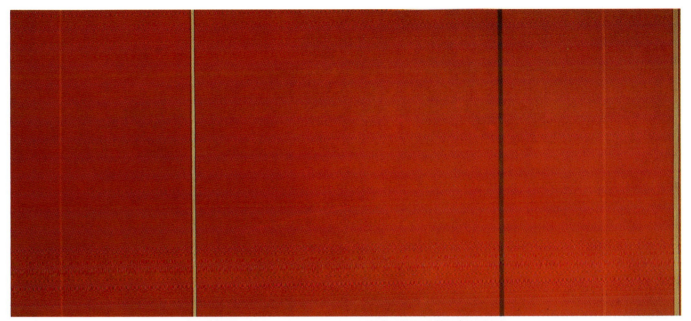

15.52 Barnett Newman, *Vir Heroicus Sublimis*, 1950–51. Oil on canvas, 7 ft 11⅜ ins × 17 ft 9¼ ins (2.42 × 5.14 m). Collection Museum of Modern Art, New York. Gift of Mr. and Mrs. Ben Heller.

Abstractionists) typically used open, relatively flat but fluid imagery created impersonally by pouring dyes onto unsized canvas, as in the work of Helen Frankenthaler (5.26). Hard-edge painters created flat, unvarying areas of pigment with immaculately sharp boundaries, sometimes with even nonobjective imagery reduced to a bare minimum. As Barnett Newman suggests by naming the hard-edged painting shown here (**15.52**) *Vir Heroicus Sublimis* ("Heroic, Elevated Man"), such works may have a sublime, Classical effect of ordered perfection and grandeur. But if you stare at his painting for a while, those fine stripes—which Newman called "zips" of light—may begin to create extra optical effects that transcend the flatness of the colossal red field.

In fact, hard-edged paintings are called **Op Art** when they deliberately use the peculiarities of human vision to make people see things that have not actually been physically placed on the canvas. The artist steps back, allowing the experience of the work to take form in the perceptions of the viewer. Josef Albers, highly influential as a teacher as well as an artist, evoked optical color phenomena in his *Homage to the Square* series (2.124). Some Op Art even creates illusions of color, space, and movement in black and white compositions, such as Bridget Riley's *Crest* (2.146) and Victor Vasarely's *Supernovae* (**15.53**).

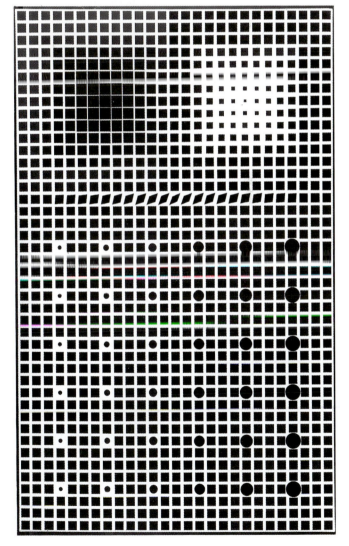

15.53 (right) Victor Vasarely, *Supernovae*, 1959–61. Oil on canvas, 8 ft 1½ ins × 5 ft (2.42 × 1.52 m). Tate Gallery, London.

Pop Art

Another mid-century direction in modern art emerged in London and has encompassed some artists in the United States. This trend, called **Pop Art**, uses objects and images from popular, commercial culture—from cartoons to beer cans—rather than the rarefied imagery of the fine arts. Some of the work is hostile toward contemporary throw-away culture; some presents it as having a rather zany aesthetic validity. As we have seen, Claes Oldenburg's monuments to the banal (such as his giant clothespin, 4.3) are humorously conceived. Some of Andy Warhol's famous pop creations, such as the well known painting of 200 Campbell's soup cans or his later self-portraits (6.31), reflect the repetitive visual patterns of the modern marketplace—a reminder of the aesthetic realities of modern life that one can interpret as one pleases. Roy Lichtenstein, one of the major early figures of the movement, exaggerated cheap printing techniques by rendering pop culture images with blown-up dot screens. He has carried this approach into the present with works such as *Mural with Blue Brushstroke* (**15.54**). It is his desire, he says, for his art to appear impersonal.

15.54 Roy Lichtenstein, study for *Mural with Blue Brushstroke*, 1985. Cut-and-pasted paper, pen and ink, pencil, 34¼ × 17½ ins (87 × 44.5 cm). © The Equitable Life Assurance Society of the United States.

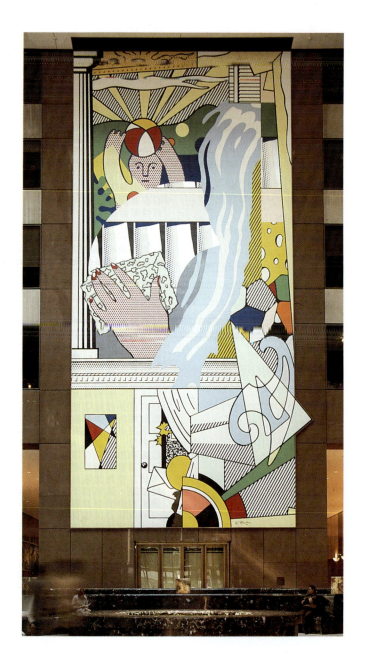

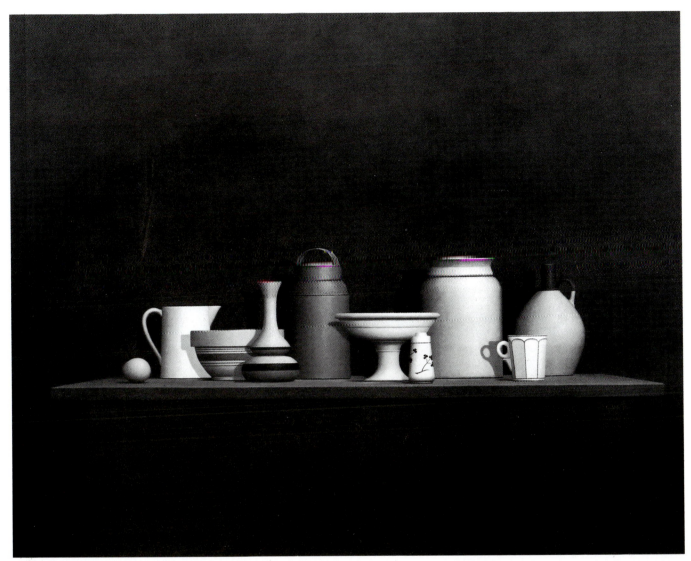

15.55 William Bailey, *Monte Migiana Still-Life*, 1979. Oil on canvas, 4 ft 6 ins × 5 ft (1.37 × 1.52 m). Pennsylvania Academy of Fine Arts, Philadelphia, Pennsylvania.

New Realism

Alongside the nonobjective and pop trends in modern art, a number of artists have continued or returned to more realistic treatments of actual objects. Their subjects have not necessarily been traditional ones, however. Many have explored the visual facts of industrialized life—the neon-lit shops, fast-food places, city streets, automobiles, depressed or overweight people. In recent years, this investigation has become *super-realistic* or **Photorealistic** in the hands of artists such as Chuck Close (5.25) and Richard Estes (2.101). Some are finding beauty in close investigations of features of the environment such as William

Beckman's *Power Lines* (1.25) and Bill Martin's *Abalone Shells* (5.24). William Bailey (11.14) has turned from abstraction to figurative subjects in his painting, but with sensitivities developed from modern art, rather than traditional representative paintings. Using objects painted from memory and references to the actual objects, but without setting up a still-life, he works with aesthetic issues such as the meanings of groupings, intervals, tensions between the flatness of the picture plane and the illusion of space, and inferences of diagonals projecting into space. Bailey says, "I wanted a painting that was silent and unfolded slowly, that offered a contemplative situation."[16]

Technological Art

Although many named twentieth-century art movements have centered on painting styles, technological changes have brought changes in all the arts and have enabled the development of art forms that did not even exist in the past. As we have seen, there are new building materials and synthetic substitutes for traditional two- and three-dimensional media. In addition, industrial technologies have spilled over into art in an entirely new way. In the new arts of computer graphics (9.6, 9.11) and laser shows (2.105), foreshadowed by the lovely light projections of Thomas Wilfred onto translucent screens (**15.56**), the hand of the artist at work has disappeared. Now it is a machine that directly creates the art, with the artist one step removed—building, programming, or operating the machine. Sometimes it is even the *observer* who seems to create the art, activating art-producing devices merely by being present in a certain space.

At one time, art and religion were closely linked in the West; now art and science are forming new alliances, and some very exciting contemporary art is coming out of the high-technology research laboratories, created by people whose skills and sensitivities encompass both science and art. Developments in fields such as fiber optics and communications may in the future be used to create arts that stimulate the senses in ways yet unimagined.

15.56 Thomas Wilfred, from *Lumia Suite*, op. 158, 1963–64. Third movement, elliptical, Lumia composition (projected light on translucent screen). Three movements, lasting 12 minutes, repeated continuously with almost endless variations. Screen 6 × 8 ft (1.8 × 2.44 m). Collection Museum of Modern Art, New York. Commissioned by the Museum through Mrs. Simon Guggenheim Fund.

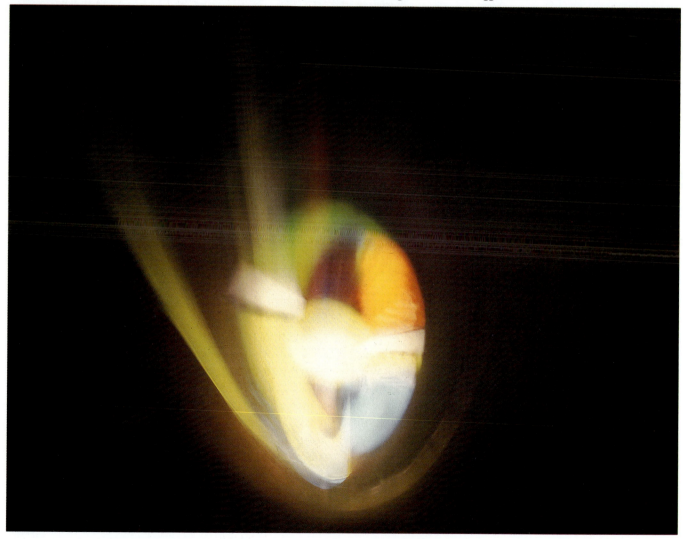

1945–2000 At the Turn of the Twenty-First Century	Events	Works of art
1945 1912–55 Abstract and Nonobjectivism Abstract Expressionism	1944 computer technology developed 1945 atomic bomb dropped on Hiroshima, Japan 1946 xerography invented 1950–53 Korean War	1950s Jackson Pollock painting, New York (*15.51*) 1950–51 Newman, *Vir Heroicus Sublimis*, U.S.A. (*15.52*) 1956 Rothko, *Green on Blue*, New York (*1.18*) 1956–73 Utzon, Sydney Opera House, Australia (*13.37*) 1959–61 Vasarely, *Supernovae*, France (*15.53*)
1960 Minimal Art Op Art Pop Art	1961 Berlin Wall built, East/West Germany 1961–73 Vietnam War 1969 first manned moon landing	1968 Noguchi, *Red Cube*, New York (*1.10*) 1964 Riley, *Crest*, England (*2.146*) 1967 Newman, *Voice of Fire*, New York (*1.40*) 1967 Oldenburg, *Clothespin*, New York (*4.3*) 1967 Warhol, *A Set of Six Self-Portraits*, New York (*6.31*) 1968–69 Close, *Frank*, U.S.A. (*5.25*)
1970 Earthworks New Realism Installation and performance art Conceptual Art	1970 Greer *The Female Eunuch* 1973 first test-tube baby born in England 1978 personal computers become available	1970 Smithson, *Spiral Jetty*, Utah (*10.24*) 1971–78 Piano/Rogers, Pompidou Center, Paris (*13.42*) 1972 Heizer, *City Complex One*, Nevada (*2.35*) 1973 Frankenthaler, *Hint from Bassano*, Toronto (*5.26*) 1976 Christo, *Running Fence*, California (*2.8*) 1977–84 Hodgkin, *Interior with Figures*, England (*15.59*) 1976 Estes, *Double Self-Portrait*, U.S.A. (*2.101*)
1980 Neo-Expressionism Technological Art	1982 first artificial heart implanted 1986 Chernobyl accident in Soviet Union 1989 fall of communist governments in eastern Europe	1982 Disney Productions, *Tron*, U.S.A. (*9.6*) 1983–84 Kiefer, *Athanor*, Germany (*2.61*) 1989 Minkowitz, *Lotus*, U.S.A. (*11.22*)
1990 Recognition of women's art Multicultural art Art at the millennium Computer graphics	1990 Gulf War 1990 Reunification of Germany 1991 Ethnic war shatters Yugoslavia 1996 Hubble telescope opens our universe	1992 Csuri, *Wondrous Spring*, U.S.A. (*9.11*) 1994 Hirst, *James*, England (*1.4*) 1995 Safdie, Vancouver Library Square, Canada (*1.48*) 1995 Viola, *Buried Secrets*, U.S.A. (*8.30*)

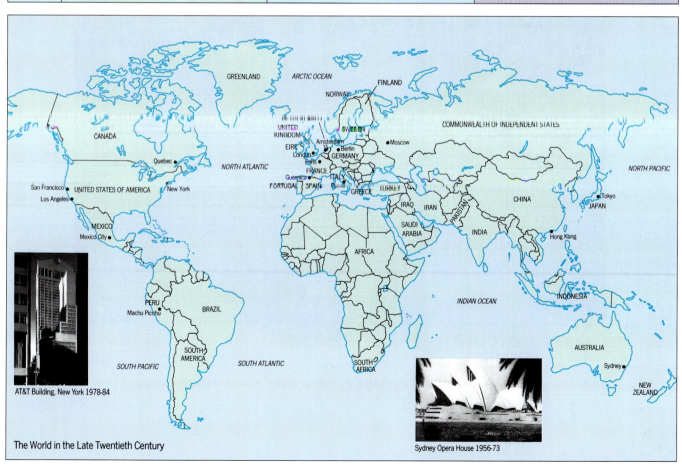

AT&T Building, New York 1978-84

The World in the Late Twentieth Century

Sydney Opera House 1956-73

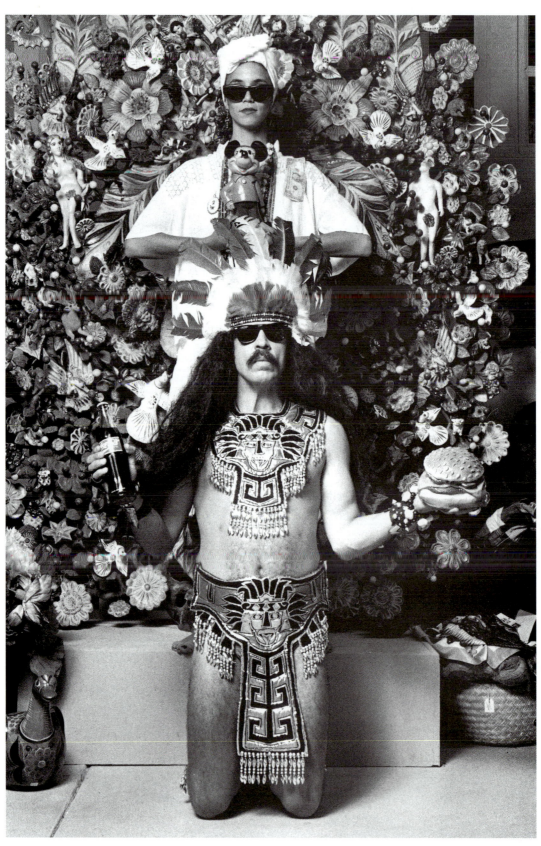

15.57 Guillermo Gomez-Pena and Coco Fusco making "ritual offerings" to welcome Columbus, performance piece at Mexican Museum, San Francisco, 1990. Courtesy of the artists.

Installations, Performance Art, Earthworks, and Conceptual Art

Already the definition of art is being continually expanded: today art is whatever an artist declares to be art. Never until now would animal parts in formaldehyde (see 1.4) have been categorized as art.

Galleries and museums now display **installation pieces**. These are three-dimensional designed environments often set up only as temporary experiences, such as Stephen Antonakos' 24-foot-long (7.4-m) *Green Neon from Wall to Floor* (2.104).

Performance art features the artist as actor. When performance and video art (see 9.7) made their appearance in the 1970s, they were promoted as a way of ending the traditional emphasis on art as object, bringing art to viewers more directly as a sheer visual experience. It is now difficult to define the boundary between performance art, experimental theater, street theater, and "happenings." During the 1980s Guillermo Gomez-Pena organized a collective of Mexican and American artists—the Border Arts Workshop—to put on interdisciplinary performance pieces about cultural and psychological boundaries. They performed not only in galleries but also at checkpoints, in the streets of San Diego, and across the border, illegally sharing food and holding hands. To encourage people to re-evaluate the "discovery" of America by Columbus, Gomez-Pena and writer/artist Coco Fusco staged "counter-Columbus" political performance pieces (**15.57**). Although much contemporary performance art is purposely shocking, non-mainstream, and political, Gomez-Pena asserts:

The great challenge of incorporating politics into art is to do it in a way that pleases aesthetically. I don't believe performance artists should be marginal. In North America, marginality—the European myth of the artist as a marginal bohemian—is still very prevalent. I aspire to speak from the center, to be active in the making of culture. The same is true for gays, women, and artists of color, who can't afford to be marginalized anymore. Performance art is the one place where this can happen—where ritual can be reinvented, and where boundaries can be crossed.[17]

In **earthworks**, the surface of the earth becomes the sculptor's medium, for such massive alterations as Robert Smithson's *Spiral Jetty* (10.24). And in **conceptual art**, idea is more important than form, which may be as ephemeral as Geyer and McMillin's *Surface Erosion* (2.159), which was destroyed as soon as the high tide returned.

If the idea of a conceptual work takes physical form, the form is relatively inconsequential and may be preserved only in photographs. Joseph Kosuth, who considers himself the founder of conceptual art, often uses words as visual ideas, as in *Zeno at the Edge of the Known World* (15.58). Their meanings are to be read between the lines, as it were. Kosuth explains that in conceptual art:

We don't work with forms and color and other devices. Materials and those other things are simply the vehicles through which one produces meaning. [The important thing] is the thinking. Anybody can buy paint and canvas ... I don't want the people who see my work to be passive consumers. Work like mine demands completion by the viewers.[18]

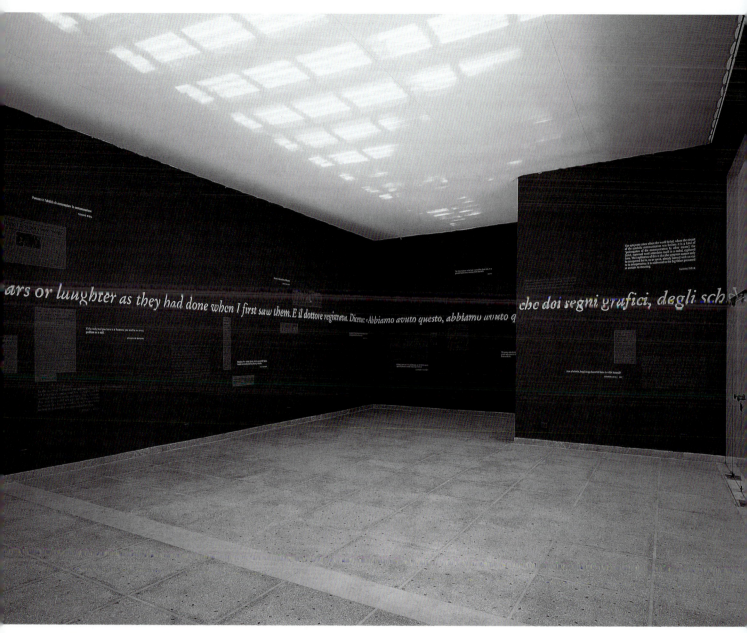

15.58 Joseph Kosuth, *Zeno at the Edge of the Known World*, 1993. Venice Biennale, The Hungarian Pavilion, Venice.
Photo courtesy of the artist.

Neoexpressionism

In the continuing replay of earlier movements, with new twists, a major current redirection in painting is called **Neoexpressionism**. Its adherents around the world are using painting to express their own emotions, as the Abstract Expressionists did, but now with figurative imagery that is distorted by those emotions. Images are often derived from the mass media, and the emotional content is typically violent or anguished, charged with energy, as in Anselm Kiefer's *Athanor* (2.61). Howard Hodgkin's *Interior with Figures* (**15.59**) is a relatively quiet example, but even here the feelings expressed seem charged with sexual energy. Hodgkin tries to recapture the emotion of an experience through evocative objects, colors, and spatial effects. He says, "I want to include more because the more feeling and emotion you include in the painting, the more it will come out the other side to communicate with the viewer."[19]

15.59 Howard Hodgkin, *Interior with Figures*, 1977–84. Oil on wood, 4 ft 6 ins × 5 ft (1.37 × 1.53 m). Saatchi Collection, London.

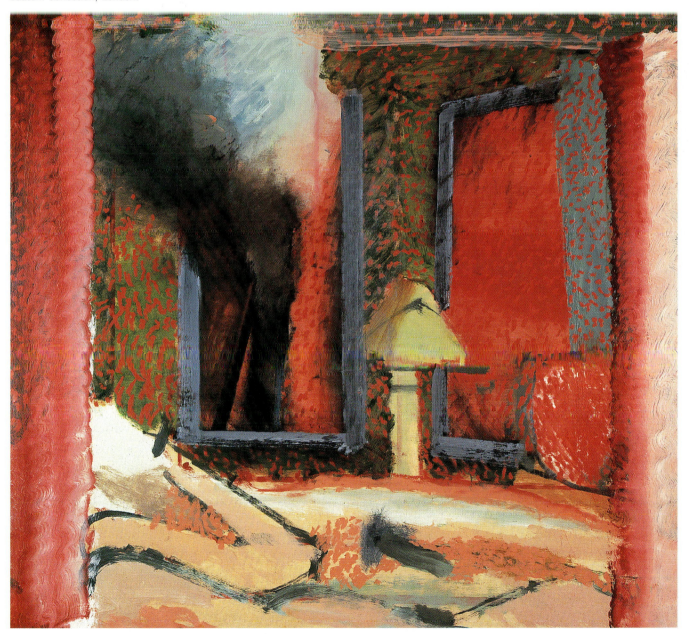

The Craft Object

In the current redefining of the boundaries of art, one interesting direction is the merger of the fine and applied arts. Industrial design, for example, is benefiting from a sculptural approach, and handcrafts are being collected and shown as works of art. Exhibitions of applied design are of great popular interest, and new museums are arising that deal in applied disciplines alone. At the same time, a number of artists trained in traditional crafts are carrying their knowledge and skills into the creation of art for art's sake.

15.60 Ryoichi Yoshida, Doll (detail), 1990.

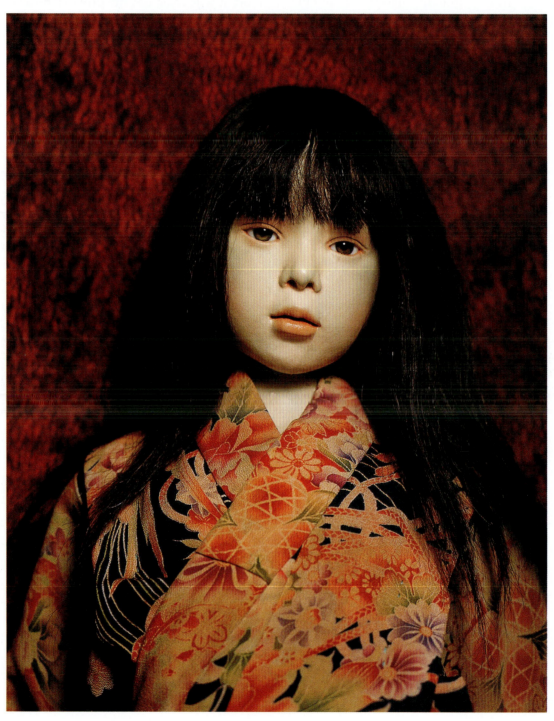

Dollmaking, for example, has been purloined from its traditional use in children's toymaking, and handmade dolls such as those by master dollmaker Ryoichi Yoshida (15.60) are now treated as valuable collectors' items. At costs of up to $20,000 each, handmade dolls are treated as unique pieces of sculpture rather than as playthings. Yoshida has taken great pains with details such as lifelike painting of the doll's eyes. Contemporary dollmakers go to great lengths to create not only the doll's body but also its clothing and accessories in delightful miniature scale.

The crossover between functional and fine arts has resulted in entirely new approaches to two- and three-dimensional design. Norma Minkowitz (11.22) crochets three-dimensional forms, shellacs them to a hard state, and colors their surfaces, thus creating see-through sculptures that are unlike any that can be developed using traditional sculptural media.

Many pieces bridge crafts and fine arts because although they may be built with craft techniques, they are nonfunctional, meant only to be experienced. Art quilts are often deliberately made too small to fit on any bed; they demand to be hung on a wall and responded to like a painting. As art critic Edward Lucie-Smith observes:

> Craft objects increasingly tend to be used in precisely the same way as paintings and sculptures in domestic and other interiors—as space modulators and as activators of particular environments, lending their own emotional coloring. We respect and value them as totems and touchstones as we do fine art.[20]

Recognition of Women's Art

Simultaneously with the acceptance of craft pieces as art objects has come a growing appreciation of art created by women. Since women have long been devalued in most cultures, so has their art. In the past, relatively few women received art education or recognition as fine artists and their craft works have not been valued as art. One major art history textbook commonly used in the United States contained not a single woman artist in its first edition.

This situation is undergoing change. Art historians are now trying to unearth evidence of art by women from the past, and contemporary women artists are receiving more attention from the world of collectors, galleries, museums, and art critics.

As women's art gains recognition, some women are developing art explicitly about their personal experiences as women. One of the heroines of this movement is Frida Kahlo, who married Diego Rivera twice and died at the age of forty-four after a life of chronic pain. She had polio as a child, was further crippled by a terrible accident, suffered a miscarriage, and had her leg amputated shortly before her early death. Her own intense experiences are the main subject of her paintings, most of which are self-portraits. *The Broken Column* (15.61), for instance, explicitly reveals the cross of pain she carries from a broken spine.

As other women are socially freed to discover their own identity, distinct from cultural roles prescribed for them, many are searching and creating art depicting previously taboo aspects of female life, such as menstrual blood and the vagina, and affirming and celebrating their sexuality.

15.61 Frida Kahlo, *The Broken Column*, 1940. Oil on canvas, 15¾ × 12¼ ins (40 × 30.7 cm). Mexico City, Museo Frida Kahlo. Collection of Lola Olmedo.

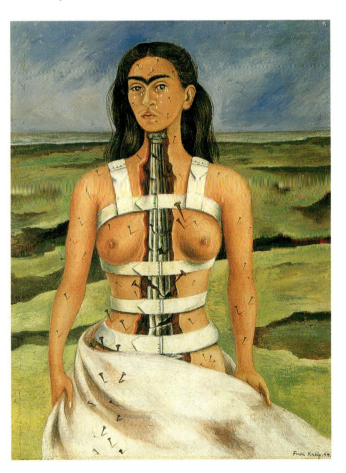

Recognition of Multi-Cultural Art

Another huge section of the world's population has long been ignored by the Western art establishment: the art of non-European people of color. Asian art was "discovered" hundreds of years ago by the dominant European and then the North American white cultures, but historical art by Africans and Native Americans was described as "primitive," and contemporary artists in Africa and Latin America were largely overlooked.

This situation is changing rapidly. In North America's multicultural society the art world is beginning to appreciate the contributions of non-European cultures, and there are now major museums and galleries devoted solely to the art of these previously neglected cultures. Others place multicultural art on a par with that of famous "white" artists, such as Mexico's new Museo de Arte Contemporaneo in Monterrey (15.62). Despite economic difficulties, Latin American countries are developing partnerships between business, government, and the art world to train and show the work of their own artists and to research and preserve artifacts from their cultural heritage. Even world maps are being revised to show the true size of the neglected continents; equal-area projections, for example, reveal the immensity of Africa in contrast to the smallness of Europe.

15.62 Museo de Arte Contemporaneo de Monterrey, with Juan Soriano's *The Dove*, 1991. Courtesy Marco.

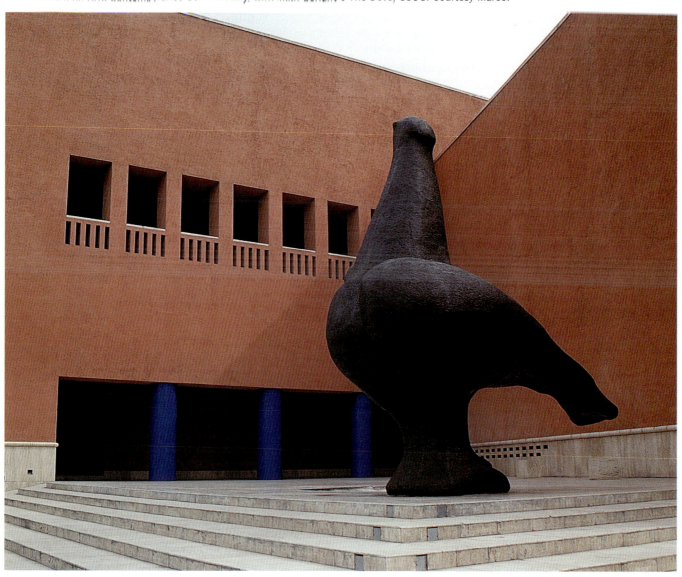

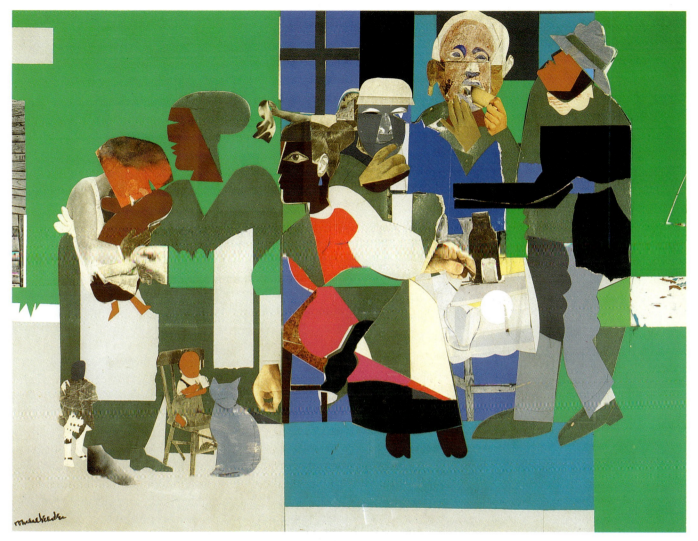

15.63 Romare Bearden, *Family Dinner*, 1968. Collage on board, 30 × 40 ins (76.2 × 101.4 cm).
ACA Galleries, New York.

There is a particular poignancy to the work of those whose cultural heritage and sense of self, as well as economic and social freedom, have been historically repressed. Sometimes the humanity of the oppressed is revealed in anger; sometimes it is as quietly moving as the montage paintings of the late Romare Bearden (**15.63**). Bearden said:

I work out of a response and need to redefine the image of man in the terms of the Negro experience I know best. I cannot divorce myself from the inequities that are around me.[21]

DEBORAH MUIRHEAD
on ART AS ANCESTRAL EXPLORATION

Deborah Muirhead was born in Bessemer, Alabama, in 1949 into an African-American family. She grew up in Chicago, where she spent every Saturday strolling through the Art Institute looking at the paintings and sculpture. She particularly recalls standing before a Georgia O'Keeffe painting of clouds which "made me feel like I was soaring, floating in a sea of blue mist alone and quite safe." Muirhead is now a respected East Coast artist and art professor whose dark abstract paintings (**15.64**) evoke similar sensations of "something felt and experienced."[22] Their abstract subject-matter arises from her compelling interest in researching her roots. She has done extensive genealogical research in census records, county courthouses, and also in novels, poems, and texts on slave history, folklore, folk culture, and life in the agrarian South. She wonders:

"Who were these people in the eighteenth century? What did they believe in, and how much of their belief system survived? The cultural continuities from Africa began to merge with both Native American and Anglo beliefs to form a distinctly new culture.

As I began researching all of that my paintings got darker and darker. The genealogical research provided a correspondence to the paintings, a mystery, a kind of searching in the dark. I was so immersed in the research that I literally dreamed about these people. They were with me all the time, almost guiding me. The dark paintings challenge the notion of darkness as void; for me, the dark paintings were full of richness and life. They were about history with all its tragic consequences for people. But they also were about life, and continuity.

I've been inspired by specific folklore legends, although I try not to illustrate. There is also a continuing legacy of the important effect of water in the lives of West Africans and then of African Americans. Water is traditionally one of the resting places of the ancestral world. The spirits reside in rivers, ponds, and streams. Africans of many tribal groups with this belief system came here and put down roots in this country, continuing belief in water's special spiritual significance. I was interested in the way that belief system combined with new religion which influenced many African Americans: Christianity, particularly Southern Baptist influence, in which there is total water immersion in baptism. The notion that you are a sinner, that you die in the water during total immersion, your sins are washed away, and you are reborn a new person free of your sins combined powerfully with the beliefs of second- or third-generation African Americans in the spirit world in the water.

One of the things I've tried to do in this series of paintings is to create a surface that could resemble a watery surface, with undefinable objects, forms, or implements. They seem to arise mysteriously from all of this stuff that I'm thinking about and reading about and totally immersed in. I think in part they are farm implements and objects that might be devices of torture or fragments that might have some archaeological significance if you knew its context but now are just fragments with no known context.

Just after I visited the plantation where my people were slaves, the paintings became incredibly dark and opaque. There was almost no point in them in which you could find a light source. In the last year or two there have been more openings in the paintings. I want people to be moved by them—to find their haunting power. Some are moved by an overwhelming sense of tragedy, but you can move through that to something more significant, something about survival. I think because the dark surface also

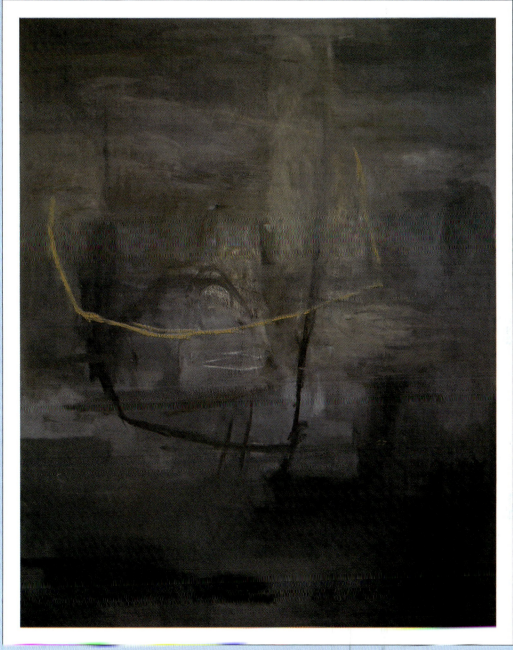

15.64 Deborah Muirhead, *Water World Voices from the Deep*, 1991. Oil on canvas, 5 ft × 4 ft (1.52 × 1.22 m). Courtesy of the artist.

resembles land or soil, it feeds a sense that life is always there, always coming back, always able to provide something.

I have all this ancestral research stuff swimming around in my head but the hard thing is to do a painting that is also about painting—that is about color, value, and chroma, and works formally, but not too formally, because if they do, then you've assembled the puzzle too neatly. I try to use as many colors as possible, and keep them really dark, working with the structure of low value and low intensity of color. People who spend a little bit longer time with them are amazed at what they begin to see. They are so elusive, like shadows on a landscape.

One of my former grad students said, 'I can smell these. These are like dirt.' It's the smell I love, in the spring after it rains. . . . So they're about a lot of things, and hopefully they're about paint, too."[23]

RECOGNITION OF OUTSIDER ART

As these "discoveries" are breathing new life into the art world, one of the hottest trends is the embracing of **outsider art** by galleries, museums, and collectors. In contrast to **folk art**, in which relatively untrained artisans are working within a cultural tradition, outsider artists are those sheer individualists who are self-taught and are working totally outside of both community traditions and establishment ideas about what constitutes good art.

This nonconformist work is highly personal, spontaneously expressive, and often spiritual. The artist may begin by creating art as a private act, not for the eyes of others, and certainly not for sale. Bessie Harvey was a cleaning woman in a hospital, quietly

following her inner spiritual calling to make sculptures of found wood for patients to help them heal, before people began noticing, loving, and collecting her work (**15.65**). Her inspirations come from vision and the spirits she senses in the wood:

> I talk to God for advice, not my neighbors. I talk to trees, weeds, and animals. I see things in dreams and when I close my eyes before sleep. I thought everyone was like that. When I meditate and close my eyes, faces and people begin to pass by—like watching a movie. Then one face stays. So I get up and try to draw it out or capture it in a piece of wood. All nature is crying out to tell us things.[24]

The first "insider" to laud such work was the Swiss painter Jean Dubuffet. At mid-century he collected a whole museum full of such pieces, which he termed "art brut" ("raw art"). In it lay true life, he felt; cultural conditioning had asphyxiated all other art:

> Simplifying, unifying, making uniform, the cultural machine, based on the elimination of flaws and scrap, on the principle of sifting in order to retain only the purest essence from its raw material, finally manages to sterilize all germination. For it is precisely from flaws and scrap that thought derives sustenance and renewal. A fixative of thought, the cultural machine has got lead in its wings.[25]

Dealers who have "discovered" outsider art are now swamping the outsider artists, snapping up cart loads of work, typically at prices that are only a fraction of their resale value in galleries. The exploitation of these sincere, eccentric artists is a serious scandal in the art world. Some have learned the hard way how to insist on honest pay for their efforts. Bessie Harvey asserts both her economic rights and the integrity of her own motivation as an artist:

> I'm not educated, but I'm not dumb. I've got a free spirit and I won't be under nobody's thumb. What they've taken from me they can have, but they can't have me. I'd rather be at peace with a biscuit and butter than to live in hell with steak and gravy.[26]

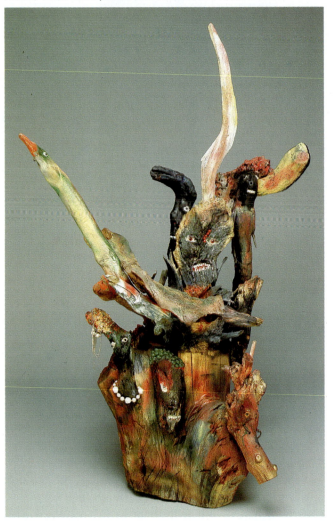

15.65 Bessie Harvey, *Tribal Spirits*, 1988. Mixed media, 45 × 26 × 20 ins (114.3 × 66 × 50.8 cm). Dallas Museum of Art, Dallas, Texas. Metropolitan Life Foundation Purchase Grant.

JON SERL
inside AN OUTSIDER'S MIND

Jon Serl (1894–1993) was discovered and his work highly sought after by the collectors of outsider art, but he continued to live as he had for decades, in a home-made 25-room ramshackle house in a small town in southern California, with chickens and dogs roaming through the dusty rooms. For the most part, he kept to himself and didn't sell his paintings, but they are now shown in major galleries and museum collections (**15.66**). After years of a variety of jobs, Serl discovered his calling as an artist when he was fifty-five:

"I wanted a painting for a big wall in that house, but I didn't have any money, so I got a board and painted my own. I didn't think it was any good, but then a man who'd traveled around the world saw it and said, 'Where'd ya get that Rousseau?' And you see what happened? Man—pat him on the back and watch him purr. From that point on, painting took over my life. I don't own a radio or watch television—all I do is paint.

I paint all day, every day. The most difficult part of it is when you have to sign a painting and admit it's yours. Then you have to rake up everything in you and ask yourself: is this what I wanted? I paint on wood now because when I was painting on canvas, I wound up putting a knife through most of my work. I no longer do that, but lately I've been burning quite a few.

[When I started painting] it was during the war. There was no art material available. Discarded soldier clothing boxes were used for panels—stains from berries and flower petals—even bark and roots gave color. I even used pulverized earth. I made my own charcoal—I still do! Later the town dump was the total source of supply. No used can of house paint was overlooked. Almost from the beginning, the fierce drive I feel from within demanded a constant search for supplies, so I could tell it while it was fresh. At times, the hillside mustard greens from my food plate had to be sacrificed for green stain needed on a canvas. Perhaps this seems drastic and fanatical, but there was no other way.

No one day is ever exactly like the day before. The position and intensity of the sun, the atmosphere, the green of trees, or color of distant buildings, dust, fog, and especially sudden rain storms all blend to offer a new and ever-changing canvas. And that is why the work I do is forever new.

If only a person will take time to observe. So much of our life is spent in sorrow and regret. All this is really waste, when with a bit more effort, all sorrow can be made a healthy happening. The world must be a gladsome place. At least, that is the way I see it.

Instead of listening to professors 'earn their keep' in schools or watching other painters copy each other into frustration, I looked as the caveman looked, to nature. 'Out there,' I found all answers to all things.

[I haven't had any art education.] Well, maybe in the fifth grade. The teacher said, 'One flower.' I bent it. She hit me on the hand with the ruler and said, 'Straight, straight.' I tore it up. Maybe that's when I became an artist.

I don't know why I've lived so long, because everyone in my family died young. Everybody's dead now and I wonder why I'm still living. I'm tired and I'm not glad to be alive because it's very hard. I'd like to be free and if it weren't for my paintings, I probably would've died long ago."[27]

15.66 Jon Serl, *Man and Papaya*, 1988. Oil on board, 48 × 32 ins (122 × 81.3 cm). Photograph courtesy of Jamison-Thomas Gallery.

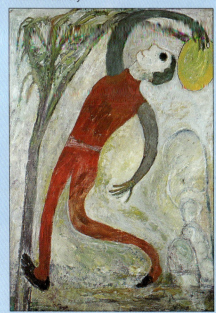

ART ISSUES
ART AS INVESTMENT

When Japanese businessman Ryoei Saito bought van Gogh's *Portrait of Dr. Gachet* for $82.5 million in 1990, he called the price "very reasonable."[28] Prices of artworks up for auction had reached extraordinary heights at that time, driven by international wealth and an increasing trend on the art scene. Instead of being purchased by people who primarily love and live with art, works by artists who are in vogue are more than ever before being bought as investments, for later auction at a higher price. Art has become a sought-after commodity because the prices that people are willing to pay for art have rapidly escalated. Not surprisingly, this situation raises many new issues, both for artists and for those who buy art.

For buyers of art offered for resale at auctions, there are the risks of buying on speculation—being sure that one is buying an original rather than a copy, assessing its quality, preserving its condition, insuring it, and then at a later date arranging to sell it for much more than was paid for it. In 1990, prices had become so inflated that the market for artworks crashed. However, the art market is heating up again, with especially high prices being paid for Impressionist paintings. As the supply of Impressionist art dwindles, people are paying huge sums for mediocre or little-known works by famous artists. In 1996, Christie's in New York sold a van Gogh painting of empty tables at a restaurant, with a few people in the background, for $10.3 million. The auction house explained that this might be the last van Gogh interior ever to come up for auction. In 1995, a small but lovely Degas monotype measuring only 31 by 37 cm brought £1,074,000 ($1,718,400) at auction at Sotheby's in London; even a rather clumsy Degas painting of a woman stepping out of a bathtub (**15.67**) was auctioned for £903,500 ($1,445,600). A reporter notes that:

"The body seems to be lunging forward and one leg simply melts down at the bottom, as if the painter could not be bothered to fit it with a foot. In the top corner left, the head of a maid bringing a cup of tea is awkwardly chopped off by the edge of the paper. Add the heavy dark colors and no wonder the work was left lying in the studio, as witnessed by the stamped signature added after the artist's death to all the works forming part of his estate."[29]

In sales of both pre-owned art through auctions and new art through galleries, prices are determined by a star system. It is ruled by what one artist characterizes as:

"a headless entity consisting of auctions, rumors, the media, newspapers, art magazines, interviews and so on. If you're out, you're out—you simply don't count. There is no opposition, no different opinion. [In this system] a painting which consists of a few square inches of paper can cost more than a building. The building is much larger and, when it rains, people can go inside. But nobody asks what this is all about."[30]

15.67 Edgar Degas, *Le Petit Déjeuner après le bain*, c. 1895–98. Pastel on paper laid down on board, 32⅝ × 31½ ins (83 × 80 cm). Courtesy of Christie's Images.

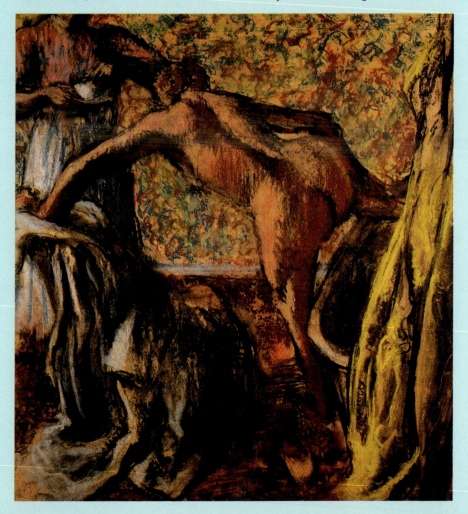

For living artists, the lure of big money may lead people to concentrate on making art that sells rather than art that comes from the urge to create. And should they receive a percentage of profits that buyers make on reselling their work? Are they only economic pawns in a high-risk game?

Where do museums stand in this game? With prices so high, small museums cannot compete with the larger ones. There are only a limited number of true masterpieces, but museums may nevertheless try to have something from every period and many famous artists in their collections. Some observers therefore think that museums have become repositories of second-rate art. Furthermore, some pieces in museum collections are antiquities taken out of other countries without permission. And some works may not have been executed by the famous artists whose names they bear. In the workshop system, which is not uncommon even today, the master artist creates the visual idea but employs helpers and apprentices for jobs such as—in the case of paintings—preparing the supports, grounds, and paints, painting the underlayers, painting certain details such as clouds and horses, and perhaps executing the whole painting under the master's supervision. Leonardo da Vinci was originally such an assistant in the studio of the Florentine artist Verrocchio. Rubens had a large studio since his work was so popular, and even when he traveled abroad, the production of paintings continued in his absence. In the output of Rembrandt's workshop, we do not now know which pieces were created solely by the hand of the master or what the "Rembrandt" signature meant at the time. The Rembrandt Research Project suggests that of the 711 existing works that were thought in 1920 to be created by Rembrandt (**15.68**), perhaps fewer than 300 were actually done by Rembrandt himself.

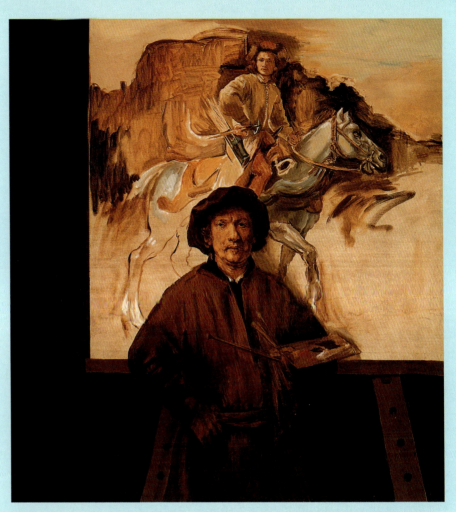

15.68 Russell Connor, *Hands Off the Polish Rider*, 1990–93. Oil on canvas, 68 × 64 ins (173 × 163 cm). Doubt has been cast on the attribution to Rembrandt of *The Polish Rider*, belonging to the Frick Collection in New York. This spoof by Russell Connor, published in *The New Yorker* magazine, pretends to be a newly discovered painting by Rembrandt's "star pupil," proving that Rembrandt himself painted *The Polish Rider*. Connor artfully copied a Rembrandt self-portrait and placed the artist before a clever approximation of *The Polish Rider* in progress.

When there is doubt about a work, museum curators may label it "attributed to" (meaning that the work is considered to be by the artist who is named), "in the manner of" (meaning that the work is by an unknown person imitating the artist who is named), or "in the school of" (meaning that the real artist's identity is not known, but that he or she is clearly influenced by the practices or style of the artist or region named, such as the Florentine school). These gray areas pose problems for investors under the star system. The question arises: if a work of art is truly great, does its value nonetheless depend on who executed it?

Many people have the perception that time is accelerating, for every-thing seems to happen very quickly these days. Artists and periods move in and out of favor very rapidly, and investors tend to resell pieces for fast and sure profits instead of keeping them in family collections. Nevertheless, there are still those who quietly buy art for the sake of good art, whether it is in vogue or not. Art that remains from the past is art that someone liked enough to keep. After one hundred years, two hundred years, another millennium, who will be the van Goghs whose work never sold during their lifetime but whose value was later declared? Will twentieth-century art be in or out? Will Western art command the highest prices or will the great art traditions of other cultures come to the fore?

16
UNDERSTANDING ART ON ALL LEVELS

Thus far we have looked at works of art from one perspective at a time—seeing, feeling, awareness of technical skill or design qualities, historical knowledge, or understanding of the content. When we have the opportunity to see actual works of art, however, our appreciation is richest if we can bring all these levels into play more or less simultaneously. In this chapter we will look at four monumental works of art:

- a painting (Pablo Picasso's *Guernica*)
- a piece of sculpture (Auguste Rodin's *Gates of Hell*)
- a ceiling fresco (Michelangelo's Sistine Chapel ceiling)
- a new public building (Moshe Safdie's Vancouver Library Square).

We have followed these key works throughout this book, but now we will look at each of them in greater depth. In the course of time, Picasso's *Guernica*, Rodin's *Gates of Hell*, and the Sistine Chapel ceiling painted by Michelangelo have been judged as great works of art. Moshe Safdie's Vancouver Library Square is as yet new and quite controversial. The process of assessing its ultimate value only began quite recently. By considering its pros and cons on the basis of the understanding of art that you have developed in this book, you become part of this process.

PICASSO'S *GUERNICA*

Pablo Picasso's *Guernica* (16.1) is thought to be the most looked-at painting of the twentieth century. It was commissioned by the Spanish Government in Exile during the Spanish Civil War, to be displayed in the 1937 Paris International Exhibition. At Picasso's request, it was then placed in the Museum of Modern Art in New York for safekeeping until "public liberties" were reestablished in his homeland, Spain. In 1981, after Franco's fascist regime had ended, the painting was moved to the Reina Sofia Museum of Modern Art in Madrid. For fourteen years it was kept behind security glass, lest it be attacked. But now the glass has been removed so that it can again be clearly seen. It stands as a monument not only to the genius of the most prolific and influential artist of the twentieth century but also to human questioning of the sufferings caused by war.

The incident Picasso chose as his subject occurred less than a week before he began work on the painting. It was the bombing of Guernica, capital and symbolic heart of the Basque provinces. To break Basque resistance, Hitler's forces, who were supporting Franco's war against the Loyalist government, carried out one of the world's first experiments in saturation bombing of a civilian population. They dropped over 3000 incendiary bombs over a period of three hours and machine-gunned the people as they tried to flee. The world was aghast, and Picasso had his subject. But the way in which he presented it is symbolic of all wars, all repression. It is not at all a literal representation of the actual bombing of the city or its aftermath (16.2). The figures are highly allegorical, abstracted in Cubist style; and the use of blacks, whites, and grays rather than more colorful hues erases any racial or nationalistic associations. The horror of Guernica becomes the horror of all war, an epic presentation that struck home in an age that thought itself too sophisticated for sentimentality.

Despite its evocation of the chaos of surprise attack, *Guernica* is held together by its triangular compositional devices. The major triangle runs from the open palm of the dead warrior at the lower left, up to the lamp held by the woman at upper center, down to the outstretched foot of the kneeling woman on the right. A secondary triangle on the left contains the head of the bull, facing away from the disaster, and the upturned head of the wailing woman with the dead baby hanging limp in her arms. There is also a bird on a table, with the same upward-turned imploring head as that of the mother. To the right, the outer triangle

16.1 Pablo Picasso, *Guernica*, 1937. Oil on canvas, 11 ft 5½ ins × 25 ft 5¼ ins (3.49 × 7.75 m). Reina Sofia Museum of Modern Art, Madrid.

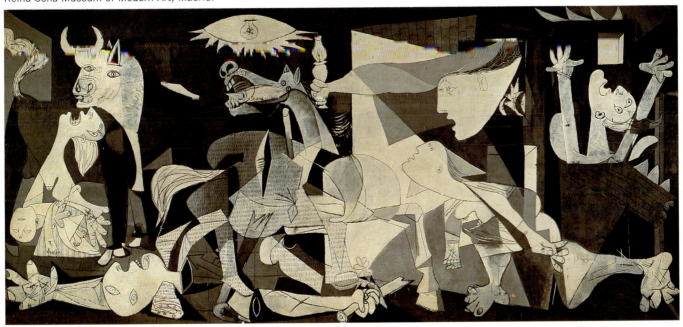

encompasses the agony of the burning woman—whose pose mirrors that of the woman with the dead baby—and the powerful questioning form of the woman thrusting a light into the scene.

Within the central triangle, there is a jumble of fragmented parts. The body of the dead warrior stretches across the base of the triangle, visually sharing the right leg with the kneeling woman. In the center is the horse with the gaping wound, whom Picasso in a rare moment of explanation identified as the spirit of the people.

The strong diagonals send the eye zipping around through the painting, searching for understandable forms and clues. We note that most of the people are women and children; this is not an heroic battle scene but the aftermath of an assault on civilians. Above all the figures is a sun or ceiling lamp or an eye—or perhaps all of these—watching, and shedding some light on the scene.

What do these images mean? Picasso generally refused to explain his symbols, insisting that viewers respond through personal, subconscious associations and emotions rather than impersonal logic:

> This bull is a bull, this horse is a horse. ... It is necessary that the public, the spectators, see in the horse, the bull, symbols that they interpret as they understand them. These are animals. These are massacred animals. That is all, for me; let the public see what it wants to see.[1]

The painting rivets our attention and involves us by making us ask questions. It does not answer them. Is the bull, for example, a symbol of unthinking brutality, the detached and stupid presence of repression, pushing down all the human forces that are trying to rise? Is he the representative of humanity, affected by but yet isolated from what happens to each person? Is he the eternal power of Spain, reassuringly solid even in the midst of devastation? Or does he represent sheer force, power that is in itself neither good nor evil? The possibilities—and there are others—have intrigued viewers of the painting for decades, and whole books have been written about the subject.

16.2 The city of Guernica after bombing by Nationalist forces, 1937.

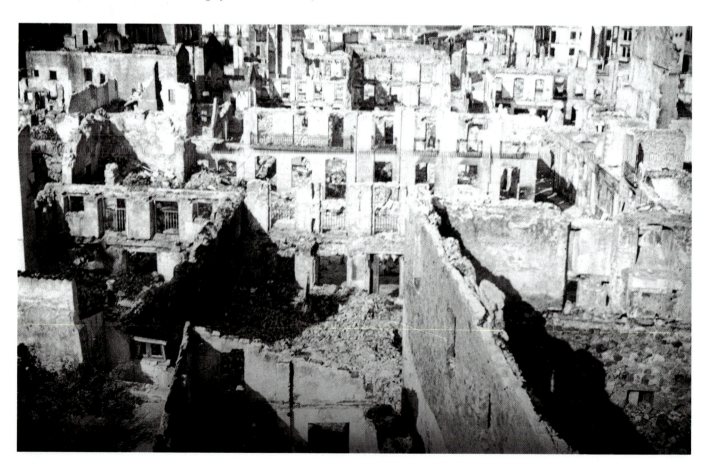

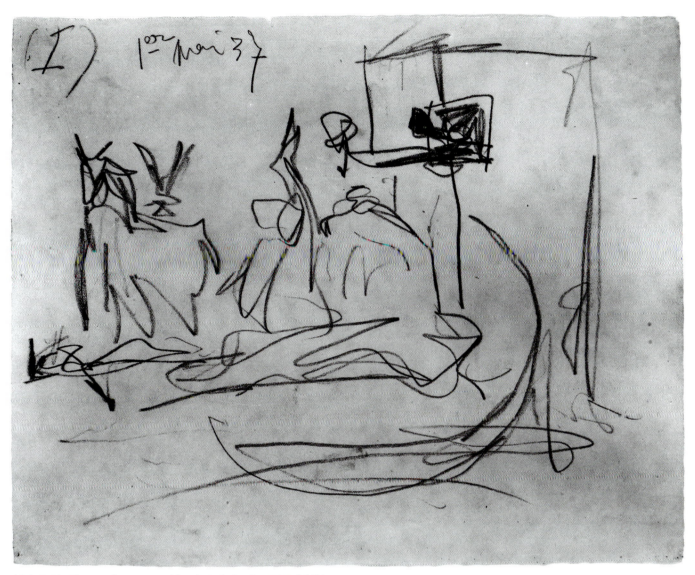

16.3 Pablo Picasso, first compositional study for *Guernica*, 1937.
Pencil on blue paper, 8¼ × 10⅝ ins (21 × 26.9 cm). Reina Sofia Museum of Modern Art, Madrid.

Picasso himself approached *Guernica* with an open, extremely flexible mind, continually changing its form. Quite aware of the historic significance of his attempts, he dated the scores of sketches in which he worked out the images and composed the powerful whole of the finished painting, leaving tracks for us to follow. From the very first compositional study (**16.3**), Picasso knew much of the basic structure. In this simplified visual note to himself, we can readily make out the woman with the lamp, the bull, and the horizontal shape of the dead soldier.

By the end of the first day, after five preliminary sketches, Picasso had worked out the compositional study shown in Figure **16.4**. The woman with the lamp already has her distinctive cometlike shape. The fallen soldier is wearing a classical centurion's helmet; the spirit of the horse escapes through the wound in its side. At this point, the figures are fairly representational and drawn with curving lines, in contrast to their fragmented, straight-edged appearance in the final version, and there is a sense of three-dimensional space receding to the rear.

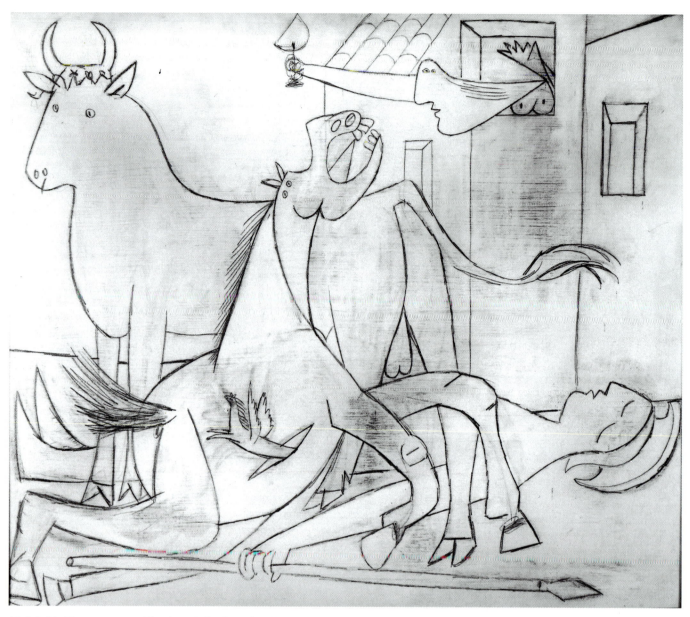

16.4 Pablo Picasso, compositional study for *Guernica*, May 1, 1937.
Pencil on gessoed wood, 25½ × 21⅛ ins (64.7 × 53.6 cm). Reina Sofia Museum of Modern Art, Madrid.

Picasso then introduced some new elements. A major group he added is the mother and the dead baby (**16.5**). Throwing her head back into a reverse scream makes her plight all the more hideous. The baby's eyes seem partially aware here; its blood oozes through the mother's fingers. By the final painting, the baby's eyes are mere empty half-moons and the blood is gone, making it the most peaceful figure in the general agony of the scene. Before Picasso worked out the fully extended reverse scream posture, he had experimented with bringing the mother and baby into the painting on bended knee at the right (**16.6**). At this point, Picasso also began to introduce the triangular shapes that play such an important role in the final composition. Three human corpses now lie on the ground, clenched fists rise heavenward, and the horse writhes into a new position.

In addition to the innovations in the sketches, Picasso continued to reassemble, add, and eliminate figures directly on the mural itself. Seven states preceding the final mural were photographed, giving us further insight into the evolution of the artist's thoughts. In the second state of the painting (**16.7**), the woman with the lamp is thrust into greater prominence than before: She is larger and brought forward by the flattening out of the crowded space of the picture. The flaming woman with upraised arms has appeared to fill the space at the far right. Triangles are everywhere elaborated. Perhaps the most striking—later abandoned—aspect of this state is the hopeful, defiant fist of the dead soldier, raised with a patch of Spanish turf against a luminous sun. This dramatic gesture is reduced to a subtle sign of hope that must be discovered in the final version: the small flower in the soldier's hand. And the sun dwarfs the light brought to the situation by the woman with the lamp, who seems to have been needed from the first as a call to the world to witness what has happened.

In the final mural, all those who are suffering are imploring upwards or looking to the left, while the eyes of the centurion have swiveled around to face us, staring blankly even in death. The other eyes that face us are those of the bull—and what do we read in them? Although the bull turns away from the violence, he is clearly involved with it on some level. And so are we. No one can see this huge mural, full of larger-than-life suffering figures, without being deeply affected by it. Most people walk toward it until it fills their peripheral vision and then stop, held back by the jagged points and the pain that is more felt than seen.

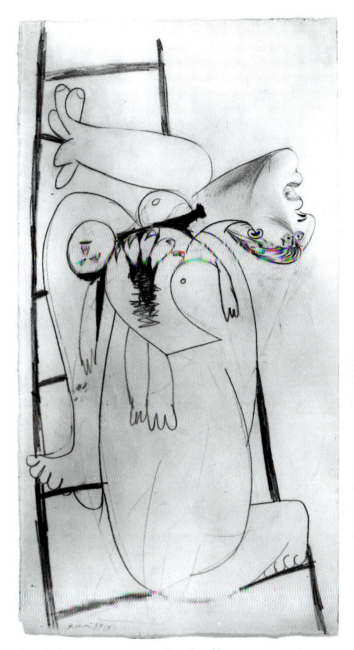

16.5 Pablo Picasso, study for *Guernica, Mother with Dead Child on Ladder*, May 9, 1937. Pencil on white paper, 9½ × 17⅞ ins (24.1 × 45.4 cm). Reina Sofia Museum of Modern Art, Madrid.

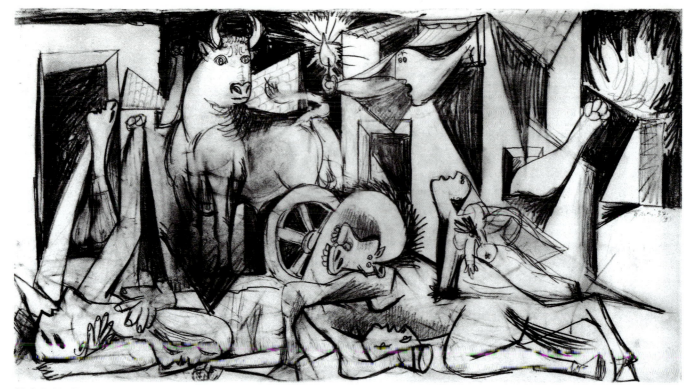

16.6 Pablo Picasso, compositional study for *Guernica*, May 9, 1937. Pencil on white paper, 9½ × 17⅞ ins (24.1 × 45.4 cm). Reina Sofia Museum of Modern Art, Madrid.

Even at a distance it is impossible to grasp the whole composition at once or to resolve the meaning of the whole. Its ambiguities, even on the most basic level (for instance, is this scene inside or outside?), keep us exploring and feeling our way through the work. It is quite likely that this painting will still be studied hundreds of years from now. Showing only the effects and not "the enemy," it stands as an incredibly powerful illumination of the suffering that we humans are capable of inflicting. In this compassionate awareness lies some hope for change.

16.7 Pablo Picasso, State II of *Guernica*, 1937. Reina Sofia Museum of Modern Art, Madrid.

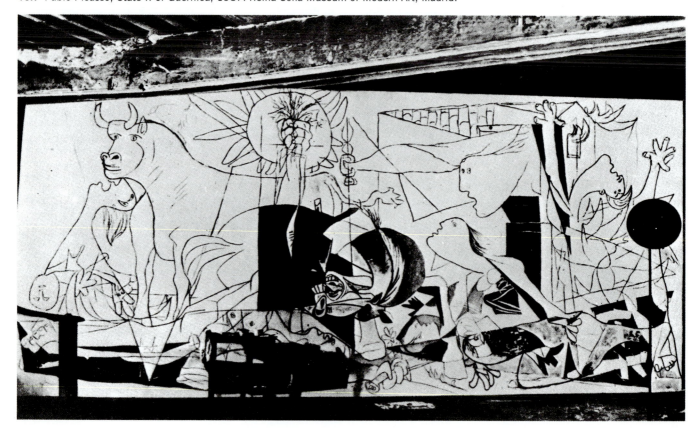

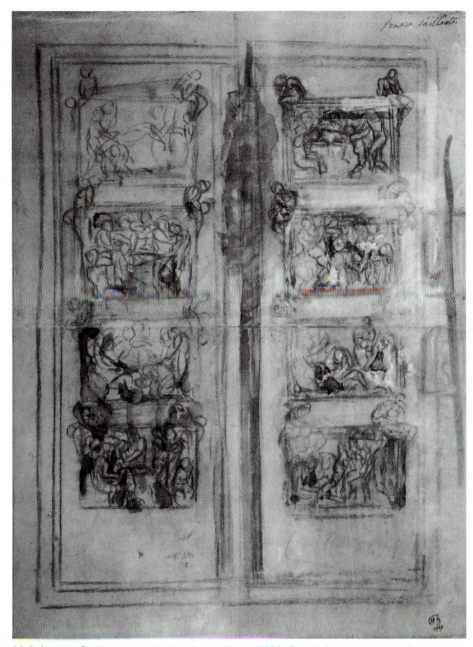

16.8 Auguste Rodin, sketch for *The Gates of Hell*, 1880. Pencil, ink wash, and white gouache. Musée Rodin, Paris.

RODIN'S *GATES OF HELL*

What may have been the greatest sculpture of the nineteenth century was never displayed until well into the twentieth. This work—*The Gates of Hell* by Auguste Rodin, who reinvigorated the art of sculpture at a time when most significant work was being done in painting—occupied the artist intermittently from 1880 to 1900 but was not cast in bronze until 1926, nine years after his death. It had been commissioned for the proposed Museum of Decorative Arts in Paris,

which was never built. Rodin welcomed the opportunity to prove his stature as a skilled and imaginative sculptor after charges that his earlier lifesized sculptures were so realistic that they must have been cast from live models. His proposal for the great door was a sculptural image of *The Inferno* from Dante's *Divine Comedy*, whose allegorical account of the soul's return to God had deeply moved Rodin. He peopled his portal with nearly 200 fluidly expressive bodies, all smaller than life. Some are modeled in such low relief that they disappear into the swirling inferno; some reach out in full three-dimensionality toward the viewer. All bear witness to the profundity of Rodin's vision and his ability to use the human body to express the full drama of existence.

Historical precedents for *The Gates of Hell* included Ghiberti's Renaissance *Gates of Paradise* (15.21), which Rodin had seen in Florence. Rodin started out with a similar concept. His first architectural sketches, such as the one shown in Figure 16.8, divide the massive width of such a door into eight symmetrical panels. Yet even here, the organic forms they contain are starting to spill over their boundaries, until, in its final form, the straight lines of the architectural framework are mated to, and in places obscured by, the multitude of sensual figures.

Rodin soon abandoned any attempt at a literal, compartmentalized depiction of the levels of Hell described by Dante. An early terracotta study for *The*

16.9 Auguste Rodin, terracotta study for *The Gates of Hell*, Musée Rodin, Paris.

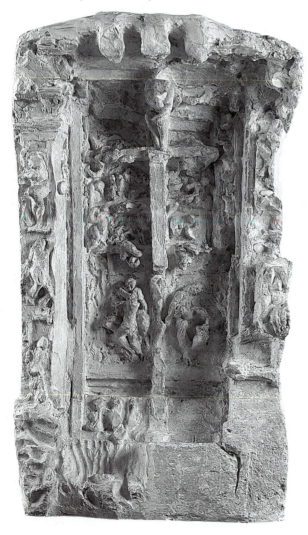

Gates of Hell (16.9) suggests its final form: a quasi-architectural framework with a cross at its center, topped by the seated figure later known as *The Thinker*. Rodin eventually executed *The Thinker* as an isolated sculpture; indeed, many of his sculptures first appeared in his preparations for *The Gates of Hell*. He worked with the malleability of clay, using live models moving freely as inspiration for gestures expressing their own inner lives. The figures and groupings thus developed were attached to a large wooden frame, on which clay was built up in relief. Plaster casts were then made of areas of the work, with the intention of using them as the basis for bronze lost-wax casts. Only one of the casts that were ultimately made was done by the fine lost-wax process. Rodin actually dreamed of having the side jambs carved in marble, with the central panels cast in bronze.

Even the plaster casts themselves (1.46) reveal the extraordinary dynamism of Rodin's sculpture. Figures move far out and way back in space, creating areas of light and shadow that undulate continually through the piece. Extremely busy passages alternate with quieter ones, weaving another dimension into the visual rhythm of the piece. At the very top are the figures called *The Three Shades*. Like *The Thinker*, they were also cast and shown as a sculpture in themselves. They are actually the same figure cast three times and shown from three different angles. Their gestures keep directing the viewer's glance down into the turmoil below.

After absorbing an impression of the whole 18-foot (5.5-m) structure, viewers are inevitably drawn in to try to decipher individual forms blended into the writhing turmoil. Among the inhabitants of Hell—which Rodin conceived as a state of mind rather than a place in the hereafter—is Count Ugolino (16.10). He and his sons were historical figures who had been locked in a tower to starve. There is an ambiguous suggestion in Dante's account that Ugolino ate his sons' corpses in his hunger. The horror of their torment is expressed physically, with the aristocratic count reduced to the crawling stance of a beast. They are placed on the left panel at the viewer's eye level, making their agony inescapable.

Below the Ugolino group are the historical figures of Francesca da Rimini and her lover, Paolo, brother of the man she had married for family political reasons. Her husband, who was deformed and ugly, killed the pair when he found them out. Rodin treats their forbidden love sympathetically, if tragically. In Rodin's

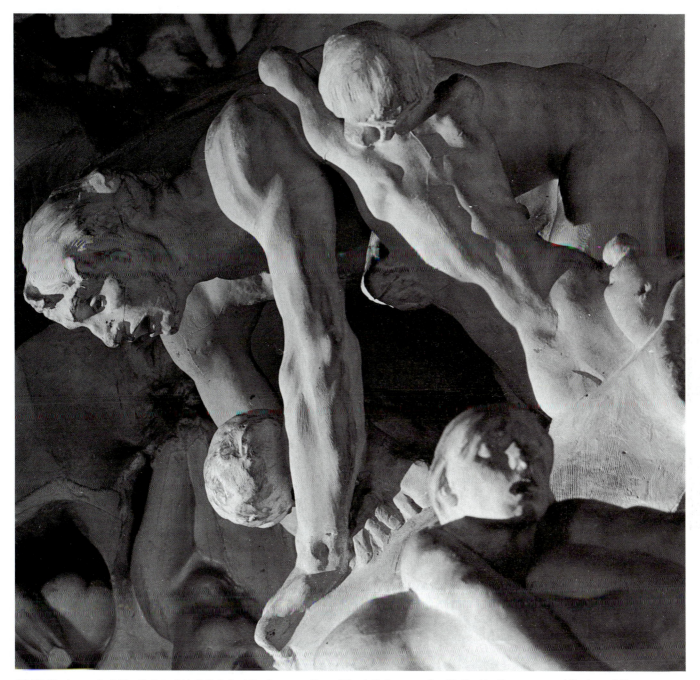

16.10 Plaster cast of *The Gates of Hell*. Detail of the lower section of the left door panel, with the Ugolino group and Paolo and Francesca.

Hell, it is humanity that torments itself with its frustrated longings and inability to find peace.

The only still figure in the work is that of *The Thinker*. Many observers consider him a self-portrait of the artist. We can imagine that Rodin is describing his own experience of the creative process when he describes his *Thinker* as:

> a naked man, seated upon a rock, his feet drawn under him, his fist against his teeth; he dreams. The fertile thought slowly elaborates itself within his brain. He is no longer dreamer, he is creator.[2]

All about *The Thinker* bodies are struggling and climbing, only to fall—even the angels (**16.11**). Within the maelstrom, some try to help and console each other; others are physically touching but isolated in their individual pain. As observers, we stand equal to the fallen, looking upward to the barrier one would have to cross to reach the level of *The Thinker*, who

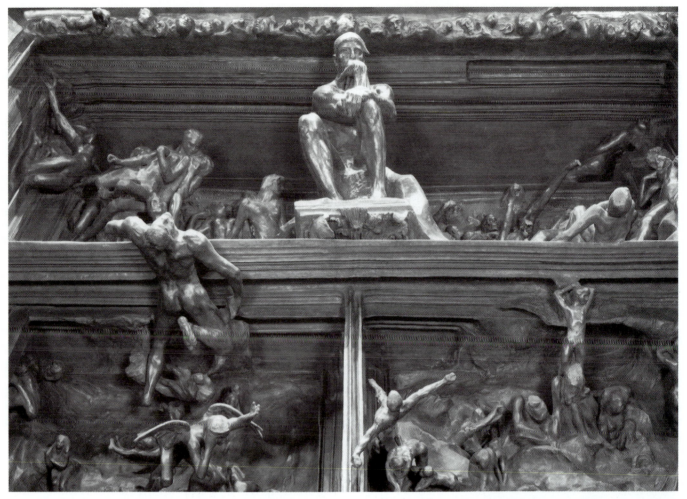

16.11 Auguste Rodin, *The Gates of Hell* (detail). *The Thinker*, with portions of the door panels and tympanum. Bronze. Stanford University Museum of Art. Gift of B. Gerald Cantor Collections.

16.12 Auguste Rodin, sketch for *The Gates of Hell*, with architectural setting, c. 1880–81. Pencil. Musée Rodin, Paris.

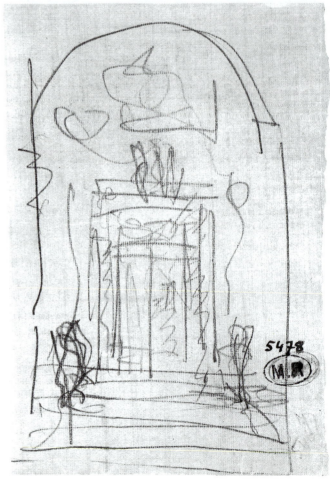

separates himself enough from the endless motion of human strivings to see the whole picture, wondering why.

To complete this epic depiction of the human condition, Rodin had intended that his sculptures of Adam and Eve be placed on either side of *The Gates of Hell*, as suggested in one of his early sketches (**16.12**). This sketch also reveals his vision of the doors as a portal at the top of a flight of stairs, framed by an arch. If this were so, if *The Gates of Hell* had actually been installed architecturally as doors, imagine what it would feel like to walk up to and then through them, as if entering the world they describe. When *The Gates of Hell* are set up with the lifesized sculptures of Adam and Eve (**16.13**), a strongly triangular composition results from the obvious reading from Adam to the Three Shades to

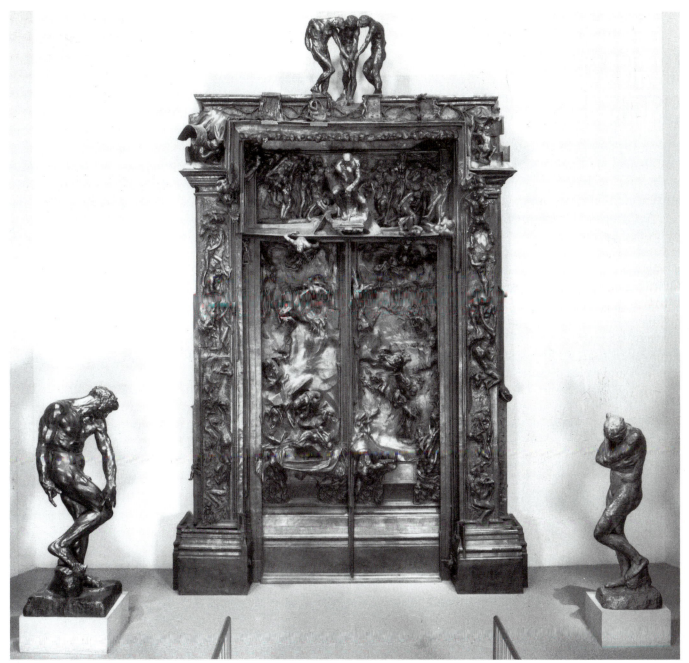

16.13 Auguste Rodin, *The Gates of Hell*, with *Adam and Eve*, 1880–1917. Bronze (Coubertin Fondeur Cast no. 5), 251 × 158 × 33 ins (638 × 401 × 84 cm). Stanford University Museum of Art. Gift of B. Gerald Cantor Collections.

Eve, justifying the large scale of the Shades. And to enter Hell by passing reminders of the idea of original sin—one explanation for human suffering—extends the logic of the whole.

Keenly aware of the pain of human existence, Rodin himself died of cold in an unheated villa, as intrigues and manipulations swirled around his bequest of his art to France.

Despite the difficulties of his own situation and the frequent rejections of his work by more conventional minds, Rodin was passionately fond of art—and of what it reveals to us of life.

Great works of art, which are the highest proof of human intelligence and sincerity, say all that can be said on man and on the world, and, besides, they teach that there is something more that cannot be known. . . We [artists] are misunderstood. Lines and colors are only to us as the symbols of hidden realities. Our eyes plunge beneath the surface to the meaning of things, and when afterwards we reproduce the form, we endow it with the spiritual meaning which it covers. An artist worthy of the name should express all the truth of nature, not only the exterior truth, but also, and above all, the inner truth.[3]

MICHELANGELO'S SISTINE CHAPEL CEILING

The next piece of art that we will explore in depth in this chapter is earlier than the first two, but it is by no means less "evolved." The complexity of its conception and execution is staggering.

At the age of thirty-three, Michelangelo was commissioned by Pope Julius II to paint a fresco to decorate the ceiling of the Sistine Chapel in the Vatican, which was used for devotions and ceremonial purposes by the pope and those surrounding him, such as cardinals and archbishops. At the time, 1508, the ceiling was already painted to look like the blue heavens, studded with stars (16.14), with scenes from the lives of Jesus and Moses painted below the high windows and painted statues of the popes between the windows. Several years later, Raphael was commissioned to design tapestries which were hung in the place of the fictitious painted drapes near the floor.

Michelangelo was reluctant to accept the ceiling commission, for he was embroiled in sculpting a tomb in which the same pope was to be buried eventually (a project which plagued him for the rest of his life, in continual wranglings with the authorities over funds and design). Furthermore, he considered himself a sculptor rather than a painter, and the difficulties he would face in painting the immense ceiling for the exaltation of its august visitors were staggering.

Michelangelo faced a vast curving surface 118 feet (38.5 m) long, broken by triangular arches over each window. He also had to create images that could be seen and make sense to people standing 70 feet (21 m) below on the floor. Fresco is a very demanding medium even on a vertical surface, and to work on the ceiling, Michelangelo had to perch on a scaffolding, apparently with his head continually thrown back and paint falling onto his face and beard. It was his first major attempt at fresco.

What he created under these extraordinarily difficult conditions is one of the world's greatest works of art. He painted it in two portions, during the winter of

16.14 G. Tagnettis, reconstruction of the 15th-century Sistine Chapel before Michelangelo's frescoes. Vatican Museums, Vatican City.

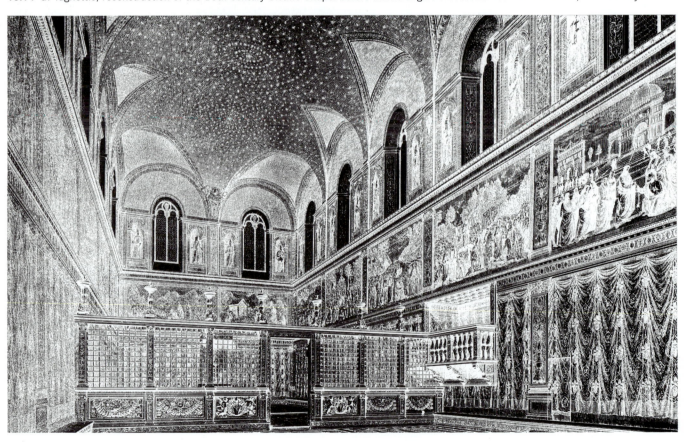

1508 to 1509—when work stopped for lack of further funds, seemingly absorbed by the military operations of the Vatican—and then again from 1511 to 1512. He tried using assistants but soon gave up and worked mostly alone in the Chapel, in pain and exhaustion, but apparently also driven by some kind of inner inspiration. We know from his letters that he dedicated himself as an artist to the service of religion and beauty, and that the two were not different in his mind. One of his sonnets explains:

> Beauty was given at my birth to serve
> As my vocation's faithful exemplar ...
> To sense the Beauty which in secret moves
> And raises each sound intellect to Heaven![4]

And in conversations recorded by a visiting Portuguese miniature painter, Michelangelo reportedly said in reference to Italian painting:

> With discreet persons nothing so calls forth and fosters devotion as the difficulty of a perfection which is bound up in union with God. For good painting is nothing but a copy of the perfections of God and a recollection of His painting; it is a music and a melody which only intellect can understand, and that with great difficulty. And that is why painting of this kind is so rare that no man may attain it.[5]

Michelangelo's own surviving letters give us no clues as to what he was attempting aesthetically and theologically in the vast work. The pope had originally suggested that he paint the Twelve Apostles, with false painted architectural decorations about them, but Michelangelo argued that the Apostles wouldn't make good subjects because they were "too poor." He won, and the pope gave him a free hand. What evolved probably exceeded anybody's wildest expectations.

The sculptor as fresco painter conceived the ceiling as an illusionary continuation of the architectural details of the building, within which over 300 figures tell the Christian story of the human situation. The panels in the crown of the vault contain the events recounted in Genesis, beginning over the altar with God's separating of the darkness and the light, proceeding through the stories of Adam and Eve, and ending with Noah, the flood, and Noah's drunkenness (**16.15**). The drama expresses God's creative power and humankind's unworthiness and need for divine salvation. Surrounding these panels

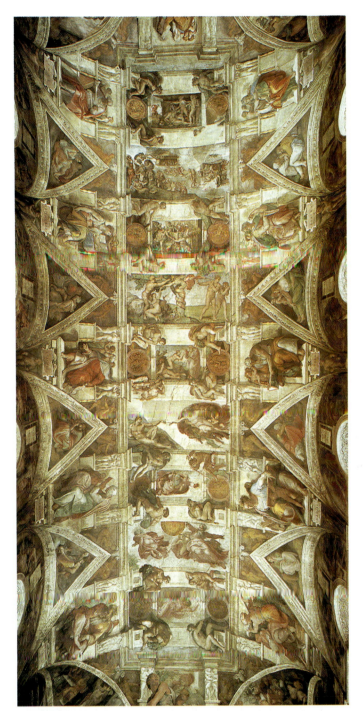

16.15 Michelangelo Buonarroti, Sistine Chapel ceiling (before restoration), Vatican Palace, Rome, 1508–12.

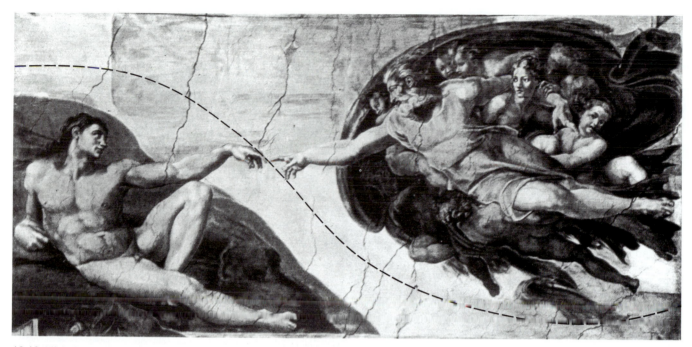

16.16 Michelangelo Buonarroti, Sistine Chapel ceiling, 1508–12, detail of the *Creation of Adam* with an overlay showing the "S" composition.

are the *ignudi*, enigmatic nude male figures in a great array of poses. Michelangelo treated the curving sides of the vault as thrones for those who prophesied the coming of Christ (the Prophets and Sibyls), with the real architectural triangles between them housing the ancestors of Christ. Between these concave triangles he painted illusionary "columns" of figures and stone ribs that seem to support the upward curve of the ceiling.

The scale of the figures changes continually, with God smaller than the Prophets and Sibyls along the sides, and with scale changes from one panel to the next through the center. Even our point of view switches from looking at God overhead to looking at God as if we were alongside, in witnessing the *Creation* and *Fall of Adam and Eve*. But rather than being disunified, these variations have the effect of a great symphonic work with many voices and recurring themes.

The major story carried through the center devotes three panels to God's creation of the world, three to the creation and fall of Adam and Eve, and three to the story of Noah, with the flood, Noah's sacrifice to God, and Noah's drunkenness. The first three portray the omnipotence of God, depicted as a gray-haired man who hovers and zooms above the spectator in the first three panels, bringing the sun and the moon into being with a gesture of his hand.

The next panel is the most famous portion of the whole ceiling: the *Creation of Adam* (**16.16**). It is said to have been the first thing Michelangelo painted when he returned to it in 1511. The use of unfilled space draws our attention in contrast with all the busy details surrounding it, and the use of outstretched fingers that almost touch, but not quite, conveys an electrical sense of the infusion of the legendary first man with life. The actual Biblical reference has God breathing life into Adam, but artistic license serves Michelangelo well here, for we can almost "see" the implied line as the spark of life jumps the gap between God and Adam. Compositionally, the panel is designed as a long horizontal "S," a device known as "the line of beauty" and used repeatedly by Michelangelo and other Renaissance artists in posing single figures and composing scenes.

The male prophets of the Old Testament alternate along the sides with female Sibyls, who were prophetesses from the pre-Christian traditions of Classical Greek and Roman culture. The Renaissance brought a resurgence of interest in these Classical civilizations and attempts to embrace them within the fold of Christianity. To this end, oracles ascribed to the Sibyls prophesied the coming of Christ, and Michelangelo places them on equal footing with the Old Testament Prophets in this regard. Although they are supposed to

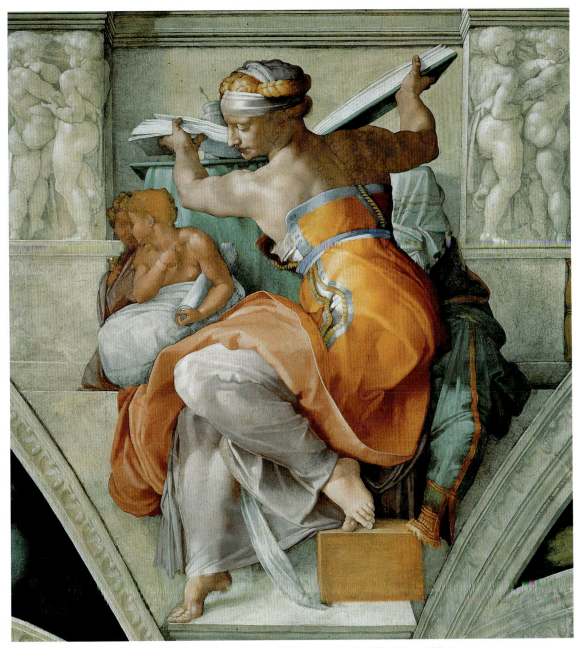

16.17 Michelangelo Buonarroti, Sistine Chapel ceiling, 1508–12, detail of *The Libyan Sibyl*.

be females, in Michelangelo's hands they become androgynous figures with the heavy musculature more characteristic of men. The Libyan Sibyl (16.17) is particularly famous as an idealized combination of the beauty of both sexes. Her exaggerated spiraling contrapposto pose and arched feet, like many of the great variations of poses in the ceiling, are thought to be precursors to the theatrics of Mannerist painting. On the other hand, some see Michelangelo as reaching backward in time to Classical interest in depictions of the nude male body, accentuated by poses involving strain, thrust, and counterthrust.

The Prophet Jonah (16.18) seems flung backward from his perch above the altar, perhaps in awe of God, who hovers just above on the ceiling. Michelangelo's genius with foreshortening is particularly evident here, for we perceive the figure as leaning away in space even though architecturally this area curves forward. Notice, for instance, how Michelangelo has shortened Jonah's trunk and right thigh to help us "see" them as

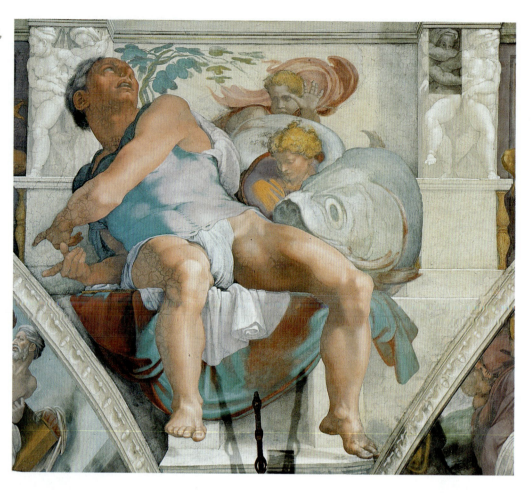

16.18 Michelangelo Buonarroti, Sistine Chapel ceiling, 1508–12, detail of *The Prophet Jonah*.

extending back from us in space. Notice also Michelangelo's strong use of complementary colors, with the green of the drape heightening the lively red glow of the skin.

Michelangelo's colors are currently the source of great controversy. For centuries the Sistine Chapel ceiling was so dulled by candle smoke and darkened varnish that people tended to assume that Michelangelo used muted, unsaturated colors. Many liked the ceiling that way. But there were clues that these were not the original colors. For instance, one observer who saw the ceiling when it was new wrote about its unprecedented luminosity. Despite international protests, a team of restorers began trying in 1980 to repair minute paint flaking and to remove the layers of old varnish without damaging the original fresco. Twelve years of painstaking work revealed surprisingly bright and glowing colors beneath (**16.19**). The contrast is striking, as can be seen in comparing before-and-after-cleaning photos of one of the lunettes over the windows (**16.20**).

The drastic cleaning may have removed too much, however. Comparison of the lunette in Figure 16.20 before and after cleaning reveals that the new effect is much flatter than before cleaning. The woman's cloak, for instance, is rather flat across the back, whereas before cleaning it had deep shadows, lending it more three-dimensionality and more distance from the background, and giving the work a certain rhythm and balance in its subtle use of values. The major argument still being passionately debated is whether or not Michelangelo had worked *a secco*, adding darker values for spatial modeling after the plaster was dry. The proponents of restoration claim that Michelangelo worked almost exclusively in the pure Florentine *buon fresco* tradition, applying paint directly to a fresh layer of wet plaster, the *intonaco*. They say that he rarely made corrections *a secco*, on dried plaster, a much less durable technique. They also speculate that he painted huge areas each day. Each of the lunettes, for example, was painted in only three days, with each day's work said to have covered about 54 square feet (5 square

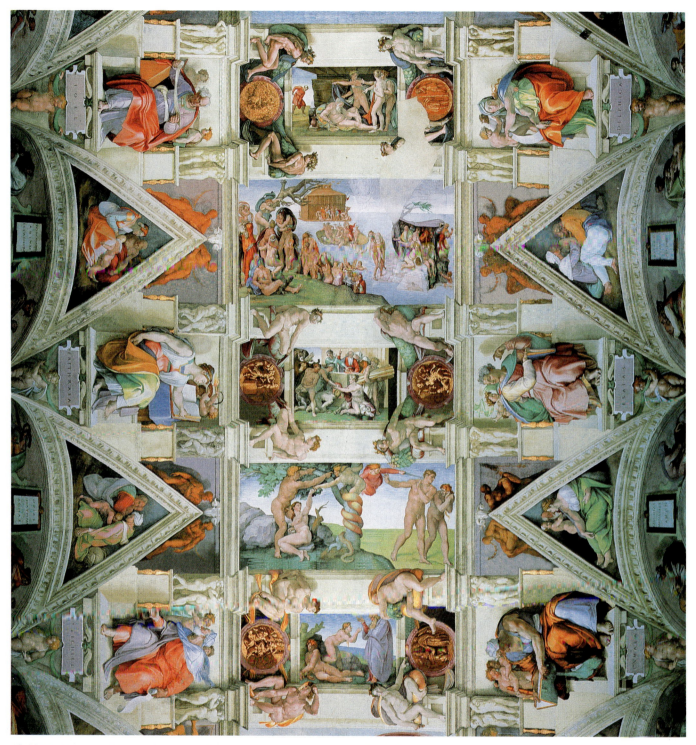

16.19 Michelangelo Buonarroti, Sistine Chapel ceiling (after restoration), 1508–12.
Detail of the ceiling showing the *Intoxication of Noah* to the *Creation of Eve*.
© Nippon Television Network Corporation, Tokyo, 1991.

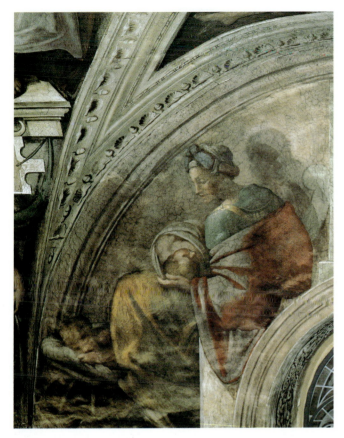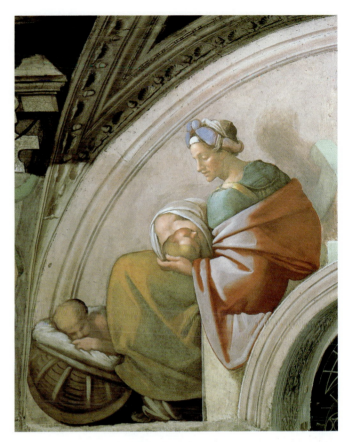

16.20 Michelangelo Buonarroti, Sistine Chapel ceiling, 1508–12, detail of a lunette before and after restoration.

meters). There is no evidence that he used a cartoon in these areas, but rather he seems to have been painting directly and freely. According to the restorers, he limited his palette to those colors that worked well in *buon fresco*, laying them side by side and often allowing the ground to show through for added brilliance. Figure 16.19 reveals that Michelangelo also boldly juxtaposed complementary colors—especially red-oranges and blue-greens—to give a stunningly vibrant effect to the figures.

Those who think that Michelangelo made *a secco* amendments to the fresco have the anguished feeling that the great fresco has been inalterably ruined by the restoration, for it took away all layers down to the *intonaco*. They question whether such a drastic cleaning was justified, and they also raise questions about commercial aspects of the restoration. It was funded by the Nippon Television Network Corporation, which tightly controlled the rights of photographing and reproducing pictures of the work in progress and the cleaned paintings and then made them available only at high prices.

The Sistine Chapel's commercial exploitation—or accessibility, depending on one's point of view—was further expanded in 1996 by introduction of its frescoes on interactive CD-ROM,. A user can select any of the parts of the Chapel ceiling, zoom in to see its details magnified, or request information including Biblical quotations and art critics' writings about the work. The paintings can even be extracted for use on one's business calendar, with angels surrounding happy events and devils marking difficult appointments. One cannot imagine how Michelangelo would respond to all of this, but the Vatican explains that it is offering CD-ROMs of its art treasures in order to better share them with the world. Cardinal José Castillo Lara told a news conference:

> We are moved to do this because the Vatican belongs to everyone but not everyone can enjoy it. Throughout its history, the Vatican has become the depository and custodian of priceless art works. We now bring these treasures into people's homes.[6]

MOSHE SAFDIE'S VANCOUVER LIBRARY SQUARE

The final piece we will consider in depth is the library and office tower completed in central Vancouver in 1995 (3.43 and **16.21**). Vancouver is considered by many to be one of the world's most beautiful cities, largely because of its environment: a clear bay with mountains rising beyond and a moist climate that supports lush vegetation. Although cosmopolitan, its urban core lacked visual coherence. To meet the needs of the public and also to provide a strong architectural symbol in the midst of Vancouver, city planners therefore held a competition for a new city library, combined with an office center for Public Works Canada. It was to be "the most important civic facility in the downtown core." The site chosen was surrounded by an undistinguished mixture of hotels, warehouses, offices, and parking lots; it sloped almost two stories toward the southeast corner of the plot.

The public was invited to help in the choice of architectural plans. Some 7000 people commented on the three final proposals, and seventy per cent of them preferred the plan crafted by Israeli architect Moshe

16.21 Moshe Safdie, Vancouver Library Square at dusk, Vancouver, British Columbia, opened May 1995. Photo by T. Hursley.

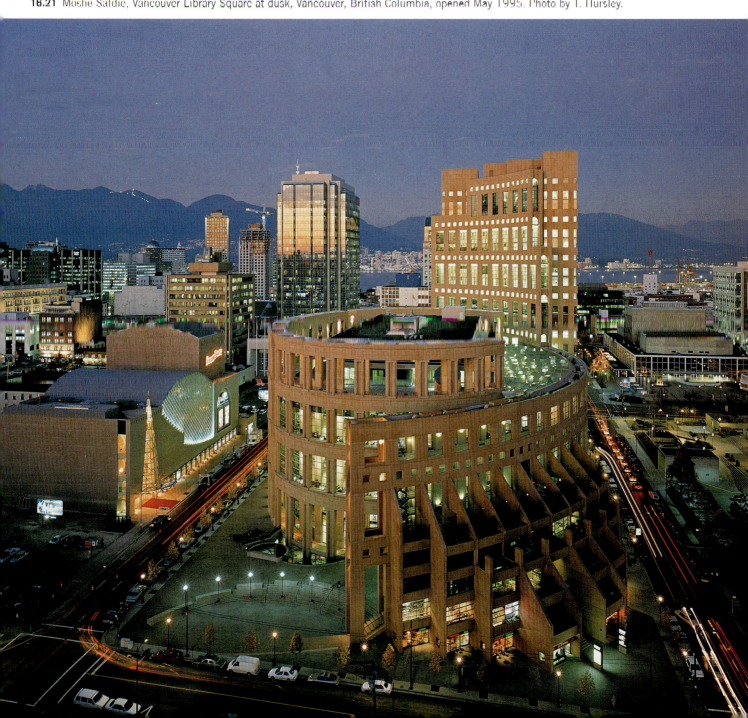

Safdie and his associates. Safdie has offices in Jerusalem, Boston, Toronto, and Montreal, and has designed many major cultural centers, public housing complexes, academic institutions, and communities in Israel, the United States, and Canada. His extensive work is now documented on CD-ROM, from a McGill University archive of 100,000 of his architectural drawings, plans, sketches, models, and slides. He also speaks, writes, and teaches about architecture as a visual language, and he has given deep thought to the way in which architecture can serve public needs.

Safdie's solution for the sloping Vancouver site was to build an eight-story glass box in the center for the book stacks and to wrap an arcade of individual reading nooks around it in a freestanding elliptical wall, reached by catwalks. Another higher curving wall approaches the library stack and arcade from the east side, creating a high open concourse and entry foyer for the library, with retail shops at floor level in the eastern wall.

The curving walls open at either side into an outer plaza, providing "instant orientation" welcoming people into the inner concourse between the library and the outer wall. This glass-roofed space bordered by shops and cafés creates an indoor gathering place for the public, sheltered from the damp climate. The downhill side of the hilly site is deeply buttressed, with retail shops and children's play area nestled within the buttresses. Just as the elliptical library wall is played against the outer freestanding wall, the semi-curve motif is again repeated in an amphitheater carrying the ramp and providing a spatial transition to street level. In accordance with the competition parameters, the office tower is functionally separate from the library but united with it by the plaza at street level and developing outward from the curving wall defining the concourse (16.22). In contrast to the aggregate from local granite used to clad the concrete walls, the northeast side of the tower is an all-glass inset with sweeping views of the city, harbor, and mountains.

16.22 Site plan of Moshe Safdie's Vancouver Library Square, Vancouver, British Columbia, opened May 1995.

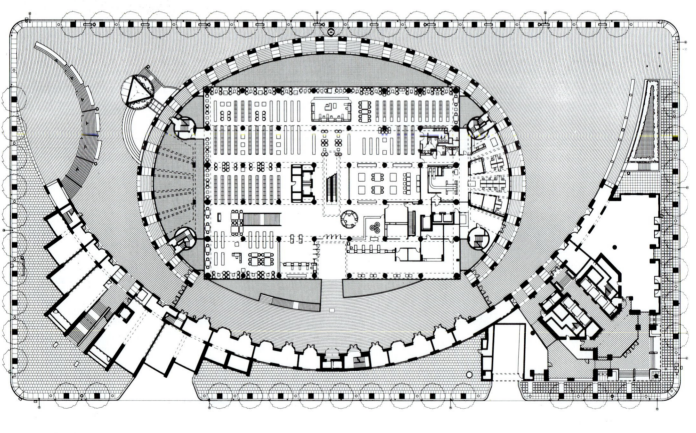

Ground Floor Plan

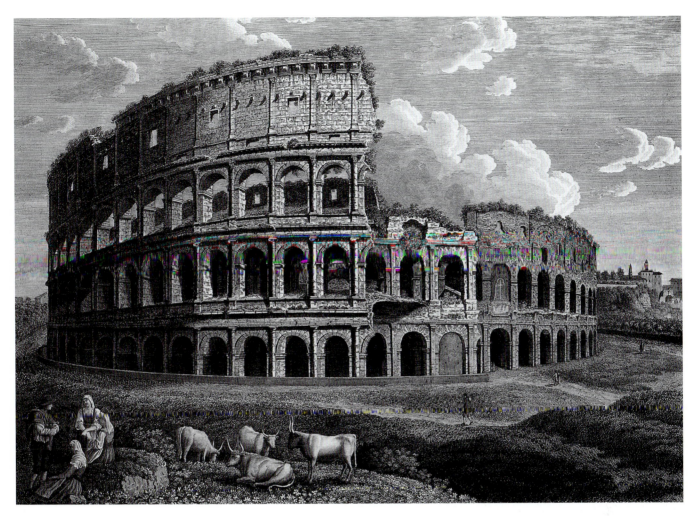

16.23 The Colosseum, Rome. Print by Franco Morelli. The O'Shea Gallery, London.

After winning the competition, Safdie was sharply criticized for the similarity to the ruins of the Colosseum in Rome, where violent deaths had been staged as public spectacle. This resemblance is quite noticeable in the precast columns and abstract frieze of the inner ellipse and the outer "ghost wall" which looks remarkably like the highest remaining wall in the ruins of the Colosseum (16.23). Critics dubbed the Library Square "a modern ruin" and compared the effect to Disneyland. The *Vancouver Province* ran an editorial (16.24) questioning, "How did a Roman-designed building erected 2000 years ago for the main function of suppressing new ideas win out as a design for a twenty-first century library and seat of learning?"[7]

The vehemence of the objections reveals the power of symbolic imagery. The objections were not directed toward the aesthetic form of the building but to its apparent historical reference. The competition parameters for the project had sought "to create facilities which have symbolic meaning," but critics objected that this was entirely the wrong symbol for Vancouver, as well as the wrong architectural style for a city dominated by modern "West Coast" architecture.

Surprisingly, Safdie insists that this similarity to the Colosseum had appeared "completely unconsciously" in the course of developing the design. Under criticism, Safdie experimented with eliminating the similarity. He found that the Classical form actually functioned better than any other solutions:

> We developed a number of schemes: one replaced the double columns with a series of free-standing columns that made it like a forest of columns rising eight stories high—like a bunch of West Coast redwoods; a second scheme had a very flat, taut façade of metal and glass; a third was all glass. But the test was

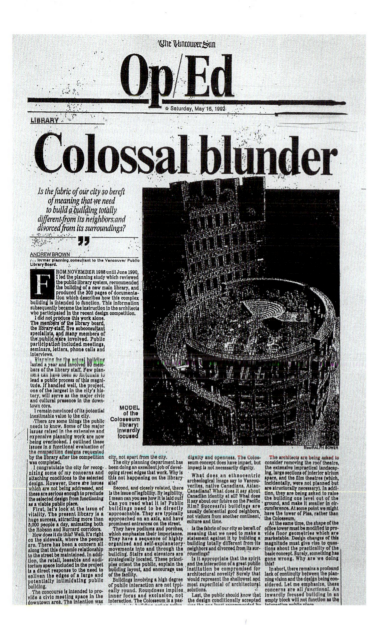

16.24 (left) Newspaper article ("Colossal Blunder...") on Moshe Safdie's Vancouver Library Square, Vancouver, British Columbia, opened May 1995. Photo by M. Ronnen Safdie.

16.25 (opposite) Readers in Vancouver Library Square carrels. Photo by T. Hursley.

when we started making models and tried to imagine placing reading tables and people in that free-standing wall. The glass schemes made you feel like you were up there on exhibit; they created no *place* at all. The metal and glass schemes could create solidity, but at the same time they lacked any scale that could make you feel comfortable.

It became absolutely obvious that the solidity of the original scheme made a place to be inside of, to read, to look out to the city, that was more compelling than any of the other schemes (**16.25**). It was a real lesson in classicism as a scale-making, humanizing device in space.[8]

After all the fracas over the design, it has been vindicated by its success with the public. Compared to the old library which it replaced, the new Vancouver Library Square brought so many new users into the library that its circulation tripled, leaving shelves bare.

The point of the design was to invite public visitation and easy access to the collection, and it is doing so. Safdie had insisted that the architect's role is to design for others, rather than oneself, by imagining how the users will experience the building. So empathetic is this design that the Canadian press now calls the Library Square "the city's living room."

Speaking prophetically three years before becoming engaged in the library project, Safdie alluded to "a sense of authenticity in a work of architecture from which it can derive an elusive quality of timelessness. As beautifully stated by August Peret, 'Will the building make a beautiful ruin?'"[9]

It is this elusive quality of authenticity and timelessness that characterizes all great art. Perhaps it cannot be fully explained or understood. But the more we know and the more we look, the deeper will be the impact of great art upon us.

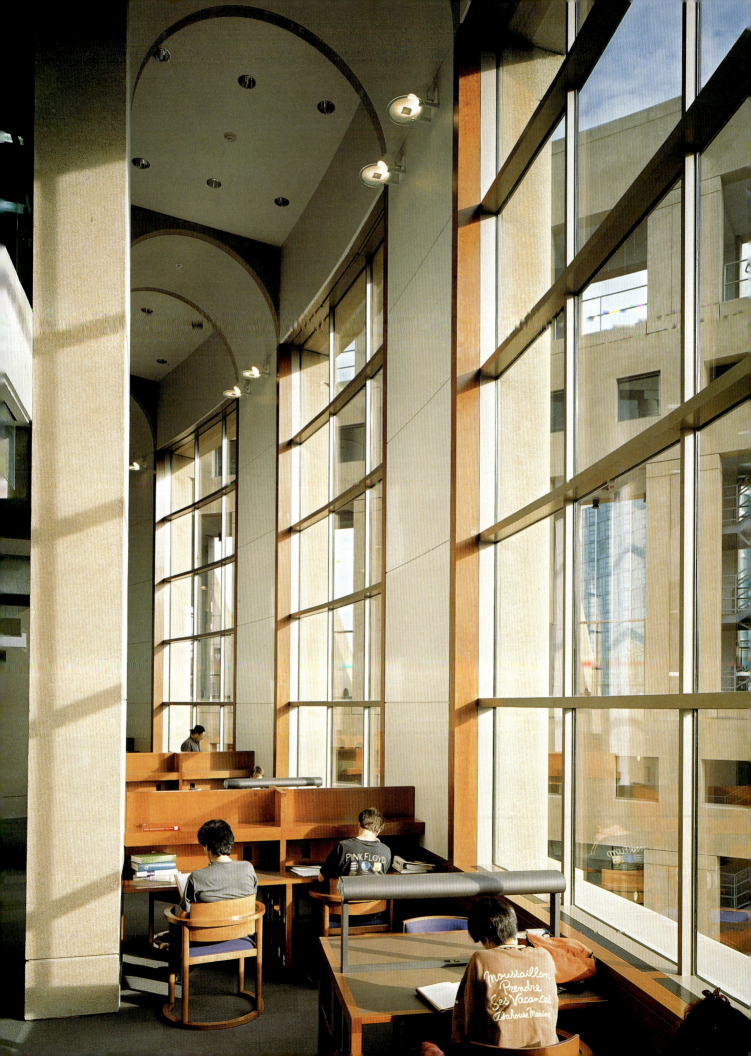

NOTES

Chapter One

1 Pat Ward Williams interviewed by Maurice Berger, "Speaking Out: Some Distance to Go," *Art in America*, September 1980, p. 83.

2 Quoted in *National Geographic Magazine*, May 1985, p. 557.

3 Written in 1918 and quoted by Eleanor S. Greenhill, *Dictionary of Art*, Laurel/Dell, New York, 1974, p. 283.

4 From Klee's Jena lecture, 1924, quoted in Will Grohmann, *Paul Klee*, Harry N. Abrams, New York, p. 367.

5 Quoted in S. Rodman, *Conversations with Artists*, first published by Devin-Adair, New York, 1957, reprinted by Capricorn Books, New York, 1961.

6 Interview with Lisa Bradley, March 1990.

7 Letters 596 and 381 excerpted from W. H. Auden, ed., *Van Gogh: A Self-Portrait*, New York Graphic Society, 1961. Letters 504 and 507 excerpted from Alfred H. Barr, Jr., ed., *Vincent van Gogh*, Museum of Modern Art, New York, 1935.

8 Quoted in Lucy R. Lippard, *Eva Hesse*, New York University Press, New York, 1976, pp. 24–25.

9 Georgia O'Keeffe, "Some Memories of Drawing," Atlantis Editions, New York, 1974. Quoted in *Georgia O'Keeffe*, Viking Press, New York, 1976, p. 1.

10 Quoted in Jack Coward and Juan Hamilton, *Georgia O'Keeffe: Art and Letters*, letters selected by Sarah Freenough, National Gallery of Art, Washington, D.C., 1987, pp. 202, 266, 242–43.

11 Quoted in Herbert Read, *A Concise History of Modern Sculpture*, Oxford University Press, New York, 1964, p. 14.

12 Conversation with Erik Satie, quoted in Carola Giedion-Weleker, *Brancusi*, Editions du Griffon, Neuchâtel, Switzerland, 1959, 31, p. 1.

13 Quoted by C. G. Guilbert, "Propos de Brancusi," *Prisme des Arts*, no. 12, 1957, p. 7, trans. by Mary Pat Fisher.

14 Felix Holtmann, quoted in "Canada Museum Imports Trouble," *Artworld*, June 1990, p. 208.

15 Shirley Thomson, quoted in April Lindren, "MP Questions Art Purchase," *Calgary Herald*, July 16, 1993, p. C4.

16 Brydon Smith, quoted in "National Gallery Buys Abstract Red-Stripe Painting for $1.8m," *Montreal Gazette*, March 8, 1990, p. F3.

17 *Miller vs. California*, US Supreme Court ruling 1973.

18 As quoted in Robin Cembalest, "The Obscenity Trial," *ARTnews*, December 1990, p. 138.

19 Ibid., p. 137.

20 Gaye, *Carteggio Inedito*, vol. ii, p. 500, as quoted in Anthony Blunt, *Artistic Theory in Italy 1450–1600*, The Clarendon Press, Oxford, 1940, p. 119.

21 Quoted in "Decadent, Un-German, Morally Offensive," *ARTnews*, May 1991, p. 123.

22 *Le Charivari* on Renoir's *Mother and Children*, 1874, now in the Frick Collection, New York. Quoted in *Portfolio Art*, New Annual #2, 1960.

23 *L'Art* on Cézanne's *The Suicide House*, 1873, now in the Louvre, Paris. Quoted in *Portfolio Art*, New Annual #2, 1960.

24 Quoted in Barbara MacAdam, "Anyone Who Doesn't Change his Mind Doesn't Have One," *ARTnews*, November 1993, p. 149.

25 Quoted in MacAdam, ibid., p. 145.

26 Daryl Chin, "Some Remarks on Racism in the American Arts," *M/E/A/N/I/N/G*, #3, May 1988, pp. 22, 25.

27 Interview with Joyce Scott, April 16, 1992.

28 "Vancouver Library Square Competition," *Canadian Architect*, July 1992, vol. 37, no. 7, p. 20.

Chapter Two

1 Holland Carter, *Art in America*, April 1989, p. 257.

2 Agnes Martin, in Joan Simon, "Perfection Is in the Mind: An Interview with Agnes Martin," *Art in America*, May 1996, p. 85.

3 Quoted in Jonathan Fineberg, "Theater of the Real: Thoughts on Christo," *Art in America*, December 1979, p. 96.

4 *Barbara Hepworth: A Pictorial Autobiography*, 1978 edition published by Moonraker Press, Bradford-on-Avon, Wiltshire, p. 27.

5 Henry Moore, "The Sculptor Speaks," article in *The Listener*, vol. XVIII, no. 449, August 18, 1937, pp. 338–40. Quoted in *Henry Moore on Sculpture*, ed. Philip James, Viking Press, New York, 1967, p. 62.

6 Henry Moore in H. Felix Man, *Eight European Artists*, Heinemann, London, 1954. Quoted in James, op. cit., p. 118.

7 Henry Moore in Donald Hall, "An Interview with Henry Moore," article in *Horizon, A Magazine of the Arts*, November 1960, vol. iii, no. 2, American Horizon, New York, 1960. Interview quoted without omissions in James, op. cit., p. 119.

8 Letters to Emile Bernard, Aix-en-Provence, July 25, 1904 and April 15, 1904, quoted in Robert Goldwater and Marco Treves, eds., *Artists on Art*, Pantheon Books, New York, third edition, 1958, pp. 364, 363.

9 Excerpted from Arshile Gorky, "Toward a Philosophy of Art," translated extracts from his letters in Armenian by Karlen Mooradian, reproduced in *Arshile Gorky: Drawings to Paintings*, Archer M. Huntington Art Gallery, The University of Texas at Austin, Austin, Texas, 1975, pp. 31–36.

10 Arshile Gorky (Vosdanik Adoian), interviewed by Malcolm Johnson, "Café Life in New York," *New York Sun*, August 22, 1941, as quoted in *Arshile Gorky: Drawings to Paintings*, The University of Texas at Austin, Austin, Texas, p. 67.

11 Helen Frankenthaler, as interviewed by Emile de Antonio, in *Painters Painting: The New York Art Scene 1940–70*, 1972, 116 minute video, Montauk, New York: Mystic Fire Video.

12 Al Held, personal communication, September 28, 1989.

13 Quoted in Barbara Rose, *Claes Oldenburg*, The Museum of Modern Art/New York Graphic Society, New York, 1970.

14 Personal communication, February 2, 1987.

15 Mark Rothko, quoted in Bonnie Clearwater, "How Rothko Looked at Rothko," *Art News*, November 1985, p.102.

16 Wassily Kandinsky, *Concerning the Spiritual in Art*, trans. M. T. H. Sadler, Dover Publications edition, New York, 1977, p. 25.

17 Quoted in Isamu Noguchi, *The Isamu Noguchi Garden Museum*, Harry N. Abrams, New York, 1987, p. 98.

18 Quoted in Robert Goldwater and Marco Treves, eds., op. cit., pp. 409–10.

19 Simon Calver, Managing Director of Pepsi UK, quoted in Roger Cowe and Edward Pilkington, "Purple Prose in Cola War," *The Guardian*, April 3, 1996, p. 2.

20 Johann Wolfgang von Goethe, *Theory of Colors*, trans. Charles Lock Eastlake, The MIT Press, Cambridge, Mass., 1970, p. 317.

21 Josel Albers, *Search Versus Re-Search*, Trinity College Press, Hartford, Connecticut, 1969, p. 17.

22 Josef Albers, *Interaction of Color*, revised edition, Yale University Press, New Haven, Connecticut and London, 1975, pp. 1, 3, 5, 12, 34, 41, 42.

23 Quoted in Paul Gsell, *Art by Auguste Rodin*, trans. by Romilly Fedden, Small, Maynard and Company, Boston, 1912, pp. 66–78.

24 Umberto Boccioni, Carlo Carrà, Luigi Russolo, Giacomo Balla, Gino Severini, "Futurist Painting: Technical Manifesto 1910," in Umbro Apollonio, ed., *The Documents of 20th Century Art: Futurist Manifestos*, Viking Press, New York, 1973 (English language translation copyright 1973 by Thames and Hudson Ltd., London), pp. 27–28.

25 Jackson Pollock, "Unframed Space," *New Yorker*, August 5, 1950, p. 16.

Chapter Three

1 Quoted in John Dornberg, "One Way to Create Fine Art is to Take the Greatest Risks," *Smithsonian*, April 1985, p. 118.

2 Emily Carr, quoted by Christopher Varley in *Emily Carr: Oil on Paper Sketches*, Edmonton, Alberta, Edmonton Art Gallery, 1979.

3 Quoted in "The Courage to Desecrate Emptiness," *ARTnews*, March 1986, p. 108.

4 Quoted in Wassily Kandinsky, *Concerning the Spiritual in Art*, trans. M. T. H. Sadler, Dover Publications, New York, 1977 (from *The Art of Spiritual Harmony*, Constable and Company Ltd., London, 1914).

5 Moshe Safdie, quoted in *Moshe Safdie Monograph*, "Moshe Safdie in Conversation with Wendy Kohn," November 1996.

6 Quoted in Frank Lloyd Wright, *An Organic Architecture: The Architecture of Democracy*, Lund Humphries, London, 1939, and in Edgar Kaufmann, Jr., ed., *An American Architecture*, Horizon Press, New York, 1955, as quoted in *Frank Lloyd Wright: In the Realm of Ideas*, ed. Bruce Brooks Pfeiffer and Gerald Norland, Southern Illinois University Press, Carbondale, Illinois, 1988, pp. 32, 43.

Chapter Four

1 Personal communication, October 1986.

Chapter Five

1 Quoted in Martin Kemp and Margaret Walker, eds., *Leonardo on Painting*, Yale University Press, New Haven and London, 1989, pp. 15, 97, 98, 162.

2 Diego Rivera, in Juan O'Gorman, *Diego Rivera: Fifty Years of His Work*, "Report on a Dissertation by Diego Rivera Concerning the Techniques of Encaustic and Fresco Painting," Department of Plastic Arts, National Institute of Fine Arts, Mexico City, undated, p. 269.

3 Pinin Brambilla Barcilon, quoted in Ken Shulman, "Like Seeing Leonardo for the First Time," *ARTnews*, November 1991, p. 53.

4 Pierre Rosenberg, quoted in Ginger Danto, "What Becomes a Legend Most," *ARTnews*, Summer 1989, p. 153.

5 James Beck with Michael Daly, *Art Restoration: The Culture, the Business, and the Scandal*, W. W. Norton and Company, New York, 1996, p. 194.

6 Helen Frankenthaler, as quoted by Barbara Rose, *Frankenthaler*, Harry N. Abrams, New York, 1970, p. 85.

7 Robert Rauschenberg, as interviewed by Emile de Antonio, in *Painters Painting: The New York Art Scene 1940–70*, 1972, Montauk, New York: Mystic Fire Video.

Chapter Six

1 Fritz Eichenberg, "Eulogy to the Woodblock," in *The Wood and the Graver: The Work of Fritz Eichenberg*, Clarkson N. Potter, Inc., New York, 1945, p. 178.

2 Stephen Alcorn, from his introduction to *Lincoln: In His Own Words*, ed. by Milton Meltzer, illustrated by Stephen Alcorn, Harcourt, Brace and Company, New York, 1993.

3 Personal communications, April 25, 1987, and June 20, 1996.

4 Frank Boyden, interviewed June 20, 1989.

5 Interview with Janet Cummings Good, January 1992.

Chapter Seven

1 Interview with Peter Good, November 1991.

2 Paul Rand, *Paul Rand: A Designer's Art*, Yale University Press, New Haven, Connecticut and London, 1985, pp. xiii, 7.

3 Quoted in Hermann Zapf, *Manuale Typographicum*, M.I.T. Press, Cambridge, Massachusetts and London, 1954 and 1970, p. 101.

4 William Morris, *The Ideal Book, Essays and Lectures on The Arts of the Book*, William S. Peterson, ed., University of California Press, Berkeley and Los Angeles, 1982, p. 73.

Chapter Eight

1 Quoted in Susan Weiley, "New Light on Color," *ARTnews*, October 1985, p. 88.

2 Excerpted from Nancy Newhall, ed., *The Daybooks of Edward Weston*, vol. 2, Horizon Press, New York, in collaboration with the George Eastman House, Rochester, 1966, pp. 13, 10, 18, 114, 206, 37.

3 Interview with Elizabeth Sunday, April 20, 1992.

4 William E. Parker, personal communication, April 7, 1992.

5 Susumu Endo, as quoted by Richard Thornton, "Space Transformations," *Print* magazine, January/February 1991, p. 91.

6 Stephen Dalton, *At the Water's Edge: The Secret Life of a Lake and Stream*, Century Hutchinson Ltd, London, 1989, p. 158.

7 David Hockney, quoted in David Sheff, "David Hockney: But is it art?", *Publish*, December 1991, p. 128.

8 Dean Devlin, quoted in Tim Prokop, "Fireworks," *Cinefex*, no. 87, September 1996, p. 60.

9 Bill Viola, in Edward Gomez, "Bill Viola," *Art and Antiques*, November 1995, p. 112.

Chapter Nine

1 Melvin L. Prueitt, Los Alamos National Laboratory, "Scientific Applications of Computer Graphics," *The Visual Computer*, 1986, vol. 2, p. 189.

2 Charles Csuri, quoted in Paul Trachtman, "Charles Csuri is an 'Old Master' in a New Medium," *Smithsonian*, pp. 57–58.

3 John Andrew Berton, Jr., "Film Theory for the Digital World: Connecting the Masters to the New Digital Cinema," *Journal of the International Society for the Arts, Sciences, and Technology*, Leonardo Supplemental Siggraph Issue 1990, pp. 6, 9.

Chapter Ten

1 Michelangelo Buonarroti, *Rime*, a cura di Enzo Noe Girardi Bari: Laterza, 1960, no. 151: 1–4, p. 82. As translated by Eugenio Garin in *The Complete Work of Michelangelo*, Reynal and Company/William Morrow and Company, New York, undated, p. 525.

2 Excerpted from *The Letters of Michelangelo*, trans. E. H. Ramsden, vol. 1, Stanford University Press, Stanford, California, 1963, pp. 108, 110, 112, 148.

3 Henry Moore, as quoted by Tom Hopkinson, "How a Sculptor Works," *Books and Art*, London, November 1957, reprinted in *Henry Moore on Sculpture*, Philip James, ed., Viking Press, New York, 1967, p. 123.

4 Donna Forma, personal communication, October 11, 1989.

5 Interview with Linda Howard, April 26, 1992.

6 Excerpted from Charles Hope, ed., and Alessandro Nova, *The Autobiography of Benvenuto Cellini*, from the translation by John Addington Symonds, St. Martin's Press, New York, pp. 179–181.

7 Quoted in "Stankiewicz, Richard (Peter)," *Current Biography Yearbook 1967*, The H. W. Wilson Company, New York, 1967, p. 398.

8 Judy Pfaff, quoted in "Sculptors' Interviews," *Art in America*, November 1985, p. 131.

9 Michael Heizer, as quoted by Bertram Gabriel, "Works of Earth," *Horizon*, January/February 1982, p. 48.

10 Robert Smithson, conversation with Dennis Wheeler, quoted in Eugenie Tsai, *Robert Smithson Unearthed*, Columbia University Press, New York, 1991, p. 105.

Chapter Eleven

1 Interview with Paula Winokur, April 21, 1992.

2 George Nakashima, essay in Derek Ostergard, *George Nakashima: Full Circle*, Weidenfeld and Nicolson, a Division of Wheatland Corporation, New York, 1989, pp. 104–5, 90–91, 109.

3 Maurice Marinot, as quoted in Robert A. Cohen, "Origins of the Studio Glass Movement," *Glass Studio*, no. 32, p. 37.

4 Susye Billy, as quoted by Ralph T. Coe, *Lost and Found Traditions*, University of Washington Press, Seattle, 1986, p. 232.

5 Norma Minkowitz, personal communication, October 23, 1989.

6 Sandra Sider, quoted in "New Works," *Fiberarts*, Summer 1991, p. 12.

Chapter Twelve

1 Eric Chan, quoted by Steven Holt in "The Art of Design," *ARTnews*, April 1990, p. 123.

2 Quoted in Jack Cocks, "The Man Who's Changing Clothes," *Time*, October 21, 1985, pp. 77–78.

Chapter Thirteen

1 Richard Swibold, personal communication, January 4, 1990.

2 Quoted in Edgar Kaufmann, ed., *Frank Lloyd Wright: An American Architecture*, Horizon Press, New York, 1955, p. 106.

3 Excerpted from Hassan Fathy, *Architecture for the Poor: An Experiment in Rural Egypt*, University of Chicago Press, Chicago and London, 1973, pp. 9–11.

4 Le Corbusier. Plans, 12 February 1932, p. 40, as quoted in William J. R. Curtis, *Modern Architecture Since 1900*, Prentice-Hall, Inc., Englewood Cliffs, New Jersey, 1987, p. 177.

5 Excerpted from R. Buckminster Fuller, "Conceptuality of Fundamental Structures," in Gyorgy Kepes, *Structure in Art and in Science*, George Braziller, New York, 1965, p. 68.

6 Quoted in Cathy Newman, "Pompidou Center, Rage of Paris," *National Geographic*, October 1980, p. 469.

7 William Rees-Mogg, quoted in Alan Riding, "London Museum Plan Sparks Uproar," New York Times Service in *International Herald Tribune*, July 4, 1996, pp. 1, 8.

8 Alvar Aalto, "The Humanizing of Architecture," *Technology Review*, 1940. As quoted on p. 78 of *Sketches, Alvar Aalto*, ed. by Goran Schildt, trans. Stuart Wrede, MIT Press, Cambridge, Massachusetts and London, 1985. Reprinted with permission from *Technology Review*, copyright 1940.

9 Alvar Aalto, "The Egg of the Fish and the Salmons," *Architectural Design*, vol. 49, no. 12, pp. 16–17. Originally published in *Alvo Aalto: An Architectural Monograph*. Reproduced here by permission of Academy Editions, London.

10 The Aga Khan, as quoted by David Holmstrom, "Architecture with a Human Touch," *The Christian Science Monitor*, January 5, 1990, p. 16.

Chapter Fourteen

1 Quoted in ed., Bruce Brooks Pfeiffer and Gerald Nordland, *Frank Lloyd Wright: In the Realm of Ideas*, Southern Illinois University Press, Carbondale and Edwardsville, 1988, p. 24.

2 Patricia Johanson, quoted in Robin Cembalest, "The Ecological Art Explosion," *ARTnews*, Summer 1991, p. 99.

3 Lawrence Halprin, *Cities*, Reinhold Publishing Corporation, New York, 1963, p. 9.

4 John Lyle, from "Can Floating Seeds Make Deep Forms?", *Landscape Journal*, vol. 10, no. 1, 1991, pp. 39–40.

5 Peter Schumann, Flyer from Bread and Puppet Theater, Glover, Vermont.

6 Elka Schumann, personal communication, October 25, 1989.

Chapter Fifteen

1 From the *Commentaries* of Lorenzo Ghiberti, quoted in Robert Goldwater and Marco Treves, eds., *Artists on Art*, Pantheon Books, New York, third edition, 1958, pp. 28–30.

2 Johann Joachim Winckelmann, *Thoughts on the Imitation of Greek Works of Art*, Dresden, 1755, English translation 1765, quoted in Hugh Honour and John Fleming, *The Visual Arts: A History*, Prentice-Hall, Inc., Englewood Cliffs, New Jersey, second edition, 1986, p. 496.

3 "Open Letter to a Group of Prospective Students," Paris, 1861, quoted in Goldwater and Treves, eds., op. cit., p. 296.

4 Conversation with Ambroise Vollard, quoted in Goldwater and Treves, op. cit., p. 322.

5 Quoted in Robert Goldwater, *Paul Gauguin*, Abrams, New York, undated, p. 13.

6 Ibid.

7 Ibid., p. 118.

8 Ibid., p. 114.

9 Excerpted from *Paul Gauguin's Intimate Journals*, trans. Van Wyck Brooks, Crown Publishers, New York, 1936, pp. 92–97.

10 Quoted in Faber Birren, *History of Color in Painting*, Reinhold Publishing, New York, 1965, p. 332.

11 "Reflections on Painting," Paris, 1917, quoted in Goldwater and Treves, op. cit., p. 422.

12 An interview with Pablo Picasso, quoted in Goldwater and Treves, op. cit., p. 417.

13 Umberto Boccioni, Carla Carrà, Luigi Russolo, Giacomo Balla, Gino Severini, "Manifesto of the Futurist Painters 1910," in Umbro Apollonio, ed., *The Documents of 20th Century Art: Futurist Manifestos*, op. cit., p. 26, trans. Robert Brain.

14 Anonymous article in *The Blind Man*, published in May 1917 by Marcel Duchamp, Beatrice Wood, and H. P. Roche, quoted in *Marcel Duchamp*, eds. Anne D'Harnoncourt and Kynaston McShine, The Museum of Modern Art, New York, and Philadelphia Museum of Art, 1973, p. 283.

15 Barnett Newman, as quoted in Thomas B. Hess, *Barnett Newman*, exhibition catalog, The Museum of Modern Art, New York, 1971, p. 38.

16 Personal communication, May 19, 1987.

17 Guillermo Gomez-Pena, as quoted by Margot Mifflin, "Performance Art—What is it and Where is it Going?", *ARTnews*, April 1992, p. 89.

18 Joseph Kosuth, quoted by Barbara A. MacAdam, "A Conceptualist's Self-Conceptions," *ARTnews*, December 1995, pp. 126–27.

19 Quoted in Judith Higgins, "In a Hot Country," *ARTnews*, Summer 1985, p. 65.

20 Quoted in Edward Lucie-Smith, "Craft Today: Historical Roots and Contemporary Perspectives," introductory essay for *American Craft Today: Poetry of the Physical*, American Craft Museum, New York, 1986, p. 37.

21 Romare Bearden, as quoted by John A. Williams, in M. Bunch Washington, *The Art of Romare Bearden: The Prevalence of Ritual*, Harry N. Abrams, New York, 1972, pp. 9, 11.

22 Deborah Muirhead, personal communication, March 1996.

23 Interview with Deborah Muirhead, April 9, 1992.

24 Bessie Harvey, in interview July 1988, Alcoa, Tennessee, in "Spirit in the Wood/Spirit in the Paint," curated by Sal Scalora, Artspace exhibit, New Haven, Connecticut, 1989.

25 Jean Dubuffet, quoted in Roger Cardinal, *Outsider Art*, Praeger, New York, 1972, p. 26.

26 Bessie Harvey, as interviewed by Eleanor E. Gaver, "Inside the Outsiders," *Art and Antiques*, Summer 1990, p. 85.

27 Jon Serl, as interviewed in Kristine McKenna, "Inside the Mind of an Artistic Outsider," *Los Angeles Times*, November 12, 1989, p. 86; Sullivan Gallery catalog for "The World of Jon Serl's Paintings," December 12, 1981–February 7, 1982; Dorrit Kirk Fitzgerald, "Four Viewpoints: Florence Arnold, Helen Lundberg, Jon Serl, and Beatrice Wood," Irvine Fine Arts Center.

28 Ryoei Saito, quoted in Charles Danziger, "Where the Buyers Are," *Art in America*, July 1990, p. 55.

29 Souren Melikian, "The Shrinking of the Impressionist Market," *International Herald Tribune*, December 2–3, 1995, p. 9.

30 Sandro Chia, quoted in "Making Art, Making Money," *Art in America*, July 1990, p. 138.

Chapter Sixteen

1 Quoted in Frank D. Russell, *Picasso's Guernica*, Allanheld and Schram, Montclair, New Jersey, 1980, p. 56.

2 From a letter written by Auguste Rodin to Marcel Adam, published in *Gil Blas*, July 7, 1904.

3 Auguste Rodin, *Art*, Small, Maynard and Company, Boston, 1912, pp. 181, 178, translated from the French of Paul Gsell by Mrs. Romilly Fedden.

4 Michelangelo Buonarroti, sonnet "On Beauty," quoted in Robert Goldwater and Marco Treves, eds., *Artists on Art*, op. cit., pp. 59–60.

5 Michelangelo Buonarroti, "Conversations with Vittoria Colonna as recorded by Francisco de Hollanda," quoted in *Artists on Art*, op. cit., pp. 68–69.

6 Cardinal José Castillo Lara, quoted by Philip Pullella, "Click, and thou shalt see angels on the Vatican's CD-ROM" (Reuter News Service), *Asian Age*, January 18, 1996, p. 1.

7 *Vancouver Province*, quoted in "A Public Affair," *The Canadian Architect*, July 1992, p. 20.

8 Moshe Safdie, quoted in "Moshe Safdie in Conversation with Wendy Kohn," *Moshe Safdie Monograph*, November 1996 (in press).

9 Moshe Safdie, "The Language and Medium of Architecture," lecture delivered at Harvard University Graduate School of Design, November 15, 1989, p. 9.

GLOSSARY/ PRONUNCIATION GUIDE

Most words are accompanied by a guide to pronunciation. Syllables are separated by a space and those that are stressed are underlined. Letters are pronounced in the usual manner for English unless they are clarified in the following list.

a	flat
aa	father
aw	saw
ay	pay
ai	there
ee	see
e	let
i	pity
ī	high
o	not
oo	food
oy	boy
ō	no
ow	now
yoo	you
u	but
er, ir, or, ur	fern, fir, for, fur
ă, ĕ, ĭ, ŏ, ŭ	about, roses, (to) suspect: (unaccented vowels represented by "shwa" in some phonetic alphabets)
ch	church
j	jet
kh	guttural aspiration (ch in Welsh and German)
ng	sing
sh	shine
wh	where
y	yes
zh	beige

A

Abstract   Referring to the essence rather than the surface of an object, often by stripping away all nonessential characteristics.

Abstract Expressionism   The post-World War II movement centered in New York in which paint was freely applied to a large canvas, expressing the energy and feelings of the artist *nonobjectively*, usually with no emphasized **focal point**.

Acoustics   The science of planning the properties of sound in architecture.

Acrylic (ă krĭl ik)   A water-based synthetic **medium** for painting, also called *acrylic emulsion*.

Action Painting   A style of painting, most notably practiced by Jackson Pollock, in which paint is dribbled and splashed onto the **support** with broad gestural movements.

Actual Texture   The true physical feeling of a form's surface.

Additive Color Mixing   The combination of **refracted** colors.

Additive Sculpture   That which is created by a process of building up or combining materials.

Adze   A woodcarving tool with both chiselling blade and axlike handle.

Aerial View   A downward perspective on an image.

Aesthetic   Pertaining to a sense of the beautiful.

Aesthetic Distance   The spatial relationship between the viewer and a work of art.

Aesthetics   Theories of what is beautiful.

Airbrush   A tool used for blowing a fine spray of paint onto a surface, to allow smooth graduations of **values** and **hues**.

Alla Prima (al a / pree ma)   See **direct painting**

Analogous Colors   Those lying near each other on the **color wheel**, combined in a color.

Anneal (ă neel)   To heat metal to make it more malleable, to counteract the hardening typical as metal is worked.

Antique Glass   Sheets of glass that have been handblown as a cylinder, cut, and heated to flatten it, often characterized by bubbles and warps.

Applied Arts   Disciplines in which functional objects are created.

Apse   In church architecture, the semicircular end of the building.

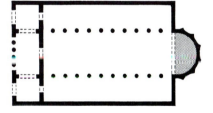

Aquatint   An **intaglio** printmaking technique, producing grainy tones rather than lines, that uses acid to penetrate areas of a metal plate that are covered by porous powdered resin.

Arch   A curving or pointed structural device supporting an opening, doorway, or bridge.

Archaic Period   In Greek arts, the 700 to 480 BC age during which interest in depicting the natural human body flourished.

Armature (aar mă ch ŭr)   An inner skeleton that supports a sculpture made of some malleable material.

Art Brut (aart / broot)   "Raw Art," Jean Dubuffet's term for **outsider art**.

Artisan   A person who is skilled at a certain **craft**.

A Secco   Referring to paint applied to the surface of a fresco after the plaster has dried, in contrast to **buon fresco**.

Assemblage (ă sem blij)   A combination of varying materials to create a three-dimensional work of art.

Asymmetrical Balance Distribution of dissimilar visual weights in such a way that those on either side seem to offset each other, also called *informal balance*, in contrast to **symmetrical** or **formal** balance.

Atmospheric Perspective   The illusion—and illusionary device—that forms seen at great distance are lower on **value** contrast and less sharply defined than objects close to the viewer.

Axis   An imaginary straight line passing centrally and/or longitudinally through a figure, form, or composition.

B

Balance   The distribution of apparent visual weights through a composition. See **asymmetrical balance**.

Balloon Frame Construction Framing for a building in which relatively small pieces of wood are nailed together rather than heavy timbers connected by joinery.

Baroque (bă rōk)   Seventeenth-century artistic styles in Europe, characterized by swirling composition,

sensuality, emotionality, and exuberant sculptural and architectural ornamentation.

Barrel Vault   A ceiling in the form of an unbroken tunnel.

Bas Relief (bas / ri leef)   See **Low Relief**.

Bearing Wall Construction A support system in which the weight of ceiling and roof is borne by the entirety of the walls.

Binder   The material used in paint and some drawing **media** to bind the particles of **pigment** together and enable them to stick to the **support**.

Bitmap   A matrix of pixels (dots in the computer's memory) of which an image may be composed in computer graphics.

Blind Embossing   Pressing an uninked, cut plate of metal against paper to create a sculptured, uninked image.

Bracelet Modeling   The use of oval lines disappearing over an edge to create the illusion of rounded form on a two-dimensional surface.

Buon Fresco (booawn / fres kō) "True fresco" in which paint is spread on wet plaster and becomes part of the wall surface itself as it dries.

Burin (byoor in)   A bevelled steel rod used for cutting lines in **line engravings** or **wood engravings**.

Burl   A woody circular knob on the trunk of certain trees, prized for its whorled lines in woodworking.

Burnish   Rub to a shiny finish.

Buttress   An external supporting structure built against a wall to counteract the thrust of an arch or vault. See **flying buttress**.

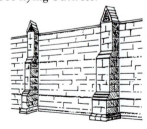

Byzantine   Referring to art of the Byzantine period in the eastern half of the Roman Empire, from AD 330 to the mid-fifteenth century. This art was primarily religious and characterized by **stylized** elongated human forms and rich ornamentation.

C

Calligraphy (kă li grā fee)   The art of fine writing.

Camera Obscura (kam er ă / ŏb skyoor ă)   A dark chamber in which the image of an object enters through a lens or small opening and is focused on a facing wall.

Cantilever (kant ĭ leev ĕr)   A projection from a building or sculpture which is supported, anchored, or balanced at only one end.

Capital   The head of a column which bears the weight of the structure above.

Cartoon   A full-sized drawing for a two-dimensional work, such as a **fresco**, which is transferred to the **support** at the preparatory stage.

Casting   The creation of a three-dimensional form by pouring into prepared molds a molten or liquid material that will later harden.

Ceramics   The art of making objects of clay and **firing** them in a **kiln**.

Chalk   Naturally deposited calcium carbonate, ground to a powder and reconstituted with a **binder** for use as a drawing **medium**.

Charcoal   Charred vine or wood used in sticks as a soft drawing **medium**.

Chiaroscuro (kee aar ă skoor ō)   The depiction in two-dimensional art of the effects of light and shadow, highly developed in **renaissance** paintings as a means of rendering the solidity of bodies.

Chroma (krō mă)   See **saturation**.

Cinematography   The artistic and technical skills involved in creating motion pictures.

Cire Perdue (<u>seer</u> / pair <u>doo</u>)   See **lost-wax**.

Classical   The art and culture of ancient Greece and Rome.

Classical Period   Greek art from c. 500 to 323 BC, characterized by serene balance, harmony, idealized beauty, and lack of extraneous detail.

Classicism   Movements, periods, and impulses in Western art that prized qualities of harmony and formal restraint and claimed direct inspiration from **Classical** models. Traditionally contrasted with **Romanticism**.

Closed Form   In sculpture, an unbroken volume with no projections or **voids**.

Coffer (<u>kaw</u> fer)   A recessed panel, often repeated as a pattern, in a ceiling or vault.

Coil Building   A method of building a form of clay by rolling it into long ropes which are coiled in a spiraling pattern to raise the sides of the piece.

Cold Color   (or "cool color") A hue traditionally thought to suggest low temperature and peacefulness, chiefly blues and greens.

Collage (kŏ <u>laazh</u> or kō <u>laai</u>)   A two-dimensional technique in which materials are glued to a flat surface.

Color Wheel   Relationships among **hues** expressed in a circular two-dimensional model.

Complementary Hues   Colors lying opposite each other on a **color wheel**.

Compositional Line   A line that leads the eye through a work, unifying figures or parts of figures.

Compressive Strength   In architecture, the amount of downward pressure a structural material can withstand without breaking.

Computer Graphics   Various techniques of creating two-dimensional artworks by computer.

Conceptual Art   Art which deals with ideas and experience rather than permanent form.

Conté Crayon (kon <u>tay</u> / <u>kray</u> on)   A fine-textured non-greasy stick of powdered graphite and clay with red ocher, soot, or blackstone added for color, used as a drawing tool.

Content   The subject-matter of a work of art and the emotions, ideas, symbols, stories, or spiritual connotations it suggests. Traditionally contrasted with **form**.

Contour   The outer edge of a three-dimensional form or the two-dimensional representation of this edge.

Contrapposto (con tra <u>pōs</u> tō)   In figurative works, counterpoised **asymmetrical balance** between parts of the body, with most of the weight on one leg and an S-curve in the torso, first used by **classical** Greek sculptors.

Contrast   Abrupt change, as when opposites are juxtaposed.

Control   To determine how an area will be seen or experienced.

Cool Colors   Those from the blue and green side of the **color wheel** thought to convey a feeling of coldness.

Corinthian (kō <u>rin</u> thee ăn)   In **classical** Greek architecture, the lightest and most ornate order, with the appearance of outward-curling acanthus leaves on the capital.

Crafts   Disciplines in which functional objects are made by hand.

Crop   To delete unwanted peripheral parts of a design.

Cross-Hatching   Crossed parallel lines used to create the illusion of form on a two-dimensional surface, by suggesting shadows and rounding in space.

Cubism (<u>kyoob</u> iz ĭm)   An early twentieth-century art movement dominated by Picasso and Braque distinguished by its experiments with analyzing forms into planes seen from many sides at once and by liberation of art from representational depictions.

Cyberspace (<u>sī</u> ber spays)   The "world" of communication through international computer networks.

D

Dada (<u>daa</u> daa)   An anti-rational, anti-**aesthetic** art movement begun in 1916.

Daguerreotype (dă ger ō tīp)   An early photographic process invented by Louis Daguerre.

Deconstructionist   Referring to contemporary architecture which deliberately gives the impression of chaos and instability rather than order and stability.

Decorative Line   Line that embellishes a surface.

Defensive Grid   Our ability to screen out unnecessary stimuli.

Descriptive Line   Line that tells the physical nature of an object.

Digitize   In computer graphics, to convert an image into computer language so that it can be projected or manipulated by computer.

Diptych (<u>dip</u> tik)   A work consisting of two panels side by side, traditionally hinged to be opened and closed.

Directional   Telling the eye which way to look.

Direct Painting   Application of paint directly to a **support** without **underlayers**, in contrast with **indirect painting**. Also called **alla prima**.

Divisionism   See **Pointillism**.

Dome   A hemispherical vault over a room or building.

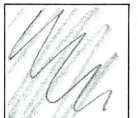

Graphite

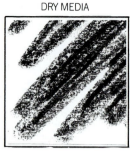

Conté

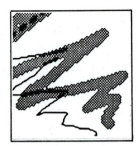

Computer printer

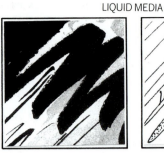

Brush and ink

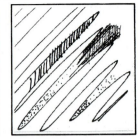

Pen and ink

Doric (<u>daw</u> rik)   In **classical** Greek architecture, the simplest order, with a heavy, fluted column, a dish-shaped capital, and no base.

Dry Media   A means of drawing such as graphite pencil, charcoal, pastel, conté crayon, or computer printer ribbon, in which the base that carries the **pigments** is not fluid. As shown in the drawing, each of these media creates a different line quality.

Drypoint   An **intaglio** printmaking technique, often used in combination with **etching**, in which lines are scratched directly into the metal plate with a sharp-pointed tool.

Ductility (duk <u>til</u> ĭ tee)   The capacity for being drawn out into wires or hammered into sheets, a varying property of metals. Gold and copper are noted for their especially high ductility.

Dynamic Form   A mass that appears to be in motion.

E

Earthenware   **Ceramics** made from porous, coarse-textured clays such as terracotta.

Earthwork   A large-scale sculpture in which the surface of the earth is the **medium**.

Economy   Use of as few means as possible to achieve a desired visual result.

Edge   A boundary where two areas treated differently meet.

Elements of Design   The basic components of the visual arts: line, shape or form, space, texture, lighting, color, and perhaps time.

Emphasis   Predominance of one area or element in a composition.

Enamel   A colored glassy coating heat-fused to metal.

Encaustic (en <u>kaws</u> tik)   A painting technique in which **pigment** is mixed with a **binder** of hot wax.

Engraving   An **intaglio** printmaking technique in which lines are cut on a metal or wood printing surface with a sharp tool.

Entablature   The horizontal member atop a column, supporting what lies above.

Entasis (<u>en</u> tă sis)   A slightly convex curve given to the shaft of a column to correct the illusion of concavity produced by a perfectly straight shaft.

Environmental Design   The art of manipulating outdoor areas for practical and aesthetic purposes, from landscaping to relationships among buildings in urban settings.

Ergonomics (ur gō <u>naam</u> iks)   The study of the mechanics and proportions of the human body, with the aim of designing products with which the body can interact efficiently and comfortably.

Etching   An **intaglio** printmaking technique in which lines are produced by scratching away a protective covering of wax on a copper plate, which is then bathed in acid that bites channels where the metal has been exposed.

Expressionism   An art movement particularly strong in Germany prior to World War I, in which the artist reports inner feelings rather than outer realities.

Expressive   Giving form to emotions.

Exterior Contour   The outside form of a three-dimensional piece.

Eye Level Line   In **linear perspective** drawings, the horizon line.

Eyeline   The implied line along which the eyes of a human figure in a work of art seem to be looking.

F

Façade (fă <u>saad</u>)   The front or principal elevation of a building.

Fantasy   Imagery existing only in the imagination.

Fat   Referring to a painting medium, such as oil, that can be piled up in thick gobs and that dries slowly.

Fauvism (<u>fō</u> viz ĭm)   An art movement of the first decade of the twentieth century, using color boldly to express the inner qualities rather than superficial appearance of things.

Fax Technology by which a facsimile of text or line art is transferred electronically from one location to another via telephone connections.

Figurative Referring to artworks based on images of identifiable objects.

Figure-Ground Relationship In two-dimensional art, seeing images as having been applied over a background.

Figure-Ground Reversal A two-dimensional work in which it is difficult to discern which is figure and which is ground, because they are visually interchangeable.

Fine Arts The nonfunctional art disciplines, such as painting and sculpture.

Fire To heat **ceramics** to make them durable.

Flying Buttress A **buttress** in the form of strut or segmented arch that transfers thrust to an outer support.

Focal Plane Shutter A common type of camera in which there is a double curtain of shutters close to the film; when a flash is used, the film must be exposed at a relatively slow speed because the double shutters take some time to open and close.

Focal Point The area of a composition to which the viewer's eye is most compellingly drawn.

Folk Art Works created by aesthetically untrained artists working somewhat within a community tradition.

Forced Perspective The exaggerated illusion of deep space, often employed in setmaking for theatrical performances.

Foreground In two-dimensional work, the area of a composition that appears closest to the viewer.

Foreshortening Contraction of the length and adjustment of the contours of a figure perpendicular to the viewer. This is done to counteract the perceptual distortion of proportions of objects receding from the viewer into the distance.

Forge To hammer heated metal over an anvil to shape it.

Form 1. The mass or volume of a three-dimensional work or the illusion of volume in a two-dimensional work. 2. The physical aspects of a work, as opposed to its emotional and intellectual **content**.

Formal balance See **symmetrical balance**.

Found Object An object that is presented as a work of art or a part of one, but which was not originally intended as art; also called *objet trouvé*.

Fractal Geometry Mathematical modeling of natural forms, often used in computer graphics.

Frame Construction Building systems in which spaced horizontal and vertical members are interlocked to form a solid skeleton to which an outer skin is added.

Fresco (fres kō) A wall painting technique in which **pigment** in a water base is applied directly to fresh, still-damp plaster, into which it is absorbed.

Frontal Referring to sculpture designed to be seen only from the front.

Full Round Referring to sculpture that exists in fully three-dimensional space, unattached to a backing.

Full Tonal Range A term used chiefly in black and white photography to signify representation of all values in a single picture, from black through mid-grays to white.

Futurism A movement initiated in Italy in 1909 to sweep aside all artistic conventions and capture the qualities of modern industrialized life.

G

Geodesic (jee ō des ik) **Dome** A structural framework of small interlocking polygons forming a **dome**.

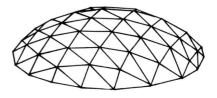

Geometric Having mathematically regular contours, such as a circle, square, or rectangle.

Geometric Period A stylistic phase of ancient Greek art between c. 800 and 700 BC characterized by abstraction of forms to geometric elements.

Gesso (jes ō) A fluid white coating of plaster, **chalk** and **size** used to prepare a painting surface so that it will accept paint readily and allow controlled brushstrokes.

Gestural A style of painting or drawing in which the artist's arm and hand movements are apparent in the finished piece.

Glaze 1. A thinned, transparent layer of oil paint. 2. A mineral solution, applied to a **ceramic** piece, that vitrifies to a glossy and water-resistant coating when **fired**.

Golden Rectangle A rectangle the lengths of whose sides correspond to **golden section** proportions. Much used as a compositional and format-establishing device in **Renaissance** painting.

Golden Section or **Mean** In ancient Greek **aesthetic** theory, an ideal proportional relationship between parts, whereby the smaller is to the greater as the greater is to the whole. This ratio cannot be worked out mathematically, but is approximately 5:8, or 1:1.618.

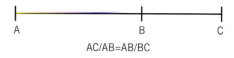

A   B   C

AC/AB=AB/BC

Gothic A style of European art from the mid-twelfth to mid-fifteenth centuries, especially noted for its soaring vertical cathedrals, three-dimensional sculptures, and the sense of depth and emotion in two-dimensional paintings.

Gouache (gwaash) An opaque water-soluble painting **medium** bound with gum arabic, the lighter tones being mixed with Chinese white watercolor.

Graphic Design The arts involved in creating two-dimensional images for commercial purposes. Graphic designers often work with type as well as illustrations; the printed surface may range from paper to fabrics.

Graphite A soft carbon used in drawing pencils.

Groin Vault In architecture, two intersecting, identical **barrel vaults**.

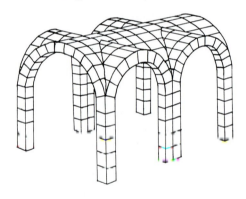

Ground 1. See **figure-ground relationship**. 2. The surface on which a two-dimensional work is developed.

H

Hard-Edged A term used chiefly in referring to twentieth-century paintings in which clean, sharp edges are formed where areas of different colors meet.

Hatching Fine, short parallel lines used in two-dimensional arts to create the effect of shadow on three-dimensional forms. See also **cross-hatching**.

Hellenistic Period Greek art from 323 to 100 BC or later, characterized by greater dynamism, emotional drama, and naturalism than that of the **Classical Period**.

High Contrast Polarization of the normal ranges of **values** towards the extremes of light and dark.

Highlight A spot of highest (lightest) **value** in a work—usually white.

High Relief Sculpture in which figures emerge three-dimensionally from a flat surface to half or more than half of their natural depth.

High Renaissance The years between roughly 1490 and 1520 in Italy, productive of some of the world's greatest art, informed by but not bound to **Classical** traditions.

High-Tech Revival A late twentieth-century return to machine-like architectural structures.

Hue The property of a color that enables us to locate its position in the **spectrum** or on the **color wheel** and thus label it as "red" or "blue," etc. This is determined by its wavelength.

I

Icon A two-dimensional depiction of a sacred figure or figures, thought to work miracles, particularly characteristic of **Byzantine** sacred art.

Iconography (ī kŏ naa grǎ fee) Visual conventions and symbols used to portray ideas in a work of art.

Idealized Referring to art in which **representational** images conform more closely to ideal **aesthetic** standards than to real life.

Impasto (im pas tō) Thickly applied paint—mainly oil or acrylic.

Implied A line, shape, or form that is suggested to the eye but not actually present.

Impressionism An art movement originating in late nineteenth-century France, in which the artist attempts to capture what the eye actually sees before the brain interprets the image. This may be a surface broken by fragmented lights or an ephemeral moment in time.

Indirect Painting Using a series of layers to produce a desired final effect, in contrast with **direct painting**.

Industrial Design The art of creating functional products that also have **aesthetic** appeal.

Installation Piece A three-dimensional designed environment set up (often temporarily) as a work of art.

Intaglio (in tal yō) A category of printmaking processes in which the desired image is cut into the surface of a plate, which is inked and then wiped, leaving ink only in the cut channels. Dampened paper is forced against the plate, picking up the ink.

Intensity See **saturation**.

Interior Contour The form of the inside of a three-dimensional piece.

Interior Design The art of decorating the insides of human environments.

International Style An architectural style, originating in Europe after World War I, characterized by rectangular forms, white walls, large windows, flat roofs, and the absence of ornament.

Interpretive Color Color chosen to represent an emotional atmosphere or idea rather than the visual reality of an object.

Interpretive Values Lights and darks used to convey an atmosphere or idea rather than a literal description of the actual **values** of a real scene.

Intonaco (in ton ă kō) In **fresco** technique, the final layer of plaster, to which paint is applied during the course of the day.

Investment   A heat-resistant outer mold packed around a **lost-wax casting**.

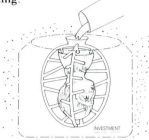

INVESTMENT

Ionic (ī aan ik)   In **classical** Greek architecture, an order characterized by fluted columns topped by scroll-like spirals.

K

Keystone   The central wedge-shaped piece of masonry in an arch, added last to lock the structure in place.

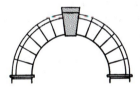

Kiln   A special oven or furnace for **firing ceramics**.

Kinetic (kin e tik) **Sculpture**   Three-dimensional work that moves.

L

Laminate (lam i nayt)   To unite flat layers of the same or different materials, such as bonded plates of wood, paper, or plastics.

Late Gothic   Work produced in Europe toward the end of the **gothic** period, characterized by increasing **naturalism** and expressiveness and by the fine details and luminosity of oil paintings.

Lead Crystal   High-quality, exceptionally clear and colorless glass in which a large percentage of the formula is lead oxide.

Lean   Referring to a **medium** that forms a uniform thin film, such as **tempera**, in contrast to a **fat** medium.

Light Well   A shaft that allows daylight to enter the interior of a building, or the optical illusion of a visual pool of light created by contrast with surrounding darker areas.

Limited Palette   Highly selective use of only a few colors.

Line Engraving   A **print** made by cutting lines into a plate of metal, forcing ink into them, and printing the cut lines.

Linear Perspective   The illusion of deep space in a two-dimensional work through convergence of lines perpendicular to the **picture plane**, toward a **vanishing point** in the distance.

Linocut (lī nō kut)   A **print** made by gouging away areas of a linoleum block that are not to be inked and printed.

Liquid Medium   A fluid base used to carry pigments for painting or drawing, such as ink, oil, or acrylic emulsion.

Lithography (li thaa grā tee)   A printmaking technique in which a flat stone or metal or plastic plate is drawn on with a greasy substance that retains ink when the wettened plate is inked for printing.

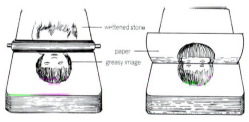

wettened stone
paper
greasy image

Local Color   The color usually associated with an object, as seen from nearby under normal daylight without shadows or reflections.

Local Value   The degree of light or darkness seen on an actual surface.

Logo   A graphic or typographic image that identifies a business or group.

Lost-Wax   A **casting** process in which wax is used to coat the insides of molds and then melted away when the molds are assembled, leaving an empty space into which molten metal is poured; also called **cire perdue**.

Low Relief   Sculpture in which figures exist on almost the same **plane** as the background.

M

Malleability (mal ee ă bil ĭ tee)   The capacity for being shaped by physical pressure, as in hand modeling or hammering.

Mannerism   An artistic style in Italy from approximately 1525 to 1600 in which artists developed a more subjective, emotional, theatrical approach than in the preceding **High Renaissance** period.

Maquette (ma ket)   A small model used for planning and guiding the creation of a sculpture.

Mass   The solid content of a three-dimensional form.

Medium   (plural *media*)   1. The material or means of expression with which the artist works. 2. The liquid solvent, such as water or linseed oil, in which **pigment** is suspended to make paint fluid and workable.

Mezzotint (mez ō tint)   An **intaglio** printmaking technique in which an overall burr is raised on the surface of the metal plate and then smoothed in places, creating various tones and textures.

Miniature   A work of art done on a much smaller scale than the object being represented.

Mixed Media   Combined use of several different techniques—such as drawing, painting, and printmaking—in a single work of art.

Mobile   See **kinetic art**.

Modeling   1. In two-dimensional art,

the depiction of three-dimensional form, usually through indications of light and shadow. 2. In sculpture, creating a form by manipulating a soft **medium**, such as clay.

Modular Construction   A building system developed from preconstructed and perhaps preassembled parts.

Monochromatric (maan ŏ krō ma tik) Having a color scheme based on **values** of a single **hue**, perhaps with accents of another color or neutral colors.

Monotype   A printmaking process in which an image is painted directly onto a sheet of metal or glass and then transferred onto paper. The process can be repeated with some repainting of the plate, but this is basically a means of creating relatively few prints of an image.

Montage (mŏn taazh) 1. A composite two-dimensional image produced by assembling and pasting down cut or torn sections of photographs or drawings. 2. In cinematography, the composition of a sequence of short shots of related meaning.

Mosaic (mō zay ik)   Two-dimensional art created by attaching small pieces (tesserae) of ceramic tile, glass, pebbles, marble, or wood to a surface.

Motif (mō teef)   A recurring pattern in a work of art.

Mural (myoor ăl)   A painting, usually large, done on a wall.

N

Naive Art   That which is created by artists with no formal training.

Narrative   Referring to art with a storytelling quality.

Naturalism   A style of art that seeks to represent accurately and faithfully the actual appearance of things.

Nave (nayv)   In church architecture, the central hall.

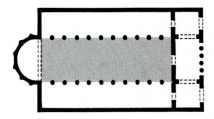

Negative Space   Unfilled areas in the design.

Neo-Classicism   The late eighteenth- and early nineteenth-century return to **Classical aesthetics** in Europe.

Neo-Expressionism   A contemporary art movement in which painting is used to express the artist's feelings, projected as distorted images from the exterior world.

Nonobjective   Referring to art that does not represent any known object.

Nonrepresentational   See nonobjective.

Northern Renaissance   Referring to German art from c. 1500, when the individualistic and rational aspects of the Italian **Renaissance** were adopted and adapted to Northern styles.

O

Offset Lithography   A commercial printmaking process in which the inking of illustrations and text is offset from the plate onto a rubber-covered cylinder that transfers them to paper so that the printed image reads the same way as the original, rather than being reversed.

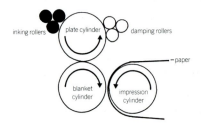

One-Point Perspective   In **linear perspective**, the representation of parallel lines converging to a single point on the horizon, to create the illusion of deep space.

Op Art   Paintings that produce visual phenomena in the perception of the viewer that do not actually exist on the canvas.

Opalescent (ō păl es ĕnt) **Glass** Opaque glass used for art objects, with color oxides swirled through it as it is poured in a molten state into sheets.

Open Form   In sculpture, a volume broken by projections and/or **voids**.

Open Palette   Use of an unlimited range of colors in juxtaposition.

Optical Color Mixtures   Those in which colors are mixed in the viewer's perception rather than in physically mixed **pigments**.

Outsider Art   Unique works created by untrained people who do not fit into any aesthetic tradition.

Overlapping   Hiding of part of one figure by another, a device used to suggest depth in space.

Overpainting   The final layers in an indirect painting, such as glazes or scumbling.

P

Pastel   A chalky stick of powdered **pigment**, calcium carbonate filler, and **binder**, used as a drawing **medium**.

Pattern   An all-over design created by repetition of figures.

Pediment   In **classical** architecture, the triangular area at the front of a building; also a similarly-shaped area used decoratively over a window, door, or **portico**.

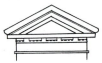

Performance Art Art in which the medium of expression is the artist's own body and its coverings.

Perspective See **aerial perspective**; **linear perspective**.

Photocopy A photographic reproduction of graphic material, in which a negative image is quickly taken and electronically transferred to paper as a positive.

Photogram One of the precursors of modern photography, an image made by laying objects on light-sensitive paper and exposing it to sunlight, leaving the masked areas white while the rest of the paper turns dark.

Photorealism Art that is as **representational** as a photograph, but created by other media; also called **super-realism**.

Picture Plane The flat surface of a two-dimensional work, often conceived as a transparent window into three-dimensional space. See **linear perspective**.

Pigment Powdered colored material used to give **hues** to paints and inks.

Pinching A simple means of using the hands to shape a ceramic vessel from a lump of clay.

Pixel (piks ĕl) In computer graphics, one of many tiny points on the computer screen determined by intersections of x and y axis.

Placement In two-dimensional art, the positioning of images on the **picture plane**, often used with reference to the illusion of three-dimensionality.

Plane A flat surface.

Planish To hammer metal smooth.

Planographic (play naa gra fik) Referring to a printmaking technique in which images are transferred from a flat surface, as in **lithography**.

Pointed Arch An arch formed by the intersection of two curves of greater radius than that of the opening; an innovation introduced in **Gothic** architecture.

Point of View The place from which a two-dimensional scene is reported.

Pointillism (pwan tĭ liz ĭm) A technique of painting using dots of **primary** and **secondary hues** in close juxtaposition to make them mix in the viewer's perception. Also called **divisionism**.

Pop Art A movement beginning in the mid-twentieth century that uses objects and images from the commercial culture.

Porcelain **Ceramics** made from the finest clays, which produce an extremely smooth, glossy surface when fired.

Portico (por ti kō) A covered colonnade at the end of a building in **classical** architecture.

Positive Space Filled areas in a design, or those intended to be seen as figures.

Post and Lintel An architectural construction system in which upright members support horizontal members, or lintels.

Post-Impressionism Transcendence of the perceived limitations of **Impressionism** by mid-nineteenth- and early twentieth-century artists such as Cézanne, Seurat, Gauguin, and van Gogh.

Post-Modernism An architectural movement of the 1970s and 80s, countering the glass boxes of the **International Style** with more historically eclectic forms.

Post-Painterly Abstraction Various mid-twentieth-century styles of creating **nonobjective** paintings that evoke certain responses in viewers, with the hand of the artist less obvious than in **Abstract Expressionism**.

Primary Colors The set of three basic **hues** from which all other hues can be mixed; in **refracted** colors, red, green, and blue; in **reflected** colors, red, yellow, and blue.

Primary Contours The outer edges of a **form**.

Principles of Design The organizing factors in the visual arts, including repetition, variety, **contrast**, **rhythm**, **balance**, compositional **unity**, **emphasis**, **economy**, **proportion**, and relationship to the environment.

Print An image made by transferring ink from a worked surface onto a surface, usually paper, and usually in multiples.

Proportion Size relationships of parts to each other and to the whole.

Proscenium (prō see nee ĭm) 1. The part of a stage for theatrical production that projects in front of the curtain. 2. In ancient Greek theater, the whole of the stage.

Proscenium Arch The arch that frames the stage, hiding its mechanics.

Putti (singular *putto*) (poot tee :poot tō) Chubby nude male babies often depicted in Italian art from the fifteenth century onward.

Q

Quilting Making blankets or other covers of two layers of fabric stitched together with padding in between, in which both the pieces of fabric and the pattern of stitching offer vehicles for aesthetic creativity.

R

Raise In metalworking, to hammer a flat sheet over a stake to bring up the sides of a vessel and work them inward.

Read To see and assign meaning to aspects of a design.

Realism The attempt in art to capture the appearance of life as it is, as opposed to **stylized** or **romanticized**

portrayals. In mid-nineteenth-century France, the artistic movement of this name concentrated on subjects from everyday, and often working-class, life.

Reduction Print   A color relief print in which portions of a single block are cut away in stages, with each stage overprinted in another color, rather than creating a series of registered blocks for the various colors.

Reflected Colors   **Hues** seen when light is reflected from a **pigmented** surface.

Refracted Colors   **Hues** seen in light.

Reinforced Concrete   Concrete into which metal mesh or rods have been embedded so that the two interact to strengthen the structure.

Reliefs   1. A sculptured work in which an image is developed outward or inward from a two-dimensional surface.   2. A printmaking category in which areas that are not to be inked are carved away, leaving the image raised on the block.

Renaissance (ren ĭ saans)   A movement beginning in fifteenth-century Italy to recapture the harmony, symmetry, and rationality of **Classical** works, with an elaboration of **linear perspective**.

Repoussé (rĕ poo say)   The working of a sheet of metal from the back to create designs in relief on the front.

Representational   Referring to artworks that aim to present likenesses of known objects.

Resist   The waxy, acid-resistant substance used to coat the metal plate used for **etching**, into which the lines of the image are drawn.

Rhythm   The visual equivalent of notes and pauses in music, created by repetition, variety, and spacing in a design.

Ribbed Vault   In architecture, a

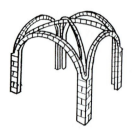

masonry ceiling in which arched diagonal ribs form a framework that is filled with lighter stone.

Rococo (rŏ kō kō)   The late **Baroque** period, particularly in France, southern Germany, and Austria, characterized by extremely ornate, curvilinear forms in architectural decoration and delicacy and looseness in painting.

Romanesque (rō mă nesk)   A style of European art from about the eleventh century to the beginning of the **Gothic** period, most notable for its architecture of rounded arches, thick walls and columns, and stone relief carvings.

Romanticism   The tendency to emphasize emotion and imagination rather than logic, occurring at many times in the history of Western art, including the first half of the nineteenth century. Traditionally contrasted with **Classicism**.

Round Arch   An arch formed by a semicircle; an innovation introduced by Roman architecture and much used in **Romanesque** architecture.

S

Sans Serif (sanz / ser if)   Referring to a **typeface** that has no fine lines finishing the major strokes.

Saturation   The relative brightness or dullness of a color, also called **chroma** or **intensity**.

Scale   Relative size.

Screen Print   See **silk screen**.

Scumbling   In oil painting, putting one layer of opaque paint on top of another in such a way that the

underlayers partially show through.

Secondary Colors   **Hues** produced by combining two **primary** hues.

Secondary Contours   Forms developed across the surface of a larger form.

Serif (ser if)   In **typography**, the fine lines used to finish the heavier main strokes of letters; also used of a **typeface** that has this feature

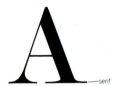

Serigraph (ser ĭ graf)   See **silk screen**

Sfumato (sfoo maa tō)   Softly graded tones in an oil painting, giving a hazy atmospheric effect, highly developed in the work of Leonardo da Vinci.

Shading   Darkening of an area in a two-dimensional work to suggest curving of a three-dimensional form away from a light source.

Shape   A flat, defined area.

Silk Screen   A printmaking process in which ink is pressed through a fine screen in areas that are not masked by a stencil or other material; also called **serigraph**.

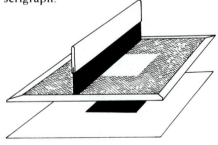

Silverpoint   A drawing **medium** in which a finely pointed rod of silver encased in a holder is used to make marks on a slightly abrasive surface; the minute deposit of metal darkens by oxidation.

Simulated Texture   The illusion that an image would feel a certain way if touched, in contrast to the reality of its actual texture.

Size or Sizing   A coating of glue or resin to make a surface such as canvas less porous so that paint will not sink into it.

Skene (skeen)   In early Greek theaters, the building at the back of the performance area from which actors entered and exited, also used as a changing room and as a backdrop for the action.

Slab Building   The process of building a form of clay by attaching flat shapes to each other.

Slip   A mixture of clay and water.

Soft-Edged   In two-dimensional work, blending of **hues** where they meet, so that no hard line forms a boundary between them.

Space   The area occupied, activated, or suggested by a work of art.

Spectrum   See **visible spectrum**.

Stained Glass   Art glass colored with chemical colorants heated in a kiln with the glass base.

State   One of the stages of an **etching**, if printed separately.

Static Form   A mass that appears inert.

Still-Life   A two-dimensional representation of a group of inanimate objects such as fruit, flowers, and vessels.

Stoneware   Ceramics made from clays that become very hard when **fired** at high temperatures.

Stylized   Referring to distortion of **representational** images in accordance with certain artistic conventions or to emphasize certain design qualities.

Stylobate (stī lŏ bayt)   In **classical** Greek architecture, the flat base on which a series of columns rests.

Subtractive Color Mixing   The combination of **reflected** colors.

Subtractive Sculpture   That which is created by the process of carving away material to reveal the desired **form**.

Super-realism   See **photorealism**.

Support   The solid material base on which a two-dimensional work of art is executed, such as canvas or panel in the case of a painting.

Surrealism   Art based on dreamlike images from the subconscious, appearing as a recognized movement beginning in the 1920s.

Symmetrical Balance   Distribution of equal forces around a central point or **axis**, also called **formal balance**.

Synergistic Color Mixing   A system of **optical color mixing** in which new **hues** are created in the spaces between colored figures.

Synthetic Media   Liquid media in which industrially-created chemicals, such as acrylic emulsion, are used to carry the pigments.

T

Tapestry   A heavy, handwoven textile with pictures woven into the surface of the fabric, usually used as a wall hanging.

Tempera   A painting **medium** in which **pigments** are mixed in water with a glutinous material such as egg yolk, usually yielding a fast-drying, matte finish that cannot be blended.

Tensile Strength   A measure of the ability of a material to be stretched without breaking.

Tertiary Color   **Hues** that are a mixture of a **primary** and a **secondary hue** lying next to each other on the **color wheel**.

Tesserae (singular *tessera*) (tes ĕr ee : tes ĕr ă)   The small cubes of colored glass, **ceramic**, or stone used in **mosaics**.

Texture   The surface quality of a form or the illusion that it would feel a certain way if touched.

Three-Dimensional   Having length, height, and width.

Throwing   See **wheel-throwing**.

Tokonoma (tō kŏ nō mă)   In a traditional Japanese home, an alcove devoted to contemplation of a single scroll painting, perhaps accompanied by a flower arrangement.

Tonal Range   The degree to which a work (particularly a photograph) approaches the full range of **values** from black through grays to white.

Transition   Abrupt or gradual change from one portion of a design to another.

Triad Color Scheme   The use of three **hues** lying at equal distances from each other on the **color wheel**.

Trompe L'ocil (tromp / lōyee)   Work that "deceives the eye" into believing it sees something other than the reality of a surface, such as architectural forms on what is actually a flat wall or ceiling.

Truss   In architecture, a framework of wood or metal beams, usually based on triangles, used to support a roof or bridge

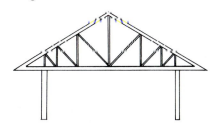

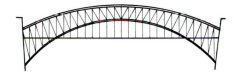

Two-Dimensional   Existing on a flat surface with only length and height but no depth in space

Two-Point Perspective   In linear perspective drawings, the representation of a three-dimensional form viewed from an angle, so that the lines formed by its horizontal edges will appear to diminish to two different **vanishing points** on the horizon.

Typeface   One of many styles of letter design, in which the entire alphabet is rendered with certain repeating characteristics.

Typography   The art of designing, sizing, and combining letterforms on a printed page.

U

Ukiyo-e (yoo kee yō ĕ)   Japanese representations of everyday life, usually **woodcut prints** but also paintings.

Underpainting   The initial layers of paint in **indirect painting**.

Unity   Visual coherence in a work of art; also used sometimes to refer to repetition of similar motifs in a design, in contrast to **variety**.

Unsized   Referring to canvas that has not been treated with a glaze or filler, leaving it porous to paint.

V

Value   Degree of dark or light.

Value Scale   A graded representation of differences in **value**.

Vanishing Point   The seen or implied spot in the distance where all lines perpendicular to the **picture plane** would appear to meet if extended. In real life, a vanishing point can only be seen where one can look across a great distance; in art, if lilies

appear to converge rapidly to a vanishing point there will be an impression of great depth.

Variety   Change rather than sameness in design elements.

Vellum (vel ŭm)   A fine parchment prepared from the skin of a calf, kid, or lamb.

Veneer (vĕ neer)   A thin surface layer, such as a fine wood placed over other woods.

Video   A process of creating moving pictures by laying down images and sound as tracks on magnetic tape.

Video Raster Graphics   Computer-generated and -manipulated **video** images.

Virtual Reality   Computer graphics in which the operator interacts with a scene as if existing within it.

Visible Spectrum   The color frequencies that humans can see; the distribution of colors produced when white light is dispersed, *e.g.* by a prism. There is a continuous change in wavelength from red, the longest wavelength, to violet, the shortest.

Visual Weight   The apparent heaviness of an area of design.

Void   In sculpture, a hole through a work.

Voussoirs (voo swaar)   The wedge-shaped stones in an arch.

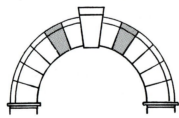

W

Walk-Through   Referring to large sculptures that the viewer can move through as well as around.

Warm Colors   Colors from the red and yellow side of the **color wheel**, associated with heat.

Watercolor   A transparent water-soluble painting **medium** consisting of **pigments** bound with gum.

Wheel-Throwing   A method of creating forms of clay by centering a mass of clay on a circular slab and then pulling the sides up from it with the hands as this wheel is turned.

Woodcut   A **print** made by carving away areas of a wood block and inking the remaining **relief** surfaces.

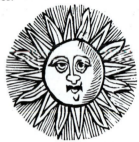

Wood Engraving   A **print** made by cutting the end-grain of a piece of wood, capable of rendering finer lines than the lengthwise grain used for **woodcuts**.

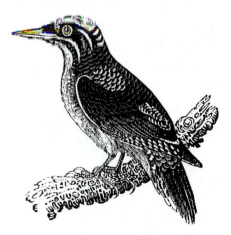

Wrought Iron   Iron that is shaped in a heated state with hand tools.

ARTISTS' PRONUNCIATION GUIDE

Aalto, Alvar   (aal tō)

Abakanowicz, Magdalena   (maag daa lay nǎ / aa baa kaa nō vich)

Albers, Josef   (yō sef / aal berz)

Anuszkiewicz, Richard   (aa nus ke vich)

Bernini, Gianlorenzo   (jaan lō ren zō / bair nee nee)

Boccioni, Umberto   (oom bair tō / bō kee ō nee)

Bonnard, Pierre   (peeair / bon aar)

Botticelli, Sandro   (san drō / bōt ee chel ee)

Bouguereau, William   (bu grō)

Brancusi, Constantin   (kaan stan teen / braan koo see)

Braque, Georges   (zhorzh / braak)

Bronzino, Agnolo   (ang nō lō / bron zee nō)

Brueghel, Pieter   (pee tair / broo gǐl)

Buonarroti, Michelangelo   (mee kěl an jě lō / booawn ǎ rōt ee)

Caravaggio, Michelangelo   (mee kěl an jě lō / kaa raa vaa geeō)

Cartier-Bresson, Henri   (an ree / kar teeay / bres on)

Cellini, Benvenuto   (ben ve noo tō / che lee nee)

Cézanne, Paul   (pōl / say zan)

Christo   (krees tō)

Cimabue   (chee mǎ hoo ny)

Claude Lorraine   (klōd / lor en)

Corot, Jean-Baptiste Camille   (zhaan / bap teest / ka mee / kō rō)

Correggio, Antonio   (an tō nee ō / kō re geeō)

Courbet, Gustave   (goos taav / koor bay)

Cranach, Lucas   (craw nok)

Csuri, Charles   (tshoo ree)

Daguerre, Louis Jacques Mande   (loo ee / zhaak / man day / daa gayr)

Dalí, Salvador   (sal vaa dōr / daa lee)

David, Jacques-Louis   (zhaak / loo ee / dǎ veed)

Degas, Edgar   (ed gaar / day gaa)

Derain, André   (aan dray / de ran)

Dubuffet, Jean   (zhaan / doo boo fay)

Duchamp, Marcel   (mar sel / doo shaan)

Dürer, Albrecht   (aal brekht / door ěr)

Escher, M. C.   (esh ěr)

Eyck, Jan van   (yaan / van / īk)

Fathy, Hassan   (has ǎn / fat hee)

Fortuny, Mario   (maar ee ō / for too nee)

Fragonard, Jean-Honoré   (zhaan / aw nō ray / fraw gō naar)

Frankenthaler, Helen   (fraank ěn taal ěr)

Gaudí, Antonio   (aan tō neeō / gow dee)

Gauguin, Paul   (pōl / gō gan)

Gentile da Fabriano   (gen tee lě / da / fab ree aan ō)

Géricault, Theodore   (tay ō dōr / je ree cō)

Ghiberti, Lorenzo   (lō ren zō / gee bair tee)

Giacometti, Alberto   (aal bair tō / jeeaa cō met ee)

Giotto   (jeeō tō)

Glaser, Milton   (mil ton / glay ser)

Gogh, Vincent van   (vin sent / van / gō)

Gorky, Arshile   (ar sheel / gōr kee)

Goya, Francisco   (fraan sis cō / goy aa)

Greco, El   (el / gre kō)

Grotell, Malja   (mǐ yǎ / gro tel)

Grünewald, Matthias   (maa tee ǎs / groon ě vaalt)

Heizer, Michael   (hītz ěr)

Hokusai   (hō kě sī)

Holbein, Hans   (haans / hōl bīn)

Ingres, Jean Auguste Dominique
        (zhaan / ō goost / dōm en eek / ǎn grě)

Isozaki, Arata   (i sō zǎ kee / ǎ rǎ tǎ)

Kahlo, Frieda   (free dǎ / kaa lō)

Kandinsky, Wassily   (vaa see lee / kan din skee)

Kiefer, Anselm   (an selm / keef ěr)

Klee, Paul   (klay)

Kollwitz, Käthe   (kay tě / kōl vits)

Kooning, Willem de   (wil ěm / d ě / koo ning)

Lachaise, Gaston   (gas ton / la shes)

Lalique, René   (re nay / la leek)

Le Corbusier   (lĕ / cōr boo zeeay)

Leonardo da Vinci   (lay ō naar dō / daa / vin chee)

LeWitt   (lĕ wit)

Lichtenstein, Roy   (likh ten shtīn)

Lin, Maya Ying   (mī yă / ying / lin)

Lorenzetti, Ambrogio   (am brō jeeō / lor en zet ee)

Lubalin, Herb   (loo ba lĭn)

Manet, Edouard   (ayd waar / ma nay)

Martinez, Maria   (ma ree ă / mar tee nez)

Masur   (ma zoor)

Mantegna, Andrea   (aan dray ă / maan tayn yaa)

Matisse, Henri   (aan ree / ma tees)

Mies van de Rohe, Ludwig   (loot tik / mees / van / dair / rō ĕ)

Miró, Joan   (hō awn / mee rō)

Miyake, Issey   (mee yă kay)

Modigliani, Amadeo   (a me dayō / mō dee glee an nee)

Mondrian, Piet   (peet / mōn dree aan)

Monet, Claude   (klōd / mon ay)

Mu-ch'i   (moo chee)

Munch, Edvard   (ed vart / moonkh)

Munsell, Albert   (al bert / mun sl)

Nakshima, George   (nă kă shee mä)

Nervi, Pier Luigi   (peeair / loo ee jee / nair vee)

Nevelson, Louise   (ne vĕl sn)

Newman, Barnett   (bar net / noo man)

Noguchi, Isamu   (i să moo / nō goo chee)

O'Keefe, Georgia   (jōr jeea / ō keef)

Oldenburg, Claes   (klaas / ōl den burg)

Orozco, José   (hō say / ōr ōs kō)

Otto, Frei   (frī / aa tō)

Palladio, Andrea   (an dray ă / pa la deeō)

Panini, Giovanni Paolo   (jeeō van ee / paō lō / pa nee nee)

Perugino (Pietro Vanucci)   (pay trō / va noo kee / pe roo jee nō)

Picasso, Pablo   (pab lō / pi ka sō)

Pollaiulo, Antonio del   (an tō neeō / pō la eeō lō)

Pollock, Jackson   (paal uk)

Raphael   (raf fī el)

Rauschenberg, Robert   (row shen bairg)

Redon, Odilon   (ō di lo / rĕ do)

Rembrandt, Van Rijn   (rem brant)

Renoir, Auguste   (ō goost / ren waar)

Rigaud, Hyacinthe   (ee aa sant / ree gō)

Rivera, Diego   (dee aa gō / ree ver ă)

Rodin, Auguste   (ō goost / rō dan)

Rosetti, Dante Gabriel
       (daan tay / gab ree el / rō se tee)

Rothko, Mark   (roth kō)

Rousseau, Henri   (aan ree / roo sō)

Rubens, Peter Paul   (roo benz)

Saarinen, Eero   (saa ree nen)

Safdie, Moshe   (saf dee)

Scamozzi, Vincenzo
       (vee chen sō / ska mō see)

Schwitters, Kurt   (schvit airs)

Seurat, Georges   (zhorzh / syoo raa)

Stankiewicz, Richard   (stan kee ay vich)

Steichen, Edward   (shtī khĕn)

Stieglitz, Alfred   (shteeg litz)

Thonet, Gebrüder   (ton et)

Tiffany, Louis Comfort   (ti fă nee)

Tinguely, Jean   (zhaan / ta glee)

Tintoretto, Jacopo   (ja kō pō / tin tō re tō)

Tomazewski, Henryk   (tō ma shev skee)

Toulouse-Lautrec, Henri   (an ree / too looz / lō trek)

Ugolino di Nerio   (oo gō lee nō / dee / ner ō)

Varo, Remedios   (re me dee ōs / vaa rō)

Vasarely, Victor   (vaa saa ray lee)

Velázquez, Diego   (deeay gō / vay las kes)

Vermeer, Jan   (yaan / vair meer)

Voisard   (vwaa zar)

Warhol, Andy   (an dee / wor haal)

Weyden, Roger van der   (way dĕ)

Wyeth, Andrew   (wayth)

Zapf, Hermann   (her maan / zapf)

Zelanski, Paul   (ze lan skee)

CREDITS

1.1 Vatican Museums and Galleries, Vatican City, Italy/Bridgeman Art Library, London
1.2 Musées des Antiquités Nationales, St German-en-Laye
1.3 Andrew W. Mellon Collection, © 1998 Board of Trustees, National Gallery of Art, Washington, D.C.
1.4 Photo: Stephen White/Private Collection, London
1.5 Chris Mellor/Telegraph Color Library
1.6 ©1972 Aileen and W. Eugene Smith (Black Star/New York)
1.7 Collection of the artist
1.8 National Park Service, Washington, D.C.
1.9 Aerofilms Ltd., Borehamwood
1.10 Isamu Noguchi, New York
1.11 Arteaga Photos Ltd.
1.12 Library of Congress, Washington, D.C.
1.13 The Mansell Collection, London
1.14 Photograph: South Australia Museum
1.15, 1.16, 1.21 and Part Opener 1, 1.31 Photograph © 1998 The Museum of Modern Art, New York
1.17 Courtesy of the artist
1.18 © ARS, NY and DACS, London 1998
1.19 Courtesy of the artist
1.21 Dave Brinicombe/The Hutchison Picture Library, London
1.22 Photograph © 1998, The Art Institute of Chicago. All rights reserved/© The Estate of Eva Hesse
1.23 Anil S. Mobi/Images of India Picture Library/DPA
1.24 The Nelson-Atkins Museum of Art, Kansas City, Missouri/Photograph by E.G. Schempf
1.28 Alte Pinakothek, Munich
1.32 Pace Primitive Art, New York
1.33 © ARS, NY and DACS, London 1998
1.34 Photograph © 1998 The Museum of Modern Art, New York/© ADAGP, Paris and DACS, London 1998
1.38 Takeshi Nishikawa
1.39 Archivi Alinari
1.40 © ARS, NY and DACS, London 1998
1.41 Archivi Alinari/Art Resource, NY
1.42 Photograph © 1998 The Museum of Modern Art, New York/© ARS, NY and DACS, London 1998
1.44 Courtesy of the artist
1.46 Photo courtesy of Musée Rodin
1.47 Museo Nacional Centro de Arte Reina Sofia, Madrid/Giraudon/Bridgeman Art Library, London/© Succession Picasso/DACS 1998
1.48 © Timothy Hursley
2.1 Private Collection, London
2.2 Private Collection, photo courtesy Pace-Wildenstein
2.3 Exxon Corporation, for Public Broadcasting Great Performances
2.4 Riksantikvaren. Directorate for Cultural Heritage, Norway
2.5 © ARS, NY and DACS, London 1998
2.7 © ADAGP, Paris and DACS, London 1998
2.8 © Christo and Jeanne-Claude 1998
2.9, 2.73, 2.76 V&A Picture Library
2.11, 2.29 The Mansell Collection, London
2.12, 2.45, 2.78, 2.82 © British Museum, London

2.16, 2.46, 2.80, 2.91 Photograph © 1998 The Museum of Modern Art, New York
2.17 Courtesy of the artist
2.19 V&A Picture Library/© ADAGP, Paris and DACS, London 1998
2.27 © Timothy Hursley
2.28 Photo by Ricardo Barros, courtesy of Grounds for Sculpture
2.34, 2.79 Reproduced by permission of the Henry Moore Foundation
2.35 © Michael Heizer, courtesy Xavier Fourcade Inc., New York
2.41 © Succession H. Matisse/DACS 1998
2.43 (detail) Museo Nacional Centro de Arte Reina Sofia, Madrid/Giraudon/Bridgeman Art Library, London/© Succession Picasso/DACS 1998
2.44 © ADAGP, Paris and DACS, London 1998
2.49 Courtesy Macmillan-Bloedel Ltd., Vancouver
2.50, 2.86 Hirmer Fotoarchiv, Munich
2.51 William L. Macdonald, New York
2.52 © The Joseph and Robert Cornell Memorial Foundation
2.53 Oil and Steel Gallery, New York
2.54 Japan National Tourist Organisation, London
2.56 Courtesy of the artist
2.57 Daitokuji, Kyoto, Japan
2.58 The Estate of Romare Bearden/© VAGA, New York and DACS, London 1998
2.61 Photo © Thijs Quispel
2.65 © Al Held/DACS, London/VAGA, New York 1998
2.67 Courtesy of Nancy Hoffman Gallery, New York
2.68 Courtesy of the artist
2.72 Popperfoto, Northampton
2.74, 2.117 The Nelson-Atkins Museum of Art, Kansas City, Missouri (Purchase: Nelson Trust)
2.75 Archivi Alinari, Florence
2.77 M.C. Escher's "Relativity" © 1998 Cordon Art--Baarn--Holland. All rights reserved
2.81 Werner Forman Archive, London
2.84 Reprinted by kind permission of David R. Goding, Inc.
2.87 O.K. Harris Works of Art, New York
2.92 Courtesy of the artist
2.93 Reprinted with permission of Joanna T. Steichen
2.94, 2.132 Courtesy of Milton Glaser
2.99 Scala, Florence
2.100 Norman McGrath, New York
2.101 Photograph © 1998 The Museum of Modern Art, New York/© Richard Estes/DACS, London/VAGA, New York 1998
2.103 Sakamoto Photo Research Laboratory, New York
2.104, 2.107 Sonia Halliday
2.105 Jeff Myers, University of Iowa
2.106 A.F. Kersting, London
2.109 British Library, London
2.114 Photograph © 1998 The Museum of Modern Art, New York/© ARS, NY and DACS, London 1998
2.115 The Tintometer Ltd., Salisbury
2.116 Shigeo Anzai, courtesy of The Isamu Noguchi Foundation, Inc.
2.119 Photograph © 1998, The Art Institute of Chicago. All rights reserved
2.120 Photograph © 1998, The Art Institute of Chicago. All rights reserved/© Succession Picasso/DACS 1998
2.121 Photograph © 1998 The Museum of Modern Art, New York/© Succession H. Matisse/DACS 1998
2.122 Courtesy of the artist/photo by Eduardo Calderon
2.124 Photograph © 1998 The Museum of Modern

Art, New York/© DACS 1998
2.123 © The Guardian, photo by Garry Weaser
2.126 Courtesy of the artist
2.128 Photograph © 1998 The Museum of Modern Art, New York
2.130 © ECART, Paris
2.133 Fotografia cedida y autorizada por El Patrimonio Nacional
2.135 © Richard Anuszkiewicz/DACS, London/VAGA, New York 1998
2.137 © Larry Poons/DACS, London/VAGA, New York 1998
2.140 © 1962 Ives Sillman, New Haven, CT. Collection of Arthur Hoener/Photo Beverly Dickinson/© DACS 1998
2.142 Photograph © 1998 The Museum of Modern Art, New York/© ARS, NY and DACS, London 1998
2.143 © Succession Picasso/DACS 1998
2.144 Leonard von Matt, Buochs, Switzerland
2.145 Philip Johnson and John Burgee
2.146 Juda Rowan Gallery, London
2.148 Photograph © 1998 The Museum of Modern Art, New York/© ADAGP, Paris and DACS, London 1998
2.149 © ADAGP, Paris and DACS, London 1998
2.150 John Olbourne, Swanbourne, Western Australia
2.151 © ADAGP, Paris and DACS, London 1998
2.153 Photograph © 1998, The Art Institute of Chicago. All rights reserved
2.154 © Association de Amis de J.H. Lartigue, Paris
2.155 Courtesy of Nancy Hoffman Gallery, New York
2.156 Giraudon, Paris
2.158 Photograph John Bigelow Taylor, New York
2.159 Libby Jennings
3.1 Manufactured by Memphis/Tino Cosmo, Italy
3.2 © Magdalena Abakanowicz/DACS, London/VAGA, New York 1998
3.3, 3.44 Photograph ©1998 The Museum of Modern Art, New York
3.5 (detail) Museo Nacional Centro de Arte Reina Sofia, Madrid/Giraudon/Bridgeman Art Library, London/© Succession Picasso/DACS 1998
3.7 Zefa Picture Library, London
3.10 Winfrid Zakowski, Helsinki
3.11 Scala, Florence
3.15 Photograph courtesy of Christie's, New York
3.17 © British Museum, London
3.18 The National Trust, London
3.19 V&A Picture Library
3.22 © Estate of Nancy Graves/DACS, London/VAGA, New York 1998
3.24 Andrew W. Mellon Collection, © 1998 Board of Trustees, National Gallery of Art, Washington, D.C.
3.27 Palazzo Ducale, Urbino/Scala, Florence
3.29 Photo Vatican Museums
3.31 The Mansell Collection, London
3.38 Archivi Alinari, Florence
3.41 © ADAGP, Paris and DACS, London 1998
3.42 Japan National Tourist Organisation, London
3.43 © Timothy Hursley
4.5 Jerry Mathiason, Minneapolis
4.7 Rosenwald Collection, ©1998 Board of Trustees, National Gallery of Art, Washington, D.C.
4.8 Joseph Szaszfai
4.15 © Succession Picasso/DACS 1998
4.14, 4.16 © British Museum, London
5.1 Margaret Courtney-Clarke
5.7 Bob Shalkwijk/AMI
5.8, 5.11, 5.16, 5.30 Scala, Florence
5.10 Mexicolore, London
5.15 Photo: © Mauritshuis, The Hague, inv. no. 670

INDEX

A

Aalto, Alvar 392–393; Vuoksenniska Church **13.44**

Abakanowicz, Magdalena: *Backs* 171, 175, **3.2**

Abalone Shells (B. Martin) 237, 471, **5.24**

Aboriginal art 21, 23, 92, **1.14**, **2.55**

Abraham's Hospitality and the Sacrifice of Isaac (mosaic) 425, **15.13**

abstract art 464, 516; *see also* abstraction; nonobjective art

Abstract Expressionism 467–468, 477, 516

Abstract Imagists 468–469

abstraction 33, 38, 464

Abstraction Blue (O'Keeffe) 129, **2.114**

Abu Temple, Tell Asmar: statuettes 420, **15.4**

Accused/Blowtorch/Padlock (Williams) 16, **1.7**

Acoma ware 41, 84, **1.35**

acoustics 372, 516

Acropolis *see* Athens

acrylic paintings 238–239, 516, **1.14**, **1.22**, **1.40**, **2.2**, **2.65**, **2.67**, **2.136**, **2.137**, **2.139**, **5.4**, **5.25**, **5.26**

Action Painting (drip painting) 48, 167, 173, 167–468, 516, **1.42**, **15.51**

Adam and Eve (Rodin) 498, **1.46**, **16.13**

Adams, Ansel 282, 284, 467; *Clearing Winter Storm, Yosemite National Park* 282, **8.12**

Adams, Eddie: *Execution of a Vietcong officer* 298, **8.29**

Adobe Magazine: Reader service card **9.1**

Adoration of the Magi, The (Gentile da Fabriano) 167, **2.157**

Adoration of the Magi, The (Leonardo) 229, **5.17**

advertisements 20, 272; *see* graphic design(ers); poster art

Aegean civilizations 419

aerial perspective *see* perspective

aerial views 100, 516

African art 69, 216, 325, 456, 461; masks 108, 177, **2.78**, **3.9**

After the Bath (Degas) 211–212, **4.10**

Aga Khan Award for Architecture 394, **13.24**, **13.25**, **13.45**

airbrushing 238, 516

Airport (film) 296

Akan people: Akua'ba wood figure 69, **2.23–2.25**

Akhenaton 421

Akua'ba wood figure, Ghana 69, **2.23–2.25**

Albers, Josef 150–151; *Homage to the Square* series 138, 150, 469, **2.124**, **2.140**

Alberts, Ton: bank complex, Amsterdam 369, 371, **13.8**

Alcalacanales: La Corrida de Cannes 292, **8.20**

Alcorn, John 251; *The Scarlet Letter* 56–57, 61, **2.3**

Alcorn, Stephen 251; *Don Juan* 252, **6.11**

Alice's Adventures in Wonderland (Moser engravings) 275, **7.13**

Allegory of Peace (Lorenzetti) 224–225, **5.8**, **5.9**

Alling, Katherine: *Feathers #22* 116, **2.92**

Alphabet no. 101 (Schulte) 64–65, **2.17**

alphabet sampler (Zapf) 271, **7.9**

Altar of the Hand (Benin bronze) 325, **10.16**

Altar for Peace (Nakashima) 342, **11.14**

altars/altarpieces 190–191; Isenheim (Grünewald) 442, **15.27**

Americans, Native 135, 480; baskets 349, **11.21**; ceramics 41, 84, 334; Kotlean robe 362–363, **12.12**; Tlingit Moon House post 67, **2.20**

amphora (attrib. Euphiletos painter) 335, **11.4**

Amsterdam, Netherlands: bank complex (Alberts) 369, 371, **13.8**

And There Is No Remedy (Goya) 266, **6.32**

Anderson, Charles Spencer: packaging 267, **7.2**

Angelico, Fra: *Annunciation* 433–434, **15.19**

annealing 338, 516

Annunciation (Angelico) 433–434, **15.19**

Anteor (Brooks) 219, **5.4**

Antonakos, Stephen: *Green Neon from Wall to Floor* 125, 475, **2.104**

Anuszkiewicz, Richard: *Splendor of Red* 146, **2.135**

Apollonius: *Seated Boxer* 325, 423, **10.17**

applied arts 40–42, 516

apse 516

aquatints 259–260, 266, 516, **6.27**, **6.32**; sugar 260

aqueducts, Roman 376, **13.19**

arch construction 376–377, 429, 516, **13.18**; ceramic (Zimmerman) 322, **10.12**

Archaic period (Greek art) 422, 517

architecture 18, 20, 44, 90, 364, 366, 394; Baroque 448; Byzantine 88, 376, 425; deconstructionist 391; and environment and function 199–200, 367, 369, 371, 380–381; Gothic 125, 372, 376, 377, 429–430; Greek 194–195, 375–376, 422; high tech revival 390–391; humanizing 392–393; International Style 384–385; and light 121, 123, 125; post-modern 389; Rococo 448, 450; Roman 376, 425, *see also* Rome; Romanesque 376, 429; sacred 190–191, 373, *see also* Gothic; Shaker 364; structural materials and techniques 374–377, 379, 380–381, 383–385, 387, 389; and variety 175; *see also* interior design; Safdie, Moshe

Ardèche Valley, France: cave paintings 418–419

Arena Chapel, Padua: *The Lamentation* (Giotto) 430–431, **15.17**

Aristide Bruant dans son cabaret (Toulouse-Lautrec) 269, **7.5**

armatures 320, 517

"art brut" 484, 517

Art Nouveau 76

Art of Painting, The (Vermeer) 77, **2.37**

Artichoke Halved (Weston) 288, **8.15**

Artist's Garden at St. Clair, The (Cross) 114, 115, **2.89**

Asaf Khan: Nishat Bagh 401, **14.6**

assemblages 90, 108, 110, 328–329, 517, **2.52**, **2.80**, **2.83**

Assumption of the Virgin, The (Rubens) 448, **15.30**

AT&T Building, New York (Johnson and Burgee) 389–390, **13.41**

At the Circus Fernando (Toulouse-Lautrec) 163, **2.153**

Athanor (Kiefer) 95–96, 477, **2.61**

Athenodorus *see* Hagesandrus

Athens, Greece 422; Acropolis 422, **15.9**; Erechtheum 375, **13.16**; Parthenon 194–195, 422, 438, **3.38**, **15.9**

"*Atlas*" *Slave* (Michelangelo) 312, **10.1**

atmospheric perspective 98–99, 517

Audi advertisement 272, 275, **7.11**

Augustus of Primaporta (marble) 425, **15.11**
Australian Aborigines *see* Aboriginal art
axis 517
Azarian, Mary: *T Is for Toad* 111, **2.84**

B

Backs (Abakanowicz) 171, 175, **3.2**
Baier, Fred, and Rose, Chris: refectory table 341, **11.12**
Bailey, William 471; *Monte Migiana Still-Life* 471, **15.55**
Bakst, Marni: stained-glass doors 139, **2.127**
balance (of design elements) 30, 170, 517; asymmetrical (informal) 184–185, 517, **3.20**; radial 183–184; symmetrical (formal) 182–183, 526, **3.16**
Balega mask 177, **3.9**
ballet 410
balloon-frame construction 383, 517, **13.29**
Balzac, Honoré de: Rodin's monument to 157, **2.147**
Bangladesh Housing Programme, Bangladesh 384, **13.45**
banner of Las Navas de Tolosa 145, **2.133**
Barcelona, Spain: Palau de la Música Catalana (Domènech i Montaner) 243, **5.32**; Sagrada Familia church (Gaudí) 175, **3.7**
bark paintings, Aboriginal 92, **2.55**
Barnes, Dorothy Gill: North Beach Rocks 352, **11.23**
Baroque style 49, 209, 444, 448, 517; *see also* Bernini, Gianlorenzo
bas relief (low relief) 67, 522
Baskerville typeface 270–271, **7.7**
basketry 41, 349, 352, **11.21**
BAT ("*bon à tirer*") 262
Batetela mask 108, **2.78**
Battle of Issus, The (mosaic) 242, 423, **5.30**, **5.31**
Battle of the Ten Nude Men (Pollaiuolo) 245–246, **6.1**, **6.2**
Bayadère, La (Royal Ballet Company, London) 401, **14.18**
bead sculptures 50, **1.44**
Bear Run, Pennsylvania: Kaufmann House (Wright) 200, 387, **3.44**
Bearden, Romare 481; *Family Dinner* 481, **15.63**; *She-Ba* 83, **2.58**
Beardsley, Aubrey: cover for *The Forty Thieves* 202, **4.1**
Beautiful Bird Revealing the Unknown to a Pair of Lovers, The (Miró) 237, **5.23**
beauty, ideals of 30
Beck, Professor James 233
Beckman, William: *Power Lines* 32, 471, **1.25**
Beggarstaff Brothers: poster 59, **2.9**
Benin bronzes 325, **10.16**
Bernini, Gianlorenzo: *The Ecstasy of St. Teresa* 21, 23, 49, 444, **1.13**; St. Peter's Piazza, Rome 402, **14.7**
Berton, John Andrew, Jr 309

Bierstadt, Albert: *The Rocky Mountains, Lander's Peak* 98, **2.64**
Bikini (Thiebaud) 31, **1.24**
Billy, Susye: basket 349, **11.21**
binders 216, 517
Bird in Space (Brancusi) 40, 191, **1.34**
Birth of Venus, The (Botticelli) 434, **15.20**
bitmap scanning 303, 517, **9.4**
Bittleman, Arnold: *Martyred Flowers* 63, **2.14**
Black Wall (Nevelson) 328, **10.20**
Blake, William 451; *The Last Judgment* 183, **3.18**
Blaue Reiter, Der ("The Blue Rider") 458
Bloom, Hyman: *Fish Skeletons* 213, **4.13**
"Blue Rider, The" (group) 458
Boating Party, The (Renoir) 189, **3.28**
Boccioni, Umberto: *Unique Forms of Continuity in Space* 463, **15.45**
Body Sculpture in Rattan (Miyake) 361, **12.10**
Bonnard, Pierre: *Nude in a Bathtub* 218–219, **5.3**
Book 4 (Samaras) 108, 328, **2.80**
Book of Kells 429, **15.14**
Books of Hours 164, 167, 245, **2.156**
Border Arts Workshop 475
Bosch, Hieronymus: *The Carrying of the Cross* 100, **2.69**
Botanical Specimens (Talbot) 276, **8.1**
Botticelli, Sandro: *The Birth of Venus* 434, **15.20**
Bouguereau, William 49; *Nymphs and Satyr* 60, **1.43**
Boyden, Frank: *Changes # IV* 260, **6.28**
Boyka Fable (Sobol-Wejmen) 259, **6.27**
bracelet modeling 63, 79, 517
Bradley, Lisa 27; *The Moon Cannot Be Stolen* **1.19**
Brambilla Barcilon, Pinin 232
Brancusi, Constantin: *Bird in Space* 40, 191, **1.34**
Brandom, Joseph L.: utensils and rack 338, **11.7**
Braque, Georges: *The Portuguese* 461, **15.44**
Brassempouy, France: ivory bust 12, **1.2**
Bread and Puppet Theater: *Passion Play for a Young Tree* 412, **14.21**
"Bridge, The" (group) 458
Brigden, Timothy: pewter chalice 195, **3.39**
British Columbia Landscape (Carr) 181, **3.14**
British Library Reading Room, London 397, **14.1**
Broken Column, The (Kahlo) 479, **15.61**
Broken Obelisk (Newman) 57, **2.5**, **2.6**
bronze, casting 73, 323, **10.14**, **10.15**
bronze sculptures 323, 325; Benin 325, **10.16**; Boccioni 463, **15.45**; Brancusi 40, 191, **1.34**; Cellini 326–7, **10.18**; Danish 73, **2.32**; Degas 322, **10.13**; Giacometti 57, **2.7**; Greco-Roman 60–61, 325, **2.11**, **10.17**; Lachaise 116, **2.91**; Moore 74, **2.34**; Rodin 157, **2.147**, *see also* Gates of Hell
Bronzino, Angelo: *Portrait of a Young Man* 218, 442, **5.2**
Brooks, James 468; *Anteor* 219, **5.4**

Brücke, Die ("The Bridge") 458
Bruegel, Pieter, the Elder: *Hunters in the Snow* 95, **2.59**
brush and ink drawings 215, **4.16**
Buddha, Polonnaruwa, Sri Lanka 103, **2.72**
Buddhist Temple in the Hills after Rain (attrib. Li Cheng) 105, **2.74**
Buñuel, Luis, and Dalí, Salvador: *Un Chien andalou* 294–295, 466, **8.23**
Burgee, John *see* Johnson, Philip
Buried Secrets (Viola) 300, **8.30**
burins 253, 517
burls 341, 517
Burne-Jones, Edward: *Works of Geoffrey Chaucer* 275, **7.12**
burnishing 227, 517
burr 255
Burrowing Skink Dreaming at Parikirlangu (Jampijimpa) 21, 23, **1.14**
Bust of a Woman after Cranach the Younger (Picasso) 253, **6.12**
Bust of a Young Girl (Houdon) 320, **10.10**
buttresses 517; flying 377, 520, **13.21**, **13.22**
Byzantine art and architecture 88, 376, 379, 425, 517, **13.27**

C

Cabinet of Doctor Caligari, The (Wiene) 294, 460, **8.22**
CAD wire-frame drawings 316, **10.6**
Calder, Alexander 158; *Lobster Trap and Fish Tail* 158, **2.148**
Calligrates *see* lettering
calligraphy 55–56, 114, 181, 517, **2.88**
Calling of St. Matthew, The (Caravaggio) 444, **15.28**
Camara, Silla: wall painting 216, **5.1**
camera obscura 276, 517
Cameron, Julia Margaret 278; *Iago* 278–279, **8.4**
Campagna Landscape (Claude Lorraine) 215, **4.14**
cantilevers 387, 517, **13.35**
canvases 216, 219
capitals 376, 517
Caravaggio, Michelangelo Merisi da 444; *The Calling of St. Matthew* 444, **15.28**; *The Conversion of St. Paul* 121, **2.99**
Caress, The (Cassatt) 255, **6.25**
carpets 349; Persian 349, **11.20**
Carr, Emily 180–181; *British Columbia Landscape* 181, **3.14**
Carrying of the Cross, The (Bosch) 100, **2.69**
Cartier-Bresson, Henri 281; *Sunday on the Banks of the Marne* 282, **8.11**
cartoons 209, 224, 517, **5.9**
carving processes 312–315
Cassandre, A. M.: poster 65, **2.19**
Cassatt, Mary: *The Caress* 255, **6.25**
casting 517; bronze 73, 323, **10.14**, **10.15**; glass 347

Caswell, Stuart: *Chain Link Disaster* 206, **4.5**
cathedrals 125, 429; Chartres 372, 430, **13.11**, **13.20**, **15.16**; Notre Dame 377, **13.21**; Rouen 454, **15.37**; St. Basil's, Moscow 369, **13.5**; St. Paul's, London 448, **15.31**; Santiago de Compostela, Spain 429, **15.15**
cave paintings, prehistoric 418–419, **15.1**
CBS album cover (Crocker) 65, **2.18**
Cellini, Benvenuto: *Perseus with the Head of Medusa* 326–327, 442, **10.18**
censorship 46–47
Centerpeace (Howard) 316, **10.5**
ceramics 41, 42, 193, 333, 422, 517, **1.35**, **1.37**, **3.35**, **15.7**; see clay
Cerulean Sky (J. Good) 266, **6.33**
Cézanne, Paul 48–49, 79, 455, 461; *Mont Sainte-Victoire seen from Les Lauves* 79, **2.40**; *Still-Life with Apples* 455, **15.38**
Chain Link Disaster (Caswell) 206, **4.5**
chair, Thonet 64, **2.16**
chalk drawings 202, 209, 211, 279, 517, **4.2**, **4.9**, **8.6**
Chan, Eric 354; toaster 354, **12.1**
Changes # IV (Boyden) 260, **6.28**
Changing the Fractal Dimension (Voss) 304, **9.5**
charcoal drawings 206, 208–209, **4.7**, **4.8**
Chartres Cathedral, France 372, **13.11**, **13.20**; rose window 430, **15.16**
chiaroscuro 120–121, 220, 436, 517
Chien andalou, Un (Buñuel and Dalí) 294–295, 466, **8.23**
Chihuly, Dale 347; *No. 2 Sea Form Series* 347, **11.16**
Chin, Daryl 50
Chinese artworks 42, 61, 105, 132, 145, 181, 192, 193, **1.37**, **2.12**, **2.74**, **2.117**, **3.34**, **3.35**
Ch'ing dynasty: stemcup 42, **1.37**
Christina's World (Wyeth) 467, **15.50**
Christo 203; *Running Fence* 57–58, **2.8**
chroma see color(s), saturation of
Chromatic Abstractionists 468–469
Cimabue: *Madonna Enthroned with Angels and Prophets* 105, **2.75**
cinematography 293–294, 518, see film
cire perdue see lost-wax casting process
Citizen Kane (Welles) 295, 296, **8.24**
City Bird (Stankiewicz) 328, **10.19**
City Complex One (Heizer) 76, 331, 332, **2.35**
Città Castellana (Corot) 205–206, **4.4**
Classical Period (Greek art) 422, 518
Classicism 518
Claude Lorraine: *Campagna Landscape* 215, **4.14**
clay 333, 335; coil building 334, 518, **11.2**; modeling 320, 322; pinching 333, 524, **11.1**; slab building 334, 526; wheel-throwing 334–335, 527, **11.3**
cleaning paintings 232–233, 504–506
Clearing Winter Storm, Yosemite National Park (A. Adams) 282, **8.12**
clock, wrought-iron (Szabo) 338–339, **11.9**

Close, Chuck 471; *Frank* 238, **5.25**
closed forms (sculpture) 73, 518
clothes 358–359, 361–363; *Delphos* dress (Fortuny) 361, **12.9**; Mandingo gown 84, **2.45**; Nigerian dress 361, **12.8**; ritual and theatrical costumes 409, **14.17**
Clothespin (Version Two) (Oldenburg) 203, **4.3**
Coady, Judy and Pat: townhouse interior 139, **2.127**
Coca-Cola bottle (Samuelson) 41, **1.36**
coffers 379, 518
Cohen, Harold 308; *Untitled* **9.10**
coil-building (clay) 334, 518, **11.2**
collages 93, 240–241, 481, 518, **2.58**, **5.28**, **5.29**, **15.63**; see also *Snail, The* (Matisse)
Collegium (King) 328, **10.21**
color(s) 30, 127; additive 128, 516; advancing 142–143; Albers on 150–151; analogous 145, 516; applied 132; artists' palettes and 152; balancing 184; combinations and interactions 143, 145–146, 148–149, 150, **2.129**, **2.136**, **2.141**; complementary 129, 131, 132, 145, 518; cool 138–139, 518; emotional effects of 135, 137–138; Goethe on 118; Hoener's theory on 148–149; impressionistic 134; interpretive 134–135, 521; local 134; Munsell's color tree 129, 131, **2.113**, **2.115**; natural 131–132; Newton's color wheel 128, 129, **2.109**; optical mixtures of 148–149, 523; primary 128, 129, **2.110**, **2.111**; receding 142–143; reflected 129, 525, **2.112**; refracted 128, 525, **2.110**; saturation of 129, 131, 525; secondary 128, **2.110**, **2.111**; spectrum 127–128, **2.108**; synergistic mixing of 148–149, 526; tertiary 129, 526, **2.111**; triad schemes 145–146, 526; value and 129, 146, **2.136**; warm 138–139, 527
color scanners 262
color separation process 262, 264, **6.30**
color wheels 128, 129, **2.109**, **2.111**
Colosseum, Rome 509, **16.23**
Composition in Blue, Yellow, and Black (Mondrian) 464, **15.47**
compositional unity see unity, compositional compressive strength 374, 518
computers: graphics 215, 301, 303, 307–310, 472, 518; imaging (in films) 296, 297; painting 303–305; and photography 290; and sculpture design 316; video graphics 305–306; virtual reality systems 306–307
conceptual art 29–30, 169, 475, 518
Concourse of the Birds, The (Habib Allah) 118, **2.96**
concrete: reinforced 387, 525, **13.35**; Roman 379
Connecticut Remembered (Zelanski) 240, **5.28**
Connor, Russell: *Hands Off the Polish Rider* 487, **15.68**
Constable, John 451
Constantine, Emperor 425
conté crayon drawings 212, 518, **4.11**
content 14–15, 518

contours 71, 79, 116, 518; modeling of 79, 522–523
contrapposto 318, 423, 518
contrast 518; of design elements 30, 170, 177–179; in value 118, 146, **2.136**
Conversion of St. Paul, The (Caravaggio) 121, **2.99**
copper 338; raised vessels 339, **11.10**
copyright: and cyberspace networks 310
Core Pieces # 1, # 2 (Noguchi) 131–132, **2.116**
Corinthian order 376, 518, **13.17**
Cornell, Joseph 90; *The Hotel Eden* 90, **2.52**
Corot, Jean Baptiste Camille: *Città Castellana* 205–206, **4.4**
Correggio, Antonio: *Danae* 229, 442, **5.16**
Corrida de Cannes, La (Alcalacanales) 292, **8.20**
costumes see clothes
Counter-Reformation 51
Courbet, Gustave 453; *The Stone Breakers* 453, **15.35**
crafts 41, 333, 350, 478–479, 518
Cranach, Lucas, the Younger: *Portrait of a Woman* 253, **6.13**
crayon drawings 212, **4.11**, **4.12**
Creation (Rivera) 223, **5.7**
Creation of Adam (Michelangelo) 12, 21, 202, 502, **1.1**, **4.2**, **16.16**
Crest (Riley) 156, 469, **2.146**
critics and critical opinions 48–49, 51; and race and gender 50
Crocker, John: CBS album cover 65, **2.18**
Cross, Henri-Edmond: *The Artist's Garden at St. Clair* 114, 115, **2.89**
cross-hatching 63, 213, 247, 418
Crucifixion with Saints, The (Perugino) 187, **3.24**–**3.26**
Crystal Palace, London (Paxton) 303; engraving (Cuff) 96, **2.63**
Csuri, Charles 307–308; *Wondrous Spring* 308, **9.11**
Cubism 461, 518
Cuff, R. P.: *The Crystal Palace* (engraving) 96, **2.63**
cyberspace 301, 518; art in 309–310
Cycladic figurines 419, **15.3**
Czech postage stamps 270, **7.6**

D

Dada 465–466, 518
Daguerre, Louis Jacques Mandé 276; *A Parisian Boulevard* 276, **8.2**
daguerreotypes 276, **8.2**
Dalí, Salvador: *Un Chien andalou* (with Buñuel) 294–295, 466, **8.23**; *The Persistence of Memory* 466, **15.49**
Dallas, Texas: *Fair Park Lagoon* (Johanson) 404–405, **14.12**; skyline 384, **13.31**
Dalton, Stephen 290–291; *Spores Falling from the Common Horsetail* 291, **8.19**
Danae (Correggio) 229, 442, **5.16**

dance 410

Dancer with a Bouquet (Degas) 99–100, **2.66**

Danto, Arthur 49

David (Michelangelo) 313, 318, 438, **10.2**

David, Gerard: *The Resurrection* 134, **2.118**

David, Jacques-Louis: *The Oath of the Horatii* 450, **15.33**

Dead Christ (Mantegna) 226, **5.11**

deconstructionist architecture 391, 518

Deductive Object (Soo-ja Kim) 25, **1.17**

Degas, Edgar 163, 279, 454, 455, 486; *After the Bath* 211–212, **4.10**; *Dancer with a Bouquet* 99–100, **2.66**; *Horse Galloping on Right Foot* 322, **10.13**; *Le Petit Déjeuner après le bain* 486, **15.67**

Déjeuner sur l'herbe, Le (Manet) 453, **15.36**

de Kooning, Willem 468

Delphos dress (Fortuny) 361, **12.9**

Demoiselles d'Avignon, Les (Picasso) 461, **15.43**

Derain, André: *The Pool of London* 460, **15.42**

design: elements of 30, 55; principles of 30, 170; unity of 30, 170, 187, 189

Devlin, Dean 296; *Independence Day* 297, **8.28**

Diebenkorn, Richard: *Ocean Park #115* 37, **1.31**

digitizing 301, 518

diptychs 518

Dipylon Vase 422, **15.7**

Disney Productions: *Tron* 305, **9.6**

Ditko, Steve *see* Shepherd, Barry

divisionism *see* pointillism

Diziani, Gaspare: *Dawn* **14.2**

documentary films 297

dolls 479, **15.60**

Domènech i Montaner, Lluís: Palau de la Música Catalana 248, **6.32**

domes 367, 379, 518; geodesic 387, **13.34**; "onion" 367, 369, **13.5**

Don Juan (S. Alcorn) 252, **6.11**

Doric order 376, 519, **13.17**

Doryphorus *see* Spear Bearer

Double Self-Portrait (Estes) 123, **2.101**

Double wall Bowl (Hoogland, Senn, and Leitru) 123, **2.102**

Dove, The (Soriano) **15.62**

drawing 202–203; brush and ink 215; chalk 209, 211, 517; charcoal 206, 208–209, 517; computer 301, 303; crayon 212; graphite pencil 205, 206; paper for 203, 204; pastel 203, 211–212; pen and ink 213, 215; silverpoint 206

Dream, The (Rousseau) 23, 25, **1.15**

Dreaming, the 21

drip paintings 48, 167, 173, 467–468, **1.42**, **15.51**

drypoint: etchings 255, **6.19**–**6.24**; prints 255, 519, **6.25**

Dubuffet, Jean 484

du Cerceau, Jean-Jacques Androuet 340, **11.11**

Duchamp, Marcel: *The Fountain* 465–466, **15.48**; *Nude Descending a Staircase #2* 159, 463, **2.151**

ductility 338, 519

Duffy Design Group: packaging 267, **7.2**

du Pasquier, Nathalie: fabric 171, 172, 175, **3.1**

Dürer, Albrecht 442; *Head of an Apostle* 61, 63, **2.13**; *Saint Christopher* 248, **6.6**; *Underweisung der Messung...* 271, **7.8**

dynamic forms 76, 519

E

earthenware 333, 519

earthworks 57–58, 76, 331–332, 475, 519, **2.8**, **2.35**

Eastman, George 293

Ecclesiastes, "And in her mouth was an olive leaf" (Eichenberg) 250, **6.10**

Echo, L' (Seurat) 201, 212, **4.11**

economy 30, 170, 192–193, 519

Ecstasy of St. Teresa, The (Bernini) 21, 23, 49, 444, **1.13**

Eddy, Don: *Imminent Desire/Distant Longing II* 100, **2.67**

edges 57, 519; *see also* hard-edged painters

Efendi, Sami 56; *Levha in Celi Sülüs* 55–56, 181, **2.1**

Egypt: ancient art and sculpture 73, 315, 421, **2.30**, **15.6**; Coptic encaustic painting 222, **5.6**; modern architecture 380–381, **13.24**, **13.25**; pyramids 420–421, **15.5**

Eichenberg, Fritz 250; *Ecclesiastes, "And in her mouth was an olive leaf"* 250, **6.10**

Eiffel Tower, Paris 391

Eisenstein, Sergei 295

Elgin "marbles" 438

embossing, blind 247, 517

emphasis 30, 170, 190–191, 519

enamel 338, 519, **11.8**; mural 403, **14.10**

encaustic painting 33, 216, 222–223, 425, 519, **1.27**, **5.6**, **5.7**, **15.12**

Endo, Susumu 290; *Space and Space Forest 91A* 290, **8.18**

engravings 519; colored 246, line 95, 167, 245–246, 253, 522, **2.63**, **2.76**, **6.1**, **6.2**, **6.15**, **6.17**; wood 250, 252, 275, **6.9**, **6.10**, **7.13**

entablatures 195, 376, 519

entasis 195, 519

Entry to Sukhum (Winokur) 336, **11.6**

envelope, Ottoman embroidered 146, **2.134**

environment: and architecture 199–200, 367, 369, 371, 380–381; and art 170, 198

environmental design 401–407, 519

ephemeral artworks 168

Ephesus, Turkey: theatre 408, **14.14**

Equestrienne, L' (Toulouse-Lautrec) 212, **4.12**

Equestrienne (At the Circus Fernando) (Toulouse-Lautrec) 163, **2.153**

Equivocal (Albers) 150, **2.140**

Erechtheum, Athens 375, **13.16**

ergonomics 356, 519

Escher, M. C.: *Relativity* 107, **2.77**

Essence Mulberry (Frankenthaler) 177, **3.8**

Estes, Richard 471; *Double Self-Portrait* 123, **2.101**

etchings 253, 255, 266, 519, **6.18**–**6.24**, **6.32**

Euphiletos painter (attrib.): amphora 335, **11.4**

Evolution (Scott) 50, **1.44**

Execution of a Vietcong officer (E. Adams) 298, **8.29**

Expressionism 294, 458, 460, 519

Eyck, Jan van 431; *Marriage of Giovanni Arnolfini and Giovanna Cenami* 433, **15.18**

eye-level line 95, 519

eyelines 60–61, 519

F

f/64 group 282, 288

fabric designs 171, 172, 174, **3.1**; *see also* clothes

"Fallingwater" (Kaufmann House) (Wright) 200, 387, **3.44**

Family Dinner (Bearden) 481, **15.63**

Farm Security Administration, USA 280

fat (of paint) 228, 519

Fathy, Hassan: New Gourna, Egypt 380–381, **13.24**, **13.25**

Fauvism 460, 519

fax art 292, 520

Feathers #22 (Alling) 116, **2.92**

Feder, Eudice: *Swarm* 303, **9.2**

fiber arts 347, 349, 350, 352, **11.22**

Fibonacci series 195

figurative art 32, 520

figure-ground relationship 92, 520

figure-ground reversal 92, 520

film 293–298; computerized special effects 296–297; documentary 297; Expressionist 294, 460

fine arts 40, 520

firing clay 335, 520

Finnan (Bakun) 114, **2.88**

Fish Skeletons (Bloom) 213, **4.13**

Flagellation of Christ (Piero della Francesca) 187, **3.27**

Flaherty, Robert: *Nanook of the North* 297, **8.27**

flask (Marriot) 71, 72, **2.29**

Flemish painting 431, 433

Floor Show (J. Good) 100, **2.68**

Florence, Italy: Baptistery *Gates of Paradise* (Ghiberti) 434, 496, **15.21**; San Marco fresco 433–434, **15.19**

Flower Day (Rivera) 33, **1.27**

Flower-form Vase (Tiffany) 76, **2.36**

Flowering Apple Tree (Mondrian) 33, 37, 55, **1.30**

flying buttresses 377, 520, **13.21**, **13.22**

focal plane shutter 163, 520

focal points 190, 191, 520

Focus on the Belvedere (Sider) 352–353, **11.24**

folk art 484, 520

foreground 520
foreshortening 520
forging 338, 520
form 30, 65, 520; two-dimensional illusion of 77, 79
Forma, Donna: *Ode to Life* 315, **10.4**
Fort Worth, Texas: Water Garden (Johnson and Burgee) 155–156, **2.145**
Fortuny, Mario: *Delphos* dress 361, **12.9**
found objects 90, 328, 520
Fountain, The (Duchamp) 465–466, **15.48**
four-color presses 262
Four Pears (O. Parker) 285, **8.13**
Fox Trot A (Mondrian) 59–60, 464, **2.10**
fractal geometry 304, 520
Fragonard, Jean-Honoré 448; *The Swing* 163, 167, **2.152**
frame construction 383, 520
Francis, Darlene: chair and chifforobe 356, 358, **12.5**
Franco, General Francisco 52, 489
Frank (Close) 238, **5.25**
Frank, Mary: *Untitled* 247, **6.4**
Frankenthaler, Helen 239, 469; *Essence Mulberry* 177, **3.8**; *Hint from Bassano* 238–239, **5.26**; *Mauve District* 84–85, **2.46**
Franklin, Aretha: poster of (Glaser) 145, **2.132**
Frasconi, Antonio: *Portrait of Woody Guthrie* 249, **6.7**
French Academy 48, 49, 453
frescoes 190, 224–225, 430–431, 433–434, 441, 520, **3.31**, **5.8–5.10**, **15.17**, **15.19**, **15.25**; buon fresco 224, 517; *see also* Sistine Chapel frescoes
Freud, Sigmund 466
frontal works 67, 520
Fuller, Richard Buckminster: geodesic dome 387, **13.34**
funerary art, Roman 425
furniture 64, 340, 341, 356, 358, 395, 399, **2.16**, **11.11**, **11.12**, **12.15**
Fusco, Coco *see* Gomez-Pena, Guillermo
Futurism 159, 463, 520

G

Gainsborough, Thomas: *Mr. and Mrs. Andrews* 184–185, **3.21**
gardens 401; Japanese 90, **2.54**; water 155–156, **2.145**
Gates of Hell, The (Rodin) 40, 52, 67, 183, 495–499, **1.46**, **2.22**, **16.11**, **16.13**; plaster cast **16.10**; sketches **16.8**, **16.12**; terracotta study **16.9**
Gates of Paradise (Ghiberti) 434, 496, **15.21**
Gaudí, Antonio: Sagrada Familia church, Barcelona 175, **3.7**
Gauguin, Paul 455, 456–457; *The Spirit of the Dead Watching* 456, **15.39**
Gellée, Claude *see* Claude Lorraine
gender: and art criticism 50

Gentile da Fabriano: *The Adoration of the Magi* 167, **2.157**
geodesic domes 387, 520, **13.34**
Geometric Period (Greek art) 422, 520
geometric shapes 59, 84, 458, 520
Géricault, Théodore: *The Raft of the Medusa* 451, 453, **15.34**
gesso 219, 227, 520, **5.12**, **5.27**
gestural style 64–65, 520
Geyer, George, and McMillin, Tom: "Surface Erosion," *Laguna Beach* 169, 475, **2.159**
Ghiberti, Lorenzo 434; *Gates of Paradise* 434, 496, **15.21**
Giacometti, Alberto: *Walking Man* 57, **2.7**
Gill, Eric 271
Gill Sans typeface 271, **7.7**
Giotto: *The Lamentation* 430–431, **15.17**
Girl with a Pearl Earring (Vermeer) 228–229, **5.15**
Giza, Egypt: pyramids 420–421, **15.5**
Glaser, Milton: logo for Russian Tea Room, New York 267, **7.1**; poster of Aretha Franklin 145, **2.132**; poster for Monet Museum 117–118, **2.94**
glass/glassware 344, 347; antique 347, 516; cast 347, **11.17**; lead crystal 522; opalescent 347, 523; plate 369; sculpture 137, 347, **2.122**, **11.16**; stained 125, 139, 347, 430, **2.106**, **2.107**, **2.127**, **11.18**, **15.16**; studio 344, **11.15**; Tiffany 76, **2.36**
glazes: ceramic 335, 520; oil paints 229, 520, **5.27**
Goethe, Johann W. von 148
Gogh, Vincent van 28, 48, 180, 218, 455, 458, 486; *Portrait of Dr. Gachet* 48, 486; *The Starry Night* 11, 27, 28–29, 218, **1.21**
gold 338, **11.8**
gold leaf, applying 227
golden rectangle 193–194, 520, **3.37**
golden section (or mean) 195, 520
Gomez-Pena, Guillermo, and Fusco, Coco: performance art 475, **15.57**
Gonzales, Juan: *Sara's Garden* 164, **2.155**
Good, Jane Cummings: *Cerulean Sky* 266, **6.33**; *Floor Show* 100, **2.68**
Good, Peter 268; logo for Hartford Whalers 193, **3.36**; logo for Special Olympics **7.3**; poster 264, **6.30**
Good Spirit (Manaipik) 88, **2.49**
Gorky, Arshile 82–83; *Making the Calendar* 81, **2.44**
Gothic style 521; cathedrals 125, 372, 376, 377, 429–430, **13.11**, **13.20**, **13.21**; painting 430–431; sculpture 431
gouache, painting in 216, 237, 521, **2.17**, **2.42**, **5.23**, **5.24**
gouges 247
Goya, Francisco de: *And There Is No Remedy* 266, **6.32**
Grainstacks (Monet) 134, **2.119**
Grameen Bank Housing Programme, Bangladesh 384, **13.45**
Grand Prix of the Automobile Club of France (Lartigue) 164, **2.154**

graphic design(ers) 41, 193, 267–70, 521; *see also* logos; poster art; typography
graphite 521, *see* pencil
Grausman, Philip: *Leucantha* 71, **2.28**
Graves, Nancy: *Trace* 185, **3.22**
Gray Tree, The (Mondrian) 33, 37, 55, **1.29**
Grear (Malcolm) Designers: poster for Guggenheim Museum 118, **2.95**
Greco, El: *View of Toledo* 145, **2.131**
Greece, ancient: amphora 335; architecture 193–5, 375–6, 422; encaustic painting 222; sculpture 73, 132, 179, 422–423; theater 408; wax modeling 322
Green on Blue (Rothko) 25, **1.18**
Green Neon from Wall to Floor (Antonakos) 125, 475, **2.104**
Gregg, Glenn, Linburg, Virginia, and McKernan, Virginia: Canberra Industries offices, Connecticut 399, **14.5**
Grotell, Maija **11.3**
grounds 92, 230, 521
Grünewald, Matthias: *The Isenheim Altarpiece* 442, **15.27**
Guanyin (wood statue) 132, 145, **2.117**
Guernica (Picasso) 52, 54, 80–81, 173, 310, 413, 439, 489–494, **1.47**, **2.43**, **3.5**, **16.1**; State II 493, **16.7**; studies for **16.3–16.6**
Guggenheim Museum: poster 118, **2.95**
Gulf Stream, The (Homer) 234, **5.22**

H

Habib Allah: *The Concourse of the Birds* 118, **2.96**
Hagesandrus, Athenodorus, and Polydorus: *Laocoön* 189, **3.29**, **3.30**
Hagia Sophia, Istanbul 88, 425, **2.50**, **2.51**
Haida culture: chest 182, **3.17**
Halprin, Lawrence 405; *Sea Ranch* 403–404, **14.11**
hammering metal 338, 339
Hands Off the Polish Rider (Connor) 487, **15.68**
Hang-up (Hesse) 29, 30, **1.22**
Hanson, Duane: *Museum Guard* 31, **1.24**
hard-edged painting 85, 469, 521
Hardouin-Mansart, Jules: Palace of Versailles 18, **1.9**
Hardwick Hall, Derbyshire: table 340, **11.11**
Harper's Magazine: Beggarstaff Brothers' poster 59, **2.9**
Harvey, Bessie 484; *Tribal Spirits* **15.65**
hatching 63, 205, 213, 247, 521
Hawaiian art 110, **2.82**
Head of an Apostle (Dürer) 61, 63, **2.13**
Head of a Virgin (Weyden) 206, **4.6**
Head of a Woman (Modigliani) 318, **10.8**
Headspring, a Flying Pigeon Interfering (Muybridge) 293, **8.21**
Heizer, Michael: *City Complex One* 76, 331, 332, **2.35**
Held, Al: *Vaporum VI* 99, **2.65**

Hellenistic Period 423, 521; bronzes 60–61, 325, **2.11**, **10.17**; mosaic 242, **5.30**, **5.31**; sculpture 113, 189, **2.86**, **3.29**, **3.30**; theater 408, **14.14**

Helsinki: Taivallahti church (T. and T. Suomalainen) 177, **3.10**

Henderson, Victor *see* Los Angeles Fine Arts Squad

Henry VIII (after Holbein) 359, 361, **12.7**

Hepworth, Barbara 72; *Pendour* 73, **2.33**

Hersey, William *see* Moore, Charles

Hesira, portrait panel of 421, **15.6**

Hesse, Eva 29–30; *Hang-up* 29, 30, **1.22**

Hicks, David: sitting room 139, **2.126**

highlights 116, 521

high relief 67, 521

high-tech revival architecture 390–391, 521

Hint from Bassano (Frankenthaler) 238–239, **5.26**

Hiroshima Series: Boy with Kite (Lawrence) 80, 85, **2.42**

Hirst, Damien: *James (The Twelve Disciples)* 14, **1.4**

Hitler, Adolf 20

Hoagland, Labbar, Soria, Alfonso Soto, and Leites, Pedro: *Double-wall Bowl* 123, **2.102**

Hockney, David 292

Hodgkin, Howard: *Interior with Figures* 477, **15.59**

Hoener, Arthur 148–149; *Tenuous* 149, **2.139**

Hofmann, Hans 468; *Rhapsody* 230, **5.18**

Hogarth, William: frontis. to Kirby's *Perspective* 105, **2.76**

Hohlwein, Ludwig: poster 20, **1.12**

Hokusai 246–247; *Southerly Wind and Fine Weather* 246, **6.3**

Holbein, Hans, the Younger: (after) *Henry VIII* 359, 361, **12.7**; *Jane Small* 105, **2.73**

Holt, Nancy: *Sun Tunnels* 120, **2.97**, **2.98**

Homage to the Square series (Albers) 138, 150, 469, **2.124**, **2.140**

Homer, Winslow: *The Gulf Stream* 234, **5.22**

Horse and Sun Chariot (bronze) 73, **2.32**

Horse Galloping on Right Foot (Degas) 322, **10.13**

Hotel Eden, The (Cornell) 90, **2.52**

Houdon, Jean-Antoine 450; *Bust of a Young Girl* 320, **10.10**

Howard, Linda 316; CAD wire-frame drawings 316, **10.6**; *Centerpeace* 316, **10.5**

Howell, Jim and Sandy: living room 139, **2.125**

hues 128–129, 521, *see* color(s)

hummingbird, Nasca 331, **10.23**

Hunters in the Snow (Bruegel the Elder) 95, **2.59**

I

Iago (Cameron) 278–279, **8.4**

Ichikawa, Ennosuke, III 411, **14.20**

icons 425, 521, **15.12**

Ictinus and Callicrates: Parthenon, Athens 194–195, **3.38**

idealization 32, 521

illusion: and color 146, 148, **2.136**; and form 77, 79; and line 59–60; of movement 157, 159; and space 105, 107; *trompe l'oeil* 113–114; *see also* texture, simulated

illustrations, book 245, 272, 275

Imminent Desire/Distant Longing II (Eddy) 100, **2.67**

Imatra, Finland: Vuoksenniska Church (Aalto) 392, **13.44**

impasto 218, 230, 521

Impressionism, French 48, 49, 134, 453–454, 458, 521

Improvisation No. 30 (Kandinsky) 464, **15.46**

Independence Day (Devlin) 297, **8.26**

India: kanna hut 367, **13.3**; laws of architecture 373, **13.12**; Nishat Bagh 401, **14.16**; rock-cut temples 374, **13.13**; Taj Mahal 15, 30, **1.5**, **1.23**

industrial design 41, 354, 356, 358, 478, 521

Ingres, Jean Auguste Dominique: *Portrait of the Princesse de Broglie* 111, **2.85**; *Two Nudes* 79, **2.39**

ink drawings/paintings 61, 63, 93, 101, 105, 192, 213, 215, **2.12**, **2.57**, **2.68**, **2.70**, **2.74**, **3.34**, **4.13**–**4.15**

installation pieces 25, 125, 475, 521

intaglio printmaking 253, 255, 259–260, 521

intellectual concepts 27–30

interior design 139, 143, 395, 397–399, 401, 521, **2.125**–**2.127**, **2.130**

Interior with Figures (Hodgkin) 477, **15.59**

International Style (architecture) 384–385, 521

Internet 309–310

intonaco 224, 521, **5.9**

investment (in casting) 323, 522

investment, art as 45, 486–487

Iona, monastery of 429

Ionic order 376, 522, **13.17**

Iris Lake (Rosenquist) 262, **6.29**

Irish Bells and Sentinels (Tiffany) 347, **11.18**

iron 338; wrought 338–339, 527, **11.9**

Isenheim Altarpiece, The (Grünewald) 442, **15.27**

Isle of California (Los Angeles Fine Arts Squad) 403, **14.10**

Istanbul: Hagia Sophia 88, 425, **2.50**, **2.51**

ivory bust (prehistoric) 12, **1.2**

Izumita, Ronald *see* Lyle, John

J

Jacobs, Herbert: "Solar Hemicycle" house (with Wright) 398–399, **14.4**

jade, carving 319; vase 319, **10.9**

Jahangir, Emperor 401

James (Hirst) 14, **1.4**

Jampijimpa, Darby: *Burrowing Skink Dreaming at Parikirlangu* 21, 23, **1.14**

Japan: architecture 372, 389, **13.10**, **13.40**; film 295–296, **8.25**; gardens 90, 198, **2.54**, **3.42**; *kabuki* actors 410–411, **14.20**; kimonos 353, 362, **11.25**, **11.26**; merchant's home 397–398, **14.3**; painting 100–101, 181; temple 124, **2.103**; *tokonoma* alcoves 42, 44, 398, **1.38**; woodcut prints 246–247, 249, **6.3**

Jefferson National Expansion Memorial (Saarinen) 20, **1.11**

Jelling, Denmark: Rune Stone 110, **2.81**

Johanson, Patricia: *Pteris Multifida*, Fair Park Lagoon, Dallas 404–405, **14.12**

Johnson, Philip: AT&T Building (with Burgee) 389–390, **13.41**; Johnson House, New Canaan 385, **13.33**; Seagram Building (with Mies van der Rohe) 385, **13.32**; Water Garden, Fort Worth, Texas (with Burgee) 155–156, **2.145**

Julius II, Pope 51, 313, 500

junk sculpture 328

Justinian, Emperor 425

K

kabuki actors 410–411, **14.20**

Kahlo, Frida 479; *The Broken Column* 479, **15.61**

Kalachakra Sand Mandala 168, **2.158**

Kandinsky, Wassily 47, 127, 196: *Improvisation # 30 (Cannons)* 464, **15.46**; *Painting # 199* **3.41**

Karnes, Karen: stoneware pot 335, **11.5**

Katsura (Stella) 152, **2.142**

Kaufmann House, Bear Run, Pennsylvania (Wright) 200, 387, **3.44**

Kawasaki, Kazuo: wheelchair 356, **12.3**

Kelly, Ellsworth: *Spectrum III* 142, 143, **2.128**

Kelmscott Press 275, **7.12**

keystones 376, 522

Kiefer, Anselm: *Athanor* 95–96, 477, **2.61**

Killed by the Army (Webb) 281, **8.10**

Kim, Soo-ja: *Deductive Object* 25, **1.17**

kimonos 362; (Kubota) 353, **11.25**, **11.26**

kinetic sculpture 158, 522, **2.148**, **2.149**

King, William: *Collegium* 328, **10.21**

Kirishima International Concert Hall, Kagoshima, Japan (Maki) 372, **13.10**

Klee, Paul 23; *Twittering Machine* 23, **1.16**

Knees (Weston) 288, **8.14**

Kollwitz, Käthe: *Self-portrait with a Pencil* 208, **4.7**

Kosuth, Joseph 475; *Zeno at the Edge of the Known World* 475, **15.58**

Kotlean robe (Samuel) 362–363, **12.12**

Kouros (marble) 422, **15.8**

Kubota, Itchiku: kimonos 353, **11.25**, **11.26**

Kukailimoku (Hawaiian war-god) 110, **2.82**

Kurokawa, Kisho: Nakagin Capsule Building, Tokyo 389, **13.40**

Kurosawa, Akira: *Rashomon* 295–296, **8.25**

Kyoto, Japan: Byodoin Temple, Uji 124, 2.103; Katsura Palace garden 90, 2.54; merchant's home 397–398, 14.3; Ryoanji temple rock garden 198, 3.42

L

Lachaise, Gaston: *Standing Woman* 116, 2.91
Lady of Fashion, A (Voisard) 359, 12.6
La Farge, John 347
Lalique, René 347; glass vase 347, 11.17
Lamentation, The (Giotto) 430–431, 15.17
laminate 318, 522
lamp (Morishima) 356, 12.4
landscape design, contemporary 403–405
landscapes 180–181, 215, 3.14, 4.14; Chinese 105, 2.74; computer painted 304; photographic 282, 284, 8.12; Romantic 451
Landscape with Rainbow (Rubens) 32, 1.26
Lange, Dorothea 467; *Migrant Mother* 280 281, 8.9
Laocoön (Hagesandrus, Athenodorus, and Polydorus) 189, 3.29, 3.30
Lara, Cardinal José Castillo 506
Lartigue, Jacques Henri: *Grand Prix of the Automobile Club of France* 164, 2.154
Lascaux, France: cave paintings 418, 419, 15.1
laser images 125, 472, 2.105
Last Judgment, The (Blake) 183, 3.18
Last Judgment, The (Michelangelo) 46, 233, 1.41, 5.19
Last Supper, The (Leonardo) 190, 232, 441, 3.31, 3.32
Last Supper, The (Tintoretto) 442, 15.26
Last Supper, The (Ugolino) 180, 226–227, 3.13, 5.12
Latham, William: *Ornamental Mutation* 303, 9.3
Lautrec *see* Toulouse-Lautrec, Henri de
Law, David (with Vignelli Associates): dinner set 354, 356, 12.2
Lawrence, Jacob: *Hiroshima Series: Boy with Kite* 80, 85, 2.42
lean (of paint) 228, 522
Le Corbusier 385; Notre-Dame-du-Haut, Ronchamp 125, 2.107
Leda and the Swan (Tintoretto) 178–179, 187, 229, 442, 3.11, 3.12
Leites, Pedro *see* Hoagland, Labbar
Leonardo da Vinci 220, 222, 436, 441, 487; *The Adoration of the Magi* 229, 5.17; *The Last Supper* 190, 232, 441, 3.31, 3.32; *Mona Lisa* 220, 233, 438, 5.5, 15.24; *The Virgin and Child with St. Anne and St. John the Baptist* 209, 211, 4.9; *The Virgin of the Rocks* 211, 229, 436, 15.23
Leucantha (Grausman) 71, 2.28
Le Vau, Louis: Palace of Versailles 18, 1.9
Levha in Celi Sülüs (Efendi) 55–56, 181, 2.1
Levine, Marilyn: *Two-toned Golf Bag* 113–114, 2.87

Lewis, Lucy 11.2; water jar 41, 84, 1.35
Li Bo, portrait of (Liang Kai) 192, 3.34
Li Cheng (attrib.): *Buddhist Temple in the Hills after Rain* 105, 2.74
Liang Kai: *The Poet Li Bo* 192, 3.34
Liberia: gown (Mandingo) 84, 2.45
Lichtenstein, Roy 470; *Mural with Blue Brushstroke* 470, 15.54
Liebeskind, Daniel: addition to Victoria and Albert Museum 391, 13.43
Life's Embrace (Sunday) 288, 8.16
light(ing) 118, 120–121, 123; and environment 401; as medium 124–125; projections 472, 15.56; reflected 123–124; and value 114–116; *see also* chiaroscuro; laser images; neon art
light wells 193, 522
Lily-White with Black (O'Keeffe) 38, 1.33
Limbourg Brothers: *Les Très Riches Heures du Duc de Berry* 164, 167, 245, 2.156
Lin, Maya Ying: Vietnam Veterans' Memorial 17, 1.8
Linburg, Virginia *see* Gregg, Glenn
Lindquist, Mark: *Toutes Uncommon Bowl* 311, 11.13
line engravings 96, 105, 245–246, 253, 522, 2.63, 2.76, 6.1, 6.2, 6.15, 6.17
line(s) 30, 55–57; decorative 61, 518; descriptive 61, 518; directional 65, 518; expressive 63–65, 519, 2.15; implied 59–61, 521; lyrical 65; *see also* bracelet modeling; calligraphy; cross-hatching; hatching
linocuts 251, 252–253, 522, 6.11, 6.12
lithography 65, 107, 260, 262, 269, 522, 2.19, 2.77, 6.28, 6.29, 7.5; offset lithography 262, 290, 523, 8.18
Littleton, Harvey 347; vase 344, 11.15
Lobster Trap and Fish Tail (Calder) 158, 2.148
logos 193, 267, 522, 3.36, 7.1, 7.3
London: British Library Reading Room 397, 14.1; Crystal Palace (Paxton) 96, 383, 2.63; St. Paul's Cathedral (Wren) 448, 15.31; Victoria and Albert Museum 391, 13.43
Looking out to Sea: A Whale Aground (Turner) 234, 5.21
Lorenzetti, Ambrogio: *Allegory of Peace* 24–225, 5.8, 5.9
Los Angeles Fine Arts Squad: *Isle of California* 403, 14.10
lost-wax casting process 323, 522, 10.14, 10.15; for glass 347
Lotus (Minkowitz) 350, 352, 11.22
Louis XIV, King of France 18
Louis XV, King of France 448
low relief 67
Lubalin, Herb: cover for *U&lc* 272, 7.10
Lucie-Smith, Edward 479
Lumia Suite (Wilfred) 472, 15.56
Lyle, John 406–407; (with Izumita) Center for Regenerative Studies 406, 14.13
Lytle, Richard 208–209; *Norfolk* 208, 4.8; *Spring Thaw on Goose Pond* 234, 5.20

M

Machine Tractor Driver and Collective Farm Girl (Mukhina) 27, 1.20
Machu Picchu, Peru 374–375, 13.14
McKernan, Virginia *see* Gregg, Glenn
McMillin, Tom *see* Geyer, George
McNutt, David: "Master Harold" ... and the Boys 92, 2.56
Madonna (encaustic on wood) 425, 15.12
Madonna Enthroned with Angels and Prophets (Cimabue) 105, 2.75
Magnolia vase (jadeite) 319, 10.9
Mahabalipuram, India: rock-cut temples 374, 13.13
Maids of Honor, The (Velázquez) 444, 15.29
Mainot, Maurice: flask 71–72, 2.29
Maki, Fumihiko: Kirishima International Concert Hall, Kagoshima, Japan 372, 13.10
Making the Calendar (Gorky) 81, 2.44
malleability 338, 522
Man and Papaya (Serl) 485, 15.66
Manaipik, Manasie: *Good Spirit* 88, 2.49
Mandala, Kalachakra Sand 168, 2.158
Mandelbrot, Benoit 304
Mandingo, the: gown 84, 2.45
Manet, Edouard: *Le Déjeuner sur l'herbe* 453, 15.36
manière noire 260
Mannerism 179, 442, 522
Mantegna, Andrea: *Dead Christ* 226, 5.11
manuscripts, illuminated 164, 167, 245, 429, 2.156, 15.14
Mapplethorpe, Robert 46
maps: 1. prehistoric and ancient world 415; 2. Europe (early 12th c.) 427; 3. Renaissance Italy 440; 4. Northern Europe (mid 17th c.) 446; 5. Europe (mid 19th c.) 452; 6. World (late 20th c.) 478
maquettes 314, 318, 522, 10.5
Marabar (E. Zimmerman) 70, 2.26
marble: carving 312, 318; quarrying 313
Marinot, Maurice 347
marionettes 411–412, 14.21
Marquesan art 456, 457
Marriage of Giovanni Arnolfini and Giovanna Cenami (van Eyck) 433, 15.18
Martin, Agnes 56; *Untitled X* 56, 2.2
Martin, Bill: *Abalone Shells* 237, 471, 5.24
Martinez, Maria 11.1
Martyred Flowers (Bittleman) 63, 2.14
masks: Balega 177, 3.9; Batetela 108, 2.78
mass 61, 65, 522
"Master Harold" ... and the Boys (McNutt) 92, 2.56
Matisse, Henri 460; *The Red Studio* 137, 460, 2.121; *The Snail* 80, 84, 187, 2.41; *Young Woman, Goldfish, and Checkered Cloth* 253, 6.18
Matthew's Lily (Raffael) 249, 6.8
Mauve District (Frankenthaler) 84–85, 2.46
Maya culture: urn incensario 320, 322, 10.11

media 202, 216; dry 205–212, 519; liquid 213–215, 522; mixed 244, 265–266, 522; painting 216; synthetic 526

Memphis design group 171

Meninas, Las (Velázquez) 444, **15.29**

Merz 19 (Schwitters) 241, **5.29**

metal, working with 338–339, **11.10**; *see* bronze sculpture

Meta-Matic No. 9 (Tinguely) 158, **2.149**

México del Presente (Rivera) 225, **5.10**

mezzotints 255, 259, 522, **6.26**

Michelangelo Buonarroti 14, 313, 436; *"Atlas" Slave* 312, **10.1**; *David* 313, 318, 438, **10.2**; *Pietà* 313, 436, 438, **15.22**; Sistine Chapel frescoes 12, 21, 46, 51–52, 54, 202, 232, 233, 436, 500–502, 504–506, **1.1**, **1.41**, **1.45**, **4.2**, **5.19**, **16.15–16.20**

Middleton, Wisconsin: "Solar Hemicycle" house (Wright) 398–399, **14.4**

Mies van der Rohe, Ludwig, and Johnson, Philip: Seagram Building, New York 385, **13.32**

Migrant Mother (Lange) 280–281, **8.9**

miniatures 105, 522, **2.73**; Persian 77, 118, **2.38**, **2.96**

minimalism 29–30, **1.22**

Minkowitz, Norma 350, 479; *Lotus* 350, 352, **11.22**

Miró, Joan: *The Beautiful Bird Revealing the Unknown to a Pair of Lovers* 237, **5.23**; mixed media 244; printmaking 265–266

Miyake, Issey 361–362; *Body Sculpture in Rattan* 361, **12.10**

mobiles 158, **2.148**

modeling: clay 320, 322; plaster 320; wax 322

modeling of contours 79, 522–523

Modigliani, Amedeo: *Head of a Woman* 318, **10.8**

modular construction (architecture) 389, 323

Mona Lisa (Leonardo) 220, 233, 438, **5.5**, **15.24**

Mondrian, Piet 464; *Composition in Blue, Yellow, and Black* 464, **15.47**; *Flowering Apple Tree* 33, 37, 55, **1.30**; *Fox Trot A* 59–60, 464, **2.10**; *The Gray Tree* 33, 37, 55, **1.29**; *Tree II* 33, 37, 55, **1.28**

Monet, Claude 48, 454, 458, **5.27**; *Grainstacks (End of Summer)* 134, **2.119**; *Rouen Cathedral* 454, **15.37**

Monet Museum, Giverny: poster 117–118, **2.94**

monochromatic combinations 143, 523

Monogram (Rauschenberg) 244, **5.33**

monotype prints 247, 523, **6.4**

Mont Sainte-Victoire seen from Les Lauves (Cézanne) 79, **2.40**

montage 295, 299, 482, 523, **15.63**

Monte Migiana Still-Life (Bailey) 471, **15.55**

Monterrey, Mexico: Museo de Arte Contemporaneo 480, **15.62**

Montreal, Canada: German Pavilion (Otto) 389, **13.39**

Monument to Balzac (Rodin) 157, **2.147**

Moon Cannot Be Stolen, The (Bradley) 27, **1.19**

Moonrise, Mamaroneck, New York (Steichen) 279, **8.7**

Moore, Charles (and William Hersey): Piazza d'Italia, New Orleans 121, 123, **2.100**

Moore, Henry 74; maquettes 314, **10.3**; *Reclining Figure* 108, **2.79**; *Sheep Piece* 74, **2.34**

Morishima, Hiroshi: *Wagami Andon* (lamp) 356, **12.4**

Morris, Jane 279, **8.5**, **8.6**

Morris, William 275; *Works of Geoffrey Chaucer* 275, **7.12**

mosaics 242–243, 425, **5.30–5.32**, **15.13**

Moscow: St. Basil's Cathedral 369, **13.5**

Moser, Barry (illus.): *Alice's Adventures in Wonderland* 275, **7.13**

movement (in artworks): actual *see* kinetic sculpture; illusionary 157, 159; and photography 163–164

movies *see* film

Mr. and Mrs. Andrews (Gainsborough) 184–185, **3.21**

Mughal turban jewel 311, 338, **11.8**

Muirhead, Deborah 482–483; *Water World Voices from the Deep* **15.64**

Mukhina, Vera: *Machine Tractor Driver and Collective Farm Girl* 27, **1.20**

multicultural art 480–481

Munch, Edvard: *The Scream* 458, **15.41**

Munsell, Albert: color tree 129, 131, **2.113**, **2.115**

Muqi: *Six Persimmons* 93, **2.57**

Mural with Blue Brushstroke (Lichtenstein) 470, **15.54**

murals 523; enamel 403, **14.10**; encaustic 223, **5.7**; *see* frescoes; wall paintings

Museum Guard (Hanson) 31, **1.24**

Muybridge, Eadweard 293; *Headspring, a Flying Pigeon Interfering* 293, **8.21**

Myers, Katherine 310, **9.12**

N

naive art 23, 523

Nakashima, George 342; *Altar for Peace* 342, **11.14**

Nangulay, Dick: *Spirit Figure* 92, **2.55**

Nanook of the North (Flaherty) 297, **8.27**

Napoli, Jana 356

Narcissus (after Zhu Da) 61, **2.12**

narrative artworks 21, 23, 167, 523

Nasca hummingbird 331, **10.23**

Nation, The 49

Naturalism 453, 523

nautilus shell 195, **3.40**

naves 377, 523, **13.20**

Nazi regime 20, 46–47, 52, 489

Neoclassicism 450, 451, 523

Neoexpressionism 477, 523

neon art 121, 123, 125, **2.100**, **2.104**

Nervi, Pierre Luigi: aircraft hangar 387, **13.36**

Neumann, Balthasar: Vierzehnheiligen Church 448, 450, **15.32**

Nevelson, Louise: *Black Wall* 328, **10.20**

New Canaan, Connecticut: Johnson House 385, **13.33**

New Gourna, Egypt 380–381, **13.24**, **13.25**

New Orleans: Piazza d'Italia (Moore and Hersey) 121, 123, **2.100**

New York: AT&T Building (Johnson and Burgee) 389–390, **13.41**; chapel (Cloisters) 190–191, **3.33**; Greenacre Park (Sasaki) 403, **14.9**; *Red Cube* (Noguchi) 18, **1.10**; Seagram Building (Mies van der Rohe and Johnson) 385, **13.32**; Whitney Museum of American Art 30–31, 50, **1.24**

New York School 467, 468

Newman, Barnett 468; *Broken Obelisk* 57, **2.5**, **2.6**; *Vir Heroicus Sublimis* 469, **15.52**; *Voice of Fire* 45, 198, **1.40**

Newton, Sir Isaac: color wheel 128, 129, **2.109**

Nicholson, William *see* Beggarstaff Brothers

Niépce, Joseph-Nicéphore 276

Nigerian traditional dress 361, **12.8**

Nikolais, Alwin: *Sanctum* 410, **14.19**

Nîmes, France: Pont du Gard 376, **13.19**

Nishat Bagh, India 401, **14.6**

Noguchi, Isamu 193; *Core Piece #1, Core Piece #2* 131–132, **2.116**; *Red Cube* 18, **1.10**; *Small Torso* 131–132, **2.116**

nonobjective/nonrepresentational art 25, 37, 48, 464, 523

Norfolk (Lytle) 208, **4.8**

North Beach Rocks (Barnes) 352, **11.23**

Norwegian door panels 57, **2.4**

Nostalgia (Tarkovsky) 298, **8.28**

Notre Dame Cathedral, Paris 377, **13.21**

Nude Descending a Staircase #2 (Duchamp) 159, 463, **2.151**

Nude in a Bathtub (Bonnard) 218–219, **5.3**

Number 1, 1948 48, **1.42**

Nymphs and Satyr (Bouguereau) 49, 60, **1.43**

O

Oath of the Horatii, The (David) 450, **15.33**

Ocean Park #115 (Diebenkorn) 37, **1.31**

oculus 379

Ode to Life (Forma) 315, **10.4**

offset lithography 262, 290, 523, **8.18**

oil painting 216, 218, 228–230, 237

O'Keeffe, Georgia 38–39, 482; *Abstraction Blue* 129, **2.114**; *Lily-White with Black* 38, **1.33**

Old Guitarist, The (Picasso) 134, 135, 461, **2.120**

Oldenburg, Claes 101, 103, 470; *Late Submission to the Chicago Tribune Competition of 1922: Clothespin (Version Two)* 203, **4.3**; *Soft Saxophone* 30, **1.24**; *Stake Hitch* 103, **2.71**

Op Art 146, 156, 469, 523
open forms 73, 523
optical illusion *see* illusion
Orange Crush (Poons) 148, **2.137**
Orbello, Italy: aircraft hangar (Nervi) 387, **13.36**
orders, Greek 376, **13.17**
Ornamental Mutation (Latham) 303, **9.3**
Orozco, José Clemente: *Zapatistas* 172, **3.3**, **3.4**
Orpheus (Redon) 85, 145, **2.47**
Otto, Frei 389; German Pavilion, Montreal 389, **13.39**
Ottoman embroidered envelope 146, **2.134**
outlines 61
outsider art 484, 485, 523
overlapping 77, 93, 523
overpainting 218, 229, 523

P

Padua, Italy: Arena Chapel frescoes (Giotto) 430–431, **15.17**
painting 216; direct 218–219, 518; indirect 218, 521, *see specific media*
Painting #199 (Kandinsky) 196, **3.41**
palettes: limited 152; open 152, 523
Palladio, Andrea 448; Teatro Olimpico, Vicenza 408–409, **14.15**, **14.16**
Palos Verdes, Calif.: Wayfarers' Chapel (Wright, Jr.) 369, **13.7**
Panini, Giovanni Paolo: *Interior of the Pantheon* **13.26**
Pantheon, Rome 367, 379, **13.4**, **13.23**, **13.26**
paper 203–204
Papuan costume 100, **14.17**
Paris, France: Eiffel Tower 391; Notre Dame Cathedral 377, **13.21**; Pompidou Center (Piano and Rogers) 390–391, **13.42**; Sainte-Chapelle 125, **2.106**
Parisian Boulevard, A (Daguerre) 276, **8.2**
Parker, Olivia 284, 285; *Four Pears* 285, **8.13**
Parker, William E.: *Der Wilde Mann* series 290,
Parthenon, Athens 194–195, 423, 438, **3.38**, **15.10**
Passion Play for a Young Tree (Bread and Puppet Theater) 412, **14.21**
pastels 32, 85, 99–100, 203, 211–212, 216, 523; **1.25**, **2.47**, **2.66**, **4.10**
patronage 20, 44–45, 51, 52
pattern 174, 523
Paxton, Joseph: *The Crystal Palace* 96, 383, **2.63**
pediments 376, 523
pen and ink drawings 63, 213, 215, **2.14**, **4.13–4.15**
Pen Argyl Myth, The (Stuart) 110, **2.83**
pencil (graphite) drawings 79, 164, 205–206, **2.39**, **2.155**, **4.4**, **4.5**
Pendour (Hepworth) 73, **2.33**

Pepsi Corporation: advertising 138–139, **2.123**
Peret, Auguste 510
performance art 475, 524, **15.57**
performing arts 408–412
Pericles 422
Perkins, Danny: *White Square 2*, 137, **2.122**
Perseus with the Head of Medusa (Cellini) 326–327, 442, **10.18**
Persian miniatures 77, 118, **2.38**, **2.96**
Persian rugs 349, **11.20**
Persistence of Memory, The (Dalí) 466, **15.49**
perspective: aerial/atmospheric 98–99, 517; forced 408, 409, 520; linear 79, 95, 433, 522; multipoint 99; one-point 95, 523, **2.60**; two-point 96, 527, **2.62**
Perugino (Pietro Vanucci): *The Crucifixion with Saints* 187, **3.24–3.26**
Petipa, Marius: *La Bayadère* 410, **14.18**
Petit Déjeuner après le bain, Le (Degas) 486, **15.67**
Pfaff, Judy 329; *3D* **10.22**
photocopying (xerox art) 291–292, 524, **8.20**
photograms 276, 524
photography 276; action 163–164, 293; of colored artworks 114; computer manipulation of 290; documentary 280–282; high-speed 290–291; landscape 282, 284; "Pictorialist" movement 279–280; political 15–16; portrait 278–279; and realism 284–285, 467; and values 116–117; and viewpoints 99, 100, 163; Weston on 286
photorealism 471, 524
Piano, Renzo, and Rogers, Richard: Pompidou Center, Paris 390–391, **13.42**
Picasso, Pablo 240, 251, 269, 414, 456, 461; *Bust of a Woman after Cranach the Younger* 253, **6.12**; *Les Demoiselles d'Avignon* 461, **15.43**; *Guernica* 52, 54, 80–81, 173, 310, *413*, 439, 489–494, **1.47**, **2.43**, **3.5**, **16.1–16.7**; *The Old Guitarist* 134, 135, 461, **2.120**; *Three Female Nudes Dancing* 213, **4.15**; *A Woman in White* 152, **2.143**
Picnic, The (Manet) 453, **15.36**
Pictorialist movement 279–280
picture plane 95, 524
Piero della Francesca: *Flagellation of Christ* 187, **3.27**
Pietà (Michelangelo) 313, 436, 438, **15.22**
pigments 216, 524
Pine Trees (Tohaku) 101, **2.70**
Pittsfield, Massachusetts: Shaker barn 364, 366, **13.1**, **13.2**
pixels 301, 524
placement 93, 524
planishing 338, 524
planographic processes 260, 262, 264, 524
plaster, modeling 320
Poet Li Bo, The (Liang Kai) 192, **3.34**
Pointillism 148, 458, 524
points of view 99–100, 524

Polish Rider, The (Rembrandt) 487, **15.68**
political content (of artworks) 15–17, 50, 52
Pollaiuolo, Antonio del: *Battle of the Ten Nude Men* 245–246, **6.1**, **6.2**
Pollock, Jackson 48, 167–168, 173, 467–468, **15.51**; *Number 1, 1948* **1.42**
Polonnaruwa, Sri Lanka: Buddha 103, **2.72**
Polyclitus (after): *Spear Bearer* 32, 73, 423, 425, **2.31**
Polydorus *see* Hagesandrus
Pont du Gard, Nîmes, France 376, **13.19**
Pool of London, The (Derain) 460, **15.42**
Poons, Larry: *Orange Crush* 148, **2.137**
Pop Art 264, 470, 524
porcelain 42, 193, 333, 524, **1.37**, **3.35**
Port Mulgrave, Yakutat: Moon House post (Tlingit) 67, **2.20**
porticoes 367, 524
Portrait of Dr. Gachet (van Gogh) 48, 486
Portrait of a Landowner (anon. photograph) 278, **8.3**
Portrait of the Princesse de Broglie (Ingres) 111, **2.85**
Portrait of a Woman (Cranach the Younger) 253, **6.13**
Portrait of Woody Guthrie (Frasconi) 249, **6.7**
Portrait of a Young Man (Bronzino) 218, 442, **5.2**
portraits 279, *and see above*; miniature 105, **2.73**; photographic 278–279, **8.3–8.5**
Portuguese, The (Braque) 461, **15.44**
post and lintel construction 375, 524, **13.15**
postage stamps 270, **7.6**
poster art 20, 59, 65, 85, 87, 92, 117–118, 145, 264, 268, 269–270
Post-Impressionists 48, 148, 455–458, 524
post-modern architecture 389–390, 524
Post-Painterly Abstraction 468, 524
pottery *see* ceramics; clay
power, art and 18, 20
Power Lines (Beckman) 32, 471, **1.25**
prehistoric art 418–419
prints and printmaking 245; intaglio 253, 255, 259–260, 521; mixed media 265–266; monotypes 247, 523; planographic 260, 262, 264, 524; relief 246, 247–253, 525; stenciling 264–265
propaganda, art and 20
Prophet Mohammad with the Archangel Gabriel Meeting Moses in Heaven (Persian miniature) 77, **2.38**
proportion 170, 193–195, 198
proscenium 408, 524
proscenium arch 409, 524
Prueitt, Melvin L. 305
Pryde, James *see* Beggarstaff Brothers
Pueblo potters *see* Acoma ware
puppetry 411–412, **14.21**
Putman, Andrée: interior design 143, **2.130**
pyramids, Egyptian 420–421, **15.5**

Q

Qing-de-zhen ware vase 193, **3.35**
Queen Charlotte Island: Haida chest 182, **3.17**
quilting 352–353, **11.24**

R

race: and art criticism 50
radiotherapy, virtual reality 307, **9.9**
Raffael, Joseph: *Matthew's Lily* 249, **6.8**
Raft of the Medusa, The (Géricault) 451, 453, **15.34**
raising metal vessels 339, 524, **11.10**
Rakim, Mustafa: *Firman* 114, **2.88**
Rand, Paul 269; catalog cover 269, **7.4**
Raphael 441; *The School of Athens* 441, **15.25**
Rashomon (Kurosawa) 295–296, **8.25**
Rauschenberg, Robert 244; *Monogram* 244, **5.33**
Ravenna, Italy: S. Vitale (mosaic) 425, **15.13**
realism 32, 524; 19th-c. 453, 525; 20th-c. 32, 467, 471
Reclining Figure (Moore) 108, **2.79**
Red Cube (Noguchi) 18, **1.10**
Red Studio, The (Matisse) 137, 460, **2.121**
Redon, Odilon 85, 251; *Orpheus* 85, 145, **2.47**
reduction prints 253, 525
reflections 123–124
Relativity (Escher) 107, **2.77**
relief printmaking processes 247–253, 525
relief sculpture 67, 315, 525; high 67, 521; low 67, 522
Rembrandt van Rijn 13, 414, 448, 487; *The Polish Rider* 487, **15.68**; *Self-Portrait* 13, 15, 117, 121, **1.3**; *Sleeping Girl* 215, **4.16**; *The Three Crosses* 255, **6.19–6.24**
Renaissance art 95, 120–121, 179, 209, 224, 326–327, 433–434, 436, 441, 525
Renoir, Pierre Auguste 18, 48, 454, 455; *The Boating Party* 189, **3.28**
repetition 30, 170, 171–174
repoussé 339, 525
representational art 32, 525
resists 253, 525
restoration of artworks 51–52, 54, 232–233, 504–506
Resurrection, The (David) 134, **2.118**
Resurrection, The (Grünewald) 442, **15.27**
Rêverie (Rossetti) 279, **8.6**
Rhapsody (Hofmann) 230, **5.18**
rhythm 30, 170, 180–181, 525
Riley, Bridget: *Crest* 156, 469, **2.146**
Rivera, Diego 222–223, 479; *Creation* 223, **5.7**; *Flower Day* 33, **1.27**; *México del Presente* 225, **5.10**
rocking chair (Thonet) 64, 180, **2.16**
Rocky Mountains, Lander's Peak (Bierstadt) 98, **2.64**
Rococo style 209, 448, 450, 525

Rodin, Auguste 40, 52, 157, 499; *Adam and Eve* **1.46**; *Gates of Hell* 40, 52, 67, 183, 495–499, **1.46, 2.22, 16.8–16.13**; *Monument to Balzac* 157, **2.147**; *The Thinker* 496, 497, **16.11**; *The Three Shades* 496, 498–499
Rodin: The Thinker (Steichen) 117, **2.93**
Rogers, Richard: Pompidou Center, Paris 390–391, **13.42**
Roman art and architecture 67, 132, 222, 223, 322, 376, 425; *see also* Rome
Romanesque architecture 376, 429, 525
Romanticism 451, 525
Rome: Arch of Constantine 44, **1.39**; Colosseum 509, **16.23**; Pantheon 367, 379, **13.4, 13.23, 13.26**; St. Peter's Piazza (Bernini) 402, **14.7**; Trajan's Column 155, **2.144**; *see also* Bernini: *Ecstasy of St. Teresa*; Sistine Chapel frescoes
Ronchamp, France: Notre-Dame-du-Haut (Le Corbusier) 125, **2.107**
Roosevelt, Franklin D. 20
Rose, Chris *see* Baier, Fred
Rosenberg, Pierre 233
Rosenquist, James: *Iris Lake* 262, **6.29**
Rossetti, Dante Gabriel: *Jane Morris* 279, **8.5**; Rêverie 279, **8.6**
Rothko, Mark 120, 468; *Green on Blue* 25, **1.18**
Rouen Cathedral (Monet) 454, **15.37**
Rousseau, Henry 23; *The Dream* 23, 25, **1.15**
Royal Ballet Company, London: *La Bayadère* 410, **14.18**
Rubens, Peter Paul 487; *The Assumption of the Virgin* 448, **15.30**; *Landscape with Rainbow* 32, **1.26**
rugs 349; Persian 349, **11.20**
Rune Stone, Jelling, Denmark 110, **2.81**
Running Fence (Christo) 57–58, **2.8**
Rupert, Prince: *The Standard Bearer* 259, **6.26**

S

Saarinen, Eero: Jefferson National Expansion Memorial 20, **1.11**
Safdie, Moshe 508; Vancouver Library Square 52, 54, 71, 199, 371, 488, 507–510, **1.48, 2.27, 3.43, 13.9, 16.21, 16.22, 16.24, 16.25**
Sagredo, Zaccaria 397
St. Basil's Cathedral, Moscow 369, **13.5**
Saint Christopher (Dürer) 248, **6.6**
Sainte-Chapelle, Paris 125, **2.106**
St. Louis, Missouri: Jefferson National Expansion Memorial (Saarinen) 20, **1.11**
St. Paul's Cathedral, London (Wren) 448, **15.31**
Samaras, Lucas: *Book 4* 108, 328, **2.80**
Samuel, Cheryl: Kotlean robe 362–363, **12.12**
Samuelson, Alex: Coca-Cola bottle 41, **1.36**
San Vitale, Ravenna: wall mosaic 425, **15.13**

Sanctum (Nikolais) 410, **14.19**
sans serif typefaces 270, 271, 525
Santiago de Compostela Cathedral, Spain 429, **15.15**
Sara's Garden (Gonzales) 164, **2.155**
sarcophagus, Roman (marble) 67, **2.21**
Sasaki, Hideo: Greenacre Park, New York 403, **14.9**
scale 93, 95, 101, 103, 105, 525
Scamozzi, Vincenzo: Teatro Olimpico, Vicenza 408–409, **14.15, 14.16**
Scarlet Letter, The (Alcorn) 56–57, 61, **2.3**
Schjeldahl, Peter 49
School of Athens, The (Raphael) 441, **15.25**
Schoonhoven, Terry *see* Los Angeles Fine Arts Squad
Schulte, Eliza: *Alphabet no. 101* 64–65, **2.17**
Schumann, Elka 412
Schumann, Peter 412; puppets **14.21**
Schwitters, Kurt 241; *Merz 19* 241, **5.29**
Scott, Joyce: *Evolution* 50, **1.44**
Scream, The (Munch) 458, **15.41**
sculpture. assemblages 90, 328–329; asymmetrical 185; bead 50; carving processes 312–315, 318–319; casting processes 323, 325–327; closed forms 73, 518; and color 131–132; and compositional lines 189; computer-aided designs 316; contours 71–72; crocheted 350, Cycladic 419; Egyptian 73, 421; and eyelines 60–1, 189; fiber 171; and focal points 191; glass 137, 347; Gothic 431; Greek 73, 113, 132, 189, 422, 423; and illusion of movement 157; kinetic 158, 522; and light 116, 117; and line 57; Mannerist 442; minimalist 29–30; modeling 320, 322; open forms 73, 523; prehistoric 418; relief 67, 315; Roman 425; and shape 65; and space 74; Sumerian 420; and texture 113; *see also* bronze sculpture; Rodin, Auguste
scumbling 230, 525
"Sea dog" table 340, **11.11**
Sea Form Series, No. 2 (Chihuly) 347, **11.16**
Sea Ranch (Halprin) 403–404, **14.11**
Seated Boxer (Apollonius) 325, 423, **10.17**
Seated Model (Seurat) 148, **2.138**
Self-Portrait (Rembrandt) 13, 15, 117, 121, **1.3**
Self-portrait with a Pencil (Kollwitz) 208, **4.7**
Self-portraits, A Set of Six (Warhol) 264, **6.31**
Senmut with Princess Nefrua (sculpture) 73, **2.30**
serif typefaces 270, 525
serigraphs *see* silkscreen printing
Serl, John 185; *Man and Papaya* **15.66**
serpentinata 179
Set of Six Self-portraits, A (Warhol) 264, **6.31**
Seurat, Georges 48, 148, 455, 456; *L'Echo* 201, 212, **4.11**; *Seated Model* 148, **2.138**; *A Sunday Afternoon on the Island of La Grande Jatte* 458, **15.40**
sfumato 211, 233, 441, 525
shading 79, 525
Shaker barn 364, 366, **13.1, 13.2**

shanshui 193

shape(s) 30, 65, 80–81; and emotion 85, 87; geometric 59, 84, 458, 520; hard-edged 85; positive 84; soft-edged 85

She (di Suvero) 90, **2.53**

She-Ba (Bearden) 93, **2.58**

Sheep Piece (Moore) 74, **2.34**

Shepherd, Barry, and Ditko, Steve: Audi advertisement 272, 275, **7.11**

Sider, Sandra: Focus on the Belvedere 352–353, **11.24**

Sigriste, Guido 163

silk 145, 171, **2.133**, **3.1**; painting 105, **2.74**

silkscreen printing 150, 264–265, 525, **2.10**, **6.31**

silverpoint drawings 206, 525, **4.6**

silverwork 123, **2.102**

Sistine Chapel frescoes, Rome 12, 21, 46, 51–52, 54, 202, 232, 233, 436, 500–502, 504–506, **1.1**, **1.41**, **1.45**, **4.2**, **16.15–16.20**

Six Persimmons (Muqi) 93, **2.57**

sizing 230, 526

skene 408, 526

skyscrapers 384–385, **13.30–13.32**

slab building (clay) 334, 526

Sleeping Girl (Rembrandt) 215, **4.16**

slip 322, 526

Small, Jane: portrait (Holbein) 105, **2.73**

Small Torso (Noguchi) 131–132, **2.116**

Smith, W. Eugene: Tomoko in a Bath 15, **1.6**

Smithson, Robert: Spiral Jetty 331, 332, 475, **10.24**

Snail, The (Matisse) 80, 84, 187, **2.41**

Snow Storm: Steamboat off a Harbor's Mouth (Turner) 453, **6.14–6.17**

Sobol Wajman, Anna: Roorka Fable 259, **6.27**

Soft Saxophone (Oldenburg) 30, **1.24**

"Solar Hemicycle" house, Wisconsin (Wright) 398–399, **14.4**

Soria, Alfonso Soto see Hoagland, Labbar

Soriano, Juan: The Dove **15.62**

Southerly Wind and Fine Weather (Hokusai) 246, **6.3**

space 30; and illusion 105, 107; negative 57, 523; positive 57, 524; and three-dimensional art 88, 90; and two-dimensional art 92–93, 95–96, 98–101

Space and Space Forest 91A (Endo) 290, **8.18**

Spain: Palau de la Música Catalana (Domènech i Montaner) 243, **5.32**; Sagrada Familia church (Gaudí) 175, **3.7**; Santiago de Compostela Cathedral 429, **15.15**

Spear Bearer (after Polyclitus) 32, 73, 423, 425, **2.31**

spectrum, visible 127–128, 527, **2.108**

Spectrum III (Kelly) 142, 143, **2.128**

Spinario (bronze) 60–61, **2.11**

Spiral Jetty (Smithson) 331, 332, 475, **10.24**

Spirit Figure (Nangulay) 92, **2.55**

Spirit of the Dead Watching, The (Gauguin) 456, **15.39**

Splendor of Red (Anuszkiewicz) 146, **2.135**

split fountain technique 265

Spores Falling from the Common Horsetail (Dalton) 291, **8.19**

Spring Thaw on Goose Pond (Lytle) 234, **5.20**

Staffelstein, Germany: Vierzehnheiligen Church (Neumann) 448, 450, **15.32**

stained glass 125, 347, 430, 526, **11.18**, **15.16**, **2.106**, **2.107**, **2.127**

Stake Hitch (Oldenburg) 103, **2.71**

stamps, postage 270, **7.6**

Standard Bearer, The (Prince Rupert) 259, **6.26**

Standing Woman (Lachaise) 116, **2.91**

Stankiewicz, Richard 328; City Bird 328, **10.19**

Starry Night, The (van Gogh) 11, 127, 28–29, 218, **1.21**

states (of etchings) 255, 526

static forms 76, 526

Steakley, Douglas: copper vessels 339, **11.10**

Steichen, Edward: Moonrise, Mamaroneck, New York 279, **8.7**; Rodin: The Thinker 117, **2.93**

Stella, Frank: Katsura 152, **2.142**

stemcup (Ch'ing dynasty) 42, **1.37**

stenciling 264–265

Stieglitz, Alfred 279, 467; The Terminal 280, **8.8**

Still Life no. 24 (Wesselmann) 31, **1.24**

Still-Life with Apples (Cézanne) 455, **15.38**

still lifes 526; see also Bailey, William and above

stippling 213

Stone Breakers, The (Courbet) 453, **15.35**

stone, carving 318; tools **10.7**

stoneware 333, 335, 334, 550, **11.5**, **12.2**

Stuart, Michelle: The Pen Argyl Myth 110, **2.83**

stylization 32–33, 526

stylobates 376, 526

sugar aquatints 260

Suger, Abbot 429

Sumerian art 420

Sun Tunnels (Holt) 120, **2.97**, **2.98**

Sunday, Elizabeth 288; Life's Embrace **8.16**

Sunday Afternoon on the Island of La Grande Jatte, A (Seurat) 458, **15.40**

Sunday on the Banks of the Marne (Cartier-Bresson) 282, **8.11**

Suomalainen, Timo and Tuomi: Taivallahti church, Helsinki 177, **3.10**

Supernovae (Vasarely) 469, **15.53**

super-realism see photorealism

supports (paint surfaces) 216, 526, **5.27**

Suq al-Ainau, Yemen: packed-mud houses 369, 374, **13.6**

Surrealism 466, 526

Suvero, Mark di: She 90, **2.53**

Swarm (Feder) 303, **9.2**

Swibold, Professor Richard 366

Swing, The (Fragonard) 163, 167, **2.152**

Sydney Opera House (Utzon) 387, **13.37**

Symbolists 85

synthetic media 238–239, 526

Szabo: wrought-iron clock 338–339, **11.9**

T

T Is for Toad (Azarian) 111, **2.84**

tables: refectory (Baier and Rose) 341, **11.12**; "Sea dog" 340, **11.11**

Taivallahti church, Helsinki (T. and T. Suomalainen) 177, **3.10**

Taj Mahal 15, 30, **1.5**, **1.23**

Talbot, William Henry Fox 276; Botanical Specimens 276, **8.1**

tapestries 347, 349, 526, **11.19**

Tarkovsky, Andrei 298; Nostalgia **8.28**

television 298–300

tempera, painting in 105, 167, 180, 183, 187, 216, 226–227, 434, 467, 526, **2.75**, **2.157**, **3.13**, **3.18**, **3.27**, **5.11–5.14**, **15.20**, **15.50**

Temperaments, The (Parker) 290, **8.17**

tensile strength 314, 526

Tenuous (Hoener) 149, **2.139**

Terminal, The (Stieglitz) 280, **8.8**

tesserae 242, 526

textiles see clothes; fabric design; fiber art; tapestries

texture(s) 30, 108, 526; actual 110, 516; simulated 111, 113–114, 526

thangka, Tibetan 183–184, **3.19**

theater 408–409, **14.14–14.16**

Thiebaud, Wayne: Bikini 31, **1.24**

Thinker, The (Rodin) 117, 496, 497, **2.93**, **16.11**

Thonet, Gebrüder: Reclining rocking chair with adjustable back 64, 180, **2.16**

Thorn Puller (bronze) 60–61, **2.11**

Three Crosses, The (Rembrandt) 255, **6.19–6.24**

3D (Pfaff) 329, **10.22**

three-dimensional artworks 30–31, 67, 69–71; characteristics 71–73; dynamic 76, 519; static 76, 526; see sculpture

Three Female Nudes Dancing (Picasso) 213, **4.15**

Three Shades, The (Rodin) 496, 498–499

Tibetan monks: sand mandala 168, **2.158**

Tiffany, Louis Comfort 347; Flower-form Vase 76, **2.36**; Irish Bells and Sentinels 347, **11.18**

time: and a captured moment 163–164; and deterioration of artworks 169; as subject 164, 167–168; for viewing artworks 155–156

timelines 414, 415, 427, 440, 446, 452, 473

Tinguely, Jean: Meta-Matic No. 9 158, **2.149**

Tintoretto, Jacopo: The Last Supper 442, **15.26**; Leda and the Swan 178–179, 187, 229, 442, **3.11**, **3.12**

Tivoli, Italy: Water Organ, Villa d'Este 158, **2.150**

Tlingit, the: Moon House post 67, **2.20**

toaster (Chan) 354, **12.1**

Tohaku, Hasegawa: *Pine Trees* 101, **2.70**

tokonoma alcoves 42, 44, 398, 526, **1.38**

Tokyo, Japan: Nakagin Capsule Building (Kurokawa) 389, **13.40**

Tolland, Gregg 295

Tomaszewski, Henryk 268, 270; poster 85, 87, **2.48**

Tomoko in a Bath (Smith) 15, **1.6**

tonal range 526; full 116, 520

Toronto, Canada: Nathan Phillips Square 402, **14.8**

Toulouse-Lautrec, Henri de: *Aristide Bruant dans son cabaret* (poster) 269, **7.5**; *Equestrienne (At the Circus Fernando)* 163, **2.153**; *L'Equestrienne* 212, **4.12**

Toutes Uncommon Bowl (Lindquist) 341, **11.13**

Toward the Tower (Varo) 181, **3.15**

Trace (Graves) 185, **3.22**

Trajan's Column, Rome 155, **2.144**

transitions 177, 526

transparencies 262

Tree II (Mondrian) 33, 37, 55, **1.28**

Trent, Council of (1563) 51

Très Riches Heures du Duc de Berry (Limbourg Brothers) 164, 167, 245, **2.156**

triad color schemes 145–146, 526

triangles (in compositional unity) 187, 441, **3.23**, **3.25**, **3.26**

Tribal Spirits (Harvey) 484, **15.65**

trompe l'oeil 113–114, 526

Tron (Disney Productions) 305, **9.6**

Trundholm, Zealand, Denmark: Horse and Sun Chariot (bronze) 73, **2.32**

trusses 383, 526, **13.28**

Turner, Joseph Mallord William 451; *Looking out to Sea: A Whale Aground* 234, **5.21**; *Snow Storm: Steamboat off a Harbor's Mouth* 253, **6.15–6.17**

Twittering Machine (Klee) 23, **1.16**

two-dimensional artworks 30, 51, 527; and illusion of form 77, 79; and illusion of movement 159; and line 59–60, 61, 63, 64; and shape 65; and space 92–93, 95–96, 98–101

Two Nudes (Ingres) 79, **2.39**

Two-toned Golf Bag (Levine) 113–114, **2.87**

typefaces 270–271, 272, 527, **7.7**, **7.9**, **7.10**

typography 270–272, 527

U

U&lc (newsletter) 272, **7.10**

Ugolino di Nerio: *Last Supper* 180, 226–227, **3.13**, **5.12**

ukiyoe woodcut prints 246–247, 249, 527, **6.3**

underpainting 218, 227, 229, 527, **5.12**

Underweisung der Messung... (Dürer) 271, **7.8**

Unicorn Tapestries 349, **11.19**

Unique Forms of Continuity in Space (Boccioni) 463, **15.45**

unity, compositional 30, 170, 187, 189, 527

Untitled (Cohen) 308, **9.10**

Untitled (Frank) 247, **6.4**

Untitled X (A. Martin) 56, **2.2**

urban planning 401–405

Urnes, Norway: church door panels 57, **2.4**

Uttar Pradesh, India: kanna hut 367, **13.3**

Utzon, Jorn: Sydney Opera House 387, **13.37**

V

value(s) (of light and dark) 114, 527; and color 129, **2.113**; and contrast 146, **2.136**; gradations 115, 211, **2.90**; interpretive 116–117, 521; local 116

van der Weyden, Roger *see* Weyden, Roger van der

van Eyck, Jan *see* Eyck, Jan van

van Gogh, Vincent *see* Gogh, Vincent van

Vancouver Library Square (Safdie) 52, 54, 71, 199, 371, 488, 507–510, **1.48**, **2.27**, **3.43**, **13.9**, **16.21**, **16.22**, **16.24**, **16.25**

vanishing point 95, 527

Vaporum VI (Held) 99, **2.65**

variety 30, 170, 175, 177, 527

varnishing 232–233, **5.27**

Varo, Remedios: *Toward the Tower* 181, **3.15**

Vasarely, Victor: *Supernovae* 469, **15.53**

vases 76, 193, 319, 335, 344, 347, 422, **2.36**, **3.35**, **10.9**, **11.4**, **11.15**, **11.17**, **15.7**

Vastushastra (laws of architecture) 373, **13.12**

vaults **13.18**: barrel 377, 517; groin 377, 521; ribbed 377, 525

Velázquez, Diego 444; *Las Meninas (The Maids of Honor)* 444, **15.09**

vellum 255, 527

veneers 341, 527

Venus de Milo (marble) 113, 423, **2.86**

Venus of Willendorf 418, **15.2**

Vermeer, Jan: *The Art of Painting* 77, **2.37**; *Girl with a Pearl Earring* 228–229, **5.15**

Versailles, Palace of 18, **1.9**

Vicenza, Italy: Teatro Olimpico (Palladio and Scamozzi) 408–409, **14.15**, **14.16**

Victoria and Albert Museum, London: addition (Liebeskind) 391, **13.43**

Victory of Samothrace 423, **15.10**

video 298, 299–300, 527

video graphics 305–306, 527

Vietnam Veterans' Memorial (Lin) 17, **1.8**

View of Toledo (Greco) 145, **2.131**

viewing time 155–156

Vignelli Associates (Lella and Massimo Vignelli) 354; dinner set 354, 356, **12.2**

Village Voice, The 49

Viola, Bill: *Buried Secrets* 300, **8.30**

Vir Heroicus Sublimis (Newman) 469, **15.52**

Virgin, The (Wyeth) 227, **5.14**

Virgin and Child with St. Anne and St. John the Baptist (Leonardo) 209, 211, **4.9**

Virgin of the Rocks, The (Leonardo) 211, 229, 436, **15.23**

virtual reality 306–307, 310, 527, **9.8**, **9.9**

visual weight 182, 527

Voice of Fire (Barnett) 45, 198, **1.40**

Voisard: *A Lady of Fashion* (engraving) 359, **12.6**

volume 61, 65

Voss, Richard: *Changing the Fractal Dimension* 304, **9.5**

Voulkos, Peter 336

voussoirs 376, 527

W

Walking Man (Giacometti) 57, **2.7**

walk-through works 70, 527, **2.26**

wall-paintings: African 216, **5.1**; *see* frescoes; murals

wallpaper (Wilson) 174, **3.6**

Warhol, Andy 470; *A Set of Six Self-portraits* 264, **6.31**

washes 215

Washington, DC: Vietnam Veterans' Memorial (Lin) 17, **1.8**

Water Garden, Fort Worth, Texas (Johnson and Burgee) 155–156, **2.145**

Water Organ, Villa d'Este, Tivoli 158, **2.150**

Water World Voices from the Deep (Muirhead) 482, **15.64**

watercolor painting 23, 105, 114, 216, 234, 527; **1.16**, **2.73**, **2.89**, **5.20–5.22**

Watteau, Antoine 448

wax, modeling 322

weaving 347, 349

Webb, Alex: *Killed by the Army* 281, **8.10**

weight 61; visual 182, 527

Welles, Orson: *Citizen Kane* 295, 296, **8.24**

Wesselmann, Tom: *Still Life no. 24* 31, **1.24**

Weston, Edward 286; *Artichoke Halved* 288, **8.15**; *Knees* 286, **8.14**

Weyden, Roger van der: *Head of a Virgin* 206, **4.6**

Whale Aground, A (Turner) 234, **5.21**

Wheel of Life, Buddhist 183–184, **3.19**

wheelchair (Kawasaki) 356, **12.3**

wheel-throwing (clay) 334–335, 527, **11.3**

White Square (Perkins) 2, 137, **2.122**

Whitington, Trent: column **2.127**

Wiene, Robert: *The Cabinet of Doctor Caligari* 294, 460, **8.22**

Wilde Mann series, Der (W. Parker) 290, **8.17**

Wilfred, Thomas: *Lumia Suite* 472, **15.56**

Willendorf, Austria: Venus 418, **15.2**

Williams, Pat Ward 16–17; *Accused/Blowtorch/Padlock* 16, **1.7**

Wilson, Henry: wallpaper 174, **3.6**

Winckelmann, Johann: *Thoughts on the Imitation of Greek Works of Art* 450
Winokur, Paula 336–337; *Entry 1: Sakkara* 336, **11.6**
Woman from Brassempouy (ivory) 12, **1.2**
Woman in White, A (Picasso) 152, **2.143**
women's art 479; and criticism 50
Wondrous Spring (Csuri) 308, **9.11**
wood: carving 315, 318, **10.7**; handcrafting 340–342; *also see below*
woodcuts 111, 177, 247–250, 442, 527, **2.84**, **3.8**, **6.9**; *ukiyoe* 246–247, 249, 527, **6.3**
wood engravings 250, 252, 275, 527, **6.9**, **6.10**, **7.13**
World Wide Web 309–310
Wren, Christopher: St. Paul's Cathedral, London 448, **15.31**
Wright, Frank Lloyd 369; Kaufmann House ("Fallingwater") 200, 387, **3.44**;

"Solar Hemicycle" house, Wisconsin 398–399, **14.4**
Wright, Frank Lloyd, Jr.: Wayfarers' Chapel, Palos Verdes, Calif. 369, **13.7**
wrought-iron 338; clock 338–339, **11.9**
Wyeth, Andrew: *Christina's World* 467, **15.50**; *The Virgin* 227, **5.14**

X
xerox art *see* photocopying

Y
Yagi, Hiroshi: *No. 27 Time Space Passage* 306, **9.7**
YA/YA: furniture 356, 358, **12.5**
Yemen packed-mud houses 369, 374, **13.6**
Yoruba, the 409; divination bag 37, **1.32**

Yoshida, Ryoichi: dolls 479, **15.60**
Young Woman, Goldfish, and Checkered Cloth (Matisse) 253, **6.18**
Young Woman with a Gold Pectoral (Egypto-Romano encaustic) 222, **5.6**

Z
Zapatistas (Orozco) 172, **3.3**, **3.4**
Zapf, Hermann 271; alphabet 271, **7.9**
Zelanski, Paul: *Connecticut Remembered* 240, **5.28**
Zeno at the Edge of the Known World (Kossuth) 475, **15.58**
Zhu Da (after): *Narcissus* 61, **2.12**
Zimmerman, Arnold: ceramic arch 322, **10.12**
Zimmerman, Elyn: *Marabar* 70, **2.26**
zoetropes 293